An Introduction to Labor and Employment Law

Michael Evan Gold

2018

Cornell University

DEDICATION

I dedicate this work to Sarah Dogbe Gold,

who truly values the opportunity for education.

MEG

Ithaca, New York

November, 2018

Published by SUNY OER Services

State University of New York Office of Library and Information Services

10 N Pearl St

Albany, NY 12207

Distributed by State University of New York Press

Cover photo by Tingey Injury Law Firm on Unsplash

ISBN: 978-1-64176-050-8

Table of Contents

CHAPTER 3: EMPLOYMENT DISCRIMINATION LAW

SEX DISCRIMINATION IN COMPENSATION: THE EQUAL PAY ACT OF 1963

DISCRIMINATION BASED ON RACE, COLOR, RELIGION, SEX, OR NATIONAL ORIGIN: TITLE VII OF THE CIVIL RIGHTS ACT OF 1964

DISCRIMINATION BASED ON DISABILITY:
THE AMERICANS WITH DISABILITIES ACT

APPENDIX

CONSTITUTION AND STATUTES

GLOSSARY

Table of Cases and Materials

CHAPTER 1: LABOR LAW BEFORE THE LABOR ACT

CASES

MATERIALS

CHAPTER 2: MODERN LABOR LAW

CASES [*]

---

* When the first party in the name of a case is the National Labor Relations Board, the case is listed according to the adverse party. Thus, *NLRB v. Jones & Laughlin* is listed as "*Jones & Laughlin adv. NLRB.*"

MATERIALS

CHAPTER 3: EMPLOYMENT DISCRIMINATION LAW

CASES

CHAPTER 1

LABOR LAW BEFORE THE LABOR ACT

The Colonial Period

The Background of the Early American Labor Cases

The system of laissez-faire capitalism that we take for granted today was not the economic or political system in Europe or America in the Seventeenth Century, when the American Colonies were founded, or even in the Eighteenth Century, when the Colonies rebelled. In those days, both business and labor were accustomed to government regulation. This was particularly true in the early colonial days: economic activity was regulated in the interest of a religious and political program. The entrepreneur did not believe one was free to carry on one's business any way one saw fit; the desire to make money was often subordinated to other values. Nor did the worker believe one was free to withhold one's labor and demand whatever wages and working conditions one desired. The notion of a market for labor may explain a great deal of the behavior of employers and workers today, but it explains much less of the relationship between masters and servants of two and three hundred years ago. (Those today who argue that the U.S. Constitution should be interpreted strictly according to the views of the Founders of the Republic might do well to keep in mind the differences between the economies and societies of the early Eighteenth Century and the early Twenty-first Century.)

The colonial experience was rooted in English mercantilism, which was the dominant theory of political economy from the Sixteenth Century until it was replaced by the laissez-faire economics of the Industrial Revolution. The objective of mercantilism was to create a secure, prosperous, and self-sufficient nation or empire. Mercantilists believed that prosperity could be attained and preserved by maintaining a strong national defense, by accumulating a store of precious metals, by subsidizing home industries and protecting them against foreign competition, and by competing successfully in foreign markets. In order to compete overseas, the mercantilists sought to assure that their industries had the necessary raw materials and that the costs of production were low. A supply of raw materials could be obtained from colonies. From the point of view of the parent country, the main purpose of colonies was to send raw materials home in exchange for finished products manufactured in the parent country. The interests of the colonies were consistently subordinated to the interests of the parent country. (This practice eventually became a major cause of the American Revolution.) Production costs could be kept down by guaranteeing the entrepreneur an inexpensive, yet adequate supply of labor. Workers should receive a subsistence wage—high enough to guarantee the long-term supply of labor, but no higher. Subsistence wages were thought to have other virtues as well: they kept the laboring class in its place, and, because a laborer with extra money in one's pocket was prone to substitute leisure for work, subsistence wages kept workers from falling into indolence and other vices.

English mercantile policy towards labor rested on the Statute of Artificers, enacted in the Sixteenth Century; this statute modified the Statute of Laborers, enacted in the Fourteenth Century. The Statute of Laborers was enacted after the bubonic plagues had drastically reduced the supply of labor; in some areas of Europe, as many as two-thirds of the peasantry died. When the supply of labor went down, the price went up. The aristocracy did not like the idea and responded in several ways in the Statute of Laborers. In general, the statute assumed that the lord of the manor had jurisdiction over the lives of one's workers and that the workers were a sort of property possessed by the lord. In particular, the statute prohibited workers from refusing to work. The statute also prohibited workers from combining with one another in pursuit of higher wages. The statute prohibited a lord from enticing away the servant of another lord. And the statute established for the entire nation maximum wage scales for various jobs. Wages were set by the day; hourly wages were not introduced until the Industrial Revolution. After half a century, this wage structure proved to be too rigid, and it was replaced towards the end of the Fourteenth Century by a decentralized structure in which justices of the peace fixed wages according to the local price of food. Being men of property, the justices were none too generous in the level of wages they fixed. Half a century later, wages were once again set nationally.

The Statute of Artificers of 1563 returned wage fixing to the local level. The length of the working day was also fixed; it was, in essence, dawn to dusk. The statute also required people of certain classes, such as vagabonds, beggars, peddlers, and gypsies, to take jobs. Young men of these classes who refused to serve as apprentices could be impressed into the military. Laborers who refused to work for the ordinary rate of pay were guilty of a crime, the punishment for which included a whipping and a term of labor in jail. Women and children were required to work as well. Thus, in the early Seventeenth Century, when a certain spinster refused to enter into service, that is, become a servant in someone else's household, the overseers of the town of Turvile committed her to the workhouse because she set an "ill example to lazy and thriftless people."

The American Colonies readily adopted a program of compulsory labor. The Colonies went further than England in the classes of people who were required to work. Whereas England required only vagabonds, beggars, and gypsies to work, the Colonies required labor of all able-bodied men and, occasionally, of women as well. Sometimes, the requirement was a response to an emergency. For example, a Massachusetts act of 1646 required artificers and handicraftsmen "to work by the day for their neighbours in mowing, reaping of corn, and inning thereof"; the reason was that the harvests of hay, corn, flax, and hemp fell so closely to one another that the crops might otherwise have been lost. During the Pequot War of 1637 and King Philip's War of 1675, civilians in Massachusetts were required to maintain the farms of soldiers engaged in the hostilities; a similar practice was observed in the southern Colonies.

More commonly, the requirement of work arose on a regular basis. All males between ages sixteen and sixty were required to serve in the militia. They were also required to work on public projects, the foremost of which was the construction and repair of roads; other examples were forts, bridges, dams, dikes, ponds, meeting houses, prisons, river channels — all the social capital that we have inherited and take for granted. In the northern Colonies, the amount of work that a man owed was often determined by the size of his land; this was, in effect, a property tax. In southern Colonies, a man could discharge his duty to work by sending a servant or slave. The requirement of work was gradually abandoned after the Revolution, but in some places remained in effect through the Nineteenth Century.

Colonists could also be required to work on private projects. In order to attract an entrepreneur to engage in an undertaking desired by the community, the authorities in a colony sometimes promised a supply of free labor. For example, in 1644 the governors of New Haven agreed to require every man to give four days of work to some entrepreneurs who were digging a channel, and in 1670 Newark induced entrepreneurs to set up a corn mill by offering three days of work of every man and woman in the town. (You might be surprised to hear that we do the same thing today, indirectly, by offering tax breaks. The new business pays lower taxes, and the rest of us, therefore, pay more taxes; so that, instead of working one hundred twenty days of the year to pay our taxes, we work one hundred twenty-two days.)

The reader may be wondering what happened if someone refused to work. Early statutes punished idleness by a whipping or a fine. For example, when Massachusetts required craftsones to help bring in the harvest, the men were paid for this work; but, if they failed to work, they were fined double the usual daily wage. If a man failed to appear for his share of public work, some towns authorized the constable to impress another worker, and fined the absent man the wages of that worker and of the constable; other towns allowed a man to pay a fee in lieu of working. Later statutes prescribed forced labor or commitment to a workhouse.

We will consider below why the Colonies adopted a system of compulsory labor. However, having just mentioned the workhouse, we may consider this institution further.

The idea of workhouses came to the Colonies from England. We have noted the English practice of punishing some classes of people who refused to work. Punishing them was sensible so long as mercantilists believed that unemployment was the result of a defect of character. In time, however, the English recognized that factors like the enclosure of farm land, the rising cost of living, and fluctuating business cycles meant that permanent employment was not available to every willing worker. As early as 1535, therefore, a statute adopted the principle that work should be provided for the able-bodied. Thereafter, workhouses began to emerge, and an act of 1575 made them part of the national program for relief of the poor. English workhouses usually concentrated on the manufacture of textiles; sometimes they offered instruction in trades. Living conditions in workhouses were bad; contemporary reports describe them as dirty and infested with vermin.

Workhouses were transplanted to the Colonies. In 1658 Plymouth passed an ordinance providing for a house of correction where vagrants, idle residents, rebellious children, and servants who refused to work would be employed. Later in the Seventeenth Century and in the early Eighteenth Century, royal instructions required colonial governors to set up workhouses, and by the middle 1700s workhouses had been erected in Boston, New York, and Philadelphia. On the eve of the Revolution, when industry was taking root in America, private businesses could draw workers from the workhouses. Indeed, entrepreneurs sometimes built factories on the understanding that they would be staffed with labor from workhouses. In Boston in 1768 a spinning mill was established for the very purpose of employing the poor, and funds were provided for setting up spinning schools for children. The undertakers of this enterprise disclaimed any motive to profit from it; rather, they said they hoped to reduce the number of poor in almshouses (in which paupers were fed and sheltered) and to "habituate the People to Industry, and preserve their Morals, who, instead of their continuing a burden to society, will become some of its most useful Members." A similar project had been started in Philadelphia four years earlier.

Colonial workhouses always had a moral quality to them; vagrancy, idleness, and refusal to work were vices. Vice is not far removed from crime, and the Colonists quickly perceived that workhouses could serve a dual function. In 1735 a grand jury in Charleston, South Carolina complained that, due to the absence of a workhouse in which to punish the idle, the poor were flocking to the town. Thus workhouses also became houses of correction for miscreants, and minor offenses were frequently punished with terms in the workhouse.

Now let us attempt to explain why the Colonies adopted compulsory labor. Three reasons may be suggested. One was simply that the Colonists brought English law with them. The laws of England continued to be influential in America through the Nineteenth Century.

A second reason for compulsory labor in the Colonies was the Puritan ethic, which strongly condemned idleness. Colonial almanacs were studded with aphorisms on the sinfulness of being unemployed. The Ameses reminded their readers, "Toil and be strong," and Poor Richard advised, "Leisure is the Time for doing something useful." Colonial children wrote in their copybooks, "By the sweat of thy brow, thou shalt eat thy bread." On the eve of his execution, a burglar exhorted the good citizens of Boston to

> "Shun vain and idle Company;
>   They'll lead you soon astray;
> From ill-fam'd Houses ever flee,
>   And keep yourselves away.
>
> With honest Labor earn your Bread,
>   While in your youthful Prime;
> Nor come you near the Harlot's Bed,
>   Nor idly waste your Time.
>
> The dreadful Deed for which I die
>   Arose from small Beginning;
> My idleness brought poverty,
>   And so I took to Stealing."

The settlers of the middle and southern Colonies were not Puritans, but they also discountenanced idleness. For example, William Penn's Frame of Government provided that "all children within this province of the age of twelve years, shall be Taught some useful trade or skill, to the end that none may be idle, but the poor may work to live, and the rich, if they become poor, may not want." Southern towns prohibited the sale of liquor to servants or slaves lest they waste their time in drinking.

A third reason for compulsory labor was that the Colonies were chronically short of labor. This shortage was perhaps the salient fact of economic life in the Colonies for many years, and it deserves careful attention. Let us consider the reasons for the shortage and then turn to some of its effects.

Why the Colonies were short of labor in the early years of colonization is obvious: there were only so many ships available to carry immigrants, and each ship could transport only so many people. Whereas the reader was born into a secure community with a fully developed capital stock — productive farms and factories, sturdy houses, paved roads, etc. — the Colonists arrived in a completely undeveloped land that was peopled by not always friendly natives. Everything had to be built from scratch, and sometimes defended against attack. There were never enough hands for the work that needed to be done.

Why the Colonies <u>continued</u> to be short of labor for a century and a half is not so obvious. Indeed, the shortage itself may be surprising. Having studied economics, the reader has probably been thinking that the shortage of labor should have had two consequences: first, the price of labor should have risen; second, workers should have flocked to the Colonies. The reader is probably correct about the price of labor. Many scholars believe that wages in the Colonies were 30 to 100 percent higher than in Europe, and this situation obtained through at least the Revolution. (By the way, wages in the Colonies were often calculated by the project. For example, John Pynchon of Springfield, Massachusetts recorded that he had "Agreed with Thomas Barber [for Barber] to Build me a Barne over the great River, [the barn to be] 50 foote long and 24 feete wide, with a leantoe all along the back side," the project "to be compleated [by] Harvest next," for which "I am to allow him £21." Wages were also calculated by the day, week, or month, but rarely by the hour.) The belief that wages were higher in the Colonies than in Europe is based on <u>nominal</u> wages, as measured in pounds and shillings; these were indeed higher in the Colonies. But one must note that this belief has been disputed in recent years. Some scholars argue that <u>real</u> wages, as measured by productivity and buying power, were no higher in the Colonies than in Europe. We need not choose between the competing bodies of scholarship, for the point is not important for our purposes. The reason is that, because people knew that nominal wages were higher in the Colonies than in England, and because one may doubt that workers in the Seventeenth and Eighteenth Centuries appreciated the difference between nominal wages and real wages, English and Continental workers must have <u>believed</u> that they could earn more money in the Colonies. So why didn't they jump on ships bound for America and glut the labor market? The explanation lies in reasons internal and external to the Colonies.

The <u>internal</u> reason was very powerful. It was the ready availability of land. To a European in the Seventeenth Century, owning land was the crowning achievement of life. It meant personal independence and high social status. Ambitious immigrants who arrived in the Colonies saved their wages, bought land as soon as they could — and thereby took themselves out of the labor market for a good deal of the year. If real wages in the Colonies were in fact fifty or seventy-five percent higher than in Europe, this process would have occurred very quickly; but it would have occurred even if real wages in Europe and in the Colonies were equal.

One reason <u>external</u> to the Colonies for the shortage of labor was the unwillingness of people to leave home for distant shores. To draw an equally distant analogy, the median starting salary for students graduating

college with a bachelor's degree last June was
approximately $40,000. How many of them would seriously
consider taking a job in the developing world, for
example, West Africa, for $60,000? Of those who would
consider it, how many would go if they might never return
home?

Another external reason for the shortage of labor in
the Colonies was the policy of the British government,
which, for a good part of the colonial period,
discouraged — and even forbade — emigration. Now, this
was not so in the beginning. In the early years of
settlement, emigration to the Colonies was encouraged.
It was widely believed that England was overpopulated and
that shipping the poor and vagrant classes to America
(many haughty American families have humble European
origins) would yield a triple benefit: these undesirables
would no longer burden English society; they would behave
like good mercantilists by extracting raw materials and
sending them back to England for processing; and they
would become consumers of England's products. Skilled
workers, though in demand at home, were also permitted to
emigrate to America, perhaps based on the belief that a
modicum of skills was necessary to establish permanent
settlements; certainly farmers, called "husbandmen," were
essential. Thus, the passenger manifests of two ships
arriving in Virginia in 1623 listed twenty-five
tradesmen, four husbandmen, one student, one servant, and
only ten "gentlemen." (This low proportion of immigrants
from the upper classes of England lasted — perhaps to the
good fortune of the Colonies — throughout the colonial
period.) A great majority of the passengers arriving
with John Winthrop in Massachusetts in 1630 belonged to
the families of artisans or farmers, and a list of the
Colonists in New England in 1634, though incomplete,
reveals a heavy majority of cloth workers and husbandmen.
As a result, even frontier communities were often served
by a variety of tradesones.

But policy changed when fledgling colonial industry
began to compete with English industry. As early as
1666, King Charles II prohibited the transportation of
knitting frames to the Colonies. At the start of the
next century, the English Board of Trade urged Parliament
to restrict workers engaged in the manufacture of woolen
goods from leaving the country. England actually began
restricting the emigration of skilled artisans in 1718.
Fearing the loss both of skilled workers and of the trade
secrets they would take with them, Parliament in 1765
forbade the emigration of all trained machine operators

and made it a crime, punishable by fine and imprisonment, to entice an operative to emigrate. Soon thereafter, it became criminal to export textile machinery, plans, or models. Criminals and vagabonds were shipped over until the eve of the Revolution, but even they were restrained by a prohibitive per capita tax in 1774. These measures were the seventh of the twenty-seven specific grievances set forth in the Declaration of Independence:

> "He {namely, King George III} has endeavoured to prevent the population of these States; for that purpose obstructing the Laws of Naturalization of Foreigners; refusing to pass other[] [laws] to encourage their migration hither, and raising the conditions of new Appropriation of Lands."

By the 1780s (which, though after the Revolution, was still within the period of an insufficient supply of labor) the restricted classes included all workers in textile plants, in plants that manufactured textile machinery, in the iron and steel industry, and in coal mines.

The restrictions were only partially effective. Ship captains became adept at avoiding them, and many skilled workers came from the Continent instead of England. The Virginia Company brought over Dutch workers to erect sawmills. Polish workers were imported to start the naval stores industry, and Italians, to establish a glassworks. Peter Hasenclever, a Prussian ironmaster, transported from Germany over five hundred miners, foreones, colliers, carpenters, masons, and laborers, together with their wives and children. Other skilled artisans who managed to reach the Colonies included flaxworkers from the north of Ireland, who developed the linen industry in New England, the Eastern Shore of Maryland, and South Carolina; Huguenots, who pioneered the manufacture of salt and the production of indigo in South Carolina; and Italians trained in silk culture, who helped establish that industry in Georgia. Nonetheless, although the restrictions were not fully effective, they did hold down immigration substantially.

To these reasons for the shortage of labor in the Colonies, an additional reason should be added. The Colonials were industrious people. In consequence, the economies of the Colonies grew quickly, and with them grew the demand for workers.

In sum, the following causes contributed to the chronic shortage of labor in the Colonies: the availability of land and the desire of immigrants to own land; the unwillingness of workers to leave their native countries; English restrictions on emigration; and the rapid growth of the colonial economies. The shortage of labor, together with the influence of English law and the Puritan ethic, explain why the Colonies adopted a program of compulsory labor.

The shortage of labor in the Colonies had other effects as well. One was a desperate need for skilled workers. Some colonial projects failed for want of skilled workers. There was no point in importing machinery unless it was accompanied by a skilled mechanic who could assemble and repair it. Because of this need, the Colonials resorted to a variety of means to attract craftsones. A few were willing to come as indentured servants; they agreed to work for a period of years in exchange for their transportation and maintenance. But most indentured servants were simple laborers; craftsones in Europe usually lived well enough that they had to be lured to the Colonies. Among the lures were substantial bounties paid to the worker and to the family that was often left behind for a few years. Exemptions from taxes, military service, and compulsory labor on public projects were also dangled before skilled Europeans to induce them to immigrate. Perhaps the strongest inducement for many was the opportunity to own land or set up businesses of their own. Some Colonies also tried to attract skilled workers from the other Colonies.

The shortage of labor in the Colonies led them, as it had led England, to control the price of labor. In the earliest days of settlement, the tiny Colonies had general wage fixing: the price for each and every task was set by the community as a whole or by its leaders. Hours of work were also regulated. For example, Massachusetts prescribed a 10-hour day for field workers and a 12-hour day for craftsones. The Colonies grew, and during most of the Seventeenth Century, only maximum wages were established. When this practice was abandoned, the Colonies continued to set the wages of quasi-public jobs like porters, millers, smiths, chimney sweeps, and grave diggers. Fees for public services like slaughtering, grinding, and sawing were also set by law. Despite wage controls, the scarcity of labor meant that its price was high.

If wages are controlled, prices must also be controlled lest they grow so high that workers can no longer buy the products. In turn, controlling the price of products prevents the wages of labor from rising lest the cost of making the products exceed the allowable price for them. Thus, the prices of necessities like bread, leather, and bricks were widely regulated in the Colonies, as were the prices that taverns and inns could charge for liquor, food, and lodging. Some of the Colonies, particularly in the South, also regulated the quality and measure of products, and the amounts that could be made and sold.

Another consequence of the shortage of labor in the Colonies was a number of laws that prohibited workers from changing jobs. In Virginia in the Seventeenth and Eighteenth Centuries, craftsones were required to work at their trades and were not permitted to turn to husbandry, that is, buy and work on their own farms. This flat prohibition proved difficult to enforce, but as late as 1748 persons imported as tradesones or wage workers were penalized by extra service if they refused to work at their trades. Rhode Island required workers in the building trades who left their work to pay a substantial fine to their former employers.

Restrictions like these, though eventually abandoned, were especially burdensome because, as I have mentioned, most immigrants dreamed of the status and personal independence that came with owning land. A law prohibiting artisans from leaving their trades frustrated this dream, and must have made them deeply discontent. This signifies something important about the colonial mind. In order to enforce laws forbidding tradesones to leave their occupations, and to live with the resulting resistance, the Colonials must have had a strong sense of obligation to the community, a strong appreciation of the need for individuals to make sacrifices for the good of the group. Of course, there may also have been an element of exploitation in their motivation, or perhaps of thinking something like, "These are our colonies. If you want to join us, you have to pay our price." Nor need one deny that another element of their motivation might have been a sense of justice: the artisans were wooed because their skills were needed, and it was unfair for them not to provide what they had promised. But neither exploitation nor justice seems sufficient to explain these restrictions. It must be added that the Colonials genuinely believed that, in some cases, individual good must give way to the good of the community.

This belief, which Americans have largely discarded, was a contributing cause of another colonial policy, one that is particularly relevant for present purposes. That policy was embodied in rules against workers combining for the purpose of raising their wages — that is, as we would say today, against labor unions. The English had prohibited combinations of workers since the Fourteenth Century, and the Colonies — facing a shortage of labor and believing in the individual's duty to the community — followed suit.

If a worker had to work, an employer had to employ. Under the Tudor industrial code, English employers, known as masters, could not fire employees, known as servants, without just cause during the term of employment, which was typically one year. On a number of occasions in the Sixteenth and Seventeenth Centuries, the English government required manufacturers to continue producing, even though there was no market for their goods. A servant could not quit a job before its term expired, nor could another master hire a servant who quit prematurely. The reason for such laws was not altogether humanitarian. A parish was responsible to care for its poor. An unemployed worker and one's dependents were likely to become indigent — and, therefore, charges on the public purse. Throughout this period, the prohibition on workers' combining for higher wages remained in effect in England. Workers who could not leave their jobs or bargain for higher wages were open to exploitation. As a result, whether from humane concern for the suffering of workers or from economic concern for an adequate supply of labor, the Tudor industrial code also restrained unconscionable practices by land owners against workers.

The Colonies generally had similar laws, both as to employment and as to the poor. In Rhode Island a master could not dismiss a covenant servant before the end of the agreed term without reasonable and sufficient cause plus the written approval of the chief officer of the town and "three or foure able and discreet men of the Common Council." In 1657 Boston required employers who set servants at liberty "to see after their imployment, and to secure the Town from any charge that might otherwise be occasioned by such." Even free workers could not be dismissed irresponsibly lest they become burdens on the public. In 1642 a Massachusetts court awarded one Thomas Marvin not only wages for the period he had worked, but also twenty shillings "for being turned away in winter, unprovided." (Of course, some

Colonials did work for others for short periods of time, for example, to help bring in a harvest. Nonetheless, the doctrine of employment-at-will, under which an employer or a worker can sever the employment relationship at any time and for any reason, is a recent development.)

Colonial masters also had to provide medical care for servants. A master was responsible for medical, surgical, and nursing care for an injured servant and could not discharge a servant who contracted an incurable illness.

Still another consequence of the shortage of labor was that women and children became unskilled and semi-skilled workers. This practice was the norm on the European Continent, and it was known, though not so widespread, in England. In Germany a child might be sent to a spinning school at the age of six; one observer lauded a system like this in which "a man that has most children lives best." Daniel Defoe was gratified that, in the vicinity of the town of Taunton, there was not a child five years of age but could, if properly trained, "earn its own bread."

In the Colonies, women and children were employed in many occupations. The demand for child labor, particularly on the frontier, created an incentive, if any were needed, for the high birth rate and large families of colonial times. If a family fell into hard times, daughters could be placed in service in the household of a more fortunate neighbor. For example, in 1684 John Pynchon of Springfield entered in his account book: "Goodwife Jefferys being here and proffering her daughter Hannah to come to us: I treated with her and shee yielded to our having [Hannah] (whom she says is 12 years old and since last August) till shee be 18 yeares old." Pynchon agreed to provide "her cloathes which she now needs to wear" and a pair of shoes, her wage to be about £6 per year. Sons were also hired out, though generally for shorter periods of time.

No one worked harder than an adult Colonial woman. While a man might rest after cutting hay, or potter about the barn in the winter, a woman was responsible on a daily basis for cooking, cleaning house, spinning thread, making and repairing clothes — and washing them with soap she also made; for gardening, preserving food, milking cows, churning butter, and pressing cheese; as well as for bearing, nursing, and educating children — in addition to which she was known to hire out at harvest time. Colonial girls and women surely heard in church, and knew they were expected to live up to, the expectations of the Book of Proverbs (31:10-31):

"A woman of valour, who can find?
          For her price is far above rubies.
"The heart of her husband doth safely trust in her,
          And he hath no lack of gain.
"She doeth him good and not evil
          All the days of her life.
"She seeketh wool and flax,
          And worketh willingly with her hands.
"She is like the merchant ships:
          She bringeth her food from afar.
"She riseth also while it is yet night,
          And giveth food to her household,
          And a portion to her maidens.
"She considereth a field, and buyeth it;
          With the fruit of her hands,
          she planteth a vineyard.
"She girdeth her loins with strength,
          And maketh strong her arms.
"She perceiveth that her merchandise is good;
          Her lamp goeth not out by night.
"She layeth her hands to the distaff,
          And her hands holdeth the spindle.
"She stretcheth out her hand to the poor;
          Yea, she reacheth forth her hands to the needy;
"She is not afraid of the snow for her household;
          For all her household are clothed with scarlet.
"She maketh for herself coverlets;
          Her clothing is fine linen and purple.
"Her husband is known in the gates,
          When he sitteth among the elders of the land.
"She maketh linen garments and selleth them;
          And delivereth girdles unto the merchant.
"Strength and dignity are her clothing;
          And she laugheth at the time to come.
"She openeth her mouth with wisdom;
          And the law of kindness is on her tongue.
"She looketh well to the ways of her household,
          And eateth not the bread of idleness.
"Her children rise up, and call her blessed;
          Her husband also, and he praiseth her;
"Many daughters have done valiantly,
          But thou excellest them all.
"Grace is deceitful, and beauty is vain;
          But a woman that feareth the Lord
          she shall be praised.
"Give her of the fruit of her hands;
          And let her works praise her in the gates."

Background of the Early American Labor Cases

The scarcity and resulting high cost of labor had still further consequences. One consequence was that they were a brake on expansion of colonial production. Colonial products cost so much to make that they generally could not compete with European-made products; this was often true even when the cost of shipping across the ocean was added to the price of the European items. To protect local producers, the Colonies resorted to non-importation agreements. Another consequence of the scarcity and high cost of labor was that the colonial worker enjoyed a higher standard of living than one's European counterpart. A third consequence was that Colonials frequently worked in more than one craft. Sometimes the crafts were related: a blacksmith might also be a toolmaker, and a carpenter might also be an undertaker. At least as often, the crafts were unrelated: Joshua Hempstead of New London, Connecticut was a farmer, surveyor, house and ship carpenter, stonecutter, sailor, trader, and an attorney. John Julius Sorge advertised in New York that he manufactured cleaning fluid, toilet water, soap, candles, insecticides, and wine; he also made artificial fruit and removed hair from ladies' foreheads and arms. Paul Revere was known not only for his midnight ride, but also as a silversmith, an engraver of copper plate, a dentist — and a manufacturer of clock faces for clockmakers, of branding irons for hatters, and of spatulas and probes for surgeons. He also set up a foundry and a mill for rolling copper into sheets. This may be part of the reason that European guilds were not transplanted to America.

Let us now focus briefly on skilled labor in the Colonies. We have noted that English mercantile policy aimed, among other things, to ensure the demand for English products in foreign markets. English products, therefore, had to be of good quality. Good quality products necessitated skilled workers. Workers learned their skills in apprenticeships. The Statute of Artificers set the period of apprenticeship at seven years. In addition, the statute allowed only children of parents who owned a specified amount of property to become apprentices. The Colonies adopted the seven-year period of apprenticeship, but they refused to impose property qualifications on parents. However, because it was customary for parents to pay masters to accept children into the more highly skilled crafts and the professions, there may have been a de facto property qualification in the Colonies.

Artisans trained in Europe were widely considered to be superior to artisans trained in the Colonies. For example, the owners of a china factory in Philadelphia advertised for workers, with the stipulation that "none will be employed who have not served their apprenticeship in England, France, or Germany." Immigrant tradesones often boasted of their European training. A tailor in Charleston advertised that he had been "foreman to the most eminent master-taylors in London and Paris, and by them acknowledged to be as compleat a workman as ever they employed, particularly in the art of cutting." A linen printer and dyer from Dublin told Bostonians that he could produce colors "as good and as lasting as any that comes from Europe." We must add, however, that not all imported workers lived up to expectations. George Cabot wrote to Alexander Hamilton in 1791 that thirty-nine of the forty workers in Cabot's cotton mill in Beverly, Massachusetts were natives of the vicinity, as the Irish artisans who had been imported for the jobs had "proved deficient in some quality essential to usefulness."

We have mentioned that many artisans plied their trades only long enough to buy land. Others had no desire to become farmers. A small amount of capital was sufficient to open a business that produced for local consumption, and high wages allowed those workers who were so inclined to own their own shops. There were constant opportunities in colonial and revolutionary times for artisans to become entrepreneurs.

A class of skilled white artisans gradually developed in the North. No such class developed in the South, where conditions were different. The land and the weather were well suited to the development of large farms or plantations that produced cash crops like tobacco. The following was written of Virginia at the close of the Seventeenth Century:

"For want of Towns, Markets, and Money, there is but little Encouragement for Tradesmen and Artificers, and therefore little Choice of them, and their Labour [is] very dear in the Country. Then a great deal of [a] Tradesman's Time being necessarily spent in going and coming to and from his Work, in dispers'd County Plantations, and his Pay being generally in straggling Parcels of Tobacco, the Collection Whereof costs about 10 per cent, and the best of this Pay coming but once a year [when the crop is harvested], so that he cannot ... [accumulate for sale] a small stock, as

Tradesmen do in England and Elsewhere, All this
occasions the Dearth of all Tradesmen's Labour, and
likewise the Discouragement, Scarcity, and
Insufficiency of Tradesmen."

Wanting artisans, southern masters trained slaves in
the skills needed on plantations. Because the wealthier
plantations also carried on industrial enterprises — a
large plantation may have had much in common with a
medieval manor — the variety as well as the number of
skilled African-Americans was great. Slaves were not
only farmers, but also carpenters, coopers, stone masons,
millers, blacksmiths, shoemakers, spinners, and weavers.
Skilled slaves were frequently hired out by their masters
to the owners of smaller plantations. White artificers
tried to check the growth of skilled slave labor, but
their efforts were futile because planters believed that
slave labor was more economical than free labor. Not
until after the Civil War were whites successful in
excluding blacks from skilled work.

There was industry in the Colonies from their early
days. The typical industrial unit established by a
colonial entrepreneur was small, composed of one or two
masters and a like number of apprentices. Corporations,
which are a means for many persons to pool their
resources in order to create a large capitalization, were
not known in colonial times. At least one reason for
this fact is that each corporation needed a special
charter from the legislature; there were no general
incorporation laws before the Nineteenth Century. Home
work was also common. For example, weaving and shoe
making were usually done in the worker's home from
materials (and sometimes implements) supplied by an
entrepreneur. However, at the time of the Revolution,
some factories were beginning to develop, as in spinning,
and, of course, this development continued thereafter.

Colonial workers tended to be independent because
they were in great demand. (The reader will understand
what this means in a few years when one tries to make a
building contractor keep to a schedule.) The scarcity of
workers, their high wages, and their personal
independence combined to yield colonial workers much more
esteem than European workers enjoyed. Even a humble
tailor like Thomas Stebbins of Springfield, if he were a
man of parts, could be elected second in command of the
town militia. Add to this the work ethic that we have
already discussed, and the ease with which workers could
become land owners or shop keepers, and the result was
that the social class structure of England did not take

deep root in American soil. Two consequences of this fact may be noted. First, respect for the worker had much to do with the growth of democracy in this country. As the reader knows, Colonials did not unanimously desire the Revolution; perhaps one-third of the population were loyalists, and another third were undecided. But the artisans were vigorous and radical supporters of independence. A second consequence of the failure of English class structure to grow in American soil is that, when workers on both sides of the Atlantic began in the Eighteenth Century to unite into associations to further their political and economic goals — that is, when labor unions started to develop — the histories of English and American unions diverged sharply. The differences may be traced partly to the greater economic democracy in the United States and the lack of a strong sense of class identity among American workers.

So far we have been describing economic and social relationships in the Colonies. Now let us turn to legal relationships, that is, how the law conceived of the economic and social relationships that have been described.

During the Eighteenth Century, and for centuries before that, the basic legal unit was the household. Simplifying somewhat, we can say that the head of the household was the man. Vis-a-vis the rest of the world, he acted for the entire household; that is, the law took cognizance only of his actions or of actions that he authorized. For example, only he could buy or sell property or enter into a contract. No one else in the household could enter into legally binding relations with the rest of the world without his consent.

More important for our purposes was the role of the head of the household vis-a-vis other members of the household. Four major types of relationship existed, namely, husband to wife, father to child, master to servant, and master to slave. Once again, the law recognized the man as the dominant figure; wives, children, servants, and slaves were subject to his orders.

Note that the locus of the master-servant and master-slave relationships was the household. There were no free-standing places of employment. Rather, work took place within the household. One typical household was a farm. Everyone worked on the land; the boundaries of the farm and of the household were the same. A household

typical of a city was a shop, say, a blacksmith or a
tailor, but once again the working and living spaces were
on the same parcel of land. Commonly, the shop was on
the ground level and the living quarters were above. If
a member of one household hired out, that is, worked in
a second household for money, the worker became, for most
legal purposes, a member of the second household, and
was, therefore, subject to the control of the master of
that household; but the money belonged to the master of
the first household.

We noted above two general ideas that were
instantiated in the Statute of Laborers in the Fourteenth
Century and the Statute of Artificers in the Sixteenth
Century, namely, that the lord of the manor had
jurisdiction over the lives of one's workers and had a
property right in their labor. These ideas persisted in
the Colonies in the Eighteenth Century, with the lord of
the manor being replaced by the head of the household.
Indeed, the law understood the household as a small
state. The head of the household had jurisdiction over
its members in much the way that the monarch had
jurisdiction over the people of the kingdom and had a
property interest in (owned) the labor of the members of
the household.

Because of this way of conceiving human
relationships, the law of the Eighteenth Century was
concerned principally with the interests of free white
males. Let us consider children first. Suppose a farmer
agreed that his daughter would work for a neighboring
farmer for a year, and that after six months she wanted
to quit, but her new master was unwilling to release her.
The dispute was not understood as one between her and her
master; the dispute was seen as one between her father,
who formerly owned her labor, and her master, who
presently owned it. Similarly, suppose a father
apprenticed his son to a silver smith for the usual
period of seven years, and that after a year or two the
boy tired of the work and returned home. The smith could
not sue the boy; rather, the smith could sue the father
for breach of contract. Or suppose business fell off and
the smith could no longer support the boy, and so turned
him out. The father, not the boy, could sue the smith.
Or suppose the boy was on the scrawny side and did not
like hefting the smith's heavy tools; but the boy had a
good mind and he liked to read, and so he left the smith
and apprenticed himself to a printer who needed help. In
this case, the smith could sue the printer for enticing
away a servant. We need hardly add that, in all of these

cases, the law focused on the interests of the parties — the fathers and the masters; the interests of the sons and daughters were neglected.

Wives were no better off than children. An unmarried woman who lived with her parents was under her father's control. If she married, she passed to the control of her husband. She could not own property. She had to work for whomever her husband designated. She could not even keep the earnings of her labor. Gradually during the Nineteenth Century, the rights of women were recognized. For example, beginning with Arkansas in 1835, statutes allowed a married woman to own property inherited from her parents; before then, the property had become her husband's. Massachusetts in 1855 and New York in 1861 permitted women to make contracts, engage in business, and sue and be sued in court. But in most states well into the Nineteenth Century, women had no civil rights.

Slaves, of course, had no rights at all; they were property. Indeed, as the Dred Scott case affirmed, Article IV of the Constitution provided that if a slave escaped and sought asylum in another state, the master's demand for return of the slave had to be honored, even if the state in which the slave was found prohibited slavery. Slaves were so completely property that their children were also the property of their masters. President Lincoln's Emancipation Proclamation freed the slaves of the Confederacy. The Thirteenth Amendment freed all the rest of the slaves in America. The Fourteenth Amendment guaranteed former slaves equal rights under the law. And the Fifteenth Amendment granted freedmen the right to vote. As a practical matter, however, the Fourteenth and Fifteenth Amendments were useless to persons of color until the middle of the Twentieth Century.

All of these relationships — parent-child, husband-wife, master-servant, and master-slave — were status relationships. As such, they were defined by law and custom. By virtue of occupying the statuses of master and servant, the master had jurisdiction over the servant and owned the servant's labor. There is another way in which relationships can be conceived. We can think of them as contractual, that is, as the result of agreement by free and independent parties. The parties in a status relationship have little power to change it. Rights and duties are fixed and inescapable. But the parties in a contractual relationship have almost complete power over it. They specify what their rights and duties are. In fact, there is no relationship at all unless the parties agree to it.

The theory of contract in general became increasingly influential during the Nineteenth Century, and the law of contract was extended to domains which had not been thought of as contractual in the past. This occurred primarily because of the growth of manufacturing and commerce, but it had effects on other areas as well. As contract became the paradigm for understanding the exchange of money for labor, the ideas waned that the master had jurisdiction over the servant and owned the servant's labor.

Of course, some relationships were not affected at all; they remain status relationships to this day. The parent-child relationship is still a status relationship in the eyes of the law. Minors have no legal right to bargain with their parents over the parents' right to control their children, and parents have no legal right to bargain with their minors over the parents' duty to support and care for the children.

Some relationships were partially modified by the growth of contract law. The husband-wife relationship today is partly status and partly contractual. For example, if one spouse dies without a will, the law provides that the surviving spouse will inherit a significant share of the property of the decedent. (This assumes that the surviving spouse did not murder the decedent, in which case the rules are a little different.) This right derives from the status of the parties. But the law allows spouses to enter into an antenuptial agreement, that is, a contract, that can modify the surviving spouse's right to inherit property.

And some relationships were wholly transformed by contract law. The employment relationship today is almost entirely contractual. It is usually established informally; the boss says, "You're hired." Therefore, we will focus on the law as it applies to this relationship, which is not based on a written contract. This law is known as "employment at will," and it has been in place since the latter part of the Nineteenth Century. The doctrine is simple: the worker may quit a job at any time and for any reason, and the employer may discharge a worker at any time and for any reason (except for a few reasons that have recently been specified by statute, for example, racial discrimination).

Employment at will is so strongly entrenched in the law that evidence that the parties intended a different result is often ignored. For example, suppose a worker is discharged and she sues, claiming that the employer offered her a permanent job. She concedes that the employer had a right to discharge her if the job were abolished or if her performance were unsatisfactory, but she claims that her performance was satisfactory and the job still exists. In almost every state, her case will be dismissed. Some exceptions to employment at will have developed in recent years, and we will consider them in due course.

In theory, employment at will is perfectly fair to both parties. The employer makes an offer of a job with certain wages and working conditions, and the worker decides whether or not to accept the offer. If a worker wants more money or easier working conditions, the worker is free to ask the employer to agree to a change — and to quit if the employer refuses to change. Similarly, if the employer wants to pay less money or demand additional work, and if the worker does not agree, the employer is free to discharge the worker and find another.

In practice, employment at will allows employers to exercise nearly all of the authority that masters formerly held over servants, but frees employers of nearly all of the duties that they formerly had to honor. As an individual, the worker's only remedy for low wages, unreasonable demands, or dangerous working conditions, is to quit; and this is not a practical remedy in many cases. Also, by permitting layoffs when business slows down, the doctrine allows employers to shift a large part of the cost of bad management decisions, or declining economic conditions, or both, from the company to the worker.

Whether fair or unfair, employment at will has been the default position of labor and employment law for the past one hundred twenty-five years. In a real way, the rest of this course is about efforts to modify employment at will.

Sources

Innes, Stephen, Labor in a New Land: Economy and Society in Seventeenth-Century Springfield (Princeton U. Press, 1983).

Morris, Richard B., <u>Government and Labor in Early America</u> (Columbia U. Press, 1946).

Steinfeld, Robert J., <u>The Invention of Free Labor</u> (U. of North Carolina Press, 1991).

QUESTIONS FOR REFLECTION

1. In what ways was the life of a colonial worker different from the life of a worker today?

2. Was the life of a colonial worker better in any way than the life of a worker today?

3. Is it possible that we would return to any of the colonial labor policies? If so, which policies and under what circumstances?

Ω

The Strike as a Criminal Conspiracy

EARLY NINETEENTH CENTURY

INTRODUCTION

Let us now take a brief look at concerted or joint action by workers in England and the colonies. The reader is familiar with medieval craft guilds. They were not unions of workers, but trade associations of master craftsones, and they exercised considerable power over the quality and price of products, the compensation of the journeyones who worked under the masters, and the system of apprenticeship by which new workers learned and entered the trade. Although guilds never took firm hold in America, in the early days, especially in the northern colonies, governments allowed some associations of craftsones, such as shoemakers, tailors, and carpenters, to exercise powers similar to those enjoyed by European guilds.

Medieval guilds were protected from non-residents' entering town and competing with local masters. There was some of this in the colonies as well, for example, building tradesones in New York City complained about low-priced competitors coming from the Jerseys. (Is there anything new under the sun?)

Another way that medieval guilds protected their members was that workers were prohibited from changing occupations. Freedom of occupational choice was restricted well into the Eighteenth Century in the colonies. Also, occupations were strictly defined. A leather tanner could not make shoes, nor could a shoemaker tan leather.

These restrictions were undermined by the growth of laissez faire philosophy. During the Eighteenth Century, the early guilds, the restrictions on competition from non-residents, and the prohibition on changing occupations disappeared in the colonies.

Although many trades were unregulated, certain trades were licensed and regulated as today's public utilities are. Licensed masters — examples are bakers, coopers, butchers, porters, carones — enjoyed a monopoly in their trades, in exchange for which the government set the prices of their products or services. Licensing of quasi-public trades, together with price-fixing, continued through the Revolution in many parts of the colonies.

Masters in both licensed and unlicensed trades sometimes withheld their labor in order to induce the government to authorize higher prices. We say "withheld their labor," rather than "struck," because we want to make clear that these were masters, not employees. Of course, masters usually worked actively at their trades, so they may properly be called workers; but they were definitely not employees.

As for combinations of journeyones, that is, of employees, instances are rare. Friendly societies appeared in the Eighteenth Century, but their purposes were to provide assistance to ill or injured workers and to pay funeral costs and benefits to the families of deceased members. Masters were permitted to join. Among the earliest combinations in the colonies of journeyones seeking higher wages were tailors and printers who struck in New York City in the 1760s and 1770s. Such strikes were the result of ad hoc groups, not of permanent labor unions. In contrast, combinations of masters to set the wages of employees were common and legal; indeed, these trade associations sometimes published their actions in newspapers.

Permanent associations of workers — that is, labor unions — emerged in America after the Revolution. The causes include the rise of the factory, the transition from custom-made items to wholesale production, the concentration of workers in the expanding industries, and the workers' realization that they were unlikely ever to earn enough money to buy land or set up their own shops. Philadelphia was the leading city in the early years of the nation, and labor union activity there was perhaps the most intense. For example, shoemakers, called "cordwainers," formed a union and struck at least three times before the end of the century.

Employers' response to organization by workers was to strengthen and increase in number the employers' trade associations. At least one of the cordwainers' strikes in Philadelphia occurred after the employers' association had lowered wages.

The following report of a case is unusual. Usually, we read one or more opinions written by the judge(s) who decided the case. In the <u>Philadelphia Cordwainers</u> case, however, we read the arguments of the parties' attorneys to the jury and the judge's charge to the jury.

The defendants in the case were journeymen cordwainers (shoe workers) who were indicted for the crime of conspiracy. A conspiracy is a combination of two or more persons to perform an unlawful act or to perform a lawful act by unlawful means. The indictment contained three charges or counts, that is, alleged three separate crimes. The counts were similar in that each count alleged the defendants had engaged in a conspiracy, but different in that each conspiracy had a different purpose. Thus, all three counts alleged that the defendants had combined in an association (a proto-labor union) to achieve a specific purpose. The unlawful purposes were

Count 1: to work only at rates set by the association
Count 2: to prevent other workers from accepting lower rates
Count 3: to refuse to work in the same shop as anyone who had broken any of the association's rules (for example, by working for lower rates).

These facts were largely true and, therefore, the issue was whether these facts amounted to a criminal conspiracy. Here follow excerpts from the arguments to the jury of the prosecution and the defense and the charge of the judge to the jury. The paragraph numbers in braces have been added by the editor for convenience of reference.

As you read the arguments and the charge to the jury, focus on the following issues:

¶ 3. Does illegal behavior by one party justify illegal behavior by the other party?

The *Philadelphia Cordwainers* Case

¶3. Had the masters previously attempted to control the price of labor?

¶¶29-30.   Does the law prohibit only physical coercion, or does the law also prohibit economic coercion?

¶¶ 29-30. Did the defendants use economic force to compel any journeyone to leave one's job or to compel any master to discharge a journeyone?

The Philadelphia Cordwainers' Case[a]
3 Commons and Gilmore, *A Documentary History of American Industrial Society* 55 ff.
(1806)

{The order of some of the paragraphs has been changed, and some paragraphs have been divided into several separate paragraphs. The numbering of the paragraphs, however, indicates their place in the original document.}

Mr. HOPKINSON {for the prosecution}

{1} ... The facts, which form the basis of this controversy, seem so well understood on both sides; so little contrariety appears in the testimony respecting them, that I may say, the dispute is more a question of principle than of evidence....

{2} The cause is an important one.... It is said on the one side to involve an important principle of civil liberty, that men in their transactions with others, have a right to judge in their own behalf, and value their labour as they please: on the contrary, we shall shew that the claims and conduct of the defendants are contrary to just government, equal laws, and that due subordination to which every member of the

---

[a] {A word about the use of brackets and braces in these materials is necessary. By convention, brackets are used by a writer to indicate additions by the writer to another person's words. For example —

"Palmadesso said, 'He [Mozart] was a great musician, but they [the Beatles] were far superior.'"

The writer of this sentence, who is anonymous, is quoting what another person, Palmadesso, said. The writer adds in brackets information that will help the reader understand what Palmadesso meant. This convention works satisfactorily when only two persons are involved, but a problem arises when three or more persons are involved — as in these materials, in which three persons may have something to say: the first person is the author of the opinion; the second is the person whose words the first person is quoting; and the third is your editor. The author of the opinion may have added to the words of the second person, and your editor may wish to add to the words of either the author or the second person. A way is needed to distinguish between additions by the author of the opinion and additions by your editor. Accordingly, in these materials brackets enclose additions supplied by the author of the opinion, and braces enclose additions supplied by your editor. For example —

"Learned Hand {who was a highly regarded judge in the first half of the Twentieth Century} is reported to have said as he sentenced a defendant to prison, 'Don't do the crime [the defendant was convicted of assault] if you can't do the time [he got five years].'"

The anonymous writer is quoting Judge Hand. Hand said, "Don't do the crime if you can't do the time." The anonymous writer added that the crime was assault and the sentence was five years. Your editor adds that Hand was a respected judge.}

community is bound to submit ... all these are essentially connected with the present prosecution.

{3} It has been attempted to be shewn {by the defendants}, that the master workmen {i.e., the employers}, associated and formed themselves into similar societies, and this they say constitutes a defence for the defendants; if the fact be so ... two wrongs never make a right. If the masters have associated in the manner stated, they are amenable to the law in the same manner as the associated journeymen. ... yet in justice to them, I must say, that all proof of this sort has failed; there has been no proof shewn, that the masters associated for unlawful, or oppressive purposes; or that when associated, they ever attempt to controul the journeymen. There is nothing like it in the constitution and minutes, that were read from the book produced. They say they associated for the convenience of the trade; nothing is said of raising or decreasing wages; nothing relative to any provision or declaration, as to the price of workmanship, &c.

{4} ... {I}t has been proved, a certain number of persons, among whom are the present defendants, associated for several distinct and criminal purposes. This is the gi(s)t of the prosecution, it is not for what any one man of them has done, that the state prosecutes: the offence is in the combination.

{5} Why a combination in such case is criminal, will not be difficult to explain: we live under a government composed of a constitution and laws ... and every man is obliged to obey the constitution, and the laws made under it. When I say he is bound to obey these, I mean to state the whole extent of his obedience. Do you feel yourselves bound to obey any other laws, enacted by any other legislature, than that of your own choice? Shall these, or any other body of men, associate for the purpose of making new laws, laws not made under the constitutional authority, and compel their fellow citizens to obey them, under the penalty of their existence? This prosecution contravenes no man's right, it is to prevent an infringement of right; it is in favour of the equal liberty of all men, this is the policy of our laws; but if private associations and clubs, can make constitutions and laws for us ... if they can associate and make by-laws paramount, or inconsistent with the state laws; What, I ask, becomes of the liberty of the people, about which so much is prated; about which the opening counsel made such a flourish!

{6} It is not intended to take away the right of any man to put his own price upon his own labour; they may ask what they please, individually. But when they associate, combine and conspire, to prevent others from taking what they deem a sufficient compensation for their labour ... and where they undertake to regulate the trade of the city, they undertake to regulate what interferes with your rights and mine. I now am to speak to the policy of permitting such associations. This is a large, encreasing, manufacturing city. Those best acquainted with our situation, believe that manufactures will, bye and bye, become one of its chief means of support. A vast quantity of manufactured articles are already exported to the West Indies, and the southern states; we rival the supplies from England in many things, and great sums are annually received in returns. It is then proper to support this manufacture. Will you permit men to destroy it, who have no permanent stake in the city; men who can pack up their all in a knapsack, or carry them in their pockets to New York or Baltimore? These manufactures are not confined to boots and shoes ... though that is very important, as you learn from Mr. Bedford, that he could export 4000 dollars worth, annually. Other articles, to a great amount, are manufactured here, and exported; such as coaches and other pleasurable carriages; windsor chairs, and particular manufactures of iron. I cannot make a calculation of the importance of manufactures to this city.

{7} If the court and jury shall decide, that journeymen may associate together, and determine that none shall work under certain prices; then, when orders arrive for considerable quantities of any article, the association may determine to raise the wages, and reduce the contractors to diminish their profit; to sustain a loss, or to abandon the execution of the orders, as was done in Bedford's case, who told you he could have afforded to execute the orders he obtained at the southward, had wages remained the same as when he left Philadelphia. When they found he had a contract, they took advantage of his necessity. What was done by the journeymen shoemakers may be done by those of every other trade, or manufacturer in the city.... A few more things of this sort, and you will break up the manufactories; the masters will be afraid to make a contract, therefore he must relinquish the export trade, and depend altogether upon the profits of the work of Philadelphia, and confine his supplies altogether to the city. The last turn-out {strike} had like to have produced that effect: Mr. Ryan told you he had intended to confine himself to bespoke work {i.e., custom-made orders}.

{8} It must be plain to you, that the master employers have no particular interest in the thing ... if they pay higher wages, you must pay higher for the articles. They, in truth, are protecting the community. Nor is it merely the advance of wages that encreases the price to the consumer, the master must have some compensation for the advance of his cash, and the credit he frequently gives. They have no interest to serve in the prosecution; they have no vindictive passions to gratify ... they merely stand as the guardians of the community from imposition and rapacity.

{9} A great rise was attempted, in 1805, on prices mutually agreed upon in 1804, without reason, in a mild winter, when wood and every necessary of life was unusually cheap.... I can see no pretext for the attempt, but the encreasing avarice of these men. They took the advantage of their masters, I mean their employers in the fall of 1805, when the business was becoming brisk; when they knew the employers must have work done for their customers; they ask{ed} from seventy-five to twenty-five cents advance on making boots, according to their quality. Is this spirit of exaction to be encouraged? Will the community be satisfied to be at the mercy of these men? Your verdict must determine, whether it is to be continued or suppressed: nor can they plead the conduct of the masters as an apology. You heard but one witness say they ever reduced the prices of workmanship in the dullest season; and he speaks only of a reduction of twenty-seven cents, viz., from two dollars seventy-seven cents to two dollars fifty.

{10} If this conspiracy was to be confined to the persons themselves, it would not be an offence against the law; but they go further. There are two counts in the indictment; you are to consider each, and to give your verdict on each. The first is for contriving, and intending, unjustly, and oppressively, to encrease and augment the wages usually allowed them. The other for endeavouring to prevent, by threats, menaces, and other unlawful means, other journeymen from working at the usual prices, and that they compelled others to join them.

{11} If these persons claim the right to put the price on their own work, if they say their labour is their own, and they are the judges of its value, why not admit the same right to others? If it is the right of Dubois, and the other defendants, is it not equally the right of Harrison and Cummings? We stand up for the right of the journeymen, as well as of the masters. The last turn-out was carried by a small majority ... 60 against 50, or thereabout: shall 60 unreasonable men, perhaps single men, having no one to provide for but themselves, distress and bring to destruction, 50 married men with their families? Let the 60 put what price they please on their own work; but the others are free agents also: leave them free, or talk no more of equal rights, of independence, or of liberty.

{12} It may be answered, that when men enter into a society, they are bound to conform to its rules; they may say, the majority ought to govern the minority ... granted ... but they ought to leave a man free to join, or not to join the society. If I go into a country I am bound to submit to its laws, but surely I may judge, whether or not I will go there. The society has no right to force you into its body, and then say you shall obey its rules under severe penalties. By their constitution you find, and from their own lips I must take the words, that though a man wants no more wages than he gets, he must join in a turn-out. The man who seeks an asylum in this country, from the arbitrary laws of other nations, is coerced into their society, though he does not work in the article intended to be raised; he must leave his seat and join the turn-out. This was Harrison's case ... he worked exclusively in shoes, they in boots; he was a stranger, he was a married man, with a large family; he represented his distressed condition; they entangle him, but shew no mercy. The dogs of vigilance find, by their scent, the emigrant in his cellar or garret: they drag him forth, they tell him he must join them; he replies, I am well satisfied as I am.... No ... they chase him from shop to shop; they allow him no resting place, till he consents to be one of their body; he is expelled {from} society, driven from his lodgings, proscribed from working; he is left no alternative, but to perish in the streets, or seek some other asylum on a more hospitable shore. To the prayers of Harrison and Dobbins, they gave this stern answer: we hear your prayer, but we will not relax ... you may perish, but we will not permit you to work.

{13} I will now proceed to shew you what the law is, and you will receive from the court more information on the subject. It will be seen, that the mere combination to raise wages is considered an offence at common law: the reason is founded in common sense. Suppose the bakers were to combine, and agree not to sell a loaf of bread, only for one week, under a dollar, would not this be an injury to the community? ... Certainly it would: and few men, unless their pockets were filled with money, could support it for any considerable length of time. All combinations to regulate the price of commodities {are} against the law. Extend the case to butchers, and all others who deal in articles of prime necessity, and the good policy of the law is then apparent.

{14} My intention, in shewing what the objects of the society were in 1799, was to convince you that the present defendants, and the majority of the society, were aiming at the same point in the turn-out of last fall. Some of the acts, stated by Harrison and Dobbins, may not have been personal acts of the defendants; but in cases of combinations and conspiracies, each must answer for the whole: the act of one is the act of each, and to this point is 2 M'Nally, p. 611. 'The existence of a conspiracy being proved, &c. each of the parties is liable.'

{15} All the defendants have been proved to have taken an active part in this combination, by giving notice to the masters, that unless they accept the terms proposed, they will be subjected to all the penalties of their club; such as were inflicted on the shops in 1799....

{16} This case has exhibited such a tissue of infractions of personal rights by the club of journeymen shoemakers, that was our state legislature to dare to pass such laws as these men have passed, it would be a just cause of rebellion. I will go further, and say, it would produce rebellion if the legislature should say, that a man should not work under a certain sum ... it would lead to beggary, and no man would submit to it. Then, shall a secret body exercise a power over our fellow-citizens, which the legislature itself is not invested with? The fact is, they do exercise a sort of authority the legislature dare not assume.

{17} It now rests with the jury, under the direction of the court to say, whether we shall in future be governed by secret clubs, instead of the constitution and laws of the state; a verdict of not guilty, will sanction combinations of the most dangerous kind; a contrary verdict will give the victory to the known and established laws of the commonwealth.

Mr. FRANKLIN for the defense

{18} Has the master then the sole right of determining the wages which are to be given for the labour of his journeymen? This would be too arbitrary a power for any man to contend for; it would be an insult to your understanding, to insist upon it. The real value of labour, in a country, must depend upon a variety of circumstances, which neither the master or his journeymen can in any way controul. As to the price which any particular employer may pay his workmen, that must be regulated by the contract between them. If they can mutually agree upon a price to be given, the master is bound to give, and the journeymen must abide by the sum stipulated. A different price will be given to different workmen; some deserve more than others, either on account of their greater industry and application, or their greater skill and ingenuity. But if the employer and journeymen cannot agree upon the work to be done, or the price to be paid, neither is bound to recede from his determination.

{19} If, then, any one man has this right, has not every other man the same privilege? If one journeyman has a right to adopt measures to prevent the effects of the obstinacy or combination of the master shoemakers, may not a number unite for the same object? A purpose innocent or lawful in one man, cannot be otherwise in a society or body of men. Supposing, therefore, that the facts charged in the first count were true; that the men refused to work but at certain prices, it is no crime, and they cannot be punished for it.

{20} But independently of those grounds, we have fully shewn, that the demand of those men was reasonable and just. The master workmen had raised the price of these very articles; this is in proof, not only on the testimony of the journeymen, but two of the masters....

{21} It is to be remembered that whatever circumstances arose from the transactions in 1799, they are not to be imputed to the journeymen, but to the master; for Mr. Harrison is proved to be mistaken in saying, that the turn-out in that year, was for an advance of wages; it is in evidence, that it was intended to prevent the masters from lowering the wages of the journeymen, which they had attempted; you must be sensible how difficult it is for the journeymen to resist the masters, who are rich, and abound in the means to support a contest; the journeymen are poor and destitute of means, though on that occasion, it appears the masters were obliged to abandon their scheme of reduction. The journeymen obtained the same wages they had had; you may, therefore, be certain they were reasonable, or they would not be given by men who could continue the resistance.

{22} Now, if any journeyman who chose to work at the rates or prices offered by the employers, contrary to the wish of other journeymen, were threatened by them, or any of them, with injury to his person or property, he has a complete and ample remedy provided for him by law without resorting to the measures which have been adopted. He might have them bound over to their good behaviour, and if they afterwards were guilty of any threats, their recognizance would be forfeited, and they would be obliged to pay the penalty. But it does not appear that either of the defendants or members of that association, uttered any menaces or were guilty of any assault. Blair said, some of his people were beaten, in 1797, but that is not brought home to either of the defendants.

{23} The third charge branches forth into three divisions. First ... Combining to make unlawful and arbitrary bye laws. What proof is there of the association having made any unlawful or arbitrary bye laws? ... None.... But supposing that such laws had been enacted by the society, are the defendants to answer for them in this way? Should it not appear clearly, that they assented to them? When the question was taken, the defendants might have been in the minority; and shall they be punished for an act of the society of which they have shewn their disapprobation? It appears in evidence, that some of the defendants opposed the adoption of the resolutions which were passed on this very occasion.

[Here he reviewed the testimony on this point.]

{24} The positions advanced by the prosecuting counsel on this subject, might be carried to a very alarming extent. If his sentiments be correct, there are many associations in this city, of high standing, which are acting illegally, and may be made the objects of a criminal prosecution. These associations are governed by rules and bye laws, which, however correct in themselves and proper for the regulation of the members of the body, are far from being conformable to the standard by which he seems to think the legality of such rules is to be tried.

{25} I will mention but one instance, and refer to your recollection for numerous other examples which might be adduced. A large and respectable society in this city has, among many excellent laws for its government, one which Mr. Hopkinson might think very arbitrary and oppressive. Some gentlemen whom I see on the jury, are well acquainted with the society and the rule to which I allude. It is to this effect: That such members as shall marry in any other mode than that prescribed by the rules of their discipline ... though it might be in strict conformity to the laws of the land ... and such as shall marry any other than members ... shall be expelled from the society ... nor can they be restored until they have made a full acknowledgment of the error of their conduct.

{26} On the trial of an indictment, against the members of this society, for combining to make arbitrary and oppressive bye laws, large room would be afforded to the gentleman for the display of his eloquence in expatiating on the impropriety of laws, which impose so severe a penalty on a legal and justifiable act ... on the impolicy of rules manifestly tending to create a restriction on the frequency of marriages, and a variety of other topics which his ingenuity would furnish. In fact, according to the doctrine which he has laid down, I know of no society which can legally exist ... if it adopt any other rules, or bye laws than the constitution or laws of the state.

{27} Second.... Refusing to work for any master or person, that should employ any journeymen who infringed the said law.

{28} Third.... Preventing by threats, menaces, or other injuries, any other workmen from working for such master.

{29} I shall consider these two subjects together. Is there the slightest evidence, that the defendants ever compelled a single journeyman to leave this employer? How did they compel? Did they use any violence? If they had, they were subject to the laws and might have been individually punished for it. But neither violence, threats, nor menaces, were used.... No man was the object of force or compulsion.... The very head and font of their offending was their refusing to work for any master who employed such journeymen as infringed the rules of the society to which they belonged.

{30} This I deny to be an offence. There is no crime in my refusing to work with a man who is not of the same association with myself. Supposing the ground of my refusal to be ever so unreasonable or ridiculous ... to be in reality, mere caprice or whim.... Still it is no crime.... The motive for my refusal may be illiberal, but it furnishes no legal foundation for a prosecution: I cannot be indicted for it. Every man may chuse his company, or refuse to associate with any one whose company may be disagreeable to him, without being obliged to give a reason for it: and without violating the laws of the land....

{31} I will conclude this part of my argument, with the remarks of a very sensible and judicious writer, which are so apposite to the subject before you, that I think it right to submit them to your consideration. 1. Smith's *Wealth of Nations*, page 89:

"Workmen desire to get as much, masters to give as little, as possible. The former are disposed to combine in order to raise, the latter in order to lower. It is not, however, difficult to foresee which of the two parties must, upon all ordinary occasions, have the advantage in the dispute, and force the other into a compliance with their terms. The masters being fewer in number, can combine much more easily; and the law, besides, authorises, or at least does not prohibit their combinations, while it prohibits those of the workmen. We have no acts of parliament against combining to lower the price of work; but many against combining to raise it. In all such disputes the masters can hold out much longer. A landlord, a farmer, a master manufacturer, or merchant, though they did not employ a single workman, could generally live a year or two upon the stocks which they have already acquired. Many workmen could not subsist a week, few could subsist a month, and scarce any a year without employment. In the long run, the workman may be as necessary to his master, as his master is to him; but the necessity is not so immediate. We rarely hear, it has been said, of the combinations of masters; though frequently of those of workmen. But whoever imagines, upon this account, that masters rarely combine, is as ignorant of the world as the subject. Masters are always and every where in a sort of tacit, but constant and uniform combination, not to raise the wages of labour above their actual rate. To violate this combination is every where a most unpopular action, and a sort of reproach to a master among his neighbours and equals. We seldom, indeed, hear of this combination, because it is the usual, and one may say, the natural state of things, which nobody ever hears of. Masters, too, sometimes enter into particular combinations to sink the wages of labour below this rate. These are always conducted with the utmost silence and secrecy, till the moment of execution, and when the workmen yield, as they sometimes do, without resistance, though severely felt by them, they are never heard of by other people."[b]

---

[b] {Immediately following this passage, Adam Smith wrote the following, which is as true today as it was in 1776.

"Such combinations, however, are frequently resisted by a contrary defensive combination of the workmen; who sometimes too, without any provocation of this kind, combine of their own accord to raise the price of their labour. Their usual pretences are, sometimes the high price of provisions; sometimes the great profit which their masters make by their work. But whether their combinations be offensive or defensive, they are always abundantly heard of. In order to bring the point to a speedy decision, they have always recourse to the loudest clamour, and sometimes to the most shocking violence and outrage. They are desperate, and act with the folly and extravagance of desperate men, who must either starve, or frighten their master into an immediate compliance with their demands. The masters upon these occasions are just as clamorous upon the other side, and never cease to call aloud for the assistance of the civil magistrate {i.e., police and judges}, and the rigorous execution of those laws which have been enacted with so much

(continued...)

{32} I feel for the situation of the court and jury, occasioned by the length of this trial; but particularly for the gentleman who is still indisposed: I will, therefore, be as short as possible in what I have to add. I had reached that part of my subject, which relates to the law of the case, and on which this prosecution is said to be grounded. 1. Hawk. p. 348, "to prejudice a third person ... to impoverish him is criminal in a confederacy." This comes within the meaning of the rule. I was willing to admit, that a conspiracy to do an illegal act was criminal. To prejudice or impoverish a third person, would be immoral and wicked in an individual, therefore, in more. But there are many acts of an individual which may, in their effects, prejudice another, which are not unlawful or indictable. For instance, there is a house not far distant from us, which is situated between a blacksmith's and tallow-chandler's shop; the tenants suffer great inconvenience from the smoke and smell. These shops also prejudice the owner, for he cannot obtain so high a rent for his house, as if they were removed. The workmen employed in them, therefore, occasion a very serious inconvenience to a third person; but who can think them criminal? And yet, according to the doctrine contended for, when carried to its full extent, if each of these shops belonged to a society, the individuals who composed it might be indicted for a conspiracy to prejudice and impoverish a third person, and be punished by fine and imprisonment at the discretion of the court. A man has a right to refuse to work or associate with another; if he refuse, it may operate an injury to the employer, but he is not answerable for that injury.

{33} ... If this be correct, what are all your town meetings, your ward committees, and your associations to support particular candidates for office? These are combinations to maintain one another in very important matters: but, if the authority cited, be law here, they are illegal ... you must discontinue them, or you render yourselves liable to an indictment for a conspiracy: they are all, all unlawful.

{34} It is lawful for a man to improve himself in any art or science, but he must not join with others for the purpose. What then becomes of the numerous

---

[b] (...continued)

severity against the combinations of servants, labourers, and journeymen. The workmen, accordingly, very seldom derive any advantage from the violence of those tumultuous combinations, which, partly from the interposition of the civil magistrate, partly from the superior steadiness of the masters, partly from the necessity which the greater part of the workmen are under of submitting for the sake of present subsistence, generally end in nothing, but the punishment or ruin of the ringleaders."

Adam Smith, *An Inquiry into the Nature and Causes of the Wealth of Nations*, v. I, pp. 84-85 (Oxford U. Press, 1976). }

literary associations which do so much honor to Philadelphia? What fate awaits the academy of fine arts, of which the learned counsel is so zealous and useful a member?

{35} It is an act of virtue to assist the poor; but to unite with others for the purpose is criminal. What then are all your charitable and benevolent societies, but unlawful combinations, and punishable by this law?

{36} It is lawful for a man to be active in the promotion and encouragement of trade, manufactures, and agriculture; but a society formed for the purpose, becomes a wicked and unlawful confederacy. Your Chamber of Commerce must therefore be closed, and your manufacturing and agricultural societies be dissolved.

{37} Our constitution says that "the citizens have a right in a peaceable manner to assemble together for the common good." If the manner, therefore, in which the defendants met for the purpose of their association was peaceable, it completely destroys the foundation of the present prosecution.

Mr. RODNEY {for the defense}

{38} It is nothing more or less than this, whether the wealthy master shoemakers of this populous and flourishing city, shall charge you and me what price they please for our boots and shoes, and at the same time have the privilege of fixing the wages of the poor journeymen they happen to employ. They may color it as they please. I care not what complection they give it, or in what specious garb they may array it, the simple and naked question is that which I have stated.

{39} You are called to decide for the first time, in this free country, and to fix the precedent, in favour of the doctrine contained in this indictment. The prosecutors,[c] not content with building costly mansions, rapidly amassing fortunes, aspire to lay up their plums annually, and they will do it, if you once give them the privilege of fixing the prices of those who are to work for them; to discover all this does not require day light; a candle, wax taper, or a lantern will be sufficient for the purpose.

{40} Let the jury take out the book of the masters' society, and they will find ample powers vested in them to regulate and fix the prices of the different articles of their trade; and to form a league to reduce the wages of their journeymen. The 5th article of their constitution, declares, that after thirty members have subscribed, none shall be admitted who offers any boots or shoes for sale in the public market, or who advertises the price of their articles in the public newspapers. Where is the harm of

---

[c] {Rather than an officer of government like the district attorney, the prosecutors of this case were the master shoemakers. — ed.}

advertising the price of boots and shoes? It is a masonic secret, they will not submit it to vulgar inspection.... Another article of the society of the 13th of April 1789, declares that the society shall consult together for the general "good of the trade, &c." ... What language can be more comprehensive or expressive than this? Within its capacious grasp there is no object! no subject of their professional interest which may not be fairly included!

{41} If it is for the general good of the trade, to raise the price of boots half a dollar a pair, and to reduce, at the same time, the journeymen's wages for making them, the other half dollar a pair, about which you find they have no squeamishness, this clause would authorize them to do it.... It is for the good of the trade and not for the good of the public that they associated.

{42} My word for it, this indictment has not originated from motives of friendship for us, nor is it thus zealously supported with a view to our interest or that of their customers. The very endeavor to impose such a belief upon you, must prove vain and fatal to their cause. Their attempt to mask their object, which they would blush to reveal; and to cover their selfish views, with the mantle of pure friendship for us; and sincere attachment to our interests; and of genuine patriotism, cannot succeed! This idle parade of merit on their part, and these hollow, empty pretensions to credit, for the disinterestedness of their conduct, will meet that fate, which they so justly deserve. This masked battery, which they have opened on us, will be turned by the jury on themselves.

...

Recorder LEVY {Judge, charging the jury}[d]

...

{43} No matter what their motives were, whether to resist the supposed oppression of their masters, or to insist upon extravagant compensation. No matter whether this prosecution originated from motives of public good or private interest, the question is, whether the defendants are guilty of the offences charged against them? A great part of the crimes prosecuted to trial in this court, are brought forward, I believe, from improper motives: for example, the prosecutions against tippling houses are generally occasioned by a difference taking place between the buyer and the seller, when the one is nearly as much in fault as the other. In the case of the crime of treason, it is often one of the parties who impeaches the other, and a quarrel about the felonious booty often leads to the detection of the thief. If the defendants are

---

[d] {The order of some of the paragraphs has been changed. — ed.}

guilty of the crime, no matter whether the prosecutor brings his action from motives of public good, or private resentment. The prosecutors are not on their trial, if they have proved the offence, alleged in the indictment against the defendants; and if the defendants are guilty, will any man say, that they ought not to be convicted: because the prosecution was not founded in motives of patriotism? Certainly the only question is, whether they are guilty or innocent. If they are guilty and were possessed of nine tenths of the soil of the whole United States, and the patronage of the union, it is the bounden duty of the jury to declare their guilt....

{44} What are the offences alleged against them? They are contained in the charges of the indictment.

[Here he recited from the indictment the first and second counts.]

{45} These are the questions for our consideration, and it lies with you to determine how far the evidence supports the charges, and how the principles of the law bear upon them.

{46.1} It is proper to consider, is such a combination consistent with the principles of our law, {or} injurious to the public welfare? The usual means by which the prices of work are regulated, are the demand for the article and the excellence of its fabric. Where the work is well done, and the demand is considerable, the prices will necessarily be high. Where the work is ill done, and the demand is inconsiderable, they will unquestionably be low. If there are many to consume, and few to work, the price of the article will be high: but if there are few to consume, and many to work, the article must be low. Much will depend too, upon these circumstances, whether the materials are plenty or scarce; the price of the commodity, will in consequence be higher or lower. These are the means by which prices are regulated in the natural course of things. To make an artificial regulation, is not to regard the excellence of the work or quality of the material, but to fix a positive and arbitrary price, governed by no standard, controuled by no impartial person, but dependent on the will of the few who are interested; this is the unnatural way of raising the price of goods or work. This is independent of the number of customers, or of the quality of the material, or of the number who are to do the work. It is an unnatural, artificial means of raising the price of work beyond its standard, and taking an undue advantage of the public.

{46.2} Is the rule of law bottomed upon such principles, as to permit or protect such conduct? Consider it on the footing of the general commerce of the city. Is there any man who can calculate (if this is tolerated) at what price he may safely contract to deliver articles, for which he may receive orders, if he is to be regulated by the journeymen in an arbitrary jump from one price to another? It renders it impossible for a man, making a contract for a large quantity of such goods, to know whether he shall lose or gain by it. If he makes a large contract for goods to-day, for delivery at three, six, or nine months hence, can he calculate what the prices will be then, if the journeymen in the intermediate time, are permitted to meet and raise their prices, according to their caprice or pleasure? Can he fix the price of his commodity for a future day? It is impossible that any man can carry on commerce in this way. There cannot be a large contract entered into, but what the contractor will make at his peril. He may be ruined by the difference of prices made by the journeymen in the intermediate time.

{46.3} What then is the operation of this kind of conduct upon the commerce of the city? It exposes it to inconveniences, if not to ruin; therefore, it is against the public welfare.

{46.5} Consider these circumstances as they affect trade generally. Does this measure tend to make good workmen? No: it puts the botch incapable of doing justice to his work, on a level with the best tradesman. The master must give the same wages to each. Such a practice would take away all the excitement to excel in workmanship or industry.

{46.6} Consider the effect it would have upon the whole community. If the masters say they will not sell under certain prices, as the journeymen declare they will not work at certain wages, they, if persisted in, would put the whole body of the people into their power. Shoes and boots are articles of the first necessity. If they could stand out three or four weeks in winter, they might raise the price of boots to thirty, forty, or fifty dollars a pair, at least for some time, and until a competent supply could be got from other places. In every point of view, this measure is pregnant with public mischief and private injury ... tends to demoralize the workmen ... destroy the trade of the city, and leaves the pockets of the whole community to the discretion of the concerned. If these evils were unprovided for by the law now existing, it would be necessary that laws should be made to restrain them.

{47} What has been the conduct of the defendants in this instance? They belong to an association, the object of which is, that every person who follows the trade of a journeyman shoemaker, must be a member of their body. The apprentice immediately upon becoming free, and the journeyman who comes here from distant places, are all considered members of this institution. If they do not join the body, a term of reproach is fixed upon them. The members of the body will not work with them, and they refuse to board or lodge with them. The consequence is, that every one is compelled to join the society. It is in evidence, that the defendants in this action all took a part in the last attempt to raise their wages.... Keimer was their secretary, and the others were employed in giving notice, and were of the tramping committee. If the purpose of the association is well understood, it will be found they leave no individual at liberty to join the society or reject it. They compel him to become a member. Is there any reason to suppose that the laws are not competent to redress an evil of this magnitude? The laws of this society are grievous to those not inclined to become members ... they are injurious to the community, but they are not the law of Pennsylvania. We live in a community, where the people in their collective capacity give the first momentum, and their representatives pass laws on circumstances, and occasions, which require their interference, as they arise.

{46.4} How does it operate upon {other workers}? We see that those who are in indigent circumstances, and who have families to maintain, and who get their bread by their daily labour, have declared here upon oath, that it was impossible for them to hold out; the masters might do it, but they could not: and it has been admitted by the witnesses for the defendants, that such persons, however sharp and pressing their necessities, were obliged to stand to the turn-out, or never afterwards to be employed. They were interdicted from all business in future, if they did not continue to persevere in the measures, taken by the journeymen shoemakers. Can such a regulation be just and proper? Does it not tend to involve necessitous men in the commission of crimes? If they are prevented from working for six weeks, it might induce those who are thus idle, and have not the means of maintenance, to take other courses for the support of their wives and children. It might lead them to procure it by crimes—by burglary, larceny, or highway robbery! A father cannot stand by and see, without agony, his children suffer; if he does, he is an inhuman monster; he will be driven to seek bread for them, either by crime, by beggary, or a removal from the city.

...

{48} ... {The law} says there may be cases in which what one man may do without offence, many combined may not do with impunity. It distinguishes between the object so aimed at in different transactions. If the purpose to be obtained, be an object of individual interest, it may be fairly attempted by an individual.... Many are prohibited from combining for the attainment of it.

{49} What is the case now before us? ... A combination of workmen to raise their wages may be considered in a two fold point of view: one is to benefit themselves ... the other is to injure those who do not join their society. The rule of law condemns both. If the rule be clear, we are bound to conform to it even though we do not comprehend the principle upon which it is founded. We are not to reject it because we do not see the reason of it. It is enough, that it is the will of the majority. It is law because it is their will — if it is law, there may be good reasons for it though we cannot find them out. But the rule in this case is pregnant with sound sense and all the authorities are clear upon the subject. Hawkins, the greatest authority on the criminal law, has laid it down, that a combination to maintain one another, carrying a particular object, whether true or false, is criminal ... the authority cited from 8 Mod. Rep. does not rest merely upon the reputation of that book. He gives you other authorities to which he refers. It is adopted by Blackstone, and laid down as the law by Lord Mansfield 1793, that an act innocent in an individual, is rendered criminal by a confederacy to effect it.

{50} In the profound system of law (if we may compare small things with great), as in the profound systems of Providence ... there is often great reason for an institution, though a superficial observer may not be able to discover it. Obedience alone is required in the present case, the reason may be this. One man determines not to work under a certain price and it may be individually the opinion of all: in such a case it would be lawful in each to refuse to do so, for if each stands, alone, either may extract from his determination when he pleases. In the turn-out of last fall, if each member of the body had stood alone, fettered by no promises to the rest, many of them might have changed their opinion as to the price of wages and gone to work; but it has been given to you in evidence, that they were bound down by their agreement, and pledged by mutual engagements, to persist in it, however contrary to their own judgment. The continuance in improper conduct may therefore well be attributed to the combination. The good sense of those individuals was prevented by this agreement, from having its free exercise.

{51.1} Considering it in this point of view, let us take a look at the cases which have been compared to this by the defendants' counsel. Is this like the formation of a society for the promotion of the general welfare of the community, such as to advance the interests of religion, or to accomplish acts of charity and benevolence? Is it like the society for extinguishing fires? or those for the promotion of literature and the fine arts, or the meeting of the city wards to nominate candidates for the legislature or the executive? These are for the benefit of third persons; {in contrast, the defendants'} society ... {seeks} to promote the selfish purposes of the members. The mere mention of them is an answer to all, that has been said on that point. There is no comparison between the two; they are as distinct as light and darkness. How can these cases be considered on an equal footing?

{51.2} The journeymen shoemakers have not asked an encreased price of work for an individual of their body; but they say that no one shall work, unless he receives the wages they have fixed. They could not go farther than saying, no one should work unless they all got the wages demanded by the majority; is this freedom? Is it not restraining, instead of promoting, the spirit of '76 when men expected to have no law but the Constitution, and laws adopted by it or enacted by the legislature in conformity to it? Was it the spirit of '76, that either masters or journeymen, in regulating the prices of their commodities should set up a rule contrary to the law of their country? General and individual liberty was the spirit of '76. It is our first blessing. It has been obtained and will be maintained ... we will not leave it to follow an ignus fatius {will o' the wisp}, calculated only to mislead our judgment. It is not a question, whether we shall have an imperium in imperio {state within a state}, whether we shall have, besides our state legislature a new legislature consisting of journeymen shoemakers. It is of no consequence, whether the prosecutors are two or three, or whether the defendants are ten thousand, their numbers are not to prevent the execution of our laws.... Though we acknowledge it is the hard hand of labour that promises the wealth of a nation, though we acknowledge the usefulness of such a large body of tradesmen and agree they should have every thing to which they are legally entitled; yet we conceive they ought to ask nothing more. They should neither be the slaves nor the governors of the community.

....

{The jury convicted the defendants, and they were fined eight dollars each plus court costs.}

The *Philadelphia Cordwainers* Case

COMMENT

The central issue in the case, though not stated baldly, was whether unions are legitimate organizations. This issue is not settled in the minds of many Americans today.

Recorder (judge) Levy had a theory of economics. He believed in the identity of interest among the principal actors in a capitalist economy, that is, among employers, non-union workers, and consumers; and he believed that this interest was opposed to the interest of union members. Such beliefs are held by many people today. Yet Levy did not subscribe to the school of classical economics that was emerging; a genuinely laissez faire philosophy requires that the government leave unions alone. (Nor do many of today's conservatives, who want to preserve regulation of unions.)

Levy paid no heed to Adam Smith's insight that accumulation of capital gives employers great power over workers, or he thought that such power was wholly legitimate. Many agree with this view today, but many disagree.

Levy also believed that unions were undemocratic because they exerted influence over workers, and this power was in his mind illegitimate. Unions do influence workers' lives, and the appropriate degree of union power is a contested issue today.

There is some question whether Levy correctly interpreted the law. The first question he faced was, what is the source of law? In particular, was the common law of England part of American law after the Revolution? In general, the answer was yes. Two (of many) reasons may be suggested to explain this fact. First, up to the Revolution, colonial law was in fact English law. Colonial judges and lawyers were familiar with English law; indeed, it was the only law they knew. Second, the colonials respected and valued English law. One of the causes of the Revolution was the colonials' belief that they were being denied the legal rights of Englishmen. The cry, "No taxation without representation," meant that the residents of England were not taxed without the agreement of their representatives in Parliament, and the colonials demanded the same right. This demand, of course, implied a fundamental acceptance of English political institutions. Connected with respect for English political institutions was respect for English economic institutions. England industrialized before the Colonies did and quite naturally served as a model for young America. While reserving the right to adapt English law to American conditions, American judges followed English precedents because the results they had produced in England were satisfactory. Respect for English political and economic institutions led to respect for English legal institutions.

Believing that English law was incorporated into American law, Levy faced a second question: What is the law of criminal conspiracy? Was it a crime for workers to strike? The answer to this question is unclear. Some scholars argue that Levy misinterpreted the law; other scholars argue that he read the law correctly. Without entering this debate, we may note that the law was ambiguous enough (and the arguments of the defendants' lawyers were strong enough) that Levy could have found the law to favor the workers if he had wanted to.

Whether or not Levy stated the law correctly, he stated the law in a way that would be convincing to the jury. Why should a judge have to convince a jury about the law? In those days, juries had much more power than they have today, for juries used to decide not only the facts of a case, but also the law. This fact explains why the lawyers in the Philadelphia Cordwainers case argued about the law to the jury. Recorder Levy told the jury what he thought the law was, but the jury was free to reject his view and accept the defendants' interpretation. Therefore, Levy's statement reveals what he thought would be convincing to a jury of American shop keepers. And because they convicted the defendants, we may assume the jury liked the law as Levy stated it. It is likely, then, that the jury shared Levy's beliefs about economics and unions.

In "The First American Labor Case," 41 YALE LAW JOURNAL 165 (1931), Walter Nelles argues that the Philadelphia Cordwainers case reveals a conflict of ideologies that continue to compete for our allegiance. However, the implications of the ideologies on specific issues have changed to some extent.

Disciples of Alexander Hamilton (known as Tories) believed that wealth is the principal element of human welfare and that increasing wealth is desirable. It is true that, as wealth increases, its distribution becomes less even; that is, the gap between rich and poor widens. But for Hamiltonians, wealth is good, and the abilities to create and accumulate wealth are also good. Those who become wealthy are those with more ability; this ability is good; and it follows that the wealthy deserve their exalted status. But, as Hamiltonians were quick to point out, this process is not harmful to the poor. They may have less ability to create and accumulate wealth and are, therefore, inferior to wealthy people; but the poor in a rich society are, in absolute terms, better off than they would be in a poor society. The poorest person in Ithaca is far richer than one's counterpart in Bolivia, Liberia, or India; the average American lives a better life in material terms than the greatest kings of the past. Thus, the welfare of the poor depends on the welfare of the rich. (In the parlance of Ronald Reagan, this is the trickle down theory; or, as John Kennedy said, a rising tide lifts all ships.)

Applying this ideology to specific issues, we find that <u>the Hamiltonians favored an active government</u> that would promote the growth of manufacturing. They opposed the growth of unions, which subtracted from the power of capitalists. It should not surprise the reader to learn that the jury that convicted the Philadelphia cordwainers was composed of petty bourgeois, that is, shop keepers, who subscribed to the Hamiltonian ideology.

In contrast, disciples of Thomas Jefferson (called Whigs) believed that wealth was only one element of human welfare. Jeffersonians were strong individualists; they opposed efforts by the government to restrict individual liberty. But Jeffersonians also believed that the various elements of human welfare must be kept in balance, and, if one grows out of proportion and becomes harmful, it must be cut back. Thus, manufacturing may add to wealth, but it could be restricted, or even outlawed, because of its effects on individual workers. The ideal citizens in Jeffersonian ideology were the individual farmer and the master craft worker because they worked, not solely for money, but also for personal satisfaction; their labor remained creative. (Karl Marx made the same point.) Further, Jeffersonians believed that freedom in America depended on substantial equality of citizens; among equal individuals, competition is possible because no one is strong enough to destroy the others. But if the disparity of power became too great (in other words, if wealth accumulated in the manufacturing classes), the government could properly intervene to restore balance.

Applying this ideology to specific issues, we find that the Jeffersonians took a laissez-faire approach to the economy; the government should not act to encourage the growth of manufacturing. Jeffersonians were sympathetic to labor unions, which were necessary to give workers a sense of individual dignity and to counter-balance the power that accumulation of capital conferred on employers.

Today's liberals and conservatives have scrambled the ideologies of the Founders. Modern conservatives, like Hamiltonians, favor the interests of capital and employers, but, like Jeffersonians, preach individualism and laissez faire. Modern liberals, like Jeffersonians, lean towards the interests of unions and individual consumers, but, like Hamiltonians, favor an active government. The student may decide for oneself whether the political and economic philosophies of the Founders were more coherent than the philosophies of today are.

> "That which hath been is that which shall be;
> "And that which hath been done is that which
>   shall be done;
> "And there is nothing new under the sun."

Ecclesiastes i.9.

QUESTIONS FOR REFLECTION

1. Does the outcome of the Philadelphia Cordwainers case seem consistent with the colonial labor practices, or does the case mark a change in attitudes?

2. The prosecution argues that a conspiracy of bakers to raise the price of bread would be illegal, and, therefore, a conspiracy to raise the price of labor is also illegal (see ¶ 13). This argument treats labor as an article of commerce. Should labor be regarded as an article of commerce?

3. Recorder Levy told the jury that sometimes a group may not do what an individual may do (see ¶ 48). Should he have stated a standard for distinguishing between cases in which persons may act in combination and cases in which persons may not act in combination? What value would such a standard have? Should we insist that judges state standards in cases like this one?

(In fairness to Recorder Levy, we must add that he did note that the defendants drew analogies to a religious society that expels members who marry outside the religion, to a fire brigade, to a literary society, and to a nominating committee in a city ward. Levy said these analogies were improper because the societies existed to benefit third persons, whereas the union existed to benefit only its own members (see ¶ 51). This may have been Levy's attempt to state a standard. If so, it was at best partially successful. The standard works in the case of a fire brigade, which is truly altruistic. The standard does not work as well in the cases of religious societies, literary societies, and ward nominating committees (nascent political parties), which seem to serve primarily the interests of their own members, not third persons.)

4. Was Recorder Levy's charge to the jury based solely on the law? If not, what other beliefs influenced him? Is it proper for judges to be influenced by such beliefs?

5. Recorder Levy spoke at some length on the duty of jurors to accept and enforce the law (see ¶¶ 49-50). Perhaps he feared "jury nullification," in which juries ignore a law which they think will produce an unjust result. Should a jury have this right?

6. Should illegal behavior by one person excuse illegal behavior by another?

EXERCISES

1. Here is an excerpt from ¶ 46.6:

"Consider the effect it would have upon the whole community. If the masters say they will not sell under certain prices, as the journeymen declare they will not work at

certain wages, they, if persisted in, would put
the whole body of the people into their power.
Shoes and boots are articles of the first
necessity. If they could stand out three or
four weeks in winter, they might raise the
price of boots to thirty, forty, or fifty
dollars a pair, at least for some time, and
until a competent supply could be got from
other places."

Paraphrase this argument in your own words. Brevity is
a virtue.

2. Here is an excerpt from ¶ 49:

"If the rule be clear, we are bound to conform
to it even though we do not comprehend the
principle upon which it is founded. We are not
to reject it because we do not see the reason
of it. It is enough, that it is the will of
the majority. It is law because it is their
will — if it is law, there may be good reasons
for it though we cannot find them out."

Paraphrase this argument in your own words. Brevity is
a virtue.

3. Here is an excerpt from ¶ 51.1:

{51.1} Considering it in this point of view,
let us take a look at the cases which have been
compared to this by the defendants' counsel.
Is this like the formation of a society for the
promotion of the general welfare of the
community, such as to advance the interests of
religion, or to accomplish acts of charity and
benevolence? Is it like the society for
extinguishing fires? or those for the promotion
of literature and the fine arts, or the meeting
of the city wards to nominate candidates for
the legislature or the executive? These are
for the benefit of third persons; {in
contrast, the defendants'} society ... {seeks}
to promote the selfish purposes of the members.
The mere mention of them is an answer to all,
that has been said on that point. There is no
comparison between the two; they are as

       distinct as light and darkness. How can these
       cases be considered on an equal footing?"

Paraphrase this argument in your own words. Brevity is
a virtue.

$$\Omega$$

The Strike as a Criminal Conspiracy (continued)

MID-NINETEENTH CENTURY

Introduction

The facts of the following case, <u>Commonwealth v. Hunt</u>, are similar to the preceding case, the <u>Philadelphia Cordwainers</u> case. In both cases, the defendants were union members who sought to improve their wages and working conditions by enforcing the **closed shop**, which is a shop in which only members in good standing of the union are allowed to work; and in both cases, the defendants were charged with the crime of criminal conspiracy. But whereas the <u>Philadelphia Cordwainers</u> case placed about equal emphasis on harm to the economy and harm to non-members of the union, the <u>Hunt</u> case emphasized only harm to non-members.

The indictment in <u>Hunt</u> contained three counts of conspiracy; that is, the prosecution alleged that the defendants had committed three separate crimes:

I.   The first count was that the defendants conspired to form a union and agreed that no member would work for an employer who also hired non-members.

II. The second count was that the defendants conspired to force an employer to discharge a non-member named Jeremiah Horne.

III. The third count was that the defendants conspired to impoverish Mr. Horne by preventing him from practicing his trade.

ii   *Commonwealth v. Hunt*

The trial court convicted the defendants on all three counts. They appealed, arguing that what they had done was not a crime.

The student should try to infer from the opinion the elements of a conspiracy, that is, the facts which the prosecution must prove to convict the defendants. In addition, the student should attempt to identify the issue that each argument addresses.

Commonwealth v. Hunt
45 Mass. 111 (1842)

SHAW, C. J.

...

{1} ... {A} conspiracy must be a combination of two or more persons, by some concerted action, to accomplish some criminal or unlawful purpose, or to accomplish some purpose, not in itself criminal or unlawful, by criminal or unlawful means....

...

{2} ... {I}t appears to us ... necessary ... that when the criminality of a conspiracy consists in an unlawful agreement of two or more persons to compass or promote some criminal or illegal purpose, that purpose must be fully and clearly stated in the indictment; and if the criminality of the offence ... consists in the agreement to compass or promote some purpose, not of itself criminal or unlawful, by the use of fraud, force, falsehood, or other criminal or unlawful means, such intended use of fraud, force, falsehood, or other criminal or unlawful means, must be set out in the indictment....

{3} With these general views of the law, it becomes necessary to consider the circumstances of the present case ....

...

{First Count of the Indictment}

{4} The first count {of the indictment} set forth that the defendants ... being workmen and journeymen in the ... occupation of bootmakers ... formed themselves into a society, and agreed not to work for any person who should employ any journeyman or other person {who was} not a member of such society....

{5} The manifest intent of the association is to induce all those engaged in the same occupation to become members of it. Such a purpose is not unlawful. It would give them a power which might be exerted for useful and honorable purposes, or for dangerous and pernicious ones. If the latter were the real and actual object, ... it should have been specially charged. Such an association might be used to afford each other assistance in times of poverty, sickness and distress; or to raise their intellectual, moral and social condition; or to make improvement in their art; or for other proper purposes. Or the association might be designed for purposes of oppression and injustice. But in order to charge all those who become members of an association with the guilt of a criminal conspiracy, it must be averred and proved that the actual, if not the avowed, object of the association, was criminal. An association may be formed, the declared objects of which are innocent and laudable, and yet they may have secret articles, or an agreement communicated only to the members, by which they are banded together for purposes injurious to the peace of society or the rights of its members. Such would undoubtedly be a criminal conspiracy, on proof of the fact, however meritorious and praiseworthy the declared objects might be. The law is not to be hoodwinked by colorable pretences. It looks at truth and reality, through whatever disguise it may assume. But to make such an association, ostensibly innocent, the subject of prosecution as a criminal conspiracy, the secret agreement which makes it so is to be averred and proved as the gist of the offence. {Or} when an association is formed for purposes actually innocent, and afterwards its powers are abused, by those who have the control and management of it, to purposes of oppression and injustice, it will be criminal in those who thus misuse it, or give consent thereto, but not in the other members of the association. In this case, no such secret agreement, varying the objects of the association from those avowed, is set forth in this count of the indictment.

{6} Nor can we perceive that the objects of this association, whatever they may have been, were to be attained by criminal means. The means which they proposed to employ, as averred in this count, ... were, that they would not work for a person, who, after due notice, should employ a journeyman not a member of their society. Supposing the object of the association to be laudable and lawful, or at least not unlawful, are these means criminal? The case supposes that these persons are not bound by contract, but free to work for whom they please, or not to work, if they so prefer. In this state of things, we cannot perceive that it is criminal for men to agree together to exercise their own acknowledged rights, in such a manner as best to subserve their own interests. One way to test this is to consider the effect of such an agreement where the object of the association is acknowledged on all hands to be a laudable one. Suppose a class of workmen, impressed with the manifold evils of intemperance, should agree with each other not to work in a shop in which ardent spirit was furnished, or not to work in a shop with any one who used it, or not to work for an employer, who should, after notice, employ a journeyman who habitually used it. The consequences might be the same. A workman who should still persist in the use of ardent spirit would find it more difficult to get employment; a master employing such a one might, at times, experience inconvenience in his work in losing the services of a skillful but intemperate workman. Still, it seems to us that as the object would be lawful, and the means not unlawful, such an agreement could not be pronounced a criminal conspiracy.

{7} From this count in the indictment, we do not understand that the agreement was that the defendants would refuse to work for an employer, to whom they were bound by contract for a certain time, in violation of that contract; nor that they would insist that an employer should discharge a workman engaged by contract for a certain time in violation of such contract....

{Second Count of the Indictment}

{8} The second count ... alleges that the defendants ... did ... conspire ... and agree together not to work for any master or person who should employ any workman ... who should break any of {the} by-laws {of their society}, unless such workmen should pay to {the society} such {fines} as should be agreed upon as a penalty for the breach of {the bylaws}, and that by means of {this} conspiracy they did compel one Isaac B. Wait, a master cordwainer, to turn out of his employ {i.e., to discharge} one Jeremiah Horne, a journeyman boot-maker.... {This} is simply an averment of an agreement amongst themselves not to work for a person who should employ any person not a member of a certain association. It sets forth no illegal or criminal purpose to be accomplished, nor any illegal or criminal means to be adopted for the accomplishment of any purpose. It was an agreement, as to the manner in which they would exercise an acknowledged right to contract with others for their labor. It does not aver a conspiracy or even an intention to raise their wages ....

...

{9} ... If, for instance, the indictment had averred a conspiracy by the defendants to compel Wait to turn Horne out of his employment, and to accomplish that object by the use of force or fraud, it would have been a very different case; especially if it might be fairly construed ... that Wait was under obligation, by contract for an unexpired term of time, to employ and pay Horne.... To mark the difference between the case of a journeyman or a servant and {one's} master {who are} mutually bound by contract, and the {case of the} same parties when free to engage anew, I should have before cited the case of the *Boston Glass Co. v. Binney,* 4 Pick. 425. In that case, it was held actionable to entice another person's hired servant to quit his employment, during the time for which he was engaged {by contract}; but not actionable to treat with such hired servant, whilst actually hired and employed by another, to leave his service and engage in the employment of the person making the proposal when the term for which he is engaged shall expire. It acknowledges the established principle that every free man, whether skilled laborer, mechanic, farmer or domestic servant, may work or not work ... with any company or individual, at his own option, except so far as he is bound by contract. But whatever might be the force of the word "compel" {in the indictment} ... it is disarmed and rendered harmless by the precise statement of the means by which such compulsion was to be effected. It was the agreement not to work for him, by which they compelled Wait to decline employing Horne longer....

{Third Count of the Indictment}

{10} The third count, reciting a wicked and unlawful intent to impoverish one Jeremiah Horne and hinder him from following his trade as a boot-maker, charges the defendants ... with an unlawful conspiracy by wrongful ... means to impoverish said Horne and to deprive and hinder him from his ... trade and getting his support thereby, and that, in pursuance of said unlawful combination, they did unlawfully ... hinder and prevent ... and greatly impoverish him.

{11} If the fact of depriving Jeremiah Horne of the profits of his business, by whatever means it might be done, would be unlawful and criminal, a combination to compass that object would be an unlawful conspiracy....

{12} {But s}uppose a baker in a small village had the exclusive custom of his neighborhood and was making large profits by the sale of his bread. Supposing a number of those neighbors, believing the price of his bread too high, should propose to him to reduce his prices, or if he did not, that they would introduce another baker; and on his refusal, such other baker should, under their encouragement, set up a rival establishment and sell his bread at lower prices; the effect would be to diminish the profit of the former baker and, to the same extent, to impoverish him. And it might be said and proved that the purpose of the associates was to diminish his profits, and thus impoverish him, though the ultimate and laudable object of the combination was to reduce the cost of bread to themselves and their neighbors. The same thing may be said of all competition in every branch of trade and industry; and yet it is through that competition that the best interests of trade and industry are promoted. It is scarcely necessary to allude to the familiar instances of opposition lines of conveyance, rival hotels, and the thousand other instances where each strives to gain custom to himself by ingenious improvements, by increased industry, and by all the means by which he may lessen the price of commodities, and thereby diminish the profits of others.

{13} We think, therefore, that associations may be entered into, the object of which is to adopt measures that may have a tendency to impoverish another, that is, to diminish his gains and profits, and yet so far from being criminal or unlawful, the object may be highly meritorious and public spirited. The legality of such an association will therefore depend upon the means to be used for its accomplishment. If it is to be carried into effect by fair or honorable and lawful means, it is, to say the least, innocent; if by falsehood or force, it may be stamped with the character of conspiracy. It follows as a necessary consequence that, if criminal and indictable, it is so by reason of the criminal means intended to be employed for its accomplishment....

...

{The convictions of the defendants were reversed.}

COMMENTS

Commonwealth v. Hunt is important because it is one of the first cases to hold that labor unions are legitimate associations and not criminal conspiracies. Courts in other states continued for several years to convict defendants of joining unions; Hunt did not mark the turning of the tide. But it did provide the intellectual basis, a legal construct, which courts that wanted to recognize the legitimacy of unions could adopt.

Hunt is important, therefore, because of its reasoning. The author of the opinion was Chief Justice Shaw, who was widely respected in his day, and the elements of his opinion have remained relevant in labor law. Three of those elements were the defendants' purposes or ends, the defendants' means or behaviors, and the defense of competition.

The Defendants' Purpose

The law has long used an actor's end or purpose as an element of illegal behavior. If you point a gun at someone and pull the trigger, with the intent to injure or kill the person, and the person dies, you are guilty of first degree murder; and your punishment could be death. If you point a gun at someone and pull the trigger, believing the chamber is empty and intending only to amuse yourself, but unfortunately the chamber contains a bullet and the person dies, you are not guilty of first degree murder; you might be guilty of negligent homicide, and your punishment (if you were prosecuted at all) would be a term in jail. Chief Justice Shaw defined criminal conspiracy to include an element of purpose or motive. If the defendants intended to destroy an employer's business or to impoverish a non-union worker, their purpose would have been illegal, and they would have committed a crime. But if the defendants intended only to improve their own working conditions, their purpose would have been perfectly lawful.

Purpose is a malleable concept. This is so for several reasons. One reason is that a person so often has more than one purpose in mind, and a judge may choose any of those purposes, however small a part of the actor's motivation, and call it "the defendant's purpose." For example, the purpose of the neighbors in

Chief Justice Shaw's example was to lower the price of bread. Let us suppose that they were also angry at the baker for charging such high prices, and so they had a secondary purpose, viz., to punish the baker. The secondary purpose may have been a minor part of their motivation, a motive so weak that they would never have acted on it by itself. Yet a judge could rule that their act was illegal because they sought to impoverish the baker.

A second reason that purpose is malleable is that, although a person may desire a particular result, one often foresees that another result will probably occur as well. The union's purpose in the Hunt case was to improve the wages and working conditions of the members. Let us suppose they bore no ill towards Mr. Horne; they had no desire to prevent him from earning a living, and certainly no desire to impoverish him. Yet they foresaw that their refusal to work alongside of him could damage him economically. A judge could rule that foreseeable consequences, though not intended, count as purposes: in which case, the defendants' purpose was to impoverish Mr. Horne.

A third reason that purpose is malleable is that one purpose often links to another. The defendants in Hunt consciously intended —
- to induce all workers in their trade to join their society,
- to adopt rules of the society which members were supposed to obey,
- to fine or expel any member who violated the rules, and
- to refuse to work in the same shop as a non-member.

All of these purposes together served another purpose —
- to protect the defendants' wages and working conditions.

Assuming that we count foreseeable, albeit unintended, consequences as purposes, the defendants foresaw the consequences of the foregoing acts and, therefore, they also intended —
- to induce a master like Wait to discharge a non-member like Horne and
- to cause economic hardship to the non-member;

or, if the master did not discharge the non-member —
- to damage the master's business.

A judge could identify any of these acts as the defendants' purpose. The student might reply that only the last act was the defendants' end, and all the preceding acts were means. But which act was the last? The last thing the defendants did was to refuse to work alongside of Horne. Was this refusal their purpose? The last thing that happened to Horne was that he lost wages and was impoverished. Was his loss the defendants' last act? Suppose Wait had refused to discharge Horne, the defendants had walked out of the shop, and Wait had lost business. The last thing that happened to Wait would have been that he lost business. Was this loss the defendants' last act?

A fourth reason that purpose is malleable is that a judge's finding of purpose is practically beyond challenge. Purpose is a state of mind. Only the actor knows one's real purpose. Yet we can hardly trust a person accused of wrongdoing to state one's true purpose. We must trust the judge to rule on purpose. If you say your purpose was this and that, which is a legal one, but the judge says your purpose was the other thing, which was an illegal one, no one but you can disagree with the judge.

When purpose is involved, courts frequently have a choice, and the characterization they choose may depend on the result they want in the case. When Nineteenth Century judges wanted to limit unions by convicting the defendants, the judges said that the defendants were seeking to impoverish non-members. Of course, the judges might honestly have believed they could know the defendants' true purpose, and perhaps a desire to restrict union activity and an honest belief about purpose melded in judges' minds. In contrast, when Nineteenth Century judges wanted to recognize unions by exonerating the defendants, the judges said that the defendants were seeking to improve wages and working conditions. Chief Justice Shaw evidently wanted to recognize unions, and, therefore, he characterized their purpose in an acceptable way. He favored competition, and perhaps this policy influenced how he characterized the defendants' purpose.

Purpose remains an element of many legal claims today, and judges are equally able to manipulate their characterization of purposes.

The Defendants' Means

Chief Justice Shaw examined not only the purpose or end of the alleged conspiracy, but also the means adopted to achieve the end. He stated that, to establish a criminal conspiracy, the prosecution had to allege that either the means or the end was unlawful. As with purposes, examining means remains important today.

There is perhaps less room for judicial maneuvering with regard to means as compared to purposes. The reason is that means involve actions, which are susceptible of observation by many persons and, therefore, of more objectivity. Nevertheless, the <u>characterization</u> of means can be manipulated. The complaint against the defendants alleged they had compelled the employer to discharge Horne. As Shaw noted, the word "compel" is ambiguous. He said that, if the defendants compelled the employer to fire Horne by striking until he was discharged, that was not illegal; but if they compelled the discharge by force or fraud, that would have been illegal. The conviction was void, said Shaw, because the complaint failed to allege unambiguously that the defendants' means were illegal. Yet, although it was true that the defendants had not used physical force against Horne, they had used economic force. Implicitly, therefore, Shaw held that economic force was not an illegal mean. But if he had wanted the conviction to stand, he could as easily have stated that economic force is an illegal mean and, therefore, it was illegal for the defendants to strike in order to compel their employer to discharge a fellow worker. Many other judges adopted such reasoning well into the Twentieth Century.

Mean or End?

Another way in which means and ends are slippery in the law is that either can often be characterized as the other. Shaw wrote in ¶ 5 that the defendants' intent or end was to induce all bootmakers to join the union. Was this truly their end? It seems unlikely that their goal was a society comprising all bootmakers for its own sake. Was not such a society in fact a mean to their end, which was to receive more money for their labor? Similarly, Shaw wrote in ¶ 10 that the third count of the indictment alleged that the defendants' end was to deprive Horne of his trade and impoverish him. It is possible that the defendants bore Horne malice because he worked for less than union scale, and so they might have desired to impoverish him. Yet is it not more likely that depriving Horne of work was a mean to the end of receiving more money for their labor? Indeed, is it not possible that the defendants did not care what happened to Horne as long as he stopped underselling them? Was his impoverishment a collateral, and perhaps undesired, consequence of the defendants' aim of improving their wages? Would the defendants have cared in the least if he had turned to carpentry and become rich at it?

In the Hunt case, it did not matter whether an act was characterized as a mean or an end, for, whichever the act was, a conspiracy resulted if the act was illegal. But whether an act was a mean or an end might matter in another kind of case; and if it did, the judge would have wide discretion in characterizing the act.

LEVELS OF ABSTRACTION IN COMMONWEALTH V. HUNT

The student who studies Chief Justice Shaw's reasoning carefully will find a link to the idea of levels of abstraction. Recall that he was examining the indictment against the defendants. An indictment must allege a crime. The indictment alleged that inducing all bootmakers to join the defendants' association was an illegal purpose. Shaw replied that, if the defendants succeeded in this purpose, they would gain power. He seemed to believe that gaining power was a certain consequence of inducing all bootmakers to join the association. Accordingly, we may infer that he believed that the indictment alleged two facts in this connection: the defendants sought to induce all bootmakers to join the association, and the defendants would gain power. But even this additional fact did not rescue the indictment; Shaw still held that it did not allege a crime.

Why not? The reason, wrote Shaw, was that the power could be used for good or ill. FOR GOOD: the power could be used to assist members of the association in times of poverty or sickness; to raise their intellectual, moral, or social condition; or to improve their craft. FOR ILL: the power could be used for oppression and injustice. To draw a comparison, suppose a student were indicted for opening a bank account. The account could be used for good, such as paying one's bills, or for ill, such as laundering stolen funds. In both the case of the bootmakers' association and the case of the student's bank account, the indictment was written at too high a level of abstraction (was too general): it captured lawful as well as unlawful behavior. A proper indictment must allege, not the possibility of unlawful behavior, but its occurrence. Specific unlawful acts must be alleged. In other words, a proper indictment must be written at the appropriate level of abstraction, and the indictments in our cases were written at an improper level, a level too high on the abstraction ladder.[a]

Shaw made a similar argument regarding the allegation that the defendants used illegal means. The indictment alleged that the defendants refused to work in the same shop as a bootmaker who was not a member of their association. Shaw replied that the defendants were free to work, or not to work, as they pleased, and this freedom included the right to leave their jobs in pursuit of their own interests.[b] He acknowledged that if the

---

a. If Shaw had been able to think of no legitimate use of the power gained by forming a union, he would have considered such power to be intrinsically evil. In this event, the indictment would probably have been acceptable; further specificity — a lower level of abstraction — would have been unnecessary if the power could have been used only for evil.

The student may be wondering what the appropriate level of abstraction is for an indictment. Although this is not a course in criminal law, we may suggest that an indictment should be written at a low enough level of abstraction that the accused person receives fair notice of the illegal conduct. For example, "On August 1, 2004 the defendant opened a checking account at the Tompkins Trust Company and deposited into it $100,000 which the defendant knew his co-conspirator, Simon Boccanegra, had earned by the sale of illegal drugs. On August 5, 2004 the defendant moved $10,000 from the Tompkins Trust account to an account in the name of Peter Grimes at the First National Bank of Podunk for the purpose of concealing the origin of this money; moved another $10,000 from the Tompkins Trust account to an account in the name of ...."

b. Shaw mentioned an exception to this rule: if the defendants had agreed to an employment contract in which they promised to work for a definite period of time (e.g., a year),

(continued...)

defendants exercised this freedom, the bootmaker whom they shunned could have trouble finding a job, and the employer could have trouble finding a replacement for the shunned bootmaker. Accordingly, we may infer that Shaw considered these additional facts to be implied by the indictment. Even so, he held that it did not allege a crime.

Why not? Because, like the power the defendants' association would gain from inducing all bootmakers to join the association, the defendants' freedom to quit their jobs could be used for good or ill. FOR GOOD: the defendants might quit rather than work in a shop in which ardent spirits were served, or in which an intemperate co-worker was employed. FOR ILL: the defendants, by threatening to quit their jobs, might force a master to violate an employment contract by prematurely discharging a co-worker who had been engaged for a definite period of time. Therefore, the allegation that the defendants threatened to quit their jobs was too general; it did not state a crime. To say the same thing, the indictment failed because it was written at too high a level of abstraction.[c]

The Importance of <u>Hunt</u>

If the <u>Hunt</u> case was a victory for unions, it was a victory in a single battle; unions were still far from winning the war. This is true because Shaw's opinion is remarkably narrow; the defendants got off on a technicality. For, although the opinion may seem like judicial approval of unions, in fact the opinion held only that the indictment failed to allege a crime. A

---

b. (...continued)
they would not have been at liberty to quit at will.

c. It is interesting that Shaw judged the defendants' mean by the <u>end</u> which the mean might serve. He said the freedom to quit one's job was good if used to combat dipsomania, bad if used to induce an employer to breach a contract. Thus he turned the question of the legality of the defendants' mean into the question of the legality of their end. Perhaps he believed that, as a mean, quitting a job held at will was always lawful, or perhaps he simply begged the question of whether or not quitting one's job was lawful.

properly written indictment <u>would</u> have alleged a crime, and Shaw gave examples of allegations that would have stated crimes. Regarding purpose, if the indictment had alleged that the union had secret articles indicating a design to injure persons or society, or that the defendants had actually used the union for purposes of oppression or injustice, a crime would have been alleged. Regarding means, if the indictment had stated that the defendants had contracts of employment for a specific period of time, and if the defendants had violated such contracts, that is, quit before the contracts had expired; or if Mr. Horne had had such a contract, and the defendants forced the employer to fire him in violation of his contract, a crime would have been alleged. The opinion almost reads like advice to a prosecuting attorney on how to write the next indictment.

Why did Shaw write the opinion this way? One may suspect he wanted to make clear that his court was not endorsing the labor movement. In fact, the opinion put unions on a fairly short leash. They might exist, but if they went any further than a strike for higher wages, it would be easy for a judge in the future to rein them in.

We cannot resist closing this discussion of the substance of <u>Hunt</u> with a word about Chief Justice Shaw. One might be inclined to think him a liberal because he held in favor labor unions. Perhaps he was. But perhaps he was influenced by his family's holdings in manufacturing plants in which many workers were union members; during this period, American manufacturers were seeking protective tariffs and relied on the political support of their workers. Also, a few years later Shaw held that the U.S. Constitution did not prohibit Massachusetts from operating segregated schools for black pupils. <u>Roberts v. Boston</u>, 5 Cush. 198. He missed his chance to become a truly great judge.

QUESTIONS FOR REFLECTION

1. The crime of conspiracy is separate from its underlying crime. If two persons plan to commit a crime (for example, hack into their professor's computer and change their grades), and if they take at least one step in furtherance of their plan (they design a protocol appropriate to their purpose), they have committed the crime of conspiracy. This is true even if they change

their minds and abandon their plan. Do good reasons support making conspiracy a crime?

2. Why must a complaint be dismissed if it does not allege facts that constitute a crime?

3. The defendants admitted that they had committed two of the three elements of conspiracy. Thus, the prosecution proved the majority of its case. Why was this not sufficient for the prosecution to win?

4. The court said that the defendants, by creating a union, gained power that could have been used for good or for evil. Every society has the right to protect itself against harm. Does not society have the right to outlaw unions because they have the potential to harm society?

5. The complaint alleged that the defendants intended to impoverish Jeremiah Horne. May we fairly say that the defendants intended this result? The effect of the their act was to prevent non-members from working. Was this part of their purpose? We know that their main purpose was to raise their pay. Their means were to refuse to work in the same shop as non-members. These means were consciously and intentionally adopted, so it is fair to say that the means were also part of the defendants' purpose. Thus, we may say the defendants' purpose was to raise their pay by refusing to work alongside of non-members. But is it also correct to say that the defendants' purpose included preventing non-members from working? This was an effect of their action. There is no evidence that they intended this effect; they might have been perfectly content for non-members to take jobs in other shops, and surely would not have objected to non-members' taking jobs in other occupations. Nevertheless, the defendants must have realized that non-members would have trouble finding work. Therefore, one might argue that the defendants intended to impoverish non-members.

Naturally, the defense would disagree. Although it used this analogy for another purpose, the defense in the Philadelphia Cordwainers case mentioned the analogy to a blacksmith's shop that gives off smoke and fumes that annoy neighbors. We would not say that the blacksmith intended to annoy the neighbors, argues the defense; the smoke is merely an unfortunate effect of a lawful act. The defendants were performing a lawful act, namely, seeking to raise their compensation; the effect of this act on non-members was unfortunate but not intended.

This disagreement may be expressed in general terms: If an individual's purpose is to perform act A; if A is likely to cause effect A; and if the individual does not wish to cause A, but is aware that A can cause A, is it correct to conclude that the individual's purpose includes A? The prosecution thought so; the defense thought not. Which was correct?

6. The defendants refused to work for Isaac Wait as long as he employed Jeremiah Horne because Horne refused to join the union, whereupon Wait discharged Horne. Is it fair to say that the defendants compelled Wait to discharge Horne? Is it fair to say that the defendants sought to compel Horne to join the union? Should it not be illegal to compel a person to perform an act that one does not wish, and has not previously promised, to perform?

7. Review the <u>Philadelphia Cordwainers</u> case. Does it appear that the prima facie case of conspiracy was the same in that case as in <u>Hunt</u>?

8. In the example of the baker in a small village (¶ 12), why were not the neighbors guilty of conspiracy?

$$\Omega$$

The Picket Line as the Tort of Damage to Business

Introduction

The first thing to note about the following case, <u>Vegelahn v. Guntner</u>, is that it is a civil case, not a criminal case. The student should be aware of a few of the differences between criminal and civil cases.

In a criminal case, the prosecution is the government. The accused party is called the defendant or the respondent. The offense is against the public at large, and, therefore, the remedies run to the benefit of the public. Thus, a defendant who is convicted in a criminal case may be punished by a sentence in jail or by a fine payable to the government.

In a civil case, the prosecution is a private party, who is called the plaintiff or the petitioner. The accused party is called the defendant or the respondent.

The offense is against a private party (usually the plaintiff), and, therefore, the remedies run to the benefit of the plaintiff. A defendant who loses a civil case is not punished,[a] but is required to compensate the plaintiff for injuries the defendant has caused. The principal form of compensation is money, which is payable to the plaintiff. (Lawyers call such money "damages.") Another kind of remedy, which has been important in labor cases, is the injunction, the purpose of which is to stop the defendant from inflicting any further injury on the plaintiff. The court orders the defendant to stop the wrongful behavior, for example, to cease playing your stereo so loudly that the professor who lives next door to you cannot sleep.

In <u>Vegelahn</u> the plaintiff was an employer. The defendants were members of a union who were on strike and were picketing in front of the employer's shop. The employer sought an injunction against the picketing.

---

[a]An exception to this statement is punitive damages, which are designed to punish a civil defendant. Although they attract a great deal of attention, punitive damages are in fact rarely awarded.

The facts of Vegelahn differed from the facts of the
Philadelphia Cordwainers case and Commonwealth v. Hunt in
an important respect: the union in Vegelahn used a
different tactic, a picket line (which, in those days,
was called a patrol). Numerous union members marched
back and forth in front of the employer's door and tried
to dissuade other workers from entering. Sometimes the
pickets were peaceable, but sometimes they physically
blocked the door and threatened or intimidated the other
workers.

The employer filed a law suit, probably in a city or
county court, and asked the judge or, perhaps, a justice
of the peace or a magistrate, whose name is not given,
for a preliminary injunction against the strike.[b] A
preliminary injunction is a temporary one; it lasts only
until the court reaches a final decision in the case,
which usually happens after a trial. The unnamed judge
issued a preliminary injunction that not only prohibited
blocking the door and threatening other workers, but also
prohibited peaceful attempts to persuade other workers
not to enter. {¶ 1} In effect, the judge prohibited all
picketing.

Then the case went to a hearing before Justice
Holmes. He was a member of the Supreme Judicial Court of
Massachusetts, but he was, evidently, a trial judge as
well. At the end of the hearing or trial, the
preliminary injunction expired. Justice Holmes then
issued a final or permanent injunction, which would last
indefinitely, that prohibited only physical obstruction,
threats, and intimidation. {¶ 2} In other words,
Holmes's final injunction permitted peaceful picketing.

This decision was appealed to the Supreme Judicial
Court. In an opinion by Justice Allen, the majority of
the court ruled that the preliminary injunction was
correct, that is, that all picketing should have been

---

[b]Another name for a preliminary injunction is an
interlocutory injunction. In the following opinion the
injunction is sometimes called a decree.

prohibited. {¶¶ 1,6} Justice Holmes dissented, arguing that the injunction he had approved was correct.[c]

❧

---

[c]Today a judge would not sit in review of a decision the judge had previously issued. If <u>Vegelahn</u> arose today, and everything else about it were the same, Justice Holmes would recuse himself when his decision was reviewed by the Supreme Judicial Court.

Vegelahn v. Guntner
167 Mass. 92 (1896)

{1} {The defendants, who were 14 individuals and two labor unions, went on strike against an employer and set up a patrol (picket line) in front of the employer's shop. They attempted to dissuade workers from crossing the line to accept work in the shop; some such workers already had specific employment contracts with the employer, and some did not. The strikers also occasionally threatened personal injury or other harm to workers who considered crossing the line, and there may have been a technical battery (that is, an unwelcomed touch). The patrol was generally maintained by two men, but sometimes more joined and blocked the employer's door. The employer applied to an unidentified judge, who issued a preliminary injunction (also called a decree). It restrained the defendants

> from interfering with the plaintiff's business by patrolling the sidewalk or street in front or in the vicinity of the premises occupied by him, for the purpose of preventing any person or persons who now are or may hereafter be in his employment, or desirous of entering the same, from entering it, or continuing in it; or by obstructing or interfering with such persons, or any others, in entering or leaving the plaintiff's said premises; or by intimidating, by threats or otherwise, any person or persons who now are or may hereafter be in the employment of the plaintiff, or desirous of entering the same, from entering it, or continuing in it; or by any scheme or conspiracy among themselves or with others, organized for the purpose of annoying, hindering, interfering with, or preventing any person or persons who now are or may hereafter be in the employment of the plaintiff, or desirous of entering the same, from entering it, or from continuing therein.

At a subsequent hearing, another judge, Oliver Wendell Holmes, Jr., modified the preliminary injunction and issued a final or permanent injunction that permitted picketing as long as the strikers did not physically obstruct the employer's premises, use force or threats of force against workers who chose to cross the picket line, or attempt to induce workers with employment contracts with the employer to dishonor their promises. Holmes's final injunction provided that the

> defendants and each and every one of them, their agents and servants, be restrained and enjoined from interfering with the plaintiff's business by obstructing or physically interfering with any persons in entering or leaving the plaintiff's premises ... or by intimidating, by threats, express or implied, of violence or physical harm to body or property, any person or persons who now are or hereafter may be in the employment of the plaintiff, or desirous of entering or continuing in it, or by in any way hindering, interfering with, or preventing any person or persons who now are in the employment of the plaintiff from continuing therein, so long as they may be bound to do so by lawful contract.

Vegelahn v. Guntner   v

The final injunction was appealed to the Supreme Judicial Court of Massachusetts (of which Justice Holmes was a member). In an opinion by Justice Allen, the court decided that the preliminary injunction, as originally issued by the unidentified judge, was proper. Justice Holmes dissented, arguing that the final injunction he had issued was correct.}

ALLEN, J., delivered the opinion of the court.

{2} The principal question in this case is whether the defendants should be enjoined against maintaining the patrol. The report shows that, following upon a strike of the plaintiff's workmen, the defendants conspired to prevent him from getting workmen, and thereby to prevent him from carrying on his business, unless and until he should adopt a certain schedule of prices. The means adopted were persuasion and social pressure, threats of personal injury or unlawful harm conveyed to persons employed or seeking employment, and a patrol of two men in front of the plaintiff's factory, maintained from half past six in the morning till half past five in the afternoon, on one of the busiest streets of Boston. The number of men was greater at times, and at times showed some little disposition to stop the plaintiff's door. The patrol proper at times went further than simple advice, not obtruded beyond the point where the other person was willing to listen; and it was found that the patrol would probably be continued, if not enjoined. There was also some evidence of persuasion to break existing contracts.

{3} The patrol was maintained as one of the means of carrying out the defendants' plan, and it was used in combination with social pressure, threats of personal injury or unlawful harm, and persuasion to break existing contracts. It was thus one means of intimidation indirectly to the plaintiff, and directly to persons actually employed or seeking to be employed by the plaintiff, and of rendering such employment unpleasant or intolerable to such persons. Such an act is an unlawful interference with the rights both of employer and of employed. An employer has a right to engage all persons who are willing to work for him, at such prices as may be mutually agreed upon; and persons employed or seeking employment have a corresponding right to enter into or remain in the employment of any person or corporation willing to employ them.... No one can lawfully interfere by force or intimidation to prevent employers or persons employed or wishing to be employed from the exercise of these rights. In Massachusetts, as in some other States, it is even made a criminal offence for one by intimidation or force to prevent or seek to prevent a person from entering into or continuing in the employment of a person or corporation. Intimidation is not limited to threats of violence or of physical injury to person or property. It has a broader signification, and there also may be a moral intimidation which is illegal. Patrolling or picketing, under the circumstances {of this case}, has elements of intimidation like those which were found to exist in *Sherry v.*

Perkins, 147 Mass. 212 {1888}.... The patrol {in the case at bar} was an unlawful interference both with the plaintiff and with the workmen....

{4} The defendants contend that these acts were justifiable because they were only seeking to secure better wages for themselves by compelling the plaintiff to accept their schedule of wages. This motive or purpose does not justify maintaining a patrol in front of the plaintiff's premises as a means of carrying out their conspiracy. A combination among persons merely to regulate their own conduct is within allowable competition, and is lawful, although others may be indirectly affected thereby. But a combination to do injurious acts expressly directed to another, by way of intimidation or constraint, either of himself or of persons employed or seeking to be employed by him, is outside of allowable competition, and is unlawful. Various decided cases fall within the former class, for example: ... *Commonwealth v. Hunt*, 4 Met. 111.... The present case falls within the latter class.

...

{5} A question is also presented whether the court should enjoin such interference with persons in the employment of the plaintiff who are not bound by contract to remain with him, or with persons who are not under any existing contract, but who are seeking or intending to enter into his employment. A conspiracy to interfere with the plaintiff's business by means of threats and intimidation, and by maintaining a patrol in front of his premises in order to prevent persons from entering his employment, or in order to prevent persons who are in his employment from continuing therein, is unlawful, even though such persons are not bound by contract to enter into or to continue in his employment; and the injunction should not be so limited as to relate only to persons who are bound by existing contracts.

{6} In the opinion of a majority of the court the injunction {should} be in the form originally issued {i.e., the preliminary injunction was correct}.

So ordered.

HOLMES, J., dissenting.

...

{7} ... There was no proof of any threat or danger of a patrol exceeding two men, and as of course an injunction is not granted except with reference to what there is reason to expect in its absence, the question on that point is whether a patrol of two men should be enjoined. Again, the defendants are enjoined by the final decree from intimidating by threats, express or implied, of physical harm to body or property, any person who may be desirous of entering into the employment of the plaintiff so far as to prevent him from entering the same. In order to test the correctness of the refusal {of the final decree} to go further, it must be assumed that the defendants obey the express prohibition of the decree. If they do not, they fall within the injunction as it now stands, and are liable to summary punishment. The important difference between the preliminary and the final injunction is that the former goes further, and forbids the defendants to interfere with the plaintiff's business "by any scheme ... organized for the purpose of ... preventing any person or persons who now are or may hereafter be ... desirous of entering the [plaintiff's employment] from entering it." I quote only a part, and the part which seems to me most objectionable. This includes refusal of social intercourse, and even organized persuasion or argument, although free from any threat of violence, either express or implied. And this is with reference to persons who have a legal right to contract or not to contract with the plaintiff, as they may see fit. Interference with existing contracts is forbidden by the final decree....[d] It appears to me that the judgment of the majority turns in part on the assumption that the patrol necessarily carries with it a threat of bodily harm. That assumption I think unwarranted.... {I}t cannot be said, I think, that two men walking together up and down a sidewalk and speaking to those who enter a certain shop do necessarily and always thereby convey a threat of force ... especially when they are, and are known to be, under the injunction of this court not to do so. I may add that I think the more intelligent workingmen believe as fully as I do that they no more can be permitted to usurp the State's prerogative of force than can their opponents in their controversies. But if I am wrong, then the decree as it stands reaches the patrol, since it applies to all threats of force. With this I pass to the real difference between the interlocutory and the final decree.

{8} I agree, whatever may be the law in the case of a single defendant, that when a plaintiff proves that several persons have combined and conspired to injure his business, and have done acts producing that effect, he shows temporal damage and a cause of action {that is, a right to sue}, unless the facts disclose, or the defendants prove, some ground of excuse or justification. And I take it to be settled, and rightly settled, that doing that damage by combined persuasion is actionable, as well as doing it by falsehood or by force.

---

[d] {Holmes and the majority agreed that an injunction should be issued to prohibit the defendants from attempting to persuade workers who had employment contracts to violate their contracts, and Holmes's injunction prohibited this. The only additional workers to whom the majority's injunction applied were those who did not have employment contracts; these were at-will employees who, in theory, entered into a new, one-day contract of employment each morning. The point of disagreement between Holmes and the majority was whether an injunction should prohibit the defendants from attempting to persuade these at-will workers to participate in the strike. — ed.}

{9} Nevertheless, in numberless instances the law warrants the intentional infliction of temporal damage because it regards it as justified. It is on the question of what shall amount to a justification, and more especially on the nature of the considerations which really determine or ought to determine the answer to that question, that judicial reasoning seems to me often to be inadequate. The true grounds of decision are considerations of policy and of social advantage, and it is vain to suppose that solutions can be attained merely by logic and the general propositions of law which nobody disputes. Propositions as to public policy rarely are unanimously accepted, and still more rarely, if ever, are capable of unanswerable proof. They require a special training to enable any one even to form an intelligent opinion about them. In the early stages of law, at least, they generally are acted on rather as inarticulate instincts than as definite ideas for which a rational defence is ready.

{10} To illustrate what I have said in the last paragraph, it has been the law for centuries that a man may set up a business in a country town too small to support more than one, although he expects and intends thereby to ruin some one already there, and succeeds in his intent. In such a case he is not held to act "unlawfully and without justifiable cause".... The reason, of course, is that the doctrine generally has been accepted that free competition is worth more to society than it costs, and that on this ground the infliction of the damage is privileged. *Commonwealth v. Hunt,* 4 Met. 111, 134. Yet even this proposition nowadays is disputed by a considerable body of persons, including many whose intelligence is not to be denied, little as we may agree with them.

{11} I have chosen this illustration partly with reference to what I have to say next. It shows without the need of further authority that the policy of allowing free competition justifies the intentional inflicting of temporal damage, including the damage of interference with a man's business, by some means, when the damage is done not for its own sake, but as an instrumentality in reaching the end of victory in the battle of trade. In such a case it cannot matter whether the plaintiff is the only rival of the defendant, and so is aimed at specifically, or is one of a class all of whom are hit. The only debatable ground is the nature of the means by which such damage may be inflicted. We all agree that it cannot be done by force or threats of force. We all agree, I presume, that it may be done by persuasion to leave a rival's shop and come to the defendant's. It may be done by the refusal or withdrawal of various pecuniary advantages which, apart from this consequence, are within the defendant's lawful control. It may be done by the withdrawal, or threat to withdraw, such advantages from third persons who have a right to deal or not to deal with the plaintiff, as a means of inducing them not to deal with him either as customers or servants. *Commonwealth v. Hunt,* 4 Met. 111.

{12} I pause here to remark that the word "threats" often is used as if, when it appeared that threats had been made, it appeared that unlawful conduct had begun. But it depends on what you threaten. As a general rule, even if subject to some exceptions, what you may do in a certain event you may threaten to do, that is, give warning of your intention to do in that event, and thus allow the other person the chance of avoiding the consequences. So as to "compulsion," it depends on how you "compel." *Commonwealth v. Hunt*, 4 Met. 111, 133. So as to "annoyance" or "intimidation." In *Sherry v. Perkins*, 147 Mass. 212, it was found as a fact that the display of banners which was enjoined was part of a scheme to prevent workmen from entering or remaining in the plaintiff's employment "by threats and intimidation." The context showed that the words as there used meant threats of personal violence, and intimidation by causing fear of it.

{13} I have seen the suggestion made that the conflict between employers and employed is not competition. But I venture to assume that none of my brethren would rely on that suggestion. If the policy on which our law is founded is too narrowly expressed in the term "free competition," we may substitute "free struggle for life." Certainly the policy is not limited to struggles between persons of the same class competing for the same end. It applies to all conflicts of temporal interests.

{14} So far, I suppose, we are agreed. But there is a notion which latterly has been insisted on a good deal, that a combination of persons to do what any one of them lawfully might do by himself will make the otherwise lawful conduct unlawful. It would be rash to say that some as yet unformulated truth may not be hidden under this proposition. But in the general form in which it has been presented and accepted by many courts, I think it plainly untrue, both on authority and on principle. *Commonwealth v. Hunt,* 4 Met. 111.... But it is not necessary to cite cases; it is plain from the slightest consideration of practical affairs, or the most superficial reading of industrial history, that free competition means combination, and that the organization of the world, now going on so fast, means an ever increasing might and scope of combination. It seems to me futile to set our faces against this tendency. Whether beneficial on the whole, as I think it, or detrimental, it is inevitable, unless the fundamental axioms of society, and even the fundamental conditions of life, are to be changed.

{15} One of the eternal conflicts out of which life is made up is that between the effort of every man to get the most he can for his services, and that of society, disguised under the name of capital, to get his services for the least possible return. Combination on the one side is patent and powerful. Combination on the other is the necessary and desirable counterpart, if the battle is to be carried on in a fair and equal way....

{16} If it be true that workingmen may combine with a view, among other things, to getting as much as they can for their labor, just as capital may combine with a view to getting the greatest possible return, it must be true that when combined they have the same liberty that combined capital has to support their interests by argument, persuasion, and the bestowal or refusal of those advantages which they otherwise lawfully control. I can remember when many people thought that, apart from violence or breach of contract, strikes were wicked, as organized refusals to work. I suppose that intelligent economists and legislators have given up that notion to-day. I feel pretty confident that they equally will abandon the idea that an organized refusal by workmen of social intercourse with a man who shall enter their antagonist's employ is wrong, if it is dissociated from any threat of violence, and is made for the sole object of prevailing if possible in a contest with their employer about the rate of wages. The fact that the immediate object of the act by which the benefit to themselves is to be gained is to injure their antagonist, does not necessarily make it unlawful, any more than when a great house lowers the price of certain goods for the purpose, and with the effect, of driving a smaller antagonist from the business. Indeed, the question seems to me to have been decided as long ago as 1842 by the good sense of Chief Justice Shaw, in *Commonwealth v. Hunt*, 4 Met. 111....

.....

COMMENTS

Two important substantive aspects of this case are the court's ruling on the legality of the union's new tactic of patrolling and the court's authorization of an injunction. Before learning about these aspects, the student should review the NOTE ON THE PRIMA FACIE CASE AND AFFIRMATIVE DEFENSE.1.

The Legality of Patrolling

The employer in <u>Vegelahn</u> accused the strikers of committing the tort of damage to business. This tort comprised a prima facie case and an affirmative defense. The key element of the prima facie case was whether the defendants pursued the end of damaging the plaintiff's business. One of the key elements of the affirmative defense was whether the defendants' means were lawful. Thus, when labor cases were decided under the category of damage to business, the courts focused on much the same behavior as they did when the category was conspiracy.

THE PRIMA FACIE CASE OF DAMAGE TO BUSINESS

Both Justice Allen for the majority and Justice Holmes in dissent treated <u>Vegelahn</u> as a case of damage to business. The majority said that the defendants sought to prevent the employer from hiring replacement workers and to prevent replacement workers from taking jobs with the employer.[e] This end was illegal prima facie because "[a]n employer has a right to engage all persons who are willing to work for him ... and persons employed or seeking employment have a corresponding right to enter into or remain in the employment of any person or corporation willing to employ them" (¶ 3). Thus, by convincing the court that the defendants had combined to achieve an unlawful end, the employer proved a prima facie case of damage to business.

---

[e]We have previously noted that ends or purposes may be characterized in various ways and that the ability to characterize a party's ends or purposes gives judges a great deal of power. In this case, the majority could as easily have said that the defendants' end was to raise their wages, a lawful goal.

THE AFFIRMATIVE DEFENSE OF COMPETITION

The defendants asserted the affirmative defense of competition, and the majority recognized the existence of this defense. We say this for four reasons. First, the majority wrote, "A combination among persons merely to regulate their own conduct is within allowable competition, and is lawful, although others may be indirectly affected thereby" (¶ 4). This sentence seems to be a terse summary of the defense of competition. Second, after stating in ¶ 4 that the defendants relied on the defense of competition, the majority immediately moved on to discuss the defendants' means. Had the defense of competition not been accepted by the majority, it probably would have said so outright (especially because Holmes in dissent acknowledged the defense). Third, had the defense of competition not been accepted by the majority, it would have needed to discuss its own precedent of Commonwealth v. Hunt. The defendants had exactly the same purpose in Hunt as in Vegelahn, and the defendants were exonerated in Hunt. Thus, in order to have condemned the defendants' purpose in Vegelahn, the majority would have had to overrule or distinguish Hunt; and the majority did neither. And finally, Justice Holmes believed that the majority recognized the defense of competition. After using the example of setting up a second business in a town too small to support more than one such business(¶ 10), and arguing that workers and employers were in competition with one another, Holmes said he believed his brethren on the court agreed on this score (¶ 13).

Justice Holmes also accepted the defense of competition, and he developed his argument in some detail. He began by stating an idea of surpassing significance:

> "The true grounds of decision are considerations of policy and of social advantage, and it is vain to suppose that solutions can be attained merely by logic and the general propositions of law which nobody disputes" (¶ 9).

This idea, which applies to all legal cases (not merely labor law cases), has set the course for legal analysis in America to the present. Holmes asserted that social policy should determine legal categories, not the reverse. Ultimately, law is politics.

Holmes had previously indicated his acceptance of the rule that deliberately damaging another's business is prima facie illegal (¶ 8):

> "I agree ... that when a plaintiff proves that several persons have combined and conspired to injure his business, and have done acts producing that effect, he shows temporal damage and a cause of action {that is, the plaintiff has a right to bring a legal action}.... And I take it to be settled, and rightly settled, that doing that damage by combined persuasion is actionable...."

But in some circumstances this sort of damage is justified; that is, an affirmative defense or excuse exists (¶ 11):

> "{T}he policy of allowing free competition justifies the intentional infliction of temporal damage, including the damage of interference with a man's business, by {legal} means, when the damage is done, not for its own sake, but as an instrumentality in reaching the end of victory in the battle of trade.... The only debatable ground is the nature of the means by which such damage may be inflicted."

Thus, Holmes believed that a combination to damage a business was prima facie illegal, even though legal means were used; but (assuming only legal means were used) the affirmative defense of competition applied when the plaintiff and defendants were in competition with one another. The application to the case at bar was obvious. A union that struck or otherwise interfered with a business committed, prima facie, a tortious act, but the act was justified if the workers and the employer were in competition with one another. (We will consider below whether workers and employers are in competition.)

In sum, all justices of the court in <u>Vegelahn</u> believed that the defendants' end (damaging the employer's business) was prima facie illegal, but an affirmative defense applied when the damage was inflicted by workers during a labor dispute with their employer.

The affirmative defense, however, was qualified by the rule that the means of competition had to be lawful. If the defendants engaged in competition by illegal means, the defense of competition would be lost. Accordingly, the majority turned to the defendants' means.

The majority could not hold either that forming a union or that striking was an unlawful mean. Regarding forming a union, Commonwealth v. Hunt had held that unions are not illegal per se, as they may pursue lawful goals. Regarding striking, Hunt had also held that a simple strike was not unlawful. However, the majority could hold that another act of a union was unlawful: and so the court focused on the patrol.

We may assume that the defendants argued that there was really no difference between a simple strike and a strike with a patrol; that both had the same purpose, viz., to deprive the employer of workers, and both utilized the same means, viz., informing potential replacements of the labor dispute and urging them not to break the strike. The majority disagreed. Justice Allen understood the simple strike as a mean, which he characterized as a "combination among persons merely to regulate their own conduct." Thus, strikers did no more than refuse to socialize with and work next to an objectionable person. Allen stated that a strike was "within allowable competition" (¶ 4) and it remained a legal mean, even though others (the employer and the shunned worker) were damaged by the tactic.

Patrolling, however, was a different act, a different mean, in the mind of the majority. It allowed an injunction against patrolling because it was "a combination to do injurious acts expressly directed to another, by way of intimidation or restraint..." (¶ 4, emphasis added). A simple strike was a lawful mean because it was not intimidating, but a patrol was an unlawful mean because it was intimidating.

Was the majority right that strikes were not intimidating, but patrols were? We may assume that, in the days of the Hunt case, strikers did their best to make miserable the lives of workers like Jeremiah Horne. Strikers probably tried to persuade such workers to honor the strike and, failing in that, probably applied unflattering epithets to such workers and refused to socialize with them. All of this seems no different from peaceful attempts by patrolling strikers to persuade potential replacements to honor the strike. (There were surely incidents of violence and threats of violence, both in the <u>Vegelahn</u> patrol and in earlier strikes, but we shall ignore those incidents. Radicals might have thought that violence against capital was justified. That position, however, had few adherents in America, and the final decree issued by Holmes enjoined threats and violence.)

If the reasoning in the preceding paragraph be correct, the difference between a simple strike and a strike with a peaceful patrol was not the effort to cut off the supply of replacement workers or the mean of persuasion. The difference, if any, between striking and patrolling must have had something to do with the act of walking back and forth in front of the employer's shop. The majority said that patrolling was a form of moral intimidation, which was illegal. Unfortunately, the majority did not define moral intimidation or distinguish it from lawful persuasion. Perhaps the majority's idea was that violence was so closely associated with patrols that an average person who saw a patrol felt intimidated. If so, one may wonder how the majority knew this fact. Justice Holmes denied it; he accused the majority of making an unwarranted assumption (¶ 7), which is strong language for one judge to hurl at another.

<u>An Historical Explanation</u> Differing perceptions of patrolling is one explanation of why the majority and Holmes disagreed. Another explanation is possible, however (and perhaps both are true). A capitalist economy sees labor and capital in different lights. It is true that capitalism envisions labor markets, just as it envisions product markets. But whereas the capitalist system permits, encourages, in fact, depends upon accumulation of capital, the system discourages the accumulation of labor. Accumulating even a small amount of capital is good (e.g., enough to open a small business); accumulating a large amount of capital is better. Of course, accumulation may be carried too far. Too much concentration of capital may actually threaten

the capitalist system itself. But short of monopolies and oligopolies, accumulation of capital is a prominent aspect of capitalism. Labor power, however, is regarded differently by capitalism. Whereas accumulation of a small amount of capital can be useful, accumulation of a small amount of labor is irrelevant. A union is not effective if only a small percentage of the workers in a firm or in an industry belongs to the union; it is unlikely to win any concessions from employers because so many other workers will accept less than the union demands. A union is effective, and becomes a relevant actor in capitalism, only to the extent that it controls the supply of labor. Therefore, unions that matter represent an accumulation of labor power that can distort the market. Monopolies increase the price of the commodity they control. Effective unions get higher wages and better working conditions for their members than employers would pay in the absence of unions. So unions, being a form of monopoly, are an undesirable feature of a capitalist system.[f]

Why did unions begin to patrol, and what explains the <u>Hunt</u> court's acceptance of the legitimacy of strikes and the <u>Vegelahn</u> court's rejection of the legitimacy of picket lines? Perhaps the answers lie in a change in the economy between 1842 and 1896. Unions may have begun to picket towards the end of the 19th Century because they could no longer control the supply of labor merely by excluding workers like Jeremiah Horne. A cordwainer in the first half of the century was a skilled artisan who had passed through an apprenticeship and belonged to a society of cordwainers; one could not easily be replaced if one struck. So it was sufficient if union members refused to work in the same shop as non-members; the strike was effective because replacements were usually unavailable. The labor monopoly was effective. But a factory worker at the end of the century was an unskilled or semi-skilled hand who belonged to no society of

---

[f]This reasoning assumes the labor market would be competitive in the absence of unions. What if this assumption is false? What if we assume that jobs are in limited supply? Today's system of labor relations seems to make this assumption, countering the employer's monopsony of jobs with the union's monopoly of labor. Is this a fair fight? Is it rational to fight fire with fire?

workers and could be replaced readily. If the union struck, the employer could quickly replace the strikers. The labor monopoly had collapsed. This change may explain why the unions began to picket at the struck shop. They needed a new way to discourage replacements.

If the foregoing explanation be correct, it remains to explain why the courts' attitude towards union tactics changed. Perhaps skilled workers in the first half of the century (all the early labor cases involved skilled workers) had enough power to demand acceptance; after all, if their strikes were effective, they must have had some real economic power, and economic power in America has always translated into political power. But at the end of the century, unskilled workers had no such power. Perhaps, therefore, the courts ruled for the unions when they were economically strong and against them when they were economically weak.

THE GREAT GAME

Labor relations in America has long been a great game, a game of cat and mouse in which unions devise a new tactic, employers check the tactic (sometimes with the aid of the courts), unions devise a new tactic that skirts the check (a loophole in the law), employers respond, and so on. At the time of the <u>Philadelphia Cordwainers</u> case, unions had invented the simple strike for a closed shop, and employers checked it by persuading the courts to outlaw this tactic. In <u>Commonwealth v. Hunt</u> unions won the right to strike for a closed shop. The court cautioned, however, that a strike would be illegal if it sought to compel the employer to discharge a worker who had an employment contract for a definite term.

As the Industrial Revolution spread in America, factories became the center of production, work was de-skilled, and workers lost economic power; in consequence, the simple strike became less potent as a weapon of industrial warfare. Unions responded with a new tactic: the patrol in front of the entrance to the shop or factory. If the patrollers tried to persuade a worker with a contract for a term to dishonor the contract, they violated the law as announced in <u>Hunt</u>; but if they limited themselves to approaching at-will workers, the patrollers were safe within the rule of <u>Hunt</u>. Because

most workers were employed at will by the end of the 19th
Century, the unions' new tactic enjoyed some success.

Employers needed a counter-move. The unions' end
had become acceptable; it was agreed that workers could
unite to seek better terms of employment. Their end
being secure, only their means were vulnerable. They
were not inducing breach of contracts for a term, and (if
they were wise) they were not violent. Employers had to
find another way to attack the unions' means. They
happened upon the concept of moral intimidation, which
the court in Vegelahn accepted, and thereby employers
neutralized the unions' new tactic of patrolling. As the
student will see in subsequent cases, unions continued to
develop new tactics, and employers continued to respond.

Injunctions

So far, we have discussed the first important
substantive aspect of the Vegelahn case, the legality of
patrolling. Now we will turn to the second important
aspect, the injunction.

From an employer's perspective, criminal prosecution
of union members is an awkward and unreliable way to
combat unions.[g] In the first place, the government may
refuse to indict the defendants. The district attorney
may be busy with more important cases like murder and
rape and embezzlement, and the discretion of a district
attorney in deciding whether to prosecute is unreviewable
in court. Also, the district attorney may be reluctant
to prosecute union members because they will certainly
oppose one's re-election. Second, even if the government
does indict, the district attorney, and not the employer,
controls the case. The district attorney may accept a
plea bargain, or seek a light penalty, or not understand
the realities of the situation and, therefore, present
the evidence poorly. Third, criminal cases are tried by
juries, which are unpredictable. Juries are usually
selected from lists of voters. At the beginning of the
Nineteenth Century, the franchise was often limited to
property holders; recall that, in the Philadelphia

---

[g]Criminal prosecution would be awkward and unreliable in
the same ways today, and for this reason we will speak in the
present tense.

<u>Cordwainers</u> case, the jury was composed entirely of small businessmen. By the end of the century, universal white male suffrage was the norm. As more workers serve on juries, guilty verdicts are probably harder to win in labor cases. After all, it only takes one person to cause a hung jury. Fourth, the burden of proof in criminal cases is heavy. The jury must find the defendant guilty beyond a reasonable doubt. And last but far from least, criminal proceedings are slow. There must be an investigation, then an indictment, then a trial. And no penalty can be imposed until the end of the process. So, even if the defendants are eventually convicted, the strike may have continued for many weeks or months.

Each of these problems with the criminal process is eliminated if the employer can seek an injunction. It is a civil, not a criminal, case. The employer, not the government, decides whether to bring the case, and the employer, not the district attorney, controls the case, that is, decides what evidence should be presented and whether to settle. There is no jury; injunctions are ruled on by judges, and judges are generally more sympathetic to employers' interests than juries are. After all, judges usually come from the dominant classes in society and are interested in preserving the status quo from which their power derives. The burden of proof in civil cases is much lighter — preponderance of the evidence. This means that the judge rules in favor of the party whose evidence is stronger. The judge may have genuine doubts about the employer's evidence; but if it is stronger than the union's, an injunction can be issued. Injunctions can be obtained very quickly. An employer can usually get one's lawyer to bring a law suit on the same day as a strike begins, and a judge can issue an injunction, based on sworn affidavits, as soon as the suit is filed. It is not unusual to see a strike begin with mass picketing at 8:00 A.M. and an injunction limiting the number of pickets to be issued by 4:00 P.M. And an injunction is enforced by the very judge who issued it. Judges do not take kindly to union members who have violated their orders.

It is evident that the injunction is the perfect weapon for an employer to use against a union. <u>Vegelahn</u> was an early example of an injunction. The theory of the case was that the members of the union were engaged in a

civil conspiracy to violate others' rights. Thousands
upon thousands of injunctions were issued thereafter,
sometimes on a theory of civil conspiracy, sometimes on
other theories.

The Effects of the Opinions of
Chief Justice Shaw
and
Justice Holmes

Justice Holmes's dissent in Vegelahn was indebted to
Chief Justice Shaw's opinion in Hunt. Holmes's reference
to a man's opening a business in a town that is too small
to accommodate two such businesses was almost identical
to Shaw's example of the townsfolk who set up a new baker
because the prices of the existing baker are too high.
In both cases, the actors meant to harm the businesses of
other persons, yet competition was a complete defense.
Also, Holmes adopted Shaw's focus on means and ends. The
workers sought improvement in their terms and conditions
of employment; these ends were lawful. As for their
means, threats and violence were wrongful, and an
injunction could properly be issued against them; but
peaceful patrolling (which the majority called moral
intimidation) was not illegal.

Holmes was indebted to Shaw in another regard.
Holmes contended that it is wrong to harm another's
business, but competition is a defense. Shaw had
recognized the defense of competition between businesses.
Holmes carried the idea further by recognizing that
workers are in competition with their employers. Holmes
argued that workers must be allowed the same freedom to
act in concert as capital is allowed to combine into
corporations.[h]

Holmes's ideas functioned much like Shaw's opinion
in the Hunt case: it had a relatively minor impact at
the time it was announced, but, by providing a rationale,
it served as the foundation for change in the future.
Upon Shaw's thoughts grew the notion that labor unions
are not criminal conspiracies. Upon Holmes's thoughts

---

[h]As we argued above in this NOTE, Justice Allen also
seemed to have believed that workers compete with their
employers.

grew the notion that unions are not civil conspiracies. When the rest of America accepted these ideas, unions were neither criminal nor civil conspiracies; they were lawful organizations.

QUESTIONS FOR REFLECTION

1. Was the movement of labor cases from the criminal to the civil courts a desirable development?

2. Does an employer have the right to hire any willing worker? Does a worker have the right to accept an employer's offer of a job? Does a union wrongfully interfere with these rights?

3. Who are the real competitors in the labor market? Do workers compete with one another, or do workers compete with employers?

4. Justice Holmes wrote (¶ 15):

> "One of the eternal conflicts out of which life is made up is that between the effort of every man to get the most he can for his services, and that of society, disguised under the name of capital, to get his services for the least possible return. Combination on the one side is patent and powerful. Combination on the other is the necessary and desirable counterpart, if the battle is to be carried on in a fair and equal way...."

(a) How did Holmes know this? Do you think evidence to this effect was presented to the court? (b) Assuming Holmes's was correct that combinations of capital are powerful, was his prescription apt? Does the accumulation of capital by employers justify unions' attempt to create a monopoly of labor?

5. In the Philadelphia Cordwainers case Recorder Levy asserted that often times many persons may not do what one person may do, and jury agreed: for it found the defendants guilty of a crime for jointly withholding their labor in pursuit of higher wages, though everyone agreed that an individual could withhold one's labor for this purpose. In Vegelahn Justice Holmes disagreed with Levy (¶ 14):

"But there is a notion which latterly has been
insisted on a good deal, that a combination of
persons to do what any one of them lawfully might
do by himself will make the otherwise lawful
conduct unlawful. It would be rash to say that
some as yet unformulated truth may not be hidden
under this proposition. But in the general form in
which it has been presented and accepted by many
courts, I think it plainly untrue, both on
authority and on principle. Commonwealth v. Hunt,
4 Met. 111...."

Was Hunt good authority for Holmes's view? Did the
majority in Vegelahn disagree with Holmes on this score?
If so, why did the majority neglect to distinguish or
overrule Hunt; and if not, was the majority's opinion
grounded on other reasoning?

Ω

Strikes and Boycotts as Violations of Anti-trust Law

THE SHERMAN ACT OF 1890

Introduction

Danbury Hatters is an anti-trust case. The Sherman Anti-trust Act of 1890 was passed primarily to control business trusts and monopolies, but this act soon proved effective in controlling labor unions. The defendants in the case were the members of the United Hatters of North America, a labor union that had organized 70 of 82 hat manufacturers in America and that sought, as unions do, to organize the rest. In particular, the union wanted Mr. Loewe's firm to sign a union contract, but he refused: whereupon the Hatters not only struck, but also deployed two tactics that we have not previously seen in the cases, namely, primary and secondary boycotts. A **primary boycott** is a campaign against the employer's products. With the help of the American Federation of Labor, the Hatters urged all of America's union members, as well as other sympathetic persons, to refrain from purchasing Loewe's hats. A **secondary boycott** is an effort to cause other employers, who are not directly involved in the dispute (hence, they are called "secondary employers"), to cease doing business with the primary employer. Secondary boycotts come in several varieties; the one used in this case was a simple one, being a boycott of the products of firms that dealt with Loewe's (e.g., retailers who sold Loewe's hats). Again with the help of the A F of L, the Hatters warned wholesalers and retailers not to handle Loewe's hats and threatened that, if they ignored the warnings, the union would boycott their businesses as well.

Loewe v. Lawlor
(The Danbury Hatters Case)
208 U.S. 274 (1908)

{The plaintiff manufactured hats in Danbury, Connecticut. The United Hatters of North America was trying to organize the plaintiff's workers. The plaintiff sued the members of the union, accusing them of conspiring to violate the anti-trust act. Specifically, the plaintiff charged that, when he refused to sign a contract with the union, it not only prepared to strike his plant, but also conspired with the American Federation of Labor to organize a nation-wide boycott of his hats (a primary boycott). In addition, the defendants threatened to boycott any wholesaler or retailer who bought or sold the plaintiff's hats (a secondary boycott).

{Before a trial was held, the defendants moved to dismiss the case on the ground that they had done nothing wrong; in other words, even if the facts in the complaint were proved to be true, the plaintiff would lose. The District Court granted the motion to dismiss, and the Court of Appeals affirmed.}

MR. CHIEF JUSTICE FULLER delivered the opinion of the Court.

{1} This was an action brought in the Circuit Court for the District of Connecticut under § 7 of the {Sherman} Anti-Trust Act of July 2, 1890, claiming threefold damages for injuries inflicted on plaintiffs by a combination or conspiracy declared to be unlawful by the act.

...

{2} The first, second and seventh sections of that act are as follows:

1. "Every contract, combination in the form of trust or otherwise, or conspiracy, in restraint of trade or commerce among the several States, or with foreign nations, is hereby declared to be illegal. Every person who shall make any such contract or engage in any such combination or conspiracy, shall be deemed guilty of a misdemeanor, and, on conviction thereof, shall be punished by fine not exceeding five thousand dollars, or by imprisonment not exceeding one year, or by both said punishments, in the discretion of the court.

2. "Every person who shall monopolize, or attempt to monopolize, or combine or conspire with any other person or persons, to monopolize any part of the trade or commerce among the several States, or with foreign nations, shall be deemed guilty of a misdemeanor, and, on conviction thereof, shall be punished by fine not exceeding five thousand dollars, or by

imprisonment not exceeding one year, or by both said punishments, in the discretion of the court."

       7. "Any person who shall be injured in his business or property by any other person or corporation by reason of anything forbidden or declared to be unlawful by this act, may sue therefor in any Circuit Court of the United States in the district in which the defendant resides or is found, without respect to the amount in controversy, and shall recover three fold the damages by him sustained, and the costs of suit, including a reasonable attorney's fee."

{3} In our opinion, the combination described in the declaration is a combination "in restraint of trade or commerce among the several States," in the sense in which those words are used in the act, and the action can be maintained accordingly.

{4} And that conclusion rests on many judgments of this court, to the effect that the act prohibits any combination whatever to secure action which essentially obstructs the free flow of commerce between the States, or restricts, in that regard, the liberty of a trader to engage in business.

{5} The combination charged falls within the class of restraints of trade aimed at compelling third parties and strangers involuntarily not to engage in the course of trade except on conditions that the combination imposes; and there is no doubt that (to quote from the well-known work of Chief Justice Erle on Trade Unions) "at common law every person has individually, and the public also has collectively, a right to require that the course of trade should be kept free from unreasonable obstruction." But the objection here is to the jurisdiction, because, even conceding that the declaration states a case good at common law, it is contended that it does not state one within the statute....

...

{6} Nor can the act in question be held inapplicable because defendants were not themselves engaged in interstate commerce. The act made no distinction between classes. It provided that "every" contract, combination or conspiracy in restraint of trade was illegal. The records of Congress show that several efforts were made to exempt, by legislation, organizations of farmers and laborers from the operation of the act and that all these efforts failed, so that the act remained as we have it before us.

{7} In an early case, *United States v. Workingmen's Amalgamated Council*, 54 Fed. Rep. 994, the United States filed a bill under the Sherman act in the Circuit

Court for the Eastern District of Louisiana, averring the existence of "a gigantic and widespread combination of the members of a multitude of separate organizations for the purpose of restraining the commerce among the several States and with foreign countries," and it was contended that the statute did not refer to combinations of laborers. But the court, granting the injunction, said:

> "I think the Congressional debates show that the statute had its origin in the evils of massed capital; but, when the Congress came to formulating the prohibition, which is the yardstick for measuring the complainant's right to the injunction, it expressed it in these words: 'Every contract or combination in the form of trust, or otherwise in restraint of trade or commerce among the several States or with foreign nations, is hereby declared to be illegal.' The subject had so broadened in the minds of the legislators that the source of the evil was not regarded as material, and the evil in its entirety is dealt with. They made the interdiction include combinations of labor, as well as of capital; in fact, all combinations in restraint of commerce, without reference to the character of the persons who entered into them. It is true this statute has not been much expounded by judges, but, as it seems to me, its meaning, as far as relates to the sort of combinations to which it is to apply, is manifest, and that it includes combinations which are composed of laborers acting in the interest of laborers.

> ...

> "It is the successful effort of the combination of the defendants to intimidate and overawe others who were at work in conducting or carrying on the commerce of the country, in which the court finds their error and their violation of the statute. One of the intended results of their combined action was the forced stagnation of all the commerce which flowed through New Orleans. This intent and combined action are none the less unlawful because they included in their scope the paralysis of all other business within the city as well."

> ....

{The judgment of the Court of Appeals was reversed, and the case was remanded to the district court for a trial.}

The *Danbury Hatters* Case   v

COMMENTS

THE ROLE OF STATUTES

Danbury Hatters is the first case in this book to involve a statute. In the previous cases, decisions were based on the **common law**, that is, the law as made by judges.[1] Perhaps the main reason for the importance of the common law was the paucity of statutes in the Nineteenth Century. In the Twentieth Century, however, legislatures became increasingly active, passing more and more statutes.

In theory and in practice, a statute trumps the common law. If the legislature of a jurisdiction is unhappy with the law as announced by a court of that jurisdiction, the legislature — being the more democratic branch of government — may pass a statute that changes the law; and the courts are bound to honor the statute. Thus, there was a common law rule against restraint of trade, but it was superceded by the Sherman Anti-trust Act.[2]

---

[1] The common law originated in medieval England. In those days, the holder of a fief had the right to administer justice in his fiefdom. This right was important not only because of the power inherent in judging, but also because of fees the lord of the fief could charge the parties for the privilege of his justice. Given the number of fiefs, the size of the country, and the difficulty of communication (not to mention the possibilities of caprice, corruption, and irrationality), it is no surprise that rules of law varied from place to place.

During the Middle Ages, kings struggled with lesser lords for money and power. As part of their effort to increase royal revenue and influence, the kings dispatched itinerant judges to dispense the king's justice throughout the realm. Springing from a single font, the king's justice was expected to be uniform, and indeed the king's judges met regularly to discuss cases and harmonize their judgments. The law made by the king's judges became known as the "common law" because it was common throughout the land.

[2] We prefaced this paragraph with the qualifier "in theory" because it is the province of courts to interpret statutes. Thus, for practical purposes, the courts have the last word on

(continued...)

A NEW TACTIC ELICITS AN OLD RESPONSE

Several other aspects of the Danbury Hatters case deserve attention. One is that unions had developed a new tactic, and it was held illegal. The same thing had happened twice before. The unions' initial tactic, maintaining a closed shop and striking for higher wages, was outlawed in the Philadelphia Cordwainers case. The unions' next major innovation in tactics, the picket line, was outlawed in Vegelahn v. Guntner. And now boycotts were prohibited. Whether there is a pattern here, the student may judge for oneself. The student may also wish to think about how the law is likely to treat recent developments in union tactics, such as the corporate campaign and the "labor rat."

EMPLOYERS MOVE TO THE FEDERAL COURTS

Another aspect of the Danbury Hatters case worth noting is that, whereas Philadelphia Cordwainers, Commonwealth v. Hunt, and Vegelahn v. Guntner were decided by state courts, Danbury Hatters was a federal case. Thus, a few words about precedents in state and federal courts are in order. State judicial systems are independent of one another. As a result, the decision of a court in Alabama is not binding on a court in Wyoming. Nevertheless, if a court in Wyoming is considering an issue which has not previously been decided in Wyoming, a precedent on that issue from Alabama will have some persuasive force. The federal and state judicial systems are, in large part, separate as well,[3] but they overlap to a degree. If a federal court is deciding an issue of

---

[2](...continued)
the meaning of the law: if judges are dissatisfied with a statute, they can modify it by their (mis)interpretation of it. The legislature, of course, is free to amend the statute in order to correct the courts.

[3]Occasionally, federal law displaces state law on an issue; for example, a federal court may rule that a state law is preempted by a federal law or that a state law is unconstitutional under the federal constitution. Rulings of this sort are much less frequent than the degree of attention they receive might suggest.

state law,[4] the federal court (even the U.S. Supreme Court) will treat that state's precedents as binding on that issue. If the state has no precedent on the issue, the federal court will decide the issue by attempting to determine how the state would have ruled; this decision will not bind the state's courts, but may influence them. Similarly, if a state court is deciding an issue of federal law, the state court will follow federal precedents. If no federal precedent exists on the issue, the state court will decide the issue by attempting to determine how the federal courts would rule; this decision will not bind the federal courts, but may influence them.

Hierarchies also affect precedents. The higher the court, the more influential its decisions. Looking down a line of authority, the decision of a higher court is, naturally, binding on a lower court. Looking up a line of authority, the decision of a lower court, though not binding on a higher court, has some persuasive force. In Danbury Hatters the Supreme Court was not bound by the decision of the Circuit Court for the Eastern District of Louisiana in U.S. v. Workingmen's Amalgamated Council, yet the Supreme Court relied heavily on the lower court's reasoning.

AN OLD THEORY IS REVIVED

A third noteworthy aspect of Danbury Hatters is that the defendants were found liable for acting in combination for the restraint of trade. The idea of combination was important a hundred years earlier when union activity was held to be a criminal conspiracy. Anti-trust cases are civil, not criminal, cases. In Vegelahn v. Guntner, the judges began translating the doctrine of criminal conspiracy into civil conspiracy, and the Danbury Hatters case continued this process. Indeed, shortly before the Sherman Act was passed, the Supreme Court held that some kinds of union activity were criminal conspiracies. The case was Callan v. Wilson, 127 U.S. 540, decided in 1888. A musician named Krause

---

[4]Federal courts may decide issues of state law, and state courts may decide issues of federal law. It is a common mistake to believe that state courts may hear only state cases and federal courts may hear only federal cases.

evidently broke a union rule and was fined. When he refused to pay, the defendants, who were probably leaders of the union, used the Cordwainers' tactic: they directed that union members refuse to work for any employer who hired Krause; and when some musicians ignored this directive, the union directed that members refuse to work for any employer who hired these musicians as well: in short, the union blacklisted Krause and boycotted employers who hired him or his allies. The defendants were charged with criminal conspiracy. The precise holding of the Supreme Court is that the defendants were entitled to a jury trial; but, implicitly, the Court held that this sort of boycott was a crime. If the Court believed that the musicians' boycott was a criminal conspiracy, we should not be surprised to find that the Court believed that the Hatters' boycott was a civil conspiracy.

AN EXPLANATION OF THE DECISION

The holding of the Danbury Hatters case has been criticized because it authorized the courts, with no guidance from the legislature, to create a new body of law to regulate labor unions. Critics argue that courts should not engage in this kind of law making. But the courts continue to make new law when it suits them.

Why did the Court rule as it did? Why were the courts so willing to extend anti-trust law to cover unions? Willie Forbath offers this explanation: At the local level, a union has to control the supply of labor in order to organize a firm and bargain with its owner. By the start of the Twentieth Century, the judges were largely willing to tolerate this degree of monopoly. But several unions at this time had gone beyond the local level of activity. They had created national federations which were capable of organizing large-scale primary and secondary boycotts. These national unions were assuming the characteristics of trusts. Many federal judges were strongly opposed to the great trusts of the late Nineteenth Century; the trusts were monopolistic and anti-competitive. As unions began to resemble business trusts, judges became willing to invoke anti-trust law against organized labor.

THE REST OF THE STORY

The student may be curious about what happened to the Hatters. There had been no trial as yet. Rather, when Mr. Loewe, the plaintiff, filed the complaint, the defendants asked the court to dismiss the complaint on the ground that, even if every fact alleged in the complaint were proved to be true, the defendants would still win because the law did not apply to union activity. It would be as if Kalil's roommate sued him for burping too often. Kalil would move to dismiss the complaint because, even if he did it, it was not against the law.[5] The lower courts agreed with the defendants; they held that the Sherman Act did not apply to unions and, accordingly, dismissed the complaint. As you have read, the Supreme Court disagreed; it held the law did cover unions. But this holding did not mean that Mr. Loewe won. The holding only meant that, if he proved the facts he alleged in the complaint, he would win. So the case was sent back to the district court for a trial. The plaintiff won the trial. The court found the boycotts had cost his business over $80,000. Under the Sherman Act, a victim of a restraint of trade is entitled to treble damages plus court costs. As a result, Mr. Loewe was awarded $252,000, which was a huge sum in 1908. The Supreme Court affirmed this award. Lawlor v. Loewe, 235 U.S. 522 (1915). The plaintiff had sued, not the union, but the individual members of the union. The reason was that unions are unincorporated associations, which lacked legal standing in the past; they could not sue or be sued. As a result, the plaintiff started to collect this money from the workers. He attached their bank accounts and began to levy on their houses. The A F of L launched a campaign to raise money and eventually settled the case for $234,000 cash. The case, particularly the employer's attempt to seize the workers' homes, became a cause celebre, and the memory of the case influenced Congress four decades later to limit employers to collecting damages from unions, never from workers (section 301(b) of the Taft-Hartley Act).

---

[5]In this regard, Kalil's case would be analogous to Commonwealth v. Hunt, in which the court held that the indictment did not allege a crime.

QUESTIONS FOR REFLECTION

1. For the purpose of interpreting a statute —

Rule 1. A tribunal will not allow legislators to testify as to the meaning of a statute that has been enacted.

Rule 2. A tribunal will use for this purpose legislators' remarks while the bill that became the statute was being debated.

What reasons support these rules? Should either of them be changed?

2. Was the pattern noted above — unions develop a new tactic, courts outlaw it — merely a coincidence, or was it caused by something fundamental in American institutions?

3. The Court drew arguments in support of its holding from the text of the statute, the legislative history of the statute, other courts' decisions, and scholarship. Purpose of the act is also used to illuminate the will of Congress. Can these sources be ranked in a hierarchy of authority?

4. If anti-trust law as applied to unions was a species of the law of civil conspiracy, the union's means or ends must have been illegal. Which was it?

5. Labor law today provides that a judgment against a union cannot be collected from its members. Is this a good rule? Should not the members of an organization be responsible to parties whom it injures?

Ω

Strikes and Boycotts as Violations of Anti-trust Law (continued)

THE CLAYTON ACT OF 1914

Introduction

Like the <u>Danbury Hatters</u> case, the following case, <u>Duplex v. Deering</u>, involves primary and secondary boycotts. In a **primary boycott**, the union urges people to stop dealing with an employer who will not accede to the union's demands. This employer is known as the primary employer because the union's primary dispute is with this firm. Primary boycotts come in several varieties. Perhaps the most common is a consumer boycott, in which the union urges consumers not to purchase the employer's products. Although not commonly referred to as a boycott, a strike may be considered a kind of primary boycott because the union asks workers not to accept employment with the primary employer. The essence of the primary boycott is that the union seeks to apply economic pressure directly against the offending employer.

In contrast, in a **secondary boycott** the union uses economic pressure to induce other firms to cease doing business with the primary employer. These firms are known as secondary (or neutral) employers because the union has no dispute with them (except that they do business with the primary employer). Secondary employers supply goods or services to the primary employer (for example, raw materials and transportation) or buy goods or services from the primary employer (for example, finished products). A secondary boycott involves more than a mere request that a secondary firm cease dealing with a primary employer; a secondary boycott involves the union's use of economic force to compel the secondary employer to sever ties with the primary employer. Thus, a union might strike a secondary employer until it stops dealing with the primary employer, or union members who work for secondary employers might refuse to handle any goods coming from the primary employer.

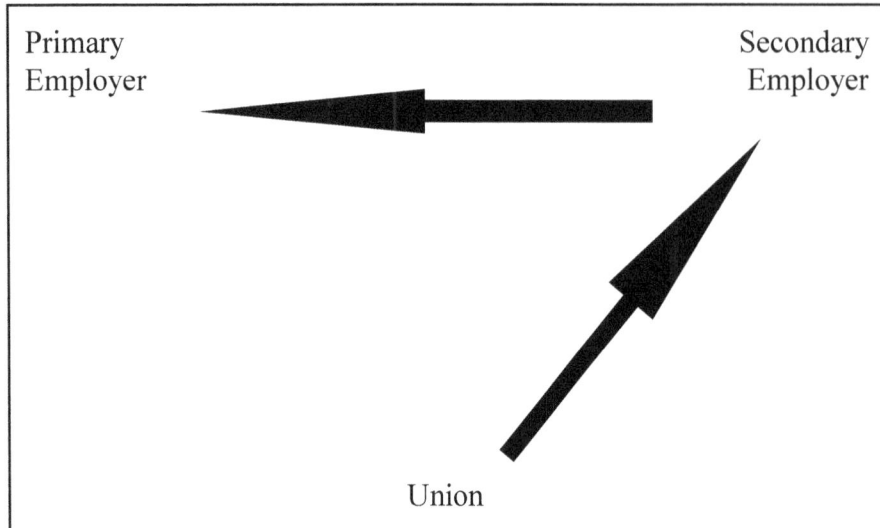

Both primary and secondary boycotts occurred in the
<u>Danbury Hatters</u> Case. The union went on strike against
the primary employer, Loewe's, which manufactured hats,
and asked consumers not to buy its hats. This was a
primary boycott. The union also urged people not to
patronize any shops that sold Loewe's hats. This was a
secondary boycott because it put economic pressure on
secondary employers (retail merchants) to induce them to
cease doing business with the primary employer.

Both primary and secondary boycotts also occurred in
the following case, <u>Duplex v. Deering</u>. The employer,
Duplex, manufactured printing presses. The union's
strike against Duplex was unsuccessful. A primary
boycott would have been worthless because the market for
printing presses was small, so the union organized
secondary boycotts. The union threatened to strike any
business that purchased presses made by Duplex. The
union threatened to organize a strike of the employees of
the trucking company that transported Duplex's presses.
The union threatened to strike repair shops that serviced
Duplex's presses, and so forth.

Duplex responded to the secondary boycotts by
seeking an injunction against them, and such an
injunction would almost surely have been issued under the

Duplex v. Deering   iii

Sherman Anti-trust Act. But the legal environment had
recently changed. After the <u>Danbury Hatters</u> case,
organized labor vigorously sought exemption from the
Sherman Act. The result was the Clayton Act of 1914,
which amended the Sherman Act. When Congress debated the
bill that became the Clayton Act, a major issue was how
anti-trust law should apply to labor unions.

Samuel Gompers hailed the Clayton Act as the
"industrial Magna Carta" for working people. Courts had
treated human labor like any other article of commerce at
least since <u>Commonwealth v. Hunt</u>, but section 6 of the
Clayton Act declared:

> "That the labor of a human being is not a
> commodity or article of commerce."

This declaration seemed to remove labor from the reach of
anti-trust law, which applies to restraint of trade: if
human labor is not a commodity or article of commerce, it
cannot be traded and a monopoly of labor is not a
restraint of trade. Section 6 continued:

> "Nothing contained in the anti-trust laws shall
> be construed to forbid the existence and
> operation of labor ... organizations ... or to
> forbid ... such organizations from lawfully
> carrying out the legitimate objects thereof;
> nor shall such organizations ... be held or
> construed to be illegal combinations or
> conspiracies in restraint of trade ...."

Gompers declared, "These words are sledgehammer blows to
the wrongs and injustices so long inflicted on the
workers."[a] And if these sledgehammer blows were not good
enough, the first paragraph of section 20 of the Clayton
Act added:

> "That no restraining order or injunction shall
> be granted by any [federal court] ... in any
> case between an employer and employees ...
> involving, or growing out of, a dispute
> concerning terms and conditions of employment,
> unless necessary to prevent irreparable injury

---

[a]Summers and Wellington, <u>Labor Law</u>, 1st ed., p. 174.

to property ...; and no such restraining order
or injunction shall prohibit any person ...
from ceasing to perform any work or labor or
from recommending, advising, or persuading
others by peaceful means so to do ... or from
ceasing to patronize ... any party to such
dispute, or from persuading others by peaceful
and lawful means so to do ...."

These words seemed to prohibit federal courts from
issuing injunctions against strikes and boycotts. The
second paragraph of section 20 concluded with the clause,
"nor shall any of the acts specified in this paragraph be
considered or held to be violations of any [federal]
law...." This clause seemed to say that strikes and
boycotts were lawful.

But the attentive student has noticed that we
consistently said that the Act seemed to do this or that.
In fact, it did not do any of this. Samuel Gompers was
wrong, as Duplex v. Deering demonstrated.

Duplex Printing Co. v. Deering
254 U.S. 443 (1921)

MR. JUSTICE PITNEY delivered the opinion of the court.

{1} This was a suit in equity brought by appellant in the District Court for the Southern District of New York for an injunction to restrain a course of conduct carried on by defendants in that District and vicinity in maintaining a boycott against the products of complainant's factory.... Complainant is a Michigan corporation and manufactures printing presses at a factory in Battle Creek, in that State, employing about 200 machinists in the factory in addition to 50 office-employees, traveling salesmen, and expert machinists or road men who supervise the erection of the presses for complainant's customers at their various places of business.....

{2} ... Complainant conducts its business on the "open shop" policy, without discrimination against either union or non-union men. The individual defendants and the local organizations of which they are the representatives are affiliated with the International Association of Machinists, an unincorporated association having a membership of more than 60,000; and are united in a combination, to which the International Association also is a party, having the object of compelling complainant to unionize its factory and enforce the "closed shop," the eight-hour day, and the union scale of wages, by means of interfering with and restraining its interstate trade in the products of the factory. Complainant's principal manufacture is newspaper presses of large size and complicated mechanism, varying in weight from 10,000 to 100,000 pounds, and requiring a considerable force of labor and a considerable expenditure of time — a week or more — to handle, haul and erect them at the point of delivery. These presses are sold throughout the United States and in foreign countries; and, as they are especially designed for the production of daily papers, there is a large market for them in and about the City of New York. They are delivered there in the ordinary course of interstate commerce, the handling, hauling and installation work at destination being done by employees of the purchaser under the supervision of a specially skilled machinist supplied by complainant. The acts complained of and sought to be restrained have nothing to do with the conduct or management of the factory in Michigan, but solely with the installation and operation of the presses by complainant's customers. None of the defendants is or ever was an employee of complainant, and complainant at no time has had relations with either of the organizations that they represent. In August, 1913 (eight months before the filing of the bill), the International Association called a strike at complainant's factory in Battle Creek, as a result of which union machinists to the number of about eleven in the factory and three who supervised the erection of presses in the field left complainant's employ. But the defection of so small a number did not materially interfere with the operation of the factory, and sales and shipments in interstate commerce continued. The acts complained of made up the details of an elaborate programme adopted and carried out by defendants and their organizations in and about the City of New York as part of a country-wide programme adopted by the International Association, for the purpose of enforcing a boycott of complainant's product. The acts embraced the following, with others: warning customers that it would be better for them not to purchase, or having purchased not to install, presses made by complainant, and threatening them with loss should they do so; threatening customers with sympathetic strikes in other trades; notifying a trucking company usually employed by customers to haul the presses not to do so, and threatening it with trouble if it should; inciting employees of the trucking company, and other men employed by customers of complainant, to strike against their respective employers in order to interfere with the hauling and installation of presses, and thus bring pressure to bear upon the customers; notifying repair shops not to do repair work on Duplex presses; coercing union men by threatening them with loss of union cards and with being blacklisted as "scabs" if they assisted in installing the presses; threatening an exposition company with a strike if it permitted complainant's presses to be exhibited; and resorting to a variety of other modes of preventing the sale of presses of complainant's manufacture in or about New York City, and delivery of them in interstate commerce, such as injuring and threatening to injure complainant's customers and prospective customers, and persons concerned in hauling, handling, or installing the presses. In some cases the threats were undisguised, in other cases polite in form but none the less sinister in purpose and effect. {The district court refused to grant an injunction and dismissed the case.} All the judges of the Circuit Court of Appeals concurred in the view that defendants' conduct consisted essentially of efforts to render it impossible for complainant to carry on any commerce in printing presses between Michigan and New York; and that defendants had agreed to do and were endeavoring to accomplish the very thing pronounced unlawful by this court in *Loewe v. Lawlor*, 208 U.S. 274; 235 U.S. 522.... {Nevertheless, the Court of Appeals affirmed the decree of the district court.}

...

{3} ... {C}omplainant's business of manufacturing printing presses and disposing of them in commerce is a property right, entitled to protection against unlawful injury or interference; ... unrestrained access to the channels of interstate commerce is necessary for the successful conduct of the business; ... a widespread combination exists, to which defendants and the associations represented by them are parties, to hinder and obstruct complainant's interstate trade and commerce by the means that have been indicated; and ... as a result of it complainant has sustained substantial damage to its interstate trade, and is threatened with further and irreparable loss and damage in the future{. These facts are} proved by clear and undisputed evidence. Hence the right to an injunction is clear if the threatened loss is due to a violation of the Sherman Act as amended by the Clayton Act.

{4} Looking first to the former act, the thing declared illegal by its first section is

> "Every contract, combination in the form of trust or otherwise, or conspiracy, in restraint of trade or commerce among the several States, or with foreign nations."

The accepted definition of a conspiracy is, a combination of two or more persons by concerted action to accomplish a criminal or unlawful purpose, or to accomplish some purpose not in itself criminal or unlawful by criminal or unlawful means. If the purpose be unlawful it may not be carried out even by means that otherwise would be legal; and although the purpose be lawful it may not be carried out by criminal or unlawful means.

{5} The substance of the matters here complained of is an interference with complainant's interstate trade, intended to have coercive effect upon complainant, and produced by what is commonly known as a "secondary boycott," that is, a combination not merely to refrain from dealing with complainant, or to advise or by peaceful means persuade complainant's customers to refrain ("primary boycott"), but to exercise coercive pressure upon such customers, actual or prospective, in order to cause them to withhold or withdraw patronage from complainant through fear of loss or damage to themselves should they deal with it.

{6} As we shall see, the recognized distinction between a primary and a secondary boycott is material to be considered upon the question of the proper construction of the Clayton Act. But, in determining the right to an injunction under that and the Sherman Act, it is of minor consequence whether either kind of boycott is lawful or unlawful at common law or under the statutes of particular States....

{7} In *Loewe v. Lawlor*, 208 U.S. 274, where there was an effort to compel plaintiffs to unionize their factory by preventing them from manufacturing articles intended for transportation beyond the State, and also by preventing vendees from reselling articles purchased from plaintiffs and negotiating with plaintiffs for further purchases, by means of a boycott of plaintiffs' products and of dealers who handled them, this court held that there was a conspiracy in restraint of trade actionable under § 7 of the Sherman Act, and in that connection said (p. 293):

> "The act prohibits any combination whatever to secure action which essentially obstructs the free flow of commerce between the States, or restricts, in that regard, the liberty of a trader to engage in business. The combination charged falls within the class of restraints of trade aimed at compelling third parties and strangers involuntarily not to engage in the course of trade except on conditions that the combination imposes."

And when the case came before the court a second time, *Lawlor v. Loewe*, 235 U.S. 522, it was held that the use of the primary and secondary boycott and the circulation of a list of "unfair dealers," intended to influence customers of plaintiffs and thus subdue the latter to the demands of the defendants, and having the effect of interfering with plaintiffs' interstate trade, was actionable.

{8} In *Eastern States Retail Lumber Dealers' Association* v. *United States*, 234 U.S. 600, {retailers of lumber wanted to prevent wholesalers from selling directly to consumers;} wholesale dealers {who persisted in selling to consumers} were subjected to coercion merely through the circulation among retailers, who were members of the association, of information in the form of a kind of "black list," intended to influence the retailers to refrain from dealing with the listed wholesalers, and it was held that this constituted a violation of the Sherman Act. Referring to this decision, the court said, in *Lawlor v. Loewe*, 235 U.S. 522, 534, "That case establishes that, irrespective of compulsion ... the circulation of a list of 'unfair dealers,' manifestly intended to put the ban upon those whose names appear therein, among an important body of possible customers combined with a view to joint action and in anticipation of such reports, is within the prohibitions of the Sherman Act if it is intended to restrain and restrains commerce among the States."

{9} It is settled by these decisions that such a restraint produced by peaceable persuasion is as much within the prohibition as one accomplished by force or threats of force; and it is not to be justified by the fact that the participants in the combination or conspiracy may have some object beneficial to themselves or their associates which possibly they might have been at liberty to pursue in the absence of the statute.

{10} Upon the question whether the provisions of the Clayton Act forbade the grant of an injunction under the circumstances of the present case, the Circuit Court of Appeals was divided; the majority holding that under § 20, "perhaps in conjunction with section 6," there could be no injunction. These sections are set forth in the margin.[a] Defendants seek to derive from them some authority for their conduct. As to § 6, it seems to us its principal importance in this discussion is for what it does not authorize, and for the limit it sets to the immunity conferred. The section assumes the normal objects of a labor organization to be legitimate, and declares that nothing in the anti-trust laws shall be construed to forbid the existence and operation of such organizations or to forbid their members from lawfully carrying out their legitimate objects; and that such an organization shall not be held in itself — merely because of its existence and operation — to be an illegal combination or conspiracy in restraint

---

[a]"Sec. 6. That the labor of a human being is not a commodity or article of commerce. Nothing contained in the antitrust laws shall be construed to forbid the existence and operation of labor, agricultural, or horticultural organizations, instituted for the purposes of mutual help, and not having capital stock or conducted for profit, or to forbid or restrain individual members of such organizations from lawfully carrying out the legitimate objects thereof; nor shall such organizations, or the members thereof, be held or construed to be illegal combinations or conspiracies in restraint of trade, under the antitrust laws."

"Sec. 20. That no restraining order or injunction shall be granted by any court of the United States, or a judge or the judges thereof, in any case between an employer and employees, or between employers and employees, or between employees, or between persons employed and persons seeking employment, involving, or growing out of, a dispute concerning terms or conditions of employment, unless necessary to prevent irreparable injury to property, or to a property right, of the party making the application, for which injury there is no adequate remedy at law, and such property or property right must be described with particularity in the application, which must be in writing and sworn to by the applicant or by his agent or attorney.

"And no such restraining order or injunction shall prohibit any person or persons, whether singly or in concert, from terminating any relation of employment, or from ceasing to perform any work or labor, or from recommending, advising, or persuading others by peaceful means so to do; or from attending at any place where any such person or persons may lawfully be, for the purpose of peacefully obtaining or communicating information, or from peacefully persuading any person to work or to abstain from working; or from ceasing to patronize or to employ any party to such dispute, or from recommending, advising, or persuading others by peaceful and lawful means so to do; or from paying or giving to, or withholding from, any person engaged in such dispute, any strike benefits or other moneys or things of value; or from peaceably assembling in a lawful manner, and for lawful purposes; or from doing any act or thing which might lawfully be done in the absence of such dispute by any party thereto; nor shall any of the acts specified in this paragraph be considered or held to be violations of any law of the United States."

of trade. But there is nothing in the section to exempt such an organization or its members from accountability where it or they depart from its normal and legitimate objects and engage in an actual combination or conspiracy in restraint of trade. And by no fair or permissible construction can it be taken as authorizing any activity otherwise unlawful, or enabling a normally lawful organization to become a cloak for an illegal combination or conspiracy in restraint of trade as defined by the anti-trust laws.

{11} The principal reliance is upon § 20. This regulates the granting of restraining orders and injunctions by the courts of the United States in a designated class of cases.... All its provisions are subject to a general qualification respecting the nature of the controversy and the parties affected. It is to be a "case between an employer and employees, or between employers and employees, or between employees, or between persons employed and persons seeking employment, involving, or growing out of, a dispute concerning terms or conditions of employment."

{12} The first paragraph ... is but declaratory of the law as it stood before {the Clayton Act was passed}. The second paragraph declares that "no such restraining order or injunction" shall prohibit certain conduct specified — manifestly still referring to a "case between an employer and employees ... involving, or growing out of, a dispute concerning terms or conditions of employment," as designated in the first paragraph. It is very clear that the restriction upon the use of the injunction is in favor only of those concerned as parties to such a dispute as is described....

{13} The majority of the Circuit Court of Appeals appear to have entertained the view that the words "employers and employees," as used in § 20, should be treated as referring to "the business class or clan to which the parties litigant respectively belong"; and that, as there had been a dispute at complainant's factory in Michigan concerning the conditions of employment there — a dispute created, it is said, if it did not exist before, by the act of the Machinists' Union in calling a strike at the factory — § 20 operated to permit members of the Machinists' Union elsewhere — some 60,000 in number — although standing in no relation of employment under complainant, past, present, or prospective, to make that dispute their own and proceed to instigate sympathetic strikes, picketing, and boycotting against employers wholly unconnected with complainant's factory and having relations with complainant only in the way of purchasing its product in the ordinary course of interstate commerce — and this where there was no dispute between such employers and their employees respecting terms or conditions of employment.

{14} We deem this construction altogether inadmissible. Section 20 must be given full effect according to its terms as an expression of the purpose of Congress;

but it must be borne in mind that the section imposes an exceptional and extraordinary restriction upon the equity powers of the courts of the United States and upon the general operation of the anti-trust laws, a restriction in the nature of a special privilege or immunity to a particular class, with corresponding detriment to the general public.... Full and fair effect will be given to every word if the exceptional privilege be confined — as the natural meaning of the words confines it — to those who are proximately and substantially concerned as parties to an actual dispute respecting the terms or conditions of their own employment, past, present, or prospective.[a] The extensive construction adopted by the majority of the court below virtually ignores the effect of the qualifying words. Congress had in mind particular industrial controversies, not a general class war. "Terms or conditions of employment" are the only grounds of dispute recognized as adequate to bring into play the exemptions; and it would do violence to the guarded language employed were the exemption extended beyond the parties affected in a proximate and substantial, not merely a sentimental or sympathetic, sense by the cause of dispute.

{15} Nor can § 20 be regarded as bringing in all members of a labor organization as parties to a "dispute concerning terms or conditions of employment" which proximately affects only a few of them, with the result of conferring upon any and all members — no matter how many thousands there may be, nor how remote from the actual conflict — those exemptions which Congress in terms conferred only upon parties to the dispute. That ... would virtually repeal by implication the prohibition of the Sherman Act, so far as labor organizations are concerned, notwithstanding repeals by implication are not favored; and in effect, as was noted in *Loewe v. Lawlor*, 208 U.S. 274, 303-304, would confer upon voluntary associations of individuals formed within the States a control over commerce among the States that is denied to the governments of the States themselves.

{16} The qualifying effect of the words descriptive of the nature of the dispute and the parties concerned is further borne out by the phrases defining the conduct that is not to be subjected to injunction or treated as a violation of the laws of the United States, that is to say:

(a) "terminating any relation of employment ... or persuading others by peaceful and lawful means so to do"; (b) "attending at any place where any

---

[a]{In other words, the phrase in § 20 "a dispute concerning terms or conditions of employment" applies only to a labor dispute between an employer and one's own employees; the term does not apply to disagreements between an employer and any other workers. As a result, the exemption from anti-trust law created by the Clayton Act protects only workers who are engaged in labor conflict with their own employer. The defendants in the case at bar, not being employees of Duplex, were not exempt from anti-trust law. —ed.}

such person or persons may lawfully be, for the purpose of peacefully obtaining or communicating information, or from peacefully persuading any person to work or to abstain from working;" (c) "ceasing to patronize or to employ any party to such dispute, or ... recommending, advising, or persuading others by peaceful and lawful means so to do"; (d) "paying or giving to, or withholding from, any person engaged in such dispute, any strike benefits..."; (e) "doing any act or thing which might lawfully be done in the absence of such dispute by any party thereto."

The emphasis placed on the words "lawful" and "lawfully," "peaceful" and "peacefully," and the references to the dispute and the parties to it, strongly rebut a legislative intent to confer a general immunity for conduct violative of the anti-trust laws, or otherwise unlawful. The subject of the boycott is dealt with specifically in the "ceasing to patronize" provision, and by the clear force of the language employed the exemption is limited to pressure exerted upon a "party to such dispute" by means of "peaceful and lawful" influence upon neutrals. There is nothing here to justify defendants or the organizations they represent in using either threats or persuasion to bring about strikes or a cessation of work on the part of employees of complainant's customers or prospective customers, or of the trucking company employed by the customers, with the object of compelling such customers to withdraw or refrain from commercial relations with complainant, and of thereby constraining complainant to yield the matter in dispute. To instigate a sympathetic strike in aid of a secondary boycott cannot be deemed "peaceful and lawful" persuasion. In essence it is a threat to inflict damage upon the immediate employer, between whom and his employees no dispute exists, in order to bring him against his will into a concerted plan to inflict damage upon another employer who is in dispute with his employees.

{17} The majority of the Circuit Court of Appeals, very properly treating the case as involving a secondary boycott, based the decision upon the {mistaken} view that it was the purpose of § 20 to legalize the secondary boycott "at least in so far as it rests on, or consists of, refusing to work for any one who deals with the principal offender." ...

...

{18} The extreme and harmful consequences of the construction adopted in the court below are not to be ignored. The present case furnishes an apt and convincing example. An ordinary controversy in a manufacturing establishment, said to concern the terms or conditions of employment there, has been held {by the union to be} a sufficient occasion for imposing a general embargo upon the products of the establishment and a nation-wide blockade of the channels of interstate commerce against them, carried out by inciting sympathetic strikes and a secondary boycott against complainant's customers, to the great and incalculable damage of many innocent people far remote from any connection with or control over the original and actual dispute — people constituting, indeed, the general public upon whom the cost must ultimately fall, and whose vital interest in unobstructed commerce constituted the prime and paramount concern of Congress in enacting the antitrust laws, of which the section under consideration forms after all a part.

...

Decree reversed....

MR. JUSTICE BRANDEIS, dissenting, with whom MR. JUSTICE HOLMES and MR. JUSTICE CLARKE, concur.

{19} The Duplex Company, a manufacturer of newspaper printing presses, seeks to enjoin officials of the machinists' and affiliated unions from interfering with its business by inducing their members not to work for plaintiff or its customers in connection with the setting up of presses made by it. Unlike *Hitchman Coal & Coke Co. v. Mitchell*, 245 U.S. 229, there is here no charge that defendants are inducing employees to break their contracts. Nor is it now urged that defendants threaten acts of violence. But plaintiff insists that the acts complained of violate both the common law of New York and the Sherman Act and that, accordingly, it is entitled to relief by injunction under the state law and under § 16 of the Clayton Act.

{20} The defendants admit interference with plaintiff's business but justify on the following ground: There are in the United States only four manufacturers of such presses; and they are in active competition. Between 1909 and 1913 the machinists' union induced three of them to recognize and deal with the union, to grant the eight-hour day, to establish a minimum wage scale and to comply with other union requirements. The fourth, the Duplex Company, refused to recognize the union; insisted upon conducting its factory on the open shop principle; refused to introduce the eight-hour day and operated for the most part, ten hours a day; refused to establish a minimum wage scale; and disregarded other union standards. Thereupon two of the three manufacturers who had assented to union conditions, notified the union that they should be obliged to terminate their agreements with it unless their competitor, the Duplex Company, also entered into the agreement with the union, which, in giving more favorable terms to labor, imposed correspondingly greater burdens upon the employer. Because the Duplex Company refused to enter into such an agreement and in order to induce it to do so, the machinists' union declared a strike at its factory, and in aid of that strike instructed its members and the members of affiliated unions not to work on the installation of presses which plaintiff had delivered in New York. Defendants insist that by the common law of New York, where the acts complained of were done, and where this suit was brought, and also by § 20 of the Clayton Act, the facts constitute a justification for this interference with plaintiff's business.

{21} First. As to the rights at common law:[b] Defendants' justification is that of self-interest. They have supported the strike at the employer's factory by a strike elsewhere against its product. They have injured the plaintiff, not maliciously, but in self-defense. They contend that the Duplex Company's refusal to deal with the machinists' union and to observe its standards threatened the interest not only of such union members as were its factory employees, but even more of all members of the several affiliated unions employed by plaintiff's competitors and by others whose more advanced standards the plaintiff was, in reality, attacking; and that none of the defendants and no person whom they are endeavoring to induce to refrain from working in connection with the setting up of presses made by plaintiff is an outsider, an interloper. In other words, that the contest between the company and the machinists' union involves vitally the interest of every person whose cooperation is sought. May not all with a common interest join in refusing to expend their labor upon articles whose very production constitutes an attack upon their standard of living and the institution which they are convinced supports it? Applying common-law principles the answer should, in my opinion, be: Yes, if as matter of fact those who so cooperate have a common interest.

{22} The change in the law by which strikes once illegal and even criminal are now recognized as lawful was effected in America largely without the intervention of legislation. This reversal of a common-law rule was not due to the rejection by the courts of one principle and the adoption in its stead of another, but to a better realization of the facts of industrial life. It is conceded that, although the strike of the workmen in plaintiff's factory injured its business, the strike was not an actionable wrong because the obvious self-interest of the strikers constituted a justification. Formerly courts held that self-interest could not be so served {e.g., the *Philadelphia Cordwainers* case}. But even after strikes to raise wages or reduce hours were held to be legal because of self-interest {e.g., *Commonwealth v. Hunt*), some courts held that there was not sufficient causal relationship between a strike to unionize a shop and the self-interest of the strikers to justify injuries inflicted. But other courts, repeating the same legal formula, found that there was justification,

---

[b]{The majority relied on the Clayton Act to issue the injunction. Consequently, the student may be wondering why Justice Brandeis discussed the common law of conspiracy. The reason may be that the plaintiff sought an injunction under *either* the common law *or* the Clayton Act. Brandeis argued below that the majority was mistaken and the Clayton Act did not allow an injunction. But even if this argument were correct, it was still possible that the plaintiff was entitled to an injunction under the common law. Therefore, Brandeis had to show that the common law did not support an injunction. — ed.}

because they viewed the facts differently. When centralization in the control of business brought its corresponding centralization in the organization of workingmen, new facts had to be appraised. A single employer might, as in this case, threaten the standing of the whole organization and the standards of all its members; and when he did so the union, in order to protect itself, would naturally refuse to work on his materials wherever found. When such a situation was first presented to the courts, judges concluded that the intervention of the purchaser of the materials established an insulation through which the direct relationship of the employer and the workingmen did not penetrate; and the strike against the material was considered a strike against the purchaser by unaffected third parties. But other courts, with better appreciation of the facts of industry, recognized the unity of interest throughout the union, and that, in refusing to work on materials which threatened it, the union was only refusing to aid in destroying itself.

{23} So, in the case at bar ... I should say, as the two lower courts apparently have said, that the defendants and those from whom they sought cooperation have a common interest which the plaintiff threatened. This view is in harmony with the views of the Court of Appeals of New York. For in New York, although boycotts like that in *Loewe v. Lawlor*, 208 U.S. 274, are illegal because they are conducted not against a product but against those who deal in it and are carried out by a combination of persons not united by common interest but only by sympathy, it is lawful for all members of a union by whomever employed to refuse to handle materials whose production weakens the union.... In my opinion, therefore, plaintiff had no cause of action by the common law of New York.

{24} Second. As to the anti-trust laws of the United States: {The Clayton Act} was the fruit of unceasing agitation, which extended over more than twenty years and was designed to equalize before the law the position of workingmen and employer as industrial combatants. Aside from the use of the injunction, the chief source of dissatisfaction with the existing law lay in the doctrine of malicious combination {i.e., conspiracy}, and, in many parts of the country, in the judicial declarations of the illegality at common law of picketing and persuading others to leave work. The grounds for objection to the latter are obvious. The objection to the doctrine of malicious combinations requires some explanation. By virtue of that doctrine, damage resulting from conduct such as striking or withholding patronage or persuading others to do either, which without more might be *damnum absque injuria* because the result of trade competition, became actionable when done for a purpose which a judge considered socially or economically harmful and therefore branded as malicious and unlawful. It was objected that, due largely to environment, the social and economic ideas of judges, which thus became translated into law, were prejudicial to a position of equality between workingman and employer; that due to this dependence upon the individual opinion of judges great confusion existed as to

Duplex v. Deering

what purposes were lawful and what unlawful; and that in any event Congress, not the judges, was the body which should declare what public policy in regard to the industrial struggle demands.

{25} By 1914 the ideas of the advocates of legislation had fairly crystallized upon the manner in which the inequality and uncertainty of the law should be removed. It was to be done by expressly legalizing certain acts regardless of the effects produced by them upon other persons. As to them Congress was to extract the element of *injuria* from the damages thereby inflicted, instead of leaving judges to determine according to their own economic and social views whether the damage inflicted on an employer in an industrial struggle was *damnum absque injuria*, because an incident of trade competition, or a legal injury, because in their opinion, economically and socially objectionable. This idea was presented to the committees which reported the Clayton Act. The resulting law set out certain acts which had previously been held unlawful, whenever courts had disapproved of the ends for which they were performed; it then declared that, when these acts were committed in the course of an industrial dispute, they should not be held to violate any law of the United States. In other words the Clayton Act substituted the opinion of Congress as to the propriety of the purpose for that of differing judges; and thereby it declared that the relations between employers of labor and workingmen were competitive relations, that organized competition was not harmful and that it justified injuries necessarily inflicted in its course. Both the majority and the minority report of the House Committee indicate that such was its purpose. If, therefore, the act applies to the case at bar, the acts here complained of cannot "be considered or held to be violations of any law of the United States," and, hence, do not violate the Sherman Act.

{26} The Duplex Company contends that § 20 of the Clayton Act does not apply to the case at bar, because it is restricted to cases "between an employer and employees, or between employers and employees, or between employees, or between persons employed and persons seeking employment, involving, or growing out of, a dispute concerning terms or conditions of employment"; whereas the case at bar arises between an employer in Michigan and workingmen in New York not in its employ, and does not involve their conditions of employment. But Congress did not restrict the provision to employers and workingmen in their employ. By including "employers and employees" and "persons employed and persons seeking employment," it showed that it was not aiming merely at a legal relationship between a specific employer and his employees. Furthermore, the plaintiff's contention proves too much. If the words are to receive a strict technical construction, the statute will have no application to disputes between employers of labor and workingmen, since the very acts to which it applies sever the continuity of the legal relationship.^c The further contention that this case is not one arising out of a dispute concerning the conditions of work of one of the parties is, in my opinion, founded upon a misconception of the facts.

{27} Because I have come to the conclusion that both the common law of a State and a statute of the United States declare the right of industrial combatants to push their struggle to the limits of the justification of self-interest, I do not wish to be understood as attaching any constitutional or moral sanction to that right. All rights are derived from the purposes of the society in which they exist; above all rights rises duty to the community. The conditions developed in industry may be such that those engaged in it cannot continue their struggle without danger to the community. But it is not for judges to determine whether such conditions exist, nor is it their function to set the limits of permissible contest and to declare the duties which the new situation demands. This is the function of the legislature....

⚜

---

^c{The "continuity of the legal relationship" is severed because, at common law, an employee who goes on strike has resigned one's job. — ed.}

COMMENTS

THE SUBSTANCE OF THE CASE

Self Interest as a Defense

Justice Brandeis argued that, although the Machinists may have damaged the plaintiff's business, their acts were justified under common law because they were taken in self defense of their economic interests. ¶¶ 21-22. This argument should be familiar to the student. It is essentially the same argument that Justice Holmes advanced unsuccessfully in Vegelahn v. Guntner: damage to business is prima facie wrong, and competition is a defense. Thus, one should not be surprised that Holmes, who had been appointed to the U.S. Supreme Court by the time Duplex was decided, joined in Brandeis's dissent.

The majority did not rebut the self-interest argument directly. Perhaps rebuttal was unnecessary; the majority authorized an injunction under anti-trust law, not the common law, and self interest is not a recognized defense under anti-trust law.[d] But perhaps the majority rebutted the self-interest argument indirectly. The majority wrote that § 20 exempts from anti-trust law only the parties to a labor dispute and that the defendants in the case, who were members of the Machinists Union in New York, had no dispute with the plaintiff, who was an employer in Michigan (¶¶ 12-14). From this it would follow that the defendants were not acting in their self interest.

Could any forceful rebuttal have been made to Brandeis's argument? If owners of capital may unite through corporations, why may not laborers unite through unions? If corporations may resist unions, why may not unions resist corporations? But perhaps these rhetorical questions are too general. The issue is usually more specific — whether a particular tactic, such as a secondary boycott, should be allowed. One may believe in

---

[d]Nearly all business decisions are made out of self interest. Thus, if self-interest were a defense to anti-trust law, the defense might swallow the rule.

the right of labor to unite and still wish to outlaw
boycotts.

Levels of Abstraction

The student should note how the arguments in the
preceding paragraph operate on different levels of
abstraction. Brandeis's argument is the more abstract:
if capital may unite, so may labor. The majority's
rebuttal is pitched at a lower level on the abstraction
ladder. The rebuttal asserts that additional facts
should be taken into account, such as the particular
tactic used by the union (the secondary boycott), because
of the effects of those facts. Which is the more
appropriate level of abstraction on which to decide this
issue? And more generally, how should we go about
choosing the appropriate level of abstraction on which to
decide an issue?

Two Fundamental Questions

The majority omitted any reference to the majestic
language of section 6, that "the labor of a human being
is not a commodity or article of commerce." This
omission is important because these words tend to refute
the majority's view that section 6 merely restated
existing law. If human labor is not an article of
commerce, it is not affected by anti-trust law. Should
labor be regarded as an article of commerce?

In ¶ 25 Brandeis wrote that the Clayton Act
"declared that the relations between employers of labor
and workingmen were competitive relations, that organized
competition was not harmful and that it justified
injuries necessarily inflicted in its course." The
student will recall that Holmes made a similar point in
<u>Vegelahn v. Guntner</u>. Should we regard the relations
between employers and workers as competitive?

Legislative History

For two reasons, we omitted from the case the
Court's extensive discussion of legislative history.
First, this book generally deletes legislative history
from cases because it is often like the Bible: various
(and sometimes contradictory) interpretations of the
text are plausible. If the student goes to law school,

one will learn how to make arguments based on legislative history; but one will not learn how to find the real intent of the legislature. Second, the legislative history of the Clayton Act is genuinely ambiguous. There are statements that support the majority's holding in Duplex and statements that support the dissent. In their book the Labor Injunction, Frankfurter and Greene state, "The Supreme Court had to find meaning where Congress had done its best to conceal meaning" (p. 145). It was irresponsible of Congress to produce a statute with such an ambiguous history. It looks as though Congress was heavily pressured by unions and management and, rather than resolve the problem, decided to pass it on to the courts. This may have been a politic solution, but it is not the way our government should operate. And, given the character of the judges in the first half of the Twentieth Century, the outcome was certain.

The Aftermath of Duplex v. Deering

The judges went right to work on organized labor as soon as Duplex was decided. The sledgehammer blows, of which Samuel Gompers had spoken, did not free workers, but forged even tighter chains. The links of the chain were both procedural and substantive; that is, they changed the procedural rules that govern how cases are tried and relief is granted, and they changed the substantive rules of law.

INJUNCTIONS

Procedurally, the Clayton Act was more damaging to unions than the Sherman Act. The Sherman Act permitted injunctions only at the behest of the U.S. government, whereas the Clayton Act allowed private parties to obtain injunctions. As Summers and Wellington have commented, the Clayton Act "hand[ed] to employers their favorite remedy in their favorite forum" — namely, injunctions issued in federal court. Labor Law: Cases and Materials (1968), p. 183.

REACH OF THE CLAYTON ACT

Substantively, the Clayton Act was applied to union activity that had previously been immune. For example, when the Shopmen struck the railroads in 1922, protesting a reduction in wages, federal judges quickly enjoined the strike on the theory that the strike interrupted interstate commerce. This theory implied that any strike that prevented goods from crossing state lines violated the anti-trust laws. Practically any strike has this effect, of course. The Supreme Court never adopted this theory — though lower courts, where most cases are decided, were more receptive to it; and perhaps the theory was more limited than our statement implies: it may have meant only that strikes by employees of firms involved in interstate transportation (such as railroads and trucking companies) were illegal. But even in this limited version, the theory outlawed straightforward strikes.

Another example of the application of the Clayton Act to unions is the two Coronado Coal opinions, both of which were written by the Supreme Court. The issue was whether a strike that prevented production of goods, and, therefore, reduced the volume of goods in interstate commerce, violated the anti-trust laws. The Mine Workers struck the Coronado coal mines in Arkansas; the strike, which was violent, was also effective, and mining and shipment of coal were stopped. The company sued and won a judgment for three quarters of a million dollars in the trial court, but in the first Coronado Coal opinion the Supreme Court sent the case back for a new trial. United Mine Workers v. Coronado Coal Co., 259 U.S. 344 (1922). The high court held that a violation of the anti-trust law was not proved merely by showing that union activity reduced the amount of coal shipped in interstate commerce.[e] What mattered was the union's motive. (The student will recall that motive had been important since Commonwealth v. Hunt.) Two motives were possible. The union might have been seeking to improve the wages and working conditions of the workers in the firm that was being struck, or the union might have been seeking to cut off the supply of non-union coal from Arkansas in order to protect unionized mines in other states. The former motive was lawful, the latter was not; and if, as was likely, both motives were at work, the outcome depended on which motive was primary. The trial court had not made the relevant findings as to the union's motives, and for this reason the case was sent back for retrial. Of

---

[e]Otherwise, every successful strike would have become illegal.

course, the union lost the retrial, and this time the trial judge made the right findings, namely, that the union's primary motive was to cut off the supply of non-union coal that undermined unionized firms elsewhere. In the second <u>Coronado Coal</u> opinion, the Supreme Court affirmed the judgment for the employer. <u>Coronado Coal Co. v. United Mine Workers</u>, 268 U.S. 295 (1925).

The Court's opinions in the <u>Coronado Coal</u> cases can be criticized. One criticism is that the opinions gave a great deal of discretion — perhaps too much discretion — to trial judges. We noted above that motive is always a sensitive inquiry: only the actor knows one's real reasons for doing what one did, and we cannot rely on the actor to tell the truth if it might incriminate oneself. As a result, if a judge says, "The defendant's motive was A," and A was illegal, there is no trustworthy person who can contradict the judge; we have to accept the judge's determination and trust in one's impartiality and professionalism. One might suggest that the federal judges were not impartial towards labor at the beginning of the Twentieth Century, and we might agree; but this is not the criticism that we have in mind: the possibility of bias always exists and is not peculiar to labor cases. Rather, our criticism is that, as the Supreme Court was fully aware, unions very often — perhaps, almost always — have <u>both</u> motives which the Court identified: they want to wrench better wages and working conditions from the employer, and they want to protect gains previously wrenched from the employer's competitors. Which of these motives is primary and which, secondary in a given case? One may doubt that union organizers themselves know most of the time, and one should have no doubt that a judge cannot find out; in fact, because the motives are likely to be equally strong, or at least because each is sufficient cause of the union's behavior, there may not exist any answer to the question. Therefore, a judge trying an anti-trust case against a union was free to choose either motive as the primary one, according to whom the judge wanted to win the case; and this choice could not be effectively reviewed on appeal.

Another criticism of the <u>Coronado Coal</u> cases is that they ignored the reality of product markets and corresponding union structures. Other things being equal (even if they rarely are), a union must organize most of the competitors in a given product market; otherwise, cheaper non-union producers will force the unionized firms to leave the market or to take back the union's gains. The <u>Coronado Coal</u> cases, therefore, prevented unions from doing what they needed to do in order to survive. The cases limited unions to bargaining for surplus value that results when other things are <u>not</u> equal. For example, if there are ten firms in a product market and all are identical, none can afford to sign a union contract for higher wages unless all sign, and the <u>Coronado Coal</u> cases made it virtually illegal for a union to try to organize them all.[f] But suppose that Firm No. 1 has an advantage over the others because of a cheap source of raw materials. A union could attempt to capture this firm's advantage and translate it into higher wages without weakening the firm's competitive position. Assuming competitive markets, this was the only possibility that the Supreme Court left open to unions.

The last anti-trust case we will consider is <u>Bedford Cut Stone Co. v. Journeymen Stonecutters Assoc.</u>, 274 U.S. 37 (1927). When the Stonecutters struck an Indiana quarry, their fellow Stonecutters across the country refused to work on stone cut by non-union workers. The Stonecutters did not involve any other crafts, as in <u>Duplex</u>, nor did they intend to reduce non-union competition, as in <u>Coronado Coal</u>. Nonetheless, the Supreme Court held that they were not acting for the purpose of improving their own terms and conditions of employment, and, therefore, they acted in restraint of trade. Thus, sympathy strikes were illegal.

Keeping the Anti-trust Law in Perspective

The federal anti-trust law was a powerful weapon against organized labor, but we should not overstate its importance. Labor faced other, even more powerful

---

[f]It might have been permissible for a union to try to organize all ten firms simultaneously, but organizing on this scale is rarely feasible. If the union tried to organize the firms one at a time, the first organizing drive would have been lawful; but the second and subsequent drives would have been vulnerable to legal attack on the theory that the union's motive was to protect the organized shop by minimizing competition from the unorganized shops.

weapons. One was the set of common law restrictions on organizing, striking, and boycotting, as exemplified by <u>Vegelahn v. Guntner</u> (also, <u>Hitchman Coal v. Mitchell</u>, which appears below). A second was the injunction. And a third was the Supreme Court's use of the federal Constitution to prevent the federal government and the states from innovating in regard to labor law. In the next case, we will turn to this third weapon, the Constitution. For the moment, we will conclude our comment on <u>Duplex v. Deering</u> with a further word about anti-trust law. By authorizing collective bargaining in the National Labor Relations Act, Congress substantially diminished labor's exposure to anti-trust violations. We will not discuss anti-trust law further in this book. Suffice it to say that anti-trust law still exists, and it can be used to limit union conduct; but most union behavior either is exempt from anti-trust law or is prohibited by the Labor Act, which takes precedence.

QUESTIONS FOR REFLECTION

1. What should a court do when the text of a statute is ambiguous in a certain application, and the legislative history either is silent or points in opposite directions?

2. Why did Brandeis take the trouble to write a dissenting opinion? Why would any judge bother?

3. The majority frequently used the words like "compel," "coerce," and "threat" to describe the defendants' acts. (See, e.g., ¶ 2 ("compelling the complainant to unionize," "coercing union men," "threatening customers with sympathetic strikes," "threatening {workers} with loss of union cards"), ¶ 5 ("intended to have a coercive effect upon complainant," "coercive pressure upon such customers"), ¶ 16 ("with the object of compelling such customers," "thereby constraining complainant," "a threat to inflict damage").) Were these words used appropriately? To what extent does the answer depend on whether secondary boycotts should be illegal?

5. Brandeis said that some judges were better acquainted than others with the facts of industrial life. Should a judge take such information into account when

interpreting a statute, or should the judge adhere to the
intent of the legislature?

$$\Omega$$

The Unconstitutionality of Government Protection of Labor

CONSTITUTIONALITY OF FEDERAL LAWS

Introduction

The origin of the following case, <u>Adair v. United States</u>, lies in the Pullman Strike of 1894, which the student may have studied in one's course on labor history and which we will say more about when we reach the <u>Debs</u> case. For present purposes, we need only say that, following the strike, President Cleveland appointed a special commission to investigate problems on the railroads. The commission recommended, among other things, that Congress protect railway workers' right to organize unions. After a great struggle in Congress, the Erdman Act of 1898, which applied only to railroads, established machinery for mediation and arbitration of disputes, banned yellow dog contracts and blacklisting, and prohibited discrimination against workers because of their membership in a union. In spite of the prohibition against discrimination (to which we will refer as "the anti-discrimination section"), William Adair, the chief of operations of the Louisville & Nashville RR., fired O. B. Coppage because the latter joined a union. Adair was prosecuted for violating the Erdman Act. Plainly, he did violate the Act. The issue before the Supreme Court was whether the anti-discrimination section was unconstitutional.

The Court found that two provisions of the Constitution applied to the case. The first provision was the Fifth Amendment, which requires the federal government to respect due process of law. The issue was whether the Erdman Act denied due process to Adair. The second provision was the Commerce Clause, which empowers Congress to regulate interstate commerce. The issue was whether the Erdman Act applied to <u>interstate</u> or intrastate commerce.

Adair v. United States
208 U.S. 161 (1908)

MR. JUSTICE HARLAN delivered the opinion of the Court.

{1} ... The 2d, 3d, 4th, 5th, 6th, 7th, 8th and 9th sections {of the Erdman Act of 1898} relate to the settlement, by means of arbitration, of controversies concerning wages, hours of labor, or conditions of employment arising between a carrier subject to the provisions of the act and its employes, which seriously interrupt or threaten to interrupt the business of the carrier. Those sections prescribe the mode in which controversies may be brought under the cognizance of arbitrators, in what way the arbitrators may be designated, and the effect of their decisions....

...

{2} The 10th section, upon which the present prosecution is based, is in these words:

> "That any employer subject to the provisions of this act and any officer, agent, or receiver of such employer, who shall require any employe, or any person seeking employment, as a condition of such employment, to enter into an agreement, either written or verbal, not to become or remain a member of any labor corporation, association, or organization; or shall threaten any employe with loss of employment, or shall unjustly discriminate against any employe because of his membership in such a labor corporation, association, or organization ... upon conviction thereof in any court of the United States of competent jurisdiction in the district in which such offense was committed, shall be punished for each offense by a fine of not less than one hundred dollars and not more than one thousand dollars."

{3} It may be observed in passing that while that section makes it a crime against the United States to unjustly discriminate against an employe of an interstate carrier because of his being a member of a labor organization, it does not make it a crime to unjustly discriminate against an employe of the carrier because of his not being a member of such an organization.[a]

...

{4} The specific charge ... was

---

[a] {In other words, the act outlawed the closed non-union shop, but permitted the closed union shop. — ed.}

"that said William Adair, agent and employe of said common carrier and employer as aforesaid, in the district aforesaid, on and before the 15th day of October, 1906, did unlawfully and unjustly discriminate against said O. B. Coppage, employe as aforesaid, by then and there discharging said O. B. Coppage from such employment of said common carrier and employer, because of his membership in said labor organization, and thereby did unjustly discriminate against an employe of a common carrier and employer engaged in interstate commerce because of his membership in a labor organization, contrary to the forms of the statute in such cases made and provided, and against the peace and dignity of the United States."

...

{The jury found the defendant guilty as charged.}

{5} May Congress make it a criminal offense against the United States — as by the tenth section of the act of 1898 it does — for an agent or officer of an interstate carrier, having full authority in the premises from the carrier, to discharge an employe from service simply because of his membership in a labor organization?

...

{6} The first inquiry is whether the part of the tenth section of the act of 1898 upon which the first count of the indictment was based is repugnant to the Fifth Amendment of the Constitution declaring that no person shall be deprived of liberty or property without due process of law. In our opinion that section, in the particular mentioned, is an invasion of the personal liberty, as well as of the right of property, guaranteed by that Amendment. Such liberty and right embraces the right to make contracts for the purchase of the labor of others and equally the right to make contracts for the sale of one's own labor; each right, however, being subject to the fundamental condition that no contract, whatever its subject matter, can be sustained which the law, upon reasonable grounds, forbids as inconsistent with the public interests or as hurtful to the public order or as detrimental to the common good. This court has said that "in every well-ordered society, charged with the duty of conserving the safety of its members, the rights of the individual in respect of his liberty may, at times, under the pressure of great dangers, be subjected to such restraint, to be enforced by reasonable regulations, as the safety of the general public may demand." *Jacobson v. Massachusetts*, 197 U.S. 11, 29, and authorities there cited.... {A}s agent of the railroad company and as such responsible for the conduct of the business of one of its departments, it was the defendant Adair's right — and that right inhered in his personal liberty, and was also a right of property — to serve his employer as best he could, so long as he did nothing that was reasonably forbidden by law as injurious to the public interests. It was the right of the defendant to prescribe the terms upon which the services of Coppage would be accepted, and it was the right of Coppage to become or not, as he chose, an employe of the railroad company upon the terms offered to him. Mr. Cooley, in his treatise on Torts, p. 278, well says: "It is a part of every man's civil rights that he be left at liberty to refuse business relations with any person whomsoever, whether the refusal rests upon reason, or is the result of whim, caprice, prejudice or malice. With his reasons neither the public nor third persons have any legal concern. It is also his right to have business relations with any one with whom he can make contracts, and if he is wrongfully deprived of this right by others, he is entitled to redress."

{7} In *Lochner v. New York*, 198 U.S. 45, 53, 56, which involved the validity of a state enactment prescribing certain maximum hours for labor in bakeries, and which made it a misdemeanor for an employer to require or permit an employe in such an establishment to work in excess of a given number of hours each day, the court {held the law unconstitutional. The court} said:

> "The general right to make a contract in relation to his business is part of the liberty of the individual protected by the Fourteenth Amendment of the Federal Constitution. *Allgeyer v. Louisiana*, 165 U.S. 578. Under that provision no State can deprive any person of life, liberty or property without due process of law. The right to purchase or to sell labor is part of the liberty protected by this amendment, unless there are circumstances which exclude the right. There are, however, certain powers, existing in the sovereignty of each State in the Union, somewhat vaguely termed 'police powers,' the exact description and limitation of which have not been attempted by the courts. Those powers, broadly stated and without, at present, any attempt at a more specific limitation, relate to the safety, health, morals and general welfare of the public. Both property and liberty are held on such reasonable conditions as may be imposed by the governing power of the State in the exercise of those powers, and with such conditions the Fourteenth Amendment was not designed to interfere.... In every case that comes before this court, therefore, where legislation of this character is concerned and where the protection of the Federal Constitution is sought, the question necessarily arises: Is this a fair, reasonable and appropriate exercise of the police power of the State, or is it an unreasonable, unnecessary and arbitrary interference with the right of the individual to his personal liberty or to enter into those contracts in relation to labor which may seem to him appropriate or necessary for the support of himself and his family? Of course the liberty of contract relating to labor includes both parties to it. The one has as much right to purchase as the other to sell labor."

Although there was a difference of opinion in that case among the members of the court as to certain propositions, there was no disagreement as to the general proposition that there is a liberty of contract which cannot be unreasonably interfered with by legislation....

{8} While, as already suggested, the right of liberty and property guaranteed by the Constitution against deprivation without due process of law, is subject to such reasonable restraints as the common good or the general welfare may require, it is not within the functions of government — at least in the absence of contract between the parties — to compel any person in the course of his business and against his will to accept or retain the personal services of another, or to compel any person, against his will, to perform personal services for another. The right of a person to sell his labor upon such terms as he deems proper is, in its essence, the same as the right of the purchaser of labor to prescribe the conditions upon which he will accept such labor from the person offering to sell it. So the right of the employe to quit the service of the employer, for whatever reason, is the same as the right of the employer, for whatever reason, to dispense with the services of such employe. It was the legal right of the defendant Adair — however unwise such a course might have been — to discharge Coppage because of his being a member of a labor organization, as it was the legal right of Coppage, if he saw fit to do so — however unwise such a course on his part might have been — to quit the service in which he was engaged, because the defendant employed some persons who were not members of a labor organization. In all such particulars the employer and the employe have equality of right, and any legislation that disturbs that equality is an arbitrary interference with the liberty of contract which no government can legally justify in a free land....

{9} As the relations and the conduct of the parties towards each other was {sic} not controlled by any contract other than a general agreement on one side to accept the services of the employe and a general agreement on the other side to render services to the employer — no term being fixed for the continuance of the employment — Congress could not, consistently with the Fifth Amendment, make it a crime against the United States to discharge the employe because of his being a member of a labor organization.

{10} But it is suggested that the authority to make it a crime for an agent or officer of an interstate carrier, having authority in the premises from his principal, to discharge an employe from service to such carrier, simply because of his membership in a labor organization, can be referred to the power of Congress to regulate interstate commerce, without regard to any question of personal liberty or right of property arising under the Fifth Amendment. This suggestion can have no bearing in the present discussion unless the statute, in the particular just stated, is within the meaning of the Constitution a regulation of commerce among the States. If it be not, then clearly the Government cannot invoke the commerce clause of the Constitution as sustaining the indictment against Adair.

Adair v. United States

...

{11} ... Manifestly, any rule prescribed for the conduct of interstate commerce, in order to be within the competency of Congress under its power to regulate commerce among the States, must have some real or substantial relation to or connection with the commerce regulated. But what possible legal or logical connection is there between an employe's membership in a labor organization and the carrying on of interstate commerce? Such relation to a labor organization cannot have, in itself and in the eye of the law, any bearing upon the commerce with which the employe is connected by his labor and services. Labor associations, we assume, are organized for the general purpose of improving or bettering the conditions and conserving the interests of its members as wage-earners — an object entirely legitimate and to be commended rather than condemned. But surely those associations as labor organizations have nothing to do with interstate commerce as such. One who engages in the service of an interstate carrier will, it must be assumed, faithfully perform his duty, whether he be a member or not a member of a labor organization. His fitness for the position in which he labors and his diligence in the discharge of his duties cannot in law or sound reason depend in any degree upon his being or not being a member of a labor organization. It cannot be assumed that his fitness is assured, or his diligence increased, by such membership, or that he is less fit or less diligent because of his not being a member of such an organization. It is the employe as a man and not as a member of a labor organization who labors in the service of an interstate carrier. Will it be said that the provision in question had its origin in the apprehension, on the part of Congress, that if it did not show more consideration for members of labor organizations than for wage-earners who were not members of such organizations, or if it did not insert in the statute some such provision as the one here in question, members of labor organizations would, by illegal or violent measures, interrupt or impair the freedom of commerce among the States? We will not indulge in any such conjectures, nor make them, in whole or in part, the basis of our decision. We could not do so consistently with the respect due to a coordinate department of the Government. We could not do so without imputing to Congress the purpose to accord to one class of wage-earners privileges withheld from another class of wage-earners engaged, it may be, in the same kind of labor and serving the same employer. Nor will we assume, in our consideration of this case, that members of labor organizations will, in any considerable numbers, resort to illegal methods for accomplishing any particular object they have in view.

{12} Looking alone at the words of the statute for the purpose of ascertaining its scope and effect, and of determining its validity, we hold that there is no such connection between interstate commerce and membership in a labor organization as to authorize Congress to make it a crime against the United States for an agent of an interstate carrier to discharge an employe because of such membership on his part....

{13} It results, on the whole case, that the provision of the statute under which the defendant was convicted must be held to be repugnant to the Fifth Amendment and as not embraced by nor within the power of Congress to regulate interstate commerce, but under the guise of regulating interstate commerce and as applied to this case it arbitrarily sanctions an illegal invasion of the personal liberty as well as the right of property of the defendant Adair.

...

{The verdict was set aside.}

MR. JUSTICE MCKENNA, dissenting.

{14} The opinion of the court proceeds upon somewhat narrow lines and either omits or does not give adequate prominence to the considerations which, I think, are determinative of the questions in the case. The principle upon which the opinion is grounded is, as I understand it, that a labor organization has no legal or logical connection with interstate commerce, and that the fitness of an employe has no dependence or relation with his membership in such organization. It is hence concluded that to restrain his discharge merely on account of such membership is an invasion of the liberty of the carrier guaranteed by the Fifth Amendment of the Constitution of the United States. The conclusion is irresistible if the propositions from which it is deduced may be viewed as abstractly as the opinion views them. May they be so viewed?

{15} A summary of the act is necessary to understand § 10. Detach that section from the other provisions of the act and it might be open to condemnation.

{16} The first section of the act designates the carriers to whom it shall apply. The second section makes it the duty of the Chairman of the Interstate Commerce Commission and the Commissioner of Labor, in case of a dispute between carriers and their employes which threatens to interrupt the business of the carriers, to put themselves in communication with the parties to the controversy and use efforts to "mediation and conciliation." If the efforts fail, then § 3 provides for the appointment of a board of arbitration — one {member} to be named by the carrier, one by the labor organization to which the employes belong, and the two thus chosen shall select a third.

{17} There is a provision that if the employes belong to different organizations, they shall concur in the selection of the arbitrator. The board is to give hearings; power is invested in the board to summon witnesses, and provision is made for filing the award in the clerk's office of the Circuit Court of the United States for the district where the controversy arose. Other sections complete the scheme of arbitration thus outlined, and make, as far as possible, the proceedings of the arbitrators judicial, and pending them put restrictions on the parties and damages for violation of the restrictions.

{18} Even from this meager outline may be perceived the justification and force of § 10. It prohibits discrimination ... or the discharge from employment of members of labor organizations "because of such membership." This the {majority} opinion condemns. The actions prohibited, it is asserted, are part of the liberty of a carrier protected by the Constitution of the United States from limitation or regulation....

...

{19} From these considerations we may pass to an inspection of the statute of which § 10 is a part, and inquire as to its purpose, and if the means which it employs has relation to that purpose and to interstate commerce. The provisions of the act are explicit and present a well coordinated plan for the settlement of disputes between carriers and their employes, by bringing the disputes to arbitration and accommodation, and thereby prevent strikes and the public disorder and derangement of business that may be consequent upon them. I submit no worthier purpose can engage legislative attention or be the object of legislative action....

{20} We are told that labor associations are to be commended. May not then Congress recognize their existence; yes, and recognize their power as conditions to be counted with in framing its legislation? Of what use would it be to attempt to bring bodies of men to agreement and compromise of controversies if you put out of view the influences which move them or the fellowship which binds them — maybe controls and impels them — whether rightfully or wrongfully, to make the cause of one the cause of all? And this practical wisdom Congress observed — observed, I may say, not in speculation of uncertain provision of evils, but in experience of evils — an experience which approached to the dimensions of a National calamity. The facts of history should not be overlooked, nor the course of legislation. The act involved in the present case was preceded by one enacted in 1888 of similar purport. 25 Stat. 501, c. 1063. That act did not recognize labor associations, or distinguish between the members of such associations and the other employes of carriers. It failed in its purpose, whether from defect in its provisions or other cause we may only conjecture. At any rate, it did not avert the strike at Chicago in 1894. Investigation followed, and, as a result of it, the act of 1898 was finally passed. Presumably its provisions and remedy were addressed to the mischief which the act of 1888 failed to reach or avert. It was the judgment of Congress that the scheme of arbitration might be helped by engaging in it the labor associations. Those associations unified bodies of employes in every department of the carriers, and this unity could be an obstacle or an aid to arbitration. It was attempted to be made an aid, but how could it be made an aid if, pending the efforts of "mediation and conciliation" of the dispute, as provided in § 2 of the act, other provisions of the act may be arbitrarily disregarded, which are of concern to the members in the dispute? How can it be an aid, how can controversies which may seriously interrupt or threaten to interrupt the business of carriers (I paraphrase the words of the statute), be averted or composed if the carrier can bring on the conflict or prevent its amicable settlement by the exercise of mere whim and caprice? I say mere whim or caprice, for this is the liberty which is attempted to be vindicated as the Constitutional right of the carriers. And it may be exercised in mere whim and caprice. If ability, the qualities of efficient and faithful workmanship can be found outside of labor associations, surely they may be found inside of them. Liberty is an attractive theme, but the liberty which is exercised in sheer antipathy does not plead strongly for recognition.

...

{21} I have said that it is not necessary to suppose that labor organizations will violate the law, and it is not. Their power may be effectively exercised without violence or illegality, and it cannot be disrespect to Congress to let a committee of the Senate speak for it and tell the reason and purposes of its legislation. The Committee on Education in its report said of the bill: "The measure under consideration may properly be called a voluntary arbitration bill, having for its object the settlement of disputes between capital and labor, as far as the interstate transportation companies are concerned. The necessity for the bill arises from the calamitous results in the way of ill-considered strikes arising from the tyranny of capital or the unjust demands of labor organizations, whereby the business of the country is brought to a standstill and thousands of employes, with their helpless wives and children, are confronted with starvation." And, concluding the report, said: "It is our opinion that this bill, should it become a law, would reduce to a minimum labor strikes which affect interstate commerce, and we therefore recommend its passage."

{22} With the report was submitted a letter from the Secretary of the Interstate Commerce Commission, which expressed the judgment of that body, formed, I may presume, from experience of the factors in the problem. The letter said: "With the corporations as employers on one side and the organizations of railway employes as the other, there will be a measure of equality of power and force which will surely bring about the essential requisites of friendly relation, respect, consideration, and forbearance." And again: "It has been shown before the labor commission of England that where the associations are strong enough to command the respect of their employers the relations between employer and employe seem most amicable. For there the employers have learned the practical convenience of treating with one thoroughly representative body instead of with isolated fragments of workmen; and the labor associations have learned the limitations of their powers."

...

MR. JUSTICE HOLMES, dissenting.

{23} I also think that the statute is constitutional, and but for the decision of my brethren I should have felt pretty clear about it.

...

{24} The ground on which this particular law is held bad is not so much that it deals with matters remote from commerce among the States, as that it interferes with the paramount individual rights, secured by the Fifth Amendment. The section is, in substance, a very limited interference with freedom of contract, no more. It does not require the carriers to employ any one. It does not forbid them to refuse to employ any one, for any reason they deem good.... The section simply prohibits the more powerful party to exact certain undertakings, or to threaten dismissal or unjustly discriminate on certain grounds against those already employed.... I turn to the general question whether the employment can be regulated at all. ... Where there is, or generally is believed to be, an important ground of public policy for restraint, the Constitution does not forbid it, whether this court agrees or disagrees with the policy pursued. It cannot be doubted that to prevent strikes, and, so far as possible, to foster its scheme of arbitration, might be deemed by Congress an important point of policy, and I think it impossible to say that Congress might not reasonably think that the provision in question would help a good deal to carry its policy along. But suppose the only effect really were to tend to bring about the complete unionizing of such railroad laborers as Congress can deal with, I think that object alone would justify the act. I quite agree that the question what and how much good labor unions do, is one on which intelligent people may differ, — I think that laboring men sometimes attribute to them advantages, as many attribute to combinations of capital disadvantages, that really are due to economic conditions of a far wider and deeper kind — but I could not pronounce it unwarranted if Congress should decide that to foster a strong union was for the best interest, not only of the men, but of the railroads and the country at large.

COMMENTS

LIBERTY OF CONTRACT UNDER THE FIFTH AMENDMENT:
ANALYZING AND EVALUATING THE COURT'S REASONING

Did Liberty of Contract Under the Fifth Amendment Include the Right to Enter into Labor Contracts?

Some aspects of the Adair case deserve comment and extension. One is that although the Court repeated a number of times that the Constitution prohibits the government from interfering with liberty of contract, the Court did not explain why liberty of contract should be included within the liberty and property protected by the Fifth Amendment. The Court cited Lochner v. New York as precedent. Lochner also said that liberty of contract is protected by the Fifth Amendment, and also did not explain why this is so, and also cited a precedent. That precedent was Allgeyer v. Louisiana, 165 U.S. 578 (1897), in which we find, at last, a justification for the holding that liberty of contract is a constitutional right.

> The liberty mentioned in {the Due Process Clause of the Fifth Amendment} ... embrace{s} the right of the citizen to be free in the enjoyment of all his faculties; to be free to use them in all lawful ways; to live and work where he will; to earn his livelihood by any lawful calling; to pursue any livelihood or avocation, and for that purpose to enter into all contracts which may be proper, necessary, and essential to his carrying out to a successful conclusion the purposes above mentioned.

165 U.S. at 589. Allgeyer also cited a precedent.

> It was said by Mr. Justice Bradley in Butchers' Union v. Crescent City ... that "the right to follow any of the common occupations of life is an inalienable right. It was formulated as such under the phrase 'pursuit of happiness' in the Declaration of Independence, which commenced with the fundamental proposition that 'all men are created equal; that they are endowed by their Creator with certain inalienable rights; and among these are life, liberty, and the pursuit of happiness." This right is a large ingredient of the civil liberty of the citizen.

<u>Allgeyer v. Louisiana</u>, 165 U.S. at 589-590, quoting <u>Butchers' Union v. Crescent City</u>, at 111 U.S. at 762.

The Court's reasoning can be analyzed into a series of legal syllogisms. By analyzing the Court's reasoning in this way, we can identify the premises and conclusions, consider whether the premises are true or well supported, and judge whether the conclusions follow logically from the premises.

I

MAJOR PREMISE: Liberty included inalienable rights.

MINOR PREMISE: The pursuit of happiness was an inalienable right. The Declaration of Independence.

CONCLUSION: Liberty included the pursuit of happiness.

The Court offered no support for the major premise, that liberty included inalienable rights. Evidently, the Court believed this proposition was self evident. It does seem to be true: a right is meaningless unless one is at liberty to exercise that right.

The Court cited the Declaration of Independence as support for the minor premise, that the pursuit of happiness is an inalienable right. This citation is striking because the Constitution, not the Declaration, established the government, delineated its powers, and listed citizens' rights against the government. Courts today rarely if ever refer to the Declaration. Whether the pursuit of happiness is an inalienable right is a question of political philosophy that depends (among other things) on how one defines "happiness" and on how one deals with rights that conflict with one another. We are often called upon to sacrifice a degree of happiness for other goods; for example, we pay taxes. Thus, the minor premise cannot be considered self evidently true, and the Court's support for it was dubious.

The logic of the syllogism was correct. If the premises were true, the conclusion followed from them.

II

MAJOR PREMISE: Liberty included the pursuit of happiness.

MINOR PREMISE: The pursuit of happiness included pursuing a lawful occupation. <u>Allgeyer v. Louisiana</u>, citing <u>Butchers' Union v. Crescent City</u>.

CONCLUSION: Liberty included pursuing a lawful occupation.

It is common in a chain of reasoning for the conclusion of one syllogism to stand as a premise in another syllogism. The major premise of the Court's second syllogism was supported by the first syllogism. Thus, whether we accept the truth of the major premise of the second syllogism depends on our evaluation of the first syllogism.

The minor premise of the second syllogism was supported by citations to the <u>Allgeyer</u> and <u>Butchers' Union</u> cases. The doctrine of precedent allows this sort of support without further discussion; issues decided in a case may be taken as settled in future cases. As parties or advocates in a law suit, we may argue that a precedent was decided incorrectly, though this sort of argument is rarely successful. But as citizens in a democracy, we are free to examine the precedent and consider whether it decided the issue correctly.

The conclusion followed logically from the premises.

III

MAJOR PREMISE: Pursuing an occupation usually included hiring workers or being hired as a worker.

MINOR PREMISE: To hire or be hired as a worker was to enter into a labor contract.

CONCLUSION: Pursuing an occupation usually included entering into labor contracts.

The Court cited no support for the major premise, but, as an empirical matter, it seems to have been a true legislative fact.

The minor premise was a rule of law. Perhaps it was so firmly established in precedent that the Court saw no need to support it with a citation, or perhaps the premise was inchoate and judges accepted it without realizing what they were doing.[b]

The conclusion followed logically from the premises.

IV

MAJOR PREMISE: Liberty included pursuing a lawful occupation.

MINOR PREMISE: Pursuing a lawful occupation included entering into labor contracts.

CONCLUSION: Liberty included entering into labor contracts.

The two premises were established by previous syllogisms. The conclusion followed logically from the premises.

V

MAJOR PREMISE: The Fifth Amendment forbade the government to deprive a person of liberty without due process.

MINOR PREMISE: Liberty included entering into labor contracts.

CONCLUSION: The Fifth Amendment forbade the government to interfere with labor contracts.

---

[b]We may note, however, that the premise could have been otherwise. As our review of Colonial practices revealed, the employment relationship may be conceived as a status relationship, governed by law, and wholly or partly protected from change by contract.

The major premise was as well supported as a legal proposition can be: it was a paraphrase of the Fifth Amendment of the Constitution. The minor premise was established by a previous syllogism. The conclusion followed logically from the premises.

VI

MAJOR PREMISE: The Fifth Amendment forbade the government to interfere with labor contracts.

MINOR PREMISE: The anti-discrimination clause of the Erdman Act interfered with labor contracts by prohibiting an employer from terminating a labor contract because a worker joined a union.

CONCLUSION: The anti-discrimination clause of the Erdman Act was unconstitutional.

The major premise was the conclusion of the fifth syllogism. The minor premise was a correct description of the anti-discrimination clause of the Erdman Act. The conclusion followed logically from the premises.

Having analyzed the Court's argument into its premises and conclusions, we can discover its strengths and weaknesses. The Court was arguing that liberty of contract, which is protected by the Fifth Amendment, included the right to enter into labor contracts. The first syllogism in this argument was probably its weakest link. Nonetheless, the argument was strong enough that Justice Holmes, who dissented from the Court's ultimate conclusion, accepted the argument. Holmes disagreed with another of the majority's arguments, to which we now turn our attention.

Did Public Policy Allow a Restriction on Liberty of Contract in this Case?

In the NOTE ON PRIMA FACIE CASE AND AFFIRMATIVE DEFENSE.1, we discussed the legal equivalent of an excuse: an act that is ordinarily prohibited may be permissible in some circumstances. The prohibited act is defined in the prima facie case; the excuse is defined in the affirmative defense. Although it would not be described

Adair v. United States

in this terminology, the Court's approach to liberty of contract under the Fifth Amendment was built on the same superstructure. A statute might have interfered with liberty of contract (the prohibited act), yet have been constitutional if the statute served a legitimate public policy (the excuse).

An example of a statute that interfered with liberty of contract, yet was excused or justified by public policy, was a case which the majority did not cite, viz., Holden v. Hardy, 169 U.S. 366 (1898). The operator of an underground mine required miners to labor in the mine for ten hours per day. This requirement violated a statute of the State of Utah that established an eight-hour day for underground mines. The operator challenged the statute on the ground that it interfered with liberty of contract. The Supreme Court conceded the interference, but upheld the statute because it served a legitimate public policy. The Court said that a state may protect the health and safety of its workers.

In his dissent in Adair, Justice Holmes might have cited Holden v. Hardy and argued that public policy justified the anti-discrimination clause of the Erdman Act.[c] He chose, however, to rest his dissent on a more general point — the proper relationship of the courts to the legislature. In order to clarify the disagreement between the majority and Holmes on this point, let us create legal syllogisms of their arguments.

MAJORITY

A

MAJOR PREMISE: In reviewing a statute that restricts liberty of contract, courts could make their own determination of whether the restriction was based on a legitimate public policy.

---

[c]In order to make such an argument, Holmes would have had to draw an analogy between Holden and Adair. The student should consider whether such an analogy would have been sound. Were Holden and Adair analogous, or were they distinguishable?

MINOR PREMISE: The anti-discrimination clause of the Erdman Act was based on the policy of promoting arbitration of disputes between railroads and labor unions.

CONCLUSION: Courts could determine whether this policy was legitimate.

B

MAJOR PREMISE: If a statute that interfered with liberty of contract was based on a policy that was not legitimate, the statute was unconstitutional.

MINOR PREMISE: Promoting arbitration of labor disputes on the railroads, on which the anti-discrimination clause of the Erdman Act was based, was not a legitimate public policy.

CONCLUSION: The anti-discrimination clause was unconstitutional.

HOLMES

MAJOR PREMISE: Courts must accept Congressional determinations of public policy unless they are irrational.

MINOR PREMISE: The anti-discrimination clause, which was based on the policy of promoting arbitration of disputes between railroads and labor unions, was not irrational.

CONCLUSION: The anti-discrimination clause was constitutional.

These syllogisms make clear that the major disagreement between the majority and the dissent was over the major premise of syllogism A in the majority's opinion and the major premise of Holmes's syllogism. Holmes believed that the legislature should determine public policy, and the courts should generally defer to legislative determinations. As a result, Holmes argued that courts should not oversee Congressional determinations of public policy (except in the rare case in which Congress acted irrationally), whereas the majority argued for more active judicial oversight. This disagreement was as much a matter of political philosophy as of law.

ARE SYMMETRICAL RIGHTS EQUAL RIGHTS?

Another aspect of the Adair case that is worthy of note is how vigorously the Court emphasized the equality of the rights of employers and employees. Each time the Court mentioned the railroad's right to purchase labor, the Court also mentioned the worker's right to sell one's labor. Here are two examples:

> It was the right of the {railroad} to prescribe the terms upon which the services of Coppage would be accepted, and it was the right of Coppage to become or not, as he chose, an employe of the railroad company upon the terms offered to him. ¶ 6.

> Of course, liberty of contract relating to labor includes both parties to it. The one has as much right to purchase as the other to sell labor. ¶ 7.

And, said the Court, these rights are not merely symmetrical; they are, in fact, equal. Here are two examples:

> In all such particulars, the employer and the employe have equality of right, and any legislation that disturbs that equality is an arbitrary interference with the liberty of contract .... ¶ 8.

> The right of a person to sell his labor upon such terms as he deems proper is, in its essence, the same as the right of the purchaser of labor to prescribe the conditions upon which he will accept such labor from the person offering to sell it. (Emphasis added.) ¶ 8.

How could the law make employer and employee more equal than by giving each the same right? Yet one may wonder whether these rights, which are equal in form, are equal in substance, that is, whether they are equally valuable.

THE MAJORITY'S STANDARD FOR JUDGING PUBLIC POLICY

A third interesting aspect of the case is the Court's standard for determining when the powers of government may be exercised to restrict liberty of contract. Quoting from <u>Lochner</u>, the Court said:

> Those powers, broadly stated and without, at present, any attempt at a more specific limitation, relate to the safety, health, morals and general welfare of the public. ... In every case that comes before this court, therefore, where legislation of this character is concerned and where the protection of the Federal Constitution is sought, the question necessarily arises: Is this a fair, reasonable and appropriate exercise of the police power of the State, or is it an unreasonable, unnecessary and arbitrary interference with the right of the individual to his personal liberty ...? ¶ 7.

As the student may already have observed, this is no standard at all. The government may restrict liberty of contract when doing so is "fair, reasonable and appropriate," but not when doing so is "unreasonable, unnecessary, and arbitrary." Such a false standard does not explain the Court's decision or provide guidance for future cases.

WAS PROTECTIVE LABOR LEGISLATION "FAIR, REASONABLE, AND APPROPRIATE"?

A few days after announcing the decision in <u>Adair</u>, the Supreme Court decided <u>Muller v. Oregon</u>, 208 U.S. 412 (1908). The State of Oregon had enacted a statute limiting the employment of women to ten hours per day. A supervisor in a laundry was convicted of requiring a woman to work in excess of ten hours. Relying on <u>Lochner v. New York</u>, which had invalidated a state law prescribing the ten-hour day in bakeries, the supervisor challenged the constitutionality of the Oregon statute. But, wrote Justice Brewer for a unanimous Court, this challenge

> assumes that the difference between the sexes does not justify a different rule respecting a restriction of the hours of labor....

... That woman's physical structure and the performance of maternal functions place her at a disadvantage in the struggle for subsistence is obvious. This is especially true when the burdens of motherhood are upon her. Even when they are not, by abundant testimony of the medical fraternity, continuance for a long time on her feet at work, repeating this from day to day, tends to injurious effects upon the body, and, as healthy mothers are essential to vigorous offspring, the physical well-being of woman becomes an object of public interest and care in order to preserve the strength and vigor of the race.

Still again, history discloses the fact that woman has always been dependent upon man. He established his control at the outset by superior physical strength, and this control in various forms ... has continued to the present.... Doubtless there are individual exceptions, and there are many respects in which she has an advantage over him; but looking at it from the viewpoint of the effort to maintain an independent position in life, she is not upon an equality.... It is impossible to close one's eyes to the fact that she still looks to her brother and depends upon him. 208 U.S. at 419, 421-422.

So-called "protective legislation" for women was evidently "fair, reasonable, and appropriate" and, therefore, constitutional. (The prohibition on sex discrimination in Title VII of the Civil Rights Act of 1964 has changed the status of such legislation.)

QUESTIONS FOR REFLECTION

1. A fundamental question in <u>Adair</u> was whether Congress had the power to regulate employment contracts. Do you think Congress should have this power?

2. Was the majority correct that both employers and workers had liberty of contract and that these rights were equal?

3. One purpose of the Erdman Act was to facilitate the unionization of railroad workers. Was this a proper purpose for Congress to pursue?

4. The gist of Justice Holmes's dissent was that the legislature, not the courts, should establish public policy. Holmes believed that procedure outranked substance, that the way a decision was made was more important than the goodness of the decision. Was he right? His view may be attractive in the context of cases like <u>Adair</u>, in which the courts were antipathetic to organized labor. Before you make up your mind, however, reflect on cases like <u>Brown v. Board of Education</u> (1954), in which the courts, not Congress or state legislatures, ordered desegregation of public schools, and <u>Lawrence v. Texas</u> (2003), in which the courts, not Congress or state legislatures, decriminalized homosexual acts between consenting adults in private.

The Unconstitutionality of Government Protection of Labor (continued)

CONSTITUTIONALITY OF STATE LAWS

Introduction

The preceding case, <u>Adair v. United States</u>, involved a constitutional challenge to a federal statute. In contrast, the next case, <u>Coppage v. Kansas</u>, involved a constitutional challenge to a state statute.

The challenge to the federal statute in <u>Adair</u> was grounded on the Fifth Amendment to the Constitution. The Fifth Amendment was not available for this purpose in <u>Coppage</u> because the Fifth Amendment applies only to the federal government, not to state governments. Instead, the challenge in <u>Coppage</u> was grounded on the Fourteenth Amendment.[a] The Fourteenth Amendment also contains a due process clause, and it is usually interpreted to limit the power of state governments in much the same way as the Fifth Amendment limits the power of the federal government.

The background of all the early American labor cases was the struggle between employers and workers. The development that precipitated both <u>Adair</u> and <u>Coppage</u> was the growing political power of organized labor. This power had been used to induce several states, including Kansas, to outlaw yellow dog contracts. Without yellow dog contracts, employers could not so easily obtain

---

[a]The first section of the Fourteenth Amendment reads:

> SECTION ONE. All persons born or naturalized in the United States and subject to the jurisdiction thereof, are citizens of the United States and of the State wherein they reside. No state shall make or enforce any law which shall abridge the privileges or immunities of citizens of the United States; nor shall any State deprive any person of life, liberty, or property, without due process of law; nor deny to any person within its jurisdiction the equal protection of the laws.

injunctions against union organizing.[b]   Therefore, although the <u>Coppage</u> case was technically about the constitutionality of a single state statute, the case was significant because it defined the role that a state government might play in the struggle between workers and employers.

We noted in connection with <u>Adair</u> that the level of abstraction at which a case is decided can affect its outcome, in particular, which prior cases will serve as precedents. In the following case, level of abstraction also plays a role. Compare how the majority characterizes the issue with how Justice Day in dissent characterizes it.

❦

---

[b]See <u>Hitchman Coal v. Mitchell</u>, below.

Coppage v. State of Kansas
236 U.S. 1 (1915)

MR. JUSTICE PITNEY delivered the opinion of the court.

{1} {A Kansas court fined the plaintiff in error (a superintendent employed by a railroad) for violating a state law that read:}

> "AN ACT to provide a penalty for coercing or influencing or making demands upon or requirements of employes, servants, laborers, and persons seeking employment....

> "SECTION 1. That it shall be unlawful for any individual or member of any firm, or any agent, officer or employe of any company or corporation, to coerce, require, demand or influence any person or persons to enter into any agreement, either written or verbal, not to join or become or remain a member of any labor organization or association, as a condition of such person or persons securing employment, or continuing in the employment of such individual, firm, or corporation.

> "SEC. 2. Any individual or member of any firm or any agent, officer or employe of any company or corporation violating the provisions of this act shall be deemed guilty of a misdemeanor, and upon conviction thereof shall be fined in a sum not less than fifty dollars or imprisoned in the county jail not less than thirty days."

{2} The judgment was affirmed by the Supreme Court of the State, two justices dissenting (87 Kansas, 752), and the case is brought here upon the ground that the statute, as construed and applied in this case, is in conflict with that provision of the Fourteenth Amendment of the Constitution of the United States which declares that no State shall deprive any person of liberty or property without due process of law.

{3} The facts, as recited in the opinion of the Supreme Court {of Kansas}, are as follows: About July 1, 1911, one Hedges was employed as a switchman by the St. Louis & San Francisco Railway Company, and was a member of a labor organization called the Switchmen's Union of North America. Plaintiff in error[c] was employed by the railway company as superintendent, and as such he requested Hedges to sign an agreement, which he presented to him in writing, at the same time informing him that if he did not sign it he could not remain in the employ of the company. The following is a copy of the paper thus presented:

---

[c]{"Plaintiff in error" is an older term meaning the appellant, i.e., the party who is appealing the judgment of the lower court. In this case, the plaintiff in error was T. B. Coppage. We do not know whether he was related to O. B. Coppage in *Adair v. U.S.*}

Fort Scott, Kansas,   , 1911.
Mr. T. B. Coppage, Superintendent Frisco Lines, Fort Scott:

We, the undersigned, have agreed to abide by your request, that is, to withdraw from the Switchmen's Union, while in the service of the Frisco Company.

(Signed)

{4} Hedges refused to sign this, and refused to withdraw from the labor organization. Thereupon plaintiff in error, as such superintendent, discharged him from the service of the company.

{5} At the outset, a few words should be said respecting the construction of the act. It uses the term "coerce," and some stress is laid upon this in the opinion of the Kansas Supreme Court. But, on this record, we have nothing to do with any question of actual or implied coercion or duress, such as might overcome the will of the employe by means unlawful without the act. In the case before us, the state court treated the term "coerce" as applying to the mere insistence by the employer, or its agent, upon its right to prescribe terms upon which alone it would consent to a continuance of the relationship of employer and employe.... There is neither finding nor evidence that the contract of employment was other than a general or indefinite hiring, such as is presumed to be terminable at the will of either party.... {T}here is nothing to show that Hedges was subjected to the least pressure or influence, or that he was not a free agent, in all respects competent, and at liberty to choose what was best from the standpoint of his own interests.... And if the right that plaintiff in error exercised is founded upon a constitutional basis, it cannot be impaired by merely applying to its exercise the term "coercion." We have to deal, therefore, with a statute that, as construed and applied, makes it a criminal offense punishable with fine or imprisonment for an employer or his agent to merely prescribe, as a condition upon which one may secure certain employment or remain in such employment (the employment being terminable at will), that the employe shall enter into an agreement not to become or remain a member of any labor organization while so employed; the employe being subject to no incapacity or disability, but on the contrary free to exercise a voluntary choice.

{6} In *Adair v. United States*, 208 U.S. 161, this court had to deal with a question not distinguishable in principle from the one now presented.... Adair was convicted upon an indictment charging that he, as agent of a common carrier subject to the provisions of the Act, unjustly discriminated against a certain employe by discharging him from the employ of the carrier because of his membership in a labor organization. The court held that portion of the Act upon which the conviction rested

Coppage v. Kansas   v

to be an invasion of the personal liberty as well as of the right of property guaranteed by the Fifth Amendment, which declares that no person shall be deprived of liberty or property without due process of law. Speaking by Mr. Justice Harlan, the court said (208 U.S., p. 174):

> While, as already suggested, the right of liberty and property guaranteed by the Constitution against deprivation without due process of law, is subject to such reasonable restraints as the common good or the general welfare may require, it is not within the functions of government — at least in the absence of contract between the parties — to compel any person in the course of his business and against his will to accept or retain the personal services of another, or to compel any person, against his will, to perform personal services for another. The right of a person to sell his labor upon such terms as he deems proper is, in its essence, the same as the right of the purchaser of labor to prescribe the conditions upon which he will accept such labor from the person offering to sell it. So the right of the employe to quit the service of the employer, for whatever reason, is the same as the right of the employer, for whatever reason, to dispense with the services of such employe. It was the legal right of the defendant Adair — however unwise such a course might have been — to discharge Coppage [the employe in that case] because of his being a member of a labor organization, as it was the legal right of Coppage, if he saw fit to do so — however unwise such a course on his part might have been — to quit the service in which he was engaged, because the defendant employed some persons who were not members of a labor organization. In all such particulars the employer and the employe have equality of right, and any legislation that disturbs that equality is an arbitrary interference with the liberty of contract which no government can legally justify in a free land.

{7} Unless it is to be overruled, this decision is controlling upon the present controversy; for if Congress is prevented from arbitrary interference with the liberty of contract because of the "due process" provision of the Fifth Amendment, it is too clear for argument that the States are prevented from the like interference by virtue of the corresponding clause of the Fourteenth Amendment; and hence if it be unconstitutional for Congress to deprive an employer of liberty or property for threatening an employe with loss of employment or discriminating against him because of his membership in a labor organization, it is unconstitutional for a State to similarly punish an employer for requiring his employe, as a condition of securing or retaining employment, to agree not to become or remain a member of such an organization while so employed.

{8} It is true that, while the statute that was dealt with in the *Adair* case contained a clause substantially identical with the Kansas act now under consideration — a clause making it a misdemeanor for an employer to require an employe or applicant for employment, as a condition of such employment, to agree not to become or remain a member of a labor organization, — the conviction was based upon another clause, which related to discharging an employe because of his membership in such an organization; and the decision, naturally, was confined to the case actually presented for decision. In the present case, the Kansas Supreme Court sought to distinguish the *Adair* decision upon this ground. The distinction, if any there be, has not previously been recognized as substantial, so far as we have been able to find....

{9} But, irrespective of whether it has received judicial recognition, is there any real distinction? The constitutional right of the employer to discharge an employe because of his membership in a labor union being granted, can the employer be compelled to resort to this extreme measure? May he not offer to the employe an option, such as was offered in the instant case, to remain in the employment if he will retire from the union; to sever the former relationship only if he prefers the latter? Granted the equal freedom of both parties to the contract of employment, has not each party the right to stipulate upon what terms only he will consent to the inception, or to the continuance, of that relationship? And may he not insist upon an express agreement, instead of leaving the terms of the employment to be implied? Can the legislature in effect require either party at the beginning to act covertly; concealing essential terms of the employment — terms to which, perhaps, the other would not willingly consent — and revealing them only when it is proposed to insist upon them as a ground for terminating the relationship? Supposing an employer is unwilling to have in his employ one holding membership in a labor union, and has reason to suppose that the man may prefer membership in the union to the given employment without it — we ask, can the legislature oblige the employer in such case to refrain from dealing frankly at the outset? And is not the employer entitled to insist upon equal frankness in return? Approaching the matter from a somewhat different standpoint, is the employe's right to be free to join a labor union any more sacred, or more securely founded upon the Constitution, than his right to work for whom he will, or to be idle if he will? And does not the ordinary contract of employment include an insistence by the employer that the employe shall agree, as a condition of the employment, that he will not be idle and will not work for whom he pleases but will serve his present employer, and him only, so long as the relation between them shall continue? Can the right of making contracts be enjoyed at all, except by parties coming together in an agreement that requires each party to forego, during the time and for the purpose covered by the agreement, any inconsistent exercise of his constitutional rights?

{10} These queries answer themselves. The answers, as we think, lead to a single conclusion: Under constitutional freedom of contract, whatever either party has the right to treat as sufficient ground for terminating the employment, where there is no stipulation on the subject, he has the right to provide against by insisting that a stipulation respecting it shall be a *sine qua non* of the inception of the employment, or of its continuance if it be terminable at will. It follows that this case cannot be distinguished from *Adair v. United States*.

{11} ... The principle is fundamental and vital. Included in the right of personal liberty and the right of private property — partaking of the nature of each — is the right to make contracts for the acquisition of property. Chief among such contracts is that of personal employment, by which labor and other services are exchanged for money or other forms of property. If this right be struck down or arbitrarily interfered with, there is a substantial impairment of liberty in the long-established constitutional sense. The right is as essential to the laborer as to the capitalist, to the poor as to the rich; for the vast majority of persons have no other honest way to begin to acquire property, save by working for money.

{12} ... We do not mean to say, therefore, that a State may not properly exert its police power to prevent coercion on the part of employers towards employes, or vice versa. But, in this case, the Kansas court of last resort has held that Coppage, the plaintiff in error, is a criminal punishable with fine or imprisonment under this statute simply and merely because, while acting as the representative of the Railroad Company and dealing with Hedges, an employe at will and a man of full age and understanding, subject to no restraint or disability, Coppage insisted that Hedges should freely choose whether he would leave the employ of the Company or would agree to refrain from association with the union while so employed. This construction is, for all purposes of our jurisdiction, conclusive evidence that the State of Kansas intends by this legislation to punish conduct such as that of Coppage, although entirely devoid of any element of coercion, compulsion, duress, or undue influence....

{13} Laying aside, therefore, as immaterial for present purposes, so much of the statute as indicates a purpose to repress coercive practices, what possible relation has the residue of the Act to the public health, safety, morals or general welfare? None is suggested, and we are unable to conceive of any. The Act ... is intended to deprive employers of a part of their liberty of contract, to the corresponding advantage of the employed and the upbuilding of the labor organizations. But no attempt is made, or could reasonably be made, to sustain the purpose to strengthen these voluntary organizations, any more than other voluntary associations of persons, as a legitimate object for the exercise of the police power. They are not public institutions, charged by law with public or governmental duties, such as would render the maintenance of their membership a matter of direct concern to the general welfare. If they were, a different question would be presented.

{14} As to the interest of the employed, it is said by the Kansas Supreme Court (87 Kansas, p. 759) to be a matter of common knowledge that "employes, as a rule, are not financially able to be as independent in making contracts for the sale of their labor as are employers in making contracts of purchase thereof." No doubt, wherever the right of private property exists, there must and will be inequalities of fortune; and thus it naturally happens that parties negotiating about a contract are not equally un-hampered by circumstances. This applies to all contracts, and not merely to that between employer and employe. Indeed a little reflection will show that wherever the right of private property and the right of free contract co-exist, each party when contracting is inevitably more or less influenced by the question whether he has much property, or little, or none; for the contract is made to the very end that each may gain something that he needs or desires more urgently than that which he proposes to give in exchange. And, since it is self-evident that, unless all things are held in common, some persons must have more property than others, it is from the nature of things impossible to uphold freedom of contract and the right of private property without at the same time recognizing as legitimate those inequalities of fortune that are the necessary result of the exercise of those rights. But the Fourteenth Amendment, in declaring that a State shall not "deprive any person of life, liberty or property without due process of law," gives to each of these an equal sanction; it recognizes "liberty" and "property" as co-existent human rights, and debars the States from any unwarranted interference with either.

...

{15} We need not refer to the numerous and familiar cases in which this court has held that the {police} power may properly be exercised for preserving the public health, safety, morals, or general welfare, and that such police regulations may reasonably limit the enjoyment of personal liberty, including the right of making contracts.... An evident and controlling distinction is this: that in those cases it has been held permissible for the States to adopt regulations fairly deemed necessary to secure some object directly affecting the public welfare, even though the enjoyment of private rights of liberty and property be thereby incidentally hampered; while in that portion of the Kansas statute which is now under consideration — that is to say, aside from coercion, etc. — there is no object or purpose, expressed or implied, that is claimed to have reference to health, safety, morals, or public welfare, beyond the supposed desirability of leveling inequalities of fortune by depriving one who has property of some part of what is characterized as his "financial independence." In short, an interference with the normal exercise of personal liberty and property rights is the primary object of the statute, and not an incident to the advancement of the general welfare. But, in our opinion, the Fourteenth Amendment debars the States from striking down personal liberty or property rights, or materially restricting their normal exercise, excepting so far as may be incidentally necessary for the accomplishment of some other and paramount object, and one that concerns the public welfare. The mere restriction of liberty or of property rights cannot of itself be denominated "public welfare," and treated as a legitimate object of the police power; for such restriction is the very thing that is inhibited by the Amendment.

{16} It is said in the opinion of the state court that membership in a labor organization does not necessarily affect a man's duty to his employer; that the employer has no right, by virtue of the relation, "to dominate the life nor to interfere with the liberty of the employe in matters that do not lessen or deteriorate the service"; and that "the statute implies that labor unions are lawful and not inimical to the rights of employers." The same view is presented in the brief of counsel for the State, where it is said that membership in a labor organization is the "personal and private affair" of the employe. To this line of argument it is sufficient to say that it cannot be judicially declared that membership in such an organization has no relation to a member's duty to his employer; and therefore, if freedom of contract is to be preserved, the employer must be left at liberty to decide for himself whether such membership by his employe is consistent with the satisfactory performance of the duties of the employment.

{17} Of course we do not intend to say, nor to intimate, anything inconsistent with the right of individuals to join labor unions, nor do we question the legitimacy of such organizations so long as they conform to the laws of the land as others are required to do. Conceding the full right of the individual to join the union, he has no inherent right to do this and still remain in the employ of one who is unwilling to employ a union man, any more than the same individual has a right to join the union without the consent of that organization. Can it be doubted that a labor organization — a voluntary association of working men — has the inherent and constitutional right to deny membership to any man who will not agree that during such membership he will not accept or retain employment in company with non-union men?[d] Or that a union man has the constitutional right to decline proffered employment unless the employer will agree not to employ any non-union man? (In all cases we refer, of course, to agreements made voluntarily, and without coercion or duress as between the parties. And we have no reference to questions of monopoly, or interference with the rights of third parties or the general public. These involve other considerations, respecting which we intend to intimate no opinion.) And can there be one rule of liberty for the labor organization and its members, and a different and more restrictive rule for employers? We think not; and since the relation of employer and employe is a voluntary relation, as clearly as is that between the members of a labor organization, the employer has the same inherent right to prescribe the terms upon

---

[d] {Compare the opinion of Recorder Levy in the *Philadelphia Cordwainers' Case.* — ed.}

which he will consent to the relationship, and to have them fairly understood and expressed in advance.

{18} When a man is called upon to agree not to become or remain a member of the union while working for a particular employer, he is in effect only asked to deal openly and frankly with his employer, so as not to retain the employment upon terms to which the latter is not willing to agree. And the liberty of making contracts does not include a liberty to procure employment from an unwilling employer, or without a fair understanding. Nor may the employer be foreclosed by legislation from exercising the same freedom of choice that is the right of the employe.

{19} To ask a man to agree, in advance, to refrain from affiliation with the union while retaining a certain position of employment, is not to ask him to give up any part of his constitutional freedom. He is free to decline the employment on those terms, just as the employer may decline to offer employment on any other; for "It takes two to make a bargain." Having accepted employment on those terms, the man is still free to join the union when the period of employment expires; or, if employed at will, then at any time upon simply quitting the employment. And, if bound by his own agreement to refrain from joining during a stated period of employment, he is in no different situation from that which is necessarily incident to term contracts in general. For constitutional freedom of contract does not mean that a party is to be as free after making a contract as before; he is not free to break it without accountability. Freedom of contract, from the very nature of the thing, can be enjoyed only by being exercised; and each particular exercise of it involves making an engagement which, if fulfilled, prevents for the time any inconsistent course of conduct.

...

Judgment reversed....

MR. JUSTICE HOLMES, dissenting.

{20} I think the judgment should be affirmed. In present conditions a workman not unnaturally may believe that only by belonging to a union can he secure a contract that shall be fair to him. If that belief, whether right or wrong, may be held by a reasonable man, it seems to me that it may be enforced by law in order to establish the equality of position between the parties in which liberty of contract begins. Whether in the long run it is wise for the workingmen to enact legislation of this sort is not my concern, but I am strongly of opinion that there is nothing in the Constitution of the United States to prevent it, and that *Adair v. United States*, 208 U.S. 161, and *Lochner v. New York*, 198 U.S. 45, should be overruled....

Coppage v. Kansas

Mr. Justice Day, with whom Mr. Justice Hughes concurs, dissenting.

...

{21} That the right of contract is a part of individual freedom within the protection of this amendment, and may not be arbitrarily interfered with, is conceded. While this is true, nothing is better settled by the repeated decisions of this court than that the right of contract is not absolute and unyielding, but is subject to limitation and restraint in the interest of the public health, safety and welfare, and such limitations may be declared in legislation of the State....

...

{22} ... Whether a given exercise of such authority transcends the limits of legislative authority must be determined in each case as it arises. The preservation of the police power of the States, under the authority of which that great mass of legislation has been enacted which has for its purpose the promotion of the health, safety and welfare of the public, is of the utmost importance....

{23} Of the necessity of such legislation, the local legislature is itself the judge, and its enactments are only to be set aside when they involve such palpable abuse of power and lack of reasonableness to accomplish a lawful end that they may be said to be merely arbitrary and capricious, and hence out of place in a government of laws and not of men, and irreconcilable with the conception of due process of law.

{24} By this it is not meant that the legislative power is beyond judicial review. Such enactments as are arbitrary or unreasonable and thus exceed the exercise of legislative authority in good faith, may be declared invalid when brought in review by proper judicial proceedings. This is necessary to the assertion and maintenance of the supremacy of the Constitution.

{25} Conceding then that the right of contract is a subject of judicial protection, within the authority given by the Constitution of the United States, the question here is, was the power of the State so arbitrarily exercised as to render its action unconstitutional and therefore void? It is said that this question is authoritatively determined in this court, in the case of *Adair v. United States*, 208 U.S. 161 {but the Court in that case did not reach the issue in the case at bar; and the issues are distinguishable.}

...

{26} There is nothing in the statute now under consideration which prevents an employer from discharging one in his service at his will. The question now presented is, May an employer, as a condition of present or future employment, require an employe to agree that he will not exercise the privilege of becoming a member of a labor union, should he see fit to do so? In my opinion, the cases are entirely different, and the decision of the questions controlled by different principles. The right to join labor unions is undisputed, and has been the subject of frequent affirmation in judicial opinions. Acting within their legal rights, such associations are as legitimate as any organization of citizens formed to promote their common interest. They are organized under the laws of many States, by virtue of express statutes passed for that purpose, and, being legal, and acting within their constitutional rights, the right to join them, as against coercive action to the contrary, may be the legitimate subject of protection in the exercise of the police authority of the States. This statute, passed in the exercise of that particular authority called the police power, the limitations of which no court has yet undertaken precisely to define, has for its avowed purpose the protection of the exercise of a legal right, by preventing an employer from depriving the employe of it as a condition of obtaining employment. I see no reason why a State may not, if it chooses, protect this right, as well as other legal rights.

{27} But it is said that the contrary must necessarily result, if not from the precise matter decided in the *Adair* case, then from the principles therein laid down, and that it is the logical result of that decision that the employer may, as a condition of employment, require an obligation to forego the exercise of any privileges because of the exercise of which an employe might be discharged from service. I do not concede that this result follows from anything decided in the *Adair* case. That case dealt solely with the right of an employer to terminate relations of employment with an employe, and involved the constitutional protection of his right so to do, but did not deal with the conditions which he might exact or impose upon another as a condition of employment.

{28} The act under consideration is said to have the effect to deprive employers of a part of their liberty of contract, for the benefit of labor organizations. It is urged that the statute has no object or purpose, express or implied, that has reference to health, safety, morals, or public welfare, beyond the supposed desirability of leveling inequalities of fortune by depriving him who has property of some part of his "financial independence."

{29} But this argument admits that financial independence is not independence of law or of the authority of the legislature to declare the policy of the State as to matters which have a reasonable relation to the welfare, peace and security of the community.

Coppage v. Kansas

...

{30} The act must be taken as an attempt of the legislature to enact a statute which it deemed necessary to the good order and security of society.... The legislature may have believed, acting upon conditions known to it, that the public welfare would be promoted by the enactment of a statute which should prevent the compulsory exaction of written agreements to forego the acknowledged legal right here involved, as a condition of employment in one's trade or occupation.

{31} It would be impossible to maintain that because one is free to accept or refuse a given employment, or because one may at will employ or refuse to employ another, it follows that the parties have a constitutional right to insert in an agreement of employment any stipulation they choose. They cannot put in terms that are against public policy either as it is deemed by the courts to exist at common law or as it may be declared by the legislature as the arbiter within the limits of reason of the public policy of the State. It is no answer to say that the greater includes the less and that because the employer is free to employ, or the employe to refuse employment, they may agree as they please....

...

{32} It may be that an employer may be of the opinion that membership of his employes in the National Guard, by enlistment in the militia of the State, may be detrimental to his business. Can it be successfully contended that the State may not, in the public interest, prohibit an agreement to forego such enlistment as against public policy? Would it be beyond a legitimate exercise of the police power to provide that an employe should not be required to agree, as a condition of employment, to forego affiliation with a particular political party, or the support of a particular candidate for office? It seems to me that these questions answer themselves. There is a real and not a fanciful distinction between the exercise of the right to discharge at will and the imposition of a requirement that the employe, as a condition of employment, shall make a particular agreement to forego a legal right. The agreement may be, or may be declared to be, against public policy, although the right of discharge remains. When a man is discharged, the employer exercises his right to declare such action necessary because of the exigencies of his business, or as the result of his judgment for other reasons sufficient to himself. When he makes a stipulation of the character here involved essential to future employment, he is not exercising a right to discharge, and may not wish to discharge the employe when, at a subsequent time, the prohibited act is done. What is in fact accomplished, is that the one engaging to work, who may wish to preserve an independent right of action, as a condition of employment, is coerced to the signing of such an agreement against his will, perhaps impelled by the necessities of his situation. The State, within constitutional limitations, is the judge of its own policy and may execute it in the exercise of the legislative authority. This statute reaches not only the employed but as well one seeking employment. The latter may never wish to join a labor union. By signing such agreements as are here involved he is deprived of the right of free choice as to his future conduct, and must choose between employment and the right to act in the future as the exigencies of his situation may demand. It is such contracts, having such effect, that this statute and similar ones seek to prohibit and punish as against the policy of the State.

{33} It is constantly emphasized that the case presented is not one of coercion. But in view of the relative positions of employer and employed, who is to deny that the stipulation here insisted upon and forbidden by the law is essentially coercive? No form of words can strip it of its true character. Whatever our individual opinions may be as to the wisdom of such legislation, we cannot put our judgment in place of that of the legislature and refuse to acknowledge the existence of the conditions with which it was dealing. Opinions may differ as to the remedy, but we cannot understand upon what ground it can be said that a subject so intimately related to the welfare of society is removed from the legislative power. Wherein is the right of the employer to insert this stipulation in the agreement any more sacred than his right to agree with another employer in the same trade to keep up prices?[e] He may think it quite as essential to his "financial independence" and so in truth it may be if he alone is to be considered. But it is too late to deny that the legislative power reaches such a case. It would be difficult to select any subject more intimately related to good order and the security of the community than that under consideration -- whether one takes the view that labor organizations are advantageous or the reverse. It is certainly as much a matter for legislative consideration and action as contracts in restraint of trade.

{34} It is urged that a labor organization — a voluntary association of working-men — has the constitutional right to deny membership to any man who will not agree that during such membership he will not accept or retain employment in company with non-union men. And it is asserted that there cannot be one rule of liberty for the labor organization and its members and a different and more restrictive rule for employers.

{35} It of course is true, for example, that a Church may deny membership to those who unite with other denominations, but it by no means follows that the State

---

[e]{An agreement between employers to set prices would violate the anti-trust law. Justice Day is arguing that if liberty of contract is not infringed by a statute outlawing contracts to set prices, liberty of contract is not infringed by a statute outlawing yellow dog contracts. — ed.}

may not constitutionally prohibit a railroad company from compelling a working-man to agree that he will, or will not, join a particular church. An analogous case, viewed from the employer's standpoint, would be: Can the State, in the exercise of its legislative power, reach concerted effort of employes intended to coerce the employer as a condition of hiring labor that he shall engage in writing to give up his privilege of association with other employers in legal organizations, corporate or otherwise, having for their object a united effort to promote by legal means that which employers believe to be for the best interest of their business?

{36} I entirely agree that there should be the same rule for employers and employed, and the same liberty of action for each. In my judgment, the law may prohibit coercive attempts, such as are here involved, to deprive either of the free right of exercising privileges which are theirs within the law. So far as I know, no law has undertaken to abridge the right of employers of labor in the exercise of free choice as to what organizations they will form for the promotion of their common interests, or denying to them free right of action in such matters.

{37} But it is said that in this case all that was done in effect was to discharge an employe for a cause deemed sufficient to the employer — a right inherent in the personal liberty of the employer protected by the Constitution. This argument loses sight of the real purpose and effect of this and kindred statutes. The penalty imposed is not for the discharge but for the attempt to coerce an unwilling employe to agree to forego the exercise of the legal right involved as a condition of employment. It is the requirement of such agreements which the State declares to be against public policy.

{38} I think that the act now under consideration, and kindred ones, are intended to promote the same liberty of action for the employe as the employer confessedly enjoys. The law should be as zealous to protect the constitutional liberty of the employe as it is to guard that of the employer. A principal object of this statute is to protect the liberty of the citizen to make such lawful affiliations as he may desire with organizations of his choice. It should not be necessary to the protection of the liberty of one citizen that the same right in another citizen be abridged or destroyed.

{39} If one prohibitive condition of the sort here involved may be attached, so may others, until employment can only be had as the result of written stipulations, which shall deprive the employe of the exercise of legal rights which are within the authority of the State to protect. While this court should, within the limitations of the constitutional guaranty, protect the free right of contract, it is not less important that the State be given the right to exert its legislative authority, if it deems best to do so, for the protection of rights which inhere in the privileges of the citizen of every free country.

{40} The Supreme Court of Kansas in sustaining this statute, said that "employes as a rule are not financially able to be as independent in making contracts for the sale of their labor as are employers in making a contract of purchase thereof," and in reply to this it is suggested that the law cannot remedy inequalities of fortune, and that so long as the right of property exists, it may happen that parties negotiating may not be equally unhampered by circumstances.

{41} This view of the Kansas court, as to the legitimacy of such considerations, is in entire harmony, as I understand it, with the former decisions of this court in considering the right of state legislatures to enact laws which shall prevent the undue or oppressive exercise of authority in making contracts with employes. In *Holden v. Hardy*, 169 U.S. 366, this court considering legislation limiting the number of hours during which laborers might be employed in a particular employment, said:

> "The legislature has also recognized the fact, which the experience of legislators in many States has corroborated, that the proprietors of these establishments and their operatives do not stand upon an equality, and that their interests are, to a certain extent, conflicting. The former naturally desire to obtain as much labor as possible from their employes, while the latter are often induced by the fear of discharge to conform to regulations which their judgment, fairly exercised, would pronounce to be detrimental to their health or strength. In other words, the proprietors lay down the rules and the laborers are practically constrained to obey them. In such cases self-interest is often an unsafe guide, and the legislature may properly interpose its authority.... But the fact that both parties are of full age and competent to contract does not necessarily deprive the State of the power to interfere where the parties do not stand upon an equality, or where the public health demands that one party to the contract shall be protected against himself. 'The State still retains an interest in his welfare, however reckless he may be. The whole is no greater than the sum of all the parts, and when the individual health, safety and welfare are sacrificed or neglected, the State must suffer.'" (Page 397.)

{42} This language was quoted with approval in *Chicago, Burlington & Quincy R. R. Co. v. McGuire*, 219 U.S. 549, 570, in which a statute of Iowa was sustained, prohibiting contracts limiting liability for injuries made in advance of the injuries received, and providing that the subsequent acceptance of benefits under such contracts should not constitute satisfaction for injuries received after the contract. Certainly it can be no substantial objection to the exercise of the police power that the legislature has taken into consideration the necessities, the comparative ability, and the relative situation of the contracting parties. While all stand equal before the law, and are alike entitled to its protection, it ought not to be a reasonable objection that one motive which impelled an enactment was to protect those who might otherwise be unable to protect themselves.

{43} I therefore think that the statute of Kansas, sustained by the Supreme Court of the State, did not go beyond a legitimate exercise of the police power, when it sought, not to require one man to employ another against his will, but to put limitations upon the sacrifice of rights which one man may exact from another as a condition of employment. Entertaining these views, I am constrained to dissent from the judgment in this case.

COMMENTS

LAISSEZ-FAIRE, SOCIAL DARWINISM, AND NATURAL RIGHTS

Adair and *Coppage* exemplify how the Nineteenth Century philosophies of laissez-faire economics and Social Darwinism combined to influence legal doctrine. Indeed, the judges wrote these philosophies into the Constitution, at least as far as they served the interests of capital.

In brief, laissez-faire doctrine calls for the government to leave the economy alone. Parties to contracts should be left free to negotiate any terms they desire. We need say little more about laissez-faire economics. It has been resurrected as neoclassical economics, which has captured the majority of economics departments in the land and which the student is advised to evaluate with care. But a few words about Social Darwinism are in order.

Social Darwinism grew out of Charles Darwin's theory that evolution is explained by survival of the fittest. Evolution is the empirical observation that the characteristics of species change over time. Survival of the fittest is the hypothesis or theory that successful changes survive. For example, fossils reveal that the creature we know as giraffe used to have a short neck, and it fed on bushes and low leaves. These creatures lived in a time when food was plentiful, and the animals increased in number. These are empirical observations and inferences based on observations. Now commences the theorizing. Short-necked giraffes increased to the point that there were not enough bushes and low leaves to support any more of them. Then something interesting happened. Some giraffes were born with necks that were a little bit longer than the rest. (We do not know why changes of this sort occur; theories abound. But the reason for changes in species is not important for our purposes.) A longer neck was an advantage because the animal could nibble on higher food as well as bushes and low leaves, so the slightly longer-necked giraffes multiplied faster than the shorter-necked giraffes with which they competed for food. In time, the longer-necked giraffes replaced all of their competitors; that is, the shorter-necked giraffes died out. And then it happened all over again: some giraffes were born with necks that were a little bit longer than the rest, and they flourished and multiplied and drove out the competition. And then it happened again and again. Other changes may have played roles as well; for example, a change in weather might have reduced the amount of bushes and low leaves, but not affected higher leaves, or other short beasts might have begun to compete with the shorter-necked giraffes for bushes and low leaves. Over a long period of time, giraffes came to have long necks. According to the theory of survival of the fittest, the longer-necked giraffes were better adaptations to the environment in which they lived than their shorter-necked cousins.

The theory smacks of tautology because fitness is defined in terms of survival. The fittest are the ones that survive because fitness simply means a species has survived. Nevertheless, the theory became widely accepted in the Nineteenth Century and was easily applied to the human race; after all, we are a species of mammal. The theory can be applied to society. The application runs like this: It has always been true that some human beings are more successful than others. Every culture has values, and some people score higher on those values than others. Hierarchies result. Consider the culture of young boys. Athletic prowess is a major value. Good athletes enjoy more prestige than poor athletes. Or consider fashions in appearance. When this writer was in junior high school, and appearance was very important to him and his peers, the coolest hair style for boys was a crew cut on top and long hair slicked back on the sides. If one had straight hair, one could enhance one's esteem by adopting this hairdo. If, like this writer, one had curly hair, one was out of luck. (White folks did not dream of straightening their hair back then.) A generation later, styles had changed, and curls were in. The children of the author's straight-haired classmates were out of style (or had to pay their hair stylists for appropriate treatments), whereas this writer's children enjoyed prestige just for being themselves. The point is that we have — probably always have had, perhaps always will have — criteria of value, and they produce hierarchies of human beings. Some criteria are stable, like athletic prowess; some are not, like hair styles.

Darwin's theory can be used to explain these hierarchies; the explanation is called Social Darwinism.

It holds that the most successful human beings are the fittest, the best adaptations to the environment. Two conclusions follow: The successful are superior to the unsuccessful, and the successful deserve their success. If one is wealthy — and wealth is the principal measure of value in modern American culture — the reason is that one has the highly valued talent of making money. Poor people lack this talent. Therefore, because one's wealth is the result of one's talent, one deserves it. Poor people are poor because they lack the talent of making money; so they are inferior, and they deserve to be poor.

Social Darwinism can be criticized. Those straight-haired youths in the 1950's were not, for this reason, better persons than this writer was; they were just luckier. Or take the case of other talents. Suppose one person invented the computer, and this person was born a hundred years earlier than she actually was. Without Twentieth Century technology, she could not have made a computer; at best she would have been considered eccentric, and she might have been considered crazy. Or suppose Achilles, the greatest of the Greek warriors, and perhaps the most famous hero of all time in the Western world, had been born today. How useful would his ability to hurl a spear be in New York or Chicago? The best he could hope for would be a spot on the Olympic team and, after that, maybe a job as a bartender or insurance sales agent or actor with a German accent. In short, a criticism of Social Darwinism is that chance is at least as important to success as talent.

Australia, New Zealand, Canada, and the United States stand as some evidence for this criticism of Social Darwinism. These nations, which are among the most prosperous on earth, were colonized and developed by the dregs of European society, including criminals. Successful persons rarely emigrate to the wilderness. Few of the ancestors of the citizens of these countries were among the elite of the lands they left, and the same is true of the United States.

Two other criticisms of Social Darwinism may be mentioned. First, the analogy between the natural world and the social world of humans is imperfect. An animal cannot change its environment, whereas humans can change their social environment. Humans can manipulate their social environment in ways to their personal advantage, so that success is no longer an objective measure of fitness. Second, Social Darwinism imagines that individual humans compete in our environment in the same way that animals compete in their environments. However, some of the most successful species of animals cooperate rather than compete. Indeed, individual members of such species may cooperate to the point of self sacrifice; for example, a soldier bee will die for the sake of the hive. It follows that competition is not the only route to success, and it may not be the best route.

In spite of these and other criticisms,[f] Social Darwinism had a powerful appeal in the Nineteenth Century, and still has today, particularly to the people at the top of the hierarchy. They want to believe that they deserve to be there; they feel they are superior to those beneath them, and they want a rationale to explain their superiority. The rationale of the early Protestants, a group that included the Puritans who founded New England, was that they were the elect, the chosen of God. That rationale ran out of force in the Eighteenth and Nineteenth Centuries. The Enlightenment made us naturalists, and today we seek scientific explanations. And so we have Social Darwinism. Survival of the fittest appears to be scientific. It applies to every living creature. If the best are on top, it is the natural order of things.

Social Darwinism can be linked with laissez-faire economics. The argument is that the economy is an

---

[f]One might add a criticism of evolutionary theory in general, not merely of its application to human society, namely, that people who apply the theory commonly assume that whatever they observe — in a living creature or a social structure — is (or was) good, or at least well adapted. But "mistakes" in evolution are bound to happen; counterproductive changes must occur. If the theory is correct, they will not endure; but a mistake might persist for a substantial period of time because the creature has other strengths that overbalance the weakness. A person at the top of a social ladder often has a number of undesirable qualities. For example, suppose a person had invented the mass production assembly line. This person would have become fabulously wealthy and powerful, and held up to others as a model, despite being paternalistic towards workers and an outspoken racist.

environment, much like the environment in which animals live, and it should be left to operate naturally so that the most able, the most productive, can become the most successful. Governmental interference will distort the economy and destroy efficiency. The beneficiaries of government interference are not the most productive, but the friends of politicians.

Social Darwinism and laissez-faire economics can be linked to the idea of natural rights, to which the authors of the Constitution subscribed. The argument is that every human being has a natural right to deal with other human beings, to bargain and enter into contracts on whatever terms are satisfactory to the parties. Because this is a natural right, the government may not interfere with it.

The cases we have been discussing used laissez-faire economics and Social Darwinism to create new natural rights, which were implied into the Constitution for the benefit of entrepreneurs. The process started with the simple notion that employment is a contract between employer and employee. That employment is contractual may seem obvious to us today, but, as the student knows, it was not obvious to the Founders of America. To them, employment was a status relationship. Masters and servants were like husbands and wives, and parents and children, and could be regulated by government. We have seen already that the government played an active role in Colonial times with regard to entering and leaving occupations, compensation, and production. But during the Nineteenth Century, the role of the government diminished, and the employment relationship came to be understood in terms of contract, not status. The cases the student has read consistently characterize employment as being the result of an offer by an employer and an acceptance by a worker, that is, as a contract.

The second step in the process of using laissez-faire economics and Social Darwinism to create new natural rights in the Constitution, was the assertion that each person has a constitutional right to be free of governmental interference in pursuing an occupation. To repeat what Justice Bradley said in the Butchers' Union case, "the right to follow any of the common occupations of life is an inalienable right." Because employment is contractual, it follows that the right to enter into employment contracts is also inalienable. As the Court held in <u>Allgeyer</u>, "The liberty mentioned in [the due process clause] ... embrace[s] the right of the citizen ... to pursue any livelihood or avocation, and for that purpose to enter into all contracts which may be proper, necessary, and essential" to this purpose. Justice Pitney explicitly made these connections in ¶ 11 of <u>Coppage</u>:

> "The principle is fundamental and vital. Included in the right of personal liberty and the right of private property — partaking of the nature of each — is the right to make contracts for the acquisition of property. Chief among such contracts is that of personal employment, by which labor and other services are exchanged for money and other forms of property."

The final step in the process was to prohibit the government from regulating the employment relationship. <u>Lochner</u> held that the government could not mandate a ten-hour maximum for bakers. <u>Adair</u> held the government could not forbid discrimination because of union membership. <u>Coppage</u> held that the government could not prohibit yellow dog contracts.

The judges were aware of what they were doing. Like all true believers, they were convinced that their philosophy was right, and they were not ashamed of it. They consciously wrote it into the Constitution. Consider the words of Justice Pitney in <u>Coppage</u>, some of which were quoted earlier:

> "As to the interest of the employed, it is said by the Kansas supreme court to be a matter of common knowledge that 'employees, as a rule, are not financially able to be as independent in making contracts for the sale of their labor as are employers in making a contract of purchase thereof.'"[g] ¶ 14.

---

[g]This curious way of saying that workers have less bargaining power than employers is reminiscent of Adam Smith's analysis that appeared in the <u>Philadelphia Cordwainers</u> case. He noted that employers are wealthier and, therefore, if a dispute arises, they can hold out longer than workers.

Justice Pitney continued:

> "No doubt, wherever the right of private property
> exists, there must and will be inequality of
> fortune; and thus it naturally happens that parties
> negotiating about a contract are not equally
> unhampered by circumstances.... And since it is
> self-evident that, unless all things are held in
> common, some persons must have more property than
> others, it is from the nature of things impossible
> to uphold freedom of contract and the right of
> private property without at the same time
> recognizing as legitimate those inequalities of
> fortune that are the necessary result of the
> exercise of those rights. But the 14th Amendment,
> in declaring that a state shall not 'deprive any
> person of life, liberty, or property without due
> process of law,' gives to each of these an equal
> sanction; it recognizes 'liberty' and 'property' as
> coexistent human rights, and debars the states from
> any unwarranted interference with either." ¶ 14.

This passage is especially interesting because it says
that inequality of wealth is a natural consequence of the
right of private property. The Constitution protects
private property; therefore, the Constitution protects
inequality of wealth. It follows that the Constitution
prohibits any attempts by the government to ameliorate
inequality of wealth, such as improving the bargaining
power of workers through labor unions.

The process of injecting laissez-faire and Social
Darwinism into the Constitution did not occur without
objection. Justice Holmes was fully aware of what was
happening, and he consistently dissented. His dissent in
Lochner (in which the majority invalidated the ten-hour
law for bakers) deserves our attention. He wrote:

> "This case is decided upon an economic theory
> which a large part of the country does not
> entertain. If it were a question of whether I
> agreed with that theory, I should desire to study
> it further and long before making up my mind. But
> I do not conceive that to be my duty, because I
> strongly believe that my agreement or disagreement
> has nothing to do with the right of a majority to
> embody their opinions in law. It is settled by
> various decisions of this court that state
> constitutions and state laws may regulate life in

many ways which we as legislators might think injudicious, or ... tyrannical.... Sunday {closing} laws and usury laws are ancient examples. A more modern one is the prohibition of lotteries. The liberty of the citizen to do as he likes so long as he does not interfere with the liberty of others to do the same, which has been a shibboleth for some well-known writers,[h] is interfered with by {mandatory} school {attendance} laws, by the Postoffice, by every state or municipal institution which takes his money for purposes thought desirable, whether he likes it or not. ✿ Some of these laws embody convictions or prejudices which judges are likely to share. Some may not. But a Constitution is not intended to embody a particular economic theory, whether of paternalism and the organic relation of the citizen to the state, or of laissez-faire. It is made for people of fundamentally differing views.... The 14th Amendment does not enact Mr. Herbert Spencer's Social Statics...."[i] {This book was a statement of Social Darwinism.} 198 U.S. at 75-76.

This dissent is somewhat disingenuous. Holmes did not need further study to make up his mind about laissez-faire economics; he believed in it, as we know from his dissent in Guntner, in which he argued that workers and employers are in competition. They compete for the surplus, that is, for the difference between the cost of producing a product and the price that consumers pay for it. If capital is allowed to combine, labor should be allowed to combine as well, and the government should leave both alone.

If he believed in laissez-faire, why did Holmes object to writing it into the Constitution? He offered one reason, and we may suggest another. He said that the majority, through the legislature, should be free to embody their economic opinions into law, and it is not the place of judges to stand in the way.

---

[h]Most notably, perhaps, John Stuart Mill in "On Liberty."

[i]The final sentence in this quotation has been moved. It appears in Holmes's opinion at the point indicated by this symbol ✿ in the quotation.

Holmes might have had another reason for dissenting in the cases we are considering. Perhaps his objection was that the majority of the Supreme Court was not truly adopting laissez-faire economics.[j] In spite of the repeated assertions that employers and employees had equal rights, the truth is that the Court was giving great freedom to entrepreneurs while at the same time severely limiting the freedom of labor unions. We have seen some of this already in the Danbury Hatters case, in which the Court initially applied the Sherman Anti-trust Act to unions, and in Duplex v. Deering, in which the Court held that the Clayton Act did not exempt labor from anti-trust law; we will see the same thing again in Hitchman Coal, which allowed an injunction against organizing in West Virginia. And we will see how the courts used injunctions to shackle unions when we turn to the Debs Case. It has occurred to many observers (including modern libertarians), and it might have been in Justice Holmes's mind as well, that the courts were not adopting laissez-faire in full. Laissez-faire called for the government, including the courts, to keep hands off actors in the economy. The courts used laissez-faire to give capital almost complete freedom from the government. However, the courts abandoned laissez-faire when they actively intervened to restrict the activity of labor unions.

A final word about the holding of Coppage. In a line of cases the student has read, the courts kept organized labor under control by outlawing private behaviors. Thus, Vegelahn v. Guntner prohibited picketing, and the Danbury Hatters case and Duplex v. Deering prohibited boycotts. Normally, the legislature has the right to the last word on whether private behavior is legal or illegal. For example, if a court ruled that homosexuals may not marry, the legislature could enact a statute permitting them to marry; if a court ruled that an employer may discharge a worker for any reason, the legislature could pass a law protecting workers against unjust discharge. Knowing that the legislature could overrule the courts on the legality of private behavior, unions went to the legislative branch of government for relief from judicial rulings; and the

---

[j]See John Roche, "Entrepreneurial Liberty and the Fourteenth Amendment," 4 Labor History 3 (Winter, 1963).

legislatures responded with statutes limiting hours of work per day and prohibiting discrimination against union members. Such statutes were meant to stymie judicial control of the private behavior of unions. In order for the courts to maintain their control of labor, it became necessary for them to develop a new strategy; and they did. As the student knows, cases like <u>Lochner v. New York</u>, <u>Adair v. U.S.</u>, and <u>Coppage v. Kansas</u> held unconstitutional statutes enacted to protect workers and unions. Thus, <u>Lochner</u>, <u>Adair</u>, and <u>Coppage</u> marked a significant shift in the relationship of the law to organized labor. To their power to control the private behavior of unions, the courts added the power to control the public acts of another branch of government.

QUESTIONS FOR REFLECTION

1. The majority held that it was not coercive for an employer to require a worker to agree to a yellow dog contract, and Kansas could not change this lawful act into coercion merely by putting a label on it. This holding was crucial to the outcome of the case because outlawing coercion is a legitimate public policy; so if demanding a yellow dog contract were coercive, the Kansas statute would have been constitutional.

The employer in <u>Coppage</u> used economic power to induce job applicants to sign yellow dog contracts. The Court held that the employer's use of economic power was not coercive and, therefore, legitimate. But earlier cases which the student has read had held that <u>workers'</u> use of economic power via unions was coercive and, therefore, illegitimate. What is coercion? Compare <u>Vegelahn v. Guntner</u>, in which the court declared that peaceful picketing was "moral intimidation," and <u>Hitchman Coal v. Mitchell</u>, in which the court held that it was coercive for the union to urge members to perform the lawful act of quitting work (striking) in order to secure higher wages. Is there a difference between identifying an act for what it is and merely putting a label on it, or was Humpty Dumpty right after all?[k]

------

[k] "'When I use a word,' Humpty Dumpty said, in a rather scornful tone, 'it means just what I choose it to mean —
(continued...)

2. The majority argued that a state had no legitimate interest in strengthening a private, voluntary association like a union. If so, why did the state have an interest in strengthening private, voluntary associations that existed for the purpose of aggregating capital, namely, corporations?

3. In Adair v. U.S. the majority said that whether a worker is willing and able to perform a job is unrelated to union membership; as a result, the government had no basis in the Commerce Clause to promote unionization of the railroads. In Coppage v. Kansas the state argued that an employer has no right to interfere with a worker's desire to join a union because union membership was unrelated to a worker's duty to one's employer (and, therefore, the state could protect the worker's right); the majority of the Court replied that union membership may well affect a member's duty to one's employer. Did the Court change its mind, or were these statements inconsistent?

4. The majority held that Adair and Coppage were indistinguishable in part on the argument that, if the anti-yellow dog contract statute were sustained, employers would evade the statute by hiring a worker regardless of one's intent to join a union (thus the employer would appear to obey the statute) and then firing the worker as soon as one joined a union. Such a course of behavior would have been illegal. Thus, the Court struck down the statute in part on the ground that citizens would violate the law. Is it proper for a court to base a ruling on the assumption that citizens will behave illegally? Did the Court make a contrary assumption in Adair?

5. Holmes argued that liberty of contract was more than symmetry of rights, but required equality of bargaining power. Do you think this argument was

---

k(...continued)
neither more nor less.' 'The question is,' said Alice, 'whether you can make words mean so many different things.' 'The question is,' said Humpty Dumpty, 'which is to be master — that's all.'" Lewis Carroll, Through the Looking-Glass, ch. 6, p. 205 (1934 edition).

correct? If so, do you also think that substantive economic rights may exist, for example, a right to a living wage or adequate medical care?

6. Adair held that an employer had a constitutional right to discharge a worker for joining a union. As a practical matter, Adair also meant that an employer could refuse to hire a union member. (The reasoning is that if an employer had to hire a union member, but was free to discharge one, the employer would hire the union member and a minute later fire the person.) Justice Day sought to distinguish Adair on the ground that a law against yellow dog contracts did not penalize an employer for discharging a worker, but for attempting to coerce a worker into abandoning one's right to join a union in the future. From the point of view of a worker, is there any difference between promising not to join a union and knowing one will be fired if one joins a union?

7. The law against yellow dog contracts aimed to protect workers from coercion in exercising their right to join a lawful private association, viz., a union. Day argued that the state could protect this right. He drew an analogy to a law that would protect employers from coercion by workers in exercising the employer's right to join a lawful trade association. Day implied that the two laws stood or fell together. Thus, Day's argument was a reductio ad absurdum within an analogy. Let us assume the analogy was sound, i.e., that a worker's joining a union was like an employer's joining a trade association. Whether the reductio was convincing depended on the implied belief that a legislature could constitutionally enact a statute that prohibited workers from using their economic power to induce an employer not to join a trade association. Was this belief justified? Would invalidation of such a law have been unthinkable?

8. A yellow dog contract deprived a worker of the liberty to join a union. The Kansas statute sought to deprive the employer of the liberty to hire only non-union workers. Were Adair and Coppage really about which party, employer or worker, would preserve freedom of action in the future?

9. Justice Day cited the precedent of <u>Holden v. Hardy</u>, in which the Supreme Court upheld a statute limiting hour of work for underground miners. The rationale of the case, according to a passage from the opinion quoted by Day (¶ 41), was that the workers lacked bargaining power and needed the protection of the law. Day also cited <u>Chicago, Burlington & Quincy R.R. Co. v. McGuire</u>, which held that a state might prohibit employers from demanding that applicants for jobs agree to a limitation on the employer's liability to them for injuries suffered on the job (¶ 42), and implied that this decision was also based on workers' lack of bargaining power. Can these decisions be distinguished from <u>Adair</u> and <u>Coppage</u>, or did the later cases implicitly overrule the earlier ones? Why did not Day also cite <u>Lochner v. New York</u>?

10. Do you think the theory of Social Darwinism has merit?

11. Would our society and economy be better off today if we adhered rigorously to laissez-faire?

Ù

Government by Injunction

JURISDICTION

Introduction

The origin of the <u>Debs</u> case is the Pullman strike of 1894. Pullman cars were special sleeping cars on trains. They were manufactured by the Pullman Co. in the company town of Pullman, Illinois, near Chicago.[a] Pullman cars were owned and operated by the Pullman Co., not by the railroads. If a traveler wanted to sleep in a Pullman car, one bought a separate ticket for this purpose. The Pullman Co. paid a fee to the railroad for hauling its cars.

Most railway workers had been organized by 1894, but Pullman refused to deal with a national union. In May of that year, Pullman cut the wages of its workers by twenty percent. When they protested, the company evicted the protesters from their houses. In response, the workers joined the American Railway Union. Eugene Debs was the president. The union had lost the strike of 1877; that strike had turned violent, and the violence had justified federal intervention to protect the flow of interstate commerce. Remembering this lesson, Debs carefully masterminded a job action directed at Pullman cars, not at the railroads themselves, so that interstate commerce (except for Pullman cars) would continue unabated. Workers were instructed not to handle Pullman cars, but otherwise to continue performing their duties. One morning in late June, Pullman cars from Michigan to California were found resting on sidings; the workers had cut them out of trains and left them behind.

President Cleveland immediately ordered the U. S. Marshal at Chicago to place special deputies on all interstate trains. Also, the railroads' managers attached U. S. mail cars to Pullman cars in the hope that

---

[a]In a company town, all the property is owned by the company, including public buildings like schools. Workers rent their homes from the company; therefore, if the company becomes dissatisfied with a worker, the worker can lose not only one's job, but also one's abode.

the mail would be stopped, and that would provide a basis for federal action. But the workers had no trouble separating mail cars from Pullman cars. The managers' next step was to refuse to run any trains that did not meet their specifications, which, of course, included Pullman cars. It was the managers, therefore, who stopped the trains. But it must be added that there was a degree of violence in some railroad yards.

On June 30th, the Attorney General of the U.S., Richard Olney, demonstrated his impartiality by appointing Edwin Walker to assist the U.S. attorney in Chicago. Walker was general counsel for the Chicago, Milwaukee, and St. Paul RR. and a legal advisor to the General Managers' Association.

With Walker's help, the government attorneys drafted an application for an injunction on July 1st and presented it to the judges the following day. The judges suggested some modifications, which the government adopted, and the injunction was issued. It prohibited a few named persons, "all persons combining and conspiring with them, and all other persons whomsoever" from interfering with or stopping the business of any of the railroads and from interfering with or stopping any mail trains or other trains, whether freight or passenger. As if this language were not inclusive enough, the injunction specifically restrained Debs and others from sending any communications that would incite or encourage or persuade any employees of the railroads to refuse to perform their duties, in other words, to continue striking. The injunction was personally served on Debs and other union leaders and published in newspapers and read aloud in railroad yards. Some historians claim that most of the violence that occurred during the strike came in response to the injunction.

Debs and his deputies did not comply with the injunction, and they were arrested on July 7th. They were held in contempt and sentenced to six months in prison.

The major issue before the Supreme Court was jurisdiction. Jurisdiction refers to the power of a court to hear and decide a case. If a court lacks jurisdiction of a case, but hears it nonetheless, the court's order is void.

Courts are organs of government; therefore, their existence and power must originate in the state or federal constitution. In some instances, the constitution creates a court and establishes its jurisdiction. In other instances, the constitution empowers the legislature to create courts and establish their jurisdiction.

The Constitution of the United States creates only one court, the Supreme Court. The Constitution gives the Supreme Court jurisdiction over a small group of cases[b] and empowers Congress to give it jurisdiction over other cases. The Constitution also allows Congress to create lower federal courts and define their jurisdiction. As a result, the federal courts are considered to be courts of **limited jurisdiction**; they may hear only those classes of cases specifically named in the Constitution or in an act of Congress.[c]

Debs argued in the Supreme Court that federal courts did not have jurisdiction to enjoin the railroad strike. Debs's argument was strong, for neither the Constitution nor any act of Congress specifically gave federal courts this sort of jurisdiction.

---

[b]See Article III, Section 2.

[c]In contrast, many state courts are courts of **general jurisdiction**, which means they are empowered to all classes of cases.

In re. Debs
158 U.S. 564 (1895)

Petition for Writ of Habeas Corpus.[d]

{At the direction of the Attorney General, the U.S. Attorney in Illinois (the petitioner) filed a petition in federal circuit court for an injunction against the defendants, who were officers of the American Railway Union. The petition contained the following allegations:

> Twenty-two railroads pass through Chicago.[e] These railroads carry passengers, freight, mail, and military troops and provisions in interstate commerce. Sleeping cars are essential to the operation of interstate railroads.

> The union is on strike against the Pullman Car Company. The defendants have conspired to boycott the Pullman Co.; they have asked members of their union, as well as sympathetic members of other railway unions, to refuse to work on trains that included Pullman cars, and this request is being honored.

> The defendants intend to take control of the railroad business and to prevent the railroads from doing their usual business. Union members have gathered in large numbers at railroad yards and, by threats and violence, prevented the railroads from hiring workers who would handle Pullman cars. Union members have also obstructed and wrecked trains by locking switches, removing spikes and rails from the tracks, destroying signals, and assaulting switchmen, and otherwise have deprived the railroad companies of the control and management of their businesses.

> As a result, supplies of coal, fuel, grain, fruits, vegetables, meat, etc. have been interrupted, to the injury of dealers in these products and consumers. Thus interstate trade in these commodities has been obstructed and destroyed.

> Defendants have threatened to continue to obstruct interstate commerce and to paralyze the operations of every railway in the country.

---

[d]{"Habeas corpus" means, literally, "you may have the body." A writ of habeas corpus is an order from a court to (often) a jailer to bring a prisoner before the court for a hearing on whether the prisoner should be freed. A petition for a writ of habeas corpus is, in effect, a request that the court consider whether to release a prisoner. — ed.}

[e]{Chicago was the principal railroad hub in the country. — ed.}

In re. Debs v

The circuit court issued an injunction commanding the defendants "and all other persons whomsoever" to desist and refrain from "interfering with, hindering, obstructing, or stopping any of the business of any of the ... named railroads" or of any other trains engaged in interstate commerce. The injunction was served on the defendants, who disobeyed it and were held in contempt and sentenced to jail.}

MR. JUSTICE BREWER delivered the opinion of the Court.

{1} The case presented by the bill is this: The United States, finding that the interstate transportation of persons and property, as well as the carriage of the mails, is forcibly obstructed, and that a combination and conspiracy exists to subject the control of such transportation to the will of the conspirators, applied to one of their courts, sitting as a court of equity, for an injunction to restrain such obstruction and prevent carrying into effect such conspiracy....

...

{2} Congress has exercised the power granted in respect to interstate commerce in a variety of legislative acts. Passing by for the present all that legislation in respect to commerce by water, and considering only that which bears upon railroad interstate transportation (for this is the specific matter involved in this case), these acts may be noticed: First, that of June 15, 1866, c. 124, 14 Stat. 66, carried into the Revised Statutes as section 5258, which provides:

> "Whereas the Constitution of the United States confers upon Congress, in express terms, the power to regulate commerce among the several States, to establish post roads, and to raise and support armies: Therefore, Be it enacted by the Senate and House of Representatives of the United States of America in Congress assembled, That every railroad company in the United States whose road is operated by steam, its successors and assigns, be, and is hereby, authorized to carry upon and over its road, boats, bridges, and ferries all passengers, troops, government supplies, mails, freight, and property on their way from any
> State to another State, and to receive compensation therefor, and to connect with roads of other States so as to form continuous lines for the transportation of the same to the place of destination."

{3} Second. That of March 3, 1873, c. 252, 17 Stat. 584, (Rev. Stat. §§ 4386 to 4389,) which regulates the transportation of live stock over interstate railroads. Third. That of May 29, 1884, c. 60, § 6, 23 Stat. 31, 32, prohibiting interstate transportation by railroads of live stock affected with any contagious or infectious disease. Fourth. That of February 4, 1887, c. 104, 24 Stat. 379, with its amendments of March 2, 1889, c. 382, 25 Stat. 855, and February 10, 1891, c. 128, 26 Stat. 743, known as the "interstate commerce act," by which a commission was created with large powers of regulation and control of interstate commerce by railroads, and the sixteenth section of which act gives to the courts of the United States power to enforce the orders of the commission. Fifth. That of October 1, 1888, c. 1063, 25 Stat. 501, providing for arbitration between railroad interstate companies and their employes; and, sixth, the act of March 2, 1893, c. 196, 27 stat. 531, requiring the use of automatic couplers on interstate trains, and empowering the Interstate Commerce Commission to enforce its provisions.

{4} Under the power vested in Congress to establish post offices and post roads, Congress has, by a mass of legislation, established the great post office system of the country, with all its detail of organization, its machinery for the transaction of business, defining what shall be carried and what not, and the prices of carriage, and also prescribing penalties for all offences against it.

{5} Obviously these powers given to the national government over interstate commerce and in respect to the transportation of the mails were not dormant and unused. Congress had taken hold of these two matters, and by various and specific acts had assumed and exercised the powers given to it, and was in the full discharge of its duty to regulate interstate commerce and carry the mails. The validity of such exercise and the exclusiveness of its control had been again and again presented to this court for consideration. It is curious to note the fact that in a large proportion of the cases in respect to interstate commerce brought to this court the question presented was of the validity of state legislation in its bearings upon interstate commerce, and the uniform course of decision has been to declare that it is not within the competency of a State to legislate in such a manner as to obstruct interstate commerce. If a State with its recognized powers of sovereignty is impotent to obstruct interstate commerce, can it be that any mere voluntary association of individuals within the limits of that State has a power which the State itself does not possess?

{6} As, under the Constitution, power over interstate commerce and the transportation of the mails is vested in the national government, and Congress by virtue of such grant has assumed actual and direct control, it follows that the national government may prevent any unlawful and forcible interference therewith. But how shall this be accomplished? Doubtless, it is within the competency of Congress to prescribe by legislation that any interference with these matters shall be offences against the United States, and prosecuted and punished by indictment in the proper courts. But is that the only remedy? Have the vast interests of the nation in interstate commerce, and in the transportation of the mails, no other protection than lies in the possible punishment of those who interfere with it? To ask the question is to answer it. By article 3, section 2, clause 3, of the Federal Constitution it is provided: "The trial of all crimes except in cases of impeachment shall be by jury; and such trial shall be held in the State where the said crime shall have been committed." If all the inhabitants of a State, or even a great body of them, should combine to obstruct interstate commerce or the transportation of the mails, prosecutions for such offences had in such a community would be doomed in advance to failure. And if the certainty of such failure was known, and the national government had no other way to enforce the freedom of interstate commerce and the transportation of the mails than by prosecution and punishment for interference therewith, the whole interests of the nation in these respects would be at the absolute mercy of a portion of the inhabitants of that single State.

{7} But there is no such impotency in the national government. The entire strength of the nation may be used to enforce in any part of the land the full and free exercise of all national powers and the security of all rights entrusted by the Constitution to its care. The strong arm of the national government may be put forth to brush away all obstructions to the freedom of interstate commerce or the transportation of the mails. If the emergency arises, the army of the Nation, and all its militia, are at the service of the Nation to compel obedience to its laws.

{8} But passing to the second question, is there no other alternative than the use of force on the part of the executive authorities whenever obstructions arise to the freedom of interstate commerce or the transportation of the mails? Is the army the only instrument by which rights of the public can be enforced and the peace of the nation preserved? Grant that any public nuisance may be forcibly abated either at the instance of the authorities, or by any individual suffering private damage therefrom, the existence of this right of forcible abatement is not inconsistent with nor does it destroy the right of appeal in an orderly way to the courts for a judicial determination, and an exercise of their powers by writ of injunction and otherwise to accomplish the same result....

{9} So, in the case before us, the right to use force does not exclude the right of appeal to the courts for a judicial determination and for the exercise of all their powers of prevention. Indeed, it is more to the praise than to the blame of the government, that, instead of determining for itself questions of right and wrong on the part of these petitioners and their associates and enforcing that determination by the club of the policeman and the bayonet of the soldier, it submitted all those questions to the peaceful determination of judicial tribunals, and invoked their consideration and judgment as to the measure of its rights and powers and the correlative obligations of those against whom it made complaint. And it is equally to the credit of the latter that the judgment of those tribunals was by the great body of them respected, and the troubles which threatened so much disaster terminated.

...

{10} We do not care to place our decision upon this ground alone. Every government, entrusted, by the very terms of its being, with powers and duties to be exercised and discharged for the general welfare, has a right to apply to its own courts for any proper assistance in the exercise of the one and the discharge of the other.... The obligation which it is under to promote the interest of all, and to prevent the wrongdoing of one resulting in injury to the general welfare, is often of itself sufficient to give it a standing in court....

...

{11} The national government, given by the Constitution power to regulate interstate commerce, has by express statute assumed jurisdiction over such commerce when carried upon railroads. It is charged, therefore, with the duty of keeping those highways of interstate commerce free from obstruction, for it has always been recognized as one of the powers and duties of a government to remove obstructions from the highways under its control.

...

{12} A most earnest and eloquent appeal was made to us in eulogy of the heroic spirit of those who threw up their employment, and gave up their means of earning a livelihood, not in defence of their own rights, but in sympathy for and to assist others whom they believed to be wronged. We yield to none in our admiration of any act of heroism or self-sacrifice, but we may be permitted to add that it is a lesson which cannot be learned too soon or too thoroughly that under this government of and by the people the means of redress of all wrongs are through the courts and at the ballot-box, and that no wrong, real or fancied, carries with it legal warrant to invite as a means of redress the cooperation of a mob, with its accompanying acts of violence.

....

{Because the injunction had been properly issued and the defendants had violated it, the petition for habeas corpus was denied.}

COMMENTS

Few decisions of the Supreme Court have been attacked so vigorously and effectively as <u>Debs</u> has been. Politicians in both parties excoriated it. It expanded the power of the executive and judicial branches of government. The president could obtain injunctions against any behavior that the courts believed to threaten the general welfare; of course, there is no limit to the concept of the "general welfare." Congress, which is supposed to make our laws, became an unnecessary appendage. As a conservative leader of the bar stated, "If the course there followed can be supported, the principles of equity jurisprudence have received an important extension which may render 'government by injunction' more than a mere epithet."[f] Although this statement may overstate the courts' assumption of power, it is certainly true that the <u>Debs</u> case brought a great deal of union activity under the jurisdiction of the federal courts; and, as we have previously suggested, employers loved being in federal court.

The disagreement between the Court that decided <u>Debs</u> and the critics of that decision may be conceived in terms of levels of abstraction. The Court argued that its jurisdiction could be inferred from federal responsibility for interstate commerce. This argument operated at a high level of generality. The significant fact would be that the Constitution created a federal interest in a field. Critics of <u>Debs</u> believed that issues of jurisdiction should be resolved at a lower level of generality. They wanted to recognize two additional facts as significant: whether a statute pertained to the parties' behavior, and whether that or another statute conferred jurisdiction on the federal courts to hear cases concerning that behavior.

Over the years, the view of the critics has prevailed.

QUESTIONS FOR REFLECTION

1. The Court compared the powers of a state to the powers of a voluntary association. "{C}an it be that any

---

[f] Frankfurter and Greene, <u>The Labor Injunction</u>, p. 88.

mere voluntary association of individuals within the
limits of that state has a power which the state itself
does not possess?" (¶ 5) Is this a convincing argument?

     2. The Court said the government deserved praise for
having asked for an injunction from a court of law rather
than sending in troops. Does this praise justify the
court's injunction?

     3. Reread the first four sentences of ¶ 6. Do they
implicitly concede the defendants' strongest argument?

Government by Injunction (continued)

ORGANIZING AS INDUCEMENT TO BREACH OF CONTRACT

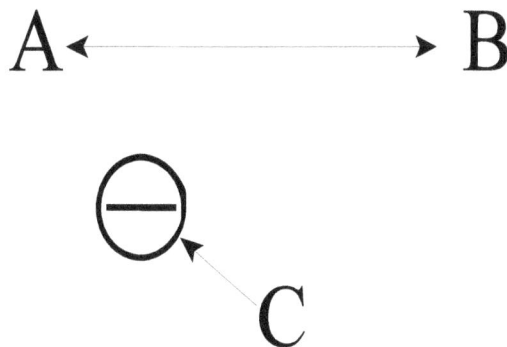

Introduction

The Constitution, as interpreted in <u>Adair v. U.S.</u> and <u>Coppage v. Kansas</u>, and the jurisdiction of federal courts, as interpreted in <u>In re. Debs</u>, greatly expanded the power of the federal courts over labor relations. This power was frequently exercised via injunctions issued in law suits brought by employers against unions based on the claim of **inducement to breach of contract**. Accordingly, let us examine this claim and see how it was applied to labor relations.

If *A* and *B* have a contract, and *C* tries to induce *A* not to perform, the courts will often issue an injunction restraining *C* from interfering with *B's* reasonable expectations.[a]

Inducement to Breach of Contract

$$A \longleftrightarrow B$$

$$\ominus$$

$$C$$

---

[a]The origin of this doctrine is rooted in the notion that an employer has a legal interest in the service of one's workers. Roman law allowed the head of a household to recover damages for injury to a member of the household, including workers. The Statute of Laborers of 1351 made it a crime for a servant to leave one's master prematurely and for an employer to hire a servant who was pledged to another employer. Curiously, the law never recognized a legal interest in a worker in one's job.

Inducement to Breach of Contract:
Between Businesses

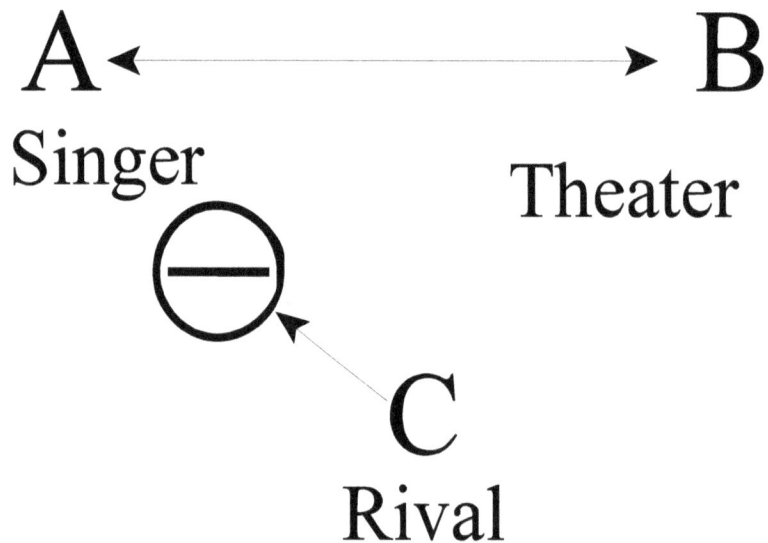

The doctrine appeared in its modern form when an opera singer (A) agreed to perform at a certain theater (B) on a certain date. Then, a rival impresario (C) persuaded her to perform for him on the same date. The court issued an injunction against the rival impresario, forbidding him from interfering with the contract between the theater owner and the singer. The court also issued an injunction against the singer, restraining her from performing at any other theater on that date.

Inducement to breach of contract became an important weapon for employers to use against unions.

Inducement to Breach of Contract:
Strike Prevents Delivery

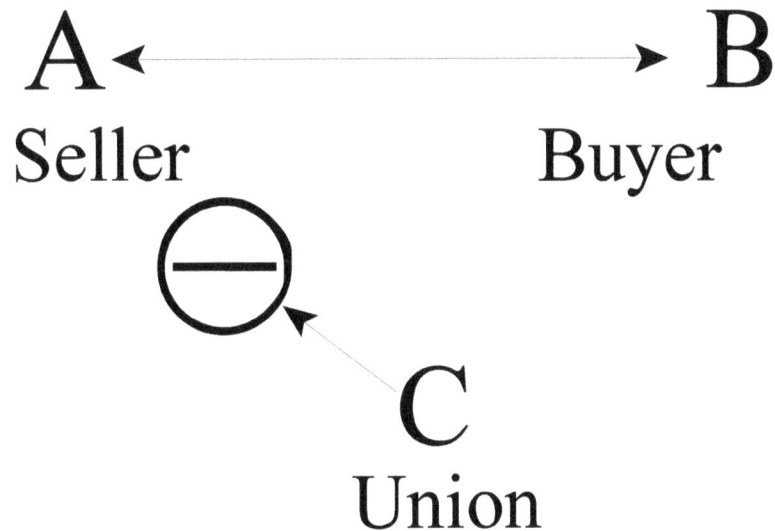

A ←————————————→ B
Seller   Buyer

⊖

C
Union

Suppose Firm A agreed to sell goods to Firm B and deliver them on a certain date, but timely delivery became problematic because Firm A's union (C) went on strike. Firm B could sue the union, claiming it was interfering with a contract for the delivery of goods, and get an injunction against the strike.

Inducement to Breach of Contract:
Contract for a Term

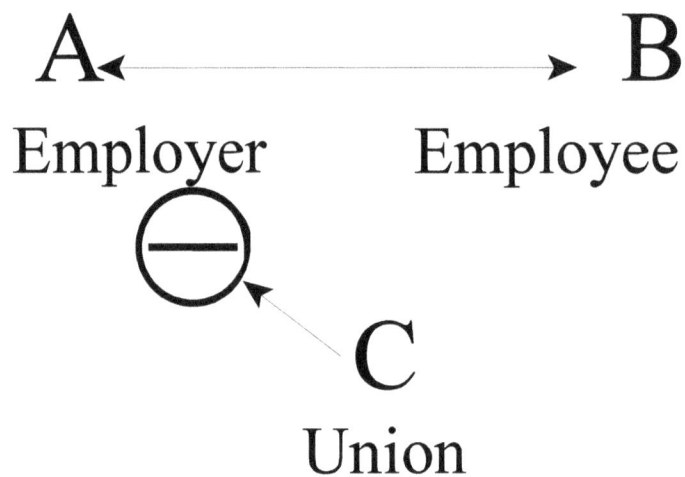

A ⟵——————————⟶ B
Employer   Employee
⊖ ⟵
C
Union

      Similarly, if a union (*c*) were trying to organize a firm (**A**), an employee (**B**) who had an employment contract for a definite term might sue the union (with a little help from the employer, of course) because, if the organizing campaign succeeded, the union would require the employer to hire only union members, and this requirement would force the employer to fire the employee before one's term expired.

Inducement to Breach of Contract:
Company Unions

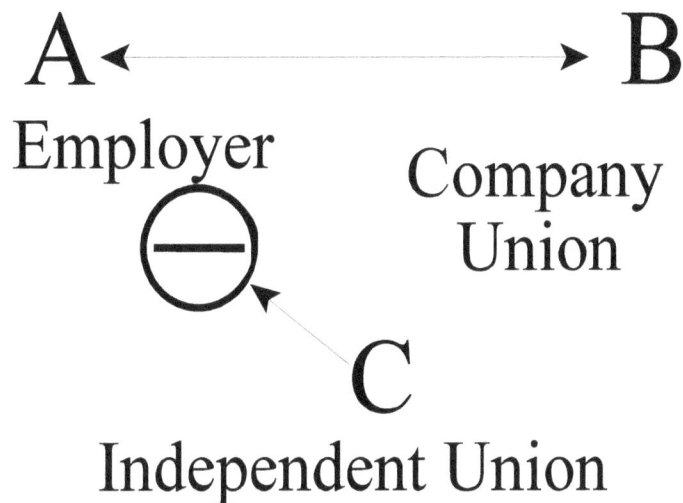

A◄──────────────► B
Employer   Company
⊖   Union

C
Independent Union

Another way that employers (A) used the law to battle unions was to create company unions (B), which the employers dominated. When an independent union (C) tried to organize the workers, the company union and the employer applied for, and received, an injunction restraining the independent union from interfering with the contract between the employer and the company union.

**Inducement to Breach of Contract:
Yellow Dog Contracts**

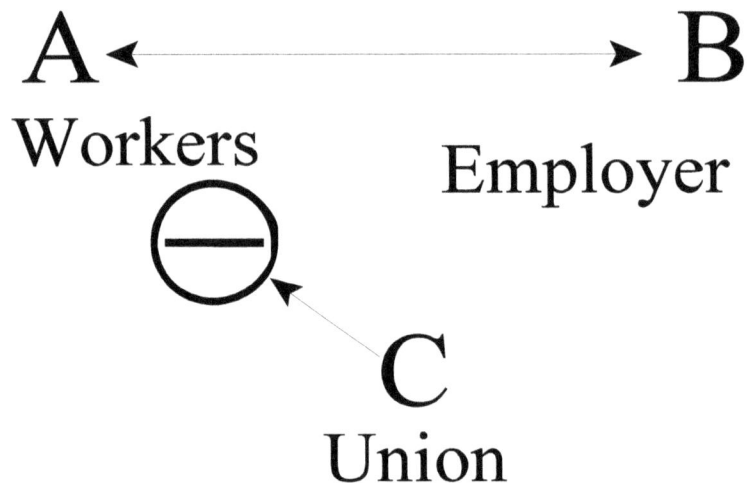

A ←————————————→ B
Workers   Employer
⊖
C
Union

Perhaps the most common instance involved yellow dog contracts. Workers (**A**) signed a contract with their employers (**B**) not to join unions. If a union (**C**) tried to organize the shop, the employer would seek an injunction to protect one's contractual expectation that one's workers would not become union members. The injunction would be granted, and the organizing campaign would be crushed.

An evenhanded approach would have allowed unions to obtain similar injunctions, but the courts were not usually willing to allow tit for tat. When a union sought to enjoin an employer's lockout, the court denied relief, saying, "The interference of a court of equity in labor disputes directed against either employer or laborer should be exercised sparingly and with caution." (It is only fair to add, however, that this was a New York decision, and New York allowed a wider scope of union activity than most other states.)

Inducement to Breach of Contract:
By Unions Against Employers

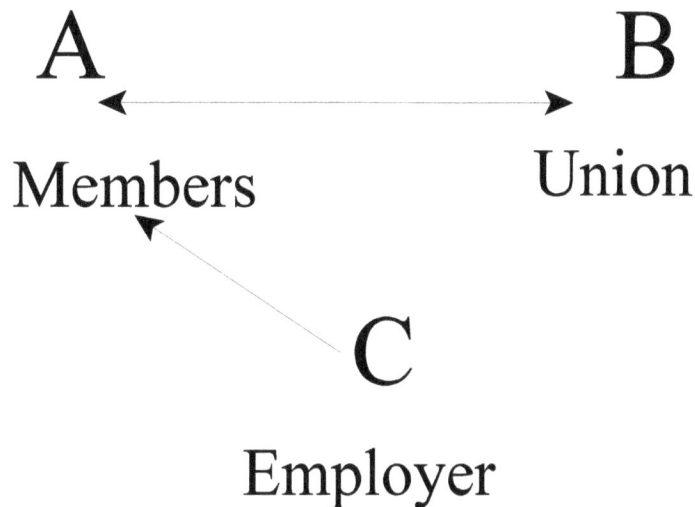

$$A \longleftrightarrow B$$

A

B

Members   Union

C

Employer

Seeing how employers used yellow dog contracts, unions (**B**) tried to apply sauce to the gander by requiring that their members (**A**) sign agreements in which they promised never to work for an employer who required a yellow dog contract. When a member who had signed such an agreement applied for a job with an employer (**C**) who required a yellow dog contract, the union sued the employer, seeking an injunction to restrain the employer from inducing the member to breach one's agreement with the union. But the court denied relief.

In Hitchman Coal v. Mitchell, the Mine Workers sought to unionize the coal mines in the panhandle of West Virginia. The union's principal motivation was to protect mines that were already organized from competition from low-wage non-union mines. One non-union mine operator had signed union contracts in the past and had endured significant labor unrest. Thereafter this operator refused to sign with the union and, further, secured yellow dog contracts from its miners. When the Mine Workers undertook to organize the employees of this operator, the union's organizer did his best to avoid the yellow dog contracts. He did not enroll any workers into the union; rather, he told them they were joining a secret order and asked them to promise only to join the union in the future. Upon learning of the organizing, the operator secured an injunction against the union. The trial court ruled that the union was a common law conspiracy in restraint of trade, that the union was also a conspiracy against the rights of non-union workers in West Virginia,[b] and that the union sought to induce the miners to breach their employment contracts with the operator.   The trial court issued an injunction restraining the Mine Workers from organizing in the entire State of West Virginia. The injunction forbade the union even from talking to workers. The Supreme Court affirmed this injunction, adding that the union was trying to enroll a sufficient number of workers that the employer, out of fear that the workers would strike, would sign a contract with the union.

⚜

---

[b]These two parts of the holding, that the union was an illegal conspiracy and that the union interfered with the rights of non-union workers, are reminiscent of the Philadelphia Cordwainers case and Vegelahn v. Guntner.

Hitchman Coal & Coke Company v. Mitchell
245 U.S. 229 (1917)

Mr. Justice PITNEY delivered the opinion of the Court.

{The plaintiff operated a coal mine in the Panhandle District of West Virginia. The defendants were officers of the United Mine Workers of America. The mine was non-union until 1903. In that year, the union threatened to strike another mine owned by the plaintiff unless the Hitchman mine were unionized. The plaintiff recognized the union, whereupon a dispute arose over compensation; the ensuing strike lasted six weeks. A two-week strike occurred during the following year. In 1906 a disagreement between the union and an association of operators with which the plaintiff was not affiliated led to yet another strike. Each strike subjected the plaintiff to heavy losses.

{During the 1906 strike, a group of employees approached the plaintiff, seeking to abandon the strike. The plaintiff allowed them to return to work on condition that they resign from the union. Thereafter, the plaintiff required each employee to agree to a "yellow dog contract" in which the employee promised that, as long as he worked for the company, he would stay out of the union. Arguing that the union's organizing campaign interfered with these contracts, the plaintiff obtained an injunction from a district court, forbidding the union to attempt to organize mine workers anywhere in the state. The Court of Appeals lifted the injunction.}

...

{1} In fact, all coal mines in the Panhandle and elsewhere in West Virginia, except in a small district known as the Kanawha field, were run "non-union," while the entire industry in Ohio, Indiana, and Illinois was operated on the "closed-shop" basis, so that no man could hold a job about the mines unless he was a member of the United Mine Workers of America. Pennsylvania occupied a middle ground, only a part of it being under the jurisdiction of the Union. Other States need not be particularly mentioned.

{2} The unorganized condition of the mines in the Panhandle and some other districts was recognized as a serious interference with the purposes of the Union in the Central Competitive Field, particularly as it tended to keep the cost of production low, and, through competition with coal produced in the organized field, rendered it more difficult for the operators there to maintain prices high enough to induce them to grant certain concessions demanded by the Union. This was the subject of earnest and protracted discussion in the annual international convention of the U.M.W.A. held at Indianapolis, Indiana, in the month of January, 1907....

...

{3} The discussion continued during three days, and at the end of it the report of a committee which expressed disagreement with Vice President Lewis' opposition to sectional settlements and recommended "a continuation in the future of the same wise, conservative business-like policies" that had been pursued by President Mitchell, was adopted by a viva voce vote.

{4} The plain effect of this action was to approve a policy which, as applied to the {case at bar}, meant that in order to relieve the union miners of Ohio, Indiana, and Illinois from the competition of the cheaper product of the non-union mines of West Virginia, the West Virginia mines should be "organized" by means of strikes local to West Virginia, the strike benefits to be paid by assessments upon the union miners in the other States mentioned, while they remained at work.

...

{5} The evidence renders it clear that Hughes was sent into the Panhandle to organize all the mines there, in accordance with the resolution of the sub-district convention.... The only defendant who testified upon the subject declared that Hughes was employed by District No. 6 as an organizer, but denied that he had power or authority to shut down the Hitchman mine.

{6} He arrived at that mine some time in September, 1907, and remained there or in that vicinity until the latter part of October, conducting a campaign of organization at the Hitchman and at the neighboring Glendale and Richland mines.

{7} The evidence shows that he had distinct and timely notice that membership in the Union was inconsistent with the terms of employment at all three mines, and a violation of the express provisions of the agreement at the Hitchman and Glendale.

...

{The plaintiff sought an injunction, which the district court granted. The defendants were restrained from persuading the plaintiff's employees to join the union without the plaintiff's consent.}

{8} The District Court based its decision upon two grounds: (1) That the organization known as the United Mine Workers of America, and its branches, as conducted and managed at the time of the suit and for many years before, was a common-law conspiracy in unreasonable restraint of trade, and also and especially a conspiracy against the rights of non-union miners in West Virginia; and (2) That the defendants, in an effort to compel the plaintiff to enter into contractual relations with the Union relating to the employment of labor and the production of coal, although having knowledge of express contracts existing between plaintiff and its employees which excluded relations with the Union, endeavored by unlawful means to procure a breach of these contracts by the employees.

...

{The court of appeals reversed the district court, holding that the union was a legal organization and was free to attempt peaceably to induce the plaintiff's employees to join the union.}

{9} In short, at the time the bill was filed, defendants, although having full notice of the terms of employment existing between plaintiff and its miners, were engaged in an earnest effort to subvert those relations without plaintiff's consent, and to alienate a sufficient number of the men to shut down the mine, to the end that the fear of losses through stoppage of operations might coerce plaintiff into "recognizing the union" at the cost of its own independence. The methods resorted to by their "organizer" were such as have been described. The legal consequences remain for discussion.

...

{10} What are the legal consequences of the facts that have been detailed?

{11} That the plaintiff was acting within its lawful rights in employing its men only upon terms of continuing nonmembership in the United Mine Workers of America is not open to question. Plaintiff's repeated costly experiences of strikes and other interferences while attempting to "run union" were a sufficient explanation of its resolve to run "non-union," if any were needed. But neither explanation nor justification is needed. Whatever may be the advantages of "collective bargaining," it is not bargaining at all, in any just sense, unless it is voluntary on both sides. The same liberty which enables men to form unions, and through the union to enter into agreements with employers willing to agree, entitles other men to remain independent of the union and other employers to agree with them to employ no man who owes any allegiance or obligation to the union. In the latter case, as in the former, the parties are entitled to be protected by the law in the enjoyment of the benefits of any lawful agreement they may make. This court repeatedly had held that the employer is as free to make non-membership in a union a condition of employment, as the working man is free to join the union, and that this is a part of the constitutional rights of personal liberty and private property, not to be taken away even by legislation, unless through some proper exercise of the paramount police power. *Adair v. United States*, 208 U.S. 161, 174; *Coppage v. Kansas*, 236 U.S. 1, 14. In the present case, needless to say, there is no act of legislation to which defendants may resort for justification.

{12} Plaintiff, having in the exercise of its undoubted rights established a working agreement between it and its employees, with the free assent of the latter, is entitled to be protected in the enjoyment of the resulting status, as in any other legal right. That the employment was "at will," and terminable by either party at any time, is of no consequence. In *Truax v. Raich,* 239 U.S. 33, 38 this court ruled upon the precise question as follows: "It is said that the [complaint] does not show an employment for a term, and that under an employment at will the complainant could be discharged at any time for any reason or for no reason, the motive of the employer being immaterial. The conclusion, however, that is sought to be drawn, is too broad. The fact that the employment is at the will of the parties, respectively, does not make it one at the will of others. The employee has manifest interest in the freedom of the employer to exercise his judgment without illegal interference or compulsion, and ... the unjustified interference of third persons is actionable although the employment is at will."

{13} In short, plaintiff was and is entitled to the good will of its employees, precisely as a merchant is entitled to the good will of his customers although they are under no obligation to continue to deal with him. The value of the relation lies in the reasonable probability that by properly treating its employees, and paying them fair wages, and avoiding reasonable grounds of complaint, it will be able to retain them in its employ, and to fill vacancies occurring from time to time by the employment of other men on the same terms. The pecuniary value of such reasonable probabilities is incalculably great, and is recognized by the law in a variety of relations.

{14} The right of action for persuading an employee to leave his employer is universally recognized — nowhere more clearly than in West Virginia — and it rests upon fundamental principles of general application, not upon the English statute of laborers.

{15} We turn to matters set up by way of justification or excuse for defendants' interference with the situation existing at plaintiff's mine.

{16} The case involves no question of the rights of employees. Defendants have no agency for plaintiff's employees, nor do they assert any disagreement or grievance in their behalf. In fact, there is none; but, if there were, defendants could not, without agency, set up any rights that employees might have. The right of the latter to strike would not give to defendants the right to instigate a strike. The difference is fundamental.

{17} It is suggested as a ground of criticism that plaintiff endeavored to secure a closed non-union mine through individual agreements with its employees, as if this furnished some sort of excuse for the employment of coercive measures to secure a closed union shop through a collective agreement with the Union. It is a sufficient answer, in law, to repeat that plaintiff had a legal and constitutional right to exclude union men from its employ. But it may be worth while to say, in addition: first, that there was no middle ground open to plaintiff; no option to have an "open shop" employing union men and non-union men indifferently; it was the Union that insisted upon closed-shop agreements, requiring even carpenters employed about a mine to be members of the Union, and making the employment of any non-union man a ground for a strike; and secondly, plaintiff was in the reasonable exercise of its rights in excluding all union men from its employ, having learned, from a previous experience, that unless this were done union organizers might gain access to its mine in the guise of laborers.

{18} Defendants set up, by way of justification or excuse, the right of workingmen to form unions, and to enlarge their membership by inviting other workingmen to join. The right is freely conceded, provided the objects of the union be proper and legitimate, which we assume to be true, in a general sense, with respect to the Union here in question. The cardinal error of defendants' position lies in the assumption that the right is so absolute that it may be exercised under any circumstances and without any qualification; whereas in truth, like other rights that exist in civilized society, it must always be exercised with reasonable regard for the conflicting rights of others....

{19} Now, assuming defendants were exercising, through Hughes, the right to invite men to join their Union, still they had plain notice that plaintiff's mine was run "non-union," that none of the men had a right to remain at work there after joining the Union, and that the observance of this agreement was of great importance and value both to plaintiff and to its men who had voluntarily made the agreement and desired to continue working under it. Yet defendants, far from exercising any care to refrain from unnecessarily injuring plaintiff, deliberately and advisedly selected that method of enlarging their membership which would inflict the greatest injury upon plaintiff and its loyal employees. Every Hitchman miner who joined Hughes' "secret order" and permitted his name to be entered upon Hughes' list was guilty of a breach of his contract of employment and acted a lie whenever thereafter he entered plaintiff's mine to work. Hughes not only connived at this, but must be deemed to have caused and procured it, for it was the main feature of defendants' plan, the sine qua non of their programme. Evidently it was deemed to be necessary, in order to "organize the Panhandle by a strike movement," that at the Hitchman, for example, man after man should be persuaded to join the Union, and having done so to remain at work, keeping the employer in ignorance of their number and identity, until so many had joined that by stopping work in a body they could coerce the employer and the remaining miners to "organize the mine," that is, to make an agreement that none but members of the Union should be employed, that terms of employment should be determined by negotiation not with the employees but with union officers — perhaps residents of other States and employees of competing mines — and that all questions in controversy between the mine operator and the miners should likewise be settled with outsiders.

{20} True, it is suggested that under the existing contract an employee was not called upon to leave plaintiff's employ until he actually joined the Union, and that the evidence shows only an attempt by Hughes to induce the men to agree to join, but no attempt to induce them to violate their contract by failing to withdraw from plaintiff's employment after actually joining. But in a court of equity, which looks to the substance and essence of things and disregards matters of form and technical nicety, it is sufficient to say that to induce men to agree to join is but a mode of inducing them to join, and that when defendants "had sixty men who had signed up or agreed to join the organization at Hitchman," and were "going to shut the mine down as soon as they got a few more men," the sixty were for practical purposes, and therefore in the sight of equity, already members of the Union, and it needed no formal ritual or taking of an oath to constitute them such; their uniting with the Union in the plan to subvert the system of employment at the Hitchman mine, to which they had voluntarily agreed and upon which their employer and their fellow employees were relying, was sufficient.

...

{21} In any aspect of the matter, it cannot be said that defendants were pursuing their object by lawful means. The question of their intentions -- of their bona fide -- cannot be ignored. It enters into the question of malice. As Bowen, L.J., justly said, in the Mogul Steamship Case, 23 Q. B. Div. 613,

> "Intentionally to do that which is calculated in the ordinary course of events to damage, and which does, in fact, damage another in that other person's property or trade, is actionable if done without just cause or excuse."

And the intentional infliction of such damage upon another, without justification or excuse, is malicious in law....

{22} Another fundamental error in defendants' position consists in the assumption that all measures that may be resorted to are lawful if they are "peaceable" — that is, if they stop short of physical violence, or coercion through fear of it. In our opinion, any violation of plaintiff's legal rights contrived by defendants for the purpose of inflicting damage, or having that as its necessary effect, is as plainly inhibited by the law as if it involved a breach of the peace. A combination to procure concerted breaches of contract by plaintiff's employees constitutes such a violation.

...

{23} It was one thing for plaintiff to find, from time to time, comparatively small numbers of men to take vacant places in a going mine, another and a much more difficult thing to find a complete gang of new men to start up a mine shut down by a strike, when there might be a reasonable apprehension of violence at the hands of the strikers and their sympathizers. The disordered condition of a mining town in time of strike is matter of common knowledge. It was this kind of intimidation, as well as that resulting from the large organized membership of the Union, that defendants sought to exert upon plaintiff, and it renders pertinent what was said by this court in the *Gompers* case (221 U.S. 418, 439), immediately following the recognition of the right to form labor unions:

> "But the very fact that it is lawful to form these bodies, with multitudes of members, means that they have thereby acquired a vast power, in the presence of which the individual may be helpless. This power, when unlawfully used against one, cannot be met, except by his purchasing peace at the cost of submitting to terms which involve the sacrifice of rights protected by the Constitution; or by standing on such rights and appealing to the preventive powers of a court of equity. When such appeal is made it is the duty of government to protect the one against the many as well as the many against the one."

{24} Defendants' acts cannot be justified by any analogy to competition in trade. They are not competitors of plaintiff; and if they were, their conduct exceeds the bounds of fair trade. Certainly, if a competing trader should endeavor to draw custom from his rival, not by offering better or cheaper goods, employing more competent salesmen, or displaying more attractive advertisements, but by persuading the rival's clerks to desert him under circumstances rendering it difficult or embarrassing for him to fill their places, any court of equity would grant an injunction to restrain this as unfair competition.

{25} Upon all the facts, we are constrained to hold that the purpose entertained by defendants to bring about a strike at plaintiff's mine in order to compel plaintiff, through fear of financial loss, to consent to the unionization of the mine as the lesser evil, was an unlawful purpose, and that the methods resorted to by Hughes — the inducing of employees to unite with the Union in an effort to subvert the system of employment at the mine by concerted breaches of the contracts of employment known to be in force there, not to mention misrepresentation, deceptive statements, and threats of pecuniary loss communicated by Hughes to the men — were unlawful and malicious methods, and not to be justified as a fair exercise of the right to increase the membership of the Union.

...

{The judgment of the Court of Appeals was reversed and the injunction, with modifications, was reinstated.}

Mr. Justice BRANDEIS, dissenting.

...

{26} The United Mine Workers of America does not appear to differ essentially in character and purpose from other international unions which, like it, are affiliated with the American Federation of Labor. Its membership is said to be larger than that of any other; and it may be more powerful. But the common law does not limit the size of unions or the degree to which individual workmen may by union increase their bargaining power. As stated in *Gompers v. Bucks Stove & Range Co.*, 221 U.S. 418, 439:

> "The law, therefore, recognizes the right of workingmen to unite and to
> invite others to join their ranks, thereby making available the strength,
> influence and power that come from such association."

We do not find either in the decisions or the statutes of West Virginia anything inconsistent with the law as declared by this court. The union is not an unlawful organization, and is not in itself an unlawful conspiracy. We have no occasion to consider the legality of the specific provisions contained in its constitution or by-laws.

...

{27} Third: The alleged conspiracy against the West Virginia mines.

{28} It was doubtless the desire of the United Mine Workers to unionize every mine on the American continent and especially those in West Virginia which compete directly with the mines of Western Pennsylvania, Ohio, Indiana, and other States already unionized. That desire and the purpose to effect it were not unlawful. They were part of a reasonable effort to improve the condition of workingmen engaged in the industry by strengthening their bargaining power through unions; and extending the field of union power. No conspiracy to shut down or otherwise injure West Virginia was proved, nor was there any averment in the bill of such conspiracy, or any issue otherwise raised by the pleadings which justified the consideration of that question by the District Court.

{29} Fourth: "Unionizing plaintiff's mine without plaintiff's consent."

{30} The fundamental prohibition of the injunction is against acts done "for the purpose of unionizing plaintiff's mine without plaintiff's consent." Unionizing a shop does not mean inducing the employees to become members of the union.[d] It

---

[d]A witness for the defendants testified as follows:

> "There is a difference between unionizing a mine and unionizing the employees in a mine; unionizing the employees is having the men join the organization; unionizing a mine is creating joint relations between the employers and employees; a mine cannot be unionized unless the employer enters into contractual relations with the union; it is not the policy or purpose of the United Mine Workers as an organization to coerce a man into doing a thing against his will; this distinction between unionizing a mine and unionizing the employees of a mine has existed since the organization came about, and this method of unionizing a mine existed in 1906 and 1907."

A witness for the plaintiff testified that

> "the term 'union,' when applied to mining, means the United Mine Workers, and a union mine is a mine that is under their jurisdiction and so recognized...." The contrary is "non-union or open shop."

And further,

> "The men might be unionized at a mine and the mine owners not recognize the union. That would in effect be an open shop. When I said 'unionize the employees' I meant practically all of the employees; but a union mine, as I understand it, is one wherein the closed shop is practically enforced."

In such case, the witness explained, the operator would be practically in contract relation with the organization.

It was also testified:

> "The difference between organizing the men at the mine and organizing the mine is that when the miners are organized the work of organizing the mine is only just started. They next proceed to meet with the operator who owns the mine, or operates it, for the purpose of making contracts or agreements. Under the constitution and methods of the United Mine Workers a mine cannot be organized without the consent of the owner, and it is not the object or purpose of the United Mine Workers to do so, and never has been; it has never been attempted as far as

(continued...)

means inducing the employer to enter into a collective agreement with the union governing the relations of the employer to the employees. Unionizing implies, therefore, at least formal consent of the employer. Both plaintiff and defendants insisted upon exercising the right to secure contracts for a closed shop. The plaintiff sought to secure the closed non-union shop through individual agreements with employees. The defendants sought to secure the closed union shop through a collective agreement with the union. Since collective bargaining is legal, the fact that the workingmen's agreement is made not by individuals directly with the employer, but by the employees with the union and by it, on their behalf, with the employer, is of no significance in this connection. The end being lawful, defendant's efforts to unionize the mine can be illegal, only if the methods or means pursued were unlawful; unless indeed there is some special significance in the expression "unionizing without plaintiff's consent."

{31} It is urged that a union agreement curtails the liberty of the operator. Every agreement curtails the liberty of those who enter into it. The test of legality is not whether an agreement curtails liberty, but whether the parties have agreed upon some thing which the law prohibits or declares otherwise to be inconsistent with the public welfare. The operator by the union agreement binds himself: (1) to employ only members of the union; (2) to negotiate with union officers instead of with employees individually the scale of wages and the hours of work; (3) to treat with the duly constituted representatives of the union to settle disputes concerning the discharge of men and other controversies arising out of the employment. These are the chief features of a "unionizing" by which the employer's liberty is curtailed. Each of them is legal. To obtain any of them or all of them, men may lawfully strive and even strike. And, if the union may legally strike to obtain each of the things for which the agreement provides, why may it not strike or use equivalent economic pressure to secure an agreement to provide them?

{32} It is also urged that defendants are seeking to "coerce" plaintiff to "unionize" its mine. But coercion, in a legal sense, is not exerted when a union merely endeavors to induce employees to join a union with the intention thereafter to order a strike unless the employer consents to unionize his shop. Such pressure is not coercion in a legal sense. The employer is free either to accept the agreement or the disadvantage. Indeed, the plaintiff's whole case is rested upon agreements secured under similar pressure of economic necessity or disadvantage. If it is coercion to

---

(...continued)

witness knows. After a mine has been organized, the agreement between the employer and the organization is paramount. The constitution of the organization has nothing to do with the workings afterwards; that agreement does not take away from the operator the control of his men."

threaten to strike unless plaintiff consents to a closed union shop, it is coercion also to threaten not to give one employment unless the applicant will consent to a closed non-union shop. The employer may sign the union agreement for fear that labor may not be otherwise obtainable; the workman may sign the individual agreement for fear that employment may not be otherwise obtainable. But such fear does not imply coercion in a legal sense.

{33} In other words an employer, in order to effectuate the closing of his shop to union labor, may exact an agreement to that effect from his employees. The agreement itself being a lawful one, the employer may withhold from the men an economic need — employment — until they assent to make it. Likewise an agreement closing a shop to non-union labor being lawful, the union may withhold from an employer an economic need — labor — until he assents to make it. In a legal sense an agreement entered into, under such circumstances, is voluntarily entered into; and as the agreement is in itself legal, no reason appears why the general rule that a legal end may be pursued by legal means should not be applied. Or, putting it in other words, there is nothing in the character of the agreement which should make unlawful means used to attain it, which in other connections are recognized as lawful.

{34} Fifth: There was no attempt to induce employees to violate their contracts.

{35} The contract created an employment at will; and the employee was free to leave at any time. The contract did not bind the employee not to join the union; and he was free to join it at any time. The contract merely bound him to withdraw from plaintiff's employ, if he joined the union. There is evidence of an attempt to induce plaintiff's employees to agree to join the union; but none whatever of any attempt to induce them to violate their contract. Until an employee actually joined the union he was not, under the contract, called upon to leave plaintiff's employ. There consequently would be no breach of contract until the employee both joined the union and failed to withdraw from plaintiff's employ. There was no evidence that any employee was persuaded to do that or that such a course was contemplated. What perhaps was intended was to secure agreements or assurances from individual employees that they would join the union when a large number of them should have consented to do so; with the purpose, when such time arrived, to have them join the union together and strike -- unless plaintiff consented to unionize the mine. Such a course would have been clearly permissible under the contract.

{36} Sixth: Merely persuading employees to leave plaintiff's employ or others not to enter it was not unlawful.

{37} To induce third persons to leave an employment is actionable if done maliciously and without justifiable cause although such persons are free to leave at their own will. It is equally actionable so to induce others not to enter the service. The individual contracts of plaintiff with its employees added nothing to its right in this connection, since the employment was terminable at will.

{38} As persuasion, considered merely as a means, is clearly legal, defendants were within their rights if, and only if, their interference with the relation of plaintiff to its employees was for justifiable cause. The purpose of interfering was confessedly in order to strengthen the union, in the belief that thereby the condition of workmen engaged in mining would be improved; the bargaining power of the individual workingman was to be strengthened by collective bargaining; and collective bargaining was to be ensured by obtaining the union agreement. It should not, at this day, be doubted that to induce workingmen to leave or not to enter an employment in order to advance such a purpose is justifiable when the workmen are not bound by contract to remain in such employment.

{39} Seventh: There was no "threat, violence or intimidation."

{40} The decree enjoined "threats, violence or intimidation." Such action would, of course, be unlawful though employed in a justifiable cause. But there is no evidence that any of the defendants have resorted to such means. The propaganda among plaintiff's employees was conducted almost entirely by one man, the defendant Hughes, a District No. 6 organizer. His actions were orderly and peaceable, consisting of informal talks with the men, and a few quietly conducted public meetings, in which he argued the benefits of organization and pointed out to the men that, although the company was then paying them according to the union scale, there would be nothing to prevent a later reduction of wages unless the men united. He also urged upon the men that if they lost their present jobs, membership in the union was requisite to obtaining employment in the union mines of the neighboring States...

{41} When this suit was filed no right of the plaintiff had been infringed and there was no reasonable ground to believe that any of its rights would be interfered with; and, in my opinion, the Circuit Court of Appeals properly reversed the decree of the District Court, and directed that the bill be dismissed.

Mr. Justice HOLMES and Mr. Justice CLARKE concur in this dissent.

COMMENTS

INJUNCTIONS AND EMPLOYMENT AT WILL

Several aspects of the Hitchman case are interesting. One is that an injunction was granted to protect yellow dog contracts signed by employees at will. In the past, courts had granted this sort of relief when employer *c* tried to woo away employer *A's* worker (*B*) only if employer *A* and the worker had a contract for a definite term, say, one year (or even one night, as in the case of the opera singer). The rationale was that, during the life of the contract, it was wrong for employer *c* to try to persuade the worker to breach the contract by quitting before its expiration. Employer *A* had a reasonable expectation that the worker would remain on the job until the contract expired, and the courts would protect this expectation. However, if employer *A* and the worker had an at-will contract, so that either one could terminate the relationship at any time and for any reason, most courts would not enjoin employer *c* from wooing the worker. The rationale was that the worker could quit at any time, so employer *c* was not trying to persuade the worker to breach the contract. Employer *A* had no reasonable expectation that the worker would remain on the job for any period of time; therefore, the courts would not intervene.

This reasoning was originally applied to yellow dog contracts. When the employer and the workers had contracts for a definite term, the courts held the employer had a reasonable expectation with which the union should not interfere; and an injunction against union organizing was issued. If the employer and the workers had only at-will contracts, the employer had no reasonable expectation, and, therefore, the union was not interfering when it solicited the workers to join the union. But the Court in Hitchman Coal ignored this reasoning.

Workers gained some power in state legislatures towards the end of the Nineteenth Century. As a result, eleven states enacted statutes outlawing yellow dog contracts. The principal effect of those laws was to prevent courts from enjoining organizing drives on the theory of inducement to breach of contract. If there was no yellow dog contract, the union was not inducing the worker to breach a contract by joining. Some states also prohibited employers from discriminating against union members, as did the federal government regarding railroads. But, as the student knows, these legislative efforts were fated to fail. In <u>Adair v. U.S.</u> and <u>Coppage v. Kansas</u> the Supreme Court held unconstitutional statutes that prohibited discrimination against union members or outlawed yellow dog contracts.

THE REACH OF <u>HITCHMAN COAL</u>

The student may be wondering how the labor movement survived after <u>Hitchman Coal</u>, <u>Duplex v. Deering</u>, <u>Adair v. U.S.</u>, and <u>Coppage v. Kansas</u>, for these cases appeared to allow employers to secure injunctions to quash any organizing drive. The answer is that <u>Hitchman Coal</u> did not reach as far as it seemed. Two years later in <u>American Steel Foundries v. Tri-City Central Trades Council</u>, 257 U.S. 184 (1921), the Court limited <u>Hitchman Coal</u> to some extent. In <u>Tri-City</u> a strike had shut down a firm. When the firm sought to reopen with replacement workers, the local trades council began to picket. The picketers sometimes threatened and assaulted the replacements, and the employer secured an injunction against these behaviors. But the injunction also prohibited persuasion and peaceful picketing directed at the replacements. Regarding this aspect of the injunction, the Court was surprisingly sympathetic to unions — up to a point. Speaking for all but one justice, Chief Justice Taft wrote:

"Is interference of a labor organization by persuasion and appeal to induce a strike against low wages, under such circumstances, without lawful excuse and malicious? We think not. Labor unions are recognized by the Clayton Act as legal when instituted for mutual help and lawfully carrying out their legitimate objects. They have long been thus recognized by the courts. They were organized out of the necessities of the situation. A single employee was helpless in dealing with an employer. He was dependent ordinarily on his daily wage for the maintenance of himself and family. If the employer refused to pay him the wages that he thought fair, he was nevertheless unable to leave the employ and to resist arbitrary and unfair treatment. Union was essential to give laborers opportunity to deal on equality with their employer. They united to exert influence upon him and to leave him in a body, in order, by this inconvenience, to induce him to make better terms with them. They were withholding their labor of economic value to him to make him pay what they thought it was worth. The right to combine for such a lawful purpose has, in many years, not been denied by any court. The strike became a lawful instrument in a lawful economic struggle or competition between employer and employees as to the share or division between them of the joint product of labor and capital. To render this combination at all effective, employees must make their combination extend beyond one shop. It is helpful to have as many as may be in the same trade in the same community united, because, in the competition between employers, they are bound to be affected by the standard of wages of their trade in the neighborhood. Therefore, they may use all lawful propaganda to enlarge their membership, and especially among those whose labor at lower wages will injure their whole guild. It is impossible to hold such persuasion and propaganda, without more, to be without excuse and malicious. The principle of maliciously enticing laborers still remains, and action may be maintained therefor in proper cases; but to make it applicable to <u>local</u> labor unions in such a case as this seems to us to be unreasonable." 257 U.S. 208-210 (emphasis added).

We have emphasized the word "local" in the last sentence because it was part of the rationale on which the Court distinguished earlier cases and limited the reach of <u>Tri-City</u>. Discussing those old friends of ours, means and ends, the Court said that both of them were illegal in <u>Hitchman Coal</u>. The end was to control the production and sale of non-union coal in West Virginia in order to protect unionized mines elsewhere. This end was illegal because it was remote from the benefit that union members would derive and because such nation-wide control of interstate commerce was dangerous. The means were deception and misrepresentation, for the union sought to induce non-union workers secretly to break their promises, join the union, and, when the employer was helpless, force agreement to unionization. <u>Tri-City</u> differed from <u>Hitchman</u> because the former involved only a local union, whose end was improvement of local wages; this end was proximate, not remote. Also, the <u>Tri-City</u> unions had not utilized any deceitful means. Thus, it appeared after <u>Tri-City</u> that local efforts at organizing would be tolerated as long as the union did not use deceitful tactics.

The Court's opinion in <u>Tri-City</u> was not faithful to the precedent set in <u>Hitchman Coal</u>. Rather, <u>Tri-City</u> interpreted <u>Hitchman Coal</u> in significant ways. <u>Tri-City</u> implied that <u>Hitchman Coal</u> turned on the defendants' means and ends; in fact, the majority scarcely mentioned them (though Justice Brandeis mentioned them in his dissent, ¶ 39). The rationale of <u>Hitchman Coal</u> was that the union was interfering with the employer's reasonable expectations deriving from his yellow dog contracts with the workers. The union was equally interfering with the employer's contractual expectations in <u>Tri-City</u>, but the Court ignored the interference. The Court in <u>Hitchman Coal</u> repudiated the argument that workers compete with their employers (¶ 25). The Court in <u>Tri-City</u> explicitly referred to "a lawful economic struggle or competition between employer and employees as to the share or division between them of the join product of labor and capital." The power to interpret is the power to change.

Nonetheless, the Court kept unions on a tight leash. The opinion in <u>Tri-City</u> distinguished a number of older cases (and, by implication, suggested that they remained good law). If the union intended to cause workers to breach their contracts with their employer (the Court had not changed its mind about enforcing yellow dog contracts), or utilized a secondary boycott, or engaged in misrepresentation or intimidation, an injunction would be appropriate. Similarly, if an employee sued a union for threatening to strike unless his employer discharged him (recall the <u>Philadelphia Cordwainers</u> case), an injunction would be in order because of "suggestions of coercion, attempted monopoly, deprivation of livelihood, and remoteness of the legal purpose of the union to better its members' condition ...." 257 U.S. at 210-211.

ORGANIZING AS COERCION

Another interesting aspect of the <u>Hitchman</u> case is that the Court characterized union organizing as coercive. The union sought to "coerce the plaintiff into 'recognizing the union,'" ¶ 9; used "coercive measures," ¶ 14; and tried to "coerce the employer and the remaining miners to 'organize the mine,'" ¶ 18.[e] Was this characterization appropriate? Coercion "may imply the exercise of physical or moral power."[f] The union did not seek to apply physical power; anyway, use of physical power would clearly have been illegal. The union may have sought to apply moral power, but the employer was evidently well steeled against it. What the union sought to apply was economic power. In the market place, use of economic power by business is usually condoned, and often praised. It is called competition. Apparently, use of economic power by workers, in the eyes of the Court, was another matter. As legal doctrine was expanded to enjoin picketing in Vegelahn v. Guntner because it was "moral intimidation," so legal doctrine was expanded in Hitchman Coal to enjoin professional organizing because it was "economic coercion."

The Court in Hitchman Coal did not justify its holding. Rather than explaining why workers should not be allowed to use economic force in the same way that businesses used it, the Court labeled union organizing as coercive. Thus, the Court expanded an existing category (coercion), which everyone agreed was illegal, to include a new phenomenon (organizing). The Court's reasoning was analogical: union organizing was similar to other kinds of coercion and, therefore, was illegal. The analogy was controversial at the beginning of the 20th Century and remains controversial at the beginning of the 21st Century.

---

[e]The Court also used the word in its more traditional sense: "Another fundamental error in the defendants' position consists in the assumption that all measures that may be resorted to are lawful if they are 'peaceable' — that is, if they stop short of physical violence, or coercion through fear of it," ¶ 22. But even here, the Court is arguing that coercion includes more than force, for the Court continued: "In our opinion, any violation of plaintiff's legal rights contrived by defendants for the purpose of inflicting damage, or having that as its necessary effect, is as plainly inhibited by the law as if it involved a breach of the peace.," ibid.

[f]Webster's Dictionary of Synonyms, G. & C. Merriam Co., Springfield, MA, 1st ed., 1951 at p. 358.

FAIRNESS, EMPLOYERS' RIGHTS, AND WORKERS' RIGHTS

Another interesting aspect of <u>Hitchman Coal</u> was that the Supreme Court granted an injunction against a union that was found to be interfering with the employer's legal right to demand yellow dog contracts. Expressed more abstractly, the Court enjoined the union from using economic force to prevent the employer from exercising a legal right. One might think that the Due Process and Equal Protection clauses of the Constitution (or perhaps the fundamental principle of fairness) would have made the Court equally willing to enjoin employers from using economic force to prevent workers from exercising their legal rights, or at least to allow legislatures to pass laws to protect workers in this way. But, as the student has seen, <u>Coppage v. Kansas</u> struck down the Kansas statute that outlawed yellow dog contracts. Was not the purpose of this statute to prevent employers from using economic force to prevent workers from exercising their legal right to join labor unions?

The Court's reply to this reasoning would have been to move the analysis to a lower level of abstraction. The union was not merely interfering with the employer's exercise of a legal right; the union was inducing workers to breach their yellow dog contracts. But even at this level of abstraction, the Court's treatment of employers and unions was not consistent. Suppose an employer discharged a worker for joining a union (a la <u>Adair</u>), or a worker joined a union, then applied for a job, and the employer conditioned the job on the workers' resignation from the union (a la <u>Coppage</u>). Would not the employer's act have been inducement to breach of contract, or something similar to it? The Court's response would have been that a legal claim had long existed for persuading an employee to leave one's employer (¶ 14), whereas no such claim existed for persuading a member to resign from an organization. The answer to this argument is straightforward. The employer's right to sue for persuading an employee to leave one's employer was created by the legislature, and the legislature should have been equally free to create a new claim for persuading a member to resign from a labor union (which is exactly what the Kansas statute attempted to do).

PRIMA FACIE CASE AND DEFENSE

Finally, it is interesting to observe that the judges continued to think of labor relations in terms of prima facie wrongs and defenses. The majority in <u>Hitchman Coal</u> wrote, quoting an English case:

> "'Intentionally to do that which is calculated in the ordinary course of events to damage, and which does, in fact, damage another in that other person's property or trade, is actionable without just cause or excuse.'" ¶ 22.

As we noted above, the Court went on to say that the union could not invoke the defense of competition because workers are not competitors of their employers. In dissent, Justice Brandeis agreed that inducing workers to leave their employer was prima facie wrong, but argued that the union's acts were lawful because it sought to improve the terms and conditions of the workers' employment by means of collective bargaining (¶¶ 38-39).

QUESTIONS FOR REFLECTION

1. Was it right for the Supreme Court to extend the claim for inducement to breach of contract to cover not only employment contracts for a term, but also employment contracts at will?

2. Unions began to make contracts with their members in which the members promised not to take jobs with employers who demanded yellow dog contracts. Why do you think unions did this?

3. The majority characterized the union's tactics as coercive. Surely it was true that the union sought to force the employer to recognize and bargain with the union. If the union had used physical force, for example, assaulted the employer, it would have been illegal. Is economic force analogous to physical force, or should they be distinguished?

4. Review ¶ 23 of the majority's opinion. Did the Court rely on good evidence?

5. Review ¶ 11 of the majority's opinion. The cases on which it relies, <u>Adair v. United States</u> and <u>Coppage v.</u>

<u>Kansas</u>, held it was unconstitutional for the government to restrict employers' liberty of contract. You know that the Constitution regulates the government, not private parties. Is the constitutional right which the Court cites an appropriate precedent for the case at bar?

6. The majority argued that the union sought to induce the workers to breach their yellow dog contracts. Brandeis argued that the union did not. Which side got the better of this argument?

7. The majority held, "the purpose entertained by defendants to bring about a strike at plaintiff's mine in order to compel plaintiff, through fear of financial loss, to consent to the unionization of the mine as the lesser evil, was an unlawful purpose ...." {¶ 25} What was the effect of this holding on recognition of unions?

8. We have observed in connection with <u>Commonwealth v. Hunt</u> that the characterization of purpose is malleable; a court can describe a party's purpose in various ways. Could the Court reasonably have characterized the defendants' purpose in another way?

Ω

CHAPTER 2

MODERN LABOR LAW

Introduction to the Norris-LaGuardia Act of 1932

The student should read the Norris-LaGuardia Act, which is printed in Chapter IV of the readings.

Comment

Injunctions were powerful weapons for employers to use against labor, and judges were allies of the employers. We have previously described how quickly injunctions can be obtained. Now we will describe some of the characteristics of labor injunctions during the half century that preceded the Norris-LaGuardia Act of 1932. In doing so, we will draw heavily on Frankfurter and Greene's book entitled The Labor Injunction, published in 1930.

Labor injunctions were often based on a complaint that was written in general terms. One judge criticized the one before him as

"a blanket complaint abounding in general conclusions but lacking in facts and circumstances .... A complaint in an action for an injunction ... should be detailed, certain, and specific, giving facts and circumstances, including time and place of each alleged act of coercion, the name of the person coerced, if known, the manner in which he was coerced, and the manner in which and the extent to which it affected or impeded the employer's right to conduct his business in a lawful way." Badger Brass v. Daly, 137 Wis. 601, 606 (1909).

Judges usually rely on affidavits to learn the facts that justify an injunction. Employers' affidavits were commonly sworn to by a "professional affidavit-maker — {that is,} the privately subsidized policeman, the private detective, {or} the 'industrial spy.'" Even the Supreme Court later commented on the probity of labor spies: "All know that men who accept such employment commonly lack fine scruples, often wilfully misrepresent innocent conduct and manufacture charges." Sinclair v. U.S., 279 U.S. 749 (1929).

Labor injunctions cast a very broad net. The injunction in the Debs case applied, not only to the

named respondents and their agents, but also to "all
persons whomsoever" who learned of its contents. Any
worker, indeed, any person, could be swept in by these
words, so long as a judge could be convinced that the
person knew about the injunction. Oftentimes, a person's
knowledge of an injunction was presumed because it had
been posted on a wall, published in a newspaper, or read
aloud to a large group of persons, even though an
individual claimed one actually knew nothing about the
injunction.

Labor injunctions prohibited a terrific range of
behavior. They were often as broad as imaginable,
prohibiting interference with an employer's business,
employees, and customers "by any means whatsoever." One
could hardly know what to do lest a judge later decide it
interfered with the business in some way. A barber was
held in contempt for putting a sign in his window saying,
"No scabs wanted here," and a newspaper was cited for
referring to strike breakers as "traitors." Injunctions
sometimes said, "Do nothing that is alleged in the
complaint." This sort of order was particularly
troublesome for two reasons: first, as noted, the
complaints were often nothing but generalities; second,
the injunction applied to anyone who had knowledge of it,
but the complaint was actually served only on the parties
named to the case.

Injunctions were also written in specifics. Perhaps
the most common act specifically prohibited was picketing
(recall Vegelahn v. Guntner); indeed, the Supreme Court
seemed to create a presumption that picketing was violent
and could be enjoined when it said, "The name 'picket'
indicated a militant purpose, inconsistent with peaceable
persuasion." American Foundries v. Tri-City Council, 257
U.S. 184 at 205 (1921). Speech was also a common target
of injunctions. The Debs and Hitchman cases restrained
any speech aimed at persuading workers to cease
performing their duties, or, in other words, to strike.
Unionists have been enjoined from publicizing strikes and
from attempting to persuade potential employees (that is,
strike breakers) not to accept work. Injunctions have
been issued against "abusive language," "bad language,"
"indecent language," "annoying language," and
"opprobrious epithets" (a term which every worker surely
understood), and sometimes particular words were
outlawed, such as "unfair," "scab," and "traitor." One

court issued an injunction against a union's holding a vote on whether or not to strike. The U.S. Attorney General asked for and obtained an injunction against threatening to strike, giving any messages regarding a strike, encouraging a strike, and paying strike benefits. An employer was enjoined from collecting dues pursuant to a check off clause in a collective bargaining agreement. A court ordered a union not to spend any money on attorney's fees, court costs, or appeal bonds; prohibited union members from congregating in a church parking lot; and restrained the members from singing any songs within the hearing of employees on the job. One injunction required that pickets be U.S. citizens who speak English.[*]

As we have previously observed, a person charged with violating an injunction — that is, of being in contempt of court — is tried by the judge who issued the injunction. The constitutional safeguards that protect defendants in criminal cases are largely absent. In the labor cases we are considering, there was no jury and no privilege against self-incrimination. The complaint and the injunction were often vague, for example, "Do not interfere with the employer's business," so that the injunction was like a dragnet, catching anyone whom the judge wished to punish. Perhaps even more important, this sort of an injunction was a scarecrow: because it was so difficult for a person to know whether any particular act was prohibited, many people refrained from perfectly legal activity out of fear that it was covered by the injunction.

Labor injunctions were effective. A strike depends on emotion, which is closely connected to timing. The first few days are the most important. If the workers lose heart, the strike is lost. Therefore, an injunction

---

[*]These requirements may have been intended to affect the union's tactics. Most of the workers were foreign-born, so not many could qualify as picketers. Also, if the pickets spoke in Polish or Italian to the workers, the employer would not understand what the pickets were saying and it would be harder to prove in contempt proceedings that the pickets violated the injunction. English-speaking citizens would be less likely to be able to speak to the workers in their native tongues.

at the right moment can win a strike for an employer. Workers respect, or at least fear, the power of judges. When a judge enjoins a strike, many workers feel a duty to obey the injunction, and many others are afraid to disobey it. During the half century beginning in 1880, a great number of strikes were crushed by injunctions. The Pullman strike was typical. In Debs's words:

> "As soon as the employees found that we {the leaders of the strike} were arrested and taken from the scene of action, they became demoralized, and that ended the strike. It was not the soldiers that ended the strike; it was not {rival unions} that ended the strike; it was simply the United States courts that ended the strike. Our men were in a position that never would have been shaken under any circumstances if we the leaders had been permitted to remain upon the field, remain among them; but once ... we were taken from the scene of action and restrained from sending telegrams or issuing the orders necessary, or answering questions ... {t}he headquarters were demoralized and abandoned.... The men went back to work, and the ranks were broken.... {T}he strike was broken by the Federal courts ... {which} restrain{ed} us from discharging our duties as officers and representatives of the employees.[*]

Efforts were made to curb the courts' abuse of injunctions, but the efforts were unsuccessful. When judges were told that they were exceeding their powers, they often made one of two replies. First, the judges said, the injunction could do no harm because it is directed only at illegal acts. But injunctions often included more than illegal acts. For example, it was not illegal to publicize a strike or persuade potential strike breakers to go elsewhere. Also, injunctions written in broad and vague terms (such as, "Do not interfere with the employer's business") often dissuaded

---

[*]The quotation is from United States Strike Commission, Report on the Chicago Strike of June-July, 1894, S. Exec. Doc. No. 7, 53d Cong. 3d Sess (1895) at XXXIX-XL, appearing in Owen Fiss, Injunctions, pp. 598-599. The facts are drawn from Fiss, pp. 596-612; John Roche, "Entrepreneurial Liberty and the Fourteenth Amendment," 4 Labor History 3 (Winter, 1963); and Frankfurter and Greene, The Labor Injunction, pp. 18, 88.

people from doing what they had a right to do. Second, the judges said, an injunction was kinder than a police officer's club; recall that the Supreme Court in <u>Debs</u> praised the government for applying for an injunction instead of sending in the army. But the police could only suppress behavior that violated the criminal law, whereas injunctions left large, undefined areas in which judges could decide whether to prohibit or permit behavior. And the protections that attach to criminal proceedings, such as a jury trial, were absent in contempt proceedings.

In the late Nineteenth and early Twentieth Centuries, some states passed laws aimed at limiting the power of judges to intervene in labor relations; but the courts held the laws were unconstitutional. We have already discussed legislative attempts to alter the substantive law, such as laws against discrimination because of union membership and yellow dog contracts; the decisions in <u>Adair</u> and <u>Coppage</u> struck down these laws. The same reasoning was used when legislatures altered the procedural law, that is, restricted the power of judges to issue injunctions in labor disputes. Anti-injunction laws in California, Arizona, and Massachusetts were invalidated on the ground that they interfered with the constitutional right to acquire and use property.

Many attempts were made to pass a bill in Congress to limit injunctions in federal courts. For example, in five successive messages to Congress, President Theodore Roosevelt urged such a law. In 1905 he said:

> "It must be remembered that a preliminary injunction in a labor case, if granted without adequate proof ... may often settle the dispute between the parties; and therefore if improperly granted may do irreparable wrong .... {T}here have undoubtedly been flagrant wrongs committed by judges in connection with labor disputes even within the last few years...."

And in 1908 he added:

> "They are blind who fail to realize the extreme bitterness caused among large bodies of worthy citizens by the use that has been repeatedly made of the power of injunction in labor disputes."

However, prior to the Norris-LaGuardia Act, to which we will turn in a moment, the only successful federal bill was the Clayton Act; yet the courts often ignored its procedural clauses. Sections 17 through 19 of the Clayton Act were intended to reform some abuses, for example, issuing injunctions without notice; but between 1914 and 1928, more labor injunctions were issued without notice than during any previous fourteen-year span. Most of these injunctions were in effect for more than ten days without a hearing at which the union could argue its case, and for this reason they violated the Clayton Act. The Act also required judges to set forth their reasons for issuing injunctions; however, when trial judges failed to do so, appellate judges held the failure was a mere error and the injunctions were still valid. (One must obey an erroneous injunction.) The Clayton Act required that injunctions be specific, but the courts held that a prohibition against "interfering in any respect" with the employer's business was specific enough. And courts continued to hold in contempt persons who were not parties to the case, but who supposedly received notice of the injunction through publication, posting, or public reading.

In 1932, during the Great Depression and the last year of the Hoover administration, the Norris-LaGuardia Act became law. It did not change the substantive law in any way. The doctrines of conspiracy, anti-trust, and inducement to breach of contract all remained in place, and, of course, the constitutional doctrine of liberty of contract was unaffected. All the Act did was to limit the authority of federal courts (but not state courts) to issue injunctions in labor disputes. Let us examine several of its sections.

Section 1 (the first paragraph) contains words that are more important than the student may realize. It states:

>"That no court of the United States[*] ... shall have jurisdiction to issue any ... injunction in a case involving or growing out of a labor dispute, except

---

[*]That is, no federal court; as opposed to state courts, over which Congress has no power.

in   strict   conformity   with   the
provisions of this Act ...."

The important idea here is jurisdiction, which refers to
the power of a court to hear a case. In general, if a
court has jurisdiction over a case, and makes a mistake,
the parties to the case are bound by that mistake; they
must obey the court unless they take an appeal and an
appellate court corrects the mistake. This rule applies
to appellate as well as trial courts. Suppose the trial
court misinterprets the law and rules in favor of the
wrong party; and the loser appeals, and the appellate
courts make the same mistake. When the last appeal is
exhausted, the case is closed.   The courts made a
mistake, and the loser has had bad luck; but one must
accept one's fate and abide by the courts' order, even if
a later case declares that the earlier one was wrongly
decided.

     This rule applies to injunctions, too.   Suppose a
trial court enjoins certain behavior by the respondent.
The injunction is erroneous; it should not have been
issued.   Nonetheless, the respondent must obey the
injunction. Of course, one may try to convince the trial
court that it made an error, and one may appeal to higher
courts; but all the while, one must continue to obey the
injunction. If one disobeys the injunction, one can be
punished for contempt of court, even if the appellate
courts later hold that the injunction should not have
been issued.

     This rule applies when the court has jurisdiction of
the case; the foregoing examples assumed that the court
had jurisdiction. A different rule applies if the court
lacks jurisdiction. In this event, the party is free to
ignore the court's order, even an injunction, because the
court had no power to issue it.

     This is a simplified explanation of jurisdiction,
which in fact is considerably more complicated, and the
rules vary according to the kind of jurisdiction that is
lacking.   This is not the place to expound upon the
niceties of personal jurisdiction, subject matter
jurisdiction, and jurisdiction in rem. As a practical
matter, if one is aware of a court order, it should be
obeyed, even if one believes the court lacked
jurisdiction to issue the order. Also, there is a great

risk in ignoring a court order because of lack of jurisdiction: if one turns out to be wrong, and the court really did have jurisdiction, one stands in contempt of court.

Our point here is that the Norris-LaGuardia Act did not merely change the federal law about injunctions. The Act did change the law; but if that were all it did, and a court issued an erroneous injunction, the parties would have been bound to obey it. The Act went further and <u>withdrew jurisdiction</u> from the courts to issue injunctions except as permitted by the Act. This is the strongest step Congress can take in regard to a court. Congress deprived the federal courts of the power to issue injunctions in labor disputes unless in strict conformity to the Act (and the words "strict conformity" appear in the Act). Therefore, if a court issues an erroneous labor injunction, the parties may ignore it because the court lacked jurisdiction.

Section 2 of the act establishes the public policy of the United States regarding labor disputes. As the student likely realized when reading this section, the ideas in the dissenting opinions of Justices Holmes and Brandeis were adopted by Congress. Section 2 states that the government allows capitalists to aggregate their property. An individual worker is practically powerless when one sells one's labor to these aggregations. Actual liberty of contract requires that the government allow workers to organize themselves into unions and collectively negotiate the terms and conditions of employment. Employers should be prohibited from interfering with workers' efforts to organize themselves. In effect, this section creates a new definition of duress or coercion, one that includes the case in which an employer has enormous bargaining power and the worker has none. The Norris-LaGuardia Act must be interpreted in light of these policies.

Section 3 forbids federal courts from enforcing yellow dog contracts. You may wonder how Congress could do this in light of the <u>Coppage</u> case, which prohibited the government from outlawing such contracts. The answer is that section 3 does not outlaw yellow dog contracts; the section only states that federal courts may not enforce them. Parties remain free to enter into yellow dog contracts, and state courts may enforce them.

There is an element of symmetry in section 3. It denies federal enforcement when employers force workers to promise not to join unions <u>and</u> when unions force employers to promise not to join employer organizations. One would test one's memory trying to recall a case in which a union sought to prevent an employer from joining the Chamber of Commerce or National Association of Manufacturers, but the possibility exists. As the student will recall from <u>Adair v. U.S.</u> and <u>Coppage v. Kansas</u>, the principle of symmetry (though not equality) is important in labor law.

Section 4 prohibits federal courts from enjoining specific behaviors in connection with labor disputes, such as striking, joining and supporting a union, and peaceably urging others to do the same. Obviously, this section was aimed at the injunctions that judges too readily issued against these activities.

Not so obviously, however, the section addresses the fundamental question in labor law: What is the limit of legitimate union activity? Once again, we find ourselves back to Chief Justice Shaw's opinion in <u>Commonwealth v. Hunt</u>: we examine means and ends. Section 4 deals with means. Permissible means include striking, joining and supporting a union, urging others to do the same, and the other actions listed in the section, so long as the acts are taken in consequence of a labor dispute.

Permissible ends are discussed in Section 13, so let us examine that section now. It makes sense if we recall Justice Holmes's opinion in <u>Vegelahn</u>. Unions do inflict injuries on other persons, such as employers and non-union workers, and inflicting injury on others is wrong unless it is justified. Holmes thought that the workers' self-interest was a sufficient justification. Section 13 may be thought of as defining a union's legitimate self-interest. The section establishes that the injuries a union inflicts (by the means listed in section 4) are justified so long as they "involve or grow out of a labor dispute." A labor dispute is defined by two elements: who the parties are and what they disagree about. A labor dispute exists if the parties are in the same industry, trade, craft, or occupation; or are employees of the same employer; or are members of the same organization of workers or employers: and if the controversy between the parties is occasioned by the terms and conditions of employment or by the representation of workers by unions, regardless of whether the disputants in the controversy are an employer and one's employees.

This is a broad description of permissible ends. Recall that in the <u>Duplex</u> case the Court held that the Clayton Act exempted unions from anti-trust law only when the parties were an employer and one's employees. Section 13 is explicitly more generous to workers; it is a labor dispute, and a federal court may not issue an injunction, even if the disputants in the controversy are an employer and someone else's employees. Also, a great many secondary boycotts are beyond the reach of federal injunctions. So long as the basic dispute is over recognition of a union or the terms and conditions of employment, and the workers are in the same industry, or work for the same employer, or belong to the same union, it is a labor dispute. In effect, section 13 enacts, as far as federal injunctions are concerned, Justice Brandeis's dissent in <u>Duplex</u>. He argued:

> "When centralization in the control of business brought its corresponding centralization in the organization of workingmen, new facts had to be appraised. A single employer might ... threaten the standing of the whole organization and the standards of all its members; and when he did so, the union, in order to protect itself, would naturally refuse to work on his materials wherever found .... {Courts must appreciate} the facts of industry {and} {recognize} the unity of interest throughout the union, and that, in refusing to work on materials which threatened it, the union was only refusing to aid in destroying itself." 254 U.S. at 482.

But there is a limit, namely, where the union's self-interest stops and it is acting only in sympathy with another union. It is not a labor dispute, and federal courts may issue injunctions, if the parties are not in the same industry or union.

Section 5 prohibits federal injunctions from being issued on the ground that a union is an unlawful combination or conspiracy because its members did any of the acts listed in section 4. Also, section 4 mentions that the acts listed in it may be performed "singly or in

concert." The purpose of this phrase and of section 5 is
to curb the doctrine that strikes and boycotts are
illegal conspiracies.

Section 7 requires federal courts to hold hearings,
with witnesses and cross-examination, before injunctions
are issued in labor disputes. An injunction can be
issued only if the court finds that the respondent has
committed or threatened to commit unlawful acts and that
the local police cannot provide adequate protection to
the complainant. (The complainant is usually an
employer, and the respondent is usually a union; so we
will refer to employers and unions from now on.) The
local chief of police must be notified of the hearing.

Section 7 also requires the court to find, with
regard to each item of relief (that is, with regard to
each act which the injunction prohibits), that the
employer would suffer more injury if the injunction is
denied than the union would suffer if the injunction is
granted. This requirement needs some explanation. The
theory of a preliminary injunction is to preserve the
status quo for both parties until the court can decide
the dispute. Suppose a woman loans her great
grandmother's wedding dress to her cousin for the
latter's wedding. It is very special to the woman
because her grandmother, her mother, and her aunt were
also married in it, and she plans the same. But then she
learns that her cousin plans to alter the dress in
various ways to make it more modern; and when she demands
that the cousin return it, the latter refuses, claiming
she has as much right to the dress as the woman does.
The woman could sue her cousin and ask for a preliminary
injunction, forbidding her to alter the dress until the
judge can decide the case. The injunction would preserve
the status quo as far as both parties to the case are
concerned and would probably be granted.

A labor injunction, however, does not fit well into
the theory of preserving the status quo. The injunction
works well for the employer, who continues doing business
and resisting the strike. But for the union, as we have
previously seen, the injunction stops the strike cold;
the time, money, and effort put into organizing and
motivating the workers are lost. Even if the injunction
is lifted later because it was erroneously granted, the
strike usually cannot be revived. Before 1932, the

federal courts were very solicitous of the employer's
interests and expressed deep concern over injuries that
strikes and boycotts caused to businesses. But the
judges paid no heed to the harm done to a union by an
injunction. For this reason, section 7 of Norris-
LaGuardia requires the court to give fair consideration
to the interests of both the union and the employer. An
injunction can be issued only if the harm from which it
will save the employer exceeds the harm which it will
cause the union.

We have mentioned that section 7 requires the court
to hold a hearing before issuing an injunction. There is
an exception to that requirement. The court may issue a
temporary restraining order, without a hearing, without
notice to the union, and based on affidavits alone, if
the employer can convince the judge that the union is
threatening very serious and immediate injury. Such a
restraining order may last for no longer than five days.
In the past, restraining orders had been allowed to stand
for weeks and months before a hearing was held. In the
Hitchman Coal case, for example, the restraining order
was in effect for seven months before a hearing was held.

Finally, for our purposes, section 11 provides that
a person charged with contempt in a labor case is
entitled to a jury trial.

A point that we made at the beginning of this
comment, and that we tried to keep in the student's
attention by our choice of words as we discussed various
sections of the act, deserves reemphasis. That point is
that Norris-LaGuardia did not change the substantive law
in any way; the act merely restricted the power of
federal judges to issue injunctions in labor disputes.
Therefore, based on the doctrines of conspiracy, anti-
trust, and inducement to breach of contract, federal
courts remained free to award money damages to employers
for injuries caused by unions; and state courts continued
to issue injunctions and to award damages.

Nevertheless, Norris-LaGuardia was an improvement as
far as unions were concerned, particularly in states,
such as New York, whose laws permitted a substantial
range of union activity. Before the Norris-LaGuardia
Act, federal judges in these states enjoined union
conduct that state courts would not have enjoined. In

these states, therefore, removal of the federal judges' jurisdiction to issue injunctions was important to unions. But states like New York were few in number, and the need remained for more fundamental and substantive revision of labor law.

QUESTIONS FOR REFLECTION

1. During a labor dispute, how can strikers be notified of an injunction?

2. Are there circumstances in which a union would want an injunction to be issued against a strike?

$$\Omega$$

The Constitutionality of the Labor Act

Introduction

NLRB v. Jones & Laughlin concerns the power of the
government to regulate labor relations. Ours is a
government of limited powers. The reason is our belief
that political power belongs to the people. We have
chosen to delegate some of that power to the government
(reserving the rest for ourselves). Thus, the government
has only the powers conferred on it by the Constitution.
If one of the branches of the government exceeds its
powers, its act is unconstitutional and void. The final
arbiter of whether an act is constitutional — that is,
within the powers granted by the Constitution — is
usually the courts.

Is the National Labor Relations Act a constitutional
exercise of the power of Congress? This question was
raised by employers in five cases decided by the Supreme
Court soon after the Labor Act was passed. The argument
based on the Due Process Clause was that it protects the
liberty and property of citizens from the government. By
requiring employers to bargain with unions instead of
individual workers, and by prohibiting employers from
discriminating against workers because of union
membership, the Act infringed on employers' liberty and
property rights. The argument based on the Commerce
Clause was that it authorizes Congress to regulate
interstate commerce, but not intrastate commerce.
Because manufacturing and labor relations were intrastate
commerce, the Act exceeded the power of Congress under
the Commerce Clause.

The facts of Jones & Laughlin are typical of all
five cases. The Labor Board held that the employer
discharged several workers because they belonged to a
union, and by the discharges coerced and intimidated
other employees in the exercise of their right to self
organization. The Board ordered the employer to cease
and desist from discrimination and coercion and to offer
reinstatement with back pay to the discharged workers.
The employer refused to comply with the Board's order,
whereupon the Board petitioned the Court of Appeals to
enforce the order. The Court of Appeals denied the
petition on the ground that the Labor Act was

NLRB v. Jones & Laughlin and *Associated Press v. NLRB*

unconstitutional. The Board then asked the Supreme Court to review the decision, and the Court took the case.

Although the Supreme Court gave its answer to the question of constitutionality in <u>Jones & Laughlin</u>, some of the Labor Board's arguments on the issue appeared in the Board's brief in <u>Associated Press v. NLRB</u> as well. Here follow excerpts from the briefs of the Board in <u>Associated Press</u> and <u>Jones & Laughlin</u> and from the brief of the employer in <u>Jones & Laughlin</u>.

The arguments in these briefs are sophisticated treatments of constitutional law that would normally exceed the grasp of students at the beginning of their first course on law. But these arguments are based on <u>Adair v. U.S.</u> and <u>Coppage v. Kansas</u>, which the student has already studied in Part I of this book; and so the student should be able to identify, understand, and paraphrase the arguments.

National Labor Relations Board v. Jones & Laughlin
301 U.S. 1 (1937)

Associated Press v. National Labor Relations Board
301 U.S. 103 (1937)

FROM THE BRIEF OF THE LABOR BOARD

{The briefs are signed by Homer Cummings, Attorney General of the U.S.; Stanley Reed, Solicitor General of the U.S.; Charles E. Wyzanski, Jr. and A. H. Feller, Special Assistants to the Attorney General; Charles A. Horsky, attorney; J. Warren Madden, Chair of the NLRB; Charles Fahy, General Counsel of the NLRB; Robert B. Watts, Associate General Counsel; and Philip Levy, Laurence A. Knapp, Malcolm F. Halliday, and David A. Moscovitz, attorneys.}

{THE DUE PROCESS ARGUMENT}

Subsections (1) and (3) of Section 8 of the National Labor Relations Act Are ... Consistent With The Fifth Amendment

...

... With respect to the provisions which are here involved, the Board contends ... that their validity under the Fifth Amendment is sustained by the decision in *Texas & New Orleans R. Co. v. Brotherhood of Railway Clerks*, 281 U.S. 548....

... The *Texas & New Orleans* case arose under the Railway Labor Act of 1926. That statute, in order to prevent industrial disputes on the railroads, established machinery for mediation, negotiation, and collective bargaining. In that Act (as it read when the *Texas & New Orleans* case was decided) Congress, in Section 2, subdivision third, had provided:

> Representatives, for the purposes of this Act, shall be designated by the respective parties in such manner as may be provided in their corporate organization or unincorporated association, or by other means of collective action, *without interference, influence, or coercion exercised by either party over the self-organization or designation of representatives by the other.* [Italics supplied.]

In the *Texas & New Orleans* case, the Brotherhood filed a bill of complaint alleging that the railroad had intimidated members of the Brotherhood and persuaded and coerced them to withdraw from membership, and prayed that the railroad be

iv   *NLRB v. Jones & Laughlin* and *Associated Press v. NLRB*

restrained from such interference, influence, or coercion in violation of the statute.

In response to the carrier's argument that if the statute authorized the decree it was invalid under the Fifth Amendment, this Court ... stated (p. 570):

> ... Congress may facilitate the amicable settlement of disputes which threaten the service of the necessary agencies of interstate transportation. In shaping its legislation to this end, Congress was entitled to take cognizance of actual conditions and to address itself to practicable measures. The legality of collective action on the part of employees in order to safeguard their proper interests is not to be disputed. It has long been recognized that employees are entitled to organize for the purpose of securing the redress of grievances and to promote agreements with employers relating to rates of pay and conditions of work. Congress was not required to ignore this right of the employees but could safeguard it and seek to make their appropriate collective action an instrument of peace rather than of strife. Such collective action would be a mockery if representation were made futile by interferences with freedom of choice. Thus the prohibition by Congress of interference with the selection of representatives for the purpose of negotiation and conference between employers and employees, instead of being an invasion of the constitutional right of either, was based on the recognition of the rights of both.

The provisions of the National Labor Relations Act here involved ... correspond in every manner material to the due process issue with Section 2, third, of the Railway Labor Act.... We submit, therefore, that their validity under the Fifth Amendment is established by the decision of this Court in that case.

{The employer} relies upon *Adair v. United States*, 208 U.S. 161, and *Coppage v. Kansas*, 236 U.S. 1. In the *Texas & New Orleans* case this Court considered both these cases and expressly rejected them as inapplicable (281 U.S. at 570-571):

> The {employers} invoke the principle declared in *Adair v. United States*, 208 U.S. 161, and *Coppage v. Kansas*, 236 U.S. 1, but these decisions are inapplicable. The Railway Labor Act of 1926 does not interfere with the normal exercise of the right of the carrier to select its employees or to discharge them. The statute is not aimed at this right of the employers but at the interference with the right of employees to have representatives of their own choosing. As the carriers subject to the Act have no constitutional right to interfere with the freedom of the employees in making their selection, they cannot complain of the statute on constitutional grounds.

The Court thus held that the discharge of employees because of activity in the Brotherhood was not a "normal exercise of the right" to hire or discharge employees which is protected under the due process clause of the Fifth Amendment. Likewise under the present Act, as the court below pointed out, there is no interference with the normal right to hire or discharge, for inefficiency or any other reason satisfactory to the employer, "provided he does not use the power of discharge as a weapon for interfering with the right of employees to organize and bargain collectively."

The *Adair* and *Coppage* cases need not be extensively analyzed here. It is sufficient to say that both decisions were vigorously urged by the carrier in the *Texas & New Orleans* case. The facts of the latter case are so similar to those of the case at bar that the earlier cases, if inapplicable there, cannot be applicable here.

{THE COMMERCE CLAUSE ARGUMENT}

Subsections (1) and (3) of Section 8 of the Act, As Applied to Interstate Enterprises, Bear a Reasonable and Direct Relation to the Protection of Interstate Commerce from the Burden of Industrial Strife, and Consequently Are a Valid Exercise of the Commerce Power

...

The basic validity of the Act presents two problems. First, does industrial strife in interstate enterprises constitute a burden on interstate commerce which Congress may remove or prevent? Second, does the present Act invoke appropriate means for the mitigation or elimination of that burden?

INDUSTRIAL STRIFE IN INTERSTATE ENTERPRISES CONSTITUTES A BURDEN ON INTERSTATE COMMERCE WHICH CONGRESS MAY REMOVE OR PREVENT

That industrial disputes in an industry or business engaged in interstate commerce may and very frequently do burden and interrupt the flow of such commerce is a fact of common knowledge. A strike or lockout ordinarily means a complete or partial suspension of business. That such an effect is so direct and substantial as to be within the scope of Congressional power has been settled by *Texas & New Orleans R. Co. v. Brotherhood of Railway Clerks*, 281 U.S. 548, where this Court in a unanimous opinion upheld Section 2, third of the Railway Labor Act of 1926, which prohibited interference with the self-organization of employees and their free choice of representatives for collective action. The Court said (p. 570):

We entertain no doubt of the constitutional authority of Congress to enact the prohibition. The power to regulate commerce is the power to enact "all appropriate legislation" for its "protection and advancement" (*The Daniel Ball*, 10 Wall. 557, 564); to adopt measures "to promote its growth and insure its safety" (*County of Mobile v. Kimball*, 102 U.S. 691, 696, 697); to "foster, protect, control and restrain" (*Second Employers Liability Cases*, 223 U.S. 1, 47). Exercising this authority, Congress may facilitate the amicable settlement of disputes which threaten the service of the necessary agencies of interstate transportation.

The Railway Labor Act was thus upheld by this Court "upon the express ground that to facilitate the amicable settlement of disputes which threatened the service of the necessary agencies of interstate transportation tended to prevent interruptions of service and was therefore within the delegated power of regulation." *Railroad Retirement Board v. Alton R. Co.*, 295 U.S. 330, 369. It is apparent that in like fashion industrial strife threatening the operation of various other forms of commercial intercourse among the States, such as motor and water transportation, pipe lines, freight agency services, and communication by wireless, telephone, telegraph or radio, would directly affect interstate commerce and hence fall within Congressional power to mitigate or eliminate.

{The employer's} contention that the principle of the *Texas & New Orleans* case is limited to instrumentalities of commerce {e.g., railroads} cannot stand. Such instrumentalities are not the only form of interstate commerce, and cases under the Sherman Act make clear that the Federal power extends to the elimination of labor disputes burdening interstate commerce in other forms. It cannot be questioned, therefore, that Congress acted within its constitutional power in adopting special preventive means to avoid such burdens at least where, as Congress found in Section 1 of the Act, they are caused by industrial strife "(a) impairing the efficiency, safety, or operation of the instrumentalities of commerce," or "(b) occurring in the current of commerce" ...

The existence of a power in Congress to protect interstate commerce from these burdens is in no way inconsistent with the statement that "the relation of employer and employee is a local relation." *Carter v. Carter Coal Co.*, 298 U.S. 238, 308. That statement cannot be understood as in conflict with the cases in which Congress has subjected that relationship to valid regulation. Thus, on the very subject matter here involved, although it be said that the right to join a labor organization is, standing alone, a local matter, that right may be protected by Congress where its protection will assist in maintaining the orderly conduct of interstate commerce, and in furthering the peaceful settlement of disputes which threaten it. *Texas & New Orleans R. Co. v. Brotherhood of Railway Clerks*, 281 U.S. 548....

We submit, therefore, that beyond any question industrial strife, at least in enterprises in interstate or foreign commerce, constitutes a burden on that commerce which Congress may remove or prevent. The remaining question is whether the means employed here are appropriate to that end.

SUBSECTIONS (1) AND (3) OF SECTION 8 OF THE NATIONAL LABOR RELATIONS ACT PROVIDE A REASONABLE MEANS OF ELIMINATING THE BURDENS ON INTERSTATE COMMERCE ARISING OUT OF INDUSTRIAL STRIFE

Industrial disputes are of two basic types. The first type arises out of employer resistance to the attempt of employees to form and maintain labor organizations, to obtain recognition of these organizations, to bargain collectively, and the like — briefly, the struggles to organize and establish the procedure of collective bargaining. The second type of dispute arises over the substantive terms of the employment contract, such as rate of wages, hours of work, or other matters of working conditions.

Subsections (1) and (3) of Section 8 of the Act, which are the only provisions invoked against {the employer}, bear upon both types of industrial controversies, by eliminating the causes of the first, and by affording a basis for the amicable and permanent adjustment of the second through the procedure of voluntary negotiation and collective bargaining conducted by freely chosen representatives of the employees.

THE ACT ELIMINATES INDUSTRIAL STRIFE GROWING OUT OF THE EFFORTS OF EMPLOYEES TO ORGANIZE AND BARGAIN COLLECTIVELY BY REMOVING THE CAUSES OF SUCH STRIFE

... {The brief discusses instances in which employers' opposition to unionization led to industrial strife.}

viii   *NLRB v. Jones & Laughlin* and *Associated Press v. NLRB*

THE ACT FACILITATES THE PREVENTION AND ADJUSTMENT OF INDUSTRIAL STRIFE ARISING OUT OF DIFFERENCES OVER TERMS AND CONDITIONS OF EMPLOYMENT

... {The brief discusses instances in which collective bargaining averted industrial strife.}

The {Employer} Is Engaged in Interstate Commerce

{The brief discusses the employer's business, stressing that it brings huge quantities of raw materials across state lines, processes them into finished products, and ships those products across state lines.}

We believe that the Board would have been justified in concluding from the facts with respect to {the employer}, without more, {that it is engaged in interstate commerce and} that industrial strife in that enterprise would have the necessary effect of burdening or injuring interstate commerce....

FROM THE BRIEF OF THE EMPLOYER

{The brief is signed by Earl F. Reed of Pittsburgh, PA; Charles Rosen of New Orleans, LA; and W. D. Evans and John E. Laughlin, Jr.}

{THE DUE PROCESS ARGUMENT}

The Provisions of the National Labor Relations Act Which the National Labor Relations Board Seeks to Apply to This Respondent Are Invalid and Void Under the Fifth Amendment to the Constitution of the United States.

THE DECISIONS OF THIS COURT IN *ADAIR V. UNITED STATES* AND *COPPAGE V. KANSAS* ARE DETERMINATIVE IN THE PRESENT CASE.

The real issue in the present case, from a factual standpoint, is the alleged commission by the respondent of unfair labor practices in the discharge of union employees. The portion of the statute involved is Section 8(3), which prohibits discrimination in regard to hire or tenure of employment or of any term or condition of employment to encourage or discourage membership in any labor organization. We believe that this provision constitutes an arbitrary interference with the respondent's freedom of contract and therefore violates the due process requirements of the Fifth Amendment to the Federal Constitution.

...

One of the foremost rights protected by the Constitution is the right to enter or refrain from normal contractual relations. It is a necessary corollary that the law must also respect the individual's freedom to contract concerning the normal incidents of his employment. Similarly, the employer enjoys a corresponding right to conduct his business in an orderly fashion, free from unjustifiable restraints and regimentation.

These rights have not been enforced in derogation of the Government's power to enact police[a] measures for the protection of the health, safety and well-being of the citizens. Consequently, State laws regulating hours of labor, working conditions and the payment of wages have been upheld, to protect the physical well-being of employees and to prevent fraud and oppression. But once the Government has gone beyond police measures and deliberately interfered with freedom of contract, to force its temporary economic conceptions upon its citizens, the Court has scrutinized its legislative efforts with the greatest of care. The present statute clearly falls into this category. Its provisions relating to majority rule for purposes of collective bargaining and to unfair labor practices are not designed to protect the property of employers or the well-being of employees, but are rather intended to force a novel economic policy into the relations of employees with each other and with their employers. Therefore, it is proper to consider whether or not they infringe upon the freedom of the parties to such an extent as to render them subject to attack.

In *Adair v. United States,* 208 U.S. 161 (1908), similar legislation of Congress prohibiting discrimination by an employer against union members was invalidated, because it conflicted with the principle of *Allgeyer v. Louisiana,* 165 U.S. 578, *supra,* the Court stating:

> "The right of a person to sell his labor upon such terms as he deems proper is, in its essence, the same as the right of the purchaser of labor to prescribe the conditions upon which he will accept such labor from the person offering to sell it."

> "In all such particulars the employer and the employee have equality of right, and any legislation that disturbs that equality is an arbitrary interference with the liberty of contract which no government can legally justify in a free land." (pp. 174, 175)

---

[a]{The legal name for the power of government to protect the health, safety, and well being of citizens is the "police power." The word "police" derives from a Middle French word meaning the conduct of public affairs; this word derived from the Latin word for state and the Greek word for city, "polis." — ed.}

Subsequently, in *Coppage v. Kansas*, 236 U.S. 1 (1914), the Court reexamined the *Adair* case. Again the conclusion was reached that such legislation constituted an unjustifiable interference with the freedom of contract, the Court declaring:

> "Included in the right of personal liberty and the right of private property — partaking of the nature of each — is the right to make contracts for the acquisition of property. Chief among such contracts is that of personal employment, by which labor and other services are exchanged for money or other forms of property. If this right be struck down or arbitrarily interfered with, there is a substantial impairment of liberty in the long-established constitutional sense."
>
> ...
>
> "And can there be one rule of liberty for the labor organization and its members, and a different and more restrictive rule for employers? We think not; and since the relation of employer and employee is a voluntary relation, as clearly as is that between members of a labor organization, the employer has the same inherent right to prescribe the terms upon which he will consent to the relationship, and to have them fairly understood and expressed in advance." (pp. 14, 20)

The provisions of the Labor Act which are in controversy in the present case present a much greater menace to the employer's freedom of contract than the enactments which were denied validity in the *Coppage* and *Adair* cases. In the *Adair* case the Court had before it a Federal statute prescribing, as a criminal offense, the discharge of an employee because of union activities, while the Kansas statute, which was involved in the *Coppage* case, merely prohibited employment contracts which required the employee to renounce his membership in a labor organization. The National Labor Relations Act not only prohibits the discharge of employees because of union activities, but it also pretends to give the petitioner authority to require the employer to restore employment. The dangerous implications of such procedure ... are apparent. The employer may be compelled to continue a relationship which is not of his own seeking, and his discretion in hiring and retaining employees is completely overridden.

Thus in *Chas. Wolff Packing Co. v. Court of Industrial Relations*, 262 U.S. 522 (1923), a Kansas statute creating an industrial court with power to hear disputes between employer and employees over wages and other terms of employment was involved. The statute was confined in operation to employers engaged in the business of manufacturing food and certain other more or less essential industries, the determination of the public character of the employer's business being vested in the industrial court. Th{is} Court said of the statute:

"It curtails the right of the employer on the one hand, and of the employee on the other, to contract about his affairs. This is part of the liberty of the individual protected by the guaranty of the due process clause of the Fourteenth Amendment. *Meyer v. Nebraska*, 262 U.S. 390 (1923). While there is no such thing as absolute freedom of contract, and it is subject to a variety of restraints, they must not be arbitrary or unreasonable. Freedom is the general rule, and restraint the exception." (p. 534)

...

THE PETITIONER'S ACTION CONSTITUTES AN UNLAWFUL INTERFERENCE WITH THE NORMAL RIGHT OF THE RESPONDENT TO MANAGE ITS OWN BUSINESS.

The text of this brief might well be taken from the paragraph of the majority opinion in *Railroad Retirement Board v. The Alton Railroad Co., et al.*, 295 U.S. 330 (1935),[b] where, in speaking of the *Texas & New Orleans Railroad* decision, it was said:

"The railroad labor act was upheld by this court upon the express ground that to facilitate the amicable settlement of disputes which threatened the service of the necessary agencies of interstate transportation tended to prevent interruptions of service and was therefore within the delegated power of regulation. *It was pointed out that the act did not interfere with the normal right of the carrier to select its employees or discharge them. Texas & New Orleans R. Co. v. Brotherhood of Railway & S.S. Clerks*, 281 U.S. 548, 570, 571." (Italics supplied) (p. 369)

Apply this to the instant case and the results are convincing that the decision of the Labor Board cannot be sustained {for the National Labor Relations Act is a much deeper intrusion on an employer's rights than is the Railway Labor Act}. In questions of employer-employee relationships, the law has always been hesitant to interfere. Courts of equity from time immemorial have refused to compel specific performance of an employment contract as against either the employer or the

---

[b]{The facts of the case are that Congress established a compulsory retirement and pension program for all carriers subject to the Interstate Commerce Act. Even though the Supreme Court had long approved of federal regulation of railroads, the Court invalidated this statute. Justice Roberts for the majority concluded that pensions were not related to interstate transportation. In response to the argument that pensions improve morale and make workers more efficient, he replied that, if this argument were accepted, there would be no limit to the field of such regulation. The statute was aimed at the social welfare of the worker, which was a local matter. — ed.}

employee.[c] From the standpoint of the employee, the law has recognized that he should not be forced into a relationship which may be distasteful to him. From the standpoint of the employer, the courts have recognized that the right to judge the capabilities of his employees is absolutely essential to the proper management of a business. A variety of reasons may lead an employer to discharge an employee. It may be a question of efficiency, of application, or discipline. On other occasions the employer may be required to take action to protect the morale of his other employees, to prevent dissatisfaction of other workers, or to put an end to suspected theft, sabotage or other undesirable conditions. In such cases, it may be preferable, for obvious reasons of policy, to withhold disclosure of the cause of the discharge. In any case the question of judgment is a delicate one which the law has always seen fit to rest in the personal discretion of the employer. If it is proper for the law to deprive the employer of his right to judgment and to rest the function in a board of this character, and then to *compel* the employer to restore the employee who has been discharged, there is an end to efficient management.

{THE COMMERCE CLAUSE ARGUMENT[d]}

The National Labor Relations Act Is a Labor Act and Not a True Regulation of Interstate Commerce.

Under this aspect of the case it is necessary to make an inquiry into the objects of the National Labor Relations Act, to determine whether it represents an honest endeavor to regulate commerce among the several states, or an usurpation of the reserved powers of the separate states to control questions of internal policy. As a consequence, the question resolves itself into two subsidiary questions, the first dealing with the scope of Congressional power over interstate commerce, and the second with the nature and objects of the statute involved.

---

[c]{Specific performance is a remedy for breach of contract in which the court directs the defaulting party to do what has been promised. (The alternative remedy is to pay damages.) If you sign a contract to buy a house and, on the closing date, the seller refuses to sign the deed, you may ask the court for an order of specific performance, requiring the seller to sign the deed. Courts generally will not order specific performance of employment contracts. — ed.}

[d]{Some of the employer's arguments on the Commerce Clause have been reordered. — ed.}

THE POWER OF THE CONGRESS OF THE UNITED STATES UNDER THE INTERSTATE COMMERCE CLAUSE OF THE CONSTITUTION IS LIMITED TO THE BONA FIDE REGULATION OF INTERSTATE COMMERCE.

The problem of measuring the constitutional validity of the National Labor Relations Act, in its application to the industrial relations of the {employer}, is greatly simplified if the inquiry begins with the Constitution itself and pays true heed to the literal requirements of the document....

...

The Constitution provides in Section 8 of Article I, "The Congress shall have power ... to regulate Commerce with Foreign nations and among the several States, and with the Indian Tribes...."

The draftsmen of the Constitution foresaw that if economic and political intercourse between the States was to be fostered, and the welfare of the nation protected, it would be necessary to curb the selfish interests of the individual States where they might easily conflict with the interests of the federation as a whole. Therefore, jurisdiction over interstate commerce — a fertile field for controversy among individual States — was granted to the Federal Government. Its jurisdiction involves the power to *regulate, restrict and protect interstate commerce, but it does not include, and was not designed to include, the right to use such jurisdiction as a pretext to interfere with the local sovereignty of the States.* If this one premise is carefully borne in mind, the apparent confusion which sometimes arises as to the limitations on the powers of each of the concurrent governments and which pervades the {Labor Board's} argument is to a large extent removed.

Breadth and meaning were given to the Commerce Clause in *Gibbons v. Ogden*, 9 Wheat. 1 (1824). It is apparent from the language of the case, considered as a whole, that Chief Justice Marshall, although a firm believer in a strong centralized government, had no thought but that the Commerce Clause meant just what it says, that is, that Congress may regulate "commerce among the States." Even under the most careful scrutiny, the opinion proceeds solely on the principle that Congress has been accorded power over commerce, that is, the movement of persons and commodities among the several States, and not over farming or mining or manufacturing, — *things which may precede or follow, but are not commerce.*

The true meaning of the Commerce Clause, as exemplified by this decision, has sometimes been lost sight of in recent years. The argument is often made, as in the {Labor Board's} brief, that the nation has come to a new conception of commerce, that business has outgrown the State and has become a matter of national concern, and that our purely internal political, economic{} and social life is so intimately connected with our national commerce that it has been swallowed up in the latter's importance. On this hypothesis, it is not difficult to argue that the wages of a newsboy, the prices of a grocer and the advertising policies of a local dentist in some degree affect incomes and business. The impact may be slight, but in the end, it may be contended, it either encourages or discourages commerce among the States.

Despite this confusion of issues, the Constitution, in the last analysis, still requires the separation of State and Federal power. The decision of this Court in *A. L. A. Schechter Poultry Corporation, et al., v. United States*, 295 U.S. 495 (1935), is a mandate that the literal requirements of the Constitution must not be ignored.[e] It may be true that purely internal affairs do indirectly affect interstate commerce, just as interstate commerce bears indirectly upon internal affairs; but while this might be urged as a reason for altering our Constitutional form of government, it is not an excuse for attempting to obliterate the Constitutional distinction between commerce and that which is not.

...

---

[e]{The National Industrial Recovery Act of 1933 was one of the major pillars of the New Deal. Designed to revive the economy, the Recovery Act envisioned that employers would form trade associations which would write codes that regulated unfair trade practices (i.e., eliminated cut-throat price competition among firms), set minimum wages and maximum hours, and required collective bargaining if the workers desired it. The Act authorized the president, upon application by a trade association, to promulgate its code, after which violating it was a misdemeanor.

{In the *Schechter* case, a wholesale poultry market in Brooklyn was found guilty of violating the wage and hour provisions of the Code of Fair Competition for the Live Poultry Industry of Metropolitan New York. Ninety-six percent of the poultry marketed in this area came from other states. Schechter purchased poultry from commission men in New York City, and the poultry was trucked to Schechter's slaughterhouses in Brooklyn. Schechter sold only to local dealers.

{Schechter argued he was not engaged in interstate commerce. The government replied that he was part of the "stream of commerce," or at least that his operations "affected commerce." The Supreme Court rejected the government's arguments and held the Recovery Act unconstitutional . Schechter was not in the stream of commerce because interstate transactions ended when the poultry reached the Brooklyn slaughterhouses; the slaughtering and subsequent sales were local transactions. The wages and hours of Schechter's employees had no direct relation to interstate commerce; they may have affected commerce indirectly, but they did not affect it directly. — ed.}

These decisions provide a sound basis for discussing the constitutionality of the National Labor Relations Act, because they enable us to perceive the real issue. The line between the divergent jurisdictions is defined by our political charter; it must be obeyed and neither the state nor the federal government may crowd the other from its allotted territory by an appeal to a broader construction than the instrument will bear. The federal government may regulate and protect the streams of commerce and the beds through which they run, but *it may not say that all activities are commerce, or concern commerce, and thereby hope to intrude in matters which are traditionally the concern of the separate states.*

THE FACT THAT THE {EMPLOYER} RECEIVES AND TRANSMITS RAW MATERIALS AND PRODUCTS IN INTERSTATE COMMERCE DOES NOT SUBJECT ITS INDUSTRIAL RELATIONS AND ACTIVITIES TO CONGRESSIONAL LEGISLATION.

It is admitted that raw materials are brought from several States to the {employer's} plant at Aliquippa. We are equally ready to concede that a large percentage of its manufactured products has found its way to States other than the State of Pennsylvania. But we cannot yield to the proposition that these factors suffice to subject the production activities of the (employer} to the regulation of Congress.

...

Arkadelphia Milling Co. v. St. Louis Southwestern Railways Co., 249 U.S. 134 (1918) arose out of actions by certain shippers and railway companies to enjoin the enforcement of intrastate railways rates fixed by a state railway commission. The facts indicated, in one of the cases, that the shipper was engaged in transporting logs from its lumber operation in the state to its mills, where the logs were processed and manufactured into staves and other products and held in storage to be sold and shipped in accordance with the demands of the market. Almost 95% of the finished articles were eventually delivered to points outside of the state. The court found that the interstate movement did not begin until the sale and delivery of the finished products, declaring:

> "It is not merely that there was no continuous movement from the forest to the points without the State, but that when the rough material left the woods it was not intended that it should be transported out of the State, or elsewhere beyond the mill, until it had been subjected to a manufacturing process that materially changed its character, utility, and value." (p. 151)

Similarly in *Oliver Iron Co. v. Lord,* 262 U.S. 172 (1923), {the Court declared} that mining "like manufacturing, is a local business" ....

... {L}ocal activities such as mining, manufacturing, warehousing, processing and the like are not withdrawn from the jurisdiction of the states {i.e., are not interstate commerce} because of subsequent or precedent movements in interstate commerce. The first of these decisions is *Kidd v. Pearson*, 128 U.S. 1 (1888). The argument was advanced that the state had transgressed beyond its proper jurisdiction in prohibiting the manufacture of intoxicants, because the statute restricted the movement of interstate commerce. In pointing out the fundamental distinction between local activities and commerce, the court declared:

> "No distinction is more popular to the common mind, or more clearly expressed in economic and political literature, than that between manufactures and commerce. Manufacture is transformation — the fashioning of raw materials into a change of form for use. The functions of commerce are different." (p. 20)

> ...

> "The reach and consequences of the contention repel its acceptance. If the possibility, or, indeed, certainty of exportation of a product or article from a State determines it to be in interstate commerce before the commencement of its movement from the State, it would seem to follow that {it} is in such commerce from the instant of its growth or production, and in the case of {minerals}, as they lie in the ground. The result would be curious. *It would nationalize all industries, it would nationalize and withdraw from state jurisdiction and deliver to federal commercial control the fruits of California and the South, the wheat of the West and its meats, the cotton of the South, the shoes of Massachusetts and the woolen industries of other States, at the very inception of their production or growth*, that is, the fruits unpicked, the cotton and wheat ungathered, hides and flesh of cattle yet 'on the hoof,' wool yet unshorn, and coal yet unmined, because they are in varying percentages destined for and surely to be exported to States other than those of their production." (Italics supplied). (p. 259)

{THE FACT THAT THE EMPLOYER'S BUSINESS HAS AN EFFECT ON INTERSTATE COMMERCE DOES NOT SUBJECT ITS ACTIVITIES TO CONGRESSIONAL LEGISLATION.}

It was this danger of the destruction of the powers of the States which seems to have evoked the following statement in the *Schechter* case:

"But where the effect of intrastate transactions upon interstate commerce is merely indirect, such transactions remain within the domain of state power. If the Commerce Clause were construed to reach all enterprises and transactions which could be said to have an indirect effect upon interstate commerce, the federal authority would embrace practically all the activities of the people, and the authority of the state over its domestic concerns would exist only by sufferance of the federal government. *Indeed, on such a theory, even the development of the state's commercial facilities would be subject to federal control."* (Italics supplied) (p. 546)

... Congress [unsuccessfully sought to} to justify the Agricultural Adjustment Act {on the ground of effects on the national economy}. This Court was urged to find that the decrease in farm prices, incident to the depression, had seriously affected the national income and therefore the general welfare. In other words, it was contended that farming had become a national problem, just as it is contended in the instant case, that the {employer's} relations with its employees have been converted into a matter of national concern because of the size of the {employer's} operations and the magnitude of the steel industry in general. The tremendous mass of data and opinion received in evidence by the {Labor} Board to show the past history of the steel industry and its industrial relations had this object in view: to convince this Court that the need of organization in the steel industry is a matter of national importance. The majority opinion in *United States v. Butler, et al.*, 297 U.S. 1 (1936), makes short shrift of this argument in the simple statement:

"*It does not help to declare that local conditions throughout the nation have created a situation of national concern;* for this is but to say that whenever there is a widespread similarity of local conditions, Congress may ignore constitutional limitations upon its own powers and usurp those reserved to the states." (pp. 74-75)

... There is no better way to demonstrate our conclusions than by a reference to the opinion of Chief Justice Hughes in the *Schechter* case:

"The argument of the government proves too much. If the federal government may determine the wages and hours of employees in the internal commerce of a state, because of their relation to cost and prices and their indirect effect upon interstate commerce, it would seem that a similar control might be exerted over other elements of cost, also affecting prices, such as the number of employees, rents, advertising, methods of doing business, etc. All the processes of production and distribution that enter into cost could likewise be controlled. If the cost of doing an intrastate business is in itself the permitted object of federal control, the extent of the regulation of cost would be a question of discretion and not of power." (p. 549)

xviii   *NLRB v. Jones & Laughlin* and *Associated Press v. NLRB*

THE EMPLOYER'S RELATIONS AND TRANSACTIONS WITH ITS PRODUCTION
EMPLOYEES ARE NOT IN OR CONNECTED WITH INTERSTATE COMMERCE.

The distinction which we have emphasized between the local activities of a
business and its subsequent or precedent participation in interstate commerce, has
been maintained in the field of labor relations.

The labor provisions of the Bituminous Coal Conservation Act were almost
identical with the provisions of the National Labor Relations Act. It, too, was
prefaced with a legislative declaration of policy that the right of mine workers to
organize and bargain collectively for wages, hours of labor and conditions of
employment should be guaranteed in order to prevent constant wage cutting and
disparage labor costs detrimental to fair interstate competition and in order to avoid
obstructions to interstate commerce that occur in industrial disputes over labor
relations at the mine. The Bituminous Coal Conservation Act likewise provided for
the creation of a Labor Board to administer the labor provisions of the Code which
was imposed by the statute on the producers of coal. Among the required provisions
of the Code was a clause that "employees shall have the right to organize and bargain
collectively through representatives of their own choosing, and shall be free from
interference, restraint or coercion of employers, or their agents, in the designation of
such representatives or in self-organization or in other concerted activities for the
purpose of collective bargaining or other mutual aid or protection; and no employee
and no one seeking employment shall be required, as a condition of employment, to
join any company union."

Other provisions {of the Coal Act} assured the right of peaceable assemblage
to workers and authorized the Labor Board to determine whether or not an
organization of employees was controlled or dominated by an employer and to certify
the freely chosen representatives of the employees. Additional labor provisions
provided for the negotiation of agreements covering hours of labor and wages by the
chosen representatives of the employers and employees.

The majority opinion in *Carter v. Coal Company, et al.*, 298 U.S. 238 (1936),
gave careful consideration to these provisions and found the conclusion inescapable
that labor relations are not in or a part of interstate commerce and therefore cannot
be subject to regulation by Congress. In this connection, it was said:

> "One who produces or manufactures a commodity, subsequently
> sold and shipped by him in interstate commerce, whether such sale and
> shipment were originally intended or not, has engaged in two distinct and
> separate activities. So far as he produces or manufactures a commodity, his
> business is purely local. So far as he sells and ships, or contracts to sell and
> ship, the commodity to customers in another state, he engages in interstate

commerce. In respect of the former, he is subject only to regulation by the state; in respect of the latter, to regulation only by the federal government. *Utah Power & L. Go. v. Pfost*, 286 U.S. 165, 182. Production is not commerce, but a step in preparation for commerce. *Chassaniol v. Greenwood*, 291 U.S. 584, 587.

We have seen that the word 'commerce' is the equivalent of the phrase 'intercourse for the purposes of trade.' Plainly, the incidents leading up to and culminating in the mining of coal do not constitute such intercourse. *The employment of men, the fixing of their wages, hours of labor and working conditions, the bargaining in respect of these things — whether carried on separately or collectively — each and all constitute intercourse for the purposes of production, not of trade.* The latter is a thing apart from the relation of employer and employee, which in all producing occupations is purely local in character. Extraction of coal from the mine is the aim and the completed result of local activities. Commerce in the coal mine is not brought into being by force of these activities, but by negotiations, agreements, and circumstances entirely apart from production. Mining brings the subject matter of commerce into existence. Commerce disposes of it.

A consideration of the foregoing, and of many cases which might be added to those already cited, renders inescapable the conclusion that the effect of the labor provisions of the act, including those in respect of minimum wages, wage agreements, collective bargaining, and the Labor Board and its powers, primarily falls upon production and not upon commerce; and confirms the further resulting conclusion that production is a purely local activity. It follows that none of these essential antecedents of production constitutes a transaction in or forms any part of interstate commerce. *Schechter Corp. v. United States, supra*, p. 542 *et seq.* Everything which moves in interstate commerce has had a local origin. Without local production somewhere, interstate commerce, as now carried on, would practically disappear. Nevertheless, the local character of mining, of manufacturing and of crop growing is a fact, and remains a fact, whatever may be done with the products." (Italics supplied) (pp. 303-304)

...

The case of *Texas and New Orleans Railroad Co. v. Brotherhood of Railway and Steamship Clerks, et al.,* 281 U.S. 548 (1930), furnishes no precedent for the National Labor Relations Act. This case arose under the Railroad Labor Act of 1926, which set up machinery for the voluntary adjustment and arbitration of labor disputes before boards of adjustment and boards of arbitration. The plaintiff union had a controversy with the Railroad before a board of adjustment; pending the decision, the defendant railroad created a rival union, by indulging in alleged coercive and oppressive tactics. The union brought injunction proceedings under the section of the

NLRB v. Jones & Laughlin and *Associated Press v. NLRB*

Act which declared that "representatives, for the purposes this Act, shall be designated by the respective parties ... without interference, influence or coercion...." The District Court expressly held that the statute was constitutional and granted an injunction. The Circuit Court of Appeals affirmed the District Court, stating:

> "We think that under the power to regulate interstate commerce it is competent for Congress to make provision for the settlement of disputes between interstate carriers and their employees with reference to rates of wages, rules, and working conditions, to the end of preventing such disputes resulting in the interruption or stopping of the movement in interstate commerce of freight or passengers." (33 F.(2d) 13, 16).

This Court accepted the argument of the Circuit Court and sustained the Act as a regulation of commerce with the statement, "Congress may facilitate the amicable settlement of disputes which threaten the service of the *necessary agents of interstate transportation.*"

We submit that the distinction between the present case and ... the *Texas & New Orleans Railroad Company* case is implicit in the opinion of this Court. The transportation of persons and commodities between states is, of course, the very essence of interstate commerce. As a consequence, congressional regulation of rates, transportation facilities, equipment, personnel and related matters has been uniformly sustained. It would be indeed difficult to find a more comprehensive and thorough program of legislation than that developed in the Halls of Congress to govern the operations of carriers and communication systems....

Even assuming that participation by an employer in interstate commerce might subject certain of his activities to congressional regulation, nevertheless the relationship between the employer and his employees is purely a local matter. Although an employee may be employed in indirectly assisting the movement of interstate commerce, his relationship to his employer is not a part of commerce. It is a status existing wholly within the State, whose incidents, such as wages, hours of labor and the like, are purely domestic in character. It may be true that congressional regulation of the local incidents of employment in cases involving interstate carriers {e.g., railroads} has been sustained, where the Court has found the true object of Congress to be the protection of interstate commerce. But there is no precedent for interference where the real purpose of the regulation is deliberately to interfere in matters which are not the concern of the Federal Government. If the proposition should be accepted that the most insignificant participation in interstate commerce subjects all of the activities and all of the relationships of an employer to congressional measures, then there would be nothing to prevent congressional entry into the field of fire and building regulations, safety requirements, and a thousand similar measures, local in character. Yet no one would argue that regulations governing the erection and operation of factories, the hours and wages of employees, and the conditions of safe employment should be functions of the central government.

COMMENT[f]

CURRENT AND COUNTER-CURRENT

Our study of labor law before the enactment of the National Labor Relations Act may have suggested a pattern: Each time workers developed a new tactic, the courts outlawed it. The strike was held to be a criminal conspiracy in the <u>Philadelphia Cordwainers</u> case. The picket line was enjoined in <u>Vegelahn v. Guntner</u>. Secondary boycotts were held a violation of anti-trust law in the <u>Danbury Hatters</u> case.

Another pattern may also be identified. It was a counter-current, one that validated the efforts of workers to organize themselves and bargain collectively. This counter-current flowed primarily in legislative channels, though it also moved in judicial channels (chiefly in dissenting opinions). Eventually, the counter-current predominated.

The first tributary feeding the counter-current was <u>Commonwealth v. Hunt</u>, which approved the strike. Only a few courts followed the lead of Massachusetts. However, state legislatures undertook the task. In the last years of the Nineteenth Century and the first years of the Twentieth Century, several state legislatures enacted statutes providing that labor unions were not criminal conspiracies.

A major tributary was Justice Holmes's dissent in <u>Vegelahn v. Guntner</u>, which argued that peaceful picketing is justified by the workers' self-interest. Holmes's opinion played much the same role as Chief Justice Shaw's opinion in <u>Hunt</u>: as Shaw provided the conceptual basis on which unions would later be exonerated from the charge of criminal conspiracy, so Holmes provided the theoretical basis on which unions would later be exonerated from the charge of civil conspiracy.

Next came the Clayton Act. It may be argued that Congress intended the act to reverse the holding in the

---

[f]Citations to pages in this comment refer to the lower-case Roman numerals at the top of the page (not to the Arabic numerals at the bottom of the page) of <u>Jones & Laughlin</u>.

<u>Danbury Hatters</u> case that anti-trust law applies to unions, though it must be admitted that the legislative history of the Clayton Act looks in both directions. Nonetheless, we do find evidence of legislative support for collective bargaining. And Justice Brandeis's dissent in <u>Duplex v. Deering</u> is evidence of judicial support for the same goal.

Then the counter-current became stronger. Both Congress and state legislatures attempted to prohibit employers from discriminating against union members and to outlaw the yellow dog contract. If yellow dog contracts were illegal, courts could no longer grant injunctions against union organizing on the theory of inducement to breach of contract. The Supreme Court held these statutes were unconstitutional in <u>Adair</u> and <u>Coppage</u>. Yet once again we find evidence of judicial support for the aims of workers in the dissenting opinions of Justices Holmes, McKenna, and Day; and the legislative support for this end, which produced clearly pro-labor statutes, was strong.

Finally, the Norris-LaGuardia Act limited the jurisdiction of federal courts to issue injunctions in labor disputes. Several states passed "Little Norris-LaGuardia" acts as well.

An interesting aspect of the counter-current is that it was composed of specific reactions to specific problems. The <u>Hunt</u> case reacted to earlier cases that held unions to be criminal conspiracies, and later state legislatures enacted laws saying that unions were not criminal conspiracies. Sections 6 and 20 of the Clayton Act were a reaction to the <u>Danbury Hatters</u> case, which held that unions are covered by federal anti-trust law. Federal and state statutes prohibiting employers from discriminating because of union membership were a reaction to unsavory behavior by employers. Federal and state statutes barring the yellow dog contract were a reaction to injunctions that prohibited organizing as a form of inducement to breach of contract. And the Norris-LaGuardia Act was a specific reaction to the specific problem of injunctions issued by federal judges who were antipathetic to labor unions.

The counter-current, then, was a piecemeal approach to labor policy. Except for the dissenting opinions of

Holmes and Brandeis, which formulated the broad principle of labor self-interest, it appears that, through 1932, few persons saw a need for a comprehensive solution to the labor problem.

The administration of Franklin Roosevelt, which took office in 1933, brought a wider vision to government. Its primary goal was to end the Depression. Whereas the Hoover administration believed that recovery would come naturally, and that all that was necessary were band-aid programs like welfare — more specific reactions to specific problems — Roosevelt's "brain trust" was convinced that systematic intervention by government was necessary. The National Industrial Recovery Act created a new agency, the National Recovery Administration, the purpose of which was to stimulate production and consumption. The Agricultural Adjustment Act, which created another new agency, the Agricultural Adjustment Administration, had a similar purpose. Underpinning the creation of these and other agencies was the theory that the government could — and, given the crisis of the times, should — formulate and implement policies that would lead the country out of the Depression. Roosevelt, then, envisioned an active government, one that identified important goals and established institutions to achieve those goals.

Those institutions were administrative agencies, which were a developing phenomenon. It is doubtful that the old methods of government would have worked. A law requiring higher production or prohibiting lay offs would have had little effect. What was needed was the ability to take account of the multiplicity of reality in a nation of 3.5 million square miles and 125 million living souls. But Congress simply could not make a law for the shoe industry, another law for the steel industry, another for potato farms, another for cotton growers, and so on. An administrative agency, however, with power to make regulations that were binding on the public at large — that is, in effect, the power to make laws — could deal with the myriad of issues that arise as a policy is applied in the world. The great innovation of the Roosevelt administration was that Congress set the overall policies, and the administrative agencies applied them. Congress created the skeleton, and the agencies put the flesh on it.

This notion of government informed the National Labor Relations Act of 1935 (NLRA) (often called the Wagner Act after its chief sponsor in the Senate). The student is advised to read the act, which is in Part IV of the readings. In brief, the NLRA guaranteed to workers the right to engage in concerted activity, that is, to form, join, and assist labor unions, and to bargain collectively through agents of their own choosing. Any state laws to the contrary were preempted. To protect against employers' infringing on these rights, the act created a number of unfair labor practices. It became illegal for an employer to discriminate against union members or to refuse to bargain with a union that represented a majority of workers. An employer who was accused of committing an unfair labor practice would be tried before the National Labor Relations Board, which had power to order a guilty employer to cease the unfair labor practice and to compensate workers for monetary losses caused by the illegal behavior. Decisions of the Labor Board could be reviewed in the courts. It was anticipated that problems would arise over bargaining agents. Do the workers truly want to be represented by a union, or do they prefer to bargain individually with their employer? If they want a union, do they prefer union A or union B? The Labor Board was empowered to investigate and decide questions concerning representation as well.

NLRB v. JONES & LAUGHLIN

Employers were unhappy with the Labor Act. It represented a significant abridgment of the freedom they had formerly enjoyed. The act also gave workers, through unions, a degree of power. Accordingly, employers immediately challenged the constitutionality of the act. The case that reached the Supreme Court was Jones & Laughlin, and it appeared that employers had a good chance of winning it. As the student knows from reading Adair v. U.S. and Coppage v. Kansas, Supreme Court cases had limited the power of government, both federal and state, to regulate labor relations. The cases followed two lines: those prohibiting both state and federal governments from interfering with the liberty of contract, and those prohibiting the federal government from legislating regarding local, as opposed to interstate, commerce.

LIBERTY OF CONTRACT

To review briefly, in <u>Lochner v. N.Y.</u> a state prescribed maximum daily hours for bakery workers. The Supreme Court held the statute was unconstitutional under the Fourteenth Amendment because it interfered with liberty of contract and was not a reasonable exercise of the state's police power. In <u>Adair v. U.S.</u> Congress made it a crime for a railroad to discriminate against an employee because of membership in a labor union. The Supreme Court held this law violated the Fifth Amendment by infringing on liberty of contract. In <u>Coppage v. Kansas</u> a state outlawed the yellow dog contract. The Supreme Court struck down this law as a violation of liberty of contract.

<u>The Labor Board's Argument</u>   <u>Lochner</u>, <u>Adair</u>, and <u>Coppage</u> were a major problem for the Labor Board as it tried to vindicate the Labor Act. The solution to the problem lay in a case decided in 1935, <u>Texas & New Orleans RR. Co. v. Brotherhood of Ry and SS Clerks</u>, in which the Supreme Court upheld the constitutionality of the Railway Labor Act. Without saying so explicitly, the Board argued that <u>Texas & New Orleans RR.</u> had overruled the older cases.[g] Here is how the Board presented these arguments.

The Board quoted a passage from <u>Texas & New Orleans RR.</u> (p. ii) in which the Court said that

- workers' collective action was not only a lawful act, but also a right that Congress could protect from infringement;
- protection of this right was not an invasion of the employer's rights, but a recognition of the rights of employers and employees; and

---

[g]Perhaps deeming it unwise to say expressly to the Supreme Court that it had overruled itself, the Board's brief subtly implied as much by stating, "The <u>Adair</u> and <u>Coppage</u> cases need not be extensively analyzed here. It is sufficient to say that both decisions were vigorously urged by the carrier in the <u>Texas & New Orleans</u> case. The facts of the latter case are so similar to those of the case at bar that the earlier cases, if inapplicable there, cannot be applicable here" (p. iii).

- Congress could seek to make collective bargaining an instrument for achieving labor peace.

The Board's brief argued that this rationale applied to the case at bar: the brief implied that if workers on railroads had a right to collective action, and if Congress could protect this right, the same was true for other workers; and that if Congress could seek to promote collective bargaining as an instrument of labor peace on the railroads, Congress could use the same instrument to promote labor peace for other industries.

It remained for the Board to deal with <u>Adair</u> and <u>Coppage</u>. Fortunately for the Board, the Court itself had dealt with those cases in <u>Texas & New Orleans RR.</u> (pp. ii-iii). In that case, the Court stated that section 2, third of the Railway Labor Act

> does not interfere with the normal exercise of the right of the carrier to select its employees or to discharge them. The statute is not aimed at this right of the employers but at the interference with the right of employees to have representatives of their own choosing. ... {Employers} have no constitutional right to interfere with the freedom of the employees in making their selection....

The Board put a touch of gloss on this statement. The employer in <u>Texas & New Orleans RR.</u> had been accused (as had the employer in <u>Jones & Laughlin</u>) of discharging workers because of their union activity. The Board wrote, "The Court thus held that the discharge of employees because of activity in the {union} was not a 'normal exercise of the right' to hire or discharge employees which is protected under the due process clause of the Fifth Amendment."

The Board implied that the reasoning of <u>Texas & New Orleans RR.</u> was this: <u>Adair</u> and <u>Coppage</u> established that employers had a constitutional right to hire and fire workers. No right is absolute, however; one right stops where another begins. The employer's right to hire and fire does not preempt the workers' right to collective action. When protecting the workers' right from interference, Congress did not infringe on the employer's right because that right never included interfering with workers' rights.

The lynchpin of the Board's argument was the workers' right to collective action; indeed, the Board's argument was plausible only if such a right existed. If the right did exist, the employer's and the workers' rights overlapped one another and needed to be accommodated. Thus, the Board took the position that Texas & New Orleans RR. had overruled Adair and Coppage. The Board argued that earlier cases may have held that Congress could not restrict an employer's right to hire and fire, but Texas & New Orleans RR. held the opposite. If the Board's argument were correct, it was no longer unconstitutional for the government to prohibit an employer from discharging a worker for joining a union.

The Employer's Argument   The employer's brief reminded the Court of doctrine as it existed before Texas & New Orleans RR.: The Constitution safeguards liberty of contract, and the government may not regulate wages, hours of work, or other terms of employment except to safeguard the health or safety of workers or to prevent fraud of oppression. In support of this doctrine, the employer cited cases like Adair and Coppage.

Then the brief argued that the Labor Act infringed on liberty of contract even more than the Erdman Act had in Adair. The Erdman Act prohibited discharge of a worker for joining a union; the Labor Act not only prohibited such a discharge, but also required the employer to reinstate the worker. If the statute in Adair was unconstitutional, the Labor Act was even more so.

This argument assumed the continuing vitality of Lochner and its ilk, and ignored the Board's contention that Texas & New Orleans RR. had overruled those cases. But the employer's brief could not ignore Texas & New Orleans RR. altogether, and the employer's next argument addressed this case. At this point the employer confronted a major obstacle: The Board had a strong argument that Texas & New Orleans RR. had overruled Lochner, etc. How could the employer get around Texas & New Orleans RR.? As the student learned in the comment following the Philadelphia Cordwainers Case, one way to handle an adverse precedent is to argue that it was wrongly decided. If the Board had been reluctant to argue that <u>Texas & New Orleans RR.</u> had overruled older cases like <u>Lochner</u> and <u>Adair</u>, the employer must have been even more reluctant to argue that the recent case of <u>Texas & New Orleans RR.</u> was wrongly decided. And yet this is exactly what the employer did; and like the Board, the employer did it subtly. The employer's strategy was to emphasize the merit of the older cases. By implication, if they were correct, <u>Texas & New Orleans RR.</u> was wrong.

Courts, argued the employer, had always been reluctant to require specific performance of employment contracts or otherwise to interfere in the relationship of employer and employee. For a variety of reasons, this reluctance remains good policy. The government should not get involved in employment. By depriving the employer of the right to make judgments about workers, the Labor Act would put an end to efficient management of business. This argument was essentially a justification for the decisions in <u>Lochner</u> and <u>Adair</u>, an argument that they should not be overruled. Of course, if they remained good law, the Labor Act was unconstitutional.

INTERSTATE COMMERCE

The Supreme Court had a long and clear line of precedent on the difference between interstate and local commerce, and some of the precedents were recent. In <u>Schechter Poultry v. U.S.</u>, the National Industrial Recovery Act — a pillar of the Roosevelt Administration's effort to pull the nation out of the Depression — was invalidated on the ground that the statute regulated local, not interstate commerce. The Schechter Poultry Company was located in New York City. Even though 96% of the poultry in New York City came from across state lines, the Court held that slaughtering was a local matter. Any effect that slaughtering had on interstate commerce was indirect and beyond the reach of the federal government.[h]   In <u>U.S. v. Butler</u>, the Agricultural

---

[h]The statute was held unconstitutional on another ground as well, viz., that Congress had wrongfully delegated legislative responsibility by authorizing private industry, through the National Recovery Administration, to formulate "Codes of Fair

(continued...)

Adjustment Act — another pillar of the New Deal — was held unconstitutional because it regulated farming, which was a local matter and not an aspect of interstate commerce. And in <u>Carter v. Carter Coal Co.</u> — decided the very year before the <u>Jones & Laughlin</u> case — the Court struck down the Bituminous Coal Conservation Act of 1935. The act forgave tax on sales of coal by mines if the operators of the mines agreed to charge a minimum price for coal, to abide by minimum wages and maximum hours for miners, and to bargain collectively with the miners' union. The Supreme Court invalidated the statute on the ground that employment is local, not interstate commerce. The Court reasoned that employment is an aspect of production, and production is a local affair that Congress may not regulate.

<u>The Labor Board's Argument</u>   The Commerce Clause cases summarized above weighed heavily against the Labor Board, but once again <u>Texas & New Orleans RR.</u> provided a ray of hope. In that case, the Supreme Court had stated (and had later repeated in <u>Alton RR.</u>) that Congress could promote settlement of disputes that threatened the "necessary agencies of interstate commerce" (p. iv). The Board's task became characterizing the Jones & Laughlin company as a necessary agency of interstate commerce.

The Board undertook this task in two steps. The first was easy and obvious: The necessary agencies of interstate commerce, wrote the Board, included not only the railroads, but also "other forms of commercial intercourse among the States" (p. iv), such as motor and water transportation, and radio, telephone, and telegraph. It was indisputable that Congress could regulate these forms of transportation and communication because they were so closely analogous to railroads, and so the courts had held.[i]

----

[h](...continued)
Competition."   This ground was not relevant to <u>Jones & Laughlin</u>.

[i]The Board's brief cited cases in support of this proposition, but we omitted them from the excerpts of the brief printed above.

The Board's second step was to argue that Jones & Laughlin's business was similar to businesses that were indisputably involved in interstate commerce. The Board's problem here is apparent: a steel mill is not a form of transportation or communication. For this reason, the Board attempted to broaden the category of businesses involved in interstate commerce. The brief made this attempt with both subtle and forthright moves.

The subtle move was a shift in terminology. Compare the key sentence in the Supreme Court's opinion in Texas & New Orleans RR. with the paraphrase of that sentence in the Board's brief:

Texas & New Orleans RR.
Congress may facilitate the amicable settlement of disputes which threaten the service of the necessary agencies of interstate commerce.

The Labor Board's Brief
It is apparent that in like fashion industrial strife threatening the operation of various other forms of commercial intercourse among the States, such as motor and water transportation, pipe lines, freight agency services, and communication by wireless, telephone, telegraph or radio, would directly affect interstate commerce and hence fall within Congressional power to mitigate or eliminate.

(p. iv)   The Supreme Court's sentence seemed to say that

- Congress could regulate the necessary agencies of interstate commerce
- railroads were necessary agencies of interstate commerce
- the Railway Labor Act regulated railroads, and therefore
- the Railway Labor Act was constitutional.

The Board's sentence, however, suggested a different interpretation of the rationale of Texas & New Orleans RR:

- Congress could protect interstate commerce from interruption
- industrial strife threatened to interrupt interstate commerce
- Congress could, therefore, seek to mitigate industrial strife
- railroads were part of interstate commerce
- the Railway Labor Act sought to mitigate or eliminate labor strife on the railroads, and therefore
- the Railway Labor Act was constitutional.

Thus, by a subtle change in wording, the Board argued that Congress could regulate, not merely the necessary agencies of interstate commerce, but all of interstate commerce. Congress could regulate the railroads because they were a part of interstate commerce, and the same thing could be said of Jones & Laughlin's steel mill. Because it was involved in interstate commerce, and because the Labor Act sought to mitigate industrial strife that would affect interstate commerce, the Labor Act was constitutional.

The Board's more forthright move to broaden the category of interstate commerce was to draw on cases decided under the Sherman and Clayton Anti-trust Acts (p. iv). Somewhat expanded, the Board's argument began with the accepted proposition that Congress may regulate only interstate commerce. The anti-trust statutes, therefore, regulated interstate commerce. These statutes had been applied to industrial strife involving labor unions. Hence, industrial strife must have directly affected interstate commerce. It followed that Congress could seek to mitigate industrial strife that affected interstate commerce. Jones & Laughlin was a large company that received raw materials and shipped finished goods across state lines. The company was part of the national economy and, therefore, industrial strife in the company would directly affect interstate commerce.

<u>The Employer's Argument</u>   The employer's brief advocated close adherence to the traditional understanding of interstate commerce. The understanding had two main parts. The first part pertained to the nature of the employer's business, and the second, to the nature of the employment relationship, regardless of the business.

Beginning with the nature of the business, the employer argued that farming, mining, and manufacturing were local, and their status remained local however they affected commerce in other places; only the movement of goods and persons across state lines was interstate commerce. So held <u>Gibbons v. Ogden</u> as long ago as 1824, and so held <u>Schechter Poultry v. U.S.</u> as recently as 1935. If commerce changes from local to interstate merely because of its effects elsewhere, "the wages of a newsboy, the prices of a grocer and the advertising policies of a local dentist" become interstate commerce because "in some degree {they} affect incomes and business" (pp. xi-xii).

Then the employer replied to the Board's argument that the steel mill was in interstate commerce because it received raw materials from, and shipped products to, other states. In <u>Arkadelphia Milling v. St. Louis Southwestern RR.</u> a company shipped 95 percent of its finished products across state lines. Nevertheless, the Supreme Court held that its manufacturing process remained local. In <u>Kidd v. Pearson</u>, a state outlawed the manufacture of intoxicating beverages. A distillery argued the law was unconstitutional because it regulated interstate commerce. But the Supreme Court held that manufacturing was local and, therefore, within the power of a state to regulate or prohibit. Were the rule otherwise, said the Court,

> {i}t would nationalize all industries, it would nationalize and withdraw from state jurisdiction and deliver to federal commercial control the fruits of California and the South, the wheat of the West and its meats ... the shoes of Massachusetts and the woolen industries of other States, at the very inception of their production or growth ... because they are in varying percentages destined for and surely to be exported to {other} States ...

(p. xiv; italics omitted). Nor did it matter, continued the employer's brief, that local commerce affected commerce elsewhere. As the Court had stated in <u>Schechter Poultry</u>:

If the Commerce Clause were construed to reach

> all enterprises and transactions which would be
> said to have an indirect effect on interstate
> commerce, the federal authority would embrace
> practically all the activities of the people
> ...

(p. xv). Even if many local matters accumulated into a national problem, they were still local matters. Per <u>U.S. v. Butler</u>:

> It does not help to declare that local
> conditions throughout the nation have created
> a situation of national concern; for this is
> but to say that whenever there is a widespread
> similarity of local conditions, Congress may
> ignore constitutional limitations upon its own
> powers and usurp those reserved to the states

(p. xv; italics omitted).

Turning to the second part of the traditional understanding, the employer argued that the Labor Act was regulation of employment, and employment was not interstate commerce. The whole relationship of employer to employee — hiring, firing, and all the terms and conditions of employment — was local. Therefore, Congress had no power to regulate employment. The Supreme Court had reaffirmed this principle as recently as 1936 in <u>Carter v. Carter Coal Co.</u>, in which the Bituminous Coal Conservation Act was held unconstitutional. This act was invalidated because, said the Court, employment is an aspect of production, and production is local. The employer's brief noted that the Bituminous Coal Conservation Act had created a scheme of labor relations that was similar to the scheme in the Labor Act, and it followed that the Labor Act was also unconstitutional.

Then the brief addressed <u>Texas & New Orleans RR.</u>, which had sustained the Railway Labor Act. The employer conceded that the provisions of this act were analogous to the provisions of the Labor Act, but argued that this similarity did not mean that the Labor Act was constitutional. Rather, a significant distinction between these acts existed: the Railway Labor Act applied to the interstate carriers. The Court had based its ruling that the Railway Labor Act was constitutional on this very distinction, writing, "Congress may facilitate the amicable settlement of disputes which threaten the service of the <u>necessary agents of interstate transportation</u>" (p. xviii). Thus, <u>Texas & New Orleans RR.</u> was a narrow holding that applied only to employment on the agents of interstate commerce like railroads. In contrast, the Labor Act applied to all businesses; therefore, the Labor Act could not be sustained on the authority of <u>Texas & New Orleans RR.</u> For all businesses that were not interstate carriers, employment remained local and beyond the power to Congress to control.

EVALUATION OF THE ARGUMENTS

The Labor Board had precedent on its side on the liberty-of-contract argument. The older cases like <u>Adair</u> and <u>Coppage</u> had been undermined by <u>Texas & New Orleans RR</u>. If the Fifth Amendment rights of a railroad are not infringed by the requirements of collective bargaining under the Railway Labor Act, the Fifth Amendment rights of other private employers were not infringed by the National Labor Relations Act.

The employer had precedent on its side on the Commerce Clause argument. The distinction between local and interstate commerce was well established, and employment had always been a local matter. The Labor Board's two arguments — that labor relations had become a national problem, and that the flow of interstate commerce was affected by labor unrest — had both been rejected by the Supreme Court in earlier cases. The <u>Texas & New Orleans RR</u> case held that the employment practices of a railroad could be regulated, so employment was no longer a purely local matter; but the ground of the holding was that railroads were the very instrumentalities of interstate commerce. As railroads carried products across state lines, they were pure interstate commerce. Regulation of the employment practices of railroads in order to keep interstate commerce open was plainly different from regulating the labor relations of a steel mill.

THE SUPREME COURT'S DECISION

In <u>NLRB v. Jones & Laughlin</u> the Supreme Court upheld the constitutionality of the Labor Act. The Court accepted the Board's arguments that the act regulated interstate commerce (disapproving earlier cases like <u>Carter Coal</u>) and did not infringe on liberty of contract (following <u>Texas & New Orleans RR.</u>).

QUESTION FOR REFLECTION

1. <u>Texas and New Orleans RR.</u> overruled a long line of cases which had held that liberty of contract prevents the government from regulating the employment relationship (except in extraordinary circumstances), and <u>Jones & Laughlin</u> overruled an equally long line of cases which had held that employment was a local matter and not part of interstate commerce. When the Supreme Court announces a rule of constitutional law, should the Court adhere to that rule forever (unless, of course, the Constitution is amended)? If not, what justifies overruling a constitutional precedent? Does it suffice that the current Supreme Court believes that the earlier decision was mistaken, or must there be a stronger reason?

2. <u>Jones & Laughlin</u> held that workers have a right to collective action, and Congress may prevent employers from interfering with this right. Plainly, the Supreme Court's view of this right and of its relationship to employers' rights had changed since <u>Adair</u> and <u>Coppage</u>. Why did this change occur?

3. In <u>Texas & New Orleans RR.</u> the Supreme Court sustained the Railway Labor Act because it was not aimed at the "normal exercise of the right of the carrier to select its employees or to discharge them ... but at the interference with the right of employees to have representatives of their own choosing." Was this a sound argument?

4. Does the National Labor Relations Act, which promotes unionization, make sense today when work can be relocated to other countries where the cost of labor is much lower?

Ω

Coverage of the Labor Act

SUPERVISORS

SUPERVISORS AS EMPLOYEES

Introduction

Every statute intends to protect certain classes of persons. Some statutes protect all persons. For example, a statute against battery protects all persons from being struck intentionally. Other statutes are limited in scope, protecting specific classes of persons. The Labor Act falls into the latter category. First of all, the Act applies only to employees; thus, it does not apply to independent contractors, who are self employed, for example, a gardener who serves many customers. But the Labor Act is even more limited than this, for it does not protect some classes of workers who are generally regarded as employees, for example, agricultural workers. Foreones are employees. Should they be covered by the Labor Act? The courts and Congress have disagreed on this question.

⚜

ii

Packard Motor Co. v. NLRB
330 U.S. 485 (1947)

Mr. Justice JACKSON delivered the opinion of the Court.

The question presented by this case is whether foremen are entitled as a class to the rights of self-organization, collective bargaining, and other concerted activities as assured to employees generally by the National Labor Relations Act. The case grows out of conditions in the automotive industry, and, so far as they are important to the legal issues here, the facts are simple.

The Packard Motor Car Company employs about 32,000 rank and file workmen. Since 1937 they have been represented by the United Automobile Workers of America affiliated with the Congress of Industrial Organizations. These employees are supervised by approximately 1,100 employees of foreman rank consisting of about 125 "general foremen," 643 "foremen," 273 "assistant foremen," and 65 "special assignment men." Each general foreman is in charge of one or more departments, and under him in authority are foremen and their assistant foremen. Special assignment men are described as "trouble-shooters."

The function of these foremen in general is typical of the duties of foremen in mass production industry generally. Foremen carry the responsibility for maintaining quantity and quality of production, subject, of course, to the overall control and supervision of the management. Hiring is done by the labor relations department, as is the discharging and laying off of employees. But the foremen are provided with forms and with detailed lists of violations of discipline, and initiate recommendations for promotion, demotion and discipline. All such recommendations are subject to the reviewing procedure concerning grievances provided in the collectively-bargained agreement between the Company and the rank and file union.

The foremen as a group are highly paid and, unlike the workmen, are paid for justifiable absence and for holidays, are not docked in pay when tardy, receive longer paid vacations, and are given severance pay upon release by the Company.

These foremen determined to organize as a unit of the Foremen's Association of America, an unaffiliated organization which represents supervisory employees exclusively. Following the usual procedure, after the Board had decided that "all general foremen, foremen, assistant foremen, and special assignment men employed by the Company at its plants in Detroit, Michigan, constitute a unit appropriate for the purposes of collective bargaining within the meaning of § 9(b) of the Act," the Foremen's Association was certified as the bargaining representative. The Company asserted that foremen were not "employees" entitled to the advantages of the Labor Act, and refused to bargain with the union. After hearing on charge of unfair labor practice, the Board issued the usual cease and desist order. The Company resisted and challenged validity of the order. The judgment of the court below decreed its enforcement, and we granted *certiorari*.

The issue of law as to the power of the National Labor Relations Board under the National Labor Relations Act is simple, and our only function is to determine whether the order of the Board is authorized by the statute.

The privileges and benefits of the Act are conferred upon employees, and § 2(3) of the Act, so far as relevant, provides, "The term 'employee' shall include any employee...." The point that these foremen are employees both in the most technical sense at common law as well as in common acceptance of the term, is too obvious to be labored. The Company, however, turns to the Act's definition of employer, which it contends reads foremen out of the employee class and into the class of employers. Section 2(2) reads: "The term 'employer' includes any person acting in the interest of an employer, directly or indirectly...." The context of the Act, we think, leaves no room for a construction of this section to deny the organizational privilege to employees because they act in the interest of an employer. Every employee, from the very fact of employment in the master's business, is required to act in his interest. He owes to the employer faithful performance of service in his interest, the protection of the employer's property in his custody or control, and all employees may, as to third parties, act in the interests of the employer to such an extent that he is liable for their wrongful acts. A familiar example would be that of a truck driver for whose negligence the Company might have to answer.

The purpose of § 2(2) seems obviously to render employers responsible in labor practices for acts of any persons performed in their interests. It is an adaptation of the ancient maxim of the common law, *respondeat superior*, by which a principal is made liable for the tortious acts of his agent and the master for the wrongful acts of his servants. Even without special statutory provision, the rule would apply to many relations. But Congress was creating a new class of wrongful acts to be known as unfair labor practices, and it could not be certain that the courts would apply the tort rule of *respondeat superior* to those derelictions. Even if it did, the problem of proof as applied to this kind of wrongs might easily be complicated by questions as to the scope of the actor's authority and of variance between his apparent and his real authority. Hence, it was provided that in administering this act the employer, for its purposes, should be not merely the individual or corporation which was the employing entity, but also others, whether employee or not, who are "acting in the interest of an employer."

Packard v. NLRB

Even those who act for the employer in some matters, including the service of standing between management and manual labor, still have interests of their own as employees. Though the foreman is the faithful representative of the employer in maintaining a production schedule, his interest properly may be adverse to that of the employer when it comes to fixing his own wages, hours, seniority rights or working conditions. He does not lose his right to serve himself in these respects because he serves his master in others. And we see no basis in this Act whatever for holding that foremen are forbidden the protection of the Act when they take collective action to protect their collective interests.

The company's argument is really addressed to the undesirability of permitting foremen to organize. It wants selfless representatives of its interest. It fears that if foremen combine to bargain advantages for themselves, they will sometimes be governed by interests of their own or of their fellow foremen, rather than by the company's interest. There is nothing new in this argument. It is rooted in the misconception that because the employer has the right to wholehearted loyalty in the performance of the contract of employment, the employee does not have the right to protect his independent and adverse interest in the terms of the contract itself and the conditions of work. But the effect of the National Labor Relations Act is otherwise, and it is for Congress, not for us, to create exceptions or qualifications at odds with its plain terms.

Moreover, the company concedes that foremen have a right to organize. What it denies is that the statute compels it to recognize the union. In other words, it wants to be free to fight the foremen's union in the way that companies fought other unions before the Labor Act. But there is nothing in the Act which indicates that Congress intended to deny its benefits to foremen as employees, if they choose to believe that their interests as employees would be better served by organization than by individual competition.[2]

. . .

We are invited to make a lengthy examination of views expressed in Congress while this and later legislation was pending to show that exclusion of foremen was intended. There is, however, no ambiguity in this Act to be clarified by resort to legislative history, either of the Act itself or of subsequent legislative proposals which

---

2. If a union of vice presidents, presidents or others of like relationship to a corporation comes here claiming rights under this Act, it will be time enough then to point out the obvious and relevant differences between the 1100 foremen of this company and corporate officers elected by the board of directors.

failed to become law.

Counsel also would persuade us to make a contrary interpretation by citing a long record of inaction, vacillation and division of the National Labor Relations Board in applying this Act to foremen. If we were obliged to depend upon administrative interpretation for light in finding the meaning of the statute, the inconsistency of the Board's decisions would leave us in the dark.[3] But there are difficult questions of policy involved in these cases which, together with changes in Board membership, account for the contradictory views that characterize their history in the Board. Whatever special questions there are in determining the appropriate bargaining unit for foremen are for the Board, and the history of the issue in the Board shows the difficulty of the problem committed to its discretion. We are not at liberty to be governed by those policy considerations in deciding the naked question of law whether the Board is now, in this case, acting within the terms of the statute.

It is also urged upon us most seriously that unionization of foremen is from many points bad industrial policy, that it puts the union foremen in the position of serving two masters, divides his loyalty and makes generally for bad relations between management and labor. However we might appraise the force of these arguments as a policy matter, we are not authorized to base decision of a question of law upon them. They concern the wisdom of the legislation; they cannot alter the meaning of otherwise plain provisions.

The judgment of enforcement is affirmed.

Mr. Justice DOUGLAS, with whom the Chief Justice and Mr. Justice BURTON concur, dissenting.

First. Over thirty years ago Mr. Justice Brandeis, while still a private citizen, saw the need for narrowing the gap between management and labor, for allowing labor greater participation in policy decisions, for developing an industrial system in which cooperation rather than coercion was the dominant characteristic. In his view,

---

3. The Board had held that supervisory employees may organize in an independent union, *Union Collieries Coal Co,* 44 NLRB 165, and in an affiliated union, *Godchaux Sugars, Inc.,* 44 NLRB(F) 874. Then it held that there was no unit appropriate to the organization of supervisory employees. *Re. Maryland Drydock Co.,* 49 NLRB 733 (1943).... [I]n *Re. California Packing Corp.,* 66 NLRB(F) 1461, the Board re-embraced its earlier conclusions with the same progressive boldness it had shown in the *Union Collieries* and *Godchaux Sugars* cases. In none of this series of cases did the Board hold that supervisors are not employees.

Packard v. NLRB

these were measures of therapeutic value in dealing with problems of industrial unrest or inefficiency.

The present decision may be a step in that direction. It at least tends to obliterate the line between management and labor. It lends the sanctions of federal law to unionization at all levels of the industrial hierarchy. It tends to emphasize that the basic opposing forces in industry are not management and labor but the operating group, on the one hand, and the stockholder and bondholder group, on the other. The industrial problem as so defined comes down to a contest over a fair division of the gross receipts of industry between these two groups. The struggle for control or power between management and labor becomes secondary to a growing unity in their common demands on ownership.

I do not believe this is an exaggerated statement of the basic policy questions which underlie the present decision. For if foremen are "employees" within the meaning of the National Labor Relations Act, so are vice-presidents, managers, assistant managers, superintendents, assistant superintendents — indeed, all who are on the payroll of the company, including the president; all who are commonly referred to as the management, with the exception of the directors. If a union of vice-presidents applied for recognition as a collective bargaining agency, I do not see how we could deny it and yet allow the present application. But once vice-presidents, managers, superintendents, foremen all are unionized, management and labor will become more of a solid phalanx than separate factions in warring camps. Indeed, the thought of some labor leaders that if those in the hierarchy above the workers are unionized, they will be more sympathetic with the claims of those below them, is a manifestation of the same idea.

I mention these matters to indicate what tremendously important policy questions are involved in the present decision. My purpose is to suggest that if Congress, when it enacted the National Labor Relations Act, had in mind such a basic change in industrial philosophy, it would have left some clear and unmistakable trace of that purpose. But I find none.

Second. "Employee" is defined to include "any" employee. § 2(3). If we stop there, foremen are included as are all employees from the president on down. But we are not warranted in stopping there. The term "employee" must be considered in the context of the Act. When it is so considered, it does not appear to be used in an all-embracing sense. Rather, it is used in opposition to the term "employer." An employer is defined to include "any person acting in the interest of an employer." § 2(2). The term "employer" thus includes some employees. And I find no evidence that one personnel group may be both employers and employees within the meaning of the Act. Rather, the Act on its face seems to classify the operating group of industry into two classes; what is included in one group is excluded from the other.

It is not an answer to say that the two statutory groups are not exclusive because every "employee" while on duty — whether driving a truck or stoking a furnace or operating a lathe — is "acting in the interest" of his employer and is then an "employer" in the statutory sense. The Act was not declaring a policy of vicarious responsibility of industry.[a] It was dealing solely with labor relations. It put in the employer category all those who acted for management not only in formulating but also in executing its labor policies.

Foremost among the latter were foremen. Trade union history shows that foremen were the arms and legs of management in executing labor policies. In industrial conflicts they were allied with management. Management indeed commonly acted through them in the unfair labor practices which the Act condemns. When we upheld the imposition of the sanctions of the Act against management, we frequently relied on the acts of foremen through whom management expressed its hostility to trade unionism.

Third. The evil at which the Act was aimed was the failure or refusal of industry to recognize the right of workingmen to bargain collectively. In § 1 of the Act, Congress noted that such an attitude on the part of industry led "to strikes and other forms of industrial strife or unrest" so as to burden or obstruct interstate commerce. We know from the history of that decade that the frustrated efforts of workingmen, of laborers, to organize led to strikes, strife, and unrest. But we are pointed to no instances where foremen were striking; nor are we advised that managers, superintendents, or vice-presidents were doing so.

Indeed, the problems of those in the supervisory categories of management did not seem to have been in the consciousness of Congress. Section 1 of the Act refers to "wage rates," "wage earners," "workers." There is no phrase in the entire Act which is descriptive of those doing supervisory work. Section 2(3) exempts from the term "employee" any "agricultural laborer." But if "employee" includes a foreman, it would be most strange to find Congress exempting "agricultural laborer" but not "agricultural foremen." The inference is strong that since it exempted only agricultural "laborers," it had no idea that agricultural "foremen" were under the Act.

---

a. {Vicarious liability means that one person is responsible for the acts of another person. The owner of a company is vicariously liable (responsible for) the negligence of the company's truck drivers. —ed.}

Packard v. NLRB

If foremen were to be included as employees under the Act, special problems would be raised — important problems relating to the unit in which the foremen might be represented.[b] Foremen are also under the Act as employers. That dual status creates serious problems. An act of a foreman, if attributed to the management, constitutes an unfair labor practice; the same act may be part of the foreman's activity as an employee. In that event the employer can only interfere at his peril. The complications of dealing with the problems of supervisory employees strongly suggest that if Congress had planned to include them in its project, it would have made some special provision for them. But we find no trace of a suggestion that when Congress came to consider the units appropriate for collective bargaining, it was aware that groups of employees might have conflicting loyalties. Yet that would have been one of the most important and conspicuous problems if foremen were to be included. The failure of Congress to formulate a policy respecting the peculiar and special problems of foremen suggests an absence of purpose to bring them under the Act. And the notion is hard to resist that the very absence of a declaration by Congress of its policy respecting foremen is the reason the Board has been so much at large in the treatment of the problem under the Act. See the cases collected in note 3 of the opinion of the Court.

Fourth. When we turn from the Act to the legislative history, we find no trace of Congressional concern with the problems of supervisory personnel. The reports and debates are barren of any reference to them, though they are replete with references to the function of the legislation in protecting the interests of "laborers" and "workers."

Fifth. When we turn to other related legislation, we find that when Congress desired to include managerial officials or supervisory personnel in the category of employees, it did so expressly. The Railway Labor Act, § 151, defines "employee" to include "subordinate official." The Merchant Marine Act, which deals with maritime labor relations as a supplement to the National Labor Relations Act, defines "employee" to include "subordinate official." And the Social Security Act, § 1301,

---

b. {One possible problem is that, if foreones and workers were in the same bargaining unit, the foreones, because of their authority at work, would dominate the union meetings and exert a disproportionate influence on the rank-and-file members. The reverse problem is also possible: because foreones have little economic power (if they strike, they are easily replaced), they would depend heavily on support from, and therefore become beholden to, the rank-and-file. A third possible problem is that foreones, for fear of being punished by their union, would be reluctant to enforce discipline on the job against workers who were members of the same bargaining unit. — ed.}

includes an officer of a corporation in the term employee. The failure of Congress to do the same when it wrote the National Labor Relations Act has some significance, especially where the legislative history is utterly devoid of any indication that Congress was concerned with the collective bargaining problems of supervisory employees.

Sixth. The truth of the matter is, I think, that when Congress passed the National Labor Relations Act in 1935, it was legislating *against* the activities of foremen, not on their behalf. Congress was intent on protecting the right of free association — the right to bargain collectively — by the great mass of workers, not by those who were in authority over them and enforcing oppressive industrial policies. Foremen were instrumentalities of those industrial policies. They blocked the wage earners' path to fair collective bargaining. To say twelve years later that foremen were treated as the victims of that anti-labor policy seems to me a distortion of history.

If we were to decide this case on the basis of policy, much could be said to support the majority view. But I am convinced that Congress never faced those policy issues when it enacted this legislation. I am sure that those problems were not in the consciousness of Congress. A decision on these policy matters cuts deep into our industrial life. It has profound implications throughout our economy. It involves a fundamental change in much of the thinking of the nation on our industrial problems. The question is so important that I cannot believe Congress legislated unwittingly on it. Since what Congress wrote is consistent with a restriction of the Act to workingmen and laborers, I would leave its extension over supervisory employees to Congress.

. . .

What I have said does not mean that foremen have no right to organize for collective bargaining. The general law recognizes their right to do so. And some states have placed administrative machinery and sanctions behind that right. But as I read the Federal Act, Congress has not yet done so.

x   *Packard v. NLRB*

Comment

CONGRESSIONAL REACTION TO PACKARD

Congress disagreed with the Supreme Court's decision in Packard and amended the Labor Act to exclude supervisors from its protection. A brief legislative history of this amendment follows.

In 1947 Representative Hartley introduced H.R. 3020 to amend the Labor Act. As reported by the House Committee on Education and Labor, the bill, among other things, proposed adding a definition of the term "supervisor" and excluding supervisors from the definition of the term "employee." H.R. 3020, 80th Cong., 1st Sess., § 101 (§§ 2(3) and 2(12)), reprinted in National Labor Relations Board, Legislative History of the Labor Management Relations Act, 1947 (hereinafter cited as Leg. Hsty. 1947), pp. 33, 40-41. The majority of the committee endorsed this amendment in its report to the House of Representatives:

> When Congress passed the Labor Act, we were concerned, as we said in its preamble, with the welfare of "workers" and "wage earners," not of the boss. It was to protect workers and their unions against foremen, not to unionize foremen, that Congress passed the act. In few trades, and in none of the great mass-producing industries, were foremen unionized. It was not until about 7 years after Congress passed the Labor Act that anyone asked the Labor Board to establish a unit composed of supervisors. Notwithstanding that in the act Congress had defined as an "employer" "any person acting in the interest of an employer," the Board held, in the first such case, that supervisors in coal mines are "employees," and it certified as the bargaining agent of supervisors of Union Collieries Coal Co. a union that claimed to be "independent" but that turned out to be a stalking horse for the United Mine Workers of America, and that now is part of the catch-all District 50 of that union

(<u>Matter of Union Collieries Coal Company</u>, 41 NLRB 96 (1942)). A little later the Board certified as the bargaining agent of foremen of Godchaux Sugars, Inc., the union of rank and file workers whom the foremen were supposed to supervise (44 NLRB 874 (1942)).

As a result of the Board's certifying unions of foremen in the <u>Union Collieries</u> and <u>Godchaux Sugar</u> cases, there was introduced in Congress a bill taking foremen out of the Labor Act. (H.R. 2239, 78th Cong.). While the bill was pending in the Military Affairs Committee of the House, the Board, on May 10, 1943, in <u>Matter of Maryland Drydock Company</u> (49 NLRB 733), reversed itself, holding that, except in trades where foremen were organized in 1935, it would not find units of supervisors appropriate for the purposes of collective bargaining under the Wagner Act. The Military Affairs Committee then dropped H.R. 2239.

In deciding the <u>Maryland Drydock</u> case, the Board pointed out that unionizing foremen under the Labor Act would be bad for output, which the act was intended to promote, bad for the rank and file, and bad for the foremen themselves. In several cases, the Board confirmed its decision in the <u>Maryland Drydock</u> case. Then, in the <u>Matter of Packard Motor Car Company</u> (61 NLRB 4 (1945)), the Board changed its mind again, certifying as the bargaining agent of five ranks of Packard's foremen the Foremen's Association of America, which [the Board] had held [previously] it ought not to certify as the bargaining agent for foremen of General Motors, Murray Corp., and other companies. Later the Board certified a division of District 50 of the United Mine Workers of America as the bargaining agent of supervisors in the mines, and subjected them to discipline and control of the United Mine Workers and its leaders.

. . .

The evidence before the committee shows clearly that unionizing supervisors under the Labor Act is inconsistent with the purpose of the act to increase output of goods that move in the stream of commerce, and thus to increase its flow. It is inconsistent with the policy of Congress to assure to workers freedom from domination or control by their supervisors in their organizing and bargaining activities. It is inconsistent with our policy to protect the rights of employers; they, as well as workers, are entitled to loyal representatives in the plants, but when the foremen unionize, even in a union that claims to be "independent" of the union of the rank and file, they are subject to influence and control by the rank and file union, and instead of their bossing the rank and file, the rank and file bosses them. The evidence shows that rank and file unions have done much of the actual organizing of foremen, even when the foremen's union professes to be "independent." Without any question, this is why the unions seek to organize the foremen.

One of the most important items of evidence in this question came to light after the committee concluded the hearings. In November 1942, Ford Motor Co. recognized the Foreman's Association of America as the representative of several ranks of supervisors. In 1944, the Ford Co. made a full collective-bargaining agreement with the association. In testifying before our committee, the president of the association urged the relation between Ford and the association as ground for unionizing foremen. Other evidence showed, however, that after Ford recognized the association, there were more strikes and stoppages by foremen at Ford's than in any other company. Although the president of the association claimed that productivity was high in plants it had organized, we had quoted to us statements by Mr. Henry Ford II that productivity declined after the foremen organized, and this evidence was supported by evidence from other companies.

On April 8, 1947, Mr. John S. Bugos, vice president and director of industrial relations at Ford's, terminated Ford's contract with the Foreman's Association. His letter to the association constitutes the clearest evidence that supervisors are not properly subject to the Labor Act:

        . . .

        After 3 years' experience — a period which seems to us ample for a test — it is our conclusion that the results have been the opposite of what we have hoped for. Rather than exerting its efforts to draw foremen into closer relationship with the rest of management, your association has worked in the opposite direction. We feel that your association under the agreement has failed to meet the test of practice.

        As recently as last Saturday — April 5, 1947 — 33 foremen, all except 3 from the River Rouge rolling mill, walked off the job without permission, and contrary to specific instructions to remain. They stayed off the job about 2 ½ hours, attending a meeting of the association. This unauthorized absence involved grave risks to our employees in the rolling mill. The fact that no damage came to men or property was fortunate, but it is something which the absent members of your association could not guarantee.

        Efforts were made — we are glad to say unsuccessfully — to induce foremen in the open hearth department to leave their jobs at the same time. There is no need to point out the risk to men and property in leaving open hearth furnaces unattended.

Your association recently instructed its members not to comply with company requirements that they check employees under their supervision at various locations away from the job where they were felt to be loitering. Spokesmen for your association did not agree with the company as to the proper technique for handling an admittedly bad situation. It is clearly the responsibility of the company, and not of your association, to determine the procedure in such situations.

. . .

The essential characteristic of management is responsibility. It follows that the characteristic which distinguishes a foreman is a sense of responsibility. It is our observation that the activities of your association under our agreement has tended to lead our foremen away from management responsibility, and has in fact opposed efforts of the company in this direction.

. . . .

If management is to be free to manage American industry as in the past and to produce the goods on which depends our strength in war and our standard of living always, the <u>Congress must exclude foremen from the operation of the Labor Act, not only when they organize into unions of the rank and file and into unions affiliated with those of the rank, but also when they organize into unions that claim to be independent of the unions of the rank and file</u>.

The committee received in evidence about 200

letters that the Foreman's Association had exchanged with unions of the rank and file. They showed a closer and more intimate relation between the association and the unions of men the foremen supervise than one ordinarily finds between unions affiliated together in the same federation, and a subservience of the association to unions of the rank and file that is rare among unions.

The evidence shows that foremen's unions are, and must be, wholly dependent upon rank-and-file unions and under constant obligation to them. The foremen cannot strike without the support of the rank and file and its agreement not to do the work of striking foremen. The association admits that it has such an agreement with the CIO. The association has adopted a formal "policy" forbidding <u>its</u> members, when the rank-and-file unions strike, to enter the struck plants and protect and maintain them without the consent of the rank-and-file unions.

The evidence further shows that rank-and-file unions tell the foreman's union when the foremen may strike and when they may not, what duties the foremen may do and what ones they may not, what plants the foreman's union may organize and what ones it may not. It shows that rank-and-file unions have helped foremen's unions, not for the benefit of the foremen, but for the benefit of the rank and file, at the expense of the foreman's fidelity in doing his duties. The chairman of a rank-and-file pit committee summed the matter up when he said:

> Well, we are trying to get them (the supervisors) to join the union, the bosses to join the union, and then we'll be their bosses. We'll be their bosses.

That most foremen themselves see the impropriety of their unionizing, and its danger for their own status, is clear from the fact that, although the Foreman's Association of America is the largest union of foremen, only about 1 percent of the foremen have joined it.

<u>Management, like labor, must have faithful agents</u>. — If we are to produce goods competitively and in such large quantities that many can buy them at low cost, then, just as there are people on labor's side to say what workers want and have a right to expect, there must be in management and loyal to it persons not subject to influence or control of unions, not only to assign people to their work, to see that they keep at their work and do it well, to correct them when they are at fault, and to settle their complaints and grievances, but to determine how much work employees should do, what pay they should receive for it, and to carry on the whole of labor relations.

. . .

Supervisors are management people. They have distinguished themselves in their work. They have demonstrated their ability to take care of themselves without depending upon the pressure of collective action. No one forced them to become supervisors. They abandoned the "collective security" of the rank and file voluntarily because they believed the opportunities thus opened to them to be more valuable to them than such "security". It seems wrong, and it is wrong, to subject people of this kind, who have demonstrated their initiative, their ambition and their ability to get ahead, to the leveling processes of seniority, uniformity and standardization that the Supreme Court recognizes as being fundamental principles of unionism. (<u>J. I. Case Co. v. National Labor Relations Board</u>, 321 U.S. 332 (1944).) It is wrong for the foremen, for it discourages the things in them that made them foremen in the first place. For the same reason, that it discourages those best qualified to get ahead, it is wrong for industry, and particularly for the future strength and productivity of our country.

. . .

The bill does not forbid anyone to organize. It does not forbid any employer to recognize a union of foremen. Employees who, in the past, have bargained collectively with supervisors may continue to do so. What the bill does is to say what the law always has said until the Labor Board, in the exercise of what it modestly calls its "expertness," changed the law: That no one, whether employer or employee, need have as his agent one who is obligated to those on the other side, or one whom, for any reason, he does not trust.

H. Rep. 245, 80th Cong., 1st Sess., pp. 13-17, reprinted in Leg. Hsty 1947, pp. 304-308.

The minority of the committee argued against this amendment in its report to the House of Representatives:

It is estimated that there are between 4 and 5 million men and women working in supervisory jobs in this Nation's industry. The right of these employees to organize and bargain collectively in a manner which is insured to other workers will be materially impaired by the proposed bill. The recognition of the necessity for organization by workers as a means of achieving a fair share of the country's wealth is the gravamen of the National Labor Relations Act. The rejection of this principle in the case of supervisory employees can be considered only in terms of discrimination against such employees.

Supervisory employees, it is true, play a dual role in our industrial life. The fact that they are, for some purposes, the agent of management does not derogate from the companion fact that even agents have an interest to protect against their principal. The identity of supervisors with management is far from complete. Their working conditions, wages, and tenure are determined by management policy which in the absence of organization they are in an unfavorable position to oppose.

The issue of the inability of the supervisory employee, who is unionized, to discharge his functions with loyalty and competency is constantly raised. This issue may be partially met by providing that supervisors are entitled to organize and bargain collectively with their employers provided that they do not belong to the union to which the production employees of the employer belong, or to any union dominated or controlled by the union to which the production employees belong. The record of industries where the unionization of supervisors is prevalent, such as the building industry, the maritime industry, the printing industry, and the railroad industry, refute the suspicion of conflict and betrayal on the part of such supervisors. The essential loyalties required of supervisors in the effective accomplishment of their duties are no more inconsistent with their interest in the conditions of their employment than is true in the case of other employees.

Recognition by the National Labor Relations Board of the right of supervisors to organize and bargain collectively has reduced the number of strikes by this class of employee. To withdraw this recognition and with it the orderly machinery for achieving organization will not eliminate unionism among supervisors. It will force them instead to the alternative of economic self-help, and in this state of affairs there is no incentive for supervisory employees to create unions which would be truly autonomous and separated from the pressures of union groups subordinate to them in the employment structure.

H .Rep. 245, 80th Cong., 1st Sess., pp. 71-72, reprinted in <u>Leg. Hsty. 1947</u>, pp. 362-363.

A few days later, Senator Taft introduced S. 1126. This bill also proposed, among other things, to exclude supervisors from the protection of the Labor Act, though the bill included a different definition of "supervisor." S. 1126, 80th Cong., 1st Sess., §§ 2(3) and 2(11), reprinted in <u>Leg. Hsty. 1947</u>, pp. 102-103, 104.

The House passed the Representative Hartley's bill, and the Senate passed Senator Taft's bill. The two bills were referred to a conference committee, which recommended Senator Taft's proposal on supervisors. H. Rep. 510, 80th Cong., 1st Sess., p. 35, reprinted in <u>Leg. Hsty. 1947</u>, p. 539. Section 2 of the Labor Act now reads in pertinent part:

> Sec. 2. When used in this Act —
>
> . . .
>
> (3) The term "employee" ... shall not include ... any individual employed as a supervisor....

Congress also added § 2(11) to the Act. It contains a list of criteria for deciding whether a worker is a supervisor or an employee:

> The term "supervisor" means any individual having authority, in the interest of the employer, to hire, transfer, suspend, lay off, recall, promote, discharge, assign, reward, or discipline other employees, or responsibly to direct them, or to adjust their grievances, or effectively to recommend such action, if in connection with the foregoing the exercise of such authority is not of a merely routine or clerical nature, but requires the use of independent judgment.

OTHER CATEGORIES OF WORKERS

We have seen that the Labor Act does not cover all workers. In addition to supervisors, the following classes of employees are not protected by the Act:

- employees of federal, state, and local governments

- employees of railroads and airlines

- agricultural workers

- domestic servants working in their employer's home

- spouses and children of their employers.

Agricultural laborers, domestic servants, and spouses and children of their employers may be employees under other statutes. For example, they are covered by the federal Social Security System and by state workers' compensation laws.

At common law, if workers went on strike, they were no longer employees of the firm. Section 2(3) of the Labor Act changed this rule by defining "employee" to include strikers. As a result, a striker retains the protection of the Act. For example, it would be discrimination for an employer to discharge a worker because the worker is one of the leaders of the strike. But if a striker accepts in another firm a regular job that is substantially equivalent to the job the striker held in the struck firm, the striker becomes an employee of the second firm and is no longer an employee of the struck firm.

In some cases, employees who are not protected by the Labor Act are protected by other laws. Thus, the Railway Labor Act covers employees of railroads and airlines. Several states have laws that allow collective bargaining for their governmental employees. A few states have enacted statutes that allow for collective bargaining by agricultural workers.

QUESTIONS FOR REFLECTION

1. Do you think the 1947 amendments were a good idea, or was <u>Packard</u> a better rule for industrial relations?

2. The majority of the Court argued for one approach to the issue of coverage of supervisors, and Congress opted for a second approach. Justice Douglas's dissent argued for a third approach. Justice Douglas's approach has come to be known as the "labor nexus" test. Do you think the labor nexus test is a better way to deal with collective bargaining rights for supervisors?

3. On the issues of whether salts are employees under the Labor Act and, if so, whether they should be allowed to vote in representation elections, the employer's and the union's arguments are presented in neutral terms, but the arguments are motivated entirely by the interests of the parties. The employer wants to expel the traitor from the company and, if that effort is unsuccessful, at least to prevent the traitor from voting in the election; the unions wants the opposite. Should the law decide the issues according to the neutral arguments, or should the law take into account the interests of the parties?

4. The rules on the eligibility of strikers and replacements to vote in representation elections during strikes are stated in terms that are neutral with respect to how the worker is likely to vote. Thus, one rule says that temporary replacements may not vote, and no consideration seems to be given to how a temporary replacement would probably vote. Similarly, the governing criterion — that a worker may vote if one has a reasonable expectation of continued employment — also seems to be neutral as to how workers are likely to vote. But the purpose of an election held during a strike is anything but neutral. Its purpose is to decertify the

Packard v. NLRB

union. Everyone knows that strikers will probably vote in favor of the union, and that replacements will probably vote against it. Accordingly, employers want replacements to be allowed to vote and strikers to be prohibited from voting. Unions, of course, want just the opposite. Both sides will present those neutral-sounding arguments that serve the parties' interests. Knowing this, should we continue to debate the issues in terms of neutral arguments, or should we entertain arguments frankly based on the parties' interests?

5. On the issue of whether the Board should order a new election because one of the parties has distributed false propaganda, does one's position on this issue depend in any way on one's view of the average worker?

INDEPENDENT CONTRACTORS

Introduction

Workers and employers are engaged in a war of attack and counter-attack, move and counter-move, thrust and parry. It is the second longest war in history. Here is a summary of the history we have already observed:

• In the Eighteenth Century, master craftsones began to abandon custom-made goods in favor of mass-produced goods; this change was the background of the <u>Philadelphia Cordwainers</u> case. In connection with this change, the masters lowered the price they paid for each item produced by journeyones.[a]

• The journeyones responded by changing the character of their benevolent associations. These associations had previously helped members in time of need, e.g., by providing money to a member who was injured or to a member's family to pay for his funeral. The journeyones transformed these associations into proto-labor unions, and they invented the strike. The associations set the price the members would accept for the items which the members produced (in today's terms, they set the union scale), and they enforced the price scale by refusing to work for (i.e., striking) any master who employed a journeyone who was not a member of the association.

• The masters counter-attacked by accusing the journeyones of participating in a criminal conspiracy, and the courts held that strikes were illegal.

---

[a]The masters paid the workers who made the items, such as shoes, on a piece-rate system: x dollars for each pair of shoes. The workers typically owned their own tools and worked in their homes. Thus, the workers were not employees in the modern sense of the word, but were more like independent contractors.

•Workers, naturally, tried to convince the courts that strikes should not be considered criminal conspiracies, and eventually succeeded (<u>Commonwealth v. Hunt</u>).

•Strikers had always tried to protect their strikes by urging other workers not to accept employment, and customers not to buy goods, from the struck employer. As cities grew, strikers no longer knew other workers and customers personally, so the strikers had to find another way to protect their strikes. Perhaps drawing from their experience during the Civil War, they hit upon the idea of a patrol or picket line in front of the employer's business.

•For reasons we have mentioned, employers found criminal law less and less useful in combating strikes. Then it occurred to their lawyers that civil law could be pressed into use. The employers accused the workers of engaging in a civil conspiracy. Civil law allowed employers to secure injunctions against picketing (<u>Vegelahn v. Guntner</u>).

•And so workers tried another tactic — boycotts, both primary and secondary.

•Boycotts were effective, and employers needed to curtail them. Anti-trust law proved a handy tool for this purpose (the <u>Danbury Hatters</u> case and <u>Duplex v. Deering</u>).

•Employers began to do business on a national scale. One result was to drive down wages to the lowest wage that workers in any part of the country would accept; this became the national wage because any employer paying more could be undersold.

•Unions replied by trying to organize all of the firms in the same industry.

•Employers used anti-trust law to ban union organizing if the union's purpose was to protect unionized workers from competition from non-union firms (the <u>Coronado Coal</u> cases).

•Unions stepped up their organizing efforts.

•Employers fired any employee who joined a union and required new employees to promise not to join a union (yellow dog contract). Employers secured injunctions against union organizing that led workers to disregard their yellow dog contracts (<u>Hitchman Coal v. Mitchell</u>).

•Unions became large and powerful enough to influence the political process. They prevailed on Congress to pass the Erdman Act, which fostered collective bargaining on the railroads and prohibited discrimination against union members. They also prevailed on states like Kansas to outlaw yellow dog contracts (thus blocking injunctions against organizing).

•Employers persuaded the courts to hold unconstitutional both the Erdman Act and the statutes outlawing yellow dog contracts. The judges said that these laws infringed on liberty of contract and that employers had a constitutional right to refuse to hire or to fire a worker for joining a union. Employers also secured injunctions against union organizing on the ground that it interfered with their yellow dog contracts.

•Unions induced Congress to enact the Norris-LaGuardia Act, sharply limiting the use of injunctions from federal courts in labor disputes.

The National Labor Relations Act did not stop the war, though the act did channel some of the conflict into collective bargaining. The war continues today, as the student will notice as we examine cases under the Labor

Act. We cannot attend to all of the issues, but we can mention three of the more interesting new battle grounds. One is employers' increasing use of temporary employees, who do not have the right to organize and demand collective bargaining.

A second new battle ground is employers' increasing use of subcontracts with other firms. Instead of hiring janitors (or clerks or accountants, etc.), a firm (the "user firm" or "client firm") makes a contract with another firm (the "provider firm" or "supplier firm") under which the latter supplies janitors (or clerks, etc.) to former. The workers are hired, compensated, and fired by the supplier firm, and legally they are employees of the supplier. There is no doubt that the workers may organize and bargain collectively with the supplier firm, but such bargaining is often severely limited because of the contract between the supplier and the user; for instance, if the contract provides that the supplier will provide all janitorial work for a total of x dollars, the supplier will not agree to raising the workers' wages if the raise would cause the supplier's costs to exceed x dollars. For this reason, workers often seek to bargain collectively with the user firm as well. If the workers perform their duties <u>off</u> the premises of the user firm, they are employees only of the supplier and may not demand to bargain with the user. Often, however, the workers perform their duties <u>on</u> the premises of the user. If the user supervises their work, the law may consider the workers to be employees of <u>both</u> the supplier and the user. It is unclear, however, whether the Labor Act will allow workers to force two such employers to bargain jointly with the union.

A third new battle ground is firms' increasing use of subcontracts with individual workers, who are often called "contingent workers." Contingent workers are **independent contractors** in the eyes of the law. A firm[b]

---

[b]We use the term "firm" rather than "employer" because no employment relationship exists between a firm and an independent contractor; indeed, the firm's purpose in dealing with independent contractors is to avoid establishing an employment relationship. Whether the firm has achieved this purpose is often contested. Desiring the protection of the

(continued...)

has few obligations to an independent contractor other than the payment of money; for example, the firm owes no payroll taxes on independent contractors and usually provides them with no fringe benefits. Correspondingly, an independent contractor has few rights against the firm except to receive the contract price.

Most importantly for the purpose of labor law, an independent contractor is not an employee under the Labor Act. In consequence, an independent contractor is not protected against acts that would be unfair labor practices if committed against an employee (e.g., discharge for supporting a union), and an employer need not bargain collectively with an organization that represents independent contractors.[c] Accordingly, whether a worker is an employee or an independent contractor is a significant question.

Two types of issue lurk in the following case. One is an issue of law, and the other is an issue of application of law to fact. The student should identify each of these issues and keep separate in one's mind the arguments that apply to each of them.

---

[b](...continued)
law, workers often claim that, despite the firm's effort to characterize them as independent contractors, they are really employees. Thus, the issue in this sort of case is whether the firm is, or is not, the employer of the workers, and to use the term "employer" would be to prejudge the case.

[c]Several other consequences follow from being classified as an independent contractor instead of an employee. For example, an independent contractor is not covered by workers' compensation and unemployment insurance programs.

NLRB v. Hearst Publications et al.
322 U.S. 111 (1944)

Mr. Justice RUTLEDGE delivered the opinion of the Court.

These cases arise from the refusal of respondents, publishers of four Los Angeles daily newspapers, to bargain collectively with a union representing newsboys who distribute their papers on the streets of that city. Respondents' contention that they were not required to bargain because the newsboys are not their "employees" within the meaning of that term in the National Labor Relations Act, § 2(3), presents the important question which we granted *certiorari* to resolve.

The proceedings before the National Labor Relations Board were begun with the filing of four petitions for investigation and certification by Los Angeles Newsboys Local Industrial Union No. 75. Hearings were held in a consolidated proceeding after which the Board made findings of fact and concluded that the regular full-time newsboys selling each paper were employees within the Act and that questions affecting commerce concerning the representation of employees had arisen. It designated appropriate units and ordered elections. At these the union was selected as their representative by majorities of the eligible newsboys. After the union was appropriately certified, the respondents refused to bargain with it. Thereupon proceedings under § 10 were instituted, a hearing was held and respondents were found to have violated §§ 8 (1) and 8 (5) of the Act. They were ordered to cease and desist from such violations and to bargain collectively with the union upon request.

Upon respondents' petitions for review and the Board's petitions for enforcement, the Circuit Court of Appeals, one judge dissenting, set aside the Board's orders. Rejecting the Board's analysis, the court independently examined the question whether the newsboys are employees within the Act, decided that the statute imports common-law standards to determine that question, and held the newsboys are not employees. 136 F.2d 608.

...The findings of the Board disclose that the Los Angeles Times and the Los Angeles Examiner, published daily and Sunday, are morning papers. Each publishes several editions which are distributed on the streets during the evening before their dateline, between about 6:00 or 6:30 p.m. and 1:00 a.m., and other editions distributed during the following morning until about 10:00 o'clock. The Los Angeles Evening Herald and Express, published every day but Sunday, is an evening paper, which has six editions on the presses between 9:00 a.m. and 5:30 p.m. The News, also published every day but Sunday, is a twenty-four hour paper with ten editions.

The papers are distributed to the ultimate consumer through a variety of channels, including independent dealers and newsstands often attached to drug, grocery or confectionery stores, carriers who make home deliveries, and newsboys who sell on the streets of the city and its suburbs. Only the last of these are involved in this case.

The newsboys work under varying terms and conditions. They may be "bootjackers," selling to the general public at places other than established corners, or they may sell at fixed "spots." They may sell only casually or part-time, or full-time; and they may be employed regularly and continuously or only temporarily. The units which the Board determined to be appropriate are composed of those who sell full-time at established spots. Those vendors, misnamed boys, are generally mature men, dependent upon the proceeds of their sales for their sustenance, and frequently supporters of families. Working thus as news vendors on a regular basis, often for a number of years, they form a stable group with relatively little turnover, in contrast to schoolboys and others who sell as bootjackers, temporary and casual distributors.

Over-all circulation and distribution of the papers are under the general supervision of circulation managers. But for purposes of street distribution each paper has divided metropolitan Los Angeles into geographic districts. Each district is under the direct and close supervision of a district manager. His function in the mechanics of distribution is to supply the newsboys in his district with papers which he obtains from the publisher and to turn over to the publisher the receipts which he collects from their sales....

The newsboys' compensation consists in the difference between the prices at which they sell the papers and the prices they pay for them. The former are fixed by the publishers and the latter are fixed either by the publishers or, in the case of the News, by the district manager. In practice the newsboys receive their papers on credit. They pay for those sold either sometime during or after the close of their selling day, returning for credit all unsold papers. Lost or otherwise unreturned papers, however, must be paid for as though sold. Not only is the "profit" per paper thus effectively fixed by the publisher, but substantial control of the newsboys' total "take home" can be effected through the ability to designate their sales areas and the power to determine the number of papers allocated to each. While as a practical matter this power is not exercised fully, the newsboys' "right" to decide how many papers they will take is also not absolute. In practice, the Board found, they cannot determine the size of their established order without the cooperation of the district manager. And often the number of papers they must take is determined unilaterally by the district managers.

In addition to effectively fixing the compensation, respondents in a variety of ways prescribe, if not the minutiae of daily activities, at least the broad terms and conditions of work. This is accomplished largely through the supervisory efforts of the district managers, who serve as the nexus between the publishers and the

NLRB v. Hearst Publishing Co.

newsboys. The district managers assign "spots" or corners to which the newsboys are expected to confine their selling activities.[16] Transfers from one "spot" to another may be ordered by the district manager for reasons of discipline or efficiency or other cause. Transportation to the spots from the newspaper building is offered by each of respondents. Hours of work on the spots are determined not simply by the impersonal pressures of the market, but to a real extent by explicit instructions from the district managers. Adherence to the prescribed hours is observed closely by the district managers or other supervisory agents of the publishers. Sanctions, varying in severity from reprimand to dismissal, are visited on the tardy and the delinquent. By similar supervisory controls minimum standards of diligence and good conduct while at work are sought to be enforced. However wide may be the latitude for individual initiative beyond those standards, district managers' instructions in what the publishers apparently regard as helpful sales technique are expected to be followed. Such varied items as the manner of displaying the paper, of emphasizing current features and headlines, and of placing advertising placards, or the advantages of soliciting customers at specific stores or in the traffic lanes are among the subjects of this instruction. Moreover, newsboys are furnished with sales equipment, such as racks, boxes and change aprons, and advertising placards by the publishers. In this pattern of employment the Board found that the newsboys are an integral part of the publishers' distribution system and circulation organization. And the record discloses that the newsboys and checkmen feel they are employees of the papers; and respondents' supervisory employees, if not respondents themselves, regard them as such.

In addition to questioning the sufficiency of the evidence to sustain these findings, respondents point to a number of other attributes characterizing their relationship with the newsboys[17] and urge that on the entire record the latter cannot be considered their employees. They base this conclusion on the argument that by

---

[16]Although from time to time these "spots" are bought and sold among the vendors themselves, without objection by district managers and publishers, this in no way negates the need for the district managers' implicit approval of a spotholder or their authority to remove vendors from their "spots" for reasons of discipline or efficiency.

[17]E. g., that there is either no evidence in the record to show, or the record explicitly negatives, that respondents carry the newsboys on their payrolls, pay "salaries" to them, keep records of their sales or locations, or register them as "employees" with the Social Security Board, or that the newsboys are covered by workmen's compensation insurance or the California Compensation Act. Furthermore, it is urged the record shows that the newsboys all sell newspapers, periodicals and other items not furnished to them by their respective publishers, assume the risk for papers lost, stolen or destroyed, purchase and sell their "spots," hire assistants and relief men and make arrangements among themselves for the sale of competing or leftover papers.

common-law standards the extent of their control and direction of the newsboys' working activities creates no more than an "independent contractor" relationship and that common-law standards determine the "employee" relationship under the Act. They further urge that the Board's selection of a collective bargaining unit is neither appropriate nor supported by substantial evidence.

I

The principal question is whether the newsboys are "employees." Because Congress did not explicitly define the term, respondents say its meaning must be determined by reference to common-law standards. In their view "common-law standards" are those the courts have applied in distinguishing between "employees" and "independent contractors" when working out various problems unrelated to the Wagner Act's purposes and provisions.

The argument assumes that there is some simple, uniform and easily applicable test which the courts have used, in dealing with such problems, to determine whether persons doing work for others fall in one class or the other. Unfortunately this is not true. Only by a long and tortuous history was the simple formulation worked out which has been stated most frequently as "the test" for deciding whether one who hires another is responsible in tort for his wrongdoing. But this formula has been by no means exclusively controlling in the solution of other problems. And its simplicity has been illusory because it is more largely simplicity of formulation than of application. Few problems in the law have given greater variety of application and conflict in results than the cases arising in the borderland between what is clearly an employer-employee relationship and what is clearly one of independent, entrepreneurial dealing. This is true within the limited field of determining vicarious liability in tort. It becomes more so when the field is expanded to include all of the possible applications of the distinction.

It is hardly necessary to stress particular instances of these variations or to emphasize that they have arisen principally, first, in the struggle of the courts to work out common-law liabilities where the legislature has given no guides for judgment, more recently also under statutes which have posed the same problem for solution in the light of the enactment's particular terms and purposes. It is enough to point out that, with reference to an identical problem, results may be contrary over a very considerable region of doubt in applying the distinction, depending upon the state or jurisdiction where the determination is made; and that within a single jurisdiction a person who, for instance, is held to be an "independent contractor" for the purpose of imposing vicarious liability in tort may be an "employee" for the purposes of particular legislation, such as unemployment compensation. In short, the assumed simplicity and uniformity, resulting from application of "common-law standards," does not exist.

Mere reference to these possible variations as characterizing the application of the Wagner Act in the treatment of persons identically situated in the facts surrounding their employment and in the influences tending to disrupt it, would be enough to require pause before accepting a thesis which would introduce them into its administration. This would be true, even if the statute itself had indicated less clearly than it does the intent they should not apply.

Two possible consequences could follow. One would be to refer the decision of who are employees to local state law. The alternative would be to make it turn on a sort of pervading general essence distilled from state law. Congress obviously did not intend the former result. It would introduce variations into the statute's operation as wide as the differences the forty-eight states and other local jurisdictions make in applying the distinction for wholly different purposes. Persons who might be "employees" in one state would be "independent contractors" in another. They would be within or without the statute's protection depending not on whether their situation falls factually within the ambit Congress had in mind, but upon the accidents of the location of their work and the attitude of the particular local jurisdiction in casting doubtful cases one way or the other. Persons working across state lines might fall in one class or the other, possibly both, depending on whether the Board and the courts would be required to give effect to the law of one state or of the adjoining one, or to that of each in relation to the portion of the work done within its borders.

Both the terms and the purposes of the statute, as well as the legislative history, show that Congress had in mind no such patchwork plan for securing freedom of employees' organization and of collective bargaining. The Wagner Act is federal legislation, administered by a national agency, intended to solve a national problem on a national scale. It is an Act, therefore, in reference to which it is not only proper but necessary for us to assume, "in the absence of a plain indication to the contrary, that Congress ... is not making the application of the federal act dependent on state law." *Jerome v. United States*, 318 U.S. 101, 104. Nothing in the statute's background, history, terms or purposes indicates its scope is to be limited by such varying local conceptions, either statutory or judicial, or that it is to be administered in accordance with whatever different standards the respective states may see fit to adopt for the disposition of unrelated, local problems. Consequently, so far as the meaning of "employee" in this statute is concerned, "the federal law must prevail no matter what name is given to the interest or right by state law." *Morgan v. Commissioner*, 309 U.S. 78, 81.

II

Whether, given the intended national uniformity, the term "employee" includes such workers as these newsboys must be answered primarily from the history, terms and purposes of the legislation. The word "is not treated by Congress as a word of art having a definite meaning...." Rather, "it takes color from its surroundings ... [in] the statute where it appears," *United States v. American Trucking Assns.*, 310 U.S. 534, 545, and derives meaning from the context of that statute, which "must be read in the light of the mischief to be corrected and the end to be attained." *South Chicago Coal & Dock Co. v. Bassett*, 309 U.S. 251, 259.

Congress, on the one hand, was not thinking solely of the immediate technical relation of employer and employee. It had in mind at least some other persons than those standing in the proximate legal relation of employee to the particular employer involved in the labor dispute. It cannot be taken, however, that the purpose was to include all other persons who may perform service for another or was to ignore entirely legal classifications made for other purposes. Congress had in mind a wider field than the narrow technical legal relation of "master and servant," as the common law had worked this out in all its variations, and at the same time a narrower one than the entire area of rendering service to others. The question comes down therefore to how much was included of the intermediate region between what is clearly and unequivocally "employment," by any appropriate test, and what is as clearly entrepreneurial enterprise and not employment.

It will not do, for deciding this question as one of uniform national application, to import wholesale the traditional common-law conceptions or some distilled essence of their local variations as exclusively controlling limitations upon the scope of the statute's effectiveness. To do this would be merely to select some of the local, hairline variations for nation-wide application and thus to reject others for coverage under the Act. That result hardly would be consistent with the statute's broad terms and purposes.

Congress was not seeking to solve the nationally harassing problems with which the statute deals by solutions only partially effective. It rather sought to find a broad solution, one that would bring industrial peace by substituting, so far as its power could reach, the rights of workers to self-organization and collective bargaining for the industrial strife which prevails where these rights are not effectively established. Yet only partial solutions would be provided if large segments of workers about whose technical legal position such local differences exist should be wholly excluded from coverage by reason of such differences. Yet that result could not be avoided, if choice must be made among them and controlled by them in deciding who are "employees" within the Act's meaning. Enmeshed in such distinctions, the administration of the statute soon might become encumbered by the same sort of technical legal refinement as has characterized the long evolution of the employee-independent contractor dichotomy in the courts for other purposes. The consequences would be ultimately to defeat, in part at least, the achievement of the statute's objectives. Congress no more intended to import this mass of technicality as a controlling "standard" for uniform national application than to refer decision of the question outright to the local law.

The Act, as its first section states, was designed to avert the "substantial obstructions to the free flow of commerce" which result from "strikes and other forms of industrial strife or unrest" by eliminating the causes of that unrest. It is premised on explicit findings that strikes and industrial strife themselves result in large measure from the refusal of employers to bargain collectively and the inability of individual workers to bargain successfully for improvements in their "wages, hours or other working conditions" with employers who are "organized in the corporate or other forms of ownership association." Hence the avowed and interrelated purposes of the Act are to encourage collective bargaining and to remedy the individual worker's inequality of bargaining power by "protecting the exercise . . . of full freedom of association, self-organization, and designation of representatives of their own choosing, for the purpose of negotiating the terms and conditions of their employment or other mutual aid or protection." § 1.

The mischief at which the Act is aimed and the remedies it offers are not confined exclusively to "employees" within the traditional legal distinctions separating them from "independent contractors." Myriad forms of service relationship, with infinite and subtle variations in the terms of employment, blanket the nation's economy. Some are within this Act, others beyond its coverage. Large numbers will fall clearly on one side or on the other, by whatever test may be applied. But intermediate there will be many, the incidents of whose employment partake in part of the one group, in part of the other, in varying proportions of weight. And consequently the legal pendulum, for purposes of applying the statute, may swing one way or the other, depending upon the weight of this balance and its relation to the special purpose at hand.

Unless the common-law tests are to be imported and made exclusively controlling, without regard to the statute's purposes, it cannot be irrelevant that the particular workers in these cases are subject, as a matter of economic fact, to the evils the statute was designed to eradicate and that the remedies it affords are appropriate for preventing them or curing their harmful effects in the special situation. Interruption of commerce through strikes and unrest may stem as well from labor disputes between some who, for other purposes, are technically "independent contractors" and their employers as from disputes between persons who, for those purposes, are "employees" and their employers. Inequality of bargaining power in controversies over wages, hours and working conditions may as well characterize the status of the one group as of the other. The former, when acting alone, may be as "helpless in dealing with an employer," as "dependent ... on his daily wage" and as "unable to leave the employ and to resist arbitrary and unfair treatment" as the latter. For each, "union ... [may be] essential to give ... opportunity to deal on equality with their employer."[25] And for each, collective bargaining may be appropriate and effective for the "friendly adjustment of industrial disputes arising out of differences as to wages, hours, or other working conditions."[26] In short, when the particular situation of employment combines these characteristics, so that the economic facts of the relation make it more nearly one of employment than of independent business enterprise with respect to the ends sought to be accomplished by the legislation, those characteristics may outweigh technical legal classification for purposes unrelated to the statute's objectives and bring the relation within its protections.

To eliminate the causes of labor disputes and industrial strife, Congress thought it necessary to create a balance of forces in certain types of economic relationships. These do not embrace simply employment associations in which controversies could be limited to disputes over proper "physical conduct in the performance of the service."[27] On the contrary, Congress recognized those economic relationships cannot be fitted neatly into the containers designated "employee" and "employer" which an earlier law had shaped for different purposes. Its Reports on the bill disclose clearly the understanding that "employers and employees not in proximate relationship may be drawn into common controversies by economic forces,"[28] and that the very disputes sought to be avoided might involve "employees [who] are at times brought into an economic relationship with employers who are not

---

[25]*American Steel Foundries Co. v. Tri-City Council*, 257 U.S. 184, 209, cited in H. R. Rep. No. 1147, 74th Cong., 1st Sess. 10.

[26]The practice of self-organization and collective bargaining to resolve labor disputes has for some time been common among such varied types of "independent contractors" as musicians, actors, and writers, and such atypical "employees" as insurance agents, artists, architects and engineers. {Citations omitted.}

[27]Control of "physical conduct in the performance of the service" is the traditional test of the "employee relationship" at common law. Cf., e. g., Restatement of the Law of Agency § 220 (1)

[28]Sen. Rep. No. 573, 74th Cong., 1st Sess. 7.

their employers."[29] In this light, the broad language of the Act's definitions, which in terms reject conventional limitations on such conceptions as "employee," "employer," and "labor dispute," leaves no doubt that its applicability is to be determined broadly, in doubtful situations, by underlying economic facts rather than technically and exclusively by previously established legal classifications.

Hence "technical concepts pertinent to an employer's legal responsibility to third persons for acts of his servants" have been rejected in various applications of this Act both here (*International Association of Machinists v. Labor Board*, 311 U.S. 72, 80-81; *H. J. Heinz Co. v. Labor Board*, 311 U.S. 514, 520-521) and in other federal courts. There is no good reason for invoking them to restrict the scope of the term "employee" sought to be done in this case. That term, like other provisions, must be understood with reference to the purpose of the Act and the facts involved in the economic relationship. "Where all the conditions of the relation require protection, protection ought to be given."[33]

It is not necessary in this case to make a completely definitive limitation around the term "employee." That task has been assigned primarily to the agency created by Congress to administer the Act. Determination of "where all the conditions of the relation require protection" involves inquiries for the Board charged with this duty. Everyday experience in the administration of the statute gives it familiarity with the circumstances and backgrounds of employment relationships in various industries, with the abilities and needs of the workers for self-organization and collective action, and with the adaptability of collective bargaining for the peaceful settlement of their disputes with their employers. The experience thus acquired must be brought frequently to bear on the question who is an employee under the Act. Resolving that question, like determining whether unfair labor practices have been committed, "belongs to the usual administrative routine" of the Board. *Gray v. Powell*, 314 U.S. 402, 411.

In making that body's determinations as to the facts in these matters conclusive, if supported by evidence, Congress entrusted to it primarily the decision whether the evidence establishes the material facts. Hence in reviewing the Board's ultimate conclusions, it is not the court's function to substitute its own inferences of fact for the Board's, when the latter have support in the record. Undoubtedly questions of statutory interpretation, especially when arising in the first instance in judicial proceedings, are for the courts to resolve, giving appropriate weight to the judgment of those whose special duty is to administer the questioned statute. But

---

[29]Sen. Rep. No. 573, 74th Cong., 1st Sess. 6.

[33]*Lehigh Valley Coal Co. v. Yensavage*, 218 F. 547, 552 (C. C. A.).

where the question is one of specific application of a broad statutory term in a proceeding in which the agency administering the statute must determine it initially, the reviewing court's function is limited. . . . [T]the Board's determination that specified persons are "employees" under this Act is to be accepted if it has "warrant in the record" and a reasonable basis in law.

In this case the Board found that the designated newsboys work continuously and regularly, rely upon their earnings for the support of themselves and their families, and have their total wages influenced in large measure by the publishers, who dictate their buying and selling prices, fix their markets and control their supply of papers. Their hours of work and their efforts on the job are supervised and to some extent prescribed by the publishers or their agents. Much of their sales equipment and advertising materials is furnished by the publishers with the intention that it be used for the publisher's benefit. Stating that "the primary consideration in the determination of the applicability of the statutory definition is whether effectuation of the declared policy and purposes of the Act comprehend securing to the individual the rights guaranteed and protection afforded by the Act," the Board concluded that the newsboys are employees. The record sustains the Board's findings and there is ample basis in the law for its conclusion.

. . .

The judgments are reversed and the causes are remanded for further proceedings not inconsistent with this opinion.

Mr. Justice ROBERTS, dissenting.

I think the judgment of the Circuit Court of Appeals should be affirmed. The opinion of that court seems to me adequately to state the controlling facts and correctly to deal with the question of law presented for decision. I should not add anything were it not for certain arguments presented here and apparently accepted by the court.

I think it plain that newsboys are not "employees" of the respondents within the meaning and intent of the National Labor Relations Act. When Congress, in § 2 (3), said "The term 'employee' shall include any employee ...," it stated as clearly as language could do it that the provisions of the Act were to extend to those who, as a result of decades of tradition which had become part of the common understanding of our people, bear the named relationship. Clearly also Congress did not delegate to the National Labor Relations Board the function of defining the relationship of employment so as to promote what the Board understood to be the underlying purpose of the statute. The question who is an employee, so as to make the statute applicable to him, is a question of the meaning of the Act and, therefore, is a judicial and not an administrative question.

I do not think that the court below suggested that the federal courts sitting in the various states must determine whether a given person is an employee by application of either the local statutes or local state decisions. Quite the contrary. As a result of common law development, many prescriptions of federal statutes take on meaning which is uniformly ascribed to them by the federal courts, irrespective of local variance. This court has repeatedly resorted to just such considerations in defining the very term "employee" as used in other federal statutes, as the opinion of the court below shows. There is a general and prevailing rule throughout the Union as to the indicia of employment and the criteria of one's status as employee. Unquestionably it was to this common, general, and prevailing understanding that Congress referred in the statute and, according to that understanding, the facts stated in the opinion below, and in that of this court, in my judgment, demonstrate that the newsboys were not employees of the newspapers.

It is urged that the Act uses the term in some loose and unusual sense such as justifies the Board's decision because Congress added to the definition of employee above quoted these further words: "and shall not be limited to the employees of a particular employer, unless the Act explicitly states otherwise ..." The suggestion seems to be that Congress intended that the term employee should mean those who were not in fact employees, but it is perfectly evident, not only from the provisions of the Act as a whole but from the Senate Committee's Report, that this phrase was added to prevent any misconception of the provisions whereby employees were to be allowed freely to combine and to be represented in collective bargaining by the representatives of their union. Congress intended to make it clear that employee organizations did not have to be organizations of the employees of any single employer. But that qualifying phrase means no more than this and was never intended to permit the Board to designate as employees those who, in traditional understanding, have no such status.

QUESTIONS FOR REFLECTION

What was the issue of law in this case, and what was its resolution? What was the issue of application of law to fact, and what was its resolution?

Comment

In footnote 27, the Majority stated the common law standard:

> Control of "physical conduct in the performance of the service" is the traditional test of the "employee relationship" at common law.

Today this standard is more commonly called the "right of control" test. Congress believed that this standard, and not the majority's "economic realities" test, was the right one and included in the Taft-Hartley Act an amendment to overrule the decision in <u>Hearst</u>. The amendment was brief; the words emphasized in the following quotation were added to section 2(3):

> The term "employee" ... shall not include ... <u>any individual having the status of an independent contractor</u>....

The House report accompanying the Taft-Hartley amendment to section 2(3) summarized the difference between employees and independent contractors:

> "{E}mployees" work for wages or salaries under direct supervision. "Independent contractors" undertake to do a job for a price, decide how the work will be done, usually hire others to do the work, and depend for their income not upon wages but upon the difference between what they pay for goods, materials, and labor and what they receive for the end result, that is, profits.

This passage provides reasonably good guidance as to the factors that define an independent contractor; the report stresses the entrepreneurial aspects of the work. The report provides much less guidance as to the factors that define an employee; it says only that an employee works under "direct supervision." This term may be considered synonymous with the term "right to control" which is widely used today. In brief, if the firm has the power

to direct the worker as to when, where, and how to do the
job, the worker is an employee. (The power to direct
need not be exercised in a given case; it suffices that
the firm has the power to direct as to these details.)
But if the firm merely specifies the end product of the
job, leaving the worker to decide when, where, and how to
do the work, the worker is an independent contractor.

$$\Omega$$

The Duty of Fair Representation

Introduction

In all the free world except the United States and Canada, the principle of freedom of association implies that a worker is free to join the union of one's choice and to be represented by that union vis-a-vis the employer. Under this regime, which we may call "multiplicity of representation," there is little or no problem of tyranny of the majority. If the majority of a union made a decision that was unacceptable to a minority (for example, to bargain for a large increase in pension benefits instead of a raise in pay), dissatisfied individuals could leave the union and either choose another union to represent them or bargain for themselves as individuals.

In contrast, in the United States and Canada, the majority of workers in a bargaining unit decides whether to be represented by a union. If the majority rejects unionization, each worker must bargain as an individual with the employer.[a] If the majority chooses to unionize, it also decides which union will represent all of the workers.[b] Under this regime, which is called "exclusivity of representation," tyranny of the majority is a constant threat. Whatever the majority decides is binding on every individual; and as long as the majority of workers in the bargaining unit wants the union, it will represent all the workers, including the minority. The duty of fair representation has evolved as a measure of protection for minorities within unions.

As you read the following case, it will be helpful for you to be familiar with the doctrine of **exhaustion of remedies**. The doctrine requires that, before one may

---

[a]The worker may join a union, but the employer need not recognize the union as the worker's bargaining agent.

[b]The worker need not join this union, though non-members may be required to pay for the union's services. A worker who chooses not to join the union designated by the majority may join another union, but the employer may not recognize this union as the worker's bargaining agent.

file a lawsuit, one must invoke and exhaust any
administrative remedies that may exist. For example,
suppose state law provides that a student who believes
that a college has treated one unfairly may file a
complaint with the president of the college. If the
president's decision is unsatisfactory, the student may
appeal to the Intercollegiate Review Board, which sits in
panels of professors and administrators who are not
associated with the student's college. Now suppose a
student believes that her professor gave her a low grade
because she disagreed with the professor in class, and,
without going to the president of her university or the
Review Board, she sues the university. The court will
dismiss her case because she has not exhausted an
available administrative remedy. Suppose she complains
to the president of the college, who rules against her,
and then, without appealing to the Review Board, she
sues. The court will dismiss her case for the same
reason.

There is an exception to exhaustion of remedies: if
pursuing administrative remedies would plainly be futile,
one may sue in court at once. Thus, our student's
lawsuit would not be dismissed if she could convince the
court that the president of her college and the Review
Board were so prejudiced against her that they could not
render an impartial decision.

Collective bargaining agreements commonly contain
grievance procedures that end with binding arbitration.
These procedures are a species of administrative remedy.
Thus, the doctrine of exhaustion of remedies generally
precludes a union from filing an unfair labor practice
charge against an employer, or vice-versa, for breach of
a labor contract until the grievance/arbitration
procedure has been carried to completion.

It may also be helpful for you to know more than the
Court tells you about Smith v. Evening News. A newspaper
publisher had a valid collective bargaining agreement
with a union that represented a unit of building
maintenance workers. A clause in the agreement provided
that the newspaper would not discriminate against any
member of the unit because of membership in the union.
When another union went on strike against the newspaper,
the maintenance workers were willing to cross the picket
line and continue working; but the newspaper locked them

out. However, the newspaper did not lock out non-union employees. Smith, a maintenance worker, sued the newspaper for breach of contract, arguing the newspaper had violated the non-discrimination clause of the agreement. The newspaper moved to dismiss the suit on the ground that the federal courts lacked jurisdiction, but the Supreme Court held that § 301 of the Labor Act allows federal courts to hear cases brought by individual workers to vindicate their rights under a collective agreement. Exhaustion of remedies did not apply to the Smith case because the agreement did not contain a grievance/arbitration procedure.

As in Hearst, the Court in the following case resolves two different types of issue, an issue of law and an issue of application of law to fact. The student should identify each of these issues and separate in one's mind the arguments that apply to each of them.

Vaca v. Sipes
386 U.S. 171 (1967)

Mr. Justice WHITE delivered the opinion of the Court.

On February 13, 1962, Benjamin Owens filed this class action against petitioners as officers and representatives of the National Brotherhood of Packinghouse Workers and of its Kansas City Local No. 12 (the Union) [including the president of Local 12, Vaca], in the Circuit Court of Jackson County, Missouri. Owens, a Union member, alleged that he had been discharged from his employment at Swift & Company's (Swift) Kansas City Meat Packing Plant in violation of the collective bargaining agreement then in force between Swift and the Union, and that the Union had "arbitrarily, capriciously and without just or reasonable reason or cause" refused to take his grievance with Swift to arbitration under the fifth step of the bargaining agreement's grievance procedures.

... After a jury trial, a verdict was returned awarding Owens $7,000 compensatory and $3,300 punitive damages. The trial judge set aside the verdict and entered judgment for [the unions].... The Supreme Court of Missouri reversed and directed reinstatement of the jury's verdict. During the appeal, Owens died and respondent [Sipes], the administrator of Owens' estate, was substituted. We granted certiorari to consider whether the finding of Union liability and the relief afforded Owens are consistent with governing principles of federal labor law. ...[W]e conclude ... the governing federal standards were not applied here, and that the judgment of the Supreme Court of Missouri must accordingly be reversed.

In mid-1959, Owens, a long-time high blood pressure patient, became sick and entered a hospital on sick leave from his employment with Swift. After a long rest during which his weight and blood pressure were reduced, Owens was certified by his family physician as fit to resume his heavy work in the packing plant. However, Swift's company doctor examined Owens upon his return and concluded that his blood pressure was too high to permit reinstatement. After securing a second authorization from another outside doctor, Owens returned to the plant, and a nurse permitted him to resume work on January 6, 1960. However, on January 8, when the [Company] doctor discovered Owens' return, he was permanently discharged on the ground of poor health.

Armed with his medical evidence of fitness, Owens then sought the Union's help in securing reinstatement, and a grievance was filed with Swift on his behalf. By mid-November 1960, the grievance had been processed through the third and into the fourth step of the grievance procedure established by the collective bargaining agreement.[c] Swift adhered to its position that Owens' poor health justified his discharge, rejecting numerous medical reports of reduced blood pressure proffered by Owens and by the Union. Swift claimed that these reports were not based upon sufficiently thorough medical tests.

On February 6, 1961, the Union sent Owens to a new doctor at Union expense "to see if we could get some better medical evidence so that we could go to arbitration with his case." This examination did not support Owens' position. When the Union received the report, its executive board voted not to take the Owens grievance to arbitration because of insufficient medical evidence. Union officers suggested to Owens that he accept Swift's offer of referral to a rehabilitation center, and the grievance was suspended for that purpose. Owens rejected this alternative and demanded that the Union take his grievance to arbitration, but the Union refused. With his contractual remedies thus stalled at the fourth step, Owens brought this suit. The grievance was finally dismissed by the Union and Swift shortly before trial began in June 1964.

In his charge to the jury, the trial judge instructed that petitioners would be liable if Swift had wrongfully discharged Owens and if the Union had "arbitrarily ... and without just cause or excuse ... refused" to press Owens' grievance to arbitration. Punitive damages could also be awarded, the trial judge charged, if the Union's conduct was "willful, wanton and malicious." However, the jury must return a verdict for the defendants, the judge instructed, "if you find and believe from the evidence that the union and its representatives acted reasonably and in good faith in the handling and processing of the grievance of the plaintiff." The jury then returned the general verdict for Owens which eventually was reinstated by the Missouri Supreme Court.

It is now well established that, as the exclusive bargaining representative of the employees in Owens' bargaining unit, the Union had a statutory duty fairly to represent all of those employees, both in its collective bargaining with Swift and in its enforcement of the resulting collective bargaining agreement. The statutory duty of fair representation was developed over 20 years ago in a series of cases involving

---

[c]The agreement created a five-step procedure for the handling of grievances. In steps one and two, either the aggrieved employee or the Union's representative presents the grievance first to Swift's department foreman, and then in writing to the division superintendent. In step three, grievance committees of the Union and management meet, and the company must state its position in writing to the Union. Step four is a meeting between Swift's general superintendent and representatives of the National Union. If the grievance is not settled in the fourth step, the National Union is given power to refer the grievance to a specified arbitrator.

alleged racial discrimination by unions certified as exclusive bargaining representatives under the Railway Labor Act, and was soon extended to unions certified under the N.L.R.A. Under this doctrine, the exclusive agent's statutory authority to represent all members of a designated unit includes a statutory obligation to serve the interests of all members without hostility or discrimination toward any, to exercise its discretion with complete good faith and honesty, and to avoid arbitrary conduct. It is obvious that Owens' complaint alleged a breach by the Union of a duty grounded in federal statutes, and that federal law therefore governs his cause of action....

... For the fact is that the question of whether a union has breached its duty of fair representation will in many cases be a critical issue in a suit under § 301 charging an employer with a breach of contract. To illustrate, let us assume a collective bargaining agreement that limits discharges to those for good cause and that contains no grievance, arbitration or other provisions purporting to restrict access to the courts. If an employee is discharged without cause, either the union or the employee may sue the employer under § 301. Under this section, courts have jurisdiction over suits to enforce collective bargaining agreements even though the conduct of the employer which is challenged as a breach of contract is also arguably an unfair labor practice within the jurisdiction of the NLRB. *Smith v. Evening News Assn.*, 371 U.S. 195....

However, if the wrongfully discharged employee himself resorts to the courts before the grievance procedures have been fully exhausted, the employer may well defend on the ground that the exclusive remedies provided by such a contract have not been exhausted. Since the employee's claim is based upon breach of the collective bargaining agreement, he is bound by terms of that agreement which govern the manner in which contractual rights may be enforced. For this reason, it is settled that the employee must at least attempt to exhaust exclusive grievance and arbitration procedures established by the bargaining agreement. However, because these contractual remedies have been devised, and are often controlled, by the union and the employer, they may well prove unsatisfactory or unworkable for the individual grievant. The problem then is to determine under what circumstances the individual employee may obtain judicial review of his breach-of-contract claim despite his failure to secure relief through the contractual remedial procedures.

An obvious situation in which the employee should not be limited to the exclusive remedial procedures established by the contract occurs when the conduct of the employer amounts to a repudiation of those contractual procedures. In such a situation (and there may, of course, be others), the employer is estopped by his own conduct to rely on the unexhausted grievance and arbitration procedures as a defense to the employee's cause of action.

We think that another situation when the employee may seek judicial enforcement of his contractual rights arises if, as is true here, the union has sole power under the contract to invoke the higher stages of the grievance procedure, and if, as is alleged here, the employee-plaintiff has been prevented from exhausting his contractual remedies by the union's wrongful refusal to process the grievance. It is true that the employer in such a situation may have done nothing to prevent exhaustion of the exclusive contractual remedies to which he agreed in the collective bargaining agreement. But the employer has committed a wrongful discharge in breach of that agreement, a breach which could be remedied through the grievance process to the employee-plaintiff's benefit were it not for the union's breach of its statutory duty of fair representation to the employee. To leave the employee remediless in such circumstances would, in our opinion, be a great injustice. We cannot believe that Congress, in conferring upon employers and unions the power to establish exclusive grievance procedures, intended to confer upon unions such unlimited discretion to deprive injured employees of all remedies for breach of contract. Nor do we think that Congress intended to shield employers from the natural consequences of their breaches of bargaining agreements by wrongful union conduct in the enforcement of such agreements.

...

A breach of the statutory duty of fair representation occurs only when a union's conduct toward a member of the collective bargaining unit is arbitrary, discriminatory, or in bad faith. There has been considerable debate over the extent of this duty in the context of a union's enforcement of the grievance and arbitration procedures in a collective bargaining agreement. Some have suggested that every individual employee should have the right to have his grievance taken to arbitration. Others have urged that the union be given substantial discretion (if the collective bargaining agreement so provides) to decide whether a grievance should be taken to arbitration, subject only to the duty to refrain from patently wrongful conduct such as racial discrimination or personal hostility.

Though we accept the proposition that a union may not arbitrarily ignore a meritorious grievance or process it in perfunctory fashion, we do not agree that the individual employee has an absolute right to have his grievance taken to arbitration regardless of the provisions of the applicable collective bargaining agreement. In § 203 (d), Congress declared, "Final adjustment by a method agreed upon by the parties is ... the desirable method for settlement of grievance disputes arising over the application or interpretation of an existing collective-bargaining agreement." In providing for a grievance and arbitration procedure which gives the union discretion to supervise the grievance machinery and to invoke arbitration, the employer and the union contemplate that each will endeavor in good faith to settle grievances short of arbitration. Through this settlement process, frivolous grievances are ended prior to the most costly and time-consuming step in the grievance procedures. Moreover, both sides are assured that similar complaints will be treated consistently, and major problem areas in the interpretation of the collective bargaining contract can be isolated and perhaps resolved. And finally, the settlement process furthers the interest of the union as statutory agent and as coauthor of the bargaining agreement in representing the employees in the enforcement of that agreement.

If the individual employee could compel arbitration of his grievance regardless of its merit, the settlement machinery provided by the contract would be substantially undermined, thus destroying the employer's confidence in the union's authority and returning the individual grievant to the vagaries of independent and unsystematic negotiation. Moreover, under such a rule, a significantly greater number of grievances would proceed to arbitration. This would greatly increase the cost of the grievance machinery and could so overburden the arbitration process as to prevent it from functioning successfully. It can well be doubted whether the parties to collective bargaining agreements would long continue to provide for detailed grievance and arbitration procedures of the kind encouraged by § 203(d) if their power to settle the majority of grievances short of the costlier and more time-consuming steps was limited by a rule permitting the grievant unilaterally to invoke arbitration. Nor do we see substantial danger to the interests of the individual employee if his statutory agent is given the contractual power honestly and in good faith to settle grievances short of arbitration. For these reasons, we conclude that a union does not breach its duty of fair representation, and thereby open up a suit by the employee for breach of contract, merely because it settled the grievance short of arbitration.

...

Applying the proper standard of union liability to the facts of this case, we cannot uphold the jury's award, for we conclude that as a matter of federal law the evidence does not support a verdict that the Union breached its duty of fair representation. As we have stated, Owens could not have established a breach of that duty merely by convincing the jury that he was in fact fit for work in 1960; he must also have proved arbitrary or bad-faith conduct on the part of the Union in processing his grievance. The evidence revealed that the Union diligently supervised the grievance into the fourth step of the bargaining agreement's procedure, with the Union's business representative serving as Owens' advocate throughout these steps. When Swift refused to reinstate Owens on the basis of his medical reports indicating reduced blood pressure, the Union sent him to another doctor of his own choice, at Union expense, in an attempt to amass persuasive medical evidence of Owens' fitness for work. When this examination proved unfavorable, the Union concluded that it could not establish a wrongful discharge. It then encouraged Swift to find light work for Owens at the plant. When this effort failed, the Union determined that arbitration would be fruitless and suggested to Owens that he accept Swift's offer to send him to a heart association for rehabilitation. At this point, Owens' grievance was suspended in the fourth step in the hope that he might be rehabilitated.

In administering the grievance and arbitration machinery as statutory agent of the employees, a union must, in good faith and in a nonarbitrary manner, make decisions as to the merits of particular grievances. In a case such as this, when Owens supplied the Union with medical evidence supporting his position, the Union might well have breached its duty had it ignored Owens' complaint or had it processed the grievance in a perfunctory manner. But here the Union processed the grievance into the fourth step, attempted to gather sufficient evidence to prove Owens' case, attempted to secure for Owens less vigorous work at the plant, and joined in the employer's efforts to have Owens rehabilitated. Only when these efforts all proved unsuccessful did the Union conclude both that arbitration would be fruitless and that the grievance should be dismissed. There was no evidence that any Union officer was personally hostile to Owens or that the Union acted at any time other than in good faith. Having concluded that the individual employee has no absolute right to have his grievance arbitrated under the collective bargaining agreement at issue, and that a breach of the duty of fair representation is not established merely by proof that the underlying grievance was meritorious, we must conclude that that duty was not breached here.

Mr. Justice BLACK, dissenting.

The Court today opens slightly the courthouse door to an employee's incidental claim against his union for breach of its duty of fair representation, only to shut it in his face when he seeks direct judicial relief for his underlying and more valuable breach-of-contract claim against his employer. This result follows from the Court's announcement in this case, involving an employee's suit against his union, of a new rule to govern an employee's suit against his employer. The rule is that before an employee can sue his employer under § 301 of the [Labor Act] for a simple breach of his employment contract, the employee must prove not only that he attempted to exhaust his contractual remedies, but that his attempt to exhaust them was frustrated by "arbitrary, discriminatory, or ... bad faith" conduct on the part of his union. With this new rule and its result I cannot agree.

... {Justice Black criticized the majority's holding that a worker like Mr. Owens may sue one's employer for breach of the collective bargaining agreement only if the worker succeeds in proving that the union breached its duty of fair representation in dealing with the worker's claim. As a result of this holding, even if the employer infringed on the worker's right by breaching the collective agreement, the worker's suit against the employer must be dismissed if the union observed its duty of fair representation. Justice Black contended that whether the employer breached the contract was not in any way related to whether the union satisfied the duty of fair representation.}

... Today the Court holds that an employee with a meritorious claim has no absolute right to have it either litigated or arbitrated. Fearing that arbitrators would be overworked, the Court allows unions unilaterally to determine not to take a grievance to arbitration—the first step in the contract grievance procedure at which the claim would be presented to an impartial third party—as long as the union decisions are neither "arbitrary" nor "in bad faith." The Court derives this standard of conduct from a long line of cases holding that "[a] breach of the statutory duty of fair representation occurs only when a union's conduct toward a member of the collective bargaining unit is arbitrary, discriminatory, or in bad faith." What the Court overlooks is that those cases laid down this standard in the context of situations where the employee's sole or fundamental complaint was against the union. There was not the slightest hint in those cases that the same standard would apply where the employee's primary complaint was against his employer for breach of contract and where he only incidentally contended that the union's conduct prevented the adjudication, by either court or arbitrator, of the underlying grievance. If the Court here were satisfied with merely holding that in this situation the employee could not recover damages from the union unless the union breached its duty of fair representation, then it would be one thing to say that the union did not do so in making a good-faith decision not to take the employee's grievance to arbitration. But if, as the Court goes on to hold, the employee cannot sue his employer for breach of contract unless his failure to exhaust contractual remedies is due to the union's breach of its duty of fair representation, then I am quite unwilling to say that the union's refusal to exhaust such remedies—however nonarbitrary—does not amount to a breach of its duty. Either the employee should be able to sue his employer for breach of contract after having attempted to exhaust his contractual remedies, or the union should have an absolute duty to exhaust contractual remedies on his behalf. The merits of an employee's grievance would thus be determined by either a jury or an arbitrator. Under today's decision it will never be determined by either.

And it should be clear that the Court's opinion goes much further than simply holding that an employee has no absolute right to have the union take his grievance to arbitration. Here, of course, the union supervised the grievance into the fourth step of the contract machinery and dropped it just prior to arbitration on its belief that the outcome of arbitration would be unfavorable. But limited only by the standard of arbitrariness, there was clearly no need for the union to go that far. Suppose, for instance, the union had a rule that it would not prosecute a grievance even to the first step unless the grievance were filed by the employee within 24 hours after it arose. Pursuant to this rule, the union might completely refuse to prosecute a grievance filed several days late. Thus, the employee, no matter how meritorious his grievance, would get absolutely nowhere. And unless he could prove that the union's rule was arbitrary (a standard which no one can define), the employee would get absolutely no consideration of the merits of his grievance—either by a jury, an arbitrator, the employer, or by the union. The Court suggests three reasons for giving the union this almost unlimited discretion to deprive injured employees of all remedies for breach of contract. The first is that "frivolous grievances" will be ended prior to time-consuming and costly arbitration. But here no one, not even the union, suggests that Benjamin Owens' grievance was frivolous. The union decided not to take it to arbitration simply because the union doubted the chance of success. Even if this was a good-faith doubt, I think the union had the duty to present this contested, but serious, claim to the arbitrator whose very function is to decide such claims on the basis of what he believes to be right. Second, the Court says that allowing the union to settle grievances prior to arbitration will assure consistent treatment of "major problem areas in the interpretation of the collective bargaining contract." But can it be argued that whether Owens was "fit to work" presents a major problem in the interpretation of the collective bargaining agreement? The problem here was one of interpreting medical reports, not a collective bargaining agreement, and of evaluating other evidence of Owens' physical condition. I doubt whether consistency is either possible or desirable in determining whether a particular employee is able to perform a particular job. Finally, the Court suggests that its decision "furthers the interest of the union as statutory agent." I think this is the real reason for today's decision, which entirely overlooks the interests of the injured employee, the only one who has anything to lose. Of course, anything which gives the union life and death power over those whom it is supposed to represent furthers its "interest." I simply fail to see how the union's legitimate role as statutory agent is undermined by requiring it to prosecute all serious grievances to a conclusion or by allowing the injured employee to sue his employer after he has given the union a chance to act on his behalf.

Henceforth, in almost every § 301 breach-of-contract suit by an employee against an employer, the employee will have the additional burden of proving that the union acted arbitrarily or in bad faith. The Court never explains what is meant by this vague phrase or how trial judges are intelligently to translate it to a jury. ... {T}oday's decision, requiring the individual employee to take on both the employer and the union in every suit against the employer and to prove not only that the employer breached its contract, but that the union acted arbitrarily, converts what would otherwise be a simple breach-of-contract action into a three-ring donnybrook. It puts an intolerable burden on employees with meritorious grievances and means they will frequently be left with no remedy. Today's decision, while giving the worker an ephemeral right to sue his union for breach of its duty of fair

xii   *Vaca v. Sipes*

representation, creates insurmountable obstacles to block his far more valuable right to sue his employer for breach of the collective bargaining agreement.

Comment

A worker who believes the duty of fair representation has been violated can pursue either of two remedies. One remedy is to file a lawsuit against the union. If the employer is involved in the dispute, the worker may also sue the employer. For example, suppose Akiko is fired for insubordination; she claims she was fired because she rebuffed her supervisor's sexual advances. She files a grievance, but it cannot be settled. The question then becomes whether the union should take the case to arbitration. The grievance committee votes to drop the matter. The committee says its reason is that it believes an arbitrator would deny the grievance; Akiko believes the true reason is bad blood between her and some members of the committee. Thus, she believes that the employer violated the contract by firing her without just cause and that the union breached the duty of fair representation by refusing to arbitrate the matter. One remedy she has is to sue them both in court. The other remedy is to file a charge against the union with the Labor Board. This is possible because the Board has held that a union's breach of the duty of fair representation is an unfair labor practice. A Labor Board charge could not be filed against the employer in a case like this, however, because a breach of contract is usually not an unfair labor practice.

Which is the better remedy for the worker? Three considerations apply. First, the worker who goes to the Labor Board incurs no cost because the government pays for the investigation and trial, whereas the worker who hires an attorney to file a private lawsuit is likely to incur substantial costs. Second, the Labor Board usually will not act against an employer in a fair representation case. Third, if the employer is not a party to the case, the only relief the worker can get is from the union. Therefore, if the union is at fault and it can provide adequate relief to the worker, a charge filed with the Labor Board might be sufficient. For example, suppose a woman believes that she is not getting jobs through the union's hiring hall because of her gender. If so, the union could provide complete relief: it could compensate her for money she lost from jobs to which she was not referred, and it could refer her fairly in the future. But if the employer has also acted wrongfully, only a lawsuit can provide complete relief. If Akiko wishes to be reinstated to her job, she must go to court and sue both the union and the employer.

QUESTIONS FOR REFLECTION

1. What was the issue of law in <u>Vaca</u>, and what was its resolution? What was the issue of application of law to fact, and what was its resolution?

2. The Court creates the impression that the outcome of the case was dictated by the legal doctrine of exhaustion of remedies. Do you agree? What argument could one make that Owens did exhaust his remedies and, therefore, was free to sue in court?

3. Were Justice Black's criticisms well taken? In particular, were his criticisms of the majority's three reasons convincing? (See the penultimate paragraph of his opinion.)

Ω

Concerted Activity

Introduction

The heart of the Labor Act is section 7. The central idea of section 7 is to give workers the legal right to negotiate with their employer as a group instead of as individuals. Congress created this right because individuals have little bargaining power when they deal with employers, particularly large corporations. The result of this lack of power is that workers can be forced to accept low wages and poor working conditions. But if workers can band together and, as a group — usually, through a union — negotiate with their employer, they have a better chance to achieve a living wage and decent working conditions.

To reach these goals, section 7 guarantees employees the right to engage in **concerted activity**, which means the right to act together to improve their working lives. The right to concerted activity includes the rights to assist and to join labor unions. Employers are forbidden to interfere with these activities. For example, it would be an unfair labor practice for an employer to fire a worker for going to talking to a union representative.

Congress recognized that some workers prefer not to engage in concerted activity. Therefore, section 7 also guarantees employees the right to refrain from assisting and joining unions. Unions and employers are forbidden to interfere with this right as well (except to the extent that union security is lawful). For example, it would be an unfair labor practice for a union to threaten to use violence against a worker who refused to support the union in a representation election.

Now let us take a closer look at section 7. It states:

> "Employees shall have the right to self-organization, to form, join, or assist labor organizations, to bargain collectively through representatives of their own choosing, and to engage in other concerted activities for the purpose of collective bargaining or other mutual aid or protection, and shall also have the right to

Jefferson Standard

refrain from any or all of such activities...."

The several rights protected by section 7 are commonly referred to collectively as the "right to concerted activity."[a] <u>Only workers who are engaged in concerted activity are protected by the Labor Act</u>.

Concerted activity has two separate elements. The first element is that the workers' activity must be **concerted**. This element has two parts. (1) The workers' act must be the joint or mutual effort of at least two workers (or of one worker on behalf of others), and (2) the act must pertain to the terms or conditions of employment. (1) Thus, an individual worker, acting in one's own behalf, is not engaged in concerted activity and is, therefore, not protected by § 7. For example, if Juanita asks her employer for a raise, and is fired because she asks, she will find no relief in the Labor Act. But two or more workers acting together are protected. If Juanita and Zbigniew together ask their employer for a raise, or if Juanita asks on behalf of herself and Zbigniew, and either is disadvantaged because of the request, the employer has committed an unfair labor practice. (2) It is also necessary that the workers' joint or mutual act pertain to the terms of their employment. If Juanita and Zbigniew together ask their employer to donate the firm's profits to the Nature Conservancy, and they are fired because they asked, they will get sympathy but not action from the Labor Board.

The examples in the preceding paragraph illustrate the truism that the end points of a continuum are often agreed upon easily. The dividing line is often more controversial. The Supreme Court's decision in <u>NLRB v. Washington Aluminum</u>, 370 U.S. 9 (1962) provides some help in drawing the line. It was an extraordinarily cold day in Baltimore, and the furnace in the shop failed to

---

[a] A more complete term would be the "the right to <u>protected</u> concerted activity" because, as explained in the text below, some activity is concerted but not protected. When one is focusing on whether an act is concerted (as we are now), one tends to speak of the right to concerted activity. When one is focusing on whether a concerted act is protected, one tends to speak of the right to protected activity.

start. The workers, who were not represented by a union, stood around in their jackets for a while, grumbling as you might expect, and then several of them decided it was too cold to work and they left. They were discharged for leaving work without permission. The Labor Board held the discharges were illegal because the workers were engaged in concerted activity. The Supreme Court agreed. The workers were engaged in a joint effort, and their focus was one of the conditions of employment. It was irrelevant that no union was present, desired, or even contemplated. The Act seeks to promote collective bargaining, which requires a union; but it is not unusual for workers, with no thought of unionizing in mind, to begin a process that eventually leads to unionization. It was also irrelevant that the workers never presented a specific demand to their employer. Their behavior may have been rash and unwise, but the Labor Act does not require workers to conform to judges' notions of reasonable behavior. And it was irrelevant that the workers broke a rule (left work without permission) because the rule, as applied in this context, was illegal. No employer may have a rule against workers' engaging in concerted activity, else every employer would have a rule against joining a union or going on strike.

The second element of concerted activity is that the workers' activity must be **protected**, that is, within the scope of the protection of section 7. It is obvious that Congress did not intend for section 7 to protect all kinds of joint or mutual activity that pertains to employment. If two workers get angry and beat their foreone with their fists, or steal tools, or bomb the factory, they may be acting in concert concerning the terms of their employment, but they are not protected by the Act. Which concerted acts are protected, and which are not, is the subject of the Jefferson Standard case.

It may be helpful for the student to know more about some of the cases to which the majority and dissenting opinions allude. In NLRB v. Peter Cailler Kohler Swiss Chocolate, the company used milk in making chocolate candy. The company bought the milk at a favorable price from a farmers' cooperative named the Dairymen's League. In 1939 a rival farmers' cooperative, the Dairy Farmers' Union, organized a "milk holiday" or "milk strike," in which it sought to increase the price of milk by withholding it from the market. The League opposed the milk holiday and wished to defeat it by making up for the milk withheld by the Dairy Farmers' Union; the company aided the League by releasing it from its obligation to supply milk for chocolate so the League could send more milk to market. In 1940 the Dairy Farmers' Union proposed another milk holiday. At the instigation of an employee of the company, the labor union that represented the company's workers passed and publicized a resolution supporting the Dairy Farmers' Union. The company fired the instigator. When charged with an unfair labor practice, the company argued that the resolution was not protected concerted activity because it did not deal with the terms and conditions of employment; but the Board and Court of Appeals held the resolution was protected.

In Hoover Co., the employer and Local 709 of the Electrical Workers signed a series of collective bargaining agreements before 1948; but, when the one ending in 1948 expired, the parties could not agree on a new contract. On April 28, 1948 the employer withdrew recognition of Local 709 on the ground that it no longer represented a majority of the workers.[b] For the purpose of regaining recognition, Local 709 called a strike on June 10th and began a consumer boycott of the employer's products on July 13th. On July 20th, Local 709 voted to abandon the strike — but not the boycott — and most of the strikers returned to work. The employer, however, refused to reinstate the members of Local 709's executive committee because of the boycott. The employer was charged with an unfair labor practice for refusing to reinstate the members of the executive board. The central issue was whether the consumer boycott was protected concerted activity. The Board held that the boycott was concerted activity and that the employer was guilty of an unfair labor practice. Meanwhile, as the strike and boycott were in progress, a rival union was trying to win the support of the workers. On July 13th the rival union filed a petition with the Board, requesting certification as the exclusive bargaining agent. (Although the fact is not relevant to the outcome of the case, the rival union won the election.)

---

[b]If Local 709 in fact no longer represented a majority of the workers, the employer was permitted — indeed, required — to cease bargaining with the local.

In <u>NLRB v. Fansteel</u>, 306 U.S. 240 (1939), workers staged a sit-down strike, that is, they occupied the plant (thus they committed trespass) and refused to leave, even after the employer secured an injunction (thus they committed contempt of court). The employer fired the leaders of the strike. The Labor Board ordered their reinstatement, finding they were engaged in protected activity because they had been provoked into the sit-down strike by the employer's severe and repeated unfair labor practices. The Supreme Court, however, held that the strikers' conduct was not protected by § 7. In <u>NLRB v. Southern Steamship</u>, 316 U.S. 31 (1942), sailors called a strike while on board a ship, which was tantamount to a mutiny. The Supreme Court held their conduct was not protected by § 7. In <u>American News Co.</u>, 55 NLRB 1302 (1944), workers struck for a raise in pay that would have violated federal wage and price controls during World War II, and they were discharged. The Board held their strike was not protected by § 7.

As you read <u>Jefferson Standard</u>, in addition to reflecting on whether the majority of the Board, the dissent, or Justice Burton presented the best arguments, try to determine exactly what took the workers' conduct outside the protection of the Act.

⚜

Jefferson Standard Broadcasting Company
94 NLRB 1507 (1951)

...

On September 3, 1949, Respondent [Jefferson Standard] discharged 10 of its technical employees for having published and distributed the so-called "second-class" handbill, set forth {below in n. 9}, in the course of peaceful picketing sponsored by the Union which was otherwise concededly lawful and protected under the Act. The Trial Examiner found that by this action Respondent violated Section 8(a)(1) and (3) of the Act because, he concluded, the handbill to which the Company took exception was a protected ... concerted activity. The question before us is whether this conclusion rests upon a proper construction of Section 7 of the Act. That section guarantees to employees the right to engage in "concerted activities for the purpose of collective bargaining or other mutual aid or protection." However, as this Board and the courts have long held, it does not embrace concerted activity undertaken for an unlawful objective, or protect employees against discharge for resorting to "indefensible" means (such as sit-down strikes, sabotage, "violence or similar conduct") in pursuit of their collective ends, however lawful.

The facts essential to an appraisal of the objectives sought by the employees in this case, and the means they adopted, are as follows:

The Union, which had represented the technical employees at the Company's radio transmitters for several years, began negotiations for a new contract in or before January 1949, and on May 9, 1949, was certified by the Board as the statutory representative of the employees in the bargaining unit. Early in July, the Union and the Company reached an impasse and suspended negotiations because of their inability to agree upon a provision covering arbitration of disputes over the discharge of employees for "cause." On or about July 9, the Union commenced picketing Respondent's downtown place of business in Charlotte, without calling a strike. By placards and handbills, the pickets appealed to the public, in the name of the Union, to support the employees' stand in the labor dispute. This pressure evidently proved unavailing, for within a few weeks after the Company had placed its newly installed television broadcast facilities into operation, the Union resolved to get "tough," and published the "second-class" handbill which provoked the discharges.

The thesis of this handbill, which the Union distributed during a 10-day period beginning on August 24, was that Respondent was mulcting the public by furnishing technically inadequate, "second-class," television service.[9] Its text made no reference

---

[9]The text of the handbill was:

(continued...)

to the labor dispute which had occasioned the picketing. It was distributed widely throughout the business section of Charlotte, not only at the picket line, but elsewhere, in places such as busses, barber shops and restaurants. Although drafted and approved by the Union's officers and executive committee, the handbill did not bear the Union's name, but was signed simply "WBT TECHNICIANS." It occasioned widespread comment in the community, and caused Respondent to apprehend a loss of advertising revenue due to dissatisfaction with its television broadcasting service.

In short, the employees in this case deliberately undertook to alienate their employer's customers by impugning the technical quality of his product. As the Trial Examiner found, they did not misrepresent, at least wilfully, the facts they cited to support their disparaging report. And their ultimate purpose — to extract a concession from the employer with respect to the terms of their employment — was lawful. That purpose, however, was undisclosed; the employees purported to speak as experts, in the interest of consumers and the public at large. They did not indicate that they sought to secure any benefit for themselves, *as employees*, by casting discredit upon their employer.

In our judgment, these tactics, in the circumstances of this case, were hardly less "indefensible" than acts of physical sabotage. The Board has held, and we reaffirm, that the Act protects employees against employer reprisal when they speak freely "on organizational matters" (to borrow the Trial Examiner's expression), and in one way or another denounce their employer for his conduct of labor relations or affairs germane to the employment relationship. Moreover, employees acting in

---

[9](...continued)

Is Charlotte a Second-Class City?

You might think so from the kind of Television programs being presented by the Jefferson Standard Broadcasting Co. over WBTV. Have you seen one of their television programs lately? Did you know that all the programs presented over WBTV are on film and may be from one day to five years old? There are no local programs presented by WBTV. You cannot receive the local baseball games, football games or other local events because WBTV does not have the proper equipment to make these pickups. Cities like New York, Boston, Philadelphia, Washington receive such programs nightly. Why doesn't the Jefferson Standard Broadcasting Company purchase the needed equipment to bring you the same type of programs enjoyed by other leading American cities? Could it be that they consider Charlotte a second-class community and only entitled to the pictures now being presented to them?

concert may exhort consumers to refrain from purchasing their employer's product unless and until he alters his labor policy or practices. But this is a different case. Here, the subject matter of the employees' verbal attack upon the employer was not related to their interests *as employees*. And the gist of their appeal to the public was that the employer ought to be boycotted because he offered a shoddy product to the consuming public — not because he was "unfair" to the employees who worked on that product. Even in the *Peter Cailler Kohler Swiss Chocolate* case, upon which our dissenting colleague relies, the employees' broadside, superficially unrelated as it was to any labor dispute or matter pertaining to the employer's labor relations,[16] did not go so far as to suggest that consumers ought to avoid the employer's product because it was of inferior quality.[17]

For these reasons, without attempting to formulate a test which will decide every imaginable case involving similar questions as to the scope of Section 7, we hold that the employees in this case went beyond the pale when they published the "second-class" handbill.[18] We shall therefore dismiss the complaint insofar as it alleges that the Respondent violated Section 8(a)(1) and (3) of the Act by discharging those individuals who were actually implicated in the publication and distribution of that leaflet.

...

Member MURDOCK, dissenting in part:

I cannot agree with the conclusion of my colleagues of the majority that the Respondent did not commit an unfair labor practice violative of Section 8 (a) (1) and (3) of the Act when it discharged a group of employees for publication and

---

[16] 130 F. 2d 503 (C.A.2). However, the publication in that case was signed in the name of the employees' labor organization....

[17] We subscribe, of course, to the general philosophy expounded by the Court in construing and applying Section 7 in that case. But we think that Judge Learned Hand's eloquent passage, wrested from its context, does not call for literal reading here.

[18] ...

We also do not decide whether the disparagement of product involved here would have justified the employer in discharging the employees responsible for it, had it been uttered in the context of a conventional appeal for support of the union in the labor dispute.

distribution of the "second-class city" handbill....

Before discussing the issue in detail, I would note at the outset that the holding of the majority that the distribution of the "second-class city" handbill is one of the most important decisions dealing with that subject which the Board has ever issued. It should be recognized as a decision of far-reaching significance. I find it a startling decision — startling because it necessarily sets aside principles which this Board with court sanction has heretofore recognized as the proper test of protected concerted activity; startling because it has shriveled the previously recognized area of statutory protection for concerted activities and left employers, employees, and the Board itself without any certain standards to mark the remaining greatly circumscribed area.

First, what are the facts? What were the contents of the handbill, the circulation of which my colleagues find was "hardly less 'indefensible' than acts of physical sabotage"? It reads thus: [The text of the handbill appears in note 9 in the majority's opinion.] It is not denied by my majority colleagues that the facts recited in the handbill with reference to the Respondent's TV programs were substantially accurate and that those who drafted and distributed it on the picket line and elsewhere believed it to be true. It is not denied that the handbill was in fact one more union weapon (specifically so recognized by the Employer although not bearing the union name) designed to exert additional pressure upon the Employer to accept the Union's position in the pending labor dispute. This was a dispute concerning a new contract which had deadlocked over the inclusion in the contract of an arbitration provision in connection with discharges. It is not denied that the handbill did not incite or seek any violation of any law — it incited no more than a public demand for better television programs.

Inescapably we are confronted in this case with concerted and union activity for the mutual aid and protection of the technicians — activity in aid of a collective bargaining dispute with Respondent. What is the proper principle or test applicable to determine whether such presumptively protected activity nevertheless falls into one of the categories of exceptions which must be denied the protection of Section 7 of the Act? In the recent *Hoover Company* case, 90 NLRB 1614, the Board reviewed the authorities and restated the applicable principles. After referring to previously recognized exceptions, such as violent picketing, sit-down strikes, strikes against Board certifications, etc., the Board said:

> Nonetheless, it is clear that in engrafting these exceptions upon the broad language of Section 7, *the Board and the courts have been particularly careful to limit such exceptions to those instances in which the means employed involved violence or similar conduct, or*

where the objectives sought were inconsistent with the terms or the clearly enunciated policy of this act or other Federal statutes. As we have had occasion to observe in the past, in light of the history of judicial treatment of labor relations which preceded the enactment of Section 7, "it seems most improbable that Congress intended to vest this Board, or the courts in reviewing our action, with any broad discretion to determine what we or the courts might choose to consider the proper objectives of concerted activity." We are free—indeed we are compelled — to examine the objectives of concerted activity to determine whether they are independently unlawful or inconsistent with the basic policy of this Act or of other pertinent Federal statutes. *We are not free, however, to measure concerted activity in terms of whether the conduct is wise or fair, or satisfies standards which we think desirable.*

In the instant case the Respondent's argument rests wholly upon the proposition that the conduct of a consumer boycott by employees while they continue to work and receive wages from the boycotted employer is unjust and disloyal. This may well be true, as it is true, to be sure, in certain other individual instances where employees strike, picket, or engage in other forms of concerted activity. *But absent any showing that the means employed were other than peaceful or that the objectives sought were as have been held for reasons of clear public policy to be improper, we find no authority to regard the concerted activity involved herein as unprotected.* [Emphasis supplied.]

One of the main authorities relied upon by the Board in its statement of principles in the *Hoover* case was the decision of the Second Circuit Court of Appeals in the *Peter Cailler Kohler* case, 130 F. 2d 503. In an opinion by Judge Learned Hand, now widely acclaimed on his impending retirement as the foremost American jurist, that court, in language peculiarly appropriate to the facts in this case, stated the applicable rule as follows:

We agree that the act does not excuse *"concerted activities,"* themselves independently unlawful. But so long as the *"activity"* is not unlawful, we can see no justification for making it the occasion for a discharge; a union may subsidize propaganda, distribute broadsides, support political movements, and in any other way further its cause or that of others whom it wishes to win to its side. *Such activities may be highly prejudicial to its employer;* his customers may refuse to deal with him, he may incur the enmity of many in the community whose disfavor will bear hard upon him; *but the statute forbids him by a discharge to rid himself of those who lay such burdens upon him.* Congress has weighed the conflict of his interest with theirs, and has pro tanto shorn him of his powers.... [Emphasis supplied.]

It is thus clear from these decisions that concerted activity such as is here involved loses its protection only if it is "unlawful." It may be "unlawful" in the sense that the *means* used is independently unlawful. Examples of this are violence and sit-down strikes of the character involved in the *Fansteel* case, 306 U.S. 240, as well as that in the *Southern Steamship* case, 316 U.S. 31, the latter involving a violation of the Federal Mutiny Act. Even where the *means* is entirely peaceful and not independently unlawful, however, an unlawful *objective* will destroy the protection which would otherwise exist. The classic example of this second type of unlawfulness is the *American News* case, 55 NLRB 1302, involving a strike to compel an employer to violate the Wage Stabilization Act.

Applying these established principles to the facts in this case, it is plain that none of the elements necessary to cause a loss of the protection accorded concerted activity is here present. There was nothing unlawful about the means used — the distribution of handbills containing substantially truthful statements — one of the most traditional and peaceful forms of union activity in a labor dispute. There was nothing unlawful about the objective of the handbills, either from the standpoint of the likely immediate consequences of the distribution or from the standpoint of the ultimate action sought to be obtained thereby from the Employer. From the standpoint of ultimate objective, the handbill was an additional pressure technique to force the Employer to agree to an arbitration clause in a contract — a provision which the Employer clearly might accept without violating any law. The likely immediate consequences of the distribution insofar as the impact of the handbill on the public was concerned would be the stimulation of a public demand for better TV programs. Surely there is nothing unlawful or contrary to public policy in that objective.

My colleagues of the majority have meticulously avoided any discussion of the *tests* for protected concerted activity which have been laid down in the Board's *Hoover* case and the court's *Peter Cailler Kohler* decision and the result of the application of such tests to the facts of this case. In a footnote, after a passing tribute to the general philosophy expounded by the court and to Judge Hand's "eloquent passage," the majority simply brushes off the carefully phrased test laid down in the court's opinion, saying that it "does not call for literal reading here." They fail to indicate how else it can be read, or how they would read it. At the same time they specifically disavow any attempt to formulate a new standard by which to determine when protection is lost and rest their decision simply on their conclusion that the employees here went "beyond the pale." In adopting such an approach, it seems to me they are flying in the face of the limitation on our authority so recently acknowledged by the Board in the *Hoover* decision, in which it said: "We are not free, however, to measure concerted activity in terms of whether the conduct is wise or fair, or satisfies standards which we think desirable."

To the extent that it is possible to distill some limited test or standard for loss of protection from the majority decision, it would appear to stand at least for this proposition: Where concerted activity is undertaken by employees "to alienate their employer's customers by impugning the technical quality of his product," it is unprotected. Yet in a footnote which apparently has reference to the previously recited facts that "the handbill did not bear the union's name," and its text "made no reference to the labor dispute," the majority say that they do not decide whether the disparagement of product here involved would have justified a discharge if "it had been uttered in the context of a conventional appeal for support of the union in the labor dispute." Surely the protection accorded to concerted activity by the statute cannot be made to depend upon such technicalities as the format of handbills — the presence or absence at the end of such magic phrase as "Support the XYZ union in its current labor dispute with this employer!" Furthermore, I am unable to see how the mere presence of a labor dispute and the failure of the handbill to make any specific reference to it or to the union could operate to make unlawful what I consider would be protected concerted activity even if there were no union and no labor dispute in the picture. If employees under the latter circumstance concertedly decided to enlighten the public on such a matter, perhaps feeling that the public would favorably remember them when they might need help in a labor dispute with their employer, there being nothing unlawful about such conduct, it would not lose its protection as concerted activity. I am not aware that the Board has ever held that the area of protection accorded "concerted activity" of employees is any less than accorded union activity.

Even if the Board is to ignore the test of unlawfulness as the proper basis for determining loss of protection, I find it an anomaly that the majority could regard the kind of concerted activity here involved as "beyond the pale," while the kind of concerted activity involved in the *Hoover* and *Peter Cailler Kohler* cases is deemed to be within the pale and entitled to protection. In the *Hoover* case the Board held in part that a union's consumer boycott conducted in conjunction with a strike, the objective of which was to compel recognition, was a protected activity even though recognition might have resulted in a *MidWest Piping* violation of the Act by the employer.[1] Beyond that the Board held that employees were engaged in a concerted activity protected from discharge in carrying on a consumer boycott of the employer's products for a different objective after abandonment of the strike and while continuing to work.[b] Stated bluntly, the *Hoover* decision means that this Board sees nothing "beyond the pale" in employees insisting on the right to be paid to make products which they are simultaneously trying to make it impossible to sell. Yet how relatively inconsequential was any actual damage to the employer from the concerted activity involved in the instant case? These employees did no more than to point out to the public what in large measure it already knew — that the Employer's TV programs consisted largely of canned film of varying degrees of antiquity with no live local talent as in other cities; and to incite a demand for better programs and the equipment which would make them possible. Unlike the activity held protected in the *Hoover* case, this handbill did not and could not result in any present financial loss to the Respondent.[38] True, the handbill might be embarrassing to the Respondent

---

[1]{*Midwest Piping*, 63 NLRB 1060 (1945), made it an unfair labor practice for an employer to recognize one of two or more unions that are competing to represent a bargaining unit if a representation petition has previously been filed with the Board. In *Hoover* the purpose of the boycott when it was started was to force the employer to recognize Local 709; because a rival union had filed a petition for certification, the employer might have violated the *Midwest Piping* doctrine by recognizing Local 709. Murdock's point is that, if this boycott was protected concerted activity, the WBT's technicians' handbill was also protected.

{The *Midwest Piping* doctrine was not well received by the courts of appeal and was vitiated by a series of Board decisions beginning in 1982. — ed.}

[b]{The Board found that the purpose of the boycott changed after the strikers returned to work. The purpose was no longer to gain recognition, but to force the employer to reinstate the members of the executive board. — ed.}

[38]As the majority opinion indicates, the Respondent only "apprehended" the remote contingency of an inability to increase its revenues by charging higher advertising rates in the future based upon the presence of a larger number of TV sets in the area, if the handbill should discourage people who did not then own TV sets from buying them.

I should make clear that in making this comparison with the *Hoover* case I do not mean to suggest that I believe that the question of economic loss to the employer is determinative of whether concerted activity is protected or unprotected. All strikes and many forms of concerted activity necessarily result in financial loss to an employer. Yet as Judge Hand states in the *Peter Cailler Kohler* decision, the fact that the activity is "highly prejudicial" to the employer and causes him to "incur the

(continued...)

and might require it to explain its inability to present better programs or even provoke a decision to purchase equipment to televise some live local sporting events, etc. But is the right to engage in concerted activities conferred by the statute to be made so ephemeral as to be forfeited simply because the activities are embarrassing to the employer?

It should also be noted that the concerted activity held to be protected in the *Peter Cailler Kohler* case did not even occur in the course of a labor dispute between the employer and his employees as did the activity in the instant case. The employer there had acted contrary to the interests of certain dairy farmer producers (not employees) who were conducting a milk "strike," by purchasing and processing milk, not for its own manufacturing operations, but for delivery to the metropolitan market. The Kohler employees gratuitously injected themselves into this picture in which their own interests were not affected, by passing and publishing a union resolution which lambasted their employer's actions. The resolution charged the employer with having "aided and abetted" the forces who were using "every vile and vicious means" to stop the dairy farmers in the current milk "strike"; it protested the employer's action and expressed the union's support of the dairy farmers. The court upheld the Board in finding such concerted activity to be protected from discharge even though undertaken in behalf of farmer producers and not for the immediate benefit of the union members who passed the resolution.[39] If, as the Board and court held, employees who have no dispute with their own employer over wages, hours or working conditions, are entitled to be protected from discharge in lambasting their employer in this fashion in the context of the *Kohler* case, I can see no logical basis for concluding that the employees in the instant case are "beyond the pale" by reason

---

[38](...continued)
enmity of many in the community" and his customers "to refuse to deal with him" does not give the employer the right to discharge those "who lay such burdens upon him." I am suggesting, however, that if the Board approaches the issue of protection from the standpoint whether the activity is to be deemed "beyond the pale," certainly the extent of the actual injury the employer suffers is a factor to be considered in weighing his right to extinguish his employee's right to engage in concerted activity; and the Board should not incongruously hold peaceful concerted activity which results in no substantial damage to the employer unprotected, as it is doing here, while holding seriously prejudicial activity of the type involved in the *Hoover* case to be protected.

[39]The theory on this aspect of the case was that the Kohler Company employees could give support to the farmers in the belief or hope that the farmers might reciprocate if at sometime in the future a dispute arose between the Kohler Company and its employees.

of the temperate and truthful criticism of their employer made in a handbill in the course of a labor dispute in which they are seeking a concession in the form of an arbitration clause in a contract. To characterize this conduct as "hardly less `indefensible' than acts of physical sabotage," as my majority colleagues do, is to draw a patently farfetched and unwarranted analogy.

I am greatly disturbed by the impact this decision of the Board will have in analogous situations. Suppose some employees in a defense plant manufacturing war material, knowing some to be defective (as has sometimes actually happened in the past) decide to write a letter to the defense procurement agency involved or to a newspaper, pointing out the existence of defects. The employer discharges them for disparaging his product. Consistent with today's decision this Board would have to find that the concerted activity was not protected because the employees impugned the technical quality of the employer's product. A shrinking of the scope of the statutory protection afforded concerted activity to exclude the area excepted by today's decision — in effect muzzling employees who would speak out on matters of general public concern, whether they be the character of TV programs or defective war materials — in my view is not consistent either with the statute or with any salutary public policy.

★ ★ ★ ★

The union appealed the Board's decision to the Court of Appeals for the District of Columbia, which remanded the case to the Board to consider further whether the technicians' behavior contravened federal or local law or the basic policies of the Labor Act. Instead of reconsidering its decision, the Board secured a writ of <u>certiorari</u> from the Supreme Court. Here follows an excerpt from the opinion of Justice Burton.

★ ★ ★ ★

NLRB v. Local Union No. 1229, IBEW (Jefferson Standard)
346 U.S. 464, 471-477 (1953)

From the opinion of Justice BURTON.

In its essence, the issue is simple. It is whether these employees, whose contracts of employment had expired, were discharged "for cause." They were discharged solely because, at a critical time in the initiation of the company's television service, they sponsored or distributed 5,000 handbills making a sharp, public, disparaging attack upon the quality of the company's product and its business policies, in a manner reasonably calculated to harm the company's reputation and reduce its income. The attack was made by them expressly as "WBT TECHNICIANS." It continued ten days without indication of abatement. The Board found that —

> It [the handbill] occasioned widespread comment in the community, and caused Respondent to apprehend a loss of advertising revenue due to dissatisfaction with its television broadcasting service.

> In short, the employees in this case deliberately undertook to alienate their employer's customers by impugning the technical quality of his product. As the Trial Examiner found, they did not misrepresent, at least wilfully, the facts they cited to support their disparaging report. And their ultimate purpose — to extract a concession from the employer with respect to the terms of their employment — was lawful. That purpose, however, was undisclosed; the employees purported to speak as experts, in the interest of consumers and the public at large. They did not indicate that they sought to secure any benefit for themselves, as employees, by casting discredit upon their employer. 94 NLRB at 1511.

The company's letter shows that it interpreted the handbill as a demonstration of such detrimental disloyalty as to provide "cause" for its refusal to continue in its employ the perpetrators of the attack. We agree.

Section 10 (c) of the Taft-Hartley Act expressly provides, "No order of the Board shall require the reinstatement of any individual as an employee who has been suspended or discharged, or the payment to him of any back pay, if such individual was suspended or discharged for cause." There is no more elemental cause for discharge of an employee than disloyalty to his employer. It is equally elemental that the Taft-Hartley Act seeks to strengthen, rather than to weaken, that cooperation, continuity of service and cordial contractual relation between employer and employee that is born of loyalty to their common enterprise.

Congress, while safeguarding in § 7 the right of employees to engage in "concerted activities for the purpose of collective bargaining or other mutual aid or protection," did not weaken the underlying contractual bonds and loyalties of employer and employee. The conference report that led to the enactment of the law said:

> [T]he courts have firmly established the rule that under the existing provisions of section 7 of the National Labor Relations Act,

employees are not given any right to engage in unlawful or other improper conduct. . . .

. . .

... Furthermore, in section 10 (c) of the amended act, as proposed in the conference agreement, it is specifically provided that no order of the Board shall require the reinstatement of any individual or the payment to him of any back pay if such individual was suspended or discharged for cause, and this, of course, applies with equal force whether or not the acts constituting the cause for discharge were committed in connection with a concerted activity." H.R. Rep. No. 510, 80th Cong., 1st Sess. 38-39.

This has been clear since the early days of the Wagner Act. In 1937, Chief Justice Hughes, writing for the Court, said:

The Act does not interfere with the normal exercise of the right of the employer to select its employees or to discharge them. The employer may not, under cover of that right, intimidate or coerce its employees with respect to their self-organization and representation, and, on the other hand, the Board is not entitled to make its authority a pretext for interference with the right of discharge when that right is exercised for other reasons than such intimidation and coercion." *Labor Board v. Jones & Laughlin*, 301 U.S. 1, 45-46.

Many cases reaching their final disposition in the Courts of Appeals furnish examples emphasizing the importance of enforcing industrial plant discipline and of maintaining loyalty as well as the rights of concerted activities. The courts have refused to reinstate employees discharged for "cause" consisting of insubordination, disobedience or disloyalty....

The [Court of Appeals] cases illustrate the responsibility that falls upon the Board to find the facts material to such decisions. The legal principle that insubordination, disobedience or disloyalty is adequate cause for discharge is plain enough. The difficulty arises in determining whether, in fact, the discharges are made because of such a separable cause or because of some other concerted activities engaged in for the purpose of collective bargaining or other mutual aid or protection which may not be adequate cause for discharge.

In the instant case the Board found that the company's discharge of the nine offenders resulted from their sponsoring and distributing the "Second-Class City" handbills of August 24-September 3, issued in their name as the "WBT TECHNICIANS." Assuming that there had been no pending labor controversy, the conduct of the "WBT TECHNICIANS" from August 24 through September 3 unquestionably would have provided adequate cause for their disciplinary discharge within the meaning of § 10 (c). Their attack related itself to no labor practice of the company. It made no reference to wages, hours or working conditions. The policies attacked were those of finance and public relations for which management, not technicians, must be responsible. The attack asked for no public sympathy or support. It was a continuing attack, initiated while off duty, upon the very interests which the attackers were being paid to conserve and develop. Nothing could be further from the purpose of the Act than to require an employer to finance such activities. Nothing would contribute less to the Act's declared purpose of promoting industrial peace and stability.

The fortuity of the coexistence of a labor dispute affords these technicians no substantial defense. While they were also union men and leaders in the labor controversy, they took pains to separate those categories. In contrast to their claims on the picket line as to the labor controversy, their handbill of August 24 omitted all reference to it. The handbill diverted attention from the labor controversy. It attacked public policies of the company which had no discernible relation to that controversy. The only connection between the handbill and the labor controversy was an ultimate and undisclosed purpose or motive on the part of some of the sponsors that, by the hoped-for financial pressure, the attack might extract from the company some future concession. A disclosure of that motive might have lost more public support for the employees than it would have gained, for it would have given the handbill more the character of coercion than of collective bargaining. Referring to the attack, the Board said, "In our judgment, these tactics, in the circumstances of this case, were hardly less 'indefensible' than acts of physical sabotage." 94 NLRB at 1511. In any event, the findings of the Board effectively separate the attack from the labor controversy and treat it solely as one made by the company's technical experts upon the quality of the company's product. As such, it was as adequate a cause for the discharge of its sponsors as if the labor controversy had not been pending. The technicians, themselves, so handled their attack as thus to bring their discharge under § 10 (c).

The Board stated, "We ... do not decide whether the disparagement of product involved here would have justified the employer in discharging the employees responsible for it, had it been uttered in the context of a conventional appeal for support of the union in the labor dispute." *Id.* at 1512, n. 18. This underscored the Board's factual conclusion that the attack of August 24 was not part of an appeal for support in the pending dispute. It was a concerted separable attack purporting to be made in the interest of the public rather than in that of the employees.

QUESTIONS FOR REFLECTION

If workers have a duty of loyalty to their employer, should an employer have a duty of loyalty to one's workers? If so, what should the content of the employer's duty be, and how should it be enforced? What should the relief be for an employer's violation of the duty?

Ω

Discrimination

THE DEFINITION OF DISCRIMINATION

Introduction

The Labor Act makes it an unfair labor practice for an employer to discriminate against a worker because of union activity. Section 8(a)(3) reads:

Sec. 8. (a) It shall be an unfair labor practice for an employer —

(3) by discrimination in regard to hire or tenure of employment or any term or condition of employer to encourage or discourage membership in any labor organization ....

The words "membership in any labor organization" have been construed broadly to include virtually all of the concerted activity that is protected by section 7, including, e.g., discussing terms of employment with a co-worker, attempting to organize a union, and processing grievances under a labor contract.

The act also makes it an unfair labor practice for a union to cause an employer to discriminate against a worker. Section 8(b)(2) reads:

Sec. 8. (b) It shall be an unfair labor practice for a labor organization or its agents —

(2) to cause or attempt to cause an employer to discriminate against an employee in violation of subsection 8(a)(3)....

Like many concepts in the law, discrimination is similar to our everyday ideas. Until about 1970, "to discriminate" meant intentionally to disadvantage someone for an improper reason. For example, if two students submit papers of equal quality, and one receives an A because the writer is friendly with the grader while the other paper receives a C because the writer is on bad terms with the grader, we would say that the grader discriminates against the student who receives the C. This idea of discrimination was incorporated into section

8(a)(3) of the Labor Act.[a]

    Discrimination under the Labor Act has two elements (in other words, in order to establish discrimination, the General Counsel must prove): (1) the employer disadvantaged a worker in the terms and conditions of employment, and (2) the employer's conscious reason was the worker's concerted activity. As a rule, both of these elements must be satisfied. Thus, many acts by an employer are harmful to a worker — layoff, denial (or imposition) of overtime, and discharge, to name a few. Yet these acts are not discriminatory unless the motive behind them is improper. It is not an unfair labor practice for an employer to lay off a worker because business is bad, but it is illegal to lay off a worker because one has been agitating for a union. Similarly, it is not an unfair labor practice for a union to insist that Jonathan be laid off instead of Harriet because she has more seniority, but it would be illegal if the union did so because Jonathan refused to join the union.

    The following case is about discrimination. It is somewhat unusual, but representative nonetheless.

⚜

---

    [a]Since 1970, another definition of discrimination has evolved. Under this definition, which is often called "disparate impact," to discriminate means to disadvantage someone without good reason. Unlike the older definition, disparate impact does not require that the actor be aware of having an improper reason. Disparate impact has not been incorporated into the Labor Act.

Edward G. Budd Mfg. Co. v. National Labor Relations Board
138 F.2d 86 (3d Cir. 1943)

BIGGS, Circuit Judge.

{The United Auto Workers (referred to below as "the CIO union") filed charges against the employer, the Budd Mfg. Co. (the petitioner), and the Labor Board issued a complaint.} The complaint, as subsequently amended, alleges that the petitioner, in September, 1933, created and foisted a labor organization, known as the Budd Employee Representation Association, upon its employees and thereafter contributed financial support to the Association and dominated its activities. The amended complaint also alleges that in July, 1941, the petitioner discharged an employee, Walter Weigand, because of his activities on behalf of the union.... The petitioner denies these charges.... After extensive hearings before a trial examiner, the Board on June 10, 1942 issued its decision and order, requiring the disestablishment of the Association and the reinstatement of Weigand....

{The court reviewed the evidence sustaining the Board's finding that the employer illegally dominated the Association.}

Another indication of the dependent nature of the Association should be referred to. We think it is symptomatic. The petitioner treated the employee representatives with extraordinary lenience. The testimony shows to what very great lengths the employer went in its parental treatment of the Association and its officers. The petitioner permitted the employee representatives to conduct themselves about as they wished. They left the plant at will whether on personal business or on the business of the Association. Some of them did very little or no work, but they received full pay. It is clear that some of them, Walter Weigand for example, [deserved discipline but] were not disciplined because they were representatives. We can scarcely believe that the petitioner would have displayed such an attitude toward officers of an undominated "adversary" labor organization.

In our opinion the decision of the Board to the effect that the Association was and is subject to the petitioner's domination and control is amply supported by the evidence.

The case of Walter Weigand is extraordinary. If ever a workman deserved summary discharge, it was he. He was under the influence of liquor while on duty. He came to work when he chose, and he left the plant and his shift as he pleased. In fact, a foreman on one occasion was agreeably surprised to find Weigand at work and commented upon it. Weigand amiably stated that he was enjoying it.[6] He brought

---

[6]Weigand stated that he was carried on the payroll as a "rigger". He was asked

(continued...)

a woman (apparently generally known as the "Duchess") to the rear of the plant yard and introduced some of the employees to her. He took another employee to visit her and, when this man got too drunk to be able to go home, punched his time-card for him and put him on the table in the representatives' meeting room in the plant in order to sleep off his intoxication. Weigand's immediate superiors demanded again and again that he be discharged, but each time higher officials intervened in Weigand's behalf because, as was naively stated, he was "a representative." In return for not working at the job for which he was hired, the petitioner gave him full pay and on five separate occasions raised his wages. One of these raises was general; that is to say, Weigand profited by a general wage increase throughout the plant, but the other four raises were given Weigand at times when other employees in the plant did not receive wage increases.

The petitioner contends that Weigand was discharged because of cumulative grievances against him. But about the time of the discharge it was suspected by some of the representatives that Weigand had joined the complaining CIO union. One of the representatives taxed him with this fact, and Weigand offered to bet a hundred dollars that it could not be proved. On July 22, 1941 Weigand did disclose his union membership to the vice-chairman (Rattigan) of the Association and to another representative (Mullen) and apparently tried to persuade them to support the union. Weigand asserts that the next day he, with Rattigan and Mullen, were seen talking to CIO organizer Reichwein on a street corner. The following day, according to Weigand's testimony, Mullen came to Weigand at the plant and stated that Weigand, Rattigan and himself had been seen talking to Reichwein and that he, Mullen, had just had an interview with Personnel Director McIlvain and Plant Manager Mahan. According to Weigand, Mullen said to him, "Maybe you didn't get me in a jam." And, "We were seen down there." The following day Weigand was discharged.

As this court [has] stated, an employer may discharge an employee for a good reason, a poor reason or no reason at all so long as the provisions of the National Labor Relations Act are not violated. It is, of course, a violation to discharge an employee because he has engaged in activities on behalf of a union. Conversely, an employer may retain an employee for a good reason, a bad reason or no reason at all, and the reason is not a concern of the Board. But it is certainly too great a strain on our credulity to assert, as does the petitioner, that Weigand was discharged for an accumulation of offenses. We think that he was discharged because his work on behalf of the CIO had become known to the plant manager. That ended his sinecure at the Budd plant. The Board found that he was discharged because of his activities on behalf of the union. The record shows that the Board's finding was based on

---

[6](...continued)
what was a rigger. He replied: "I don't know; I am not a rigger."

sufficient evidence.

The order of the Board will be enforced.

⚜

QUESTIONS FOR REFLECTION

1. Would it have been an unfair labor practice for the employer to have favored Weigand if no union were on the scene and the boss just liked him? Why or why not?

2. Would it have been an unfair labor practice if the boss stopped liking Weigand and withdrew his benefits? Why or why not?

3. If Weigand was not entitled to the benefits he received, why was it illegal for the employer to withdraw those benefits?

4. Suppose Weigand's supervisor had two reasons for discharging Weigand. One reason was lawful (Weigand was the worst employee ever) and one reason was unlawful (Weigand became affiliated with the CIO). How should the law treat a case of "mixed motive"?

Ω

Replacement of Strikers

THE POLICY

Introduction

Over the years, several efforts have been made in Congress to overrule the *dictum* in *Mackay Radio* and prohibit employers from hiring permanent replacements for strikers. The efforts were increased after the Supreme Court's decision in *Trans World Airlines v. Independent Federation of Flight Attendants,* 489 U.S. 426 (1989), which allowed employers to treat **crossovers** as though they were permanent replacements.[a] In *TWA*, the contract between the employer and the union allowed workers to bid for job assignments, flight schedules, etc. on the basis of seniority; more senior workers were, as usual, the best protected against layoffs. The union struck after the contract expired. During the strike, the employer allowed permanent replacements and crossovers to choose jobs, flights, etc. according to the seniority provisions of the expired contract. When the strike ended, the employer refused to displace crossovers from the jobs for which they had successfully bid during the strike, with the result that many senior strikers were bumped by crossovers with less seniority. The Supreme Court held that the employer's policy was lawful under the Railway Labor Act. Because the Court discussed and rejected the union's argument that the policy would have been unlawful under the National Labor Relations Act (once again, the Supreme Court decided a question regarding the re-employment rights of strikers in *dictum*), it appears that employers under the latter statute may also treat crossovers as though they were permanent replacements.

The Cesar Chavez Workplace Fairness Act, H.R. 5, passed the House of Representatives, but not the Senate, during the 103d Congress (1993-1994). The bill would

---

[a]A crossover is a worker who is employed by a firm when a strike against the firm begins and who joins the strike for a while but returns to work ("crosses over" the picket line) before the strike ends. A worker who stays at work and never joins the strike is treated similarly to, and may be called, a crossover.

ii

have added § 8(a)(6) to the Labor Act, effectively overruling the *dicta* in *Mackay Radio* and *TWA* for employees represented by labor unions. If enacted, the relevant section of the Act would have read:

> Sec. 8. (a) It shall be an unfair labor practice for an employer—
>
> ...
>
> (6) to promise, to threaten, or to take other action—
>
>> (i) to hire a permanent replacement for an employee who—
>>
>>> (A) at the commencement of a labor dispute was an employee of the employer in a bargaining unit in which a labor organization
>>>
>>>> (I) was the certified or recognized exclusive representative, or
>>>>
>>>> (II) at least 30 days prior to the commencement of the dispute had filed a petition pursuant to section 9(c)(1) on the basis of written authorizations by a majority of the unit employees, and the Board has not completed the representation proceeding; and
>>>
>>> (B) in connection with that dispute has engaged in concerted activities for the purpose of collective bargaining or other mutual aid or protection through that labor organization; or

(ii) to withhold or deny any other employment right or privilege to an employee who meets the criteria of subparagraphs (A) and (B) of clause (i) and who is working for or has unconditionally offered to return to work for the employer, out of a preference for any other individual that is based on the fact that the individual is performing, has performed, or has indicated a willingness to perform bargaining unit work for the employer during the labor dispute.]

iv

Report of the Committee on Education and Labor of the House of Representatives on H.R. 5, the Cesar Chavez Workplace Fairness Act

Rept. No. 103-116, Part I (103d Cong., 1st Sess., 1993)

From the majority report
(urging approval of the bill)

III. BACKGROUND

A.   *The National Labor Relations Act and* Mackay

For more than half a century, the NLRA has been the principal Federal law governing labor-management relations in this country. At the core of the Act is Congress's intent to promote collective bargaining as the preferred method of resolving labor-management disputes and preserving economic stability in the private sector. To that end, the Act encourages the use of certain peaceful self-help options as each side seeks to achieve its economic objectives. Congress has viewed the resolution of economic differences through "controlled conflict" in the collective bargaining arena not only as the best solution for labor and management, but also as the solution best serving the public's interest in the free flow of commerce.

The NLRA promises workers that they shall have the right, without fear of employer discipline or discharge, to join unions, to bargain collectively, and—if no agreement can be reached—to participate in peaceful concerted activity to further their bargaining goals. The ultimate form of such peaceful concerted activity is the economic strike. It is the primary method for resolving disputes when a union and an employer are unable to agree on the terms of a contract. Moreover, the possibility of a strike is often the primary force driving both sides to settle their contractual disagreement. Employees contemplating a strike face the prospect of lost wages and benefits for the duration of their walkout. Employers must cope with the possible loss of revenue over the same time period. These economic risks, of comparable magnitude, have tended to produce a desire for compromise.

The Act expressly recognizes the central importance of the right to strike. Section 7 establishes the employees' right to engage in concerted activities for mutual aid or protection, which includes the right to withhold their labor when all other means of settlement have failed. And section 13 provides, "Nothing in this Act shall be construed so as to interfere with or impede or diminish in any way the right to strike." In short, Congress from the outset made clear that the right to strike is critical in providing the balance that makes the bargaining process work.

Notwithstanding the protection promised to striking workers, the Supreme Court, in one of its earliest decisions interpreting the NLRA, imposed a significant limit on the right to engage in an economic strike. In the case of *Labor Board v. Mackay Radio,* 304 U.S. 333, 345 (1938), the Court stated that an employer's "right to protect and continue his business" justified the hiring of permanent replacements for employees who were on economic strike. The actual dispute in the *Mackay* case did not involve permanent replacements at all. Rather, it involved an unfair labor practice charge that the employer had discriminated against active union supporters when deciding which former strikers should be reinstated to vacant positions. The Supreme Court ruled for the Board and against the employer on that issue. But in doing so, the Court stated in *dicta* that an employer had the right to fill the places left vacant by strikers, in order to "protect and continue his business," and the employer was not bound to discharge those replacements when strikers elected to resume their jobs. *Id.*

Although not part of its holding in *Mackay,* the Court's pronouncement on permanent replacements has become settled doctrine. An employer has an absolute right, in the event of an economic strike, to hire replacements on a permanent basis, thereby eliminating the jobs of striking workers.

This policy has a number of adverse consequences. It effectively allows employers to punish workers who exercise their lawful right to strike. It subverts the processes of securing union representation and negotiating a collective bargaining agreement. It encourages employers to reject cooperative labor-management relations and instead force confrontations with their employees in hopes of eliminating their union. And it tips an already skewed balance of power in labor relations even more in favor of management.

...

Professor Paul Weiler of the Harvard Law School has put the point this way in testimony before the Senate Subcommittee on Labor:

> For the last several decades, labor law classes around the country have annually broken out in laughter at the thought that lawyers and judges would draw such a spurious distinction between

vi

discharging and permanently replacing an employee in his job.[b] But to ordinary workers, this legal distinction is no joke at all. The employee may have spent twenty to thirty years with a firm, investing his whole working life building up a stake of experience and security in this enterprise that cannot possibly by duplicated somewhere else. Then, if the employee chooses to go out on strike, pursuing the course our labor law says is the only way open to try to improve (or even maintain) terms and conditions of employment, the firm's management is free to hire replacements who with less than twenty to thirty minutes on the job get a permanent claim to the position as against the striker.

"Prohibiting Discrimination Against Economic Strikers: Hearings on S. 55 Before the Subcommittee on Labor of the Senate Committee on Labor and Human Resources," 102d Cong., 1st Sess. 88, 89 (Mar. 12, 1991).

...

B. Minimal impact of permanent replacement doctrine before 1980

The *Mackay* doctrine from its inception has been viewed as incompatible with basic rights and values of Federal labor law. Yet despite widespread criticism of the decision, it is only recently that Congress has made a serious effort to address the issue of permanent replacements. The Committee concludes that there is a sound basis for the new attention being devoted to this issue. The *Mackay* decision for its first 40 years was largely an aberration with few practical consequences. But in the years since 1980, it has become a significant practical problem that now warrants legislative action.

...

2. Limited use of permanent replacements prior to 1980

Before 1980, it was extremely rare for employers to hire permanent replacements during an economic strike. Indeed, the use of such replacements was

---

[b]{An employer may not discharge a worker for going on strike because discharge would be discrimination due to concerted activity; but under *Mackay Radio* it is not considered discrimination for an employer permanently to replace a worker on strike over economic issues. Professor Weiler is saying that, to an ordinary person, the difference between being discharged and being permanently replaced is laughable.}

349

so infrequent that virtually all evidence on the subject is anecdotal. One notable exception is a study conducted by Dr. Charles Perry of the Industrial Research Unit of the Wharton Business School, together with two management labor lawyers. See Perry, Kramer and Schneider, "Operating During Strikes: Company Experience, NLRB Policies, and Governmental Regulations," Labor Relations and Public Policy Series No. 23, University of Pennsylvania (1982). (Cited [hereafter] as "Wharton Study".)

In his introduction to the Wharton Study, the Director of the Industrial Research Unit described management determinations to operate struck facilities at all as a "relatively new phenomenon," and identified the use of permanent replacements in that context as "rather unique." Wharton Study at (iii). Against this background, Dr. Perry conducted extensive interviews during 1980 with management personnel from 15 companies known to have operated a major production facility during a strike. He found that "the basic policy of virtually all of the firms studied" was "to rely exclusively on managerial and supervisory personnel in manning a struck facility." *Id.* at 64. Thus, many firms reported using "supplementary" rather than "replacement" workers: this included deferring retirement of salaried personnel; expanding use of existing on-site contractor personnel; and hiring temporary supervisors or security personnel.

The desire to avoid needless confrontation also helped determine the type of outside replacements used. Most of those who hired outside replacements "consciously avoided the use of permanent replacements either by explicitly stating that they were hiring only temporary replacements or by being silent on the subject of whether replacements were temporary or permanent." *Id.* at 64. The Wharton Study concluded: "Although the right to operate during strikes provides employers with a weapon to augment their right to take a strike in the conduct of collective bargaining, to date that weapon has only seldom been used; it has not become a basic part of the American system of collective bargaining." *Id.* at 1231.

Forty years after *Mackay*, the Wharton Study found that the option of hiring permanent replacements "remain[ed] difficult and unpopular." *Id.* at 125.

3.   *Explanation for limited use of permanent replacements*

Several factors contributed to employers' reluctance to use an economic weapon that had been held lawful by the Supreme Court. First, employers had a sound economic motive for not using permanent replacements. Productivity in the workplace is closely linked to a long-term, stable, and experienced work force, and also to high employee morale. Each of these assets is likely to be sacrificed through the upheaval and antagonism that result from the hiring of permanent replacements.

viii

As indicated in the Wharton Study, employers prior to 1980 generally were unwilling to make such a short-sighted and unproductive business decision.

Second, employers were restrained by a desire to maintain an image as corporate "good citizens." Unfair labor practices were relatively rare (fewer than 10,000 charges per year in the 1960's opposed to more than 20,000 per year in the 1980's) when compared with the lawlessness we see today. Managers tended to have long-term ties to their community and would have had to live with the divisions that use of permanent replacements could cause. Before the PATCO strike in 1981, most employers perceived that it was wrong to fire employees who had spent years working for them, helping them build the company, over a temporary economic dispute.

Third, and perhaps most important, the law governing labor-management relations during a strike initially militated against the use of permanent replacements. Significantly, unions had useful responses available that made it hazardous for employers to engage in the practice.

The *Mackay* case was decided in 1938, three years after enactment of the NLRA and six years following enactment of the Norris LaGuardia Act, which operated to restrain Federal judicial intervention in labor disputes. At the time of *Mackay*, if an employer attempted to operate with permanent replacements, the strikers had a right to pressure the struck firm's suppliers and customers–through peaceful means–to cease doing business with that firm during the strike. Thus, even if a struck employer successfully hired permanent replacements, his striking employees could continue to exert countervailing economic pressures on him through appeals to fellow workers, and sympathetic consumers, at all of the enterprises upon which the struck employer depended. These appeals could take the form of secondary strikes; peaceful consumer picketing of a struck employer's suppliers or customers; and the negotiation of "hot cargo agreements" granting bargaining unit members a contractual right to refuse to handle certain goods, such as goods produced by an employer operating during a strike. Given that these effective secondary economic pressures were available to striking employees in the early days of the NLRA, the employer who used the *Mackay* weapon did so at the risk of being economically isolated.

In addition to having available certain countervailing economic weapons, unions in 1938 also had the ability to strengthen solidarity within the bargaining unit against an employer that used permanent replacements.

The right to hire permanent replacements allows employers to break strike solidarity by coercing strikers–who are afraid of permanent job loss–to cross picket line and return to work. But at the time of *Mackay*, unions could, and often did, negotiate for the closed shop. By doing so, unions could assure that only union members who had agreed to abide by union rules–including those respecting strike solidarity–would be hired into the bargaining unit, thereby maximizing the bargaining unit's power during a strike. In addition, even when a union lost a strike, its negotiation of closed shop agreements elsewhere enabled its out-of-work members to obtain comparable employment. In both these ways, unions could reduce the power of an employer to break solidarity by threatening workers with replacement and job loss if they remained on strike.

A final factor which strengthened the effectiveness of strikes was the fact that the original Wagner Act did not exclude foremen and supervisors from the definition of employee. In the 1940's the NLRB held that foremen and supervisors had the right to engage in concerted activity such as forming a union or respecting a picket line. The Supreme Court upheld this principle in *Packard Co. v. Labor Board,* 330 U.S. 485 (1947). The strike and the threat to strike are much more potent when an employer is faced with the prospect of losing the services of supervisory employees in addition to those employees within union bargaining units.[c]

In sum, for many years under the *Mackay* doctrine, employers very rarely made use of permanent replacement. Economic factors, employer morality, and the state of the law all combined to discourage such use.

IV. NEED FOR THE LEGISLATION

A. *Recent Supreme Court decisions*

The *Mackay* doctrine was an unimportant anomaly in American labor relations during the first four decades after it was handed down by the Supreme Court in 1938. But in the last decade *Mackay* has played a far more prominent and destructive role. Two Supreme Court decisions in the 1980's gave new impetus to the *Mackay* doctrine.

In *Belknap v. Hale,* 463 U.S. 491 (1983), the Court held that workers promised permanent replacement status could enforce this promise in state court against an employer that discharged them to make room for strikers who were being

---

[c]Congress [overruled] the holding in *Packard* when it added section 2(11) to the National Labor Relations Act in 1947.

X

reinstated.[d] The Court's holding in *Belknap*–that a state law action for breach of contract was not preempted by the NLRA–increased the value attached to the "permanent replacement" promise, thereby weakening the position of workers engaged in a lawful strike.

Then, in *TWA, Inc. v. Flight Attendants,* 489 U.S. 426 (1989), the Court relied on *Mackay* to further erode the protection accorded to economic strikes. The *TWA* case extended the permanent replacement doctrine to cover employees under the Railway Labor Act (RLA). But more important was the Court's holding that junior striking employees who "cross over" a picket line to return to work may be retained at the end of the strike, or given superior positions, in preference to more senior employees who remained on strike. It cannot be disputed that this preferential treatment for so-called "crossovers" is inherently destructive of the right to strike. The employer effectively encourages junior employees to "break ranks" by offering the inducement of post-strike job placements and job security that they could not otherwise obtain....

---

[d]{As part of a strike-settlement agreement, employers sometimes discharge permanent replacements or recall all strikers and assign jobs by seniority, resulting in layoff of replacements. *Belknap* held that federal law does not prohibit states from allowing permanent replacements who are discharged or laid off to sue the employer for breach of contract. The worker's theory would be that employer promised not to discharge the worker when the strike was over.—ed.}

B.   Substantial use of permanent replacements since 1980

Whereas the Wharton Study concluded that the use of permanent replacements prior to 1980 was "rather unique" and that basic policy of all of the firms studied was "to rely exclusively on managerial and supervisory personnel in manning a struck facility," the evidence from more recent studies shows a massive change.

...

2.   Gramm study

A survey of employer responses to strikes was conducted in 1989 by Associate Professor Cynthia Gramm at the University of Alabama-Huntsville. See, C. Gramm, "Employer's Decision to Operate During Strikes: Consequences and Policy Implications" in Employee Rights in Changing Economy, 33-40 (W. Spriggs, ed. 1991) (hereinafter "Gramm study"). Professor Gramm studied two randomly drawn samples of strikes during the period 1984 to 1988. One sample included 35 strikes across the country (U.S.) and the other included 21 strikes in New York State (N.Y.). Professor Gramm compiled her data from surveys of managers who were involved in these strikes. She found that employers hired permanent replacements in about 16 percent of the U.S. strike sample, and about 24 percent of the N.Y. strike sample. Gramm found that in contrast, temporary replacements were used less frequently by employers in both samples: 6 percent of the employers in the U.S. sample, and 10 percent of employer in the N.Y. sample.

In an effort to examine whether employers have increased their use of permanent replacements during strikes, Gramm asked managers who indicated there had been previous strikes involving the same bargaining unit whether they had hired replacements during these prior strikes. As Gramm explained, "Every single manager said that this particular strike was the first attempt to hire replacement workers. This strategy appears to be a new experience for the firms in the sample." Gramm study at 35. Gramm also compared her results to those a decade earlier:

> Another study involving case studies of fifteen firms conducted by Perry, Kramer, and Schneider in the early 1980s found that managers in most of the firms explicitly chose not to hire replacement workers. If they felt they had to hire replacement workers in order to keep operating, they chose to hire temporary replacements. They did not want to hire permanent replacements. Comparing that finding with my finding that firms are hiring permanent replacements more frequently than temporary replacements

xii

suggests that the willingness of employers to hire permanent replacements has increased during the 1980s. *Id.*

Finally, Gramm examined how the use of permanent replacements affects the length of strikes. She found that strikes lasted substantially longer when permanent replacements were hired than when temporary replacements or no replacements were hired. In the U.S. sample, strikes lasted a mean duration of 363 days when the employer hired permanent replacements; this compares to a mean of 72 days when the employer hired temporary replacements, and a mean of 64 days when no replacements were hired.

...

C.   *Explanation for increased use of permanent replacements*

Each of the factors that previously contributed to employer reluctance to use permanent replacements has been affected by subsequent events. The Committee believes that changes in the attitudes and economic motivation of some employers, and in the state of labor law, all have contributed to the substantially increased use of permanent replacements during economic strikes.

President Reagan's firing and permanent replacement of 12,000 striking air traffic controllers in 1981 had a dramatic impact on the way many Americans view strikes, including the view taken by a new generation of corporate managers. Even though that strike by Federal employees was illegal, American employers did not readily make this distinction. President Reagan's action was regarded by many observers as a signal to the employer community that it was acceptable to dismiss striking workers. The events surrounding the air traffic controllers' strike ushered in a much more aggressive, and even hostile, employer strategy toward lawful strikes.

The Committee believes, however, that other factors account more directly for the increased use of permanent replacements. One such factor is a change in the structure and mobility of corporate capital. Since 1981, there has been a wave of mergers and leveraged buyouts in this country, along with a distorted focus on short-term performance. Many employers, overloaded with debt, have tended to regard workers as mere assets to be used and discarded. Because they have just taken over an enterprise, these new employers have no investment in their newly acquired work force. Frequently, their interest in short-term returns leads them to ignore or even sacrifice long-term employee interests by getting rid of a loyal, experienced work force.

This so-called "new breed of employer" does not hesitate to permanently replace a union work force. The New York Daily News advertised for permanent replacements and spent millions of dollars training them months before any labor dispute had even arisen. And Frank Lorenzo twice rushed into bankruptcy court to repudiate his firm's collective bargaining agreements. For this new breed of employer, who use and even encourage strikes in order to undermine the collective bargaining process, the basic assumption that there are economic reasons to retain a long-term work force is no longer applicable.

...

D. *Adverse consequences of permitting use of permanent replacements*

1. Mackay *undermines the rights of individual workers*

The NLRB promises workers a fair chance to engage in collective bargaining. The Act states that workers shall have the right, without fear of employer discipline or discharge, to join unions, to bargain collectively, and, if no agreement can be reached, to participate in a peaceful strike to further their bargaining goals. Section 13 of the NLRA says, "Nothing in this Act ... shall be construed to impede or diminish in any way the right to strike...."

But today, workers have not so much a right to strike as a right to quit. Workers who exercise the "right" to strike face the very real prospect of losing their jobs to "permanent replacements." Even long-term employees, who have invested decades of their lives in a firm, risk losing their jobs for doing nothing more than exercising their right to participate in a lawful and peaceful strike. From a striking employee's perspective, the fact that one has not been (illegally) discharged, but rather (legally) permanently replaced, is truly a distinction without a difference. The words of the law do not ring true. The Act's promise to workers has become a false one.

The system of collective bargaining envisioned by our labor law is premised on treating both employers and employees fairly. The ability to permanently replace a striking worker inevitably undermines this most important objective. It is impossible to convince a long-term, conscientious employee of the law's consistency after the employee has lost a job for doing no more than exercising a protected right.

The Committee has heard extensive testimony demonstrating that the impact of permanent replacements is ultimately borne by individual workers and their families. The economic and emotional impact is severe. To hardworking Americans and their families, the loss of a job can be, in the words of one witness, a form of economic execution. As explained by Chester Abbott, Secretary-Treasurer of Teamsters Local 829:

xiv

I have seen first hand what this vicious practice has done to hardworking and decent people. Members of our local have had their cars repossessed and their homes jeopardized because of mortgage payment problems. The financial and emotional stress of this tragedy has extracted personal cost[s] as well, resulting in the break-up of the members' families through separation [for example, the worker must go to another town to find a job] and divorce. The issue of permanent replacement of strikers is not some economic equation dreamt up by some company official who is only interested in the bottom line. It is not simply this debate in the halls of Congress. Rather, it is real life that often carries devastating consequences for your constituents.

"Legislative hearings on H.R. 3936, before the Subcommittee on Labor-Management Relations of the House Committee on Education and Labor," 101st Cong., 2d Sess. 69 (June 13, 1990)....

...

2. The Mackay *doctrine undermines collective bargaining*

In addition to jeopardizing the rights of individual workers, the *Mackay* doctrine has also subverted the Act's core goal of securing stable collective bargaining relationships. This subversion may occur at several different stages. During the course of an organizing campaign, employers are permitted to tell their employees that a union means the possibility of a strike and the likelihood of permanent replacements. This lawful threat of "job loss for joining a union" has a significant chilling effect on the exercise of employee free choice.

Even when a union is elected by a majority of employees and certified by the NLRB as exclusive representative, negotiation of the initial collective bargaining agreement is often a special challenge. Employers involved in a first contract negotiation may be skeptical about the benefits of having a union. In these circumstances, the use—or even the threatened use—of permanent replacements may substantially diminish the prospects for establishing a collective bargaining relationship. This frustrates the employees' desire for union representation that was expressed in the election.

Once collective bargaining has been established, maintaining a fair balance between labor and management is critical to the stability and success of the relationship. The guarantee of a right to strike is an essential part of maintaining such a balance. The ability to strike, should negotiations ultimately fail to produce an agreement, provides leverage for union negotiators and an incentive for an employer to bargain seriously. But the readiness of employers to replace strikers permanently has increasingly hovered over the bargaining table from the outset of negotiations....

...

3. *Permanent replacements lead to contentious and protracted strikes*

When striking workers are permanently replaced, the strike is converted from a limited dispute about working conditions to a broader confrontation about retention of jobs and the right of the workers to union representation. Unions understandably insist on the reinstatement of strikers as a precondition to settlement of the strike. This issue is often more difficult to resolve than the original economic dispute separating the parties....

...

The *Mackay* doctrine, itself, has become the cause of strikes.

Frequently, strikes occur because of the previously described incentive *Mackay* provides employers who wish to continually challenge the choice of employees to be represented by a union. As stated by Professor Getman: *"Mackay* motivates employers to bargain not to reach an agreement but rather to force a strike, so that it can permanently rid itself of union supporters and very possibly the union itself." "Striker Replacement Bill Hearings," supra at 138.

...

4. *Employers do not need the* Mackay *weapon.*

The permanent replacement doctrine of *Mackay* is not just bad even on its own terms. An employer who seeks "to protect and continue his business" has many alternatives to hiring permanent replacements.

An employer's options include: hiring temporary replacements, relying on supervisory or management personnel, transferring or subcontracting work, or stockpiling in advance of a strike. In addition, the Supreme Court has long held that an employer lawfully may lock out his employees as a means of controlling the timing of a work stoppage and obtaining bargaining advantage. Thus, even when the employees choose not to strike and are willing to continue working without a contract under terms that the employer unilaterally imposes, the employer can lawfully lock out the employees. The employer may choose when and how to do this to maximize its bargaining advantage.

xvi

...

5.   Mackay *undermines the development of cooperative labor-management relations*

Good will between labor and management must be nurtured if we are to keep pace with our global competitors. Many point to the economic success of Japan, Germany and other European countries in fostering harmonious labor-management relations. There is a direct correlation between efficient economic performance and cooperative working relationships between employers and employees. In each of these countries, collective bargaining is an important element in fostering cooperative labor-management relations.

Our foreign competitors have laws which recognize the importance of establishing an equitable balance between labor and management. Their laws encourage long-term bargaining relationships, promoting the stability and durability of such relationships. In each country, should bargaining fail to produce an agreement, employees have a right to strike which includes the right to reinstatement at the conclusion of the strike. Permanent replacements are not permitted.

...

V. RESPONSE TO OPPONENT'S ARGUMENTS

The opponents of H.R. 5 make a number of arguments against the bill. In the Committee's view, none of these arguments is valid.

A.   Doesn't the amended version of H.R. 5 discriminate against non-union employees?

No. This attack on the bill seems hypocritical, but more importantly, it is inaccurate. Anyone—regardless of whether they are union members—would be protected if their union-represented bargaining unit engaged in a lawful economic strike. By contrast, the mere fact of being a member of a union would not protect a worker against permanent replacement if that union were not authorized to act as his collective bargaining representative or if the union that represents him for collective bargaining purposes did not sanction the strike.

The bill does exclude from coverage non-union *workplaces.* This exclusion is intended to protect employers against undisciplined and unpredictable work stoppages by employees who might have no clearly articulated demands and no identified representative authorized to negotiate and settle their grievances.

B.   Will H.R. 5 damage cooperative labor-management relations?

Quite the contrary. Taking away management's unilateral right to destroy the union will foster cooperation, not hinder it. As former Secretary of Labor Ray Marshall put it, "It's very hard to have a cooperative relationship between parties with unequal power. Sooner or later the party with more power will exert it, and then there is no cooperative relationship anymore." The Journal of Commerce put it more colorfully when it likened the *Mackay* doctrine to bringing a loaded gun to the bargaining table and pointing it at the union's head. Journal of Commerce, 8A (Mar. 18, 1991). Intimidation does not foster cooperation.

C.   Will H.R. 5 upset a "delicate balance" in the economic weapons available to management and labor that has existed since Mackay was decided in 1938?

As explained earlier, the initial balance of the Act has been tipped in management's favor many times over the last five decades. Unions have lost the right to engage in most forms of peaceful secondary activity; they have lost the right to impose strike solidarity; they have lost the right to engage in the most effective kinds of strikes; and they have lost the unilateral right to determine the timing of work stoppages. All of these rights were protected at the time *Mackay* was decided. During the same period, employers were given new weapons, including the right to lock out the union offensively, even prior to impasse.

Passage of H.R. 5 will help to restore, not upset, the desired "delicate balance" in relative bargaining power.

D.   Don't employers need permanent replacements in order to operate during a strike?

No. Struck employers have traditionally operated through a combination of strategies including hiring temporary replacements, subcontracting the struck work, assigning bargaining unit work to non-unit employees, and stockpiling inventory. In light of the growth of the temporary employment industry and our recent chronically high unemployment rates, it is undoubtedly easier today to find temporary replacement workers for even skilled jobs than it was ten years ago, let alone 50 years ago.

E.   Won't H.R. 5 inevitably lead to more strikes?

No. Employees are reluctant to strike, even in the face of oppressive working conditions, because they give up their wages and benefits for the duration of the strike. Any increase in strike activity due to removal of the threat of permanent xviii

replacement is likely to be counterbalanced by the fact that employers will no longer use the tactic of forcing strikes in order to avail themselves of permanent replacements and, ultimately, to break the union. Studies show that the presence of permanent replacements produces longer and more bitter strikes.

F.   *Won't H.R. 5, by making strikes "risk-free," guarantee unions will win every strike and drive employers into bankruptcy?*

No. Strikes are never "risk-free" for the workers. The hardship of doing without a paycheck and health insurance puts enormous pressure on the strikers to settle a dispute as soon as possible. Most American workers have no cushion, no money socked away to make house payments and car payments, to buy food or to pay doctors' bills. Strikes are a last resort when negotiations fail, not a risk-free lark for workers and their families.

Moreover, workers have no incentive to make demands that would throw their employers into bankruptcy or otherwise cause permanent economic harm to their employers. The worker, after all, is dependent on the employer's long-term economic health. Workers realize this, and this realization significantly moderates worker demands.

Employers win many strikes in which the use of permanent replacements never occurs and is never threatened. By stockpiling product in advance, employing temporary replacements, subcontracting struck work, or using non-strikers, managers, and supervisors, employers often are able to maintain production and revenues throughout a strike. There is no dispute that the majority of employers over the years have chosen not to use permanent replacements.

G.   *Won't H.R. 5 put American companies at a disadvantage with respect to their international competitors?*

No. Our principal economic competitors and trading partners including Germany, Japan, Canada, and France have long recognized that using permanent replacements is unwise as a matter of both public policy and good business. Each country prohibits the use of permanent replacements for strikers. Moreover, we cannot hope to compete in global markets if those who labor cannot work with those who manage. Hiring permanent replacements sends an unmistakable message that workers are disposable, reducing employee morale and lowering productivity. For example, a study conducted by William N. Cooke, a Wayne State University professor of industrial relations, indicates that in the long run firms that adopt hardball, confrontational tactics such as the use of permanent strike replacements are less profitable than firms that adopt a cooperative approach to labor relations....

...

From the minority report
(urging rejection of the bill)

We oppose H.R. 5 as introduced and as reported by the Committee on Education and Labor. If enacted, H.R. 5 will upset over fifty years of accepted labor law by prohibiting the use of permanent replacement workers in economic strikes. In doing so, it will unfairly strengthen the hand of organized labor while weakening the economic power of employers. The resulting imbalance will inevitably lead to more strikes, impair labor-management relations, and threaten the economic survival of many businesses.

H.R. 5 ignores economic realities

Proponents of H.R. 5 contend that the practice of hiring permanent replacements has increased so dramatically over the last several years that its use by management in labor disputes has become nearly commonplace. Unfortunately, this contention ignores the economic realities that are inextricably linked to any employers' decision to pursue such a course of action.

Any strike, no matter how short-lived, causes some economic disruption. H.R. 5, by preventing management from hiring permanent replacement workers, would simply give organized labor little to lose in calling a strike, regardless of the issues or circumstances involved. With much of the risk removed from its participation in the collective bargaining process, there is little to temper labor's impulse to strike, and it seems inevitable that strike activity will increase. H.R. 5 allows organized labor the comfort of being able to go out on strike, with the full knowledge that as soon as the walkout causes any discomfort, striking employees can return to work to jobs that must be waiting for them.

In the meantime, business, which suffers from lost productivity and profits regardless of whether it hires temporary or permanent replacements during a strike, could be left without the ability to continue operation. Assertions of the bill's proponents notwithstanding, it is impossible for many employers to keep an operation running for any sustained period of time utilizing supervisory personnel or temporary replacements. Geographic isolation, specialized skill requirements, or the threat of union violence all may drive employers to the necessity of offering permanent employment to those who cross the picket lines.

Nonetheless, in no case does an employer make the decision to hire permanent replacements lightly, for such a decision inevitably entails many costs. These include xx

increased expenses for hiring and training, additional security costs, a decline in production until training is complete, as well as the potential loss of customer confidence and local community goodwill.

If H.R. 5 were to become law, the consequences to the economic health of this country would be enormous, as strike activity increased and employers were forced to accede to unreasonable economic demands by labor or risk going out of business. Nonunion workers in related businesses could also find themselves out of work as [part of] a domino effect of stalled industries and services respond[ing] to prolonged shutdowns by laying off employees.

We are convinced that if employers who are faced with unreasonable demands from a union cannot consider hiring permanent replacements, even as a last resort, many businesses will face [the] choice of either closing down altogether, or agreeing to union's demands and ultimately being forced out of business because of an inability to compete in the market place. Either choice will have devastating economic effects on the employees, their families, the business owners, and the communities in which they live.

H.R. 5 upsets the balance of interests and risk

We are also troubled and, frankly, perplexed by the efforts H.R. 5's proponents to overturn over 50 years of well-settled labor law. Indeed, the bill runs counter to the very purpose of our collective bargaining system, which is to facilitate the resolution of disputes between employees and employers within the general confines of a competitive market place. Fundamental to that system and its overall effectiveness, is a delicate balance that both protects the interests of labor and management and, at the same time, exposes both to certain risks.

While there may be changes to the law of labor-management relations that would improve the collective bargaining process, the current law is based on the premise that the interests of all parties in a labor dispute deserve protection. The law protects workers' right to strike, and the right of employers to continue business operations during a strike. If an employer is found to have committed unfair labor practices in the course of a strike undertaken to secure economic concessions, all economic strikers are entitled to full reinstatement and back pay. If, however, the strike is fully based on economic disagreements between labor and management, management may continue to operate with workers to whom it may offer permanent employment.

At the same time, both management and labor must confront certain risks that are inherent in any labor dispute. Put simply, besides having something to lose if they fail to reach agreement, labor is threatened with the prospect of permanent replacement if it goes on strike; and business is faced with the decline in production and profits which invariably accompany a strike, whether or not permanent replacements are employed.

This balance of protections and risks is designed to encourage settlement of labor disputes. For 55 years this balance has served labor and management very well, and has never been seriously questioned by the Congress—or by the Supreme Court, which first articulated the permanent replacement doctrine in its *Mackay* decision in 1938. The result, as noted by the General Accounting Office, has been very few instances when permanent replacements have been used, and then, only as a last resort.

Accordingly, we fail to see the merit in any proposal that would upset the delicate balance which is, and always has been, one of the underpinnings of our collective bargaining system. Unfortunately, H.R. 5 is just such a proposal and, therefore, does not deserve our support.

Our opposition to H.R. 5 however, should not be construed as advocating "union-busting" or other tactics which diminish the lawful exercise of the right to strike. Rather, we are attempting to maintain the foundation of our system of collective bargaining, which is that both parties to a labor dispute must have the means necessary—both the right to strike, and the right to permanently replace, which make the prospect of prolonged dispute costly and to be avoided by both sides.

H.R. 5 would add to the regulatory burden which impairs the ability of American businesses to compete in the global economy

Finally, we are compelled to note that H.R. 5, in addition to all its substantive shortcomings, is another in a long line of recent legislative initiatives that will add significant costs to doing business in this country. H.R. 5 cannot be considered in a vacuum. The Civil Rights Act of 1991 became effective on November 21, 1991. It was soon followed by the employment requirements of the Americans with Disabilities Act (ADA), which became effective on July 26, 1992. The ADA has been called the most significant change in workplace law in many years. And, with passage of the Civil Rights Act, punitive and compensatory damages have been added to the arsenal of plaintiffs' lawyers in labor law litigation for the first time. More recently, the Family and Medical Leave Act became law on February 5, 1993. When provisions of that new law become effective in August 5, 1993, employers will once again have to modify their labor-management practices in order to comply with another set of federal requirements. Whatever the intrinsic merits of these initiatives, it can hardly be argued that they will not, in total, add to the regulatory burden placed xxii

on employers.

These are only, of course, a few of the labor laws employers must comply with, and, indeed, even more are pending in the 103rd Congress. For instance, currently waiting in the wings of the Committee on Education and Labor is a massive bill amending the Occupational Safety and Health Act (H.R. 1280), a bill to add punitive and compensatory damages to litigation under the Employee Retirement Income Security Act (H.R. 1881), and, as if these are not enough, a bill to completely eliminate the caps on damages under the Civil Rights Act mentioned above (H.R. 224.) And, with health care reform a virtual certainty, the prospects for costly new benefit mandates are greater than ever.

This is not to suggest that Congress should never consider or pass legislation affecting the American workplace, and we acknowledge that improvements could be made in current law to improve the productivity of labor-management relations, but where will it all end? Congress cannot continue to layer one law over another into perpetuity; choices have to be made and priorities set. Not every interest group can be or should be satisfied through a legislative response. The business community can only withstand so much, and all the good intentions in the world for workers, which we all share, will mean nothing to a worker without a job.

We must, in short, be very careful before we pass yet another new restriction on American businesses, and Congress should enact new laws only when a truly pressing societal need for that law has been demonstrated. H.R. 5 not only fails to meet that test, but, we feel, will do much more harm than good, for the reasons such as above. At a time when American industry faces ever mounting competition from around the world, we believe that our nation certainly does not need legislation designed to encourage strikes and a resulting loss of competitive standing.

H.R. 5 would reverse 55 years of labor-management law which recognizes the right of employers to maintain operations during an economic strike by hiring permanent replacement workers

In the 1938 decision *NLRB v. Mackay Radio & Telegraph Co.,* the Supreme Court concluded that, although section 13 of the National Labor Relations Act (NLRA) prohibits employer interference with the right to strike:

> ... it does not follow that an employer, guilty of no act denounced by the statute, has lost the right to protect and continue his business by supplying in places left vacant by strikers. And he is not bound to discharge those hired to fill the places of the strikers, upon the election of the latter to resume their employment, in order to

create places for them. The assurance by [the employer] to those who accepted employment during the strike that if they so desired their places might be permanent was not an unfair labor practice nor was it such to reinstate only so many of the strikers as there were vacant places to be filled. 304 U.S. at 345.

The Court thus concluded that hiring "permanent" replacements during "economic" strikes was not an unfair labor practice prohibited by the NLRA. The Supreme Court emphasized that, under the Act, economic strikers continue to retain their status as employees and would have the jobs available to them when the replacement workers departed. In returning to the facts at hand, the Court determined that, in reinstating employees after the strike, the employer refused to reinstate certain strikers because of their leadership in union activities, and thus had committed unfair labor practices. The Court then affirmed the National Labor Relations Board's order to reinstate those strikers.

This decision illuminated the distinction, continued in current law, between economic strikes and unfair labor practice strikes. Economic strikes are those conducted over wages, working conditions, fringe benefits, and the like, while unfair labor practice strikes are those conducted to protest the alleged conduct of an employer in violation of the NLRA. The distinction is most significant because of the differing re-employment rights of returning strikers. ... *Mackay Radio* decision now stands for [the proposition that] economic strikers may be permanently replaced subject to a right to be recalled as vacancies occur. Unfair labor practice strikers, on the other hand, who unconditionally offer to return to work, have a right to be reinstated even if it requires the termination of replacement workers.

Proponents of H.R. 5 claim that the legislation would reverse the above-quoted portion of *Mackay*, asserting that permanent replacement of economic strikers interferes with the "right to strike." As is obvious from the quotation and the above discussion, the impact that *Mackay* had on the "right to strike" was to impose some risk on those asserting that right. *Mackay* allowed an employer "guilty of no act denounced by the statute," to continue to operate a business despite a union's attempt to achieve its own economic goals. As the subsequent development of the doctrine showed, *Mackay*, consistent with the balancing of employer and employee interests that is at the heart of the NLRA, is about weighing the steps an employer may legitimately take to maintain operations against the infringement on the right of employees to engage in concerted activities that such steps may have. The Supreme Court concluded, we believe correctly, that the right of employers to continue business operations by hiring permanent replacement workers was not an encroachment on employee rights that rose to the level of an unfair labor practice.

xxiv

The origins and development of the Mackay Radio *doctrine demonstrate that the right of employers to hire permanent replacement workers is a well-accepted facet of labor law*

Proponents of H.R. 5 urge that the Supreme Court announced the right of employers to hire permanent replacement workers during an economic strike in a discussion that was peripheral to the holding of the *Mackay* decision. They contend that this right became enshrined in precedent without a thorough examination of the issue of permanent replacement either in the decision or when the NLRA was passed.

However, this contention ignores legislative developments prior to passage of the NLRA, amendments to the NLRA subsequent to the *Mackay* decision, and the evolution of the *Mackay* doctrine though 50 years of Supreme court decision making. At the time of the decision in *Mackay Radio*, the right of employers to continue operations during an economic strike by hiring permanent replacement workers had been congressionally recognized for several years. In 1934, Senator Robert Wagner introduced the Labor Disputes Act, which was a harbinger of the later enacted NLRA. This bill contained a definition of "employee" which explicitly excluded an individual hired to replace a striking employee. This definition, which excluded permanent replacement workers from the protections of the Act, promoted vigorous debate, and the exclusion was eventually deleted in subsequent drafts.

In the following Congress, the National Labor Relations Act (also known as the "Wagner" Act) was proposed and its definition of "employee" did not exclude striker replacements. In fact, a memorandum prepared by the Senate Committee on Education and Labor comparing the Wagner Act with the earlier Labor Disputes Act specifically recognized the legitimacy of the employer's right to maintain operations by hiring permanent replacement workers. In explaining the provisions including economic strikers in the definition of the term "employee," the memorandum provided:

> [The Wagner Act] provides that the labor dispute shall be "current" and that the employer is free to hasten its end by hiring a new permanent crew of workers and running the plant on a normal basis....

> The broader definition of "employee" in [the Wagner Act] does not lead to the conclusion that no strike may be lost or that all strikers must be restored to their jobs, or that an employer may not hire new workers, temporary or permanent, at will.

Senate Committee on Education and Labor, Comparison of S. 282 and S. 1958, 74th

Cong., 1st Sess. (1935), pp. 22-22, reprinted in I Legislative History of the National Labor Relations Act, 1935, pp. 1319, 1346.

It was only several years after the passage of the Wagner Act of 1935 that the Supreme Court judicially recognized the right of employers to continue operations by hiring permanent replacement workers during an economic strike. Although proponents of H.R. 5 contend that it was not essential to the holding in *Mackay*, the Supreme Court would never have reached the question of whether an employer could discriminate against active union members in reinstating strikers if the legal requirement was that an employer had to reinstate all strikers. By analyzing the circumstances under which an employer could choose between employees in reinstatement, the Supreme Court had to make the assumption that the employer was under no obligation to reinstate the strikers.

In the years following the *Mackay* decision, there was ample evidence that the Congress did not find the doctrine of permanent replacement to be inconsistent with the goal of the NLRA. In fact, Senator Wagner, the author of the NLRA, was himself quoted as saying:

> Every step that the Supreme Court has taken toward clarifying the meaning and defining the scope of the [Wagner] Act has made it easier for workers and employers to deal successfully under its provisions.[2]

Moreover, as the NLRA was amended subsequent to the *Mackay* decisions, the permanent replacement doctrine was basically incorporated into other provisions of the Act dealing with the rights of economic strikers. Section 9(c)(3) of the NLRA, which was added by 1947 Taft-Hartley changes to the Act and amended by 1959 Landrum-Griffin changes, implicitly recognizes the right of employers to hire permanent replacement workers in an economic strike. That provision deals with the voting rights of "employees on strike who are not entitled to reinstatement" and has always been interpreted to refer to replaced economic strikers.[d]

---

[2]National Labor Relations Act and Proposed Amendments: Hearings Before the Senate Committee on Education and Labor, 76th Cong., 1st Sess (1939) (statement of Sen. Robert F. Wagner).

[d]{Whether a permanently replaced striker may vote in a representation election is important principally in the following situation: The union strikes. The employer hires many permanent replacements. The employer then doubts that the union still

(continued...)

xxvi

The Supreme Court continued to develop the doctrine of permanent replacement in numerous decisions [after] *Mackay*. In *Mastro Plastics Corp. v. NLRB*, the Supreme Court again sharply defined the distinction between economic strikes and unfair labor practice strikes, and, in the latter case, recognized that striking employees are "entitled to reinstatement with back pay even if replacements for them have been made."[3] Later, in the 1962 *Erie Resistor* decision, while concluding that an employer could not offer additional benefits to replacement workers, the Court did not question "the continuing vitality of the *Mackay* rule."[4] Again, in *National Labor*

(...continued)

represents the majority of the workers. The Labor Board holds an election in which the workers vote on whether they wish to continue being represented by the union. Under the Wagner Act, permanently replaced strikers were allowed to vote in such an election. (They usually voted for the union, so unions had a good chance to win the election.) Under the Taft-Hartley Act, permanently replaced strikers were prohibited from voting in such an election. (As a result, employers had a much better chance of winning the election.) Section 9(c)(3) of the Landrum-Griffin Act, which remains in force today, provides that permanently replaced strikers may vote in such an election *if it is conducted within 12 months of the commencement of the strike*, but not thereafter. The minority's argument is that, both in 1947 and in 1959, Congress assumed the legality of hiring permanent replacements.—ed.}

[3]350 U.S. 270, 278 (1956). {Section 8(d) provides, in relevant part, that if a collective bargaining agreement is in effect, neither party may terminate or modify the contract until 60 days after notifying the other party in writing of the desire for change and until 30 days after notifying the Federal Mediation and Conciliation Service that a labor dispute exists; and that employees who engage in a premature strike lose all their protections under the Labor Act (meaning that they can be fired). In *Mastro Plastics*, union workers struck over their employer's unfair labor practice; because they failed to give the required notices specified in § 8(d), their employer concluded they had lost the protection of the Act and fired them. The Supreme Court, however, held that the notice requirements apply only to economic strikes, not to unfair labor practice strikes, and therefore that the strikers were entitled to reinstatement with back pay, even if the employer had hired permanent replacements. The minority's argument is that, even though the Court created a special privilege for unfair labor practice strikers, the Court recognized that economic strikers could be permanently replaced.–ed.}

[4]*National Labor Relations Board v. Erie Resistor Corp.,* 373 U.S. 221, 232 (1962). {In this case, the employer, in order to attract replacements during a strike, offered 20 years worth of extra seniority to replacements. The Supreme Court held

(continued...)

Relations Board v. Fleetwood Trailer Co., the Supreme Court recognized the employer's right to continue operations by hiring permanent replacement workers while maintaining that the displaced economic striker's right to reinstatement continued until he has obtained "other regular and substantially equivalent employment."[5] As recently as 1990, in *NLRB v. Curtin Matheson Scientific, Inc.,* the Court acknowledged that employers could hire permanent replacement workers when it found that the employer cannot presume that such workers do not support the union for purposes of its duty to bargain.[6]

---

[4](...continued)

this offer of super seniority was an unfair labor practice because of its drastic effect both on the strike and on labor-management relations after the strike. The minority's argument is that the Court did not question the right of the employer to hire permanent replacements.–ed.}

[5]389 U.S. 375, 379 (1967). {In *Fleetwood Trailer*, an employer cut back operations during a strike. When the strike ended, some strikers were recalled, but there were no positions for a number of them. Six strikers who were not recalled indicated that their desire to be recalled when their jobs were reactivated. Later, when their jobs were reactivated, the employer hired six new applicants instead of recalling the strikers. The Supreme Court held that the strikers remained employees under the Act and were entitled to preference over new applicants. (However, the strikers would not have been entitled to this preference if their jobs had been abolished—that is, if the new applicants had been hired for newly created jobs—or if the strikers were no longer employees of this employer because they had accepted permanent employment at another firm.) The minority's argument is that the Court again recognized the right of a struck employer to hire permanent replacements.–ed.}

[6]110 S.Ct. 1542 (1990). {When permanent replacements are hired during a strike, the employer may doubt that the majority of employees still desires to be represented by the union. As mentioned above in n. d, an election can be held. But it is also possible for the employer simply to withdraw recognition from the union, provided the employer has a good-faith doubt as to the union's majority status. In this event, the union will file an unfair labor practice charge, accusing the employer of refusing to bargain. The central issue in the case will be whether the employer had a good-faith doubt. For the purpose of deciding this issue, both replacements and strikers are counted as employees. The Labor Board presumes that replacements support the union in the same proportion as the replaced workers did. The effect of this presumption is to place the burden on the employer to prove that the majority of employees no longer bears allegiance to the union. In *Curtin Matheson*, a collective contract expired; the union rejected the employer's last offer, and the employer

(continued...)

xxviii

As the foregoing discussion indicates, the right of employers to maintain operations during an economic strike by hiring permanent replacement workers did not evolve in the offhanded manner the proponents of H.R. 5 would have one believe. Employers were understood to retain that right prior to the passage of the National Labor Relations Act, and in numerous cases since the 1938 decision, the Supreme Court has reaffirmed the *Mackay* doctrine. Further, subsequent case law and legislative developments related to the rights of both replacement workers and economic strikers have started from the premise of the *per se* legality of permanent replacement.

The many legal protections in the NLRA that are extended to strikers ensure that permanent replacement is not the same as firing a striker

Another argument raised by supporters of the ban on permanent replacement workers is that employers have used their ability to hire such workers as a means to "bust" unions and that permanent replacement is essentially "firing" an employee for engaging in strike activity protected by section 7 of the NLRA. However, several other legal doctrines that have developed under the NLRA make it difficult for employers to use permanent replacement workers for this purpose. In the first instance, the use of permanent replacement workers as a means to eliminate a union from a workplace is thwarted by the fact that, to the extent that an employer is engaging in surface bargaining and is trying to instigate a strike so nonunion

---

[6](...continued)
locked out the 27 workers in the bargaining unit. The union responded by calling a strike. Five workers decided to cross the picket line and report for work. The employer then hired 29 permanent replacements to replace the 22 remaining strikers. The union abandoned the strike; it accepted the employer's last offer, and the strikers offered to return to work. The employer replied that the strikers had been replaced. The employer also withdrew recognition from the union, which filed an unfair labor practice charge. The Board applied its presumption that the replacements supported the union in the same proportion as the strikers and required the employer to substantiate its doubt as to the union's majority status. The Board evaluated the employer's evidence and held that it was insufficient to support a good-faith doubt. Accordingly, the Board ordered the employer to recognize and bargain with the union. The Court of Appeals refused to enforce the Board's order because the court rejected the Board's presumption that replacements support the union in the same proportion as strikers do; the court believed that the Board should presume that replacements do not support the union. The Supreme Court reversed the Court of Appeals and upheld the Board, finding the Board's presumption was justified. The minority's argument is that the Court once again acknowledged that employers may hire permanent replacements for strikers.–ed.}

replacement workers could be hired, the employer would be guilty of an unfair labor practice and could not permanently replace the strikers. Further, economic strikers remain members of the bargaining unit eligible to participate in union elections for 12 months. Thus, hiring permanent replacement workers does not provide a ready majority for voting out a union.

The National Labor Relations Board (NLRB) and the Courts have gone to great lengths to balance the rights of strikers against the rights of employers to continue to operate their businesses during strikes. In *NLRB v. Erie Resistor Corp.*, which was mentioned previously, the Supreme Court held that a struck employer may not offer inducements, such as super-seniority, to striker replacements, and to do so constitutes an unfair labor practice. The Court reasoned that although "the employer's interest must be deemed to outweigh the damage to concerted activities caused by permanently replacing strikers, it does not follow that the [employer's interest] also outweighs the far greater encroachment resulting from super-seniority in addition to permanent replacement."[8] Thus, the Supreme Court accommodated the rights of all parties in a fair and balanced manner consistent with section 7 of the NLRA. Taking its cue from the Court, the NLRB held, in *Burlington Homes, Inc.,*[9] that the employer commits an unfair labor practice when wages or benefits are offered to replacements that are higher than those offered the union during negotiations before the strike.

Strikers retain their status as employees under section 2(3) of the Act, and the Supreme Court held in *Fleetwood Trailer*[10] that, in the absence of "legitimate and substantial business justification," the employer commits an unfair labor practice if others are preferred over unreplaced "economic" strikers long after the strike has ended even though no jobs were available at the time the "economic" strikers applied for reinstatement. Expanding the *Fleetwood* protections, the Board held in *Laidlaw Corp.*[11] that economic strikers who unconditionally apply for reinstatement (1) remain employees even if their positions are held by "permanent" replacements and (2) are entitled to full reinstatement upon the departure of the "permanent" replacement, unless they have acquired regular and substantial equivalent employment, or the employer proves failure to offer full reinstatement was for legitimate and substantial business reasons. Furthermore, reinstated strikers are entitled to all benefits, including past seniority. In other words, "permanently" replaced economic strikers

[8] 373 U.S. 221, 232 (1962).

[9] 246 NLRB 1029 (1979).

[10] 389 U.S. 375 (1967).

[11] 171 NLRB 1366 (1968).

xxx

have the right to reinstatement over all others once their replacements depart, and strikers so reinstated retain all past benefits.

An employer walks a mine field in replacing strikers. If it is subsequently found that a strike was an unfair labor practice rather than an economic strike, an employer may be liable for back pay to all strikers from the time they unconditionally offered to return to work. Because of the Supreme Court's decision in *Belknap v. Hale*,[13] ... an employer must be extremely cautious in hiring "permanent" replacements who were promised permanent jobs but were later discharged to make room for returning strikers whom the employer reinstated in accordance with a settlement agreement [because the discharged replacements may sue the employer if state law allows]. Accordingly, the employer is subject to paying "damages" to "permanent replacements."

The Supreme Court's decision in *NLRB v. Curtin Matheson Scientific, Inc.* further put employers at peril if they question a union's majority status when a majority of the employees are replacements for striking employees. The Court ruled it may not be presumed that replacements do not support the striking union, and an employer commits an unfair labor practice if he refuses to bargain with the union on the claim that replacements outnumber strikers.

The many-layered protections that are extended to striking employees during a strike, at the time an employer makes a decision to hire replacement workers, and when the striking employee offers to return to work, guarantee that an employer cannot cavalierly hire permanent replacement workers as a means to "bust" a union. These protections also serve to ensure that many "permanently" replaced strikers do eventually get their old jobs back. In fact, the Bureau of National Affairs conducted a study that indicated that, even in those rare strikes involving permanent replacement workers, where the status of strikers could be determined, a majority were reinstated to their former jobs.[15] Beyond these legal protections, it should be reemphasized that sound practical considerations mitigate against hiring permanent replacement workers at all. The animosity created between labor and management, the difficulty of recruitment, and the costs of training replacement workers are but a few of the reasons why employers only reluctantly fill strike vacancies with permanent replacement workers. The sad fact is that H.R. 5 will likely lead to more job loss through the economic disruption caused by increased strike activity than will the limited use by employers of permanent replacement workers during economic strikes.

---

[13]463 U.S. 491 (1983).

[15]See "Daily Labor Report," No. 75, p. E-3 (April 17, 1992).

There was no increase in the incidence of striker replacement activity during the 1980's that would justify passage of H.R. 5

Proponents of H.R. 5 have argued that, after 55 years of coexisting with the possibility of permanent replacement, the practice has increased so dramatically in the last decade that it has become management's first and most common response to any labor dispute. Some have gone so far as to accuse employers of deliberately forcing strikes in order "bust" the union by hiring permanent replacements. Unfortunately, these contentions ignore both the facts surrounding the incidence of permanent replacement hirings, as well as the business realities of an employer's decision to resort to such a tactic.

The notion that employers cavalierly decide to replace entire units of employees contradicts the nearly universal efforts of employers to ensure workforce stability. Indeed, an experienced, well trained workforce is one of an employer's most valuable assets. In today's competitive marketplace, employers strive to hire and retain a quality workforce. Moreover, hiring permanent replacements is not only costly, in terms of recruitment, training, and productivity loss, it often is associated with strike violence, public relations problems and costly litigation. As a result, most employers involved in labor disputes will hire permanent replacements when faced with the most dire of circumstance and then, only as a last resort.

The only study of which we are aware that compares the use of permanent replacement workers prior to 1980 with the use in later years was conducted by the Employment Policy Foundation. The study, which was based on research of published cases decided from 1938 to 1989 citing the *Mackay* decision, found that the use of permanent replacements was both rare and relatively constant during that period.[16]

The rarity of an employer's resort to hiring permanent replacement workers is also borne out in a 1991 General Accounting Office study which found that permanent replacement workers were used in only 17% of recent strikes, and that only 4% of strikers were legally "replaced" in 1985. By 1989, the number of workers who were not reinstated after a strike had dropped to 3%.[17] To those who contend that the practice of hiring permanent replacements "exploded" in the 1980s, the GAO

---

[16]The study is published in "Loading the Scales: Is the Balance Between the Right to Strike and the Right to Operate in Need of Reform?" by Daniel V. Yager, Employment Policy Foundation (1993).

[17]See GAO/HRD-91-2, "Strikes and the Use of Permanent Strike Replacements in the 1970's and 1980's" (January 1991).

xxxii

has stated that there is "little supporting data" that employers have hired more permanent replacements since 1981. While the GAO did note that 45% of employers and 77% of the union representatives believed that replacement workers were hired more often in the 1980's, such unbuttressed opinion is hardly conclusive evidence on which to base a radical change in labor law.

Our Federal labor laws are designed to help resolve costly disputes between employees and employers. And while an employer's ability to hire permanent replacements is but one aspect of that design, its role in maintaining a balance between labor and management is evidenced by how little it is actually used.

Comparisons to the labor-management laws of other nations are irrelevant to the issue of whether H.R. 5 makes policy sense in the United States

Much has been made by proponents of H.R. 5 of the fact that the United States is the only industrialized nation in the world to allow the permanent replacement of striking workers. While a recent study by the United States Council for International Business and the Institute for International Human Resources casts doubt on this assertion,[18] even if it were accurate, such a comparison ignores not only the comprehensive body of statutory and regulatory labor relations law in each country, but also the economic, social, and cultural context of which any legal system is a part.

We could also pick and choose among the labor relations laws of other nations to find provisions that might be more amendable to the interests of American businesses than the system of balanced interests [in which] they must work within in this country. It would be interesting to note the position of the proponents of H.R. 5 on some of the other aspects of the labor relations laws of Great Britain, France, Germany, or the other nations whose ban on permanent replacement workers is so highly touted. Would H.R. 5's supporters favor multi-union representation of employees in the same work unit as is permitted in France, Italy and Germany? Maybe the proponents of H.R. 5 would support legislation to allow individual employee bargaining or unilateral employer action superseding collective bargaining agreement provisions as is the law in Germany, Austria, Luxembourg, Netherlands, Ireland, Spain and the United Kingdom? Perhaps Germany's ban on any strike that is severe enough to "grievously wound" a company is a provision that H.R. 5's proponents can accept? Would those who support H.R. 5 also support a Canadian-

---

[18]The 1993 study found that, of 32 countries responding [to] a survey of labor law and practices, seven countries clearly permit the use of permanent replacements, including Australia, Austria, Hong Kong, Ireland, Norway, South Africa, and the United Kingdom.

style prohibition on strikes seeking union recognition or over the interpretation of a collective bargaining agreement?[19]

A decision by any other country to include a ban on the hiring of permanent replacement workers within the fabric of their labor always tells us very little about whether that policy makes sense for the United States. The fact remains that within the context of our system of labor relations law, the collective bargaining process simply will not work with the inequality of power that will result from a ban on permanent replacement workers. Collective bargaining works because both labor and management have powerful economic tools—the right to strike and the right to hire replacement workers in an economic strike respectively—that make it in their mutual interests to hammer out an agreement. Without that balance, the concessions demanded by organized labor will become more unrealistic and more strikes will result.

H.R. 5's ban on permanent replacement workers is not limited to union workplaces

H.R. 5, as it was originally introduced in the 102nd Congress, was criticized because it covered non-union workplaces where it was asserted that the bill's protections would lead to indiscriminate and undisciplined strikes by groups of employees over minor issues. The Peterson substitute offered on the House floor during the last Congress attempted to address this issue by providing that the bill's protections apply only in union workplaces and in workplaces where a majority of employees have signed union authorization cards and the union, at least 30 days prior to the strike, has filed a petition to be recognized as the exclusive bargaining agent. H.R. 5 mimics the Peterson substitute with respect to the issue of the coverage of union versus nonunion workplaces.

Although the change in the coverage provision was purportedly designed to avoid disruption of nonunion workplaces, the ban on the use of permanent replacement workers continues to apply in the context of recognitional strikes. Essentially, any union with a "card check" majority could force an employer to recognize it as the exclusive bargaining agent simply by calling a strike. Many employers, who under the bill would be prohibited from maintaining operations by hiring permanent replacement workers, would not have the luxury of waiting for an NLRB-certified election to determine if the union in fact had majority status. Both employers and the labor community are well aware that the fact that a majority of employees have signed authorization cards is not a true indicator of the level of union support.

---

[19]See, generally, "Loading the Scales," *supra* n. 16.

xxxiv

The exemption of non-union workplaces from H.R. 5's prohibition creates an anomaly under the NLRA whereby non-union employees are ... second class citizens in terms of an employer's ability to permanently replace them. This unprecedented legal preference for union workers will surely be used as an organizational tool by labor unions struggling to increase their ranks above the paltry 12% of the private sector workforce they currently represent. The proponents of this legislation, by exempting nonunion workplaces, are recognizing that there is a legitimate use of the weapon of hiring permanent replacement workers. However, they then turn this recognition on its head by establishing a prohibition that allows them to tell nonunion employees that if they join the union, they can't be permanently replaced, whether it is legitimate or not.

...

H.R. 5 threatens the rights of employees who exercise their option not to strike.

Another decision that H.R. 5 is purportedly designed to overrule is the 1989 Supreme Court decision in *Trans World Airlines, Inc. v. Independent Federation of Flight Attendants,* 489 U.S. 426 (1989). This decision dealt with the issue of the rights of full-term strikers vis-a-vis the rights of crossover employees who did not honor the duration of the strike. In that case, at the conclusion of an economic strike, TWA refused to displace junior crossover employees who were able to bid into desirable job vacancies left open by more senior full-term strikers. Under the collective bargaining agreement, there was a seniority bidding system which would normally allow the most senior employees to select the most favorable job assignments, flight schedules and bases of operation. In essence, the returning strikers were arguing that at the conclusion of the strike, all the jobs should be re-bid so senior employees could get their previous job assignments back.

The Supreme Court held that there was no valid reason to treat crossover employees any differently than newly hired replacement workers and concluded that to do so would have the effect of penalizing workers who exercised their right not to strike. Thus, just as an employer is not bound to terminate a replacement worker to give a job to a returning striker, [an employer is] not bound to displace a crossover employee to give a specific job to a returning striker. The Court found that whether jobs were filled by crossover employees or replacement workers, they were simply not "available positions" to which returning strikers had a right to reinstatement.

The Supreme Court distinguished the *Erie Resistor* decision, which held that it is an unfair labor practice to give additional benefits to new hires or crossover employees. The employer in that case had given employees who did not honor the strike 20 years of additional seniority credit. In *Trans World Airlines,* the Supreme

Court found that full-term strikers lost no seniority either in actual or relative terms, and, in any future reduction in force, strikers could displace both junior crossover employees and new hires just as if the strike had never occurred.

The result contemplated by H.R. 5 would require employers to discriminate against those who choose not to strike, in order to benefit those who do. Such a result is entirely inconsistent with section 7 of the NLRA which, by design, protects employees' right to engage in concerted activities, as well as the right of employees to refrain from such activities.

CONCLUSION

Regardless of its duration, any strike causes some disrupt[ion] to our productive capacity, and in an increasingly competitive global economy, that is a result that none of us can favor. In those circumstances where geographic isolation or the need for special skills make it impossible to maintain business operations during a strike without hiring permanent replacement workers, the economic disruption caused by H.R. 5 will be even worse.

Moreover, our federal labor laws are predicated upon, and have consistently maintained, a balance of interests and risks between employees and employers. By prohibiting the hiring of permanent replacement workers, H.R. 5 will place so heavy a thumb on the scale in favor of labor that the foundation of our system of collective bargaining will be seriously undermined.

In conclusion, therefore, we believe that the consequences of enacting this bill are likely to be broadly felt, as more American businesses are rendered unproductive by increased work stoppages and uncompetitive by inflationary labor demands. The unfortunate result will be shrinking profitability, investment, and ultimately, jobs.

xxxvi

Questions for Discussion

1. The majority argues that H.R. 5 would promote productivity by preserving a stable and experienced work force. Is this an appropriate consideration?

2. Relying on Professor Gramm's study, the majority states that strikes last longer when permanent replacements are hired. In which direction does causality flow? In other words, has Professor Gramm reversed the cause and the effect?

3. After noting instances in which employers have used permanent replacements, the majority writes, "For this new breed of employer, who use and even encourage strikes in order to undermine the collective bargaining process, the basic assumption that there are economic reasons to retain a long-term work force is no longer applicable." Is this statement consistent with the rest of the majority's argument? If economic realities have changed, should employers adhere to old practices?

4. Based on Professor Cooke's study, the majority argues that, in the long run, firms that "adopt hardball, confrontational tactics such as the use of permanent strike replacements are less profitable than firms that adopt a cooperative approach to labor relations." In which direction does causality flow? Has Professor Cooke reversed cause and effect?

5. Should it be an unfair labor practice for an employer to break a union by forcing a strike (for example, by making a demand in bargaining that the union could not accept) and hiring permanent replacements?

THE LAW

We have noted above that, at common law, a worker who went on strike was considered to have resigned. Consequently, before 1935 an employer was at liberty to replace strikers. We have also noted that the Labor Act changed this rule so that strikers remain employees of the struck firm.

Section 8(a)(3) prohibits an employer from discriminating against a worker because of concerted activity. A strike is concerted activity. A replacement is a worker who chooses not to engage in a strike. Thus, it can be argued that hiring a replacement for a striker is to discriminate against the striker for engaging in concerted activity and in favor of the replacement for not engaging in concerted activity. In addition, at the time the following case was decided, section 13 of the Act read:

> "Nothing in this Act shall be construed so as either to interfere with or impede or diminish in any way the right to strike."[t]

Replacing strikers arguably interferes with, impedes, or diminishes their right to strike. Among other things, the following case considers whether this reasoning is sound. As you read the case, consider whether the Court's statement on replacement of economic strikers is holding or dictum.

✦

---

[t]Section 13 now reads:

> "Nothing in this Act, except as specifically provided for herein, shall be construed so as either to interfere with or impede or diminish in any way the right to strike, or to affect the limitations or qualifications on that right."

The changes in section 13 do not affect the issue in the following case.

xxxviii

National Labor Relations Board v. Mackay Radio
304 U.S. 333 (1937)

{The employer (respondent) operated facilities in several cities. The union called a nation-wide strike over economic issues. Although all of the workers in the San Francisco office heeded the call, few workers elsewhere struck. Wishing to maintain operations in San Francisco, the employer asked employees in other cities to fill in for the strikers. The employer promised that those who agreed would be allowed to remain in San Francisco if they chose. By the third day of the strike, 11 employees had transferred to San Francisco.

{Seeing the strike was unsuccessful elsewhere, the workers in San Francisco offered to return to work. The employer accepted the offer, but drew up a list of 11 strikers who would not be recalled because their jobs had been taken by replacements. Later, six of the replacements decided to return to the cities from which they came, and six of the strikers on the list were recalled.

{The union filed a charge with the Labor Board, alleging that the workers on the no-recall list were chosen because they had been the most active in the strike. The Board agreed, holding the employer had violated §§ 8(a)(1) and (3) by refusing to recall five strikers because of their concerted activity. The Board ordered the employer to reinstate the five remaining strikers. The Court of Appeals refused to enforce the Board's order. The Supreme Court granted the Board's petition for *certiorari* and upheld the Board. The Court's comments on the employer's right to hire permanent replacements for strikers follow.}

Mr. Justice ROBERTS delivered the opinion of the Court.

...

The strikers remained employees under § 2(3) of the Act, which provides: "The term 'employee' shall include ... any individual whose work has ceased as a consequence of, or in connection with, any current labor dispute or because of any unfair labor practice, and who has not obtained any other regular and substantially equivalent employment...." Within this definition the strikers remained employees for the purpose of the Act and were protected against the unfair labor practices denounced by it. Nor was it an unfair labor practice to replace the striking employees with others in an effort to carry on the business. Although § 13 provides, "Nothing in this Act shall be construed so as to interfere with or impede or diminish in any way the right to strike," it does not follow that an employer, guilty of no act denounced by the statute, has lost the right to protect and continue his business by supplying places left vacant by strikers. And he is not bound to discharge those hired to fill the places of strikers, upon the election of the latter to resume their employment, in order to create places for them. The assurance by respondent to those who accepted employment during the strike that if they so desired their places might be permanent was not an unfair labor practice, nor was it such to reinstate only so many of the strikers as there were vacant places to be filled. But the claim put forward is that the unfair labor practice indulged by the respondent was discrimination in reinstating striking employees by keeping out certain of them for the sole reason that they had been active in the union. As we have said, the strikers retained, under the Act, the status of employees. Any such discrimination in putting them back to work is, therefore, prohibited by § 8.

...

As we have said, the respondent was not bound to displace men hired to take the strikers' places in order to provide positions for them. It might have refused reinstatement on the grounds of skill or ability, but the Board found that it did not do so. It might have resorted to any one of a number of methods of determining which of its striking employees would have to wait because five men had taken permanent positions during the strike; but it is found that the preparation and use of the list, and the action taken by respondent, was with the purpose to discriminate against those most active in the union. There is evidence to support these findings.

....

♣

QUESTIONS FOR REFLECTION

1. The Court said the employer could have determined which strikers to recall by "any one of a number of methods" other than the extent of their concerted activity. Name a few methods that would not have violated the Labor Act.

2. What reasons did the Court give for saying that an employer may hire permanent replacements? How much respect does a case deserve as precedent if a court has not revealed its reasons for decision?

3. Perhaps the Court's discussion of an employer's right to hire permanent replacements is so brief because it was not an issue in the case! One reason it was not an issue is that the Labor Board did not hold that it was

an unfair labor practice for the employer to bring in permanent replacements for economic strikers. The General Counsel charged, and the Board held, only that the employer committed discrimination by deciding which strikers to recall according to how active they had been during the strike. Nevertheless, the employer argued in its brief to the Supreme Court that it had the right to hire permanent replacements, and in its reply brief, the Board conceded that employers may hire permanent replacements for economic (but not for unfair labor practice) strikers. That the parties agreed on the point is a second reason why the legality of hiring permanent replacements was not an issue before the Court. In such cases, it is normal practice for courts to refrain from commenting on the issue. Had the Court in <u>Mackay</u> followed this practice, it might have written something like this:

> The employer brought in permanent replacements for the strikers. The employer and the Board agree that an employer may hire permanent replacements for economic strikers. Assuming without deciding that this is the law, we proceed to the issue on which the parties disagree, to wit, whether the Board may order an employer to reinstate strikers as a remedy for an unfair labor practice.

What is the name for a statement like this? What effect would it probably have on subsequent cases?

4. The rule of <u>Mackay Radio</u> applies to economic strikes, that is, strikes motivated by a dispute over the terms and conditions of employment. Most strikes are economic, but some strikes are motivated by an employer's unfair labor practices. For example, in the introduction to <u>Jefferson Standard</u> we mentioned the <u>Fansteel</u> case, in which workers struck because their employer had committed serious unfair labor practices.

(a) Should unfair labor practice strikes be permitted today?

(b) If so, should an employer be allowed to replace unfair labor practice strikers?

$$\Omega$$

Solicitation on Company Property

Introduction

Property rights are among the most nearly absolute of all the rights we enjoy. For example, if you own a piece of real estate, you may exclude everyone else on earth from it, and you may allow (in legal terms, grant a license to) someone to enter only upon conditions that you specify.[a]

Property rights apply not only to real estate, but also to moveable property (known as a **chattel**), whether it be tangible, such as a pin, a bookcase, or a tractor, or intangible, such as a debt, a copyright, or the goodwill of a business.[b] In general, the same rights that apply to real estate apply to chattels.

A business is typically a combination of real estate and chattels. Part of operating a business is usually hiring workers. Workers generally must enter property in the control of the business; thus, employment involves property rights of real estate. Workers normally must handle tools that belong to the business, and often deal with intangible things like secret formulae or the names of customers; thus, employment also involves property rights of chattels. In the past, when we protected property rights to the fullest, an employer had the right to exclude a worker from the real estate on which the business was located, to license the worker to enter the property only during hours specified by the employer, and to control the behavior of the worker while on the property and while handling the employer's chattels.

---

[a]The same applies to leased property, except that the lease usually reserves to the landlord the right to enter for specific purposes, for example, to make repairs.

[b]The terms "personal property" and "personalty" are synonyms for "chattel."

NLRB v. Babcock and Wilcox

We have seen that, in the Nineteenth and early Twentieth Centuries, the property rights just mentioned were considered to be constitutional rights, and the government was prohibited from infringing them.[c] Our view of the Constitution changed during the 1930s, and today we recognize that the government may pass laws that limit, to some extent, one's property rights. When the Labor Act was held to be constitutional, employers lost the right to discriminate against workers on the basis of their concerted activity.[d] Similarly, fifty years ago, a landlord was free to refuse to rent an apartment to a person, a business was free to refuse to serve a customer, and an employer was free to refuse to hire a worker, because of the person's race. Today, however, the law prohibits racial discrimination in renting real estate, in serving the public, and in employing workers.

A result of our changing view of the importance of property rights vis-a-vis other rights is that boundaries must be re-drawn between competing legitimate interests. The law must determine where the property right of a business ends and the right of a customer or employee begins. One of the first situations in which a boundary had to be drawn involved labor relations.

In two cases decided in a single opinion, Republic Aviation v. NLRB and NLRB v. Le Tourneau, 324 U.S. 793 (1945), the Supreme Court considered the legality of employers' rules that prohibited workers from soliciting for the union on company property during rest breaks, lunch, and other non-working hours. Solicitation included wearing union insignia like buttons and speaking to co-workers. The Board had concluded that the no-solicitation rules violated section 8(a)(1). The employers' principal argument was that the Board had not followed proper procedures in reaching its conclusion,

---

[c]Recall Adair v. United States and Coppage v. Kansas.

[d]Recall NLRB v. Jones & Laughlin.

and most of the Supreme Court's opinion was devoted to rejecting this argument. But the Court also addressed the issue of whether the no-solicitation rules were lawful. It wrote:

> These cases bring here for review the action of the National Labor Relations Board in working out an adjustment between the undisputed right of self-organization assured to employees under the Wagner Act and the equally undisputed {property} right of employers to maintain discipline in their establishments. Like so many others, these rights are not unlimited in the sense that they can be exercised without regard to any duty which the existence of rights in others may place upon employer or employee. Opportunity to organize and proper discipline are both essential elements in a balanced society." 324 U.S. at 797-798.

> Not only has the Board in these cases sufficiently expressed the theory upon which it concludes that rules against solicitation or prohibitions against the wearing of insignia must fall as interferences with union organization, but, in so far as rules against solicitation are concerned, it had theretofore succinctly expressed the requirements of proof which it considered appropriate to outweigh or overcome the presumption as to rules against solicitation. In the *Peyton*

Packing Co. Case, 49 NLRB (F) 828 at 843, the presumption adopted by the Board is set forth.[10] 324 U.S. at 803.

———

    [10] 49 NLRB (F) at 843, 844: "The Act, of course, does not prevent an employer from making and enforcing reasonable rules covering the conduct of employees on company time. Working time is for work. It is therefore within the province of an employer to promulgate and enforce a rule prohibiting union solicitation during working hours. Such a rule must be presumed to be valid in the absence of evidence that it was adopted for a discriminatory purpose. It is no less true that time outside working hours, whether before or after work, or during luncheon or rest periods, is an employee's time to use as he wishes without unreasonable restraint, although the employee is on company property. It is therefore not within the province of an employer to promulgate and enforce a rule prohibiting union solicitation by an employee outside of working hours, although on company property. Such a rule must be presumed to be an unreasonable impediment to self-organization and therefore discriminatory in the absence of evidence that special circumstances make the rule necessary in order to maintain production or discipline."

It is clear, therefore, that employees may solicit one another for unionization on company property during non-working hours. May they get help from a union? That is, may a union representative, who is not an employee of the company, enter company property and do what employees themselves may do, namely, solicit employees to join the union during non-working hours? Here follow the decision of the Court of Appeals for the Fifth Circuit on this issue plus excerpts from briefs filed in the Supreme Court in the appeal of the Fifth Circuit's decision. A central issue is whether <u>Republic Aviation</u> and <u>Le Tourneau</u> are precedents for the case at bar, or whether they are distinguishable.

National Labor Relations Board v. Babcock and Wilcox Co.
222 F.2d 316 (5th Cir. 1955)

HUTCHESON, Chief Judge.

{The employer, Babcock & Wilcox (the respondent), prohibited non-employees from soliciting on company property. The rule was enforced without discrimination, that is, outsiders — whether soliciting for a union or for any other purpose — were barred. Union organizers who sought to solicit in the parking lot on company property complained to the Board, which held the employer in violation of § 8(a)(1) and ordered the employer to permit the organizers to solicit on company property. The employer refused to obey the Board's order, and the Board petitioned the court for enforcement.}

...

... Th{e} question is whether, on a record devoid of proof that any employees were disciplined or in any manner discriminatorily dealt with by the respondent, or were or desired to be members of the union, or were in any way connected with or interested in the distribution by the union representatives of its literature, the board had authority to require the respondent to institute in favor of non-employee union organizers, complete strangers to it and to its employees, a discriminatory non-enforcement of its non-distribution rule, which the proof showed and examiner and board found had always and uniformly been enforced in a completely non-discriminatory way.

... We find ourselves in full agreement too with the contention of the respondent that the orders of the board in this case are not in accordance with, but in direct violation of, the letter and spirit of the Labor Management Act, as amended. Indeed we are at a loss to understand how on this record — which contains neither findings (nor evidence furnishing a basis for findings) that the rights or interests of respondent's employees are involved or will be furthered by compelling the respondent to institute a discriminatory application in favor of a particular labor union of its non-distribution rule — the board can take to itself the power to accord the union rights which the statute does not accord it by imposing against the respondent, in favor of a particular union, a servitude on its property[e] which the law, neither in terms nor in spirit, accords to it, in a case, too, where no employee is involved, no employee is complaining, and no rights of employees have been invaded or abridged by the respondent. We think that the order is itself in violation of the Labor Management Act and of the board's duty to impartially enforce it as between union

---

[e]{A servitude is an easement, that is, the right of one person to use the property of another person for a special purpose. — ed.}

NLRB v. Babcock and Wilcox

and management in the interest of neither but only in the interest of the employees.

...

Enforcement of the Board's order is denied.

★ ★ ★ ★

```
    The Labor Board obtained a writ of certiorari from
the Supreme Court.  The Board and the employer offered
the following arguments.
```

★ ★ ★ ★

National Labor Relations Board v. Babcock & Wilcox Co.
351 U.S. 105 (1956)

From the brief of the Labor Board
(Petitioner)

{The brief is signed by Simon E. Sobeloff, Solicitor General of the U.S., and Theophil C. Kammholz, General Counsel, David P. Findling, Associate General Counsel, Dominick L. Manoli, Assistant General Counsel, and Ruth V. Reel, attorney, NLRB.}

The Board properly found that respondent violated Section 8(a)(1) of the Act by prohibiting union organizers from distributing union literature on its plant parking lot during the employees' free time.

In *National Labor Relations Board v. Le Tourneau Company,* 324 U.S. 793, this Court held that an employer prohibition against the distribution of union literature by employees on a company parking lot unlawfully interfered with the rights guaranteed employees by Section 7 of the Act because it constituted an unreasonable impediment to the employees' exercise of those rights. The only significant factual difference between the two cases, which the court below deemed decisive, is that here the employer's rule against such distribution was enforced against nonemployee union organizers. Nevertheless, we believe that the principles upon which the *Le Tourneau* decision rests also sustain the Board's ruling here that respondent violated Section 8(a)(1) of the Act in barring these union organizers from distributing union literature on its parking lot.

1. In *Le Tourneau,* as here, the employer's plant was located in a rural area. The employees' dwellings were widely scattered within a radius of 20 miles from the

plant. Contact on public ways or on noncompany property with employees at or near the plant was limited to those employees, approximately one-third of the working force, who were likely to walk across the public highway near the plant on their way to work or who would stop their private automobiles, busses or other conveyances on the public roads for communications.

The employer in that case adopted and enforced a rule prohibiting his employees from distributing union literature during their free time on a company-owned parking lot adjacent of his fenced-in plant. Although neither union bias nor a discriminatory purpose prompted the adoption or enforcement of the rule, the Board concluded that the prohibition constituted an unreasonable and therefore illegal impediment to the employees' exercise of the rights guaranteed by Section 7 of the Act. This Court upheld the Board's invalidation of the employer's rule as an appropriate "adjustment between the undisputed right of self-organization assured to employees under the ... Act and the equally undisputed right of employers to maintain discipline in their establishments." 324 U.S. at 797-798.

The underlying considerations which prompted the Board and this Court to reach that conclusion are relevant and controlling here. Insuring the right of employees to organize for mutual aid is, as this Court pointed out, a "dominant purpose" of the Act. In order that employees may effectively exercise the rights guaranteed them under the Act, there must be available to the employees adequate channels of communication for the receipt and transmittal of organizational information, both oral and written. On the other hand, due recognition must be given to the employer's property and legitimate business interests. "Like so many others, these rights are not unlimited in the sense that they can be exercised without regard to any duty which the existence of rights in others may place upon employer or employee. Opportunity to organize and proper discipline are both essential elements in a balanced society." 324 U.S. at 798. Therefore, where an employer seeks to justify a rule prohibiting organizational activities on his premises, the critical issue before the Board is whether, on balance, the injury to the organizational interests of the employees which the rule imposes outweighs the injury which the employer would sustain if the rule were abrogated.

Weighing these factors, the Board found in *Le Tourneau,* with the subsequent approval of this Court, that the prohibition against distribution of union literature on the company parking lot deprived the employees of an important avenue of communication, and therefore seriously impeded the exercise of their right to self-organization for purposes of collective bargaining....

Against the detriment to employee interests which the parking lot prohibition imposed, the Board weighed the employer's need for such a restriction to maintain production or discipline or to protect other legitimate interests. The Board had already concluded that an employer was justified in prohibiting organizational activities during working hours, and, further, that his interest in keeping a clean and orderly plant warranted a prohibition against distribution of union literature inside the plant even during nonworking hours. Noting, however, that "considerations of efficiency and order which may be deemed of first importance within buildings where production is being carried on, do not have the same force in the case of parking lots" (54 NLRB at 1261), the Board found that permitting distribution of union literature on the parking lot during nonworking hours would impose little, if any, detriment upon the legitimate interests of the employer and that the employer remained free to protect those interests by methods which did not adversely affect the rights of employees.

Thus, the employer's assertion that the rule was necessary to prevent littering of the parking lot did not justify a prohibition against distribution, because the littering could be avoided by a rule against littering. His claim that the prohibition was necessary to prevent literature from going into the plant where it might provoke controversy which might impair efficiency and safety was deemed to be equally insubstantial, since his interest in these respects could as well be safeguarded by a rule barring the carrying of literature into the plant as by a rule directed against distribution on the parking lot. Accordingly, the Board found that, on balance, the employer's business interests were insufficient to justify the impediment which the parking lot prohibition imposed upon the effective exercise of the employees' organizational rights, and that therefore the employer's proprietary interest could properly be subordinated to the employees' interest in self-organization. And this court approved the accommodation the Board had made between the competing interests.

Upon substantially identical reasoning, the Board has concluded in the instant and other cases that a similar ban against distribution of literature by *union organizers* on a company parking lot likewise constitutes an unlawful interference with the employees' organizational rights if it unreasonably restricts opportunity for their exercise. {Emphasis added.} Proceeding under the principles which this Court approved in the *Le Tourneau* case, the Board has assessed the impact of such a restriction upon the organizational interests of the employees. It has recognized that, as this Court noted in *Thomas v. Collins,* 323 U.S. 516, 533-534, adequate opportunity for employees to receive information not only from fellow employees but also from union organizers is an indispensable attribute of the right to self-organization. It has found that this right cannot, as a practical matter, be effectively realized unless the union has access to the employees in the area in the immediate vicinity of the plant. For union distributors face the same practical hardships which confront employee distributors in attempting to distribute literature to employees' homes scattered throughout a large city or over a wide rural area.

...

2. The court below distinguished *Le Tourneau* and held it inapplicable because the distributors there were *employees* while the distributors here were *nonemployee union organizers*. {Emphasis added.} Basically, the ruling below rests on the premise that, where the prohibition is against nonemployees rather than employees, it cannot be said that "rights of employees have been invaded or abridged." This premise misconceives the scope of employee rights under the Act.

The statutory guarantee of self-organization, as this Court recognized in *Thomas v. Collins,* 323 U.S. 516, 534, includes not only the right of employees "fully and freely to discuss and be informed" concerning organizational matters, but also the "necessarily correlative" right of a "union, its members and officials ... to discuss with and inform the employees" about the advantages of self-organization. The Court further noted (323 U.S. at 533) that the right "to organize freely for collective bargaining ... comprehends whatever may be appropriate and lawful to accomplish and maintain such organization." As stated in the Senate Report on Violations of Free Speech and Rights of Labor (S. Rep. No. 1150, 77th Cong., 2d Sess., Part 1, pp. 4-5):

> ... The right of self-organization and collective bargaining is a complex whole, embracing the various elements of meetings, speeches, peaceful picketing, the printing and distribution of pamphlets, news and argument, all of which, however, are traceable to the fundamental liberties of expression and assembly. So compounded, the right of self-organization and collective bargaining is fundamental, being one phase of the process of free association essential to the democratic way of life.

Obedient to the broad legislative purpose incorporated in the Act, the Board has found from the outset of its administration that "The rights guaranteed to employees by the act include full freedom to receive aid, advice, and information from others, concerning those rights and their enjoyment" (*Matter of Harlan Fuel Company,* 8 NLRB 25, 32).

Both before and after the passage of the Act it has, of course, been common practice for employees to avail themselves of the services of outside organizers. The necessity for invoking such assistance, particularly in the light of modern industrial conditions, requires little elaboration. Today, as everyone knows, it is commonly true that effective union organization can be best promoted by persons who devote their

x   *NLRB v. Babcock and Wilcox*

full time and knowledge to the task. Union representatives who specialize in organization are experienced in organizing techniques and familiar with the complexities of present day labor law. Formal training in organizational methods is increasingly an indispensable prerequisite to organizing work. Unions have more and more drawn upon colleges and graduate and law schools for the knowledge and skills required by ambitious organizing campaigns. In addition, the labor movement has developed its own training schools for organizers comparable to the salesmanship training courses of industry and the programs of business colleges and graduate schools. Employees who are unable to tap such organizational know-how gained from long experience or specialized training are manifestly handicapped in exercising their statutory right to self-organization for purposes of collective bargaining. And to the extent that otherwise appropriate channels of communication between employees and such organizers are blocked, as here, the employees' statutory rights are diminished.

Contrary to the view of the court below, it should not be significant, even assuming it to be correct, that the record in the instant case may be "devoid of proof that any employees ... were or desired to be members of the Union, or were in any way connected with or interested in the distribution by the union representatives of its literature." While the record actually suggests that the court's statement was inaccurate, the decisive point in any event is that employee rights are no less involved merely because organizational information is disseminated by the union on its own initiative rather than by the employees or upon their invitation. In either case, the distributors are "pursuing the same end, namely, to advise the workers at the plant of their rights under the Act and of the purported advantages of unionization" (Judge Healy dissenting in *National Labor Relations Board v. Monsanto Chemical Co.,* 225 F. 2d 16, 22 (C.A.9)). Where lack of interest stems from apathy or ignorance of the advantages of self-organization, employees cannot realize the benefits of the statutory guarantees unless those advantages are called to their attention. Indeed, it has been noted that "very few American employees organize themselves. They have to be organized." 93 *Cong. Rec.* 4432. Adequate opportunity to receive information from outside organizers is therefore both appropriate and essential for the exercise and enjoyment of the employees' right of self-organization, and therefore necessarily encompassed within its protection.

An employer may not restrict the exercise of that right solely on the ground that his property rights entitle him to exclude "trespassers." This Court has recognized that the grant to employees in Section 7 of the Act of the right to engage in concerted activities for purposes of self-organization may properly supersede the employer's right, as property owner, to exercise absolute dominion over the property on which such activities occur. As stated in *National Labor Relations Board v. Stowe Spinning Co.,* 336 U.S. 226, 232, "It is not 'every interference with property rights that is within the Fifth Amendment.... Inconvenience, or even some dislocation of property rights, may be necessary in order to safeguard the right to collective bargaining.'" And, of course, *National Labor Relations Board v. Le Tourneau* applies this familiar principle....

... Having opened up its property for employee use for its own advantage, respondent cannot exclude as trespassers persons whose presence is necessary for an effective exercise of the employees' statutory rights. The necessity for protecting the statutory rights of employees who use the plant parking lot affords ample basis for superseding the "dominion" which the employer-owner of a parking lot may exercise over his property. Indeed, even the court below recognized, as both the Board and the courts of appeals have generally held, that where employees live on company property the employer's proprietary interest may properly be subordinated to the employees' statutory rights so as to permit outside organizers to have access to them for the purpose of assisting them in the exercise of these rights. The premise on which such cases stand is that access is necessary to the effective exercise of the employees' rights. By the same token, the employer's proprietary interest in the instant case may properly be subordinated to the employees' interest in self-organization for purposes of collective bargaining. And, as we have shown, the Board was fully justified in concluding that access to the employees at the plant property is necessary if they are to make effective use of the statutory guarantees.

From the brief of the employer
(Respondent)

{The brief is signed by O. B. Fisher, Paris, TX.}

2.

Unions Have No Inherent Right to Distribute Union Literature in the Manner Quickest, Most Convenient and Cheapest for Them As Against the Right of Ownership of Property

Throughout Petitioner's brief, the theme is that union organizers have the right to distribute their literature and solicit union membership at the location or locations most convenient to them, in the quickest manner and with the least expense possible. Where do they get such a right? The Act does not expressly or impliedly give to non-employee organizers such right. The Board, based on a conclusion that the union could not readily distribute its literature off Respondent's premises, gave to its organizers the right to make distribution thereof on Respondent's property, the place most convenient for it.

...

Even if we are to concede that the immediate vicinity of the plant is the most convenient place for distribution of union literature and perhaps the least expensive, the Act does not give to the non-employee union organizer the inherent right to do his solicitation at the place most convenient to him, particularly at the sacrifice of the property rights of others. The Petitioner's argument, that the union cannot convey information to employees unless it has access to the employees in the immediate vicinity of the plant, is completely fallacious. Respondent is surprised at Petitioner advancing such an argument with all of the means, devices and methods of communication that we have and which were at the union's disposal here, had it desired to use them....

Respondent recognizes that employees are entitled to freedom in receiving advice and information from others concerning their rights under the Act. However, this does not give to the union organizers, ... the right to exact a servitude upon the employer's property whereby the employer is required to permit the union organizer to go on his property....

If we are to face realities, we must face the fact that labor unions in the United States are big business with substantial wealth at their control. Where do the representatives of this business get the right to use another's property in the furtherance of their efforts solely because it will be easier, cheaper and more convenient for them, as contended by Petitioner? Surely the employer is not called on to furnish a forum for the union organizer, in order to make his job easier, quicker and cheaper for him. An employer is not required to aid employees to organize, but only not to interfere.

...

The magnitude of the right to own and control property has always been recognized and jealously guarded by our courts as a necessary part of liberty and freedom. The right has never been lightly dealt with. It is of such importance to our society and democracy that it is protected and guaranteed by the *Fifth Amendment to the Constitution of the United States.* Admittedly, the exercise of the elements of enjoyment and ownership of property are subject to government regulation to the extent that the exercise of an equally valuable and important right by another shall not be denied to him. However, in each instance that our courts have found it necessary to make some dislocation of property rights in favor of strangers, it was only when the stranger had encountered an insuperable and unsurpassable hardship or difficulty in exercising some Constitutional right, for example, his freedom of communication with others.

...

5.

Board Improperly Equalizes Rights of Employees and Non-employees

The order entered by the Board, which Petitioner here seeks to have enforced, accords to non-employee union organizers exactly the same rights and privileges as is accorded unto employees. The equalization of those rights was never intended by the Act, nor by Congress. As stated by the Fifth Circuit Court of Appeals in the case of *National Labor Relations Board v. Swartz,* 146 F. 2d 773 (1945) at page 774:

> Contrary to a rather general misconception, the National Labor Relations Act was passed for the primary benefit of the employees as distinguished from the benefit of labor unions....

...

... {B}asic distinctions exist between rights accorded employees and non-employees by the Act. *Section 7 of the Act* specifically gives the rights encompassed in the Act to employees and also specifically provides that employees shall have the right to refrain from any or all of the activities provided for in the Act. Non-employees have no rights under the Act except such rights, by inference, as are necessary to prevent the rights accorded employees from being forfeited. Nevertheless, the Board here seeks to have this Court perpetuate an order of its own which would equalize the standards governing the conduct and rights of non-employee union organizers under the Act. Such equalization was never intended by Congress, and is not provided for, either expressly or impliedly by the Act. A distinction between those rights has been consistently recognized by our courts and properly so. The Petitioner here seeks to do away with that distinction. The Petitioner seeks to justify such equalization by arguing that it has put ample safeguards in the order by which it permits the employer to impose reasonable rules and regulation. Such argument is completely foreign to the question before this Court. To require that *employees* be permitted to distribute literature on the employer's parking lot, does not invade his property or abridge his rights, they being *licensees*, as does the requirement permitting non-employees to distribute literature on the employer's parking lot. The employee already has a license from the owner of the parking lot to use it. Our courts have consistently recognized basic distinctions between the rights of licensees and strangers to the use of property in a variety of situations. The courts should not entertain the thought of equalizing those rights in any situation unless and until specifically provided for by Congress. Even then serious questions under the Fifth Amendment to the Constitution would arise.

...

By its order in this case the Board would accord respondent the right to impose reasonable and non-discriminatory regulations "in the interest of plant efficiency and discipline" in respect to the use of its property for organizational purposes but not so as to deny "full access" to non-employee union organizers for the purposes of soliciting union memberships and distributing union literature. Plant efficiency and discipline make sense when related to employees, but they become sheer nonsense when they are related to non-employees. How can an employer provide for the discipline of non-employees who are trespassers as to him and over whom he can exercise neither sanction nor control?

QUESTIONS FOR REFLECTION

1. Republic Aviation and Le Tourneau held that an employer may not prohibit employees from soliciting for a union on company property during non-working hours. Can you think of any circumstances in which an employer may legitimately prohibit workers from soliciting for a union on company property during non-working hours?

2. The holding of a case is limited by the facts of the case. This is an important principle of legal doctrine, and it bears repeating. **The holding of a case is limited by the facts of the case.** The solicitation in Republic Aviation and Le Tourneau occurred before a union had been recognized as the bargaining agent for a unit of workers; therefore, the rule of those cases applies only to solicitation BEFORE a union has been recognized. But a precedent can often be stretched to apply to related cases. How should the precedent of Republic Aviation and Le Tourneau be applied AFTER a union has been recognized?

(a) For example, should employees have the right to discuss a grievance arising under a labor contract on company property during non-working hours?

(b) Another example: suppose some employees become dissatisfied with their union. Should employees have the right to criticize the union on company property during non-working hours or to solicit one another to replace the union or oust it?

3. One argument in favor of allowing union organizers on to company property is that unions experience significant difficulty in contacting workers in other places. Imagine yourself to be an experienced advocate for employers in Babcock & Wilcox. You know that sometimes a small concession can avert a great loss. Can you think of a concession that would be small in comparison to allowing union organizers on to company property, yet would mitigate the difficulty the unions have identified?

4. The employer's brief notes that unions have become "big business." So have union-busting firms, that is, professional consultants who specialize in defeating union organizing campaigns. These consultants have developed sophisticated techniques for persuading workers

to vote against unions. Also, large privately owned
shopping malls have proliferated. Because they are
private property, their owners may exclude all
solicitors, including union organizers. If Congress were
debating a statute to overrule Babcock and Wilcox, how
should these developments affect the debate?

Ω

Plant Closings

Introduction

Imagine you are the officer of the day at a regional office of the Labor Board. A union representative files a charge that says:

> "My union just won an election at the Darlington Co. Immediately after the election, we tried to schedule a meeting with management to commence bargaining. They said there was no point because the owner had decided to close the plant rather than deal with a union. He did and we all were laid off."

In your mind, you load the program entitled, "Match the Facts," and you enter the facts in the charge. Does your mental computer detect a match between the facts of an unfair labor practice and the facts in the charge?

Textile Workers v. Darlington Mfg. Co.
380 U.S. 263 (1965)

JUSTICE HARLAN delivered the opinion of the Court.

We here review judgments of the Court of Appeals setting aside and refusing to enforce an order of the National Labor Relations Board which found respondent Darlington guilty of an unfair labor practice by reason of having permanently closed its plant following petitioner union's election as the bargaining representative of Darlington's employees.

Darlington Manufacturing Company was a South Carolina corporation operating one textile mill. A majority of Darlington's stock was held by Deering Milliken, a New York "selling house" marketing textiles produced by others. Deering Milliken in turn was controlled by Roger Milliken, president of Darlington, and by other members of the Milliken family. The National Labor Relations Board found that the Milliken family, through Deering Milliken, operated 17 textile manufacturers, including Darlington, whose products, manufactured in 27 different mills, were marketed through Deering Milliken.

In March 1956 petitioner Textile Workers Union initiated an organizational campaign at Darlington which the company resisted vigorously in various ways, including threats to close the mill if the union won a representation election.[3] On September 6, 1956, the union won an election by a narrow margin. When Roger Milliken was advised of the union victory, he decided to call a meeting of the Darlington board of directors to consider closing the mill. Mr. Milliken testified before the Labor Board:

> "I felt that as a result of the campaign that had been conducted and the promises and statements made in these letters that had been distributed [favoring unionization], that if before we had had some hope, possible hope of achieving competitive [costs] ... by taking advantage of new machinery that was being put in, that this hope had diminished as a result of the election because a majority of the employees had voted in favor of the union . . . ." (R. 457.)

The board of directors met on September 12 and voted to liquidate the

---

[3]The Board found that Darlington had interrogated employees and threatened to close the mill if the union won the election. After the decision to liquidate was made, Darlington employees were told that the decision to close was caused by the election, and they were encouraged to sign a petition disavowing the union. These practices were held to violate § 8 (a)(1) of the National Labor Relations Act, and that part of the Board decision is not challenged here.

corporation, action which was approved by the stockholders on October 17. The plant ceased operations entirely in November, and all plant machinery and equipment were sold piecemeal at auction in December.

The union filed charges with the Labor Board claiming that Darlington had violated §§ 8 (a)(1) and (3) of the National Labor Relations Act by closing its plant, and § 8 (a)(5) by refusing to bargain with the union after the election.[5] The Board, by a divided vote, found that Darlington had been closed because of the antiunion animus of Roger Milliken, and held that to be a violation of § 8 (a)(3). The Board also found Darlington to be part of a single integrated employer group controlled by the Milliken family through Deering Milliken; therefore Deering Milliken could be held liable for the unfair labor practices of Darlington. Alternatively, since Darlington was a part of the Deering Milliken enterprise, Deering Milliken had violated the Act by closing part of its business for a discriminatory purpose. The Board ordered back pay for all Darlington employees until they obtained substantially equivalent work or were put on preferential hiring lists at the other Deering Milliken mills. Respondent Deering Milliken was ordered to bargain with the union in regard to details of compliance with the Board order.

On review, the Court of Appeals, sitting *en banc*, set aside the order and denied enforcement by a divided vote. The Court of Appeals held that even accepting arguendo the Board's determination that Deering Milliken had the status of a single employer, a company has the absolute right to close out a part or all of its business regardless of antiunion motives. The court therefore did not review the Board's finding that Deering Milliken was a single integrated employer. We granted *certiorari* to consider the important questions involved. We hold that so far as the Labor Relations Act is concerned, an employer has the absolute right to terminate his entire business for any reason he pleases, but disagree with the Court of Appeals that such right includes the ability to close part of a business no matter what the reason. We conclude that the cause must be remanded to the Board for further proceedings.

...

---

[5] The union asked for a bargaining conference on September 12, 1956 (the day that the board of directors voted to liquidate), but was told to await certification by the Board. The union was certified on October 24, and did meet with Darlington officials in November, but no actual bargaining took place. The Board found this to be a violation of § 8 (a)(5). Such a finding was in part based on the determination that the plant closing was an unfair labor practice, and no argument is made that § 8 (a)(5) requires an employer to bargain concerning a purely business decision to terminate his enterprise. Cf. *Fibreboard Paper Products Corp. v. Labor Board,* 379 U.S. 203.

Textile Workers v. Darlington

I.

We consider first the argument, advanced by the petitioner union ... and rejected by the Court of Appeals, that an employer may not go completely out of business without running afoul of the Labor Relations Act if such action is prompted by a desire to avoid unionization. Given the Board's findings on the issue of motive, acceptance of this contention would carry the day for the Board's conclusion that the closing of this plant was an unfair labor practice, even on the assumption that Darlington is to be regarded as an independent unrelated employer. A proposition that a single businessman cannot choose to go out of business if he wants to would represent such a startling innovation that it should not be entertained without the clearest manifestation of legislative intent or unequivocal judicial precedent so construing the Labor Relations Act. We find neither.

So far as legislative manifestation is concerned, it is sufficient to say that there is not the slightest indication in the history of the Wagner Act or of the Taft-Hartley Act that Congress envisaged any such result under either statute.

As for judicial precedent, the Board recognized that "there is no decided case directly dispositive of Darlington's claim that it had an absolute right to close its mill, irrespective of motive." 139 N. L. R. B., at 250....

The courts of appeals have generally assumed that a complete cessation of business will remove an employer from future coverage by the Act. Thus the Court of Appeals said in these cases: The Act "does not compel a person to become or remain an employee. It does not compel one to become or remain an employer. Either may withdraw from that status with immunity, so long as the obligations of any employment contract have been met." 325 F.2d, at 685. The Eighth Circuit, in *Labor Board v. New Madrid Mfg. Co.*, 215 F.2d 908, 914, was equally explicit:

> "But none of this can be taken to mean that an employer does not have the absolute right, at all times, to permanently close and go out of business ... for whatever reason he may choose, whether union animosity or anything else, and without his being thereby left subject to a remedial liability under the Labor Management Relations Act for such unfair labor practices as he may have committed in the enterprise, except up to the time that such actual and permanent closing ... has occurred."[12]

---

[12]In *New Madrid* the business was transferred to a new employer, which was held liable for the unfair labor practices committed by its predecessor before closing. The closing itself was not found to be an unfair labor practice.

The AFL-CIO suggests in its *amicus* brief that Darlington's action was similar to a discriminatory lockout, which is prohibited "'because designed to frustrate organizational efforts, to destroy or undermine bargaining representation, or to evade the duty to bargain.'" One of the purposes of the Labor Relations Act is to prohibit the discriminatory use of economic weapons in an effort to obtain future benefits. The discriminatory lockout designed to destroy a union, like a "runaway shop," is a lever which has been used to discourage collective employee activities in the future. But a complete liquidation of a business yields no such future benefit for the employer, if the termination is bona fide.[14] It may be motivated more by spite against the union than by business reasons, but it is not the type of discrimination which is prohibited by the Act. The personal satisfaction that such an employer may derive from standing on his beliefs and the mere possibility that other employers will follow his example are surely too remote to be considered dangers at which the labor statutes were aimed.[15] Although employees may be prohibited from engaging in a strike under certain conditions, no one would consider it a violation of the Act for the same employees to quit their employment *en masse*, even if motivated by a desire to ruin the employer. The very permanence of such action would negate any future economic benefit to the employees. The employer's right to go out of business is no different.

We are not presented here with the case of a "runaway shop," whereby Darlington would transfer its work to another plant or open a new plant in another locality to replace its closed plant.[17] Nor are we concerned with a shutdown where the employees, by renouncing the union, could cause the plant to reopen.[18] Such cases would involve discriminatory employer action for the purpose of obtaining some benefit from the employees in the future.[19] We hold here only that when an

---

[14] The Darlington property and equipment could not be sold as a unit, and were eventually auctioned off piecemeal. We therefore are not confronted with a sale of a going concern, which might present different considerations under §§ 8 (a)(3) and (5).

[15] Different considerations would arise were it made to appear that the closing employer was acting pursuant to some arrangement or understanding with other employers to discourage employee organizational activities in their businesses.

[17] After the decision to close the plant, Darlington accepted no new orders, and merely continued operations for a time to fill pending orders.

[18] Similarly, if all employees are discharged but the work continues with new personnel, the effect is to discourage any future union activities.

[19] All of the cases to which we have been cited involved closings found to have been

(continued...)

employer closes his entire business, even if the liquidation is motivated by vindictiveness toward the union, such action is not an unfair labor practice.[20]

II.

While we thus agree with the Court of Appeals that viewing Darlington as an independent employer the liquidation of its business was not an unfair labor practice, we cannot accept the lower court's view that the same conclusion necessarily follows if Darlington is regarded as an integral part of the Deering

---

(...continued)

motivated, at least in part, by the expectation of achieving future benefits. See cases cited in notes 16, 18, supra. The two cases which are urged as indistinguishable from Darlington are *Labor Board v. Savoy Laundry*, 327 F.2d 370, and *Labor Board v. Missouri Transit Co.*, 250 F.2d 261. In *Savoy Laundry* the employer operated one laundry plant where he processed both retail laundry pickups and wholesale laundering. Once the laundry was marked, all of it was processed together. After some of the employees organized, the employer discontinued most of the wholesale service, and thereafter discharged some of his employees. There was no separate wholesale department, and the discriminatory motive was obviously to discourage unionization in the entire plant. *Missouri Transit* presents a similar situation. A bus company operated an interstate line and an intrastate shuttle service connecting a military base with the interstate terminal. When the union attempted to organize all of the drivers, the shuttle service was sold and the shuttle drivers were discharged. Although the two services were treated as separate departments, it is clear from the facts of the case that the union was attempting to organize all of the drivers, and the discriminatory motive of the employer was to discourage unionization in the interstate service as well as the shuttle service.

[20]Nothing we have said in this opinion would justify an employer's interfering with employee organizational activities by threatening to close his plant, as distinguished from announcing a decision to close already reached by the board of directors or other management authority empowered to make such a decision. We recognize that this safeguard does not wholly remove the possibility that our holding may result in some deterrent effect on organizational activities independent of that arising from the closing itself. An employer may be encouraged to make a definitive decision to close on the theory that its mere announcement before a representation election will discourage the employees from voting for the union, and thus his decision may not have to be implemented. Such a possibility is not likely to occur, however, except in a marginal business; a solidly successful employer is not apt to hazard the possibility that the employees will call his bluff by voting to organize. We see no practical way of eliminating this possible consequence of our holding short of allowing the Board to order an employer who chooses so to gamble with his employees not to carry out his announced intention to close. We do not consider the matter of sufficient significance in the overall labor-management relations picture to require or justify a decision different from the one we have made.

Milliken enterprise. The closing of an entire business, even though discriminatory, ends the employer-employee relationship; the force of such a closing is entirely spent as to that business when termination of the enterprise takes place. On the other hand, a discriminatory partial closing may have repercussions on what remains of the business, affording employer leverage for discouraging the free exercise of § 7 rights among remaining employees of much the same kind as that found to exist in the "runaway shop" and "temporary closing" cases. Moreover, a possible remedy open to the Board in such a case, like the remedies available in the "runaway shop" and "temporary closing" cases, is to order reinstatement of the discharged employees in the other parts of the business. No such remedy is available when an entire business has been terminated. By analogy to those cases involving a continuing enterprise we are constrained to hold, in disagreement with the Court of Appeals, that a partial closing is an unfair labor practice under § 8(a)(3) if motivated by a purpose to chill unionism in any of the remaining plants of the single employer and if the employer may reasonably have foreseen that such closing would likely have that effect.

While we have spoken in terms of a "partial closing" in the context of the Board's finding that Darlington was part of a larger single enterprise controlled by the Milliken family, we do not mean to suggest that an organizational integration of plants or corporations is a necessary prerequisite to the establishment of such a violation of § 8 (a)(3). If the persons exercising control over a plant that is being closed for antiunion reasons (1) have an interest in another business, whether or not affiliated with or engaged in the same line of commercial activity as the closed plant, of sufficient substantiality to give promise of their reaping a benefit from the discouragement of unionization in that business; (2) act to close their plant with the purpose of producing such a result; and (3) occupy a relationship to the other business which makes it realistically foreseeable that its employees will fear that such business will also be closed down if they persist in organizational activities, we think that an unfair labor practice has been made out. Although the Board's single employer finding necessarily embraced findings as to Roger Milliken and the Milliken family which, if sustained by the Court of Appeals, would satisfy the elements of "interest" and "relationship" with respect to other parts of the Deering Milliken enterprise, that and the other Board findings fall short of establishing the factors of "purpose" and "effect" which are vital requisites of the general principles that govern a case of this kind. Thus, the Board's findings as to the purpose and foreseeable effect of the Darlington closing pertained only to its impact on the Darlington employees. No findings were made as to the purpose and effect of the closing with respect to the employees in the other plants comprising the Deering Milliken group. It does not suffice to establish the unfair labor practice charged here to argue that the Darlington closing necessarily had an adverse impact upon unionization in such other plants. We have heretofore observed that employer action which has a foreseeable consequence of discouraging concerted activities generally does not amount to a violation of § 8 (a)(3) in the absence of a showing of motivation which is aimed at achieving the prohibited effect.... In an area which trenches so closely upon otherwise legitimate employer prerogatives, we consider the absence of Board findings on this score a fatal defect in its decision. The Court of Appeals for its part did not deal with the question of purpose and effect at all, since it concluded that an employer's right to close down his entire business because of distaste for unionism, also embraced a partial closing so motivated.

Apart from this, the Board's holding should not be accepted or rejected without court review of its single employer finding, judged, however, in accordance with the general principles set forth above. Review of that finding, which the lower court found unnecessary on its view of the cause, now becomes necessary in light of our holding in this part of our opinion, and is a task that devolves upon the Court of Appeals in the first instance. In these circumstances, we think the proper disposition of this cause is to require that it be remanded to the Board so as to afford the Board the opportunity to make further findings on the issue of purpose and effect. This is particularly appropriate here since the cases involve issues of first impression. If such findings are made, the cases will then be in a posture for further review by the Court of Appeals on all issues. Accordingly, without intimating any view as to how any of these matters should eventuate, we vacate the judgments of the Court of Appeals and remand the cases to that court with instructions to remand them to the Board for further proceedings consistent with this opinion.

It is so ordered.

⚜

QUESTIONS FOR REFLECTION

1. We have noted that the elements of the unfair labor practice of discrimination are (1) the worker was engaged in concerted activity, (2) the employer disadvantaged the worker, and (3) the employer's reason was the worker's concerted activity. Do the facts of <u>Darlington</u> seem to match the facts of discrimination? If so, why did the Supreme Court exonerate the employer?

2. What is holding and what is dictum in the <u>Darlington</u> case?

3. Why did the Court announce the dictum in <u>Darlington</u>?

4. The Court suggests that lack of an effective remedy in the case of a total shut down is a reason to distinguish cases of runaway shops and partial closings. Is the Court right about this?

Exercises

1. Suppose a union is attempting to organize all the hourly-paid workers of a university. Before an election, the university closes its janitorial unit and contracts the work out: whereupon the union files an unfair labor practice charge. Write a brief opinion that resolves this case based on <u>Darlington</u>? Hint: an opinion is essentially an argument. Your opinion should therefore include the elements in our model of legal argument.

2. The Court distinguishes several cases in section II of its opinion. Choose one of these distinctions and express it within the model of a complete distinction.

$$\Omega$$

Promises and Benefits

Introduction

Section 8(a) of the Labor Act lists unfair labor practices which employers are forbidden to commit. The first one on the list, § 8(a)(1), is the most general; it forbids an employer

> "to interfere with, restrain, or coerce employees in the exercise of the rights guaranteed in section 7."

Interference, restraint, and coercion are broad concepts, indeed, too broad for the purposes of Labor Law. For example, suppose a worker, on company property and during working hours, wishes to solicit other workers to join the union. Not surprisingly, the employer has a rule against such solicitation. Is the rule illegal? In the ordinary English meaning of "interference," the rule does interfere with the worker's concerted activity; yet surely the Labor Act was not intended to outlaw the rule. Most Americans agree that working time is for work. Accordingly, the legal meaning of interference is narrower than its English meaning. Like many other words in statutes, "interference" is a term of art, that is, a term that has a special meaning within a discipline.

In Labor Law, deciding whether an employer's act interferes with workers' rights requires balancing the interests of the workers against the interests of the employer. Thus, in the example in the previous paragraph, it was decided that the employer's interest in insisting that workers perform their duties during working hours outweighed the worker's interest in soliciting for the union during working hours.

In the following case, the Labor Board charged the employer with interference in violation of section 8(a)(1). Therefore, the court was called upon to weigh the employer's interest against the union's interest.

⚜

National Labor Relations Board v. Exchange Parts
375 U.S. 405 (1964)

Mr. Justice HARLAN delivered the opinion of the Court.

This case presents a question concerning the limitations which § 8(a)(1) of the National Labor Relations Act places on the right of an employer to confer economic benefits on his employees shortly before a representation election. The precise issue is whether that section prohibits the conferral of such benefits, without more, where the employer's purpose is to affect the outcome of the election. We granted the National Labor Relations Board's petition for certiorari to clear up a possible conflict between the decision below and those of other Courts of Appeals on an important question of national labor policy. For reasons given in this opinion, we conclude that the judgment below must be reversed.

The respondent, Exchange Parts Company, is engaged in the business of rebuilding automobile parts in Fort Worth, Texas. Prior to November 1959 its employees were not represented by a union. On November 9, 1959, the International Brotherhood of Boilermakers, Iron Shipbuilders, Blacksmiths, Forgers and Helpers, AFL-CIO, advised Exchange Parts that the union was conducting an organizational campaign at the plant and that a majority of the employees had designated the union as their bargaining representative. On November 16 the union petitioned the Labor Board for a representation election. The Board conducted a hearing on December 29, and on February 19, 1960, issued an order directing that an election be held. The election was held on March 18, 1960.

At two meetings on November 4 and 5, 1959, C.V. McDonald, the Vice President and General Manager of Exchange Parts, announced to the employees that their "floating holiday" in 1959 would fall on December 26 and that there would be an additional "floating holiday" in 1960. On February 25, six days after the Board issued its election order, Exchange Parts held a dinner for employees at which Vice President McDonald told the employees that they could decide whether the extra day of vacation in 1960 would be a "floating holiday" or would be taken on their birthdays. The employees voted for the latter. McDonald also referred to the forthcoming representation election as one in which, in the words of the trial examiner, the employees would "determine whether ... [they] wished to hand over their right to speak and act for themselves." He stated that the union had distorted some of the facts and pointed out the benefits obtained by the employees without a union. He urged all the employees to vote in the election.

On March 4 Exchange Parts sent its employees a letter which spoke of "the *Empty Promises* of the Union" and "the *fact* that *it is the Company that puts things in your envelope....*" After mentioning a number of benefits, the letter said: "The Union can't put any of those things in your envelope—*only the Company can do that."* Further on, the letter stated: "... [I]t didn't take a Union to get any of those things and ... it won't take a Union to get additional improvements in the future." Accompanying the letter was a detailed statement of the benefits granted by the company since 1949 and an estimate of the monetary value of such benefits to the employees. Included in the statement of benefits for 1960 were the birthday holiday, a new system for computing overtime during holiday weeks which had the effect of increasing wages for those weeks, and a new vacation schedule which enabled employees to extend their vacations by sandwiching them between two weekends. Although Exchange Parts asserts that the policy behind the latter two benefits was established earlier, it is clear that the letter of March 4 was the first general announcement of the changes to the employees. In the ensuing election the union lost.

The Board, affirming the findings of the trial examiner, found that the announcement of the birthday holiday and the grant and announcement of overtime and vacation benefits were arranged by Exchange Parts with the intention of inducing the employees to vote against the union. It found that this conduct violated § 8(a)(1) of the National Labor Relations Act and issued an appropriate order. On the Board's petition for enforcement of the order, the Court of Appeals rejected the finding that the announcement of the birthday holiday was timed to influence the outcome of the election. It accepted the Board's findings with respect to the overtime and vacation benefits, and the propriety of those findings is not in controversy here. However, noting that "the benefits were put into effect unconditionally on a permanent basis, and no one has suggested that there was any implication the benefits would be withdrawn if the workers voted for the union," 304 F.2d 368, 375, the court denied enforcement of the Board's order. It believed that it was not an unfair labor practice under § 8(a)(1) for an employer to grant benefits to its employees in these circumstances.

...

We think the Court of Appeals was mistaken in concluding that the conferral of employee benefits while a representation election is pending, for the purpose of inducing employees to vote against the union, does not "interfere with" the protected right to organize.

The broad purpose of § 8(a)(1) is to establish "the right of employees to organize for mutual aid without employer interference." *Republic Aviation Corp. v. Labor Board,* 324 U.S. 793. We have no doubt that it prohibits not only intrusive threats and promises but also conduct immediately favorable to employees which is undertaken with the express purpose of impinging upon their freedom of choice for or against unionization and is reasonably calculated to have that effect. In *Medo*

Photo Supply Corp. v. Labor Board, 321 U.S. 678, this Court said: "The action of employees with respect to the choice of their bargaining agents may be induced by favors bestowed by the employer as well as by his threats or domination." Although in that case there was already a designated bargaining agent and the offer of "favors" was in response to a suggestion of the employees that they would leave the union if favors were bestowed, the principles which dictated the result there are fully applicable here. The danger inherent in well-timed increases in benefits is the suggestion of a fist inside the velvet glove. Employees are not likely to miss the inference that the source of benefits now conferred is also the source from which future benefits must flow and which may dry up if it is not obliged.[3] The danger may be diminished if, as in this case, the benefits are conferred permanently and unconditionally. But the absence of conditions or threats pertaining to the particular benefits conferred would be of controlling significance only if it could be presumed that no question of additional benefits or renegotiation of existing benefits would arise in the future; and, of course, no such presumption is tenable.... We cannot agree with the Court of Appeals that enforcement of the Board's order will have the "ironic" result of "discouraging benefits for labor." 304 F.2d, at 376. The beneficence of an employer is likely to be ephemeral if prompted by a threat of unionization which is subsequently removed. Insulating the right of collective organization from calculated good will of this sort deprives employees of little that has lasting value.

Reversed.

---

[3]The inference was made almost explicit in Exchange Parts' letter to its employees of March 4, already quoted, which said: "The Union can't put any of those ... [benefits] in your envelope—*only the Company can do that.*" (Original italics.) We place no reliance, however, on these or other words of the respondent dissociated from its conduct. Section 8(c) of the Act provides that the expression or dissemination of "any views, argument, or opinion" "shall not constitute or be evidence of an unfair labor practice under any of the provisions of this Act, if such expression contains no threat of reprisal or force or promise of benefit."

QUESTIONS FOR REFLECTION

1. What were the standards used by the Labor Board, by the Court of Appeals, and by the Supreme Court in this case, and were they objective or subjective?

2. Which tribunal's standard was most favorable to employers? to unions?

3. Suppose an employer raises pay shortly before a union election in order to match the pay increase of a competitor. In light of Exchange Parts, is the raise illegal interference?

4. Suppose an employer regularly evaluates workers and adjusts pay in December. A union organizing campaign begins in November, and an election is scheduled for January 15th. What should the employer do about the December evaluations?

5. What is the Supreme Court's view of the average worker? Do you share it?

6. Why shouldn't an employer be allowed to purchase the loyalty of workers, and why shouldn't they be allowed to sell it? Specifically, should an employer be allowed to say shortly before an election, "If you vote against the union, I'll raise your pay by $x"?

7. We saw above in the Darlington case that an employer may close a business rather than deal with a union. Suppose an employer tells one's workers, shortly before they vote in a representation election, that the business will be closed if the union wins. Has the employer made a threat in violation of section 8(a)(1)?

Ω

Authorization Cards and Bargaining Orders

Introduction

In order to move the Labor Board to schedule a representation election, a union must produce a "showing of interest," i.e., demonstrate that a substantial number of workers desires an election. For many years, the Board has accepted proof that at least 30 percent of the workers want an election as sufficient.

A showing of interest is almost always made by means of cards signed by workers. Cards come in several varieties. Three kinds are important for present purposes: membership cards, which say, in effect, "I hereby join the union"; authorization cards, which say, "I authorize the union to represent me vis-a-vis the employer (and I will decide later whether I will join)"; and election cards, which say, "I desire an election (and I will decide later whether I will vote for the union and, if it wins, whether I will join)." Membership and authorization cards demonstrate support for the union; election cards do not. Sometimes a worker is told that a membership or authorization card will be used only to get an election; in this event, the union could not use the card to prove the extent of its support. But proof as to what was said before a card was signed is problematic.

The difference between membership and authorization cards, on the one hand, and election cards, on the other hand, is important should the Board consider issuing a **bargaining order**. A bargaining order instructs an employer to recognize and bargain with a union, even though the union has not won a representation election. The Board will issue a bargaining order if an employer commits such serious unfair labor practices during the campaign preceding a representation election that the workers could not cast free and uncoerced ballots, for example, if the employer fired union supporters, spied on union meetings, threatened to reduce pay if the union won, and so forth.

The Board will issue a bargaining order only if evidence exists that, at some time before the election, the majority of workers favored representation by the

NLRB v. Gissel Packing Co.

union. Otherwise, a union might be established as the bargaining agent when only a minority of workers desires it. Election cards obviously may not be used to obtain a bargaining order, but the Board accepts authorization and membership cards for this purpose. In the following case, employers challenged this practice.

NLRB v. Gissel Packing Co.
395 U.S. 575 (1969)

{Four cases were decided in a single opinion. In each case, a union waged an organizational campaign and secured membership or authorization cards from a majority of employees. The union then demanded recognition from the employer, who refused on the ground that cards are an unreliable indicator of employee sentiment. Then the employer embarked on a vigorous antiunion campaign. In *General Steel* and *Sinclair*, the unions petitioned for elections; the unions lost the elections, but the Board set them aside because serious unfair labor practices had interfered with the employees' free choice. In *Heck's* the union petitioned for an election, but it was never held because the union filed unfair labor practice charges and the Board, following its customary procedure, postponed the election until the charges were disposed of. In *Gissel*, the union never petitioned for an election, but instead filed charges with the Board. In each case, the Board found that the union had secured valid membership or authorization cards from a majority of employees in an appropriate unit; that the employer violated §§ 8(a)(1) and (3) during the campaign opposing the union, and these violations were so serious that a fair election could not be held; and that the appropriate remedy (in addition to a cease-and-desist order and relief for specific victims) was an order requiring the employer to recognize and bargain with the union as representative of the employees in the unit. In *General Steel*, *Heck's*, and *Gissel*, the Court of Appeals for the Fourth Circuit enforced the Board's orders regarding the §§ 8(a)(1) and (3) violations, but, following its decision in *NLRB v. Logan Packing Co.*, 386 F.2d 562 (4th Cir. 1967), refused to enforce the bargaining orders because of the unreliability of authorization cards. In *Sinclair*, the Court of Appeals for the First Circuit enforced the bargaining order.}

From the Brief of the Labor Board
(Petitioner)

{The brief is signed by Erwin S. Griswold, Attorney General, and Peter L. Strauss, Assistant to the Solicitor General, of the United States; and Arnold Ordman, General Counsel, Dominick L. Manoli, Associate General Counsel, Norton J. Come, Assistant General Counsel, and Thomas E. Silfen, attorney, National Labor Relations Board.}

UNDER BOTH THE WAGNER ACT AND THE PRESENT ACT, A UNION IS NOT LIMITED TO A BOARD ELECTION AND CERTIFICATION AS THE ONLY MEANS TO ESTABLISH REPRESENTATIVE STATUS

Both Section 8(5) of the Wagner Act and Section 8(a)(5) of the present Act require an employer to bargain with the representative of his employees as defined in Section 9(a). In both, Section 9(a) refers to the representative as one "designated or selected" by a majority of the employees without specifying any particular method by which it is to be chosen. Accordingly, early in the administration of the Wagner Act, it was recognized that a union need not have been certified as the winner of a Board election to invoke the Section 8(5) bargaining obligation; it could establish majority status and thus the bargaining obligation by other means, such as cards by which the employees authorized it to represent them for collective bargaining. The existence of alternative routes to majority status, including authorization cards, has consistently been recognized under the present Act also by the courts of appeals as well as this Court.

ALTHOUGH AN EMPLOYER ACTING IN GOOD FAITH IS ENTITLED TO INSIST UPON AN ELECTION, SUBSTANTIAL EMPLOYER UNFAIR LABOR PRACTICES MAY JUSTIFY A REMEDIAL ORDER TO BARGAIN WITH A UNION WHICH HAS OBTAINED AUTHORIZATION CARDS FROM A MAJORITY OF EMPLOYEES

... [U]nfair labor practices sufficient to dissipate a union's majority also preclude the Board from conducting a fair election.... The Board's election procedures normally provide a better means of testing majority status than a check of authorization cards. However, where the employer has precluded a fair election by his unfair labor practices ... [i]f in fact the union commanded a majority when it made its demand, he may be ordered to bargain with it. As the Court of Appeals for the District of Columbia Circuit stated in *Joy Silk Mills, Inc. v. National Labor Relations Board*, 185 F.2d 732, 741,

> "The Act provides for election proceedings in order to provide a mechanism whereby an employer acting in good faith may secure a determination of whether or not the union does, in fact, have a majority.... Another purpose is to insure that the employees may freely register their individual choices concerning representation. Certainly it is not one of the purposes of the election procedure to supply the employer with a procedural device by which he may secure the time necessary to defeat efforts toward organization being made by a union...."

Accordingly, under both the Wagner Act and the present Act, the courts of appeals in every circuit, including the Fourth Circuit prior to its recent departure, have enforced Board orders to bargain where a union had obtained authorization cards from a majority of employees and the Board found that the employers' unfair labor practices which tended to dissipate the union's majority and to preclude a fair Board election.

THE CONSIDERATIONS RELIED ON BY THE COURT BELOW DO NOT WARRANT A DEPARTURE FROM THESE PRINCIPLES

In departing from these well settled principles, the Fourth Circuit has held that "absent other affirmative evidence to show employer knowledge that its employees desire union representation, an employer may properly have a good faith doubt as to the union's majority status and withhold recognition pending the result of a certification election." *National Labor Relations Board v. Bratten Pontiac Corp.*, 406 F.2d 349 (4th Cir. 1969). Its position rests upon two premises: (1) that union authorization cards are inherently unreliable as an indication that the employees want the union to represent them; and (2) that Congress, in amending the Act in 1947, intended to make a Board election the only method for resolving questions about a union's majority status. Neither of these premises is valid.

Although there have been abuses in the use of authorization cards — primarily misrepresentations as to whether by signing the card the employees were designating the union as their representative or merely authorizing it to seek an election to determine that issue — it does not follow that cards are so inherently unreliable that they may never be used to determine majority status. The Board views an election as ordinarily the most satisfactory, and indeed the preferred, method of measuring employee sentiment. But, if an employer has engaged in conduct tending to destroy the conditions necessary for a fair election, authorization cards may be the most effective method of assuring employee choice. If in a specific case union authorization cards have been misused, the proper remedy is to hold that the union did not represent a majority of the employees. To give an employer's claim of doubt presumptive validity, as the Fourth Circuit does, is to enable employers to eliminate cards as a basis for representation in all cases, and is thus to permit them to delay or prevent unionization through interference with the election process.

... [T]he court below contrasts the card check process with a secret ballot election, concluding that the lack of secrecy in the former creates an inherent unreliability. Specifically, the court dwells upon the probable ill-effects of social pressure and group psychology when the choice of a bargaining representative takes place in public view. But this argument assumes that employees who sign union authorization cards do so lightly and without any real intention of having the union represent them for collective bargaining purposes. In view of the substantial benefits of unionization, there is no warrant for this assumption. Moreover, social pressure exists in an election campaign, no less than in a card signing drive; if employees desire to sign cards only if their friends have, they will wish to vote as their friends do. The single moment of secrecy in the voting booth cannot totally eliminate all influences — from the employer, the union, and friends — that have been brought to bear during a campaign. And again, where the employer has warped the campaign by his unfair acts, the authorization cards may represent the most accurate view possible of employee sentiment.

In sum, the Fourth Circuit has overstated the deficiencies of authorization cards; its rigid rule that authorization cards are *per se* unreliable certainly does not fit cases such as those here, where the supposed infirmities of cards are not in fact present and where the employer's unfair labor practices have effectively foreclosed the preferred election route.

WHERE THE BOARD HAS FOUND A REFUSAL TO BARGAIN IN VIOLATION OF SECTION 8(a)(5), IT MAY APPROPRIATELY ENTER A BARGAINING ORDER EVEN THOUGH SUBSEQUENTLY THE UNION MAY HAVE LOST ITS MAJORITY STATUS

Upon finding that an employer refused to bargain in violation of Section 8(a)(5) of the Act, the Board is not limited to a cease-and-desist remedy; it may properly order the employer to bargain with the union without first requiring the union to show that it still represents a majority of the employees.

Where there has been a refusal to bargain accompanied by serious unfair labor practices against a union which has obtained authorization cards from a majority of employees, it is likely that its majority status will be dissipated as a result of the unfair labor practices and the time required for the Board to issue its decision and remedial order. Merely to issue a cease-and-desist order and to direct an election in this situation would both prejudice the employees' right freely to determine whether they desire a representative and profit the wrongdoing employer. The new test of the union's majority would most probably reflect an unlawfully altered picture of employee sentiment.

This would be precisely the result which the recalcitrant employer hoped to achieve by his refusal to bargain and his course of unlawful conduct. Further, such a limitation on remedy would encourage the employer to meet the new election with renewed coercion, aggravating the unlawful situation already existing. In any particular case, an effective remedy may require an order restoring the parties to the positions they occupied when the refusal to bargain took place by directing the employer to bargain with the union on the basis of its original showing of majority status.[44]

---

[44] "When the preferred method of determining employee wishes has been tampered with, it totally begs the question to say that employee rights are sacrificed by a bargaining order. Employee rights are affected whatever the result: If an

(continued...)

From the Brief of the Union
(Petitioner)

{The brief is signed by Albert Gore, Joseph M. Jacobs, and Judith A. Lonnquist, Chicago, IL.}

REPRESENTATION ELECTIONS ARE NOT NECESSARILY THE MOST RELIABLE INDICATORS OF EMPLOYEES' DESIRES

In *Logan*, the Fourth Circuit espoused its view, correlative with its holding on the inherent unreliability of cards, that a representation election under the auspices of the NLRB is the sole method reliably to determine employees' wishes. However, careful analysis of and familiarity with the election processes and the human variables incident thereto belie the validity of the Fourth Circuit's belief.

A "SECRET BALLOT" IS NO MORE INDICATIVE OF EMPLOYEES' INTENT THAN AN AUTHORIZATION CARD

The *Logan* court noted that cards are unreliable, *inter alia*, because they are "obtained before the employees are exposed to any counter-argument and without an opportunity for reflection or recantation" [386 F.2d at 566]. This conclusion overlooks the realities of the employer-employee relationship, for whereas the employee is exposed to the union's arguments only during an organizing campaign, he is subjected to daily exposure of the employer's views. From the day he is hired the employee is indoctrinated with management's views of unionization, labor economics and employer prerogative. Thus, numerous studies have demonstrated that long prior to the advent of a union organizational campaign, many employers have imbued employees with an "elemental fear of reprisal" sufficient to forestall any union activity.[104] Moreover, it should be noted that employees are acutely aware that

---

[44](...continued)

inadequate rerun remedy is routinely applied, the rights of those employees who desire collective bargaining, and whose desires were met with violations of the law, are not being protected; if a bargaining order is issued, the rights of those who oppose collective bargaining are being tramped on if ... a poll, conducted after the effects of the earlier coercion were satisfactorily dissipated, would indicate a union loss. Thus it is impossible to defend a refusal to impose a bargaining order unless one is willing to defend the adequacy of the particular remedies in fact applied in connection with the decision to direct a second election...." Lesnick, 65 Mich. L.Rev. at 862.

[104] See Bok, "The Regulation of Campaign Tactics in Representation Elections
(continued...)

if the union loses the election, it will hold no sway over their economic lives, whereas, if the union wins, the employer still maintains his economic life-and-death power over his employees.

Nonetheless, the Fourth Circuit asserts that "exposure of each employee to both sides of the issue" renders the employee's choice "when the ballot is cast — as reasoned and rational as possible," *N.L.R.B. v. Logan Packing Co.*, 386 F.2d at n. 16. However, even full exposure to both the union's and management's propaganda may be totally irrelevant to the employee's decision to designate a union whether by authorization cards or an election. A study of why workers join unions concludes:

> "Often the decision to join a union is not based on logical reasoning in which self-interest figures to a large degree, but upon expediency — a reaction to the pressures of the moment."

Other studies indicate that the decision to vote for the union is made before the election procedure is invoked and thus pre-election propaganda, whether one- or both-sided, may have little influence on the voter:

> "After extensive empirical research, various voting analysts have come to suspect that even if election propaganda is read, it will largely serve to provide rationalizations for decisions already reached on other grounds.... As some have observed: "Arguments (read or heard by the voters) enter the final stage of decision more as

---

[104](...continued)
Under the National Labor Relations Act," 78 Harv. L. Rev. 38, 125, and authorities cited therein at n. 238. See also, *Butler, op. cit.* at 136. Case studies conducted by Butler revealed that employer threats remained foremost in employees' memories, whereas recollections of other campaign propaganda faded with the passage of time:

> "The workers interviewed made no mention of any economic activities on the part of the organizer though they fairly well agreed that the management was set on keeping the union out and two remembered that he said that he would close the plant if the union came in."

In the instant *Gissel* case the evidence disclosed interference, restraint and coercion practiced in respect to employees more than three months prior to the commencement of the Union's organizing campaign. Moreover, Gissel's antiunion attitude had been instilled in many of the same employees in 1960 when the company was found to have violated sections 8(a)(1) and (3).

indicators than as *influences*. They point out, like signboards along
the road, the way to turn in order to reach a destination which is
already determined."

Further, Bok suggests that votes "as reasoned and rational as possible" may not result
in expression of majority will because few voters are able to appraise evidence
sufficiently systematically and rationally in the increasingly complex arena of labor
relations and because often the adverse arguments of labor and management will not
yield to logical analysis.[109] Accordingly, there is reason to doubt that a ballot cast in
an NLRB election is, as asserted by the Fourth Circuit, the result of a free choice, "as
reasoned and rational as possible."[110]

...

---

[109] Bok states [78 Harv. L. R. at n. 34]: "The most conscientious voter may be
unable to decide on logical grounds whether the indeterminate possibility of a five
cent increase, an expanded health insurance program, and a grievance procedure
outweighs the indeterminate chance of a strike or a relocation of the enterprise.
Moreover, legal rules will have no meaningful effect unless the questionable
campaign tactics are truly capable of affecting the decisions of enough conscientious
voters to affect the outcome of the election. And even if these conditions are
satisfied, the law will only succeed in causing the election to correspond more closely
to the values and preferences of the rational voters. If these voters represent a small
minority — as most empirical studies would have us believe — the law may still fail
to bring about an election result that will correspond to the values and desires of the
majority."

[110]It is clear that the employer engages in much conduct which, although of
seeming little moment to reviewing tribunals, nonetheless just as seriously interferes
with the free choice of employees as do unfair labor practices or other conduct
sufficient to set aside an election. For example, during a union campaign, when a
supervisor has prior thereto said, "Hello," to the employees and ceases such practice,
this affects employees' votes. When the supervisor, during the election campaign,
stands at an employee's station for a number of minutes or even seconds when it was
not his practice to do so theretofore, this affects the employee's "free choice." In such
innumerable ways of daily contact, the employees are affected in their so-called "free
choice" and, accordingly, because of the superior position of the employer, his daily
and even minute by minute contact with the employees can and does affect the
employee's vote to the extent that no "free and fair election" is ever truly possible.
It is therefore a rebuttable homily when it is said that an election is more reliable
indicator of employees' wishes than unambiguous authorization cards.

x   *NLRB v. Gissel Packing Co.*

ELECTIONS ARE SUSCEPTIBLE TO MISREPRESENTATION AND COERCION

Although the Board supposedly conducts its elections only in so-called "laboratory conditions," "no seasoned observer considers [this objective] realistic." "[E]lection campaigns are characterized by 'prattle rather than precision' and exaggerations, name calling, inaccuracies, and, to some extent, deliberate falsehoods [which] are sometimes permitted as usual electioneering devices and campaign tactics."

In addition, much objectionable conduct which interferes with the employee's "free choice" is held by the Board to be insufficient to invalidate an election. For instance, inadvertent misstatement, which under Board law will not void an election, deprives the employee of a free choice just as effectively as a fraudulent misrepresentation. Also, misinformation disseminated more than 24 hours before an election may impair the employee's freedom of choice regardless of whether there is ample time for the employees to verify it or for the union to rebut it (the Board's tests for validity). Information concerning the misrepresentation may not be communicated to the union in sufficient time for rebuttal. Employees may not have time or may be reluctant to question the union, or the union may not have sufficient access to the employees, especially close to the date of the election, whereas the employer has almost unlimited access.

Employer speeches and interrogation, even if held lawful by the Board, cannot help but have a disproportionate impact on employees.

While the Fourth Circuit imports great weight to the opportunity afforded by the election process, for employees to hear "both sides of the issue," misrepresentation, intimidation and a myriad of other influences too often render such opportunity more destructive than protective of employee rights.

Procedurally, many valid objections to conduct affecting the results of an election are never raised because they come to the union's attention, if at all, after the short period for filing objections has run. Also, many unions fail to file objections because of the expense of litigation, the unlikelihood of success in re-run elections, the potential long administrative delay and the possibility that even if the union gains certification in a re-run election, the employer may refuse to bargain to challenge the certification through a lengthy Board and Court unfair labor practice proceeding. An employer need not articulate his anti-union attitudes to "men who know the consequences of incurring [their] employer's strong displeasure" — knowledge gleaned from daily exposure to management's influence. Even the standards set by the Board to protect employees from coercive interrogation may not adequately safeguard the employee's free choice in an election.

One commentator discussed the fallibility of these standards [Bok, 78 Harv. L. R. at 109, 108]:

> "current standards ... will not suffice to rule out the existence of coercion; it is quite possible that intimidation will occur even if all, or most of the factors cut in favor of the employer.
>
> "...
>
> "... employees may be somewhat more easily intimidated if top management itself takes the trouble to inquire into their activities...."

Nonetheless many elections are upheld despite evidence of employer captive audience speeches and wholesale interrogation on the Board's theory that there is no coercive impact on employees if management gives assurances against reprisal or merely expresses opinion.

Many employer statements held by the Board to be protected by Section 8(c) have persuasive impact on employees inconsistent with free choice, *e.g.*, economically based statements concerning partial or complete plant shut down or expressions of opinion as to economic consequences of selecting a union: strikes, loss of seniority, loss of employer-employee "good will." The Board in evaluating such pre-election conduct balances the employee's right to a "free choice" in a "laboratory election atmosphere" against the employer's right vigorously to argue his side of the issue in accordance with considerations of free speech under Section 8(c). In applying this test, however, the Board too frequently does not ensure a reasoned and rational vote by failing to restrict pre-election campaigning to legitimate arguments relevant and conducive to the employee's reasoned choice. Almost universally employers utilize the pre-election period not to educate employees, but by planting fear of dire consequences in the minds of employees if the union should win, to prevent unionization of their companies by engaging in conduct inconsistent with employee free choice. In this regard the election procedure is particularly susceptible to employer manipulation to serve not the purposes of the Act, but the ends of the employer.

...

xii   *NLRB v. Gissel Packing Co.*

From the Brief of the AFL-CIO
(Amicus Curiae)

{The brief is signed by J. Albert Woll, General Counsel, and Thomas E. Harris, Associate General Counsel, of the AFL-CIO; and Robert C. Mayer and Laurence Gold, Washington, D.C.}

...

This temptation to violate the Act is enhanced by the fact that the minimum benefit which may be expected in any event is delay. An employer who litigates an unfair labor practice charge through the Courts of Appeal is assured approximately two years before any remedy at all is imposed. During an organizing campaign as during a strike, time is one-dimensional — delay inevitably works for the employer. Employees seek representation in order to deal with immediate practical problems rather than to fulfill a timeless platonic ideal. If the desire for immediate representation is frustrated by delays caused by the employer's unfair labor practices, the union's strength tends to be dissipated even though the end result of the litigation is in its favor. For there are no means at its disposal to maintain and strengthen the employees' desire for unionization. In light of this fact, it is plain that effective remedies are of the essence. If the ultimate order does nothing more than revivify the campaign years after it was thwarted, there is every reason to violate the law and none but scruple to obey it. Once this is recognized, it is plain that an order to cease and desist is obviously insufficient in itself. It is an invitation to commit unfair labor practices to secure delay, safe in the knowledge that the only cost of doing so will be an order not to repeat the violation.

...

From the Brief of Gissel Packing Co.
(Respondent)

{The brief is signed by John E. Jenkins, Jr. and C. Robert Schaub, Huntington, W.Va.}

AUTHORIZATION CARDS ARE AN UNRELIABLE INDICATOR OF AN EMPLOYEE'S ACTUAL PREFERENCE AS TO REPRESENTATION BY A LABOR ORGANIZATION

RIGHTS OF INDIVIDUAL EMPLOYEES

It is one of the oddities of these times that, in the present posture of labor-management relations, the general assumption by labor advocates is that the interests of labor and management are necessarily in opposition, with a battle line drawn between "organized labor" on the one hand and management on the other.

This view, apparently followed by the NLRB, is in direct contravention of the intent of labor legislation. The rights given are not phrased to apply to "organized labor," or labor unions. Instead, the rights to be considered are those of the individual employee. As stated in Section 7 of the NLRA:

> *"Employees* shall have the right to self-organization, to form, join or assist labor organizations... [emphasis added]."

In practice, the individual employee has become the forgotten man. The actions and decisions of the NLRB in large part involve the employee only as a prize with rules regulating the manner of his capture by unions.

The situation present in this cause strongly reflects this treatment. The NLRB has an elective process with which to determine the actual and uncoerced desire of an employee under safeguards far stronger and more protective than are those under which this nation does now, and has from inception, chosen those who are responsible for the actions and continuing existence of the nation.

The Board chooses not to believe its own statements as to elections. It says, at page 65 of the Commerce Clearing House reproduction, *Thirty-Second Annual Report of the National Labor Relations Board* (1968):

> "Board elections are conducted in accordance with strict standards designed to assure that the participating employees have an opportunity to determine, and to register a free and untrammeled

choice in the selection of, a bargaining representative."

It is apparent that the use of authorization cards to effect recognition has become more popular with unions unwilling to risk a fair and honest selection through a supervised election. In recent years, cognizance of the abuses attendant with the securing of such cards on an individual basis has become recognized by some authorities, and by some court which decline to act as rubber-stamp enforcers of Board decisions.

The reason for union reliance on any method of gaining recognition other than through fair choice is apparent when it is found that in fiscal year 1967, the latest for which figures are available, 7,882 elections were conducted by the Board, and four out of ten were lost by unions. Of the 7,882, 4,722, or 60%, were won by unions, *including* elections where the essential choice was between rival unions. Chart 12, *Thirty-second Annual Report of the National Labor Relations Board* (1968).

Doubt as to the validity of authorization cards has long been present. For instance, then Board Chairman McCullock pointed out in a speech to the American Bar Association that in 57 elections where unions presented authorization cards from over 70% of the employees, they won 43, or 75% of them; thus, unions *lost* one in four elections where employees were given a free choice, even though their card-based apparent approval would indicate that a lost election would be a statistical rarity. 1962 PROCEEDINGS, SECTION OF LABOR RELATIONS LAW, AMERICAN BAR ASSOCIATION 14-17.

The unreliability of authorization cards has been recognized by the AFL-CIO in the oft-quoted remark from the AFL-CIO *Guidebook for Union Organizers* (1961) that:

> "NLRB pledge cards are at best a signifying of intention at a given moment. Sometimes they are signed to 'get the union off my back.'"

From the brief of General Steel Products
(Respondent)

{The brief is signed by Lewis P. Hamlin, Jr., Salisbury, NC.}

UNRELIABILITY OF AUTHORIZATION CARDS

When the Board conducts elections it insists upon so called "laboratory conditions" — an unlikely term which is hardly descriptive of any election — but as a minimum it always means a closely supervised secret balloting outside the presence of both the employer and the union organizer. This "laboratory" test for elections is impossible to reconcile with the totally unsupervised solicitation of cards by union professionals, under partisan conditions, where the "voter" is required to accept or reject in full view of those who solicit him. The unreliability of such expressions has been nowhere better summarized than by the Court of Appeals for the Fourth Circuit in *National Labor Relations Board v. Logan Packing Co.*, 386 F.2d 562, 564-6 (C.A. 4). We quote a part of this opinion (footnotes omitted):

> "In stark contrast is a decisional rule that bypasses the election processes and places signed authorization cards on a parity with an affirmative vote in a secret election.

> "It would be difficult to imagine a more unreliable method of ascertaining the real wishes of employees than a 'card check,' unless it were an employer's request for an open show of hands. The one is no more reliable than the other. No thoughtful person has attributed reliability to such card checks. This, the Board has fully recognized. So has the AFL-CIO. In 1962, Board Chairman McCulloch presented to the American Bar Association data indicating some relationship between large card-signing majorities and election results. Unions which presented authorization cards from thirty to fifty per cent of the employees won nineteen per cent of the elections; those having authorization cards from fifty to seventy per cent of the employees won only forty-eight per cent of the elections, while those having authorization cards from over seventy per cent of the employees won seventy-four per cent of the elections.

> "The unreliability of the cards is not dependent upon the possible use of misrepresentations and threats, however. It is inherent, as we have noted, in the absence of secrecy and in the natural inclination of most people to avoid stands which appear to be nonconformist and antagonistic to friends and fellow employees. It is enhanced by the fact that usually, as they were here, the cards are obtained before the employees are exposed to any counter argument and without an opportunity for reflection or recantation. Most employees having second thoughts about the matter and regretting having signed the card would do nothing about it; in most situations, only one of rare strength of character would succeed in having his card returned or destroyed. Cards are collected over a period of time, however, and there is no assurance that an early signer is still of the same mind on the crucial date when the union delivers its bargaining demand.

"An employer could not help but doubt the results of a card check as an indication of the wishes of employees, for there is nothing in the process to allay it. Unless the employer is extraordinary gullible and unimaginative, he will at least suspect unreliability in the cards, and their signatures. If he has no honest doubt of the Union's claim of support by a majority of the employees, it will be because of other evidence known to him not because of the card check."

LACK OF EMPLOYEE OPPORTUNITY TO HEAR BOTH SIDES

When an election is to be held the Board now insists that the employer furnish the union in advance with a list of names and addresses of all employees. This is done to insure that the union will have a chance to communicate with them so that they may hear both sides and vote intelligently. The Board's reasoning is set out in *Excelsior Underwear, Inc.*, 156 NLRB 1236 (1966):

"Accordingly, we now establish a requirement that will be applied in all election cases. That is, within 7 days after the Regional Director has approved a consent-election agreement entered into by the parties or after the Regional Director or the Board has directed an election, the employer must file with the Regional Director an election eligibility list, containing the names and addresses of all the eligible voters. The Regional Director, in turn, shall make this information available to all parties in the case. Failure to comply with this requirement shall be grounds for setting aside the election whenever proper objections are filed.

"The considerations that impel us to adopt the foregoing rule are these: The control of the election proceeding, and the determination of the steps necessary to conduct that election fairly (are) matters which Congress entrusted to the Board alone. In discharging that trust, we regard it as the Board's function to conduct elections in which employees have the opportunity to cast their ballots for or against representation under circumstances that are free not only from interference, restraint, or coercion violative of the Act, but also from other elements that prevent or impede a free and reasoned choice. Among the factors that undoubtedly tend to impede such a choice is a lack of information with respect to one of the choices available. In other words, an employee who has had an effective opportunity to hear the arguments concerning representation is in a better position to make a more fully informed and reasoned choice. Accordingly, we think that it is appropriate for us to remove the impediment to communication to which our new rule is directed."

Surely this contrasts strangely with the Board's willingness to count authorization cards solicited at a time when no election has even been set or called for and when, more often than not, the employee has been exposed only to the union's solicitations and with no opportunity to hear what the employer or anyone else has to say about it.

EMPLOYEES ARE DENIED THE OPPORTUNITY TO CHANGE THEIR MINDS

A further evil in card check proceedings is that the *employee who signs a card is locked in*. He cannot get his card back or avoid its being counted by anything less than a formal application to the union (if this will do it). An application to the Board will not accomplish anything.

This very thing happened in the present *General Steel* case. Ten employees endeavored to intervene through counsel of their own before the Trial Examiner, declaring that they had changed their minds and had voted against the union and desired to have their cards suppressed. The motion to intervene was denied and all but two of these cards were counted for the union! Contrast this with a voter's right to change his mind even to the last minute before marking his ballot.

⚜

QUESTION FOR REFLECTION

The parties were battling about the validity of authorization cards, but this was not the real issue in the case. Cards were a minor issue. What was actually at stake?

Ω

Successorship

Introduction

It is not uncommon for one business to acquire or merge with another. In Labor Law, the acquired business is known as the "predecessor" or "predecessor employer," and the acquiring business is known as the "successor" or "successor employer." If the workers of the predecessor were represented by a union, the issue arises whether the union should continue to serve as the bargaining agent of the workers vis-a-vis the successor.

The issue of successorship presents itself in a variety of contexts. In John Wiley & Sons v. Livingston, the publishing company John Wiley & Sons acquired another publishing company, Interscience, and the latter ceased to operate as a separate entity. At the time of acquisition, John Wiley's employees were not represented by a union, but some of Interscience's employees were represented. The collective agreement between the union and Interscience did not contain a successorship clause.[a] John Wiley did not agree to assume the obligations of Interscience, but the law of the state which governed the transaction provided that a successor employer is liable for the obligations of a predecessor.[b] Wiley retained almost all of Interscience's workers, and they performed the same work on the same products as they had before the acquisition.

---

[a] A successorship clause is a provision in a labor contract in which the employer promises that, in the event it is acquired by another firm, the acquisition agreement between the two firms will specify that the successor will recognize the union as the bargaining agent of the workers in the unit and will honor the terms of the labor contract.

[b] Labor law is federal law; therefore, the state law applied to obligations like debts and promises to deliver goods, but did not apply to obligations under labor contracts.

In the absence of such a state law, whether a successor business assumes the obligations of the predecessor business is a matter for negotiation between the parties.

The contract between Interscience and the union provided the workers with typical rights, such as seniority, severance pay, and contributions to a pension fund, and also contained an arbitration clause. By its terms, that contract was to expire a few months after the acquisition.

Both before and after the acquisition, the union maintained that it continued to represent the former Interscience workers and demanded that Wiley honor certain rights in the contract. Wiley refused to recognize the union and contended that the acquisition had terminated the labor contract. Shortly before the expiration date of the contract, the union demanded that Wiley arbitrate the dispute. Wiley refused, and the union sued in court to compel arbitration.

The Supreme Court required Wiley to arbitrate the union's claims. The Court wrote:

> "We hold that disappearance by merger of a corporate employer which has entered into a collective bargaining agreement with a union does not automatically terminate all rights of the employees covered by the agreement, and that, in appropriate circumstances, present here, the successor employer may be required to arbitrate with the union under the agreement." 376 U.S. at 548.

The Court did not delineate the "appropriate circumstances" which cause the duty to arbitrate to survive the acquisition. However, the passage just quoted implies that the duty does not survive all acquisitions, as does another passage in the opinion, which states that the "lack of any substantial continuity of identity in the business enterprise before and after the change" in ownership would defeat the duty. 376 U.S. at 551. Nor did the Court hold that Wiley was obliged to honor the workers' substantive rights under the Interscience contract (and, indeed, most of the union's claims were rejected in the subsequent arbitration, 55 LA 210 (1970)).

In the following case, the Labor Board, on the one hand, and both the majority and the dissent, on the other hand, disagree about the precedential effect of <u>Wiley</u>. Did the Board or the Court use that case appropriately?

NLRB v. Burns International Security
406 U.S. 272 (1972)

Mr. Justice WHITE delivered the opinion of the Court.

Burns International Security Services, Inc. (Burns), replaced another employer, the Wackenhut Corp. (Wackenhut), which had previously provided plant protection services for the Lockheed Aircraft Service Co. (Lockheed) located at the Ontario International Airport in California. When Burns began providing security service, it employed 42 guards; 27 of them had been employed by Wackenhut. Burns refused, however, to bargain with the United Plant Guard Workers of America (UPG) which had been certified after a National Labor Relations Board (Board) election as the exclusive bargaining representative of Wackenhut's employees less than four months earlier. The issues presented in this case are whether Burns refused to bargain with a union representing a majority of employees in an appropriate unit and whether the National Labor Relations Board could order Burns to observe the terms of a collective-bargaining contract signed by the union and Wackenhut that Burns had not voluntarily assumed. Resolution turns to a great extent on the precise facts involved here.

I

The Wackenhut Corp. provided protection services at the Lockheed plant for five years before Burns took over this task. On February 28, 1967, a few months before the changeover of guard employers, a majority of the Wackenhut guards selected the union as their exclusive bargaining representative in a Board election after Wackenhut and the union had agreed that the Lockheed plant was the appropriate bargaining unit. On March 8, the Regional Director certified the union as the exclusive bargaining representative for these employees, and, on April 29, Wackenhut and the union entered into a three-year collective-bargaining contract.

Meanwhile, since Wackenhut's one-year service agreement to provide security protection was due to expire on June 30, Lockheed had called for bids from various companies supplying these services, and both Burns and Wackenhut submitted estimates. At a pre-bid conference attended by Burns on May 15, a representative of Lockheed informed the bidders that Wackenhut's guards were represented by the union, that the union had recently won a Board election and been certified, and that there was in existence a collective-bargaining contract between Wackenhut and the union.[3] Lockheed then accepted Burns's bid, and on May 31 Wackenhut was notified

---

[3] A Burns executive later admitted in the unfair-labor-practice proceeding that
(continued...)

that Burns would assume responsibility for protection services on July 1. Burns chose to retain 27 of the Wackenhut guards, and it brought in 15 of its own guards from other Burns locations.

During June, when Burns hired the 27 Wackenhut guards, it supplied them with membership cards of the American Federation of Guards (AFG), another union with which Burns had collective-bargaining contracts at other locations, and informed them that they had to become AFG members to work for Burns, that they would not receive uniforms otherwise, and that Burns "could not live with" the existing contract between Wackenhut and the union. On June 29, Burns recognized the AFG on the theory that it had obtained a card majority. On July 12, however, the UPG demanded that Burns recognize it as the bargaining representative of Burns's employees at Lockheed and that Burns honor the collective-bargaining agreement between it and Wackenhut. When Burns refused, the UPG filed unfair labor practice charges, and Burns responded by challenging the appropriateness of the unit and by denying its obligation to bargain.

The Board, adopting the trial examiner's findings and conclusions, found the Lockheed plant an appropriate unit and held that Burns had violated §§8(a)(2) and 8(a)(1) by unlawfully recognizing and assisting the AFG, a rival of the UPG; and that it had violated §§8(a)(5) and 8(a)(1) by failing to recognize and bargain with the UPG and by refusing to honor the collective-bargaining agreement that had been negotiated between Wackenhut and UPG.

Burns did not challenge the §8(a)(2) unlawful assistance finding in the Court of Appeals but sought review of the unit determination and the order to bargain and observe the pre-existing collective-bargaining contract. The Court of Appeals accepted the Board's unit determination and enforced the Board's order insofar as it related to the finding of unlawful assistance of a rival union and the refusal to bargain, but it held that the Board had exceeded its powers in ordering Burns to honor the contract executed by Wackenhut. Both Burns and the Board petitioned for *certiorari*, Burns challenging the unit determination and the bargaining order and the Board maintaining its position that Burns was bound by the Wackenhut contract, and we granted both petitions, though we declined to review the propriety of the

---

[3](...continued)
Burns was aware of the union's status, the unit certification, and the collective-bargaining contract after the May 15 meeting.

bargaining unit.

II

... Because the Act itself imposes a duty to bargain with the representatives of a majority of the employees in an appropriate unit, the initial issue before the Board was whether the charging union was such a bargaining representative.

The trial examiner first found that the unit designated by the regional director was an appropriate unit for bargaining. The unit found appropriate was defined as "[a]ll full-time and regular part-time employees of [Burns] performing plant protection duties ... at Lockheed, Ontario International Airport; excluding office clerical employees, professional employees, supervisors, and all other employees as defined in the Act." This determination was affirmed by the Board, accepted by the Court of Appeals, and is not at issue here because pretermitted by our limited grant of *certiorari*.

The trial examiner then found, *inter alia*, that Burns "had in its employ a majority of Wackenhut's former employees," and that these employees had already expressed their choice of a bargaining representative in an election held a short time before. Burns was therefore held to have a duty to bargain, which arose when it selected as its work force the employees of the previous employer to perform the same tasks at the same place they had worked in the past.

The Board, without revision, accepted the trial examiner's findings and conclusions with respect to the duty to bargain, and we see no basis for setting them aside. In an election held but a few months before, the union had been designated bargaining agent for the employees in the unit and a majority of these employees had been hired by Burns for work in the identical unit. It is undisputed that Burns knew all the relevant facts in this regard and was aware of the certification and of the existence of a collective-bargaining contract. In these circumstances, it was not unreasonable for the Board to conclude that the union certified to represent all employees in the unit still represented a majority of the employees and that Burns could not reasonably have entertained a good-faith doubt about that fact. Burns's obligation to bargain with the union over terms and conditions of employment stemmed from its hiring of Wackenhut's employees and from the recent election and Board certification. It has been consistently held that a mere change of employers or of ownership in the employing industry is not such an "unusual circumstance" as to affect the force of the Board's certification within the normal operative period if a majority of employees after the change of ownership or management were employed by the preceding employer.

It goes without saying, of course, that Burns was not entitled to upset what it should have accepted as an established union majority by soliciting representation cards for another union and thereby committing the unfair labor practice of which it was found guilty by the Board. That holding was not challenged here and makes it imperative that the situation be viewed as it was when Burns hired its employees for the guard unit, a majority of whom were represented by a Board-certified union.

It would be a wholly different case if the Board had determined that because Burns's operational structure and practices differed from those of Wackenhut, the Lockheed bargaining unit was no longer an appropriate one. Likewise, it would be different if Burns had not hired employees already represented by a union certified as a bargaining agent,[5] and the Board recognized as much at oral argument. But where the bargaining unit remains unchanged and a majority of the employees hired by the new employer are represented by a recently certified bargaining agent, there is little basis for faulting the Board's implementation of the express mandates of §8(a)(5) and §9(a) by ordering the employer to bargain with the incumbent union.

III

It does not follow, however, from Burns's duty to bargain that it was bound to observe the substantive terms of the collective-bargaining contract the union had negotiated with Wackenhut and to which Burns had in no way agreed. Section 8(d) of the Act expressly provides that the existence of such bargaining obligation "does not compel either party to agree to a proposal or require the making of a concession." Congress has consistently declined to interfere with free collective bargaining and has preferred that device, or voluntary arbitration, to the imposition of compulsory terms as a means of avoiding or terminating labor disputes. In its report accompanying the 1935 Act, the Senate Committee on Education and Labor stated:

> "The committee wishes to dispel any possible false impression that this bill is designed to compel the making of agreements or to permit governmental supervision of their terms. It must be stressed that the duty to bargain collectively does not carry with it the duty to reach an agreement, because the essence of collective bargaining is that either party shall be free to decide whether proposals made to it are satisfactory." S. Rep. No. 573, 74th Cong., 1st Sess., 12 (1935).

---

[5] The Board has never held that the National Labor Relations Act itself requires that an employer who submits the winning bid for a service contract or who purchases the assets of a business be obligated to hire all of the employees of the predecessor through it is possible that such an obligation might be assumed by the employer. However, an employer who declines to hire employees solely because they are members of a union commits a §8(a)(3) unfair labor practice.

This Court immediately noted this fundamental theme of the legislation: "[The Act] does not compel any agreement whatever... . The theory of the Act is that free opportunity for negotiation with accredited representatives of employees is likely to promote industrial peace and may bring about the adjustments and agreements which the Act in itself does not attempt to compel." *NLRB v. Jones & Laughlin Steel Corp.*, 301 U.S. 1, 45.

Section 8(d) made this policy an express statutory mandate, and was enacted in 1947 because Congress feared that "the present Board has gone very far, in the guise of determining whether or not employers had bargained in good faith, in setting itself up as the judge of what concessions an employer must make and of the proposals and counterproposals that he may or may not make. ... [U]nless Congress writes into the law guides for the Board to follow, the Board may attempt to carry this process still further and seek to control more and more the terms of collective bargaining agreements." H.R. Rep. No. 245, 80th Cong., 1st Sess., 19-20 (1947).

This history was reviewed in detail and given controlling effect in *H. K. Porter Co. v. NLRB*, 397 U.S. 99 (1970). There this Court, while agreeing that the employer violated §8(a)(5) by adamantly refusing to agree to a dues checkoff, intending thereby to frustrate the consummation of any bargaining agreement, held that the Board had erred in ordering the employer to agree to such a provision:

> "[W]hile the Board does have power ... to require employers and employees to negotiate, it is without power to compel a company or a union to agree to any substantive contractual provision of a collective-bargaining agreement.
>
> "...
>
> "... It would be anomalous indeed to hold that while §8(d) prohibits the Board from relying on a refusal to agree as the sole evidence of bad-faith bargaining, the Act permits the Board to compel agreement in that same dispute. The Board's remedial powers under §10 of the Act are broad, but they are limited to carrying out the policies of the Act itself. One of these fundamental policies is freedom of contract." 397 U.S. at 102, 108 (citations omitted).

These considerations, evident from the explicit language and legislative history of the labor laws, underlay the Board's prior decisions, which until now have consistently held that, although successor employers may be bound to recognize and bargain with the union, they are not bound by the substantive provisions of a collective-bargaining contract negotiated by their predecessors but not agreed to or assumed by them. As the Court of Appeals said in this case, "In none of the previous successorship cases has the Board ever reached that result. The successor has always been held merely to have the duty of bargaining with his predecessor's union."[8] 441 F.2d at 915.

The Board, however, has now departed from this view and argues that the same policies that mandate a continuity of bargaining obligation also require that successor employers be bound to the terms of a predecessor's collective-bargaining contract. It asserts that the stability of labor relations will be jeopardized and that employees will face uncertainty and a gap in the bargained-for terms and conditions of employment, as well as the possible loss of advantages gained by prior negotiations, unless the new employer is held to have assumed, as a matter a federal labor law, the obligations under the contract entered into by the former employer. Recognizing that under normal contract principles a party would not be bound to a contract in the absence of consent, the Board notes that in *John Wiley & Sons, Inc. v. Livingston,* 376 U.S. 543, 550 (1964), the Court declared that "a collective bargaining agreement is not an ordinary contract" but is, rather, an outline of the common law of a particular plant or industry. The Court held in *Wiley* that although the predecessor employer which had signed a collective-bargaining contract with the union had disappeared by merger with the successor, the union could compel the successor to arbitrate the extent to which the successor was obligated under the collective-bargaining agreement. The Board contends that the same factors that the Court emphasized in *Wiley*, the peaceful settlement of industrial conflicts and "protection [of] the employees [against] a sudden change in the employment relationship," *id.*, at 549, require that Burns be treated under the collective-bargaining contract exactly as Wackenhut would have been if it had continued protecting the Lockheed plant.

We do not find *Wiley* controlling in the circumstances here. *Wiley* arose in the context of a §301 suit to compel arbitration, not in the context of an unfair labor practice proceeding where the Board is expressly limited by the provisions of §8(d). That decision emphasized "[t]he preference of national labor policy for arbitration as a substitute for tests of strength before contending forces" and held only that the agreement to arbitrate, "construed in the context of a national labor policy," survived the merger and left to the arbitrator, subject to judicial review, the ultimate question of the extent to which, if any, the surviving company was bound by other provisions of the contract.

Wiley's limited accommodation between the legislative endorsement of

---

[8] When the union that has signed a collective-bargaining contract is decertified, the succeeding union certified by the Board is not bound by the prior contract, need not administer it, and may demand negotiations for a new contract, even if the terms of the old contract have not yet expired.

freedom of contract and the judicial preference for peaceful arbitral settlement of labor disputes does not warrant the Board's holding that the employer commits an unfair labor practice unless he honors the substantive terms of the pre-existing contract. The present case does not involve a §301 suit; nor does it involve the duty to arbitrate. Rather, the claim is that Burns must be held bound by the contract executed by Wackenhut, whether Burns has agreed to it or not and even though Burns made it perfectly clear that it had no intention of assuming that contract. *Wiley* suggests no such open-ended obligation. Its narrower holding dealt with a merger occurring against a background of state law that embodied the general rule that in merger situations the surviving corporation is liable for the obligations of the disappearing corporation. Here there was no merger or sale of assets, and there were no dealings whatsoever between Wackenhut and Burns. On the contrary, they were competitors for the same work, each bidding for the service contract at Lockheed. Burns purchased nothing from Wackenhut and became liable for none of its financial obligations. Burns merely hired enough of Wackenhut's employees to require it to bargain with the union as commanded by §8(a)(5) and §9(a). But this consideration is a wholly insufficient basis for implying either in fact or in law that Burns had agreed or must be held to have agreed to honor Wackenhut's collective-bargaining contract.

We agree with the Court of Appeals that the Board failed to heed the admonitions of the *H. K. Porter* case. Preventing industrial strife is an important aim of federal labor legislation, but Congress has not chosen to make the bargaining freedom of employers and unions totally subordinate to this goal. When a bargaining impasse is reached, strikes and lockouts may occur. This bargaining freedom means both that parties need not make any concessions as a result of Government compulsion and that they are free from having contract provisions imposed upon them against their will. Here, Burns had notice of the existence of the Wackenhut collective-bargaining contract, but it did not consent to be bound by it. The source of its duty to bargain with the union is not the collective-bargaining contract but the fact that it voluntarily took over a bargaining unit that was largely intact and that had been certified within the past year. Nothing in its actions, however, indicated that Burns was assuming the obligations of the contract, and "allowing the Board to compel agreement when the parties themselves are unable to agree would violate the fundamental premise on which the Act is based — private bargaining under governmental supervision of the procedure alone, without any official compulsion over the actual terms of the contract." *H. K. Porter Co. v. NLRB*, 397 U.S. at 108.

We also agree with the Court of Appeals that holding either the union or the new employer bound to the substantive terms of an old collective-bargaining contract may result in serious inequities. A potential employer may be willing to take over a moribund business only if he can make changes in corporate structure, composition of the labor force, work location, task assignment, and nature of supervision. Saddling such an employer with the terms and conditions of employment contained in the old collective-bargaining contract may make these changes impossible and may discourage and inhibit the transfer of capital. On the other hand, a union may have made concessions to a small or failing employer that it would be unwilling to make to a large or economically successful firm. The congressional policy manifest in the Act is to enable the parties to negotiate for any protection either deems appropriate, but to allow the balance of bargaining advantage to be set by economic power realities. Strife is bound to occur if the concessions that must be honored do not correspond to the relative economic strength of the parties.

The Board's position would also raise new problems, for the successor employer would be circumscribed in exactly the same way as the predecessor under the collective-bargaining contract. It would seemingly follow that employees of the predecessor would be deemed employees of the successor, dischargeable only in accordance with provisions of the contract and subject to the grievance and arbitration provisions thereof. Burns would not have been free to replace Wackenhut's guards with its own except as the contract permitted. Given the continuity of employment relationship, the pre-existing contract's provisions with respect to wages, seniority rights, vacation privileges, pension and retirement fund benefits, job security provisions, work assignments and the like would devolve on the successor. Nor would the union commit a §8(b)(3) unfair labor practice if it refused to bargain for a modification of the agreement effective prior to the expiration date of the agreement. A successor employer might also be deemed to have inherited its predecessor's pre-existing contractual obligations to the union that had accrued under past contracts and that had not been discharged when the business was transferred. "[A] successor may well acquire more liabilities as a result of *Burns* than appear on the face of a contract."[11] Finally, a successor will be bound to observe the contract despite good-faith doubts about the union's majority during the time that the contract is a bar to another representation election. For the above reasons, the Board itself has expressed doubts as to the general applicability of its *Burns* rule.

In many cases, of course, successor employers will find it advantageous not only to recognize and bargain with the union but also to observe the pre-existing contract rather than to face uncertainty and turmoil. Also, in a variety of circumstances involving a merger, stock acquisition, reorganization, or assets purchase, the Board might properly find as a matter of fact that the successor had assumed the obligations under the old contract. Such a duty does not, however, ensue as a matter of law from the mere fact that an employer is doing the same work

---

[11]Doppelt, Successor Companies: The NLRB Limits the Options — and Raises Some Problems, 20 DePaul L. Rev. 176, 191 (1971).

in the same place with the same employees as his predecessor, as the Board had recognized until its decision in the instant case. We accordingly set aside the Board's finding of a §8(a)(5) unfair labor practice insofar as it rested on a conclusion that Burns was required to but did not honor the collective-bargaining contract executed by Wackenhut.

IV

It therefore follows that the Board's order requiring Burns to "give retroactive effect to all the clauses of said [Wackenhut] contract and, with interest of 6 percent, make whole its employees for any losses suffered by reason of Respondent's [Burns's] refusal to honor, adopt and enforce said contract" must be set aside. We note that the regional director's charge instituting this case asserted that "[o]n or about July 1, 1967, Respondent [Burns] unilaterally changed existing wage rates, hours of employment, overtime wage rates, differentials for swing shift and graveyard shift, and other terms and conditions of employment of the employees in the appropriate unit...," and that the Board's opinion stated that "[t]he obligation to bargain imposed on a successor-employer includes the negative injunction to refrain from unilaterally changing wages and other benefits established by a prior collective-bargaining agreement even though that agreement had expired. In this respect, the successor-employer's obligations are the same as those imposed upon employers generally during the period between collective-bargaining agreements." This statement by the Board is consistent with its prior and subsequent cases that hold that whether or not a successor employer is bound by its predecessor's contract, it must not institute terms and conditions of employment different from those provided in its predecessor's contract, at least without first bargaining with the employees' representative. Thus, if Burns, without bargaining to impasse with the union, had paid its employees on and after July 1 at a rate lower than Wackenhut had paid under its contract, or otherwise provided terms and conditions of employment different from those provided in the Wackenhut collective-bargaining agreement, under the Board's view, Burns would have been subject to an order to restore to employees what they had lost by this so-called unilateral change.

Although Burns had an obligation to bargain with the union concerning wages and other conditions of employment when the union requested it to do so, this case is not like a §8(a)(5) violation where an employer unilaterally changes a condition of employment without consulting a bargaining representative. It is difficult to understand how Burns could be said to have *changed* unilaterally any pre-existing term or condition of employment without bargaining when it had no previous relationship whatsoever to the bargaining unit and, prior to July 1, no outstanding terms and conditions of employment from which a change could be inferred. The terms on which Burns hired employees for service after July 1 may have differed from the terms extended by Wackenhut and required by the collective-bargaining contract, but it does not follow that Burns changed *its* terms and conditions of employment when it specified the initial basis on which employees were hired on July 1.

Although a successor employer is ordinarily free to set initial terms on which it will hire the employees of a predecessor, there will be instances in which it is perfectly clear that the new employer plans to retain all of the employees in the unit and in which it will be appropriate to have him initially consult with the employees' bargaining representative before he fixes terms. In other situations, however, it may not be clear until the successor employer has hired his full complement of employees that he has a duty to bargain with a union, since it will not be evident until then that the bargaining representative represents a majority of the employees in the unit as required by §9(a) of the Act. Here, for example, Burns's obligation to bargain with the union did not mature until it had selected its force of guards late in June. The Board quite properly found that Burns refused to bargain on July 12 when it rejected the overtures of the union. It is true that the wages it paid when it began protecting the Lockheed plant on July 1 differed from those specified in the Wackenhut collective-bargaining agreement, but there is no evidence that Burns ever unilaterally changed the terms and conditions of employment it had offered to potential employees in June after its obligation to bargain with the union became apparent. If the union had made a request to bargain after Burns had completed its hiring and if Burns had negotiated in good faith and had made offers to the union which the union rejected, Burns could have unilaterally initiated such proposals as the opening terms and conditions of employment on July 1 without committing an unfair labor practice. The Board's order requiring Burns to make whole its employees for any losses suffered by reason of Burns's refusal to honor and enforce the contract cannot, therefore, be sustained on the ground that Burns unilaterally changed existing terms and conditions of employment, thereby committing an unfair labor practice which required monetary restitution in these circumstances.

Affirmed.

Mr. Justice REHNQUIST, with whom the CHIEF JUSTICE, Mr. Justice BRENNAN, and Mr. Justice POWELL join, concurring and dissenting.

Although the Court studiously avoids using the term "successorship" in concluding that Burns did have a statutory obligation to bargain with the union, it affirms the conclusions of the Board and the Court of Appeals to that effect which were based entirely on the successorship doctrine. Because I believe that the Board and the Court of Appeals stretched that concept beyond the limits of its proper application, I would enforce neither the Board's bargaining order nor its order imposing upon Burns the terms of the contract between the union and Wackenhut. I therefore concur in part and dissent in part.

...

The Court concludes that because the trial examiner and the Board found the Lockheed facility to be an appropriate bargaining unit for Burns's employees, and because Burns hired a majority of Wackenhut's previous employees who had worked at that facility, Burns should have bargained with the union, even though the union never made any showing to Burns of majority representation. There is more than one difficulty with this analysis.

First, it is by no means mathematically demonstrable that the union was the choice of a majority of the 42 employees with which Burns began the performance of its contract with Lockheed. True, 27 of the 42 had been represented by the union when they were employees of Wackenhut, but there is nothing in the record before us to indicate that all 27 of these employees chose the union as their bargaining agent even at the time of negotiations with Wackenhut. There is obviously no evidence whatever that the remaining 15 employees of Burns, who had never been employed by Wackenhut, had ever expressed their views one way or the other about the union as a bargaining representative. It may be that, if asked, all would have designated the union. But they were never asked. Instead, the trial examiner concluded that because Burns was a "successor" employer to Wackenhut, it was obligated by that fact alone to bargain with the union.

...

... The imposition of successorship in this case is unusual because the successor, instead of purchasing business or assets from or merging with Wackenhut, was in direct competition with Wackenhut for the Lockheed contract. I believe that a careful analysis of the admittedly imprecise concept of successorship indicates that important rights of both the employee and the employer to independently order their own affairs are sacrificed needlessly by the application of that doctrine to this case.

It has been aptly observed that the doctrine of "successor" employer in the field of labor law is "shrouded in somewhat impressionist approaches."[3] In *John Wiley & Sons, Inc. v. Livingston,* 376 U.S. 543 (1964), we employed a form of the "successor" doctrine to impose upon an employer an obligation to arbitrate disputes under an arbitration clause in an agreement entered into between a predecessor

---

[3]*International Assn. of Machinists v. NLRB,* 414 F.2d 1135, 1139 (1969) (Leventhal, J., concurring).

employer and the bargaining representative of the latter's employees. The doctrine has been applied by the Board and by the courts of appeals to impose upon the successor employer a duty to bargain with representatives of the employees of his predecessor, to support a finding of unfair labor practices from a course of conduct engaged in by both the predecessor and the successor, and to require the successor to remedy unfair labor practices committed by a predecessor employer. The consequences of the application of the "successor" doctrine in each of these cases has been that the "successor" employer has been subjected to certain burdens or obligations to which a similarly situated employer who is not a "successor" would not be subject.

The various decisions that have applied the successor doctrine exhibit more than one train of reasoning in support of its application. There is authority for the proposition that it rests in part at least upon the need for continuity in industrial labor relations, and the concomitant avoidance of industrial strife that presumably follows from such continuity. On examination, however, this proposition may more accurately be described as a statement of the result of a finding of successorship, rather than a reason for making that finding.

Other cases have stated the guiding principle to be whether the "employing industry" remains essentially the same after the change in ownership. Under this approach a variety of facts relating to the "employing industry" have been examined to see whether a sufficient number remain unchanged to warrant the imposition of successorship. While it cannot be doubted that a determination as to successorship will vary with different fact situations, some general concept of the reason for the successorship doctrine is essential in order to determine the importance of the various factual combinations and permutations that may or may not call for its application.

This Court's opinion in *Wiley* makes it clear that one of the bases for a finding of successorship is the need to grant some protection to employees from a sudden transformation of their employer's business that results in the substitution of a new legal entity, not bound by the collective-bargaining contract under contract law, as the employer, but leaves intact significant elements of the employer's business. The Court said there:

> "The objectives of national labor policy, reflected in established principles of federal law, require that the rightful prerogative of owners independently to rearrange their businesses and even eliminate themselves as employers be balanced by some protection to the employees from a sudden change in the employment relationship. The transition from one corporate organization to another will in most cases be eased and industrial strife avoided if employees' claims continue to be resolved by arbitration rather than by 'the relative strength ... of the contending forces'...." 376

U.S. at 549.

But other language in *Wiley* makes it clear that the considerations favoring the continuity of existing bargaining relationships are not without their limits:

> "We do not hold that in every case in which the ownership or corporate structure of an enterprise is changed the duty to arbitrate survives. As indicated above, there may be cases in which the lack of any substantial continuity of identity in the business enterprise before and after a change would make a duty to arbitrate something imposed from without, not reasonably to be found in the particular bargaining agreement and the acts of the parties involved." 376 U.S. at 551.

The conflicting implications in these portions of the opinion in *Wiley* suggest that employees are indeed entitled to a measure of protection against change in the employing entity where the new employer continues to make use of tangible or intangible assets used in carrying on the business of the first employer. They also make clear that the successorship doctrine, carried to its ultimate limits, runs counter to other equally well-established principles of labor law. Industrial peace is an important goal of the Labor Management Relations Act. But Congress has time and again refused to sacrifice free collective bargaining between representatives of the employer for a system of compulsory arbitration. As the Court said in *NLRB v. Insurance Agents,* 361 U.S. 477, 488 (1960):

> "The mainstream of cases before the Board and in the courts reviewing its orders, under the provisions fixing the duty to bargain collectively, is concerned with insuring that the parties approach the bargaining table with this attitude [good faith]. But apart from this essential standard of conduct, Congress intended that the parties should have wide latitude in their negotiations, unrestricted by any governmental power to regulate the substantive solution of their differences."

And this Court has recently held that the Board itself may not compel one of the parties in the collective-bargaining process to agree to any particular proposal of the other. Conceivably the imposition of a system of compulsory arbitration, or the granting of authority to the Board to insist that the parties at some point agree on particular terms of a potential contract, would lessen the risk of industrial strife. But Congress has plainly been unwilling to purchase industrial peace at the price of substantial curtailment of free collective bargaining by the freely chosen representatives of the employees with their employer.

There is also a natural tension between the constraints imposed on employers by the Labor Management Relations Act, and the right of those employers in competition with one another "independently to rearrange their businesses and even eliminate themselves as employers." *Wiley*, 376 U.S. at 549. An employer's ability to compete in this market is affected, of course, by the terms of whatever collective-bargaining agreement he negotiates with the representative of his employees. Aside from the direct influence on price brought about by the terms of a collective-bargaining agreement, the collective-bargaining process itself presents a certain cost factor that may affect competition between employers in the market. The national commitment to collective bargaining embodied in the Labor Management Relations Act either requires or permits many of these constraints. But quite reasonable expectations of the employees in a particular collective-bargaining unit may be disappointed by a voluntary change in the condition of the employer that is quite incapable of being remedied by any rational application of the successorship doctrine. An employer is free to cease doing business, even though he chooses to do so wholly because of anti-union animus. An employer may adamantly refuse, at the expiration of the period covered by a collective-bargaining agreement, to again consent to a particular term of the agreement that the employees regarded as significant. These examples of permissible employer conduct for which the Labor Management Relations Act provides no remedy, notwithstanding that the conduct results in the disappointment of legitimate expectations of employees, suggest that the successorship principle, like every other principle of law, has limits beyond which it may not be expanded.

Wiley speaks in terms of a change in the "ownership or corporate structure of an enterprise" as bringing into play the obligation of the successor employer to perform an obligation voluntarily undertaken by the predecessor employer. But while the principle enunciated in *Wiley* is by no means limited to the corporate merger situation present there, it cannot logically be extended to a mere naked shifting of a group of employees from one employer to another without totally disregarding the basis for the doctrine. The notion of a change in the "ownership or corporate structure of an enterprise" connotes at the very least that there is continuity in the enterprise, as well as change; and that continuity be at least in part on the employer's side of the equation, rather then only on that of the employees. If we deal with the legitimate expectations of employees that the employer who agreed to the collective-bargaining contract perform it, we can require another employing entity to perform the contract only when he has succeeded to some of the tangible or intangible assets by the use of which the employees might have expected the first employer to have performed his contract with them.

Phrased another way, the doctrine of successorship in the federal common law of labor relations accords to employees the same general protection against transfer of assets by an entity against which they have a claim as is accorded by other legal doctrines to nonlabor-related claimants against the same entity. Nonlabor-related claimants in such transfer situations may be protected not only by assumption

NLRB v. Burns Security

agreements resulting from the self-interest of the contracting parties participating in a merger or sale of assets, but also by state laws imposing upon the successor corporation of any merger the obligations of the merged corporation and by bulk sales acts found in numerous States. These latter are designed to give the nonlabor-related creditor of the predecessor entity some claim, either as a matter of contract right against the successor, or as a matter of property right, to charge the assets that pass from the predecessor to the successor. The implication of *Wiley* is that the federal common law of labor relations accords the same general type and degree of protection to employees claiming under a collective-bargaining contract.

Cases from the courts of appeals have found successorship, consistently with these principles, where the new employer purchases a part or all of the assets of the predecessor employer; where the entire business is purchased by the new employer; and where there is merely a change in the ownership interest in a partnership that operates the employing entity. Other courts of appeals have, equally consistently with these principles, refused to find a successorship where there have been no contractual dealings between the two employers, and all that has taken place is a shift in employees.

The rigid imposition of a prior-existing labor relations environment on a new employer whose only connection with the old employer is the hiring of some of the latter's employees and the performance of some of the work which was previously performed by the latter, might well tend to produce industrial peace of a sort. But industrial peace in such a case would be produced at a sacrifice of the determination by the Board of the appropriateness of bargaining agents and of the wishes of the majority of the employees which the Act was designed to preserve. These latter principles caution us against extending successorship, under the banner of industrial peace, step by step to a point where the only connection between the two employing entities is a naked transfer of employees. Justice Holmes in *Hudson Water Co. v. McCarter,* 209 U.S. 349, 355 (1908) summarized the general problem this way:

> "All rights tend to declare themselves absolute to their logical extreme. Yet all in fact are limited by the neighborhood of principles of policy which are other than those on which the particular right is founded, and which become strong enough to hold their own when a certain point is reached."

Burns acquired not a single asset, tangible or intangible, by negotiation or transfer from Wackenhut. It succeeded to the contractual rights and duties of the plant protection service contract with Lockheed, not by reason of Wackenhut's assignment or consent, but over Wackenhut's vigorous opposition. I think the only permissible conclusion is that Burns is not a successor to Wackenhut. Following its decision in this case, the Board concluded in *Lincoln Private Police*, 189 NLRB No.

103 (1971), that an employer of guards was not a successor, saying:

> "Respondent, moreover, has operated as an entirely new and independent business enterprise. It obtained its own operating capital, purchased new uniforms, vehicles, and equipment, and occupied different premises than Industrial. Additionally, there is no indication that there has been any carryover of supervisory personnel from Industrial to Respondent." 189 NLRB at __.

To conclude that Burns was a successor to Wackenhut in this situation, with its attendant consequences under the Board's order imposing a duty to bargain with the bargaining representative of Wackenhut's employees, would import unwarranted rigidity into labor-management relations. The fortunes of competing employers inevitably ebb and flow, and an employer who has currently gained production orders at the expense of another may well wish to hire employees away from that other. There is no reason to think that the best interests of the employees, the employers, and ultimately of the free market are not served by such movement. Yet inherent in the expanded doctrine of successorship that the Board urges in this case is the notion that somehow the "labor relations environment" comes with the new employees if the new employer has but obtained orders or business that previously belonged to the old employer. The fact that the employees in the instant case continued to perform their work at the same situs, while not irrelevant to the analysis, cannot be deemed controlling. For the rigidity that would follow from the Board's application of successorship to this case would not only affect competition between Wackenhut and Burns, but would also affect Lockheed's operations. In effect, it would be saddled, as against its competitors, with the disadvantageous consequences of a collective-bargaining contract unduly favorable to Wackenhut's employees, even though Lockheed's contract with Wackenhut was set to expire at a given time. By the same token, it would be benefited, at the expense of its competitors, as a result of a "sweetheart" contract negotiated between Wackenhut and its employees.[*] From the viewpoint of the recipient of the services, dissatisfaction with the labor relations environment may stimulate a desire for change of contractors. Where the relation between the first employer and the second is as attenuated as it is here, and the reasonable expectations of the employees equally attenuated, the application of the successorship doctrine is not authorized by the Labor Management Relations Act.

---

[*]{This and the preceding sentence probably mean that an employer in Lockheed's position might be advantaged or disadvantaged vis-a-vis its competitors, depending on the nature of the labor contract between the union and the predecessor employer. If that contract were overly generous to the workers, Lockheed would be paying too much for their services (though this disadvantage would expire with the labor contract). If that contract were unduly stingy to the workers (a sweetheart contract), Lockheed would be getting their services below the market rate. — ed.}

This is not to say that Burns would be unilaterally free to mesh into its previously recognized Los Angeles County bargaining unit a group of employees such as were involved here who already have designated a collective-bargaining representative in their previous employment. Burns's actions in this regard would be subject to the commands of the Labor Management Relations Act, and to the regulation of the Board under proper application of governing principles. The situation resulting from the addition of a new element of the component work force of an employer has been dealt with by the Board in numerous cases, and various factors are weighed in order to determine whether the new workforce component should be itself a separate bargaining unit, or whether the employees in this component shall be "accreted" to the bargaining unit already in existence. Had the Board made the appropriate factual inquiry and determinations required by the Act, such inquiry might have justified the conclusion that Burns was obligated to recognize and bargain with the union as a representative of its employees at the Lockheed facility.

But the Board, instead of applying this type of analysis to the union's complaints here, concluded that because Burns was a "successor" it was absolutely bound to the mold that had been fashioned by Wackenhut and its employees at Lockheed. Burns was thereby precluded from challenging the designation of Lockheed as an appropriate bargaining unit for a year after the original certification.

I am unwilling to follow the Board this far down the successorship road, since I believe to do so would substantially undercut the principle of free choice of bargaining representatives by the employees and designation of the appropriate bargaining unit by the Board that are guaranteed by the Act.

⚜

QUESTIONS FOR REFLECTION

1. How should union support among the predecessor's employees be measured? For example, suppose the predecessor employed 100 workers; 60 were members of the union, and 40 paid agency shop fees as required by the collective bargaining agreement. The successor hires 50 former employees and 40 new employees. We could assume that all of the predecessor's employees support the union, in which event the union would have majority support among the successor's workers. We could assume that the predecessor's employees supported the union in proportion to the union's membership, in which event the union would have the support of (50 x .6 =) 30 of the successor's employees — not a majority of the new work force. Or we hold a representational election. Which approach should we use?

2. Suppose a successor employer purposefully refuses to hire a predecessor's workers in order to avert the obligation to bargain with the union. Would this be an unfair labor practice? If so, what should the remedy be?

3. When a successor buys a predecessor, is the predecessor absolved of existing contractual obligations to <u>other businesses</u>? If not, why should both the predecessor and the successor be absolved of contractual obligations <u>to the union</u>?

Ω

REMEDIES FOR REFUSING TO BARGAIN

Introduction

When an individual is victimized by an unfair labor practice, the Board must order the respondent to cease and desist from the illegal conduct, and, if the individual has lost wages or seniority, the Board may also order the respondent to make the victim whole for these loses. The remedies for a refusal to bargain are parallel. The respondent is always ordered to cease violating the law, in other words, to bargain in good faith in the future. If specific losses can be proved, the Board may order the respondent to compensate the victims. For example, if an employer unilaterally cuts wages from eight dollars an hour to seven, the Board may order the employer to pay the eight-dollar rate in the future (at least until bargaining can occur) and to pay the workers one dollar for each hour they worked at the seven dollar rate.

Another common example — and a more difficult one to deal with — is the employer who violates the law by refusing to bargain in good faith during negotiations. The topic is often wages. What should the remedy be for this violation? A cease-and-desist order is appropriate, of course, but what about money? Do workers lose anything when their employer refuses to bargain with their union, and, if so, can the loss be measured with reasonable accuracy? Prior to Ex-Cell-O, the Board did not award compensation in this situation.

It will help the student to keep in mind the procedural context in which cases like Ex-Cell-O arise. If the union wins a representation election, the employer may object to the result on various grounds. For example, the employer may believe that the bargaining unit sought by the union is not appropriate, or that ineligible persons were allowed to vote in the election or eligible persons were prevented from voting, or that irregularities tainted the pre-election campaign and interfered with the workers' freedom of choice. The regional director rules on the employer's objection. If the employer is not satisfied with the director's ruling, it may be appealed to the Labor Board. Decisions of the Board in representation cases are considered to be administrative rulings and, therefore, may not be appealed to the courts. Accordingly, the decision of the Board is final — in theory.

In practice, however, if the Board denies the employer's appeal, the employer may refuse to bargain with the union. The union must then file an unfair labor practice charge against the employer.[a] When the regional office of the Board investigates the charge, it is found to be valid; after all, the employer's objection has already been overruled by both the region and the Board. So the regional director issues an unfair labor practice complaint. The employer spurns all efforts to settle the case, and a hearing is held before an administrative law judge (formerly known as a trial examiner). The employer defends on the ground that the election was invalid. The administrative law judge, knowing that the Board has already found the election was proper, summarily rules against the employer. The employer appeals to the Labor Board. The Board, of course, denies the appeal and orders the employer to bargain with the union. The order of the Board is not self-enforcing, and the employer refuses to obey it. The General Counsel must then petition the Court of Appeals to enforce the Board's order. At the hearing before the court, the employer once again argues that the election was invalid; and the court rules on this issue. Thus, the Board's decision on the representation issue, which is theoretically not appealable, is in fact appealed. If the court disagrees with the Board's decision, the election is invalidated and the employer does not have to bargain with the union. If the court agrees with Board's decision, the employer is ordered to bargain with the union.

Ex-Cell-O followed this pattern through the Board's ruling on the unfair labor practice charge. Then the case got interesting. Instead of requesting only the usual cease-and-desist order, the General Counsel asked for an order that the employer pay the workers the additional wages the union would have secured for them via collective bargaining. The administrative law judge recommended this remedy, and the Board focused on whether such a remedy was appropriate.

⚜

---

[a]Alternatively, the union could strike in protest of the employer's unfair labor practice and rely on economic power to compel bargaining.

Ex-Cell-O Corporation
185 NLRB 107 (1970)

{The union won a representation election on October 22, 1964. The employer objected to the results on the ground that the union had made misrepresentations before the election. The regional director overruled the objections on December 29, 1964, and the Board affirmed this ruling on October 28, 1965. The employer then refused to bargain with the union in order to secure judicial review of the Board's decision: whereupon, the union accused the employer of an unfair labor practice, and the Board issued a complaint on November 23, 1965. A trial was held on the complaint in June and July of 1966.}

... On March 2, 1967, the Trial Examiner issued his Decision, finding that the Company had unlawfully refused to bargain in violation of Section 8(a)(5) and (1) of the Act and recommended the standard bargaining order as a remedy. In addition, the Trial Examiner ordered the Company to compensate its employees for monetary losses incurred as a result of its unlawful conduct.

It is not disputed that Respondent refused to bargain with the Union, and we hereby affirm the Trial Examiner's conclusion that Respondent thereby violated Section 8(a)(1) and (5) of the Act. The compensatory remedy which he recommends, however, raises important issues concerning the Board's powers and duties to fashion appropriate remedies in its efforts to effectuate the policies of the National Labor Relations Act.

It is argued that such a remedy exceeds the Board's general statutory powers. In addition, it is contended that it cannot be granted because the amount of employee loss, if any, is so speculative that an order to make employees whole would amount to the imposition of a penalty. And the position is advanced that the adoption of this remedy would amount to the writing of a contract for the parties, which is prohibited by Section 8(d).

We have given most serious consideration to the Trial Examiner's recommended financial reparations Order, and are in complete agreement with his finding that current remedies of the Board designed to cure violations of Section 8(a)(5) are inadequate. A mere affirmative order that an employer bargain upon request does not eradicate the effects of an unlawful delay of 2 or more years in the fulfillment of a statutory bargaining obligation. It does not put the employees in the position of bargaining strength they would have enjoyed if their employer had immediately recognized and bargained with their chosen representative. It does not dissolve the inevitable employee frustration or protect the Union from the loss of employee support attributable to such delay. The inadequacy of the remedy is all the more egregious where, as in the recent *NLRB v. Tiidee Products, Inc.* case,[f] the court found that the employer had raised "frivolous" issues in order to postpone or avoid its lawful obligation to bargain. [As a result, the employer was ordered to compensate the union and the Board for their litigation expenses.] We have weighed these considerations most carefully. For the reasons stated below, however, we have reluctantly concluded that we cannot approve the Trial Examiner's Recommended Order that Respondent compensate its employees for monetary losses incurred as a consequence of Respondent's determination to refuse to bargain until it had tested in court the validity of the Board's certification.

Section 10(c) of the Act directs the Board to order a person found to have committed an unfair labor practice to cease and desist and "to take such affirmative action including reinstatement of employees with or without back pay, as will effectuate the policies of this Act." This authority, as our colleagues note with full documentation, is extremely broad and was so intended by Congress. It is not so broad, however, as to permit the punishment of a particular respondent or a class of respondents. Nor is the statutory direction to the Board so compelling that the Board is without discretion in exercising the full sweep of its power, for it would defeat the purposes of the Act if the Board imposed an otherwise proper remedy that resulted in irreparable harm to a particular respondent and hampered rather than promoted meaningful collective bargaining. Moreover, as the Supreme Court recently emphasized, the Board's grant of power does not extend to compelling agreement. It is with respect to these three limitations upon the Board's power to remedy a violation of Section 8(a)(5) that we examine the UAW's requested remedy in this case.

The Trial Examiner concluded that the proposed remedy was not punitive, that it merely made the employees partially whole for losses occasioned by the Respondent's refusal to bargain, and was much less harsh than a back pay order for discharged employees, which might require the Respondent to pay wages to these employees as well as their replacements. Viewed solely in the context of an assumption of employee monetary losses resulting directly from the Respondent's violation of Section 8(a)(5), as finally determined in court, the Trial Examiner's conclusion appears reasonable. There are, however, other factors in this case which provide counterweights to that rationale. In the first place, there is no contention that this Respondent acted in a manner flagrantly in defiance of the statutory policy. On the contrary, the record indicates that this Respondent responsibly fulfills its legally established collective-bargaining obligations. It is clear that Respondent merely sought judicial affirmance of the Board's decision that the election of October 22, 1964, should not be set aside on the Respondent's objections. In the past, whenever an employer has sought court intervention in a representation proceeding, the Board has argued forcefully that court intervention would be premature, that the employer had an unquestioned right under the statute to seek court review of any Board order

---

[f]426 F.2d 1243 (D.C. Cir. 1970).

before its bargaining obligation became final. Should this procedural right in 8(a)(5) cases be tempered by a large monetary liability in the event the employer's position in the representation case is ultimately found to be without merit? Of course, an employer or a union which engages in conduct later found in violation of the Act, does so at the peril of ultimate conviction and responsibility for a make-whole remedy. But the validity of a particular Board election tried in an unfair labor practice case is not, in our opinion, an issue on the same plane as the discharge of employees for union activity or other conduct in flagrant disregard of employee rights. There are wrongdoers and wrongdoers. Where the wrong in refusing to bargain is, at most, a debatable question, though ultimately found a wrong, the imposition of a large financial obligation on such a respondent may come close to a form of punishment for having elected to pursue a representation question beyond the Board and to the courts. The desirability of a compensatory remedy in a case remarkably similar to the instant case was recently considered by the Court of Appeals for the District of Columbia in *United Steelworkers [Quality Rubber Manufacturing Company, Inc.] v. NLRB*, 430 F.2d 519. There the court, distinguishing *Tiidee Products*, indicated that the Board was warranted in refusing to grant such a remedy in an 8(a)(5) case where the employer "desired only to obtain an authoritative determination of the validity of the Board's decision." It is not clear whether the court was of the opinion that the requested remedy was within the Board's discretion or whether it would have struck down such a remedy as punitive in view of the technical nature of the respondent's unfair labor practice. In any event, we find ourselves in disagreement with the Trial Examiner's view that a compensatory remedy as applied to the Respondent in the instant case is not punitive "in any sense of the word."

In *Tiidee Products* the court suggested that the Board need not follow a uniform policy in the application of a compensatory remedy in 8(a)(5) cases. Indeed, the court noted that such uniformity in this area of the law would be unfair when applied "to unlike cases." The court was of the opinion that the remedy was proper where the employer had engaged in a "manifestly unjustifiable refusal to bargain" and where its position was "palpably without merit." As in *Quality Rubber*, the court in *Tiidee Products* distinguished those cases in which the employer's failure to bargain rested on a "debatable question." With due respect for the opinion of the Court of Appeals for the District of Columbia, we cannot agree that the application of a compensatory remedy in 8(a)(5) cases can be fashioned on the subjective determination that the position of one respondent is "debatable" while that of another is "frivolous." What is debatable to the Board may appear frivolous to a court, and vice versa. Thus the debatability of the employer's position in an 8(a)(5) case would itself become a matter of intense litigation.

We do not believe that the critical question of the employer's motivation in delaying bargaining should depend so largely on the expertise of counsel, the accident of circumstances, and the exigencies of the moment.

In our opinion, however, the crucial question to be determined in this case relates to the policies which the requested order would effectuate. The statutory policy as embodied in Section 8(a)(5) and (d) of the Act was considered at some length by the Supreme Court in *H. K. Porter Co., Inc. v. NLRB,* 397 U.S. 99.[a] There the Court held that the Board had power to require employers and employees "to negotiate" but that the Board was without power to compel a company or a union "to agree to any substantive contractual provision of a collective bargaining agreement." The purpose of the act, the Court held, was to ensure that employers and their employees "work together to establish mutually satisfactory conditions." The Court noted that Congress was aware that agreement between employers and unions might not always be reached, that agreement might in some cases be impossible, or thwarted by strikes and lockouts. But it was never intended, the Court held, that the Government in such cases step in and become a party to the negotiations. Recognizing that the Board's remedial powers might be insufficient to cope with important labor problems, the Supreme Court nevertheless struck down an order requiring the respondent employer involuntarily to agree to a specific contractual provision. It was the job of Congress, not the Board or the courts, Justice Black wrote, "to decide when and if it is necessary to allow governmental review of proposals for collective bargaining agreements and compulsory submission to one side's demands."

It is argued that the instant case is distinguishable from *H. K. Porter* in that here the requested remedy merely would require an employer to compensate employees for losses they incurred as a consequence of their employer's *failure to agree* to a contract he *would* have agreed to *if* he had bargained in good faith. In our view, the distinction is more illusory than real. The remedy in *H. K. Porter* operates prospectively to bind an employer to a specific contractual term. The remedy in the instant case operates retroactively to impose financial liability upon an employer flowing from a *presumed* contractual agreement. The Board infers that the latter contract, though it never existed and does not and need not exist, was *denied* existence by the employer because of his refusal to bargain. In either case the employer has not agreed to the contractual provision for which he must accept full responsibility *as though he had agreed to it*. Our colleagues contend that a compensatory remedy is not the "writing of a contract" because it does not "specify new or continuing terms of employment and does not prohibit changes in existing terms and conditions." But there is no basis for such a remedy unless the Board finds, as a matter of fact, that a contract would have resulted from bargaining. The fact that the contract, so to speak, is "written in the air" does not diminish its financial impact upon the recalcitrant employer who, willy nilly, is forced to accede to terms never mutually established by the parties. Despite the admonition of the Supreme Court that Section 8(d) was intended to mean what it says, i.e., that the obligation to bargain "does not compel either party to agree to a proposal or require the making of a concession," one of the parties under this remedy is forced by the Government to submit to the other side's

---

[a]{The Board found the employer had refused to bargain over one specific topic, namely, the union's request for a dues checkoff clause. As a remedy, the Board ordered the employer to accept a checkoff clause. The Supreme Court affirmed the finding of a refusal to bargain, but refused to enforce the remedy. — ed.}

demands. It does not help to argue that the remedy could not be applied unless there was substantial evidence that the employer would have yielded to these demands during bargaining negotiations. Who is to say in a specific case how much an employer is prepared to give and how much a union is willing to take? Who is to say that a favorable contract would, in any event, result from negotiations? And it is only the employer of such good will as to whom the Board might conclude that he, at least, would have given his employees a fair increase, who can be made subject to a financial reparations order; should such an employer be singled out for the imposition of such an order? To answer these questions the Board would be required to engage in the most general, if not entirely speculative, inferences to reach the conclusion that employees were deprived of specific benefits as a consequence of their employer's refusal to bargain.

Much as we appreciate the need for more adequate remedies in 8(a)(5) cases, we believe that, as the law now stands, the proposed remedy is a matter for Congress, not the Board. In our opinion, however, substantial relief may be obtained immediately through procedural reform, giving the highest possible priority to 8(a)(5) cases combined with full resort to the injunctive relief provisions of Section 10(j) and (e) of the Act.

Members MCCULLOCH and BROWN, dissenting in part:

Although concurring in all other respects in the Decision and Order of the Board, we part company with our colleagues on the majority in that we would grant the compensatory remedy recommended by the Trial Examiner. Unlike our colleagues, we believe that the Board has the statutory authority to direct such relief and that it would effectuate the policies of the Act to do so in this case.

Section 10(c) of the act directs the Board to remedy unfair labor practices by ordering the persons committing them to cease and desist from their unlawful conduct "and to take such affirmative action including reinstatement of employees with or without back pay, as will effectuate the policies of the Act...." The phrase "affirmative action" is nowhere qualified in the statute, except that such action must "effectuate the policies of this Act," and indicates the intent of Congress to vest the Board with remedial powers coextensive with the underlying policies of the law which is to be enforced. This provision "did not pass the Wagner Act Congress without objection to the uncontrolled breadth of this power."[11]

But the broad language survived the challenge.

...

The declared policy of the Act is to promote the peaceful settlement of disputes

---

[11] *Local 60, Carpenters v. NLRB,* 365 U.S. 651 (concurring opinion).

Ex-Cell-O

by encouraging collective bargaining and by protecting employee rights. To accomplish this purpose, Board remedies for violations of the Act should, on one hand, have the effect of preventing the party in violation from so acting in the future, and from enjoying any advantage he may have gained by his unlawful practices. But they must also presently dissipate the effects of violations on employee rights in order that the employees so injured receive what they should not have been denied. A Board order so devised is to be enforced by the courts "unless it can be shown that the order is a patent attempt to achieve ends other than those which can fairly be said to effectuate the policies of the Act."[22]

Deprivation of an employees' statutory rights is often accompanied by serious financial injury to him. Where this is so, an order which only guarantees the exercise of his rights in the future often falls far short of expunging the effects of the unlawful conduct involved. Therefore, one of the Board's most effective and well-established affirmative remedies for unlawful conduct is an order to make employees financially whole for losses resulting from violations of the Act. Various types of compensatory orders have been upheld by the Supreme court in the belief that "Making the workers whole for losses suffered on account of an unfair practice is part of the vindication of the public policy which the Board enforces."[24] The most familiar of these is the back pay order used to remedy the effect of employee discharges found to be in violation of Section 8(a)(3) of the Act. While the cease-and-desist and reinstatement orders remedy the denial of the aggrieved employee's rights and protect the prospective exercise thereof, the back pay order repairs the financial losses which have been suffered, and, thus making the employee whole, serves to recreate, as fully as possible, the conditions and relationships that would have been, had there been no unfair labor practice.

...

The Board has already recognized in certain refusal-to-bargain situations that the usual bargaining order is not sufficient to expunge the effect of an employer's unlawful and protracted denial of its employees' right to bargain. Though the bargaining order serves to remedy the loss of legal right and protect its exercise in the future, it does not remedy the financial injury which may also have been suffered. In a number of situations the Board has ordered the employer who unlawfully refused to bargain to compensate its employees for their resultant financial losses. Thus, some employers unlawfully refuse to sign [a written contract after an oral agreement has been reached]. The Board has in these cases ordered the employer to execute the agreement previously reached and, according to its terms, to make whole the employees for the monetary losses suffered because of the unlawful delay in its effectuation.

---

[22]*Fibreboard Paper Product Corp. v. NLRB*, 379 U.S. 203, 216.

[24]*Phelps Dodge v. NLRB,* 313 U.S. 177 at 197.

Similarly, in *American Fire Apparatus Co.*,[36] the employer {had awarded Christmas bonuses for several years before the union organized the plant. The first collective bargaining agreement, signed in September, did not mention bonuses. The following Christmas, the employer} violated Section 8(a)(5) by unilaterally discontinuing payment of Christmas bonuses, and the Board concluded that only by requiring the bonuses to be paid could the violation be fully remedied. The Court of Appeals for the Eighth Circuit in enforcing the order commented, "Nor do we believe that the difficulty in computing the precise amount due each employee is a substantial reason for modifying the Board's order." In *Leeds & Northrup Co. v. NLRB*, 391 F.2d 874, which involved a related problem, the Court of Appeals for the Third Circuit reached a similar conclusion. {The employer had implemented a profit-sharing plan before the union organized the plant. Several collective bargaining agreements did not mention the plan, and the company renewed the plan annually. Then, during the term of an agreement,} the employer unilaterally altered its formula for computing its annual profitsharing bonus. The Board found that a violation of Section 8(a)(5) had occurred and ordered payment to the employees of the difference between what they had received and the amount they would have been paid under the prior method of computation. In enforcing that order, the court stated:

> The Board's back pay award in this case is supportable on the ground that the union might have successfully resisted all or a portion of the reduction in its share of profits had it been afforded an opportunity to bargain, and the employees should not be left in a worse position than they might have enjoyed if the union had been given the opportunity to bargain. While it is true that a retroactive order might afford the employees a better position than the union's bargaining might have achieved, the Board can hardly be said to be effectuating policies beyond the purposes of the Act by resolving the doubt against the party who violated the Act. Retroactive enforcement must always contain in it some element of hardship on the employer, but a failure to grant back pay imposes at least an equal hardship on the employees.

And in *Fibreboard Paper Products Corp.*, {the agreement between the employer and the union covered maintenance and other jobs in a plant. While the agreement was in force} the employer unilaterally contracted out its maintenance operations in violation of Section 8(a)(5). The Board concluded that an order to bargain about this decision could not, by itself, adequately remedy the effects of the violation. It further ordered the employer to reinstate the employees and to make them whole for any loss of earnings suffered on account of the unlawful conduct. The Supreme Court upheld the compensatory remedy and stated, "There has been no showing that the Board's order restoring the *status quo ante* to insure meaningful bargaining is not well designed to promote the policies of the Act."[38]

---

[36] 160 NLRB 1318.

[38] 379 U.S. at 216.

The question now before us is whether a reimbursement order is an appropriate remedy for other types of unlawful refusals to bargain. On the basis of the foregoing analysis regarding Section 10(c), we believe that the Board has the power to order this type of relief. Further, for the reasons set forth herein, we are of the view that the compensatory remedy is appropriate and necessary in this case to effectuate the policies of the act.

An employer's unlawful refusal to bargain completely frustrates the purposes of the Act, as it directly contravenes the congressional policy of encouraging collective bargaining and also denies the statutory right of the employees to bargain collectively through their chosen representative. It is clear from the Act itself and from its legislative history that immediate recognition of this right was contemplated; and partly to achieve this goal Congress, in originally enacting the Act in 1935, excluded Board orders in certification proceedings under Section 9(c) from direct review in the courts. This judgment was reaffirmed in 1947 when a conference committee rejected a proposed House amendment which would have permitted any interested persons to obtain review immediately after certification because "such provision would permit dilatory tactics in representation proceedings."[41] Very often, as noted by the Supreme Court, the procedural delays necessary to make a fair determination on charges of unfair labor practices have the effect of postponing indefinitely the performance of employers' statutory duty to bargain, thus depriving employees of their legal right to such collective-bargaining representation. The Board has taken various steps in an effort to relieve the wrongful effects of such delay. Thus, in *Frank Bros. Company*, for example, the Board issued a bargaining order even though the union had lost its majority before the issuance of the complaint alleging the refusal to bargain, and the Supreme Court upheld this action, commenting that to order further elections would be "providing employers a chance to profit from a stubborn refusal to abide by the law. That the Board was within its statutory authority in adopting the remedy which it had adopted to foreclose the probability of such frustrations of the Act seems too plain for anything but statement."[44]

The present remedies for unlawful refusals to bargain often fall short, as in the present case, of adequately protecting the employees' right to bargain. Recent court decisions, congressional investigations, and scholarly studies have concluded that, in the present remedial framework, justice delayed is often justice denied.

In *NLRB v. Tiidee Products, Inc.*, the Court of Appeals for the District of Columbia Circuit recently stated:[46]

While [the Board's usual bargaining] remedy may provide some bargaining

---

[41]Statement by Senator Taft, 93 *Cong. Rec.* 6444 (1947).

[44]321 U.S. 702 at 705....

[46]426 F.2d 1243.

from the date of the order's enforcement, it operates in a real sense so as to be counter productive, and actually to reward an employer's refusal to bargain during the critical period following a union's organization of his plant. The obligation of collective bargaining is the core of the Act, and the primary means fashioned by Congress for securing industrial peace.

... Employee interest in a union can wane quickly as working conditions remain apparently unaffected by the union or collective bargaining. When the company is finally ordered to bargain with the union some years later, the union may find that it represents only a small fraction of the employees. Thus the employer may reap a second benefit from his original refusal to comply with the law: He may continue to enjoy lower labor expenses after the order to bargain either because the union is gone or because it is too weak to bargain effectively.

A study by Professor Philip Ross shows that a contract is signed in most situations where the employer honors its duty to bargain without delay, but that the chance of a contract being signed is cut in half if the case must go to court enforcement of a bargaining order.[48] In the interim, of course, the employees are deprived of their rightful union representation and the opportunity to bargain over their terms and conditions of employment, while at the same time their employers may gain a monetary advantage over their competitors who have complied with their legal duty.

The present case is but another example of a situation where a bargaining order by itself is not really adequate to remedy the effects of an unlawful refusal to bargain. The Union herein requested recognition on August 3, 1964, and proved that it represented a majority of employees 2½ months later in a Board-conducted election. Nonetheless, since October 1965 the employer, by unlawfully refusing to bargain with the Union, has deprived its employees of their legal right to collective bargaining through their certified bargaining representative.[50] While a bargaining order at this

---

[48]Ross, *The Government as a Source of Union Power* 251.

[50]We find no merit in the Respondent's contention in the present case that, at least in a "technical" refusal to bargain situation, a compensatory remedy would penalize it for obtaining judicial review of the Board's representation proceedings. In *Consolo v. Federal Maritime Commission*, 383 U.S. 607 at 624, 625, the Court rejected the same contention. Relying on a case involving the Board (*NLRB v. Electric Vacuum Cleaner Company, Inc.*, 315 U.S. 685) the Court concluded, "At any rate it has never been the law that a litigant is absolved from liability for that time during which his litigation is pending" (*id.* at 624-625) and noted (at 625) that the time of appeal allowed the respondent to continue its unlawful conduct [and thus to] continue to injure the petitioner. That such a remedy would include the entire amount lost by the wronged party, instead of being reduced by the amount accruing while the violator was contesting the issue, no more makes the remedy penal in character under this Act than it does elsewhere. "The litigant must pay for his experience, like others who have tried and lost." *Life and Casualty Ins. Co. v. McCray*, 291 U.S. 566, 575.

(continued...)

time, operating prospectively, may insure the exercise of that right in the future, it clearly does not repair the injury to the employees here, caused by the Respondent's denial of their rights during the past 5 years.

In these refusal-to-bargain cases there is at least a legal injury. Potential employee losses incurred by an employer's refusal to bargain in violation of the Act are not limited to financial matters such as wages. Thus, it is often the case that the most important employee gains arrived at through collective bargaining involve such benefits as seniority, improved physical facilities, a better grievance procedure or a right to arbitration. Therefore, even the remedy we would direct herein is not complete, limited as it is to only some of the monetary losses which may be measured or estimated. The employees would not be made whole for all the losses incurred through the employer's unfair labor practice. But, where the legal injury is accompanied by financial loss, the employees should be compensated for it. The compensatory period would normally run from the date of the employer's unlawful refusal to bargain until it commences to negotiate in good faith, or upon the failure of the Union to commence negotiations, within 5 days of the receipt of the Respondent's notice of its desire to bargain with the Union, although here a later starting date could be used because this remedy would be a substantial departure from past practices. Further, the Board could follow its usual procedure of providing a general reimbursement order with the amount, if any, to be determined as part of the compliance procedure.

This type of compensatory remedy is in no way forbidden by Section 8(d). It would be designed to compensate employees for injuries incurred by them by virtue of the unfair labor practices and would not require the employer to accept the measure of compensation as a term of any contract which might result from subsequent

---

(...continued)

There is no question of the right of an employer to test the legal propriety of a Board certification or to test its legal position respecting any issue of law or fact upon which a Board bargaining order is predicated, but it should not thereby realize benefits not usually flowing from such a proceeding. In other words, should an employer choose to await court action and if its legal position be sustained, it would not only be absolved of the duty to bargain, but also of any monetary remedy arising out of the order contemplated herein; if, on the other hand, an employer be found to have rested its refusal to bargain on an erroneous view of law or fact, any loss to employees incurred by its continued adherence to that error should be borne by that employer and not by its employees. That is the risk taken by all litigants.

The employer's argument for tolling the compensatory period during the time he contests the violation is contrary to the policy of the Act in fostering the prompt commencement of collective bargaining, a policy shown explicitly in the denial of judicial review of the Board's representation proceedings. To allow the employer to avoid making his employees whole for the period bargaining was delayed by his litigating a mistaken view of the law would encourage such delay in the areas in which Congress particularly deemed speed to be essential.

collective bargaining. The remedy contemplated in no way "writes a contract" between the employer and the union, for it would not specify new or continuing terms of employment and would not prohibit changes in existing terms and conditions. All of these would be left to the outcome of bargaining, the commencement of which would terminate Respondent's liability.

Furthermore, this compensatory remedy is not a punitive measure. It would be designed to do no more than reimburse the employees for the loss occasioned by the deprivation of their right to be represented by their collective-bargaining agent during the period of the violation. The amount to be awarded would be only that which would reasonably reflect and be measured by the loss caused by the unlawful denial of the opportunity for collective bargaining. Thus, employees would be compensated for the injury suffered as a result of their employer's unlawful refusal to bargain, and the employer would thereby be prohibited from enjoying the fruits of its forbidden conduct — to the end, as embodied in the Act, that collective bargaining be encouraged and the rights of the injured be protected. It is well settled that a reimbursement order is not a redress for a private wrong, since the Act does not create a private cause of action for damages, but is a remedy created by statute and designed to aid in the achievement of the public policy embodied in the Act. Accordingly, as the reimbursement order sought herein is meant to enforce public policy, the Board's exercise of its discretion in ordering such a remedy would not be strictly confined to the same considerations which govern comparable awards in either equity courts or damage awards in legal actions. In the first place, it is well established that, where the defendant's wrongful act prevents exact determination of the amount of damage, he cannot plead such uncertainty in order to deny relief to the injured person, but rather must bear the risk of the uncertainty which was created by his own wrong. The Board is often faced with the task of determining the precise amount of a make-whole order where the criteria are less than ideal, and has successfully resolved the questions presented.[62]

---

[62]The problem most frequently arises when we must determine the amount of back pay due to unlawfully discharged employees. As we recently stated in connection with this issue (*The Buncher Company*, 164 NLRB 340):

> In solving many of the problems which arise in back pay cases, the Board occasionally is required to adopt formulas which result in back pay determinations that are close approximations because no better basis exists for determining the exact amount due. However, the fact that the exact amount due is incalculable is no justification for permitting the Respondent to escape completely his legal obligation to compensate the victims of his discriminatory actions for the loss of earnings which they suffered. In general, courts have acknowledged that in solving such back pay problems, the Board is vested with wide discretion in devising procedures and methods which will effectuate the purposes of the Act and [have] generally limited [their] review to whether a method selected was "arbitrary or unreasonable in the

(continued...)

But even if a reimbursement order were judged by legal or equitable principles regarding damages, the remedy would not be speculative. It is well established that the rule which precludes recovery of "uncertain damages" refers to uncertainty as to the fact of injury, rather than to the amount. Where, as here, the employer has deprived its employees of a statutory right, there is by definition a legal injury suffered by them, and any uncertainty concerns only the amount of the accompanying reimbursable financial loss.

From a remedial viewpoint, the present type of refusal to bargain differs from other 8(a)(5) situations where reimbursement has been ordered only in the method of proof needed to calculate the amount of financial loss, if any, which the employees may have suffered. In the cases involving employer refusals to sign agreements already reached, the employees' losses were compensated according to the terms of such agreement for the length of the delay in effectuation caused by the employer. Where the employer unilaterally discontinued a Christmas bonus, the amount of employee loss was determined by utilizing the past records of bonuses given and the methods by which they were previously calculated. In a recent case,[66] a union and multiemployer bargaining association successfully bargained to a contract. The employer subsequently refused to sign the contract and attempted to withdraw from the multiemployer bargaining association. The Board found a violation of Section 8(a)(5) and ordered the employer to cease and desist from unfair labor practices, to sign the contract, and to pay the fringe benefits provided for in that contract. The court of appeals had agreed with the Board's finding of violation and its order to cease and desist from violation and to sign the contract, but refused to enforce that part of the Board's order requiring the Respondent to pay the contractual fringe benefits as being outside the Board's powers. The Supreme Court, on writ of *certiorari*, affirmed the Board order *in toto*, finding that the provision ordering the Respondent to pay the contractual fringe benefits was within the Board's remedial power granted in Section 10(c) of the Act. In situations of unlawful unilateral discontinuance of part of an operation, the compensation is based upon the wage rates previously earned by the injured employees. It may be noted that the Supreme Court upheld the order in *Fibreboard* even though the amount of actual loss might be deemed speculative because it was not shown that, had the employer bargained lawfully, it would not have contracted out the work and discharged the employees.

As previously indicated, the injury suffered by employees is predicated upon the employees' being deprived of the right to collective bargaining as required by the Act. The burden of proof would be upon the General Counsel at the compliance stage to translate that legal injury into terms of measurable financial loss, if any, which the employees might reasonably be found to have suffered as a consequence of that injury.

---

[62](...continued)
    circumstances involved," or whether in determining the amount, a
    "rational basis" was utilized.

[66]*NLRB v. Joseph T. Strong dba Strong Roofing,* 393 U.S. 357.

A showing at the compliance stage by the General Counsel or Charging Party by acceptable and demonstrable means that the employees could have reasonably expected to gain a certain amount of compensation by bargaining would establish a *prima facie* loss, and the Respondent would then be afforded an opportunity to rebut such a showing. This might be accomplished, for example, by adducing evidence to show that a contract would probably not have been reached, or that there would have been less or no increase in compensation as a result of any contract which might have been signed.

Accordingly, uncertainty as to the amount of loss does not preclude a make-whole order proposed here, and some reasonable method or basis of computation can be worked out as part of the compliance procedure. These cannot be defined in advance, but there are many methods for determining the measurable financial gain which the employees might reasonably have expected to achieve, had the Respondent fulfilled its statutory obligation to bargain collectively. The criteria which prove valid in each case must be determined by what is pertinent to the facts. Nevertheless, the following methods for measuring such loss do appear to be valuable, although these are neither exhaustive nor exclusive. Thus, if the particular employer and union involved have contracts covering other plants of the employer, possibly in the same or a relevant area, the terms of such agreements may serve to show what the employees could probably have obtained by bargaining. The parties could also make comparisons with compensation patterns achieved through collective bargaining by other employees in the same geographic area and industry. Or the parties might employ the national average percentage changes in straight time hourly wages computed by the Bureau of Labor Statistics.

And there [are] other available significant data which may be utilized to indicate the value of the lost collective-bargaining opportunity. For example, the Bureau of Labor Statistics conducts an annual study of union wage scales in the building construction, local transit, local trucking, and printing industries. This study covers all local unions in 68 selected cities. The Bureau also issues monthly reports of wage and benefit changes under collective-bargaining agreements in manufacturing establishments employing 1,000 or more production and related workers. A related survey of wage developments in smaller manufacturing units covers both unionized and nonunionized establishments. There are other Bureau of Labor Statistics facts which may bear on the remedy. One of significance is the periodic wage and benefits survey of 50 manufacturing and 20 nonmanufacturing industries. The data collected in this program report on about 20 million employees on both a national and regional basis, usually with listings by size of establishment, size of community, collective-bargaining coverage, and type of product or plant group. Another Bureau of Labor Statistics program periodically gathers wage and benefits data on a Standard Metropolitan Statistical Area basis for more than 60 occupational categories in all but the smallest establishments. Depending on the type of industry, these surveys cover from 8 to 72 metropolitan areas. Guidance may also be forthcoming, on occasion, from other forms of data frequently cited in the collective-bargaining process, such as Consumer Price Indices and productivity statistics. Other relevant wages and benefit information will be available to the General Counsel and the parties from private sources, and their use and usefulness in the compliance process will likely vary with particular circumstances of the individual case. Furthermore, additional data could become available through new compilations which might later be undertaken by the Bureau of Labor Statistics or other agencies, including this agency, as well as by unions, employers, and private and public organizations and institutions.

In the instant case, as noted above, a *prima facie* showing of loss can readily be made out by measuring the wage and benefit increments that were negotiated for employees at Respondent's other organized plants against those given employees in this bargaining unit during the period of Respondent's unlawful refusal to bargain. Granted that the task of determining loss may be more difficult in other cases where no similar basis for comparison exists, this is not reason enough for the Board to shirk its statutory responsibilities, and no reason at all for it to do so in a case such as this where that difficulty is not present.

For the reasons set out above, we would order the Employer to make its employees whole for their measurable losses, if any, resulting from the unlawful refusal to bargain. We dissent from the Decision of the Board to the extent that it fails to direct such a remedy.

Questions for Discussion

1. One of the majority's reasons for denying monetary relief was that crucial questions could not be answered, namely, would good-faith bargaining have resulted in a raise for the workers, and, if so, how much would it have been? These are counter-factual questions; answering them would require determining what would have happened if the facts had been different. The majority balked at employing counter-factual reasoning and refused to determine what would have occurred if the employer had bargained in good faith.

Counter-factual reasoning, however, is used in other areas of labor law that we have studied. For example, suppose an applicant is not hired because the employer believes her to be a union agitator. In order to award her back pay, the Board must determine what would have occurred if she had been hired. The Board must answer counter-factual questions such as, would her work have been satisfactory, how many hours would she have worked, and would she have been laid off? The Board also answers counter-factual questions in mixed motive cases, that is, cases in which an employer has two or more reasons for an act and one of the reasons is illegal. In such cases, the General Counsel establishes a prima facie case by proving that one of the employer's reasons was illegal; but the employer may defend the case by proving that the same decision would have been made even in the absence of the illegal reason (in other words, that a lawful reason was a sufficient cause of the employer's act). The employer's defense requires counter-factual reasoning.

Why is counter-factual reasoning appropriate in back pay and mixed motive cases, but inappropriate in refusal-to-bargain cases?

2. The dissent cited American Fire Apparatus Co., Leeds & Northrup Co. v. NLRB, and Fibreboard Paper Products v. NLRB. Are these cases analogous to Ex-Cell-O, or can they be distinguished?

3. The majority argues that any change on this issue should be effected by Congress. In general, when should a tribunal itself change a policy, and when should the tribunal wait for legislative action?

    4. If the union had had sufficient economic power,
it would have forced the employer to bargain in good
faith by striking. Should the law give the union what it
lacked the bargaining power to achieve?

    5. Can you think of a remedy that would serve the
purposes of the dissent without being subject to the
objections of the majority?

    6. The elaborate procedures for appealing the
Board's initial order certifying the union may take two
years. Who benefits from the delay? Should the
procedures be modified?

Ω

Bargaining in Good Faith

Introduction

Section 8(a)(5) requires employers and § 8(b)(3) requires unions to bargain collectively with each other. Section 8(d) defines this duty as the obligation "to meet at reasonable times and confer in good faith with respect to wages, hours, and other terms and conditions of employment...." Is this an objective or a subjective standard? The words "good faith" imply a subjective standard, for good faith is an actor's state of mind. Yet the words "meet at reasonable times" imply an objective standard because, in the law, reasonableness is what an ordinary person in the actor's position would have thought (as distinguished from what the actor may actually have thought); and the words "wages, hours, and other terms and conditions of employment" also imply an objective element because the meanings of those terms are well settled and do not vary with persons. As you read the following case, try to determine whether **bargaining in good faith** is a single duty, and if so, whether it is judged by an objective or a subjective standard; or whether bargaining in good faith is several duties, some judged by objective and others judged by subjective standards.

The following case is so famous (or infamous) that the employer's strategy has acquired its own name, "Boulwarism." Named after Lemuel Boulware, the manager who devised the strategy, Boulwarism was an attempt to apply marketing techniques to labor relations. In marketing, a company researches the wants and needs of customers, designs a product that should satisfy those wants and needs, creates a demand for the product by advertising which extols the virtues of the product, and aggressively fights the competition. Similarly, in Boulwarism the employer surveyed the desires of workers, fashioned a proposal that (in the company's opinion) reasonably satisfied those desires, actively communicated the virtues of the proposal to the workers, criticized both the union and its proposals, and asserted that nothing, not even a strike, would persuade the employer to deviate from its "firm and fair" offer. One issue in the case is whether Boulwarism, taken in its totality, indicated an improper attitude towards collective bargaining. Several other, more specific issues also tax the members of the Board.

As you read the opinions, make a list of the various ways mentioned in which §§ 8(a)(5) and 8(b)(3) can be violated. Also, consider whether the opinions provide helpful guidance to employers and unions that wish "to meet at reasonable times and confer in good faith."

General Electric Company
150 NLRB 192 (1964)

The Trial Examiner found that Respondent {the employer, General Electric} had not bargained in good faith with the Union, thereby violating § 8(a)(5) and (1) of the Act, as evidenced by:

> (a) its failure timely to furnish certain information requested by the Union during contract negotiations;

> (b) its attempts, while engaged in national negotiations with the Union, to deal separately with locals on matters which were properly the subject of national negotiations, and its solicitations of locals separately to abandon or refrain from supporting the strike;

> (c) its presentation of its personal accident insurance proposal to the Union on a take-it-or-leave-it basis;

> (d) its overall approach to and conduct of bargaining.

We agree with these findings of the Trial Examiner. Because Respondent's defense of its bargaining conduct raises a fundamental question as to the requirements of the statutory bargaining obligation, we have stated for more particular emphasis the reasons why we agree with the Trial Examiner that Respondent did not bargain in good faith with the Union.

In challenging the Trial Examiner's finding that it violated § 8(a)(5), Respondent argues that an employer cannot be found guilty of having violated its statutory bargaining duty where it is desirous of entering into a collective-bargaining agreement, where it has met and conferred with the bargaining representative on all required subjects of bargaining as prescribed by statute and has not taken unlawful unilateral action, and where it has not demanded the inclusion in the collective bargaining contract of any illegal clauses or insisted to an impasse upon any nonmandatory bargaining provisions. Given compliance with the above, Respondent further argues that an employer's technique of bargaining is not subject to approval or disapproval by the Board.

Respondent reads the statutory requirements for bargaining collectively too narrowly. It is true that an employer does violate § 8(a)(5) where it enters into bargaining negotiations with a desire not to reach an agreement with the union, or has taken unilateral action with respect to a term or condition of employment or has adamantly demanded the inclusion of illegal or nonmandatory clauses in the

iv   *General Electric*

collective bargaining contract. But, having refrained from any of the foregoing conduct, an employer may still have failed to discharge its statutory obligation to bargain in good faith. As the Supreme Court has said:[8]

> ... the Board is authorized to order the cessation of behavior which is in effect a refusal to negotiate, *or* which directly obstructs or inhibits the actual process of discussion, *or* which reflects a cast of mind against reaching agreement. [Emphasis supplied.]

Thus, a party who enters into bargaining negotiations with a "take-it-or-leave-it" attitude violates its duty to bargain although it goes through the forms of bargaining, does not insist on any illegal or nonmandatory bargaining proposals, and wants to sign an agreement. For good-faith bargaining means more than "going through the motions of negotiating."[10] "... the essential thing is rather the serious intent to adjust differences and to reach an acceptable common ground...."

Good-faith bargaining thus involves both a procedure for meeting and negotiating, which may be called the externals of collective bargaining, and a bona fide intention, the presence or absence of which must be discerned from the record. It requires recognition by both parties, not merely formal but real, that "collective bargaining" is a shared process in which each party, labor union and employer, has the right to play an active role. On the part of the employer, it requires at a minimum recognition that the statutory representative is the one with whom it must deal in conducting bargaining negotiations, and that it can no longer bargain directly or indirectly with the employees.

It is inconsistent with this obligation for an employer to mount a campaign, as Respondent did, both before and during negotiations, for the purpose of disparaging and discrediting the statutory representative in the eyes of its employee constituents, to seek to persuade the employees to exert pressure on the representative to submit to the will of the employer, and to create the impression that the employer rather than the union is the true protector of the employees' interests. As the Trial Examiner phrased it, "the employer's statutory obligation is to deal with the employees through the union, and not with the union through the employees."

We do not rely solely on Respondent's campaign among its employees for our finding that it did not deal in good faith with the Union. Respondent's policy of disparaging the Union by means of the communications campaign ... was

---

[8]*NLRB v. Katz,* 369 U.S. 736 at 747.

[10]*NLRB v. Truitt,* 351 U.S. 149 at 154 (Frankfurter, J.).

implemented and furthered by its conduct at the bargaining table. Thus, the negotiations themselves, although maintaining the form of "collective bargaining," fell short, in a realistic sense, of the concept of meaningful and fruitful "negotiation" envisioned by the Act.

As the record in the case reflects, Respondent regards itself as a sort of administrative body which has the unilateral responsibility for determining wages and working conditions for employees, and it regards the union's role as merely that of a kind of adviser for an interested group—the employees. Thus, according to its professed philosophy of "bargaining," Respondent, on the basis of its own research and evaluation of union demands, determines what is "right" for its employees, and then makes a "fair and firm offer" to the unions without holding anything back for later trading or compromising. It professes a willingness to make prompt adjustments in its offer, but only if new information or a change in facts indicates that its initial offer is no longer "right." It believes that if its research has been done properly, there will be no need to change its offer unless something entirely unforeseen has developed in the meantime. Simultaneously, Respondent emphasizes, especially to employees, that as a matter of policy it will not be induced by a strike or a threat of a strike to make any change in its proposals which it believes to be "wrong."

This "bargaining" approach undoubtedly eliminates the "ask-and-bid" or "auction" form of bargaining, but in the process devitalizes negotiations and collective bargaining and robs them of their commonly accepted meaning. "Collective bargaining" as thus practiced is tantamount to mere formality and serves to transform the role of the statutory representative from a joint participant in the bargaining process to that of an adviser. In practical effect, Respondent's "bargaining" position is akin to that of a party who enters into negotiations "with a predetermined resolve not to budge from an initial position," an attitude inconsistent with good-faith bargaining.[17]

In fact Respondent here went even further. It consciously placed itself in a position where it could not give unfettered consideration to the merits of any proposals the Union might offer. Thus, Respondent pointed out to the Union, after Respondent's communications to the employees and its "fair and firm offer" to the Union, that "everything we think we should do is in the proposal and we told our employees that, and we would look ridiculous if we changed now."

In short, both major facets of Respondent's 1960 "bargaining" technique, its campaign among the employees and its conduct at the bargaining table, complementing each other, were calculated to disparage the Union and to impose

---

[17]*NLRB v. Truitt*, 351 U.S. 149 at 154 (Frankfurter, J.).

General Electric

without substantial alteration Respondent's "fair and firm" proposal, rather than to satisfy the true standards of good faith collective bargaining required by the statute. A course of conduct whose major purpose is so directed scarcely evinces a sincere desire to resolve differences and reach a common ground. For the above reasons, we adopt [the Trial Examiner's] conclusion that Respondent did not bargain in good faith with the Union, thereby violating § 8(a)(5) and (1) of the Act.

Our concurring colleague, Member JENKINS, who joins us in finding certain conduct of the Respondent inconsistent with its bargaining obligation under the statute, misreads the majority opinion and the Trial Examiner's Intermediate Report, which we affirm, in asserting that our decision is not based on an assessment of Respondent's conduct, but only on its approach to or techniques in bargaining.

On the contrary, our determination is based upon our review of the Respondent's entire course of conduct, its failure to furnish relevant information, its attempts to deal separately with locals and to bypass the national bargaining representative, the manner of its presentation of the accident insurance proposal, the disparagement of the Union as bargaining representative by the communication program, its conduct of the negotiations themselves, and its attitude or approach as revealed by all these factors.

Nothing in our decision bans fact gathering or any specific methods of formulating proposals. We prescribe no time table for negotiators. We lay down no rules as to any required substance or content of agreements. Our decision rests rather upon a consideration for the totality of Respondent's conduct.

In one central point of our colleague's comment, with all respect, we believe he is in error. His strictures in relation to our interpretation of the law's restraints on "take-it-or-leave-it" bargaining were decisively answered by the Supreme Court in its review of the nature of the bargaining obligation in *Insurance Agents*:[18]

> ... the legislative history [of Taft-Hartley] makes it plain that Congress was wary of the position of some unions, and wanted to ensure that they would approach the bargaining table with the same attitude of willingness to reach an agreement as had been enjoined on management earlier. It intended to prevent employee representatives from putting forth the same "take-it-or-leave-it" attitude that had been condemned in management.

---

[18]*NLRB v. Insurance Agents,* 361 U.S. 477 at 487.

And in Justice Frankfurter's opinion in *Truitt*,[19] upon which our colleague relies, the Justice also wrote:

> ... it [good faith] is inconsistent with a predetermined resolve not to budge from an initial position.

While we share his objective and that of our dissenting colleague of encouraging a maximum of freedom and experimentation in collective bargaining, when questions are raised under the law as construed by the courts and the Board concerning the conformity of a specific respondent's course of conduct with the requirements of the law, the Board must apply the law to the totality of that conduct in the interest of preserving and fostering collective bargaining itself. That is what we have sought to do here.

Member JENKINS, concurring:

The fundamental issues in this case have been obscured by slogans and shibboleths which have understandably led my colleagues into deciding issues which in my judgment are not presented for decision. Moreover, the Board has undertaken to describe the statutory obligation to bargain in good faith by utilizing conclusionary comments which may be justified by the facts in this case but which have such far-reaching implications as to warrant the expression of my individual views designed to limit the reach of this decision.

Stripped of verbiage, this case presents the fundamental issue of whether the course of conduct engaged in by the Employer during the 1960 contract negotiations, which led to an unsuccessful 3-week strike, fell below the standard of good-faith bargaining required by § 8(a)(5) of the Act. Certain specific conduct was alleged as the basis for finding that the Respondent's conduct violated 8(a)(5) and (1) of the Act.

This Board has repeatedly held that conduct designed to undermine the union, or to demonstrate to employees the futility of engaging in collective bargaining through a union, fails to meet the standard of good-faith bargaining. If my colleagues had been content to thus ground their finding in the instant case, I would have no reason to disagree. The record clearly supports their findings with respect to (a) the failure of Respondent to furnish certain information requested by the Union during contract negotiations, (b) the attempts to deal separately with locals on matters which were properly the subject of national negotiations, and (c) the Respondent's importuning of locals to abandon or refrain from supporting the strike authorized by the collective bargaining representative.

---

[19]351 U.S. 149 at 154.

...

In effect, I read the majority opinion to hold that the Act so regulates a party's choice of techniques in collective bargaining as to make unlawful an advance decision, and a frank communication of that decision, concerning the position from which a party is unwilling to retreat. The majority would apparently find that it is unlawful for a union to present a contract proposal on a take-it-or-leave-it basis since I assume the majority would not apply different standards to unions than to employers.

The bargaining technique often employed by unions in support of "area standards" contracts is not significantly different from the technique described as the "firm, fair offer" by an employer.* I would not find a lack of good faith bargaining where either the employer or the union entered the negotiations with a fixed position from which it proposed not to retreat, engaging in hard bargaining to maintain or protect such position, and made no concessions from that position as a result of bargaining. As one member of the Supreme Court has pointed out, good faith is not necessarily incompatible with stubbornness or even with what to an outsider may seem unreasonableness.[21]

The majority states frankly that the holding of a predetermined resolve not to budge from an initial position is incompatible with good faith bargaining. That statement seems to ignore the language in § 8(d) of the Act which makes it clear in unequivocal words that "such obligation does not compel either party to agree to a proposal or require the making of a concession."

...

I know of no decision of this Board which has sought to interpret the statute as requiring either unions or employers to follow a prescribed timetable in communicating the various shifts in position which seem desirable as a matter of self-interest. Thus, if either an employer or a union, for reasons dictated by self-interest, chooses to include in a proposal trading items which it is willing later to withdraw or, conversely, chooses to limit its proposal to items which it will never withdraw

---

*In area standards bargaining, a union seeks to achieve the same terms and conditions of employment at all firms within an area. Typically, the union chooses one employer as a target and puts all of its resources into winning the most favorable contract possible. Thereafter, as the union wins similar gains from other firms, its reluctance to accept lesser gains increases.

[21]*NLRB v. Truitt,* 351 U.S. 149, 154-155 (Frankfurter, J.).

voluntarily, the choice is its and not the Board's.

To describe the foregoing in shorthand by evocative terms provides little guidance for either unions or employers. To condemn bargaining techniques as unlawful because of the utilization of what the majority describes as "take it or leave it" is to obfuscate the issue. Basically it is our purpose to examine industrial relations against the realities that exist. It is not our function to require the adoption of a particular technique or to condemn the use of a given technique as such.

...

If free collective bargaining is to survive, both employers and unions must remain free of governmental interference with their right to formulate independently the economic positions which each desires to take and to decide without governmental compulsion whether that position shall be conveyed to the other party at the outset, at some midpoint, or at the conclusion of negotiations. To do otherwise maximizes governmental construction of the bargain and minimizes the free flow of independent economic judgment essential to a strong, independent trade union movement and a strong, independent entrepreneurial system, both of which are vital to the kind of economy envisaged by the Act which we administer.

Member LEEDOM, dissenting in part:

My colleagues have found that the Respondent failed to bargain in good faith with the Union in the 1960 negotiations, both in certain specific respects and generally. Although I agree with the specific violations found, I cannot justify the bad faith finding with respect to the Respondent's overall bargaining conduct.

On the issue as to Respondent's overall good or bad faith, it should be conceded that there are various approaches to, and tactics in, negotiations that are wholly consistent with the bargaining obligation imposed by the Act; and it seems to me that both management and labor should not be discouraged from seeking new techniques in dealing with the constantly evolving problems with which they are faced across the bargaining table. Consequently, we should take care not to create the impression that we view with suspicion novel approaches to, and techniques of, collective bargaining.

This is not an area of sharp disagreement at this Board. Rather it is a question of emphasis: Should the parties be given a wide latitude in devising their bargaining methods, or should there be careful intervention by a regulator? At this time when not only the industrial community, but some labor spokesmen as well, are urging less Government intervention in industrial relations, it seems to me the emphasis should be on freedom of action in the bargaining process. Very respectable authority seems to agree: "The law of collective bargaining will have little value to the community if the process of logical deduction from prior decisions results in wide divergence between the administrative and judicial rules and the needs of both management and labor."[22]

Notwithstanding the foregoing, I cannot fully accept Respondent's view of the breadth of the bargaining obligation imposed by the Act, nor the limitation it believes the law places on those matters which can properly be considered where good- or bad-faith bargaining is in issue. In both regards its construction seems too rigid. I nevertheless believe that both the law and good policy require that this Board not be hypercritical of what goes on at the bargaining table or in a developing situation. In order for collective bargaining to be free and to succeed, the parties themselves must, with a minimum of exceptions, have the right to resort to such tactics, and to take such positions, as they believe necessary or desirable in dealing with the matters before them. If at each step they must consider the effect of their specific words, actions, and proposals, upon some distant tribunal unacquainted with the particular problems in dispute, and with that more subtle distinction, the personalities of the negotiators themselves, they surely lose the flexibility and spontaneity necessary for free, effective bargaining. Thus they are deprived of their right to determine, free of governmental intervention, the substantive terms of their agreement, should one be reached.

No matter how much we may disclaim any intent to compel bargaining to proceed in some set form, the fact that we closely scrutinize what goes on at the bargaining table will necessarily have the effect of directing bargaining into channels which we have in the past approved, for in such channels will lie security in bargaining, if not success. Whether the substitution of our judgment as to the proper forms and content of bargaining be made directly or indirectly is a difference of no consequence insofar as it interferes with free bargaining and tends to discourage innovation both in tactics and proposals which, as I believe, could be of benefit not only to the parties but to the public as well. Consequently, good policy suggests that we leave the parties to their own devices at the bargaining table unless some compelling facts force us into the area of bargaining. As the Supreme Court stated in *Oliver*, "The purposes of the Act are served by bringing the parties together and establishing conditions under which they are to work out their agreement

---

[22]Cox and Dunlop, "Regulation of Collective Bargaining," 63 Harvard Law Review 389 at 405.

themselves."[25]

The principal facts are not disputed. Concededly, the Respondent did not intend to rid itself of the Union during the 1960 negotiations. Rather it approached the bargaining table fully intending to reach an agreement with the Union and to this end engaged in many bargaining sessions running from mid-summer to the late fall of 1960. And the end result was in fact a comprehensive agreement. To be sure, the respondent in presenting its offer on August 31 took a firm position, but that does not in itself demonstrate bad faith. In fact, the Respondent's initial attitude with respect to its offer does not appear to have been appreciably, if any, more intransigent than that of union presenting its proposed changes.

However, I find it hard to measure degrees of intransigence and have considerable doubts that balancing it out is of real significance; for whatever may have been the situation at early stages of negotiation, it is clear that as negotiations proceeded the Union backed down considerably and the Company acquiesced in a number of changes from its original proposals. Even though the Respondent's changes may not have been all that the Trial Examiner and majority may have wished, I fail to see how their alleged "inconsequential" nature is some evidence of bad faith when Respondent was not obligated to propose or agree to any change at all in its initial offer.

The majority and the Trial Examiner advert to statements by the Respondent and its representatives both at the bargaining table and in employee communications which were highly critical of the Union and its president, and some also suggesting an approach to bargaining not wholly in keeping with its statutory responsibilities. But against the background of continuing negotiations and the Union's equally inflammatory publications and comments, and its statements of "must" demands, the Respondent's role in this battle of words seems to me to lose some of its evidentiary significance. Consequently, I question whether the cause of collective bargaining is aided by the Board's taking particular comments and evaluating them in a dispassionate context so extremely different from that of which they were a part. It is too easy through such an approach to find unlawful that which is perhaps at worst only undesirable.

I do not mean to suggest that the issue of good or bad faith has any clear-cut answer here. My position is not dictated so much by strong conviction as by uncertainty. I am not persuaded by the reasons that the majority state for their finding of bad faith bargaining; and the finding itself and the supporting rationale leave me in the dark as to their practical efficacy. But I am particularly disturbed by the

---

[25]*Local 24, Teamsters v. Oliver*, 358 U.S. 283, 295 (1959).

General Electric

treatment accorded Respondent's communications. Surely the Respondent can lawfully communicate with its employees. Yet here, although the communications are held to be some evidence of bad faith, the majority, neither in its decision nor in adopting the Trial Examiner's Recommended Order, provides the Respondent with any guides by which it can with reasonable certainty determine what it can lawfully say to its employees.

In areas such as this bordering on § 8(c) of the Act and free speech, I believe that the Respondent is entitled to something more by way of clarification than the vague proscription implied in the general bargaining order. But I doubt if the facts and findings indicate what specific limitations can properly be laid down. In any event, the situation with respect to the bad faith finding is at best ambiguous, and I would, therefore, find that the General Counsel has failed to prove by a preponderance of the evidence that the Respondent did not bargain in good faith during the 1960 negotiations with the Union.

Questions for Discussion

1. The majority of the Board held that, where the national union is the recognized bargaining agent, an employer may not ask local unions not to support a strike called by the national. Yet it is permissible for an employer to ask workers not to support a strike called by their bargaining agent. Can these cases be distinguished?

2. The majority faults the employer for attempting to sell its proposal directly to the workers.

(a) Does this rule ignore the protection in section 8(c) for freedom of speech?

(b) Should the Board fault a union if it tried to sell its proposal directly to the board of directors or shareholders of a corporation?

3. Would collective bargaining be improved if the Board stopped looking inside the bargaining room?

Ω

CHAPTER 3

EMPLOYMENT DISCRIMINATION LAW

Sex Discrimination in Compensation:

The Equal Pay Act of 1963

Equal Pay, Equal Work
and
"Any Other Factor Other Than Sex"

Introduction

Like most Equal Pay Act cases, the following one involved extensive findings of fact. The first issue of fact was whether the women's pay was equal to the men's pay. If pay had been equal, the case would have been dismissed; the Equal Pay Act applies only to cases of unequal pay.[a] The court found that pay was not equal; the men's pay was greater than the women's pay. Therefore, the court moved to the next issue of fact — whether the men's work and the women's work were equal. If not, the case would have been dismissed because the Act applies only when a man and a woman perform equal work. The court found that the men's and women's work was equal. As a result, another issue of fact arose; it was pertinent to the employer's defense. The defense was that the difference between men's and women's pay was based on a factor other than sex. Accordingly, the issue of fact was, what was the basis for the pay differential? If the basis of the differential were the sex of the workers (i.e., men were paid more because they were men), the defense would have failed and the employer would have lost the case. If the basis of the differential were any factor other than sex, the defense would succeed and the employer would win the case.

Facts come in different varieties. For present purposes, we need to distinguish between material and evidentiary facts. **Material facts** are the elements of the prima facie case. The material facts of battery are that the defendant intentionally inflicted a harmful or offensive contact on the plaintiff. **Evidentiary facts** help or tend to prove material facts. In order to prove

---

[a]Indeed, as long as pay is equal, the content of the jobs is unimportant. If a woman's job calls for twice as much effort as a man's job, requires three times the degree of skill, carries four times the level of responsibility, and is performed under conditions five times worse, she has no claim if their pay is equal.

Hodgson v. Robert Hall Clothes

the material fact that a physical contact was harmful or
offensive, a plaintiff might offer the evidentiary fact
that the contact caused a bruise on his skin; in order to
prove the material fact that the contact was intentional,
a plaintiff might offer the evidentiary fact that, just
before striking the blow that caused the bruise, the
defendant said, "I'm gonna murder you."

In the following case, the student should identify
the material facts — the prima facie case — of a
violation of the Equal Pay Act. The student should also
make a list of the evidentiary facts that tended to prove
each material fact.

James D. Hodgson, Secretary of Labor

v.

Robert Hall Clothes, Inc.

326 F. Supp. 1264 (D. Del. 1971)

STEEL, J.:

...

At all relevant times, defendant Robert Hall Clothes, Inc. (Robert Hall) has been a Delaware corporation with its main office in New York and defendant Robert Hall Clothes Greenbank Corp. (Greenbank) has been a Delaware corporation having its place of business on Greenbank Road, Wilmington, Delaware. Greenbank is a wholly owned subsidiary of Robert Hall Clothes of Jamaica, Inc., which in turn is a wholly owned subsidiary of Robert Hall.

Greenbank first opened for business in September, 1962. It was and still is engaged in the operation of a retail clothing store which sells men's and boys' and ladies' and girls' clothing and apparel.

...

The men's and boys' department, and the ladies' and girls' department at Greenbank are contained in one building. All men's and boys' merchandise sold in the one-floor store is located in the men's and boys' department which is on one side of the store, and all ladies' and girls' merchandise sold in the store is located in the ladies' and girls' department which is on the other side of the store....

...

Sales personnel in the men's and boys' department (men's department) and sales personnel in the ladies' and girls' department (ladies' department) at the Greenbank store perform their activities under similar working conditions.

...

At the outset three substantive questions must be decided: (1) does the Act apply where the nature of the jobs makes it impractical for both sexes to work interchangeably; (2) are the rates of wages which Greenbank pays to saleswomen less than those paid to salesmen; and (3) do saleswomen and salesmen perform equal work. If these three questions are answered in the affirmative, a fourth question must be decided, namely, whether the wage differential is based upon any factors other than sex.

vi   *Hodgson v. Robert Hall Clothes*

(1)   Application of the Act to jobs which reasonably require performance exclusively by one sex.

The jobs performed by salesmen and salesladies, respectively, are not reasonably susceptible of performance by both sexes because of the nature of the jobs. One is a "male" job and the other a "female" job. Defendants have always had a policy of having only salesmen in the men's and boys' department because of the frequent necessity for physical contact between the salespersons and the customers which would embarrass both and would inhibit sales unless they were of the same sex.[b] ... The question arises whether the Equal Pay Act was intended to apply to jobs which require employment by one or the other of the sexes exclusively. {After reviewing the legislative history of the Act, interpretations by the Wage-Hour Administrator, and case law, the court held that the Act does apply to jobs that are segregated by sex.}

...

(2)   Pay Differential

Greenbank employs salesmen and salesladies who work regularly forty hours a week or more and salesmen and salesladies who perform their duties on a sporadic basis and work less than forty hours per week. The former are referred to as full-time and the latter as part-time employees. The full-and part-time sales employees in the men's department have always been exclusively male, and the full-and part-time sales employees in the ladies' department have always been exclusively female. When Greenbank opened in September 1962, it employed the following sales personnel: two full-time females, fifteen part-time females, four full-time males, and twelve part-time males. By January 1963, the number of full-time sales personnel was reduced to two: one man and one woman. It has since remained at that figure.

The number of part-time sales personnel was pared down gradually during 1962 and 1963. It has since varied between two and five part-time salesmen and two and five part-time saleswomen, depending on the season.

At all times from the passage of the Act, the starting salaries for full-time salesmen at Greenbank have ranged between 21% and 55% higher than starting salaries for full-time saleswomen. The starting wage rate for part-time salesmen has likewise varied between 3% and 35% higher than that paid part-time saleswomen. See Table 1.

---

[b]The parties to the case agreed that it was lawful for the employer to segregate the jobs by sex. Thus, the court did not rule on whether the job segregation was lawful.

After the commencement of their employment, progressive increases were given to both male and female personnel, part-time and full-time, at specified intervals. These increases reflected compensation differentials which favored salesmen over saleswomen, and ranged from 35% to 52% in the case of full-time personnel and between 16% and 34% for part-time personnel. See Tables 2 and 3.

The progression schedules were eliminated effective February 1, 1967 and defendants began a program of periodic merit increases in sales personnel salary and wage rates based on the recommendation of the store manager. He would base his recommendation on the employee's performance, length of service, attitude, absenteeism, time since last increase and economic factors.

Incentive compensation was also paid salesmen and salesladies. This was based upon various factors such as type, number of garments sold to a given customer at one time, price, age of garment, etc. The system in its ramifications was extremely complex. It was designed to move merchandise and increase profits. Since no incentive rate existed for all male garments and all female garments, a direct comparison of rates is not possible. Different items of merchandise carry different amounts of incentive compensation. In both the men's and ladies' departments, the sale of some low priced items of merchandise, if sold individually, will not earn the selling employee any incentive compensation; almost all of the merchandise in the store when sold in multiple units (double-header) or in combination with other items to the same customer yield incentive compensation. Additionally, the incentive earned upon the sale of merchandise from a prior season may change from season to season, depending upon the length of time an item remains in the store. The longer it remains in the store, the higher the incentive when it is sold.

The particular amount of incentive compensation placed upon a particular item of merchandise, regardless in which department it is sold, is determined not by whom the item is sold, but on the need to sell the particular item, the markup on the item, the profitability to the store on the sale of the item, the length of time the item is in the store, the ease of selling the item and its selling price. coats and suits are over $39.95. The average unit selling price of merchandise is substantially higher in the men's department than in the ladies' department.

Hodgson v. Robert Hall Clothes

Table 1—Starting						
	Full-Time (per week)			Part-Time (per hour)		
			% by which			% by which
	M	F	M exceeds F	M	F	M exceeds F
9/5/62-8/30/64	$65	$42	55%	$1.42	$1.05	35%
8/31/64-9/2/65	67	46	46%	1.47	1.15	28%
9/3/65-1/31/67	67	50	34%	1.47	1.25	18%
2/1/67-4/13/70	67	50	34%	1.47	1.25	18%

Table 2—6 Months After Starting						
	Full-Time (per week)			Part-Time (per hour)		
			% by which			% by which
	M	F	M exceeds F	M	F	M exceeds F
9/5/62-8/30/64	$67	$44	52%	$1.47	$1.10	34%
8/31/64-9/2/65	70	48	46%	1.52	1.20	27%
9/3/65-1/31/67	70	52	35%	1.52	1.30	17%

Table 3—1 Year After Starting						
	Full-Time (per week)			Part-Time (per hour)		
			% by which			% by which
	M	F	M exceeds F	M	F	M exceeds F
9/5/62-8/30/64	$71	$48	48%	$1.57	$1.20	30%
8/31/64-9/2/65	73	50	46%	1.57	1.25	26%
9/3/65-1/31/67	73	54	35%	1.57	1.35	16%

In both men's and ladies' departments the higher the price of the merchandise the greater the incentive compensation. More high priced merchandise is carried in the men's department than in the ladies' department, i.e., 60% of the men's suits and coats are over $39.95, whereas 20% of ladies'

Merchandise in the men's department remains in the store longer before it is sold than merchandise in the ladies' department. Merchandise sold in the ladies' department is more related to change in fashion, and consequently, is frequently removed and salvaged if not sold in the current season. Rarely is merchandise in the ladies' department retained which is more than two six-month seasons old. On the other hand, it is common for men's merchandise to date back four or six six-month seasons. Thus, there is reasonably a greater category breakdown in the incentive compensation payable upon the sale of men's stale merchandise than there is for ladies' stale merchandise, i.e., in the case of men's stale merchandise, there are four different age categories of merchandise; whereas in the case of ladies' stale merchandise, there are only two different age categories of merchandise; the older the merchandise within a category, the higher the incentive.

The net effect of the incentive system, however, resulted in a ratio of incentive pay to gross sales which was approximately .2% more in the case of men than women.

Under the Act the "wages" which must be paid at equal rates to both sexes if the work performed is equal include "all payments made to or on behalf of the employee as remuneration for employment." 29 C.F.R. § 800.110. The term wage "rate" used in the Act encompasses all rates of wages "whether calculated on a time, piece, job, incentive or other basis." 29 C.F.R. § 800.111. The Government has established by a preponderance of the evidence that Greenbank ... has paid saleswomen "wages" — starting, progressive and incentive — at "rates" less than those paid to salesmen.

(3) Equality of Jobs

Salesmen are engaged in selling men's and boys' apparel such as top coats, sport coats, suits, slacks, sweaters, shoes, underwear, and furnishings, in sizes 2 through adult. Salesladies engaged in selling women's and girls' and infants' apparel, such as coats, dresses, suits, slacks, skirts, pants suits, sweaters, blouses, hosiery, and undergarments, in sizes 9 months through adult.

Obviously the jobs performed by salesmen and salesladies are not identical. Salesmen sell different merchandise from salesladies and the customers of salesmen are mostly men and boys whereas the customers of salesladies are mostly women and girls. These distinctions make the job different. They do not necessarily make the job unequal within the meaning of the Equal Pay Act. The Act does not require that the jobs performed be identical but only that they be substantially equal. *Shultz v. Wheaton Glass Co.*, 421 F.2d 259 (3d Cir. 1970). This does not depend upon job classification but rather on actual job requirements. The jobs as a whole must be viewed over the entire work cycle. *Wirtz v. Rainbo Baking Co.*, 303 F. Supp. 1049, 1052 (E.D. Ky. 1967). Whether by this test the jobs of salesmen and saleswomen require substantially equal skill, effort and responsibility is the question to be resolved.

Both male and female sales personnel engage in selling the above described merchandise by applying sales techniques, basic knowledge of garments sold, materials, wearability, location of items in the store, and quality of garments stocked; by showing apparel to customers, engaging them in discussion about the merchandise, advising and answering questions as to appearance and fit, size, color, fabrics, appropriateness and quality of merchandise, all for the purpose of effecting a sale.

In hiring both male and female personnel consideration was given to the appearance of applicants and their response to questions submitted to them. There was no educational requirement for sales personnel of either sex.

Both salesmen and saleswomen perform the same inventory and stock work and housekeeping duties. They each move garments from the stockroom to the sales floor and make sure that the merchandise already on the floor is grouped according to size. After customer try-ons, both salesmen and salesladies put the garments back on the racks in their proper places.

Defendants argue that the job of selling in the men's department differs substantially from that in the women's department because of differences in the character, price, profitability, markup and markdown in the merchandise sold. Defendants also argue the job content of salesmen and saleswomen differs with respect to the type of training received, the work required of men in completing the back of the cash alterations sales slips, their alteration and fitting responsibilities and the use of sizing charts and tape measures in connection with fittings.

Generally speaking, the prices, profitability and markups were higher in men's wear than in women's wear and the markdown differences were less in the case of men's wear than in women's wear. These variances, however, were not so great as to make any significant differences in the effort, skill and responsibility required between the salesmen and salesladies in performing their jobs.

The character of the merchandise sold by salesmen and saleswomen was likewise different in that the styles, colors and materials varied. Differences of this kind do not necessarily mean that the sale of one article requires a higher degree of skill, effort and responsibility than the sale of another, see 29 C.F.R. § 800.123, and in the instant case they did not. Although men's suits are manufactured in various models which give rise to fitting and sizing problems, just as varied styles existed among women's garments which resulted in comparable sizing and fitting complexities. The skill, effort and responsibility in knowing the styles, colors and materials were not greater in the case of men than they were for women.

For the most part differences in instructions given to male and female sales personnel were occasioned by the differences in the merchandise which they were to sell. The testimony of salesmen as to the training which they received was not consistent, and at best such training as they had appeared to be perfunctory and in some instances on a day by day, on the job basis. Such training differences as existed were a minor consideration when viewed against the substantial identity of the over-all skill, effort and responsibility required of salesmen and salesladies.

As to fitting skill, effort and responsibility, some salesmen used a card which specified suit models of various types (Ivy, Bankers, Portly, etc.,) and related these types to waist and chest measurements of customers. By using the card the salesmen were able to tell at a glance which model, from a fit standpoint, would be most appropriate for a customer. This was a simple operation. The saleswomen had no such aid. They were required visually and by experience to determine sizes and types of dresses which would be best suited from a style and fit standpoint for customers to wear for a particular purpose. The sizing card furnished salesmen reduced or at least minimized the skill required of them as against that demanded for saleswomen in size selection.

Because no alterations were made by the ladies' department, whereas alterations were made in the men's department, salesmen were required to use a tape measure in measuring customers but saleswomen were not. This was but a minor variance in duties and did not distinguish the salesmen's job in any appreciable way from that performed by the saleswomen.

Nor did the knowledge of alteration possibilities on men's clothing vary importantly from the knowledge of saleswomen of the same possibilities. Although no alterations were made in the women's department, the job of saleswomen made it necessary for them to advise their customers of the "at home" alteration potentials.

The major thrust of the defendants' argument that the jobs of both sexes were substantially unequal rests upon the asserted fact that the salesmen, unlike the saleswomen, had to mark men's clothing so that the tailor would know what work he should do. The job of marking men's clothing for alterations was especially important, defendants argue, because Greenbank made it a policy to guarantee the fit of all men's clothing for the life of the garment. Hence, Greenbank was obligated to make additional alterations whenever the customer decided that the garment fitted

Hodgson v. Robert Hall Clothes

him poorly, even if this occurred long after the date of purchase.

The basic premise of defendants' argument, i.e., that salesmen as a group had the responsibility of marking clothes for alteration is not borne out by the evidence. It discloses that marking was not uniformly performed by all the salesmen and that such marking as was done by some was subject to important qualifications.

The basic policy of Greenbank since opening in September of 1962 has been for either the manager or assistant manager to be called by a salesman to perform marking whenever alterations were required. This policy existed at least until January 10, 1968, when defendants' answer to plaintiff's initial interrogatory 21 was filed. It stated that male sales personnel did not engage in marking.

It is true that at times the basic policy to have the manager or assistant manager mark the clothes has been deviated from. Such deviations as there were involved for the most part only simple and sporadic marking. Four of ten salesmen employed at the Greenbank store testified they performed no marking at all. Of the remaining six, three stated that their marking was limited to pants length, sleeve length and waist. Three other salesmen testified that they did more than this and also marked coat size, collars or crotch, but only if the manager or assistant manager were not available. The marking of cuffs, sleeves and waists was simple. At least two of the employees (Blawn and Steinebach) who performed this work did so within a few days after their employment.

The ability or inability of salesmen to mark clothes for alterations and the fact that they may have done so were not considered by defendants in fixing the wage differentials favoring salesmen. Considering the totality of the functions which salesmen and salesladies performed and the responsibilities which they assumed, such marking of clothes for alteration exclusively by salesmen as existed did not distinguish the job performed by salesmen from that performed by saleswomen to any significant degree.

Defendants point out that salesmen fill in the back of cash alteration sales slips and saleswomen do not. Again, this is a matter of job detail requiring merely the checking of spaces on the back of the alteration slip or making simple notations on it.

...

After listening to voluminous ... testimony for days on end concerning the differences and similarities between the jobs of salesmen and salesladies, the conclusion is warranted that such differences as existed were at best only incidental to the job of each when considered in its totality. The skill, effort and responsibility of each were substantially equal.

Plaintiff has borne the burden of proving by a preponderance of the evidence that defendants have discriminated between salesmen and salesladies by paying to the latter wages at a lesser rate than paid to the former for equal work on jobs that required equal skill, effort and responsibility. Plaintiff has thus made out a prima facie case against defendant for violating the Equal Pay Act. *Shultz v. Wheaton Glass Co., supra*, p. 266.

Even though this be so, if the pay differential was justified by factors other than sex, as defendants claim, defendants have a valid defense under the Act. The defense is an affirmative one which the defendants have the burden of proving. *Shultz v. Wheaton Glass Co., supra*, p. 266. This must be done by a preponderance of the evidence.

(4)   Factors Other Than Sex

Defendants contend that the Act is violated only if a wage differential is based solely on sex and is justified by no other factor. This contention is unacceptable. Properly interpreted, the Act means that if the differential in pay is, in whole or in part, based upon sex, it is not based upon factors other than sex. Only if sex plays no part in the wage differential is it beyond the condemnation of the Act. 29 C.F.R. § 800.142.

Contrary views have been expressed. In *Kilpatrick v. Sweet*, 262 F. Supp. 561, 564 (M.D. Fla. 1967) the court said that "if there were any other factors other than sex upon which a difference in wages was based, then no violation of the law could be found." See also *Shultz v. Kentucky Baptist Hospital*, 62 CCH Lab. Cas. 44,117, 44,123 (W.D. Ky. 1969). This construction of the Act is not required by its language and if adopted evasion of the Act would be easy and its remedial purpose would be thwarted.

Defendants argue that economic considerations were the sole reasons for the compensation differential between salesladies and salesmen and that sex had nothing to do with it. The difference in merchandise carried in the men's department and the relatively greater benefits which it is said that defendants experienced by the operation of that department lie at the root of this argument.

The merchandise carried in the men's department differed from that in the women's department in style, quality, price and carries a considerably higher markup and markdown. On the average more merchandise in the men's department is in the

Hodgson v. Robert Hall Clothes

higher price range and of better quality than in the ladies' department; on the average the merchandise in the men's department carries a considerably higher markup and lesser markdown than that in the ladies' department; and, of course, styles in the men's merchandise differ from styles in the ladies' merchandise.

Defendants point to the fact that the sales in the men's department exceeded by several fold those in the ladies' department, and that the percentage of gross profit to sales in the former was substantially greater than in the latter.

SCHEDULE OF SALES AND GROSS PROFITS						
BY DEPARTMENT						
Fiscal	Men's and Boys' Clothing			Ladies' and Girls' Clothing		
Year	Dept.			Dept.		
Ended		Gross	Gross		Gross	Gross
June 30	Sales	Profit	Profit %	Sales	Profit	Profit %
1963	$ 210,639.48	$ 85,328.48	40.51	$ 177,742.17	$ 58,547.13	32.92
1964	178,867.50	73,608.08	41.16	142,788.22	44,612.12	31.24
1965	206,472.93	89,930.00	43.55	148,252.90	49,608.08	33.46
1966	217,765.79	97,447.54	44.74	166,479.47	55,463.29	33.31
1967	244,922.09	111,498.79	45.52	206,680.27	69,190.04	33.47
1968	263,663.53	123,681.60	46.90	230,156.63	79,846.92	34.69
1969	316,242.41	148,001.30	46.79	254,379.22	92,686.87	36.43

In establishing pay rates Robert Hall did not consider the nature of the specific merchandise sold by individual employees and made no attempt to relate the specific wages of specific employees to specific merchandise. Silbert, the senior vice president and treasurer of Robert Hall, testified that the compensation differential at Greenbank was based upon the experience which Robert Hall had in its other stores and involved solely economic considerations which reflected the difference in merchandise sold. Greenbank was opened in 1962. In the case of every one of its other stores Robert Hall had learned that on the average each salesman generated per hour of work more sales dollars and more gross profit than the average saleswoman. Silbert said that it was solely because of this experience that Robert Hall, which fixed compensation policies for all of its retail stores, determined to pay the differential at Greenbank. He said that the decision was simply a forward judgment based upon past facts.

The defendants' prognostication that at Greenbank salesmen on the average per hour of work would sell more merchandise in terms of dollars and produce more gross profits than saleswomen was borne out by each year's operation at Greenbank.

SCHEDULE OF HOURLY SALES, EARNINGS AND GROSS PROFIT						
	Sales	Excess	Earnings	Excess	Gross Profit	Excess
Year	Per Hour	M over F	Per Hour	M over F	Per Hour	M over F
MEN'S & BOY'S						
1963	38.31	40%	2.18	25%	15.52	72%
1964	40.22	32%	2.46	32%	16.55	74%
1965	54.77	64%	2.67	48%	23.85	114%
1966	59.58	73%	2.92	50%	26.66	134%
1967	63.14	71%	2.88	45%	28.74	133%
1968	62.27	70%	2.97	47%	29.21	127%
1969	73.00	77%	3.13	45%	34.16	127%
LADIES' & GIRLS'						
1963	27.31		1.75		9.00	
1964	30.36		1.86		9.49	
1965	33.30		1.80		11.14	
1966	34.31		1.95		11.43	
1967	36.92		1.98		12.36	
1968	37.20		2.02		12.91	
1969	41.26		2.16		15.03	

This tabulation is based on averages and does not reflect individual performances by the sales personnel. Standing alone, the greater amount paid to the average salesman per hour is amply justified by the greater amount of dollar volume per hour and gross profits per hour generated by the average salesman. These average figures, however, are less meaningful than they appear to be on the surface when other statistical data of record is analyzed with an eye to performance by and pay to full-time and part-time personnel, respectively.

{These} data {are} ... for the period January 26, 1969-April 15, 1969 and for the period August 10, 1969-October 18, 1969. During these two periods Greenbank had only one full-time salesman, Robbins, and one full-time saleswoman, Donofrio. For the January 26, 1969 April 15, 1969 period Robbins earned $2.61 per hour, as against $2.14 per hour for Donofrio, incentive compensation being excluded in each instance. Robbins' compensation was, therefore, 22% more than Donofrio's. ... {F}or the same period Robbins was responsible for $83.40 per hour of sales as against $50.53 by Donofrio, or 65% more than Donofrio. A like comparison between Robbins and Donofrio for the period August 10, 1969 through October 18, 1969 reveals that whereas Robbins generated 43% more gross sales per hour his compensation per hour was only 14% more per hour than Donofrio, again excluding incentive pay.

The discussion thus far relates to a comparison between the wage rate of an individual full-time salesman and an individual full-time saleswoman for two limited periods in 1969. No comparable statistics are available of record for other periods. Sales checks made out by the individual sales employees from which dollar volumes could be ascertained were destroyed promptly after the district manager reviewed them. It was only a fortuitous circumstance which caused the sales slips ... to survive. However, there is nothing in the record to indicate that the periods in 1969 ... were not typical.

So far as full-time employees are concerned, and apart from incentive payments, the pay differential in favor of salesmen as against saleswomen (thus far only one of each) was based upon economic considerations and in no way upon sex.

The wage compensation disparity between part-time salesmen and part-time saleswomen, excluding from consideration incentive payments, presents a different story. The part-time salesmen for the period January 26, 1969 to April 15, 1969 on the average were responsible for $44.79 of sales per hour as against $37.47 by saleswomen, or 20% more. The average part-time salesman was paid $1.93 per hour in wages as against $1.61 per hour to part-time saleswomen, or 20% more. For the period August 10, 1969 to October 18, 1969 the part-time salesmen generated on the average 46.43 dollars of sales per hour as against 43 dollars by saleswomen, or 8% more. The average salesman was paid during the period $1.91 per hour in wages as against $1.65 per hour to saleswomen, or 16% more.

In the case of part-time sales personnel no records of sales per hour were introduced in evidence for periods of time other than the two discussed. There is no suggestion that there was a deliberate destruction of records by defendants other than in the normal course of business. It is reasonable to infer that, had the records been available, their disclosure would not have been significantly different from that shown by the analysis just discussed.

The conclusion is warranted that the compensation disparity (apart from incentives) in favor of the part-time salesmen cannot be supported by any economic benefits which defendants received from the job performances of the salesmen. The difference in wage rates paid to the salesmen and saleswomen was not based upon factors other than sex.

This is borne out by individual compensation and economic benefits comparisons. Two of Greenbank's part-time female employees, Alice Raker and C. Jarrell, were responsible for a higher per hour dollar volume of sales than three of the part-time male employees, McGonegal, Law and Layton, during the period from August 10, 1969 to October 18, 1969. A division of Jarrell's gross earnings (less incentive) by hours worked and a similar computation for the part-time salesmen discloses that Jarrell received a lower hourly rate than all three of these part-time salesmen, even though her gross sales per hour were more than that made by three of the five part-time salesmen. Silbert conceded that it was possible in a given location that an excellent saleswoman might generate more sales than a very poor salesman, although he said that normally this would not happen. At Greenbank this did occur.

Incentive compensation presents its own unique problem and necessitates separate consideration. Its complex nature and the purposes it was designed to serve have been previously discussed. Here it need only be noted that the incentives paid depended upon differences in the style, quality, price and markup between the merchandise sold in the two departments. Except as these factors were themselves based upon the sex of the customers, the incentive differentials were not based in any way upon sex, and were sanctioned by 29 C.F.R. § 800.116(e).[16] Although the example given in this regulation presupposes the hiring of males and females indiscriminately in each of two shoe departments, it is not for this reason irrelevant to the instant case. Were this a case in which the defendant had arbitrarily employed only females in the department paying the lower commissions, it might be. But this did not occur. Here the necessity of close bodily contact between customers and sales personnel made it logical and necessary for salesmen to be employed in the men's department and salesladies in the women's department.

In its operation the ratio of incentive pay to gross sales was only about .2%

---

[16]Section 800.116(e) reads:

(e) *Commissions*. The establishment of different rates of commission on different types of merchandise would not result in a violation of the equal pay provisions where the factor of sex provides no part of the basis for the differential. For example, suppose that a retail store maintains two shoe departments, each having employees of both sexes, that the shoes carried in the two departments differ in style, quality, and price, and that the male and female sales clerks in the one department are performing "equal work " with those in the other. In such a situation, a prohibited differential would not result from payment of a lower commission rate in the department where a lower price line with a lower markup is sold than in the other department where the merchandise is higher priced and has a higher markup, if the employer can show that the commission rates paid in each department are applied equally to the employees of both sexes in the establishment for all employment in that department and that the factor of sex has played no part in the setting of the different commission rates.

Hodgson v. Robert Hall Clothes

more in the case of salesmen than in the case of saleswomen. This compensation differential distinction was based solely upon factors other than sex.

Conclusion

Plaintiff is entitled to an injunction restraining defendants from (a) further violating the Equal Pay Act at the Greenbank store {regarding part-time women}, and (b) from withholding back wages due {part-time} salesladies at the Greenbank store because of violation of the Equal Pay Act. The parties have agreed to attempt to stipulate the amount of back wages which defendants must pay.

....

QUESTIONS FOR REFLECTION

1. What are the material facts (elements) of the prima facie case of a violation of the Equal Pay Act?

2. With respect to each material fact of the claim, state the evidentiary facts that proved the material fact.

3. The Act allows a pay differential for equal jobs if the differential is based on a factor other than sex. The court held that economic benefit to the employer is a factor other than sex. Do you agree that the Act should be interpreted in this way?

Exercise

An employer operated a health club. It was open to men and women on alternate days. On men's days, all workers were male; on women's days, all workers were female. (The parties agreed for purposes of the case that this job segregation was not illegal.) The principal duty of the managers and assistant managers of both sexes ("managers") was to sell memberships. Managers were compensated solely by commission on sales. The women's division of the business generated 50 percent more sales than the men's division. The employer paid male managers a commission that was 50 percent higher than the commission paid to female managers, with the result that male and female managers earned approximately equal pay. Assume <u>Robert Hall</u> is precedent in your jurisdiction and, using the model of legal argument, write two opinions — one holding the pay practice legal, the other holding the pay practice illegal.

Ω

Equal Work

Introduction

Two jobs can be different in the tasks they require, yet be equal in terms of skill, effort, responsibility, and working conditions. For example, the tasks of a nurse and a maintenance mechanic are different, but they may require equal levels (albeit different kinds) of skill, effort, responsibility, and be performed under similar working conditions.[a] To say that the work of two such different jobs is equal is to say that they have "comparable worth." The idea is that, because they involve equal skill, effort, etc., they are equally valuable to the employer and deserve the same rate of compensation. The text of the Equal Pay Act lends itself to an interpretation that embraces comparable worth:

> "No employer ... shall discriminate ... between employees on the basis of sex by paying wages to employees ... at a rate less than the rate at which he pays wages to employees of the opposite sex ... for equal work on jobs the performance of which requires equal skill, effort, and responsibility, and are performed under similar working conditions ...."

Congress was aware of comparable worth as the bill that became the Equal Pay Act was debated. At the time some large firms, using job evaluation plans, attempted to provide equal pay to jobs of comparable worth. The Kennedy administration urged Congress to incorporate comparable worth into the bill, but Congress refused. The legislative history seems clear that Congress

---

[a]The student may be thinking that the working conditions of nurses and mechanics are different. The Equal Pay Act specifies, however, that working conditions need only be "similar." Also, in <u>Corning Glass Works v. Brennan</u>, 417 U.S. 188 (1974), the Supreme Court held that the term "working conditions" in the Act refers only to "surroundings" and "hazards," which terms are defined technically. Surroundings are things such as toxic chemicals and fumes, and hazards are physical hazards. It is possible, therefore, that the working conditions of nurses and mechanics in a given hospital might be similar.

rejected the proposal to require that different jobs receive equal pay simply because they require equal levels of skill, effort, etc.

The courts have read the text of the Equal Pay Act in light of its legislative history. Equal work means not only equality of skill, effort, responsibility, and working conditions, but also substantial identity of tasks. Accordingly, if one of the jobs requires a task that the other does not, and if performing this additional task is a crucial aspect of the job — the chief measure of this being how much of the day the worker must devote to the task — the jobs are not equal.

The following case requires mediated application of law to fact on issues pertaining to equal pay. When a tribunal engages in mediated application of law to fact, precedents are used as rules of law. Commonly, one party urges the tribunal to use an earlier case (let us call it A v. B) as a precedent. If the other party is unhappy with A v. B as a precedent, (1) the party may argue that A v. B is distinguishable from the case at bar, in other words, that significant differences exist between the facts of A v. B and the facts of the case at bar; or (2) the other party may argue that A v. B is incorrect, in other words, it is an erroneous decision that should not be followed. Of course, the tribunal may accept or reject such arguments. To accept the argument is to decide not to use A v. B as a precedent; in this event, the tribunal will (at least, it should) state the differences in facts between the rejected precedent and the case at bar. To reject the argument is to decide to follow A v. B as a precedent; in this event, the tribunal will (should) state the similarity of facts between the precedent and the case at bar.[b]

---

[b]The student will notice that the case contains numerous citations to earlier cases. In the interest of conserving space, we have usually deleted such citations from the cases in this book. We have preserved the citations in the following case to illustrate how earlier cases are used in mediated application of law to fact. However, still being conscious of space, we have omitted all but the first citation in instances where the court has cited more than one case in support of an assertion.

Like all cases, the following one also requires direct application of law to fact. Direct application occurs when the tribunal can determine whether the material facts of the rule(s) of law are true of the case at bar. In the example of *A* in the Note on Application of Law to Fact, once the tribunal determined how fast *A's* car was moving, it was immediately obvious that *A* had exceeded the speed limit. Most cases concerning violations of the Equal Pay Act require extensive direct application of law to fact. The reason is that each element of the plaintiff's claim calls for detailed comparison of the man's job and the woman's job. The details of the jobs are evidentiary facts, which the tribunal must compare in order to determine whether the material facts of the claim, such as equal work and equal effort, are true.

Peter Brennan, Secretary of Labor
v.
Prince William Hospital Corporation
503 F.2d 282 (4th Cir., 1974)

BUTZNER, CIRCUIT JUDGE:

The Secretary of Labor appeals from the dismissal of an action against Prince William Hospital to equalize pay of male hospital orderlies and female nurses' aides in conformity with the Equal Pay Act of 1963. The district court noted that the facts were not in dispute and that the controversy centered on the inferences to be drawn from them. It found that although aides and orderlies do the same type of patient care work, the following differences exist between the jobs: the proportions of routine care tasks are not the same; aides do work which orderlies are neither required nor permitted to do; and, most important, orderlies do work, including extra tasks, which aides are neither required nor permitted to do. It concluded, therefore, that the Secretary had failed to establish that the aides and orderlies perform substantially equal work.

We believe that the district court gave undue significance to these differences because it misapprehended the statutory definition of equal work, which embraces the concepts of "skill, effort, and responsibility."[2] Since it applied an improper legal standard to the relevant facts, we reverse and remand for the entry of judgment for the Secretary.

I

In applying the Congressional mandate of equal pay for equal work on jobs which require equal skill, effort, and responsibility, there are two extremes of interpretation that must be avoided. Congress realized that the majority of job differentiations are made for genuine economic reasons unrelated to sex. It did not authorize the Secretary or the courts to engage in wholesale reevaluation of any employer's pay structure in order to enforce their own conceptions of economic worth. *See Hodgson v. Miller Brewing Co.*, 457 F.2d 221, 227 (7th Cir. 1972). But if courts defer to overly nice distinctions in job content, employers may evade the Act at will. *Hodgson v. Behrens Drug Co.*, 475 F.2d 1041, 1049 (5th Cir. 1973). The response to this dilemma has been to require the Secretary to prove substantial

---

[2] 29 U.S.C. § 206(d)(1). Congress patterned the Equal Pay Act on the principles of job classification by which many employers set wage rates. Under these principles, each job is rated in terms of the skill, effort, and responsibility required to do it, and the working conditions of the place where it is performed. *See Corning Glass Works v. Brennan* 417 U.S. 188 (1974).

equality of skill, effort, and responsibility as the jobs are actually performed. *See Hodgson v. Fairmont Supply Co.*, 454 F.2d 490, 493 (4th Cir. 1971).

One of the most common grounds for justifying different wages is the assertion that male employees perform extra tasks. These may support a wage differential if they create significant variations in skill, effort, and responsibility between otherwise equal jobs, *see, e.g. Hodgson v. Golden Isles Convalescent Homes, Inc.*, 468 F.2d 1256 (5th Cir. 1972). But the semblance of a valid job classification system may not be allowed to mask the existence of wage discrimination based on sex. The Secretary may therefore show that the greater pay received by the male employees is not related to any extra tasks and thus is not justified by them. Higher pay is not related to extra duties when one or more of the following circumstances exists:

> Some male employees receive higher pay without doing the extra work. *E.g. Shultz v. American Can Co.-Dixie Products*, 424 F.2d 356 (8th Cir. 1970).
> Female employees also perform extra duties of equal skill, effort, and responsibility. *E.g. Hodgson v. Fairmont Supply Co.*, 454 F.2d 490 (4th Cir. 1971).
> Qualified female employees are not given the opportunity to do the extra work. *E.g. Shultz v. Wheaton Glass Co.*, 421 F.2d 259 (3d Cir. 1969).
> The supposed extra duties do not in fact exist. *E.g. Hodgson v. Security National Bank*, 460 F.2d 57 (8th Cir. 1972).
> The extra task consumes a minimal amount of time and is of peripheral importance. *E.g. Hodgson v. Behrens Drug Co.*, 475 F.2d 1041 (5th Cir. 1973).
> Third persons who do the extra task as their primary job are paid less than the male employees in question. *E.g. Shultz v. Wheaton Glass Co.*, 421 F.2d 259 (3d Cir. 1969).

In all of these cases the basic jobs were substantially equal. Despite claims to the contrary, the extra tasks were found to be makeweights. This left sex — which in this context refers to the availability of women at lower wages than men — as the one discernible reason for the wage differential. That, however, is precisely the criterion for setting wages that the Act prohibits. *See Brennan v. City Stores, Inc.*, 479 F.2d 235, 241 n.12 (5th Cir. 1973).

II

Although a number of courts have applied the Equal Pay Act to hospital and nursing home aides and orderlies, varied employment practices among institutions have prevented the development of an industry-wide standard. The Act must be applied on a case by case basis to factual situations that are, for practical purposes, unique. *See Hodgson v. Golden Isles Convalescent Homes, Inc.*, 468 F.2d 1256, 1258 (5th Cir. 1972). It is therefore necessary to examine in some detail the employment practices of Prince William Hospital, even though the material facts are not in dispute.

Prince William is a 154 bed general hospital in Manassas, Virginia. It contains four medical and surgical units, intensive care and cardiac facilities, an obstetric floor with a nursery, four operating rooms, and an emergency room. Average occupancy is 120 patients, 60% female.

Floor orderlies and nurses' aides provide routine patient care under the supervision of nurses. The hospital hires only men as orderlies and only women as aides. Their numbers varied during the time covered by this case, ranging between 30-40 aides and 5-10 orderlies. When the case was tried, there were four full-time floor orderlies and thirty-four full-time aides, plus three part-time orderlies and three part-time aides. Full-time employees work five eight-hour shifts per week.

The hospital has maintained a pay differential between the two jobs since 1969. It uses a pay system with thirteen pay grades and five steps within each grade. Grades are assigned to positions and steps within grade show merit or longevity. All nurses' aides are in grade I, in which the hourly pay ranges from $1.98 to $2.31, and all orderlies are in grade II, in which the hourly pay ranges from $2.08 to $2.43, depending on the step in which the employee has been placed.

Before 1969 aides and orderlies had been paid the same wages, but the hospital had difficulty in hiring orderlies. The hospital's administrator believed that a higher wage was needed to attract orderlies because of the limited number of men willing to do housekeeping and personal care work. When the orderlies' wage was raised, they were given the additional duty of catheterizing male patients.

Hiring criteria for aides and orderlies are identical: a tenth grade education, personal cleanliness, and a desire to work with people. Experience, though desirable, is unnecessary. Although the educational level of the aides was somewhat lower, both groups included individuals who had not finished high school. The pay differential follows neither experience nor education. An aide with prior hospital experience starts in grade I step 2 ($2.06), while a completely inexperienced orderly starts in grade II step 1 ($2.08).

Aides and orderlies are the least skilled persons who care for patients. They participate in a common orientation program, but much of their training is acquired on the job. Each is assigned six to eight patients who require routine care. Whenever possible orderlies are assigned to male patients and aides to female, but the shortage of orderlies requires aides to care for males. Most of the time, aides and orderlies are occupied with tasks related to routine patient care that do not require the skills of a trained nurse.

The principal duties of both, which the hospital's director of nursing stated were identical, can be divided into four groups: patient care, which includes oral hygiene, back rubs, baths, bed-making, answering calls, giving bed pans, feeding, transporting the patient, and assistance with ambulation; minor treatment, which includes weighing, taking pulse, temperature, or blood pressure, draping and positioning the patient, administering heat pads and ice packs, assistance with dressing changes, and giving enemas; housekeeping, which includes room cleaning, equipment care and cleaning, work area cleaning, and obtaining supplies; and miscellaneous tasks, including answering the phone, running errands, and transportation to the morgue.

The hospital emphasized statistical evidence which shows that aides and orderlies do not perform all of their routine tasks with equal frequency. One of its exhibits, for example, shows that aides write charts, make beds, give baths, rub backs and fetch bed pans more often than orderlies. Orderlies, on the other hand, bring supplies, run errands and assist the nurses with their duties more often than aides. These distinctions, however, do not show any difference in skill, effort or responsibility. All of the routine tasks are relatively simple. None performed more frequently by the orderlies requires the exertion of significantly more skill, effort, or responsibility than those performed more frequently by the aides. As hired, trained, and employed, the orderlies and aides are practical substitutes for one another in the performance of their basic duties. Disproportionate frequency in the performance of the same routine tasks does not make the job unequal. *See* 29 C.F.R. § 800.123 (1973).

III

The district court also found that aides perform certain duties which orderlies do not. Specifically, it found that some of the aides work in the obstetric department and care for infants in the nursery. Orderlies were not assigned to obstetrics, according to the director of nursing, for two reasons: there were no male patients and their lifting ability was unneeded there. Aides assigned to obstetrics performed the same duties as those on the medical and surgical wards. These facts do not show any differences in skill, effort, or responsibility. Unless there is a difference of working conditions involved, which is not contended here, there is no reason why the performance of the same duties in a different location should be a significant difference in the jobs. *See* 29 C.F.R. § 800.123 (1973).

IV

The final — and in some respects the most difficult — aspect of this case pertains to extra duties throughout the hospital that are assigned to the orderlies but not to the aides. These duties are specified in the job description of the orderlies. The district court found that the following extra duties were the most significant: heavy lifting, assisting in the emergency room, performing surgical preps on male patients, providing physical security by dealing with combative or hysterical persons, and catheterization of male patients.

Job descriptions and titles, however, are not decisive. Actual job requirements and performance are controlling. *See* 29 C.F.R. § 800.121 (1973). This aspect of the case, therefore, turns primarily on the extent to which the aides and orderlies actually perform the extra duties nominally assigned to the orderlies and on the skill, effort and responsibility involved in those tasks which the orderlies alone perform.

In addition to caring for assigned patients, orderlies are required to answer calls to different parts of the hospital. On these excursions, called floating, they perform either their basic duties or the extra tasks. Floating itself adds nothing to the level of skill or responsibility, for that depends on the work done in the other locations. It might add to the degree of effort involved if the orderlies, in addition, had to perform their full basic workload. This, however, is not the case. According to the director of nursing, an orderly's routine duties at his assigned station are reassigned to other staff personnel, including the aides, when he is in another part of the hospital.[6]

The job description states that orderlies are expected to perform total lifting of heavy or helpless patients and to set up traction equipment. The district court, however, found that the same tasks are performed by aides when no orderly is available and that aides assist orderlies in these tasks. Due to the small number of orderlies, there are rarely more than two on duty each shift, and from time to time no

---

[6]In contrast, *Hodgson v. Good Shepherd Hospital*, 327 F.Supp 143, 146 (E.D. Tex. 1971), on which the hospital relies, involved orderlies without assigned patients. The court characterized their work as "continuous, demanding, and tiring, ... so rushed as to prevent rest or scheduled coffee breaks or lunch periods," which was not true of the aides' job.

orderly is available on some of the shifts. It sometimes takes more than one aide, or mechanical assistance, to replace an orderly, but there is no evidence that any heavy lifting cannot be done without male assistance.[7] The performance of tasks involving physical strength, therefore, though necessary to the operation of the hospital, is not a peculiar aspect of the orderlies' job. Strength is not a factor in the hiring of orderlies, except in the very general sense that the hospital assumes that a man usually is stronger than a woman. A large, burly woman would not be hired as an orderly, nor would a small, delicate man be hired as an aide. But the converse is not true. One of the orderlies is 5 feet 2 inches tall and weighs 125 lbs., while one aide is 6 feet 1 inch and weighs 225 lbs. The wage differential therefore can not be justified on the grounds that the hospital is maintaining a reserve of strong men for essential tasks.

Heavy lifting does not add significantly to the effort involved in the orderlies' job. In the ten working days covered by the hospital's survey of activities, the orderlies set up traction only once and lifted or assisted patients of unknown weight 54 times. Aides set up traction and lifted or ambulated patients a proportionate number of times. The extra effort, if any, is not substantial.

The emergency room is staffed by an orderly whose status is not questioned in this action. The hospital's claim that floor orderlies "assisted" there is supported only by the job description, but a mere job description without evidence of actual performance does not establish the existence of extra duties. *Hodgson v. Brookhaven General Hospital*, 436 F.2d 719, 724 (5th Cir. 1970). Aides were also called to work in the emergency room. The record proves no more than that both aides and orderlies performed their normal duties with minor variations in a different location.

All surgical preps during the day shifts are done by the operating room staff. On the evening and night shifts, surgical preps on men are done by orderlies, and on women by aides or nurses. Aides also do surgical preps in the obstetric ward. A person performing a prep explains to the patient what is about to be done, shaves the area where the incision will be made, and washes it with antiseptic soap. The skill, effort, and responsibility involved are identical regardless of the patient's sex.

---

[7]The reverse was true in *Hodgson v. Golden Isles Convalescent Homes, Inc.*, 468 F.2d 1256 (5th Cir. 1972); *Hodgson v. Good Shepherd Hospital*, 327 F.Supp 143 (E.D. Tex. 1971); and *Hodgson v. William and Mary Nursing Hotel*, 20 W.H. Cases 10 (M.D. Fla. 1972), in all of which orderlies were required to transport and set up heavy, bulky oxygen equipment which was unsafe or impossible for the aides to move. In addition, the aides in *William and Mary* were forbidden to move patients by themselves. 20 W.H. Cases at 23.

Physical security, as an extra duty, has two components. Because of his size and sex, the presence of a male orderly is claimed to reassure the other staff and exert a calming and deterrent effect on potentially violent patients or intruders. Because of his superior strength, he is given the primary responsibility for restraining actually violent persons. According to the hospital, he therefore possesses a special skill and is required to exert extra effort.

The hospital's contention, however, is contradicted by the record. Although in theory the orderly deals with disturbances, in practice the nearest staff member is expected to do so until assistance comes. Aides are expected to restrain violent or disoriented patients themselves when possible. They also deal with intruders. The hospital's tabulation of orderly and aide activity shows aides spending a larger proportion of their time than orderlies in applying restraining devices to patients. There is no evidence that orderlies do more actual physical restraint than aides.

No doubt the physical presence of a man in the house does have a comforting effect on the staff. It is doubtful, though, that this is a significant component of the orderly job. Unlike hospitals in which providing physical security has been found significant,[8] Prince William Hospital does not handle psychiatric, alcoholic, criminal, or other potentially dangerous patients. There is no evidence that episodes caused by violent or confused patients are so frequent or dangerous that orderlies are necessary for the safety of the staff. Security guards are called to deal with violent episodes even when orderlies are available. Moreover, the ability to deal with confused or violent patients, according to the director of nursing, is as much a function of attitude and experience as of size and strength. If the orderly's superior strength is an extra skill, it is a peripheral part of his employment.

The hospital places great emphasis on the fact that orderlies insert Foley catheters in male patients. It contends that the task is a highly skilled and responsible procedure, requiring 30 to 45 minutes of an orderly's time.

A Foley catheter is a sterile tube which is inserted in the patient's urethra to drain the bladder. Orderlies catheterize male patients with unobstructed urinary tracts. If any difficulty is foreseen or experienced, a physician catheterizes the patient. Nurses catheterize female patients. They are competent to catheterize males, but prefer not to do so for reasons of modesty. Since the hospital has enough nurses to

---

[8]*E.g. Hodgson v. Owensboro-Daviess County Hospital*, 21 W.H. Cases 250 (W.D. Ky. 1972) (primary care of violent patients, alcoholics, and addicts); *Hodgson v. Good Shepherd Hospital*, 327 F.Supp 143 (E.D. Tex. 1971) (violent alcoholics, addicts, and psychiatric patients in lockup cells); *Hodgson v. William and Mary Nursing Hotel*, 20 W.H. Cases 10 (M.D. Fla. 1971) (geriatric facility with many senile patients).

catheterize women, aides are not assigned this duty. The orderly's job therefore does call for the exercise of skill and responsibility which is not required of the aides.

However, no more than one or two routine catheterizations are usually performed each week. When no floor orderly is present, other qualified male personnel are available to do them. The hospital looks for no special skill in this regard from its prospective orderlies, but concedes that "any reasonably dextrous person can learn male catheterization on the job." Orderlies were assigned this duty only when the hospital decided that a higher wage rate was needed to attract men for routine care work, and new orderlies who have not yet learned to catheterize are nevertheless paid at the higher rate.

Like any other extra duty, catheterization must be evaluated as part of the entire job. In *Hodgson v. Fairmont Supply Co.*, 454 F.2d 490, 496 (4th Cir. 1972), we pointed out that when jobs were substantially equal, a minimal amount of extra skill, effort, or responsibility cannot justify wage differentials. Infrequent performance of catheterizations, unaccompanied by other extra skills and responsibilities, has never been held to support a pay differential between aides and orderlies. The orderlies in *Hodgson v. William and Mary Nursing Hotel*, 20 W.H. Cases 10 (M.D. Fla. 1971), for example, a case in which the district court found catheterization to be a significant extra duty, also moved heavy equipment, administered suction therapy, and did other demanding work not done by aides. Catheterizations, moreover, were frequent and difficult in that geriatric nursing home. Similarly, catheterization was only one element of the orderlies' duties, which differed fundamentally from the aides in *Hodgson v. Good Shepherd Hospital*, 327 F. Supp. 143 (E.D. Tex. 1971). In contrast, catheterization which only consumed a minimal amount of time was considered to be an insubstantial difference in *Shultz v. Brookhaven General Hospital*, 305 F. Supp. 424 (E.D. Tex. 1969). We conclude, therefore, that orderlies' pay differential cannot be justified on the basis of the occasional extra work involved in catheterizing male patients.

In sum, the work performed by aides and orderlies is not identical. But, as we have previously held, application of the Equal Pay Act is not restricted to identical work. *Hodgson v. Fairmont Supply Co., supra*, 454 F.2d at 493. The basic routine tasks of the aides and orderlies are equal. The variations that the district court found, when tested by the Act's standard of "equal skill, effort, and responsibility," do not affect the substantial equality of their overall work.

The judgment of the district court is reversed, and this case is remanded for entry of judgment for the Secretary.

Exercises

1. Sometimes a rule of law can be applied directly to the facts of a case without the mediation of additional rules of law. The law is sufficiently refined to decide the case. To say the same thing, mediation between the existing rule and the facts is unnecessary; no further distinctions need be drawn; we have reached the appropriate level of abstraction. Indeed, direct application of law to fact is always the final step in the process.

Find in <u>Prince William Hospital</u> at least one instance in which the court directly applies an existing rule of law to the facts of the case. State the material fact in issue, and make a list of the evidentiary facts the court uses to establish the material fact. HINT: look at the court's discussion of duties that aides performed and orderlies did not.

2. Often an existing rule of law cannot be applied directly to the facts of the case at bar; in consequence, an additional rule of law is needed to mediate between the existing rule and the facts. A court can create the needed rule, but usually prefers to find one in precedent. Find in <u>Prince William Hospital</u> an instance in which a rule was needed in addition to the existing rule of law, and the court found the additional rule in precedent. Then state the material fact in issue, and make a list of the evidentiary facts the court uses to establish the material fact. HINT: look at duties in the emergency room or at orderlies' duty to catheterize patients.

3. Parties commonly cite precedents in applying law to fact, and opposing parties try to distinguish such precedents. Find in <u>Prince William Hospital</u> two instances in which one party cited a precedent, but the court found it was distinguishable. Make a list of the facts that distinguished the precedents from the case at bar. HINT: look at orderlies' floating duties, at orderlies' duty of lifting patients and setting up traction equipment, and at orderlies' duty of providing physical security.

Tutorials

After answering the questions above, the student should read the following hypothetical case and do the interactive exercises after the hypothetical. AS background, the student should know that the Supreme Court wrote in <u>NLRB v. Babcock & Wilcox</u>, 351 U.S. 105, 112-113 (1956):

> [A]n employer may validly post his property against nonemployee distribution of union literature if reasonable efforts by the union through other available channels of communication will enable it to reach the employees with its message and if the employer's notice or order does not discriminate against the union by allowing other distribution. In these circumstances the employer may not be compelled to allow distribution. . . .
>
>   . . .
>
> The plants {in the case at bar} are close to small well-settled communities where a large percentage of the employees live. The usual methods of imparting information are available. See, e. g., note 1, <u>supra</u>.

Footnote 1, which was a quotation from the Labor Board's decision in the case, read:

> 1. <u>Other union contacts with employees</u>: In addition to distributing literature to some of the employees, as shown above, during the period of concern herein the Union has had other contacts with some of the employees. It has communicated with over 100 employees of Respondent on 3 different occasions by sending literature to them through the mails. Union representatives have communicated with many of Respondent's employees by talking with them on the streets of Paris, {Texas} by driving to their homes and talking with them there, and by talking with them over the telephone. All of these contacts have been for the purpose of soliciting the adherence and membership of the employees in the Union." 109 NLRB, at 492-493.

<u>Id</u>. at 7.

Brennan v. Prince William Hospital   XV

Hypothetical Case

Jordan, Unlimited, an employer covered by the Labor Act, owns an independent company that explores and drills for oil. After geologists identify a promising site and lawyers and executives negotiate a lease, Jordan's roughnecks sink a well and, if it is successful, pump oil from it.

At the present time, Jordan operates three offshore wells in American territory in the Gulf of Mexico. Over each well is a large floating platform on which the roughnecks work, eat, and sleep for two weeks at a time. The platform is close enough to the mainland to receive television and radio programs from Galveston, Texas, as well as satellite programs. The platform is also linked to the mainland by telephone, and mail and newspapers are delivered by helicopter daily.

The roughnecks are grouped into three crews of fifty persons. Each crew works two weeks on the platform, followed by a week's vacation. On the platform, a crew works 12 hours and rests 12 hours. The crews' weekly schedules overlap. Thus, on Platform 1, Kareem's crew (the crews are identified by the name of their foreone) worked January 1-14; Julius's crew worked January 8-21; Oscar's crew worked January 15-28; Kareem's crew worked January 22-February 4, etc. On Mondays the crews are flown by helicopter between the platform and the Galveston airport.

Few of the roughnecks live in Galveston; their homes are scattered across five states. As part of their compensation, Jordan reimburses them up to $450 towards the cost of the round-trip airfare from their homes to Galveston each two weeks. Jordan does not charge roughnecks for room or board while they are on the platform. Excluding reimbursement for airfare and the value of room and board on the platform, Jordan pays the roughnecks $1,500 per week on the platform.

Local 3 of the Chattelers, Tattlers, and Dawdlers of the World represents roughnecks employed by other companies operating near Jordan's wells. Recently, a roughneck named Greenstein approached Garland, the president of Local 3, and asked it to organize his crew. Garland said he wanted some indication that other members of the crew were interested in unionizing; he suggested that Greenstein talk to his crew mates and distribute union literature. Greenstein agreed and began doing so as soon as he returned to Platform 1. When the superintendent of the platform learned what Greenstein was doing, the former instructed the latter to cease. Garland immediately filed an unfair labor practice charge, which was sustained by the Labor Board.

Then Garland asked Jordan's permission to ride on the Monday helicopter and talk to the roughnecks on the platforms while they were off duty. Jordan refused. Garland offered to arrange his own transportation to and from the platforms for the same purpose. Jordan refused again. He added that only employees were allowed on the platforms, and this fact was true. Garland asked for a list of the names and home addresses of the roughnecks. Jordan replied that the information was confidential.

Local 3 made no further efforts to communicate with the roughnecks, but it filed a charge of unfair labor practice against Jordan. The foregoing facts were proved at a hearing before an administrative law judge.

Now do the tutorial entitled "Applying Law to Fact Without Using Precedents." When you have completed it, do the tutorial entitled "Applying Law to Fact Using Precedents."

Ω

Equal Effort and Similar Working Conditions

Introduction

One of the requirements for a plaintiff to prove a violation of the Equal Pay Act is that the man's and the woman's jobs must involve equal effort. The following case examines whether the effort needed to perform the job of heavy cleaner, held primarily by men, was equal to, or greater than, the effort needed to perform the job of light cleaner, held entirely by women.

Note how the court deals with the argument of the government that effort was equal because the total amount of effort expended by workers was equal for the two jobs, and the opposing argument of the employer that effort was not equal because the effort expended on some specific tasks of heavy cleaning exceeded the effort expended on any specific task of light cleaning. These competing arguments may be abstracted as follows:

Heavy Cleaning | Light Cleaning

Task A			Task W		
Effort per repetition:	20		Effort per repetition:	3	
No. of repetitions:	1		No. of repetitions:	10	
Effort per day:	20		Effort per day:	30	
Task B			Task X		
Effort per repetition:	5		Effort per repetition:	5	
No. of repetitions:	8		No. of repetitions:	2	
Effort per day:	40		Effort per day:	10	
Task C			Task Y		
Effort per repetition:	10		Effort per repetition:	4	
No. of repetitions:	4		No. of repetitions:	10	
Effort per day:	40		Effort per day:	40	
			Task Z		
			Effort per repetition:	2	
			No. of repetitions:	10	
			Effort per day:	20	
Total effort per day: 100			Total effort per day: 100		

We continue to examine the skill of application of law to fact. In this process, step 1 is to state the general rule of law. Step 2 is to state any additional rules of law needed to mediate between the general rule and the facts of the case at bar. (Step 2 is usually, but not always, necessary.) Step 3 is to find the facts of the case. And step 4 is to apply the law directly to the facts of the case. Pay particular attention to (step 2) how the court uses precedent to identify the mediating rules of law, and to (step 4) how the court distinguishes cases that reached different results on similar facts.

W. J. Usery, Jr., Secretary of Labor
v.
Columbia University
568 F. 2d 953 (2d Cir. 1977)

TIMBERS, Circuit Judge.

On this appeal from a judgment entered after a bench trial in the Southern District of New York, Richard Owen, District Judge, 407 F. Supp. 1370, the essential question presented is whether the work performed respectively by the heavy and light cleaners employed by Columbia University is "equal" within the meaning of the Equal Pay Act of 1963 (the Act). We agree with the district court that the work is not equal. We affirm.

I.

The Equal Pay Act prohibits an employer from discriminating "between employees on the basis of sex by paying wages to employees ... at a rate less than the rate at which he pays wages to employees of the opposite sex ... for equal work on jobs the performance of which requires equal skill, effort, and responsibility, and which are performed under similar working conditions ...."

Invoking the enforcement provisions of the Fair Labor Standards Act, the Secretary of Labor commenced the instant action against Columbia University and its president (Columbia) on March 11, 1974. The action sought to enjoin Columbia from discriminating against its female light cleaners, allegedly on the basis of sex in violation of the Equal Pay Act, by paying them at a lower hourly rate than that paid to its male heavy cleaners. The action also sought an injunction against further violations and an award of back pay.

At a 15 day bench trial during September and November 1974, the parties, focusing upon the statute's "equal ... effort" criterion, produced extensive evidence on the physical requirements of the heavy and light cleaning positions. The crux of Judge Owen's finding of fact on this critical issue is set forth in his opinion dated February 11, 1976 as follows:

> "The jobs of heavy cleaner and light cleaner are different. Going beyond the job descriptions, from the extensive testimony adduced before me at the trial, it is clear that the job of heavy cleaner involves greater effort than that of light cleaner." 407 F. Supp. at 1374-75.

Accordingly, the judge held that the Secretary had failed to sustain the burden of proving that the heavy and light cleaners perform equal work within the meaning of the Act. From the judgment dismissing the action, the Secretary has taken the instant appeal.

II.

...

For more than 30 years Columbia has divided the duties of its custodial force into "heavy" and "light" categories. At the time of trial it employed 160 heavy cleaners (designated "janitors" prior to 1972), 4 of whom were female, and 111 light cleaners (designated "maids" prior to 1972), all of whom were female. Since 1972 all heavy cleaning positions have been open to applicants of both sexes.[5] No male ever has applied for the position of light cleaner. The light cleaners always have been paid less than the heavy cleaners. The differential was 45 cents an hour at the time of trial.

Columbia assigns approximately 80% of the light cleaners to its academic buildings and the remainder to its residence halls. Each cleaner in the group assigned to the academic buildings has daily responsibility for between 1 and 5 floors, depending on the size of the building and the functions of the particular rooms included in the assignment. The functions are those one would expect at any university, including classrooms, offices, library stacks, and the like. The light cleaners dust mop or vacuum the floors of the rooms and some of the corridors; dust, polish, or dampcloth the furniture, fixtures, baseboards and windowsills; and remove small spots from the walls, floors and doors. They also empty wastebaskets and ashtrays into trash bags. These are deposited at the elevator on each floor where they are picked up by heavy cleaners. In performing their work the light cleaners use dust mops, carpet sweepers, household vacuum cleaners, toy brooms, rags, sponges and 14 quart buckets. Some of the light cleaners transport this equipment in wheeled carts which weigh 60 pounds unloaded. The equipment itself, including a vacuum cleaner, creates a 21 pound load, to which a full trash bag adds an indeterminate amount of weight up to 30 pounds.

The light cleaners assigned to the residence halls perform the same functions as those performed in the academic buildings. Each day they clean the common rooms and offices on the ground floors, and the corridors and lounges on the

---

[5]For heavy cleaning work Columbia has been paying more in cleaning wages to a limited number of women since 1949 when the classification "shower maid" first appeared in its collective bargaining agreement. This classification encompassed the female cleaners assigned to the showers and lavatories in the women's residence hall at Columbia. The classification never included more than 8 employees. At the time of trial 2 of the 4 female heavy cleaners performed the "shower maid" function.

All other heavy cleaner positions were limited to men until 1972 when Columbia opened them to women. The remaining 2 women employed as heavy cleaners at the time of the trial worked within this broad, formerly male, classification.

residential floors. Students' rooms are cleaned on a special assignment basis when unoccupied during the summer.

The heavy cleaners may be grouped roughly into four categories: (1) those assigned to public corridors, lobbies, stairways and elevators; (2) those assigned to public lavatories; (3) those permanently assigned to special projects; and (4) those assigned to certain off-campus buildings.

The primary daily responsibility of group (1) is to wet mop the corridors, lobbies, stairways, elevators, classrooms and laboratories of the academic buildings. They also collect the bags of trash left on each floor by the light cleaners and transport them to dumping areas.

The heavy cleaners in group (2) clean daily the university's public lavatories. They dust and wet mop the floors, clean the toilets and sinks, empty the trash, and wash marks from the walls. Many of the heavy cleaners in this group assist the heavy cleaners in the first group with the job of removing trash. Depending on the load, this takes from less than one-half hour to 2 hours daily.

In their wet mopping both of these groups use a dolly which carries two 44 quart buckets with wringers and cleaning solution. The dolly weighs 60 pounds empty and up to 140 pounds full. For larger areas they use mop trucks which hold 30 or 60 gallons. These weigh from 160 to 200 pounds empty and from 300 to 500 pounds full. Trash removal is accomplished by the use of trucks. These are 6 feet long, 3 feet wide and 6 feet high, and weigh 200 pounds empty and up to 800 pounds full.

The heavy cleaners in groups (1) and (2) perform additional tasks on an occasional basis. These include loading, unloading and transporting drums of cleaning solvent which hold 55 gallons of liquid and weigh from 400 to 600 pounds; climbing 14 foot ladders to clean in high places and change light bulbs; vacuuming carpets with industrial machines which weigh from 74 to 96 pounds empty and from 122 to 192 pounds full; cleaning carpets with motorized pile lifters; shoveling snow from entrance ways; and turning on and off heavy ventilation equipment.

The special projects handled by group (3) of the heavy cleaners are jobs done regularly but infrequently. These include scrubbing and stripping floors, shampooing rugs and washing Venetian blinds.

The work assignments of those classified in groups (1), (2) and (3) are not necessarily hard and fast. For example, in Avery Hall, one of the smaller buildings, one heavy cleaner wet mops all the corridors and staircases, cleans the lavatories and does any project work. (Two light cleaners handle the offices and libraries in that building). In contrast, in a large building such as Butler Library, assignments of the 5 heavy cleaners in the building are divided among the 3 classifications. (Eleven light cleaners are assigned to Butler).

The heavy cleaners in group (4) are assigned to small converted office buildings located on streets adjacent to Columbia's main campus. They primarily perform light cleaning duties. Light cleaners handled these assignments until 1974 when considerations of security prompted Columbia to substitute male employees. The buildings involved are outside of the security perimeter of the main campus and are cleaned during the midnight to 8 A.M. shift. Before the change heavy cleaners escorted the light cleaners from the main campus to these buildings and locked them in. Each light cleaner then spent the night alone in her respective building and later was escorted back to the main campus.

These off-campus buildings are the only exception to the otherwise uniform line of demarcation which Columbia maintains between "heavy" and "light" cleaning tasks. Written job descriptions listing the heavy and light cleaning tasks are incorporated in the collective bargaining agreements between Columbia and the Transport Workers' Union.[7]

The cleaners themselves are well aware of the distinction between heavy and light assignments and have not hesitated to enforce it. In 1971, for example, 8 light cleaners successfully protested an assignment to remove heavy trash. Columbia moreover has changed from "light" to "heavy" certain assignments which technically were in the "light" category but which in practice called for physical exertion comparable to that of the heavy cleaning tasks. The wastebaskets in the Journalism building, for example, frequently are filled with books, magazines and other heavy materials. After the light cleaners in the building complained of the resulting burden, the job of emptying these wastebaskets was reassigned to heavy cleaners. The heavy cleaners also collect the heavy trash which accumulates in the chemistry laboratories and the architecture drafting rooms.

The light cleaners' perception of the distinction between their duties and those of the heavy cleaners has manifested itself in other ways as well. Seven light cleaners applied for and were accepted as heavy cleaners when Columbia first opened the heavy cleaner category to women in 1972. On-the-job training commenced. By the end of 7 weeks, 4 of the 7 had transferred back to light cleaning. No light cleaners have applied for heavy cleaner openings posted since that time. At trial several light cleaners testified that they had not applied for heavy cleaning positions because heavy

---

[7]The Transport Workers' Union is the exclusive bargaining agent for all of Columbia's custodial and maintenance employees.

cleaning tasks were beyond their capacity. As one of them put it, "I cannot do a heavier job than I have already."

...

III.

Since job content is a matter determined by the particular employer, whether two job classifications entail "equal work" under the Act necessarily must be decided on a case-by-case basis. *Brennan v. Prince William Hospital Corp.*, 503 F.2d 282, 286 (4 Cir. 1974). The burden of proving that "equal work" is involved is on the Secretary. *Corning Glass Works v. Brennan*, 417 U.S. 188, 195 (1974). But in meeting that burden the Secretary does not have to prove that the duties performed are identical. A violation of the Act may be proven if the "skill, effort, and responsibility" required in the performance of the jobs is "substantially equal." *Hodgson v. Corning Glass Works,* 474 F.2d 226, 234 (1973). One court has suggested a balancing function in applying this "substantially equal" test:

> "[Congress] did not authorize the Secretary or the courts to engage in wholesale reevaluation of any employer's pay structure in order to enforce their own conceptions of economic worth .... But if courts defer to overly nice distinctions in job content, employers may evade the Act at will." *Brennan v. Prince William Hospital Corp., supra*, 503 F.2d at 285.

The "equal effort" criterion — the principal issue in the instant case — has been elaborated upon extensively in prior cases and in the interpretive bulletin promulgated by the Secretary. 29 C.F.R. § § 800.114-800.163 (1976). Under the Act, "effort" is the physical or mental exertion required in performing a job. So long as the ultimate degree of exertion remains comparable, the mere fact that two jobs call for effort different in kind will not render them unequal. *Brennan v. South Davis Community Hospital*, 538 F.2d 859, 863-64 (10 Cir. 1976). Nor will effort expended on additional tasks assigned to male employees necessarily suffice to justify a pay differential. If the additional tasks do not consume a significant total amount of all of the employees' time; or if female employees also perform duties which require additional effort, *Brennan v. Prince William Hospital Corp., supra*, 503 F.2d at 286; or if third persons who perform the additional tasks as their primary job are paid less than the male employees in question, see *Shultz v. Wheaton Glass Co., supra*, 421 F.2d at 266 — in these situations the additional effort is insufficient to differentiate the male positions under the Act.

... The Secretary contends on the facts of this case that the application of these rules requires reversal. His argument has two prongs. First, he argues that, notwithstanding the differences between the particular tasks performed by the heavy and light cleaners, they ultimately expend equivalent amounts of effort. What the light cleaners save in not having to deal with heavy equipment, so the argument goes, they expend in having to cover larger areas and in handling additional fixtures and furniture.[10] Second, he attacks the significance the district court attached to the heavy cleaners' heavier equipment. According to the Secretary, there is "nothing in the record ... to support the court's assumption ... that the [heavy cleaners'] equipment ... which was either used for infrequent periods or in combination with other [heavy cleaners] or was on wheels and could be moved easily, required any greater effort."

Turning to the first prong, it is true that the light cleaners cover a great deal of ground each night. But the evidence of distribution of work assignments among the buildings shows that the amount of ground covered by the heavy cleaners, while less extensive by some number of square feet not specified by the Secretary, cannot be dismissed so easily. The very heavy cleaners the Secretary singles out as responsible for small areas testified to difficulties in completing their daily assignments. Moreover the Secretary's own expert witness testified that the heavy cleaners' corridors, lobbies, stairways, elevators and lavatories collect a greater concentration of dirt than do the light cleaners' offices and classrooms and hence require greater cleaning effort.

As for the second prong, we believe that the district court attached appropriate significance to the heavy cleaners' equipment. The record clearly supports the inference that the heavy cleaners' principal task of wet mopping heavily traversed areas requires greater physical effort than wielding dust mops and rags. This is true not only because the surfaces are dirtier but also because the equipment is substantially bulkier and heavier.

The concept of "effort" in the Act is straightforward. It calls for a direct comparison of the amount of physical exertion required by the jobs; there is no factor added to compensate for physiological differences between men and women. Based on our careful review of the record before us, we cannot say that the district court was

---

[10]The mainstay of the Secretary's argument in this respect is a comparison between the daily responsibilities of two light cleaners and those of two heavy cleaners assigned to the public lavatories in the same academic building. Specifically, a light cleaner responsible for 60 library "cubicles," 8 carpeted offices, 5 other rooms, a classroom, a private toilet, and a flight of stairs, is compared with a heavy cleaner responsible for the 16 public lavatories, ranging in size from 1 toilet and sink to 4 toilets and sinks, and the trash detail in a building used by 10,000 people daily.

clearly erroneous in making this direct comparison and in finding as a fact that heavy cleaning involves "greater effort".

We are mindful of other cases which, in applying the Act to janitors and maids who perform the same general cleaning duties as Columbia's heavy and light cleaners, have held that the jobs involve substantially equal effort. *Brennan v. South Davis Community Hospital, supra*, 538 F.2d at 863-64; *Brennan v. Goose Creek Consolidated Independent School District*, 519 F.2d 53, 58 (5 Cir. 1975); *Brennan v. Board of Education, Jersey City, New Jersey, supra*, 374 F. Supp. at 828-29; but see *Marshall v. Marist College*, No. 74 Civ. 4713-LWP (S.D.N.Y. June 30, 1977). Close scrutiny of the facts of these cases, however, shows that the division of duties in the instant case is materially different. The cited cases follow the fact pattern which has emerged as the dominant one in cases under the Act involving all types of work. The central fact is the sharing of common responsibilities by male and female workers. The most frequently litigated question is whether additional lifting, fetching, hauling or other tasks performed by men require an amount of additional effort sufficient to foreclose a holding of substantial equality under the Act. For the most part the cases have concluded that the additional duties are either too insubstantial in amount or too inconsistently assigned to measure up to the Act's standard of substantial equality.[11]

In the instant case, by contrast, the male employees' duties consistently require greater effort. Columbia's job classifications cannot be equated with the makeweight

---

[11]In *Brennan v. South Davis Community Hospital, supra*, the janitors and maids performed common duties, except that the janitors (1) occasionally operated a floor stripping machine; (2) refilled a soft drink machine; (3) carried trash cans to an outside receptacle; (4) used ladders; and (5) shoveled snow. The maids also worked on ladders, occasionally carried trash, and had additional cleaning duties not shared with the janitors. The Tenth Circuit, while recognizing that the janitors' additional duties did require "extra effort", found the amount too insubstantial to preclude the Act's application. 538 F.2d at 863-864.

Brennan v. Goose Creek Consolidated Independent School District, supra, was to the same effect. There the employer's job description somewhat resembled the actual division of duties at Columbia. But in practice the janitors and maids did almost identical work. 519 F.2d at 58.

In *Brennan v. Board of Education, Jersey City, New Jersey, supra*, the maids and janitors both performed the basic wet mopping, sweeping, and dusting in classrooms, corridors and lavatories. The court found the janitors' yard work, snow removal, ladder work, light hauling and floor stripping either too incidental to overcome the basis in "common chores [performed] for the bulk of the workday" or balanced by additional tasks assigned to the maids. 374 F. Supp. at 828-29.

....

classifications so frequently found in the prior cases. See *Angelo v. Bacharach Instrument Co.*, 555 F.2d 1164, 1172 & n.11 (3 Cir. 1977). Moreover, since the "additional" duties of Columbia's heavy cleaners in fact comprise their entire jobs, the increment of effort involved is more "substantial" than that involved in any of the cases cited above.

  Both management and employees at Columbia for more than 30 years have recognized the existence of a material difference in the amount of effort required by heavy and light cleaning. The job classifications here involved never were entirely sex-based. Ever since 1949, long before most heavy cleaning positions were opened to women on an equal basis, Columbia has paid heavy cleaners' wages to women employed in tasks equivalent to those performed by the male cleaners. See note 5 *supra*. The record shows that the light cleaners are cognizant of the difference. It supports a finding that even today it is the additional effort demanded of heavy cleaning which has deterred the vast majority of Columbia's light cleaners from availing themselves of the opportunity to eliminate the 45 cent hourly disparity in pay.

  Based on this evidence of the understanding and experience of those most closely involved, together with the undisputed fact that heavy cleaning calls for greater effort, we hold that heavy and light cleaning are not substantially equal work within the meaning of the Act.

  In reaching this conclusion we have excluded from consideration the comparatively small number of heavy cleaners assigned to off-campus office buildings who perform work identical to that performed by the light cleaners on campus. On the face of it, this recently created category of heavy cleaners would fall within the frequently cited rule mentioned above that additional tasks must "consume a significant amount of the time of *all* those whose pay differentials are to be justified in terms of them ...." *Hodgson v. Brookhaven General Hospital, supra*, 436 F.2d at 725.

  But assuming that this strict reading of the statute applies to the heavy cleaners assigned to off-campus buildings, even though the majority of the employees in the "male" classification perform work consistently demanding greater effort than that required in the "female" classification, an additional factor precludes its application here. Judge Owen found that the light cleaning in question is performed "alone at night in off-campus buildings located outside the University's security perimeter." Taken in the context of his opinion, this necessarily implies a further finding that the off-campus work is performed in more dangerous conditions. The record does show that solicitude for the safety of the light cleaners motivated Columbia to change the assignments.

Labor and Employment Law

These circumstances call for the application of the provision of the Act which permits pay differentials between work performed under dissimilar "working conditions". As defined by the Supreme Court in *Corning Glass Works v. Brennan, supra*, 417 U.S. at 202, this concept encompasses the "hazards" of employment. Specifically, "the physical hazards regularly encountered, their frequency, and the severity of injury they can cause" are taken into account. *Id.* This case does not involve the dangers of a machine on an assembly line, but the risk of exposure to urban crime faced by women working alone and unguarded in the middle of the night. So long as the hazard is a genuine one, however, its source is not determinative under the Act.

True, the record here does not show that any light cleaner, on or off campus, has been a victim of crime while on the job. One court has demanded such tangible proof of a hazard's existence before applying the "working conditions" provision of the Act. See *Hodgson v. Daisy Manufacturing Co.*, 317 F. Supp. 538, 543-44 (W.D. Ark. 1970). In the instant case however we hold that the imposition of such a threshold requirement would be unreasonable. Columbia, a great university forced to cope with the sometimes uncongenial contemporary urban environment, is entitled to recognition of the preventive measures it takes. Moreover the university's good faith in this matter is not open to question. Only genuine concern could have motivated it to increase its custodial costs and, barely two months before the instant action was commenced, risk an adverse legal impact. Indeed, the Secretary has described Columbia's action in reassigning these buildings to the heavy cleaners as "laudable".

Nor do we attach significance to the fact that the heavy cleaners have not had these off-campus assignments during the indefinite past. Any other interpretation of the Act would deter employers who maintain job classifications in compliance with the Act from taking corrective action once they conclude that some existing security or safety arrangement is unsatisfactory.

Affirmed.

QUESTIONS FOR REFLECTION

1. How should effort on jobs be compared? In particular, should the comparison be made at the bottom line, that is, the total energy expended by workers, or should the comparison be made on a task-by-task basis?

2. In comparing effort, should the relative size and strength of the workers be taken into account? Suppose a woman performing light cleaning burns 3,000 calories, and a man performing heaving cleaning burns 4,000 calories. She weighs 120 pounds, and he weighs 160 pounds. They report being equally fatigued at the end of their shifts. Is their work equal?

3. Suppose 10 men hold job M and are paid $x per hour while 10 women hold job W and are paid $x-1 per hour. The duties of 8 of the men require more effort than the duties of all the women, but the duties of 2 of the men are substantially equal to the duties of the women. Has the employer violated the Equal Pay Act?

4. The court mentioned that some men performed light cleaning tasks in buildings off campus, but these jobs were classified as heavy cleaning. Why did the court find this permissible?

5. The Equal Pay Act was passed when it was still lawful for an employer to segregate jobs by sex. State and federal legislation has since outlawed job segregation, and employers have responded by opening jobs to members of both sexes. Therefore, if two jobs are equal but one pays better than the other, a woman in the lower-paying job may switch to the higher-paying job. Has the Equal Pay Act become an anachronism?

Ω

Discrimination Based on

Race, Color, Religion, Sex, or National Origin:

Title VII of the Civil Rights Act of 1964

Disparate Treatment

Introduction

Two principal methods of proving discrimination have evolved under Title VII of the Civil Rights Act of 1964. The first is known as **disparate treatment.**[a] It refers to intentionally denying a person an employment opportunity on the basis of the person's race, color, religion, sex, or national origin.[b] For example, an employer is guilty of disparate treatment for refusing to promote Wu to supervisor because, though she is qualified for the job, the employer believes that women should not supervise men, or cannot supervise them effectively.

Intent is crucial in a disparate treatment case. Workers are denied employment opportunities for many reasons, and Title VII is indifferent to most of those reasons. Title VII may be invoked only if the employer intentionally denies a worker an employment opportunity because of the worker's race or gender. Thus, if the employer decides not to promote Wu because she is active in the union, the NLRB might be interested, but not the EEOC. Similarly, if the employer's reason is Wu's age or disability, Title VII is not violated, though another statute might be.[c]

In the following case the court does not lay out the prima facie case of disparate treatment. Nevertheless, much of the prima facie case can be inferred from the court's opinion. To do this, the student should ask oneself, which facts in the case were material, that is,

---

[a]The other definition is called "disparate impact." We will consider it in a subsequent case.

[b]For convenience, we will use the term "race or gender" to refer to all of these bases.

[c]Disparate treatment is also a definition of discrimination under other civil rights statutes such as the Age Discrimination in Employment Act and the Americans with Disabilities Act.

ii   *Slack v. Havens*

which facts should any plaintiff in an employment
discrimination case need to prove?

Slack v. Havens
7 FEP Cases 885 (S.D. CA, 1973)

GORDON THOMPSON, JR.:—This action is brought by the plaintiffs, four Black women, who allege they were discriminatorily discharged due to their race, in violation of the Civil Rights Act of 1964.... Plaintiffs seek back pay or lost compensation ... and injunctive relief.

Defendant, a sole proprietor doing business as Havens Industries (hereinafter Industries), was the employer of the plaintiffs on February 1, 1968, the date plaintiffs' employment was terminated....

Following trial in this matter by the court sitting without a jury, counsel for the parties filed proposed findings of fact and conclusions of law. Having considered the evidence, oral argument and all the records of this case, the Court makes the following findings of fact and conclusions of law.

A. Findings of Fact

...

4. On January 31, 1968, plaintiffs Berrel Matthews, Emily Hampton and Isabell Slack were working in the bonding and coating department of defendant Industries' plant, engaged in preparing and assembling certain tubing components for defendant's product. A white co-worker, Sharon Murphy, was also assigned to the bonding and coating department on that day and was performing the same general work as the three plaintiffs mentioned above. The fourth plaintiff Kathleen Hale, was working in another department on January 31st.

Near the end of the working day, plaintiffs Matthews, Hampton and Slack were called together by their immediate supervisor, Ray Pohasky, and informed that the following morning, upon reporting to work, they would suspend regular production and engage in a general cleanup of the bonding and coating department. The cleanup was to consist of washing walls and windows whose sills were approximately 12 to 15 feet above the floor, cleaning light fixtures, and scraping the floor, which was caked with deposits of hardened resin. Plaintiffs Matthews, Hampton and Slack protested the assigned work, arguing that it was not within their job description, which included only light cleanup in their immediate work areas, and that it was too hard and dangerous. Mr. Pohasky agreed that it was hard work and said that he would check to see if they had to do it.

iv   *Slack v. Havens*

5.   On the following work day, February 1, 1968, plaintiffs Matthews, Hampton and Slack reported to the bonding and coating department along with Sharon Murphy, their white co-worker.   However, Mr. Pohasky excused Sharon Murphy to another department for the day, calling in plaintiff Kathleen Hale from the winding department where she had been on loan from the bonding and coating department for about a week.   Mr. Pohasky then repeated his announcement that the heavy cleaning would have to be done.   The four plaintiffs joined in protest against the heavy cleanup work.   They pointed out that they had not been hired to do janitorial type work, and one of the plaintiffs inquired as to why Sharon Murphy had been excused from the cleanup detail even though she had very little seniority among the ladies in the bonding and coating department.   In reply, they were told by Mr. Pohasky that they would do the work, "or else."   There was uncontradicted testimony that at sometime during their conversation Pohasky injected the statement, "Colored people should stay in their places," or words to that effect.   Some further discussion took place between plaintiffs and Pohasky and then with Gary Helming, plaintiffs' general supervisor, but eventually each of the plaintiffs was taken to the office of Mr. Helming where she was given her final paycheck and fired.   Plaintiff Matthews testified without contradiction that on the way to Mr. Helming's office Mr. Pohasky made the comment, "Colored folks are hired to clean because they clean better."

6.   The general cleanup work was later performed by newly-hired male employees.   Sharon Murphy was never asked to participate in this cleanup before or after the plaintiff termination.

7.   The day following the plaintiffs' firing, a conference was held between plaintiffs and defendant Glenn G. Havens, together with Mr. Helming, Mr. Pohasky and other company officials, but the dispute was not resolved as to the work plaintiffs were expected to do.   Apparently, the plaintiffs were offered reinstatement if they would now agree to do the same cleanup work.   They refused.

8.   Sometime later plaintiffs Matthews and Hampton received telephone calls from Mr. Helming in which he invited them to come back to the plant for job interviews.   However, neither plaintiff was extended a firm job offer.   Both declined the invitation for an interview, plaintiff Hampton expressing her attitude that all four plaintiffs should be rehired in their former jobs.

...

B. Conclusions of Law

Having concluded that defendant Industries is an "employer" under Title VII of the Civil Rights Act for the purposes of this action, we must next consider whether plaintiffs' termination amounted to unlawful discrimination against them because of their race. Defendants deny that the facts support such a conclusion, contending that plaintiffs' case amounts to nothing more than a dispute as to their job classification.

Admittedly, the majority of the discussion between plaintiffs and Industries' management on January 31 and February 1, 1968 centered around the nature of the duties which plaintiffs were ordered to perform. Plaintiffs pointed out that they had not been hired with the understanding that they would be expected to perform more than light cleanup work immediately adjacent to their work stations. They were met with an ultimatum that they do the work–or else. Additionally, no explanation was offered as to why Sharon Murphy, a white co-worker, had been transferred out of the bonding and coating department the morning that the heavy cleaning was to begin there, while plaintiff Hale was called back from the winding department, where she had been working, to the bonding and coating area, specifically for participation in the general cleanup. It is not disputed that Sharon Murphy had less seniority than all of the plaintiffs except plaintiff Hale (having been hired 8 days prior to plaintiff Hale) and no evidence of a bona fide business reason was ever educed by defendants as to why Sharon Murphy was excused from assisting the plaintiffs in the proposed cleaning project.

The only evidence that did surface at the trial regarding the motives for the decisions of the management of defendant Industries consisted of certain statements by supervisor Pohasky, who commented to plaintiff Matthews, "Colored folks were hired to clean because they clean better," and "Colored folks should stay in their place," or words to that effect. Defendants attempt to disown these statements with the argument that Pohasky's state of mind and arguably discriminatory conduct were immaterial and not causative of the plaintiffs' discharge.

But defendants cannot be allowed to divorce Mr. Pohasky's conduct from that of Industries so easily. First of all, § 701(b) expressly includes "any agent" of an employer within the definition of "employer." Secondly, there was a definite causal relation between Pohasky's apparently discriminatory conduct and the firings. Had Pohasky not discriminated against the plaintiffs by demanding they perform work he would not require of a white female employee, they would not have been faced with the unreasonable choice of having to choose between obeying his discriminatory work order and the loss of their employment. Finally, by backing up Pohasky's ultimatum, the top level management of Industries ratified his discriminatory conduct and must be held liable for the consequences thereof.

Slack v. Havens

Furthermore, defendants' contention that no top level management officials of Industries intended to discriminate against the plaintiffs is irrelevant.... [A]s District Judge McMillan put it in *United States v. Central Motor Lines, Inc.*, 338 F.Supp. 532 (W.D.N.C. 1971) at p. 559:

> In cases under Title VII, the "intent" required by the statute may be inferred from the defendants' conduct. The statute requires only that a defendant has meant to do what was done; that is, the act or practice must not be accidental.

From all the evidence before it, this Court is compelled to find that defendant Industries, through its managers and supervisor, Mr. Pohasky, meant to require the plaintiffs to perform the admittedly heavy and possibly dangerous work of cleaning the bonding and coating department when they would not require the same work from plaintiffs' white fellow employee. Furthermore, it meant to enforce that decision by firing the plaintiffs when they refused to perform that work. The consequence of the above was racial discrimination....

C. The Measure of Damages.

The Act provides that in computing back pay,

> ... interim earnings or amounts earnable with reasonable diligence by ... persons discriminated against shall operate to reduce the back pay otherwise allocable.[a]

...

...

Overriding all other considerations, of course, is the traditional legal principle that an aggrieved party should always seek to mitigate his or her damages. This principle applies to damages in Civil Rights Act cases, since the provisions for back pay are "not a penalty imposed as a sanction for moral turpitude," but as "compensation for the tangible economic loss resulting from an unlawful employment practice." *Robinson v. Lorillard Corp.*, 444 F.2d at 804. It, therefore, stands to reason that if the loss results from the employee's failure to mitigate, it should not be passed on to the employer.

---

[a]This passage now appears in § 706(g) of Title VII.

D. Individual Claims for Back Pay.

Isabell Slack: In the plaintiffs' brief on damages, plaintiff Slack claims that if she had not been wrongfully discharged by defendant Industries, she would have received at least $14,817.60 in wages from the period February 1, 1968 through January 17, 1972, the date chosen by plaintiff as the time when the corporate defendant Industries would no longer be in a position to employ her. To offset that amount plaintiff Slack admits to having received $13,040.00 in income exclusively from her employment at a cleaner's in Los Angeles. She testified that she found that job in January 1969 after seeking work in San Diego without success. She assesses her damages, therefore, at $1,777.60.

However, this fails to take into account that during April and May of 1968 plaintiff Matthews earned $692.00 and during the month of December 1968 plaintiff Hale earned $105.00. In the Court's opinion, plaintiff Slack's award should be further reduced by the sum of these figures or $797.00 as an amount "earnable with reasonable diligence." The total amount of plaintiff Slack's award should thus be $980.00

Kathleen Hale: This plaintiff claims that she would have received $14,420.00 if she had been permitted to remain in the employ of Industries and its successors. The Court's computations set plaintiff Hale's income during that period at $6,781.60 and ... would add $428.00 to that figure as "amounts earnable with reasonable diligence," in view of the additional amount earned by plaintiff Matthews during the period 1969-1970 while living in San Diego. Plaintiff Hale's award then should equal $7,210.40 since the Court is satisfied she otherwise acted diligently to mitigate her damages.

Berrell Matthews and Emily Hampton: Plaintiffs Matthews and Hampton were both telephoned less than a month after their termination and invited to return for an interview at Industries to discuss a position which was then available. Both refused to go for an interview, indicating that they were interested in nothing less than a full reinstatement of all four of the plaintiffs.

Whatever they believed to be their ultimate rights in this case under the Civil Rights Act, the plaintiffs were under an immediate duty to mitigate their economic losses. Given this opportunity for potential employment, these plaintiffs chose to ignore it for their own reasons. Such insistence on all or nothing may seem to some heroic. But the law recognizes only the reasonable man or woman, and in this statute, Congress seems to have codified this attitude in its reference to "amounts earnable with reasonable diligence." ... By failing to give the defendant an opportunity to set things right or at least to minimize its potential exposure, these plaintiffs also failed to mitigate their damages and cannot be heard to claim full back pay in the absence of a showing that they were ready, willing and available for work.

In light of the above, the Court concludes that plaintiffs Matthews and Hampton should be awarded the equivalent of six weeks' pay, six weeks being calculated to constitute a reasonable period of time within which defendant Industries could have interviewed each plaintiff and processed her for reemployment, had it been granted the opportunity to do so. In plaintiff Matthew's case, that amounts to $504.00 (assuming the revised wage of $2.10 per hour), and in plaintiff Hampton's case $468.00.

....

QUESTIONS FOR REFLECTION

1. The court held the employer responsible for the acts and statements of the supervisor, Pohasky. Was this fair? Do you think Pohasky himself should have been liable to the plaintiffs?

2. In large part, the parties to <u>Slack</u> agreed on the controlling rules of law; thus, there is little mediated application of law to fact, and most of the case involves direct application. Two issues of direct application were vigorously contested: causation (motive) and damages (back pay).

The court's opinion indicates that the employer contested the element of causation. Did race motivate the employer to assign the plaintiffs to heavy cleaning and to discharge them when they refused to do the work? If so, the plaintiffs were discriminated against. If not — for example, if the assignment to heavy cleaning had been motivated by the honest belief of the supervisor, Pohasky, that the plaintiffs, as individuals, were better suited to do the work than other employees were — the plaintiffs were not discriminated against. Both sides introduced evidentiary facts on the issue of causation, and used those facts in arguments. The evidentiary facts used by the plaintiffs were statements by Pohasky, who said, "Colored folks are hired to clean because they clean better" and "Colored folks should stay in their place." The court tells us that the employer responded that Pohasky's statements did not lead to the plaintiffs' discharge. Evidently, the employer argued that the plaintiffs were discharged because they refused to perform the work assigned to them. The evidentiary facts incorporated in the employer's argument were that the plaintiffs refused to do the work and that it was the employer's policy to fire any worker who refused to perform an assigned task.

The employer's argument raises the question, may a worker refuse to obey an illegal order? In the present context, may an employer discipline a worker for refusing to obey an order that violates Title VII?

3. Back pay was an issue in the case. It appears that the parties agreed on the legal standard: a victim of discrimination must mitigate the employer's damages;

that is, the victim must use reasonable diligence in looking for another job, and the money which the worker actually earned, or could reasonably have earned, will be deducted from the award of back pay. Is this the best standard?   What purpose(s) does it serve?   (Same question: what effects does it have?) Is there another standard that would better serve the purposes of the statute?

4. A few weeks after their discharges, Matthews and Hampton received calls from the firm, inviting them to a job interview. Both declined to attend, saying that all the women stood together and the employer had to rehire all of them or none of them; as the result, the court denied Matthews and Hampton back pay for the period of time after the calls. Was the judge's ruling fair?

5. Should the plaintiffs have been awarded "general damages" for the insult and humiliation of racial discrimination? Should they have been awarded punitive damages to punish this employer and deter others?

Ω

Sexual Harassment

Introduction

Title VII prohibits disparate treatment on the basis of sex. As we saw in <u>Slack v. Havens</u>, disparate treatment means intentionally denying an employment opportunity to a person because of the person's race or sex. A raise in pay is an employment opportunity; so is a promotion. If a person is denied a raise in pay or a promotion because of one's race or sex, the employer has violated Title VII. The working environment is also an employment opportunity. If a person is treated less favorably on the job than a person of the opposite sex, for example, subjected to physical or verbal abuse, the employer has violated Title VII.[a]

Two common misconceptions about sexual harassment need to be discarded. The first misconception is that sexual harassment comes in two varieties. It is true that, in the past, lower courts divided sexual harassment into two types of claim, depending on the type of opportunity which the victim was denied. If the victim was denied a specific opportunity such as a job, a promotion, or a raise, the claim was called "quid pro quo" sexual harassment.[b] The idea was that the woman was required to provide sexual favors as the quid pro quo for the opportunity and, when she declined, she was denied the opportunity. If the victim was denied a less specific opportunity such as being treated as respectfully as men were treated, the claim was called "hostile environment" sexual harassment. The Supreme Court, however, has disapproved of this distinction. In determining whether the statute has been violated, the issue in every case is whether the plaintiff was denied an employment opportunity because of one's sex, and the nature of the opportunity that was denied is not relevant.

The second misconception grows out of the two meanings of the word "sex": it means (a) an act of sex,

---

[a]Sexual harassment usually involves a man harassing a woman, and for this reason the victims in our examples will be women. But Title VII protects men as well as women from sex discrimination, and there have been female-on-male cases.

[b]Such an opportunity is commonly, but erroneously, called a "tangible" opportunity.

and (b) a person's status as a male or a female. Sex
discrimination has to do with status as a male or a
female, not with the act of sex; accordingly, sexual
harassment, as a kind of sex discrimination, has to do
with status as a male or a female. Thus, although sexual
harassment is often linked to acts of sex, such as
unwelcome touching or off-color speech, sexual harassment
that is not linked to acts of sex is also illegal. For
example, suppose the only female manager in an office is
criticized by her supervisor in public, whereas the male
managers are criticized in private. Further, the
supervisor uses rude (but not sexual) language in
reference to the woman, but not in reference to men, and
addresses the woman by her first name, but the men by
their surnames. This is sexual harassment, though acts
of sex are not involved.[c]

   The following case addresses a number of issues that
have arisen as Title VII has been applied to sexual
harassment on the job. It was decided before the Supreme
Court disapproved of the distinction between quid pro quo
and hostile environment sexual harassment, but the case
is instructive nonetheless.

---

[c]Given this confusion, a number of legal scholars and
practitioners speak of "gender discrimination" and "gender
harassment." However, we will refer to "sex discrimination"
because the statutes use the term "sex" and because the word
"gender" is a linguistic term referring to the rule of grammar
in some languages, such as Spanish, that nouns, verbs, and
adjectives are masculine, feminine, or neuter.

Rabidue v. Osceola Refining Co.
805 F.2d 611 (6th Cir. 1986)

Krupansky, Circuit Judge:——The plaintiff Vivienne Rabidue timely appealed the district court's judgment in favor of defendant Osceola Refining Co. (Osceola), a division of Texas-American Petrochemicals, Inc. (defendant or Texas-American), after a bench trial on plaintiff's charges of sex discrimination and sexual harassment....

A review of the record disclosed that the plaintiff entered the employ of Osceola during December of 1970....

The plaintiff initially occupied the job classification of executive secretary. In that position, she performed a variety of duties, which included attending the telephone, typing, and a limited amount of bookkeeping. In 1973, the plaintiff was promoted to the position of administrative assistant and became a salaried rather than hourly employee. Her new position entitled her to a longer lunch hour, more liberal vacation allowances, together with various other benefits. In her position of administrative assistant, the plaintiff was responsible for, among other duties, purchasing office supplies, monitoring and/or distributing incoming governmental regulations, and contacting customers. Subsequently, she was assigned additional duties as credit manager and office manager. Included in the plaintiff's new responsibilities was the authority to assign work to a number of other Osceola employees.

The plaintiff was a capable, independent, ambitious, aggressive, intractable, and opinionated individual. The plaintiff's supervisors and co-employees with whom plaintiff interacted almost uniformly found her to be an abrasive, rude, antagonistic, extremely willful, uncooperative, and irascible personality. She consistently argued with co-workers and company customers in defiance of supervisor direction and jeopardized Osceola's business relationships with major oil companies. She disregarded supervisory instruction and company policy whenever such direction conflicted with her personal reasoning and conclusions. In sum, the plaintiff was a troublesome employee.

The plaintiff's charged sexual harassment arose primarily as a result of her unfortunate acrimonious working relationship with Douglas Henry. Henry was a supervisor of the company's key punch and computer section. Occasionally, the plaintiff's duties required coordination with Henry's department and personnel, although Henry exercised no supervisory authority over the plaintiff nor the plaintiff over him. Henry was an extremely vulgar and crude individual who customarily made obscene comments about women generally, and, on occasion, directed such obscenities to the plaintiff. Management was aware of Henry's vulgarity, but had been unsuccessful in curbing his offensive personality traits during the time

544

Rabidue v. Osceola

encompassed by this controversy. The plaintiff and Henry, on the occasions when their duties exposed them to each other, were constantly in a confrontation posture. The plaintiff, as well as other female employees, were annoyed by Henry's vulgarity. In addition to Henry's obscenities, other male employees from time to time displayed pictures of nude or scantily clad women in their offices and/or work areas, to which the plaintiff and other women employees were exposed.

The plaintiff was formally discharged from her employment at the company on January 14, 1977 as a result of her many job-related problems, including her irascible and opinionated personality and her inability to work harmoniously with co-workers and customers. The immediate incidents that precipitated the plaintiff's termination included a heated argument with Charles Shoemaker, the vice-president of Osceola, concerning the implementation of certain accounting practices and procedures by the company and a subsequent, vitriolic confrontation with Robert Fitzsimmons, the vice-president of United Refineries, one of Osceola's major customers, concerning pricing schedules that existed between the companies. The latter incident proved to be highly embarrassing to Shoemaker, especially since the plaintiff intruded into his office while he was meeting with Fitzsimmons. A male employee assumed the plaintiff's former duties as administrative assistant.

...

[The Court of Appeals upheld the district court's finding that the plaintiff's discharge was not discriminatory and turned to her claim of sexual harassment due to a hostile environment.]

In addressing the issues presented by such a sexual harassment charge, this court's attention is initially directed to the guidelines issued by the Equal Employment Opportunity Commission (EEOC) as an informed source of instruction to assist its efforts to probe the parameters of Title VII sexual harassment. Those guidelines define sexual harassment in the following terms:

> (a) Harassment on the basis of sex is a violation of Sec. 703 of Title VII. Unwelcome sexual advances, requests for sexual favors, and other verbal or physical conduct of a sexual nature constitute sexual harassment when (1) submission to such conduct is made either explicitly or implicitly a term or condition of an individual's employment, (2) submission to or rejection of such conduct by an individual is used as the basis for employment decisions affecting such individual, or (3) such conduct has the purpose or effect of unreasonably interfering with an individual's work performance or creating an intimidating, hostile, or offensive working environment.

29 C.F.R. §1604.11(a) (footnote omitted).

After having considered the EEOC guidelines and after having canvassed existing legal precedent that has discussed the issue, this court concludes that a plaintiff, to prevail in a Title VII offensive work environment sexual harassment action, must assert and prove that: (1) the employee was a member of a protected class; (2) the employee was subjected to unwelcomed sexual harassment in the form of sexual advances, requests for sexual favors, or other verbal or physical conduct of a sexual nature; (3) the harassment complained of was based upon sex; (4) the charged sexual harassment had the effect of unreasonably interfering with the plaintiff's work performance and creating an intimidating, hostile, or offensive working environment that affected seriously the psychological well-being of the plaintiff; and (5) the existence of respondeat superior liability.

Thus, to prove a claim of abusive work environment premised upon sexual harassment, a plaintiff must demonstrate that she would not have been the object of harassment but for her sex. It is of significance to note that instances of complained of sexual conduct that prove equally offensive to male and female workers would not support a Title VII sexual harassment charge because both men and women were accorded like treatment.

Unlike *quid pro quo* sexual harassment which may evolve from a single incident, sexually hostile or intimidating environments are characterized by multiple and varied combinations and frequencies of offensive exposures, which characteristics would dictate an order of proof that placed the burden upon the plaintiff to demonstrate that injury resulted not from a single or isolated offensive incident, comment, or conduct, but from incidents, comments, or conduct that occurred with some frequency. To accord appropriate protection to both plaintiffs and defendants in a hostile and/or abusive work environment sexual harassment case, the trier of fact, when judging the totality of the circumstances impacting upon the asserted abusive and hostile environment placed in issue by the plaintiff's charges, must adopt the perspective of a reasonable person's reaction to a similar environment under essentially like or similar circumstances. Thus, in the absence of conduct which would interfere with that hypothetical reasonable individual's work performance and affect seriously the psychological well-being of that reasonable person under like circumstances, a plaintiff may not prevail on asserted charges of sexual harassment anchored in an alleged hostile and/or abusive work environment regardless of whether the plaintiff was actually offended by the defendant's conduct. Assuming that the plaintiff has successfully satisfied the burden of proving that the defendant's conduct would have interfered with a reasonable individual's work performance and would have affected seriously the psychological well-being of a reasonable employee, the particular plaintiff would nevertheless also be required to

Rabidue v. Osceola

demonstrate that she was actually offended by the defendant's conduct and that she suffered some degree of injury as a result of the abusive and hostile work environment.

Accordingly, a proper assessment or evaluation of an employment environment that gives rise to a sexual harassment claim would invite consideration of such objective and subjective factors as the nature of the alleged harassment, the background and experience of the plaintiff, her co-workers, and supervisors, the totality of the physical environment of the plaintiff's work area, the lexicon of obscenity that pervaded the environment of the workplace both before and after the plaintiff's introduction into its environs, coupled with the reasonable expectation of the plaintiff upon voluntarily entering that environment. Thus the presence of actionable sexual harassment would be different depending upon the personality of the plaintiff and the prevailing work environment and must be considered and evaluated upon an *ad hoc* basis. As Judge Newblatt aptly stated in his opinion in the district court:

> Indeed, it cannot seriously be disputed that in some work environments, humor and language are rough hewn and vulgar. Sexual jokes, sexual conversations and girlie magazines may abound. Title VII was not meant to—or can—change this. It must never be forgotten that Title VII is the federal court mainstay in the struggle for equal employment opportunity for the female workers of America. But it is quite different to claim that Title VII was designed to bring about a magical transformation in the social mores of American workers. Clearly, the Court's qualification is necessary to enable 29 C.F.R. §1604.11(a)(3) to function as a workable judicial standard.

Rabidue, 584 F.Supp. at 430.[5]

---

[5]Such an approach is not inconsistent with the EEOC guidelines, which emphasize the individualized nature of a probative inquiry:

> (b) In determining whether alleged conduct constitutes sexual harassment, the Commission will look at the record as a whole and at the totality of the circumstances, such as the nature of the sexual advances and the context in which the alleged incidents occurred. The determination of the legality of a particular action will be made from the facts, on a case by case basis.

29 C.F.R. §1604.11(b).

The dissent's focus on certain of the above factors in isolation is misplaced. The
(continued...)

...

In the case at bar, the record effectively disclosed that Henry's obscenities, although annoying, were not so startling as to have affected seriously the psyches of the plaintiff or other female employees. The evidence did not demonstrate that this single employee's vulgarity substantially affected the totality of the workplace. The sexually oriented poster displays had a *de minimis* effect on the plaintiff's work environment when considered in the context of a society that condones and publicly features and commercially exploits open displays of written and pictorial erotica at the newsstands, on prime-time television, at the cinema, and in other public places. In sum, Henry's vulgar language, coupled with the sexually oriented posters, did not result in a working environment that could be considered intimidating, hostile, or offensive under 29 C.F.R. §1604.11(a)(3) as elaborated upon by this court.[7] The district court's factual findings supporting its conclusion to this effect were not clearly erroneous. It necessarily follows that the plaintiff failed to sustain her burden of proof that she was the victim of a Title VII sexual harassment violation. Accordingly, the trial court's disposition of this issue is AFFIRMED.

---

[5](...continued)
district court possesses broad discretion as to the evidence to be considered in evaluating the totality of the circumstances and the context of the alleged incidents. This court has merely attempted to identify in general terms some criteria that may potentially enter into a case-by-case examination of the totality of the evidence in such a case, without inferring the weight to be accorded in the first instance by the district court to any particular factor.

[7]The precedential cases addressing a sexually hostile and abusive environment within the context of Title VII have all developed more compelling circumstances than are presented herein. In *Bundy v. Jackson,* 641 F.2d 934 (D.C. Cir. 1981), both the plaintiff's co-employees and supervisors harassed her with conduct that included continual personal and telephonic sexual propositions both at work and at her home and the plaintiff's complaints inspired her supervisor to also proposition her. 641 F.2d at 939-40. In *Henson v. Dundee,* 682 F.2d 897 (11th Cir. 1982), the plaintiff was subjected to numerous harangues and demeaning inquiries into her sexual proclivities, vulgarities, and repeated requests for sexual relations from her supervisor, the police chief. 682 F.2d at 899-901. In *Katz v. Dole,* 709 F.2d 251 (4th Cir. 1983), several supervisory personnel and co-workers bombarded the plaintiff with sexual slurs, insults, innuendo, and propositions, the plaintiff's complaints to her supervisor generated further harassment from him, and the plaintiff's supervisor admitted having heard co-workers direct obscenities to the plaintiff. 709 F.2d at 253-54. In the case at bar, the charges of sexually hostile and abusive environment were limited to pictorial calendar type office wall displays of semi-nude and nude females and Henry's off-color language. Unlike the facts of *Bundy, Henson,* and *Katz,* this case involved no sexual propositions, offensive touchings, or sexual conduct of a similar nature that was systematically directed to the plaintiff over a protracted period of time.

Rabidue v. Osceola

...

Keith, Circuit Judge, concurring in part, dissenting in part:

...

I dissent for several reasons. First, after review of the entire record I am firmly convinced, that although supporting evidence exists, the court is mistaken in affirming the findings that defendant's treatment of plaintiff evinced no anti-female animus and that gender-based discrimination played no role in her discharge. The overall circumstances of plaintiff's workplace evince an anti-female environment. For seven years plaintiff worked at Osceola as the sole woman in a salaried management position. In common work areas plaintiff and other female employees were exposed daily to displays of nude or partially clad women belonging to a number of male employees at Osceola. One poster, which remained on the wall for eight years, showed a prone woman who had a golf ball on her breasts with a man standing over her, golf club in hand, yelling "Fore." And one desk plaque declared, "Even male chauvinist pigs need love." Plaintiff testified the posters offended her and her female co-workers.

In addition, Computer Division Supervisor Doug Henry regularly spewed anti-female obscenity. Henry routinely referred to women as "whores," "cunt", "pussy" and "tits." Of plaintiff, Henry specifically remarked, "All that bitch needs is a good lay" and called her "fat ass." Plaintiff arranged at least one meeting of female employees to discuss Henry and repeatedly filed written complaints on behalf of herself and other female employees who feared losing their jobs if they complained directly. Osceola Vice President Charles Muetzel stated that he knew that employees were "greatly disturbed" by Henry's language. However, because Osceola needed Henry's computer expertise, Muetzel did not reprimand or fire Henry. In response to subsequent complaints about Henry, a later supervisor, Charles Shoemaker, testified that he gave Henry "a little fatherly advice" about Henry's prospects if he learned to become "an executive type person."

In addition to tolerating this anti-female behavior, defendant excluded plaintiff, the sole female in management, from activities she needed to perform her duties and progress in her career. Plaintiff testified that unlike male salaried employees, she did not receive free lunches, free gasoline, a telephone credit card or entertainment privileges. Nor was she invited to the weekly golf matches. Without addressing defendant's disparate treatment of plaintiff, the district court dismissed these perks and business activities as fringe benefits. After plaintiff became credit manager, defendant prevented plaintiff from visiting or taking customers to lunch as all previous male credit managers had done. Plaintiff testified that upon requesting such privileges, her supervisor, Mr. Muetzel, replied that it would be improper for a woman to take male customers to lunch and that she "might have car trouble on the road." Plaintiff reported that on another occasion, Muetzel asked her, "How would it look for me, a married man, to take you, a divorced woman, to the West Branch Country Club in such a small town?" However, defendant apparently saw no problem in male managers entertaining female clients regardless of marital status. Plaintiff's subsequent supervisor, Charles Shoemaker, stated to another female worker, Joyce Solo, that "Vivienne [plaintiff] is doing a good job as credit manager, but we really need a man on that job," adding, "She can't take customers out to lunch." Aside from this Catch-22, Mr. Shoemaker also remarked plaintiff was not forceful enough to collect slow-paying jobs. How plaintiff can be so abrasive and aggressive as to require firing but too timid to collect delinquent accounts is, in my view, an enigma.

My review of the record also shows plaintiff was consistently accorded secondary status. Plaintiff recounted that at a meeting convened to instruct clerical employees on their duties after the United States Refineries takeover, plaintiff was seated with female hourly employees. The male salaried employees, apparently pre-informed of the post-takeover procedures, stood at the front of the room. Plaintiff confronted Muetzel to express surprise at being addressed as a clerical employee and to ask what her post-takeover role would entail. Muetzel responded plaintiff would have whatever role was handed to her. At the suggestion of her former boss, Mr. Hansen, plaintiff wrote a memo summarizing her qualifications and pleading for non-sex based consideration for post-takeover positions. She received no response to this memo.

In contrast to the supervisors' reluctance to address Henry's outrageous behavior, plaintiff was frequently told to tone down and discouraged from executing procedures she felt were needed to correct waste and improve efficiency as her job required. Not only did plaintiff receive minimal support, but she was repeatedly undermined. For example, supervisor Doug Henry once directed his employees to ignore plaintiff's procedures for logging time and invoices, a particularly damaging directive given plaintiff's responsibility of coordinating the work of Henry's computer staff. In another example, plaintiff returned from her vacation to find that none of the check depositing procedures agreed upon had been implemented and that some of her duties had been permanently transferred to the male who filled in during her vacation. In contrast to the fatherly advice and the praise for potential which Henry received, plaintiff was informed she had set her goals too high. After dismissal, but prior to final notice, plaintiff received instructions not to return to the refinery. In contrast, male employees fired for embezzlement were allowed to return to clean out their desks. Upon dismissal, plaintiff reported that Shoemaker advised her to get a secretarial job.

The record establishes plaintiff possessed negative personal traits. These traits did not, however, justify the sex-based disparate treatment recounted above. Whatever undesirable behavior plaintiff exhibited, it was clearly no worse than Henry's. I conclude the misogynous language and decorative displays tolerated at the refinery (which even the district court found constituted a "fairly significant" part of the job environment), the primitive views of working women expressed by Osceola supervisors and defendant's treatment of plaintiff as the only female salaried employee clearly evince anti-female animus.

...

Nor do I agree with the majority holding that a court considering hostile environment claims should adopt the perspective of the reasonable person's reaction to a similar environment. In my view, the reasonable person perspective fails to account for the wide divergence between most women's views of appropriate sexual conduct and those of men. ... I would have courts adopt the perspective of the reasonable victim which simultaneously allows courts to consider salient sociological differences as well as shield employers from the neurotic complainant. Moreover, unless the outlook of the reasonable woman is adopted, the defendants as well as the courts are permitted to sustain ingrained notions of reasonable behavior fashioned by the offenders, in this case, men.

Which brings me to the majority's mandate to consider the "prevailing work environment," "the lexicon of obscenity that pervaded the environment both before and after plaintiff's introduction into its environs," and plaintiff's reasonable expectations upon "voluntarily" entering that environment. The majority suggests through these factors that a woman assumes the risk of working in an abusive, anti-female environment. Moreover, the majority contends that such work environments somehow have an innate right to perpetuation and are not to be addressed under Title VII....

In my view, Title VII's precise purpose is to prevent such behavior and attitudes from poisoning the work environment of classes protected under the Act. To condone the majority's notion of the "prevailing workplace" I would also have to agree that if an employer maintains an anti-semitic workforce and tolerates a workplace in which "kike" jokes, displays of Nazi literature and anti-Jewish conversation "may abound," a Jewish employee assumes the risk of working there, and a court must consider such a work environment as "prevailing." I cannot. As I see it, job relatedness is the only additional factor which legitimately bears on the inquiry of plaintiff's reasonableness in finding her work environment offensive. In other words, the only additional question I would find relevant is whether the behavior complained of is required to perform the work. For example, depending on their job descriptions, employees of soft pornography publishers or other sex-related industries should reasonably expect exposure to nudity, sexually explicit language or even simulated sex as inherent aspects of working in that field. However, when that exposure goes beyond what is required professionally, even sex industry employees are protected under the Act from nonjob-related sexual demands, language or other offensive behavior by supervisors or co-workers. As I believe no woman should be subjected to an environment where her sexual dignity and reasonable sensibilities are visually, verbally or physically assaulted as a matter of prevailing male prerogative, I dissent.

The majority would also have courts consider the background of plaintiff's co-workers and supervisors in assessing the presence of actionable work environment sex harassment. The only reason to inquire into the backgrounds of the defendants or other co-workers is to determine if the behavior tolerated toward female employees is reasonable in light of those backgrounds. As I see it, these subjective factors create an unworkable standard by requiring the courts to balance a morass of perspectives. But more importantly, the background of the defendants or other workers is irrelevant. No court analyzes the background and experience of a supervisor who refuses to promote black employees before finding actionable race discrimination under Title VII. An equally disturbing implication of considering defendants' backgrounds is the notion that workplaces with the least sophisticated employees are the most prone to anti-female environments. Assuming *arguendo*[*] this notion is true, by applying the prevailing workplace factor, this court locks the vast majority of working women into workplaces which tolerate anti-female behavior. I conclude that for actionable offensive environment claims, the relevant inquiry is whether the conduct complained of is offensive to the reasonable woman. Either the environment affects her ability to perform or it does not. The backgrounds and experience of the defendant's supervisors and employees [are] irrelevant.

Nor can I agree with the majority's notion that the effect of pin-up posters and misogynous language in the workplace can have only a minimal effect on female employees and should not be deemed hostile or offensive "when considered in the context of a society that condones and publicly features and commercially exploits open displays of written and pictorial erotica at newsstands, on prime-time television, at the cinema and in other public places." "Society" in this scenario must primarily refer to the unenlightened; I hardly believe reasonable women condone the pervasive degradation and exploitation of female sexuality perpetuated in American culture. In fact, pervasive societal approval thereof and of other stereotypes stifles female potential and instills the debased sense of self worth which accompanies

---

[*]I do not assert any correlation exists between the level of social sophistication present in a work environment and anti-female behavior.

stigmatization. The presence of pin-ups and misogynous language in the workplace can only evoke and confirm the debilitating norms by which women are primarily and contemptuously valued as objects of male sexual fantasy. That some men would condone and wish to perpetuate such behavior is not surprising. However, the relevant inquiry at hand is what the reasonable woman would find offensive, not society, which at one point also condoned slavery. I conclude that sexual posters and anti-female language can seriously affect the psychological well being of the reasonable woman and interfere with her ability to perform her job.

....

QUESTIONS FOR REFLECTION

1. How significant should it be that the plaintiff in Rabidue voluntarily entered the environment?

2. Should the background of co-workers be taken into account in deciding whether sexual harassment has occurred?

3. The standard for determining whether an environment is abusive has both objective and subjective components. Regarding the objective component, should it be judged by the opinion of a "reasonable person" (as the majority held) or by the opinion of a "reasonable victim" (as the dissent advocated)?

4. What is the subjective component of the standard for determining whether an environment is abusive?

5. How severe must harassment be in order to violate Title VII? Was the majority right that harassment is not illegal unless it affects the psychological well being of the victim?

6. Suppose a supervisor is an "equal opportunity harasser," that is, the supervisor abuses men and women alike.
   (a) Does this violate Title VII?
   (b) Suppose the abuse is sexual in nature. The supervisor touches the private parts of both men and women and uses sexual language when speaking to or about both men and women. Does this violate Title VII?

7. How should the law treat same-sex sexual harassment, i.e., the case in which the harasser and the victim are the same sex?

Ω

Bona Fide Occupational Qualifications

Introduction

The affirmative defense to disparate treatment is the **bona fide occupational qualification** (bfoq).[a] Section 703(e) allows an employer to allocate employment opportunities among workers on the basis of sex, religion, or national origin if the characteristic is a bona fide occupational qualification reasonably necessary to the normal operation of that particular business or enterprise. Note that a finding that sex, etc. is a bfoq for one "particular employer or enterprise" does not mean that sex, etc. is a bfoq for another employer; because of the variation in jobs across firms, the statute requires that decisions be made on a case-by-case basis.

In some cases, whether a characteristic is a bfoq for a job has not been controversial. The female sex is plainly a bfoq for the job of modeling women's fashions.

Other cases have been more controversial. Many of these cases have involved sex. For example, airlines contended that the female sex was a bfoq for the job of flight attendant. Their argument was that customers preferred stewardesses. Various employers maintained that the male sex was a bfoq for jobs that are dangerous or strenuous. Their argument was that men were generally stronger and more willing to take risks than women. Although district courts sometimes accepted these arguments, the Courts of Appeals unanimously rejected them. See, for example, Diaz v. Pan American World Airways, 442 F.2d 385 (5th Cir. 1971). Fearing that the exception would swallow the rule if the bfoq clause were construed broadly, the appellate courts read the clause narrowly. They held that sex, religion, or national origin constitutes a bfoq only when the task in question

---

[a]An employer may also defend the case by attacking the elements of the plaintiff's case, for example, by challenging whether the plaintiff was qualified for the opportunity in question. This strategy is analogous to the defendant in a battery case who defends by trying to show that someone else struck the plaintiff or that the blow was not harmful or offensive.

is crucial to the business, all or substantially all members of the excluded class are unable to perform the task, and individual determinations of ability are impractical.

The following case is the first in which the Supreme Court expressed its view of how the bfoq clause should be interpreted. Familiarity with the doctrine of judicial notice will enhance one's appreciation of the case. **Judicial notice** allows a court to rely on a fact as to which there is no proof in the record. A court usually reserves judicial notice for indisputable facts such as the time of sunrise or the official residence of the pope. Does the majority take judicial notice of a fact in this case? If so, is it an appropriate fact to find without evidence in the record?

Dothard v. Rawlinson
433 U.S. 321 (1977)

Mr. Justice STEWART delivered the opinion of the Court.

Appellee Dianne Rawlinson sought employment with the Alabama Board of Corrections as a prison guard, called in Alabama a "correctional counselor." After her application was rejected, she brought this class suit under Title VII of the Civil Rights Act of 1964, alleging that she had been denied employment because of her sex in violation of federal law. A three-judge Federal District Court for the Middle District of Alabama decided in her favor. We noted probable jurisdiction of this appeal from the District Court's judgment.

I

At the time she applied for a position as correctional counselor trainee, Rawlinson was a 22-year-old college graduate whose major course of study had been correctional psychology. She was refused employment because she failed to meet the minimum 120-pound weight requirement established by an Alabama statute. The statute also establishes a height minimum of 5 feet, 2 inches.

After her application was rejected because of her weight, Rawlinson filed a charge with the Equal Employment Opportunity Commission, and ultimately received a right-to-sue letter. She then filed a complaint in the District Court on behalf of herself and other similarly situated women, challenging the statutory height and weight minima as violative of Title VII and the Equal Protection Clause of the Fourteenth Amendment.[b] A three-judge court was convened. While the suit was pending, the Alabama Board of Corrections adopted Administrative Regulation 204, establishing gender criteria for assigning correctional counselors to maximum-security institutions for "contact positions," that is, positions requiring continual close physical proximity to inmates of the institution. Rawlinson amended her class-action complaint by adding a challenge to Regulation 204 as also violative of Title VII and the Fourteenth Amendment.

Like most correctional facilities in the United States, Alabama's prisons are segregated on the basis of sex. Currently the Alabama Board of Corrections operates four major all-male penitentiaries — Holman Prison, Kilby Corrections Facility, G.K. Fountain Correction Center, and Draper Correctional Center. The Board also operates the Julia Tutwiler Prison for Women, the Frank Lee Youth Center, the Number Four

---

[b]{The Supreme Court's ruling on the plaintiff's challenge to the height and weight minima is printed separately below. — ed.}

Honor Camp, the State Cattle Ranch, and nine Work Release Centers, one of which is for women. The Julia Tutwiler Prison for Women and the four male penitentiaries are maximum-security institutions. Their inmate living quarters are for the most part large dormitories, with communal showers and toilets that are open to the dormitories and hallways. The Draper and Fountain penitentiaries carry on extensive farming operations, making necessary a large number of strip searches for contraband when prisoners re-enter the prison buildings.

A correctional counselor's primary duty within these institutions is to maintain security and control of the inmates by continually supervising and observing their activities. To be eligible for consideration as a correctional counselor, an applicant must possess a valid Alabama driver's license, have a high school education or its equivalent, be free from physical defects, be between the ages of 20½ years and 45 years at the time of appointment, and fall between the minimum height and weight requirements of 5 feet 2 inches and 120 pounds, and the maximum of 6 feet 10 inches and 300 pounds. Appointment is by merit, with a grade assigned each applicant based on experience and education. No written examination is given.

At the time this litigation was in the District Court, the Board of Corrections employed a total of 435 people in various correctional counselor positions, 56 of whom were women. Of those 56 women, 21 were employed at the Julia Tutwiler Prison for Women, 13 were employed in non-contact positions at the four male maximum-security institutions, and the remaining 22 were employed at the other institutions operated by the Alabama Board of Corrections. Because most of Alabama's prisoners are held at the four maximum-security male penitentiaries, 336 of the 435 correctional counselor jobs were in those institutions, a majority of them concededly in the "contact" classification. Thus, even though meeting the statutory height and weight requirements, women applicants could under Regulation 204 compete equally with men for only about 25% of the correctional counselor jobs available in the Alabama prison system.

...

III

... Regulation 204 explicitly discriminates against women on the basis of their sex. In defense of this overt discrimination, the appellants rely on § 703(e) of Title VII, which permits sex-based discrimination "in those certain instances where ... sex ... is a bona fide occupational qualification reasonably necessary to the normal operation of that particular business or enterprise."

The District Court rejected the bona fide occupational qualification (bfoq) defense, relying on the virtually uniform view of the federal courts that § 703(e) provides only the narrowest of exceptions to the general rule requiring equality of employment opportunities. This view has been variously formulated. In *Diaz v. Pan American World Airways*, 442 F.2d 385, 388, the Court of Appeals for the Fifth Circuit held that "discrimination based on sex is valid only when the *essence* of the business operation would be undermined by not hiring members of one sex exclusively." (Emphasis in original.) In an earlier case, *Weeks v. Southern Bell Tel. & Tel. Co.*, 408 F.2d 228, 235, the same court said that an employer could rely on the bfoq exception only by proving "that he had reasonable cause to believe, that is, a factual basis for believing, that all or substantially all women would be unable to perform safely and efficiently the duties of the job involved." But whatever the verbal formulation, the federal courts have agreed that it is impermissible under Title VII to refuse to hire an individual woman or man on the basis of stereotyped characterizations of the sexes, and the District Court in the present case held in effect that Regulation 204 is based on just such stereotypical assumptions.

We are persuaded — by the restrictive language of § 703(e), the relevant legislative history, and the consistent interpretation of the Equal Employment Opportunity Commission[19] — that the bfoq exception was in fact meant to be an extremely narrow exception to the general prohibition of discrimination on the basis of sex. In the particular factual circumstances of this case, however, we conclude that the District Court erred in rejecting the State's contention that Regulation 204 falls within the narrow ambit of the bfoq exception.

The environment in Alabama's penitentiaries is a peculiarly inhospitable one for human beings of whatever sex. Indeed, a Federal District Court has held that the conditions of confinement in the prisons of the State, characterized by "rampant violence" and a "jungle atmosphere," are constitutionally intolerable. *Pugh v. Locke*, 406 F.Supp. 318, 325 (M.D. Ala 1976). The record in the present case shows that because of inadequate staff and facilities, no attempt is made in the four maximum-security male penitentiaries to classify or segregate inmates according to their offense or level of dangerousness — a procedure that, according to expert testimony, is essential to effective penological administration. Consequently, the estimated 20% of the male prisoners who are sex offenders are scattered throughout the penitentiaries' dormitory facilities.

---

[19]The EEOC issued guidelines on sex discrimination in 1965 reflecting its position that "the bona fide occupational qualification as to sex should be interpreted narrowly." 29 CFR § 1604.2(a). It has adhered to that principle consistently, and its construction of the statute can accordingly be given weight.

In this environment of violence and disorganization, it would be an oversimplification to characterize Regulation 204 as an exercise in "romantic paternalism." In the usual case, the argument that a particular job is too dangerous for women may appropriately be met by the rejoinder that it is the purpose of Title VII to allow the individual woman to make that choice for herself. More is at stake in this case, however, than an individual woman's decision to weigh and accept the risks of employment in a "contact" position in a maximum-security male prison.

The essence of a correctional counselor's job is to maintain prison security. A woman's relative ability to maintain order in a male, maximum-security, unclassified penitentiary of the type Alabama now runs could be directly reduced by her womanhood. There is a basis in fact for expecting that sex offenders who have criminally assaulted women in the past would be moved to do so again if access to women were established within the prison. There would also be a real risk that other inmates, deprived of a normal heterosexual environment, would assault women guards because they were women.[22] In a prison system where violence is the order of the day, where inmate access to guards is facilitated by dormitory living arrangements, where every institution is understaffed, and where a substantial portion of the inmate population is composed of sex offenders mixed at random with other prisoners, there are few visible deterrents to inmate assaults on women custodians.

Appellee Rawlinson's own expert testified that dormitory housing for aggressive inmates poses a greater security problem than single-cell lockups, and further testified that it would be unwise to use women as guards in a prison where even 10% of the inmates had been convicted of sex crimes and were not segregated from the other prisoners.[23] The likelihood that inmates would assault a woman because she was a woman would pose a real threat not only to the victim of the assault but also to the basic control of the penitentiary and protection of its inmates and the other security personnel. The employee's very womanhood would thus directly undermine her capacity to provide the security that is the essence of a correctional counselor's responsibility.

---

[22] The record contains evidence of an attack on a female clerical worker in an Alabama prison, and of an incident involving a woman student who was taken hostage during a visit to one of the maximum-security institutions.

[23] Alabama's penitentiaries are evidently not typical. Appellee Rawlinson's two experts testified that in a normal, relatively stable maximum-security prison — characterized by control over the inmates, reasonable living conditions, and segregation of dangerous offenders — women guards could be used effectively and beneficially. Similarly, an *amicus* brief filed by the State of California attests to that State's success in using women guards in all-male penitentiaries.

Dothard v. Rawlinson (bfoq)   vii

There was substantial testimony from experts on both sides of this litigation that the use of women as guards in "contact" positions under the existing conditions in Alabama maximum-security male penitentiaries would pose a substantial security problem, directly linked to the sex of the prison guard. On the basis of that evidence, we conclude that the District Court was in error in ruling that being male is not a bona fide occupational qualification for the job of correctional counselor in a "contact" position in an Alabama male maximum-security penitentiary.[24]

The judgment is accordingly ... reversed in part, and the case is remanded to the District Court for further proceedings consistent with this opinion.

Mr. Justice MARSHALL, with whom Mr. Justice BRENNAN joins ... dissenting in part.

... I ... agree with much of the Court's general discussion in Part III of the bona-fide-occupational-qualification exception contained in § 703(e) of Title VII. The Court is unquestionably correct when it holds "that the bfoq exception was in fact meant to be an extremely narrow exception to the general prohibition of discrimination on the basis of sex." I must, however, respectfully disagree with the Court's application of the bfoq exception in this case.

The Court properly rejects two proffered justifications for denying women jobs as prison guards. It is simply irrelevant here that a guard's occupation is dangerous and that some women might be unable to protect themselves adequately. Those themes permeate the testimony of the state officials below, but as the Court holds, "the argument that a particular job is too dangerous for women" is refuted by the "purpose of Title VII to allow the individual woman to make that choice for herself." Some women, like some men, undoubtedly are not qualified and do not wish to serve as prison guards, but that does not justify the exclusion of all women from this employment opportunity. Thus, "[i]n the usual case," the Court's interpretation of the bfoq exception would mandate hiring qualified women for guard jobs in maximum-security institutions. The highly successful experiences of other States allowing such job opportunities confirm that absolute disqualification of women is not, in the words of Title VII, "reasonably necessary to the normal operation" of a maximum security prison.

---

[24]The record shows, by contrast, that Alabama's minimum-security facilities, such as work-release centers, are recognized by their inmates as privileged confinement situations not to be lightly jeopardized by disobeying applicable rules of conduct. Inmates assigned to these institutions are thought to be the "cream of the crop" of the Alabama prison population.

What would otherwise be considered unlawful discrimination against women is justified by the Court, however, on the basis of the "barbaric and inhumane" conditions in Alabama prisons, conditions so bad that state officials have conceded that they violate the Constitution. To me, this analysis sounds distressingly like saying two wrongs make a right. It is refuted by the plain words of § 703(e). The statute requires that a bfoq be "reasonably necessary to the normal operation of that particular business or enterprise." But no governmental "business" may operate "normally" in violation of the Constitution. Every action of government is constrained by constitutional limitations. While those limits may be violated more frequently than we would wish, no one disputes that the "normal operation" of all government functions takes place within them. A prison system operating in blatant violation of the Eighth Amendment is an exception that should be remedied with all possible speed, as Judge Johnson's comprehensive order in *Pugh v. Locke*, 406 F.Supp. 318 (M.D. Ala 1976), is designed to do. In the meantime, the existence of such violations should not be legitimatized by calling them "normal." Nor should the Court accept them as justifying conduct that would otherwise violate a statute intended to remedy age-old discrimination.

The Court's error in statutory construction is less objectionable, however, than the attitude it displays toward women. Though the Court recognizes that possible harm to women guards is an unacceptable reason for disqualifying women, it relies instead on an equally speculative threat to prison discipline supposedly generated by the sexuality of female guards. There is simply no evidence in the record to show that women guards would create any danger to security in Alabama prisons significantly greater than that which already exists. All of the dangers — with one exception discussed below — are inherent in a prison setting, whatever the gender of the guards.

The Court first sees women guards as a threat to security because "there are few visible deterrents to inmate assaults on women custodians." In fact, any prison guard is constantly subject to the threat of attack by inmates, and "invisible" deterrents are the guard's only real protection. No prison guard relies primarily on his or her ability to ward off an inmate attack to maintain order. Guards are typically unarmed and sheer numbers of inmates could overcome the normal complement. Rather, like all other law enforcement officers, prison guards must rely primarily on the moral authority of their office and the threat of future punishment for miscreants. As one expert testified below, common sense, fairness, and mental and emotional stability are the qualities a guard needs to cope with the dangers of the job. Well qualified and properly trained women, no less than men, have these psychological weapons at their disposal.

The particular severity of discipline problems in the Alabama maximum-security prisons is also no justification for the discrimination sanctioned by the Court.

Dothard v. Rawlinson (bfoq)   ix

The District Court found in *Pugh v. Locke* that guards "must spend all their time attempting to maintain control or to protect themselves." 406 F.Supp. at 325. If male guards face an impossible situation, it is difficult to see how women could make the problem worse, unless one relies on precisely the type of generalized bias against women that the Court agrees Title VII was intended to outlaw. For example, much of the testimony of appellants' witnesses ignores individual differences among members of each sex and reads like "ancient canards about the proper role of women." *Phillips v. Martin Marietta Corp.*, 400 U.S. at 545. The witnesses claimed that women guards are not strict disciplinarians; that they are physically less capable of protecting themselves and subduing unruly inmates; that inmates take advantage of them as they did their mothers, while male guards are strong father figures who easily maintain discipline, and so on.[2] Yet the record shows that the presence of women guards has not led to a single incident amounting to a serious breach of security in any Alabama institution.[3] And, in any event, "[g]uards rarely enter the cell blocks and dormitories," *Pugh v. Locke*, 406 F.Supp. at 325, where the danger of inmate attacks is the greatest.

---

[2] The State Commissioner of Corrections summed up these prejudices in his testimony:

> Q. Would a male that is 5'6", 140 lbs., be able to perform the job of Correctional Counselor in an all male institution?
>
> A. Well, if he qualifies otherwise, yes.
>
> Q. But a female 5'6", 140 lbs., would not be able to perform all the duties?
>
> A. No.
>
> Q. What do you use as a basis for that opinion?
>
> A. The innate intention between a male and a female. The physical capabilities, the emotions that go into the psychic make-up of a female vs. the psychic make-up of a male. The attitude of the rural type inmate we have vs. that of a woman. The superior feeling that a man has, historically, over that of a female.

[3] The Court refers to two incidents involving potentially dangerous attacks on women in prisons. But these did not involve trained corrections officers; one victim was a clerical worker and the other, a student visiting on a tour.

It appears that the real disqualifying factor in the Court's view is "[t]he employee's very womanhood." The Court refers to the large number of sex offenders in Alabama prisons, and to "[t]he likelihood that inmates would assault a woman because she was a woman." In short, the fundamental justification for the decision is that women as guards will generate sexual assaults. With all respect, this rationale regrettably perpetuates one of the most insidious of the old myths about women — that women, wittingly or not, are seductive sexual objects. The effect of the decision, made I am sure with the best of intentions, is to punish women because their very presence might provoke sexual assaults. It is women who are made to pay the price in lost job opportunities for the threat of depraved conduct by prison inmates. Once again, "[t]he pedestal upon which women have been placed has ..., upon closer inspection, been revealed as a cage." *Sail'er Inn, In. v. Kirby*, 5 Cal. 3d 1, 20 (1971). It is particularly ironic that the cage is erected here in response to feared misbehavior by imprisoned criminals.

The Court points to no evidence in the record to support the asserted "likelihood that inmates would assault a woman because she was a woman." Perhaps the Court relies upon common sense, or "innate recognition." But the danger in this emotionally laden context is that common sense will be used to mask the "'romantic paternalism'" and persisting discriminatory attitudes that the Court properly eschews. To me, the only matter of innate recognition is that the incidence of sexually motivated attacks on guards will be minute compared to the "likelihood that inmates will assault" a *guard* because he or she is a *guard*.

The proper response to inevitable attacks on both female and male guards is not to limit the employment opportunities of law-abiding women who wish to contribute to their community, but to take swift and sure punitive action against the inmate offenders. Presumably, one of the goals of the Alabama prison system is the eradication of inmates' anti-social behavior patterns so that prisoners will be able to live one day in free society. Sex offenders can begin this process by learning to relate to women guards in a socially acceptable manner. To deprive women of job opportunities because of the threatened behavior of convicted criminals is to turn our social priorities upside down.[5]

---

[5]The appellants argue that restrictions on employment of women are also justified by consideration of inmates' privacy. It is strange indeed to hear state officials who have for years been violating the most basic principles of human decency in the operation of their prisons suddenly become concerned about inmate privacy. It is stranger still that these same officials allow women guards in contact positions in a number of nonmaximum-security institutions, but strive to protect inmates' privacy in the prisons where personal freedom is most severely restricted. I have no doubt on

(continued...)

....

(...continued)
this record that appellants' professed concern is nothing but a feeble excuse for discrimination.

As the District Court suggested, it may well be possible, once a constitutionally adequate staff is available, to rearrange work assignments so that legitimate inmate privacy concerns are respected without denying jobs to women. Finally, if women guards behave in a professional manner at all times, they will engender reciprocal respect from inmates, who will recognize that their privacy is being invaded no more than if a woman doctor examines them. The suggestion implicit in the privacy argument that such behavior is unlikely on either side is an insult to the professionalism of guards and the dignity of inmates.

QUESTIONS FOR REFLECTION

1. Is the bfoq a genuine defense?

2. Should race or color be recognized as a bfoq in an appropriate case?

3. Should a bfoq exist if members of the excluded class, on the average, are able to perform the task that justifies their exclusion, but not as well as the favored class?

4. Should a bfoq exist when individual testing is not reliable?

5. Do you think that any of your female teachers had the authority and personal presence to be a guard in a male prison in Alabama?

6. The majority finds that a woman guard in Alabama's prisons would be assaulted because of her sex. Is this a legislative or an adjudicative fact? How does the Court know this fact is true?

7. We have noted that lawyers sometimes present arguments that are not based on doctrine; such arguments are commonly referred to as "policy arguments." Central to a policy argument is an assertion of fact. Consider the following two facts, on which policy arguments in Dothard could easily have been built. Would they have affected the outcome of the case?

a. Homosexual rape is frequent in prison.

b. Rape is not a crime of sex, but of violence.

8. Does privacy justify a bfoq-male for a job that requires strip searches of male prisoners?

9. Should the law require that job duties be shuffled in order to minimize or eliminate bfoq's? For example, suppose the answer to question 7 is yes. Suppose also that in a certain prison all guards perform strip searches on a rotating basis, but jobs could be redefined so that some guards perform strip searches more often than at present and other guards never perform them. Such redefinition of jobs would eliminate the bfoq-male for the guards who do not perform strip searches. Should the law require the employer to redefine these jobs to the extent feasible?

Ω

Proof of Disparate Treatment

CONVENTIONAL PROOF OF DISPARATE TREATMENT

Introduction

When one first thinks of lawsuits under Title VII, one probably has in mind the model in which a single worker sues an employer for intentional discrimination based on race or gender. In such "one-on-one" cases, the parties' proof is usually conventional evidence, that is, documents and testimony from witnesses about what they observed.

The following case expounds perhaps the dominant pattern of prima facie cases in the second sense of disparate treatment; this pattern is applicable to one-on-one cases. (Let us call this pattern the "McDonnell Douglas formula.")

The student will naturally attend to the components of the McDonnell Douglas formula. In addition, the student should ask oneself

- Why does the formula work? Why does it tend to prove discrimination? In other words, how does the formula prove the elements of the prima facie case in the first sense?

The case also specifies the parties' burdens of production. Therefore, ask

- Who has to offer evidence of what?

Pay particular attention to the point at which the burden of production shifts from the plaintiff to the defendant.

McDonnell Douglas Corp. v. Green
411 U.S. 792 (1973)

Mr. Justice POWELL delivered the opinion of the Court.

The case before us raises significant questions as to the proper order and nature of proof in actions under Title VII of the Civil Rights Act of 1964.

Petitioner, McDonnell Douglas Corp., is an aerospace and aircraft manufacturer headquartered in St. Louis, Missouri, where it employs over 30,000 people. Respondent, a black citizen of St. Louis, worked for petitioner as a mechanic and laboratory technician from 1956 until August 28, 1964 when he was laid off in the course of a general reduction in petitioner's work force.

Respondent, a long-time activist in the civil rights movement, protested vigorously that his discharge and the general hiring practices of petitioner were racially motivated. As part of this protest, respondent and other members of the Congress on Racial Equality illegally stalled their cars on the main roads leading to petitioner's plant for the purpose of blocking access to it at the time of the morning shift change. The District Judge described the plan for, and respondent's participation in, the "stall-in" as follows:

> [F]ive teams, each consisting of four cars, would "tie up" five main access roads into McDonnell at the time of the morning rush hour. The drivers of the cars were instructed to line up next to each other, completely blocking the intersections or roads. The drivers were also instructed to stop their cars, turn off the engines, pull the emergency brake, raise all windows, lock the doors, and remain in their cars until the police arrived. The plan was to have the cars remain in position for one hour.

> Acting under the "stall in" plan, plaintiff [respondent in the present action] drove his car onto Brown Road, a McDonnell access road, at approximately 7:00 a.m. at the start of the morning rush hour. Plaintiff was aware of the traffic problems that would result. He stopped his car with the intent to block traffic. The police arrived shortly and requested plaintiff to move his car. He refused to move his car voluntarily. Plaintiff's car was towed away by the police, and he was arrested for obstructing traffic. Plaintiff pleaded guilty to the charge of obstructing traffic and was fined.

On July 2, 1965, a "lock-in" took place wherein a chain and padlock were placed on the front door of a building to prevent the occupants, certain of petitioner's employees, from leaving. Though respondent apparently knew beforehand of the "lock-in," the full extent of his involvement remains uncertain.

Some three weeks following the "lock-in," on July 25, 1965, petitioner publicly advertised for qualified mechanics, respondent's trade, and respondent promptly applied for re-employment. Petitioner turned down respondent, basing its rejection on respondent's participation in the "stall-in" and "lock-in." Shortly thereafter, respondent filed a formal complaint with the Equal Employment Opportunity Commission, claiming that petitioner had refused to rehire him because of his race and persistent involvement in the civil rights movement, in violation of §§ 703(a)(1) and 704(a) of the Civil Rights Act of 1964. The former section generally prohibits racial discrimination in any employment decision while the latter forbids discrimination against applicants or employees for attempting to protest or correct allegedly discriminatory conditions of employment.

The Commission made no finding on respondent's allegation of racial bias under § 703(a)(1), but it did find reasonable cause to believe petitioner had violated § 704(a) by refusing to rehire respondent because of his civil rights activity. After the Commission unsuccessfully attempted to conciliate the dispute, it advised respondent in March, 1968, of his right to institute a civil action in federal court within 30 days.

On April 15, 1968, respondent brought the present action, claiming initially a violation of § 704(a) and, in an amended complaint, a violation of § 703(a)(1) as well.[5] The District Court dismissed the latter claim of racial discrimination in petitioner's hiring procedures on the ground that the Commission had failed to make a determination of reasonable cause to believe that a violation of that section had been committed. The District Court also found that petitioner's refusal to rehire respondent was based solely on his participation in the illegal demonstrations and not on his legitimate civil rights activities. The court concluded that nothing in Title VII or § 704 protected "such activity as employed by the plaintiff in the 'stall in' and 'lock in' demonstrations."

On appeal, the Eighth Circuit affirmed that unlawful protests were not protected activities under § 704(a), but reversed the dismissal of respondent's § 703(a)(1) claim relating to racially discriminatory hiring practices, holding that a prior Commission determination of reasonable cause was not a jurisdictional prerequisite to raising a claim under that section in federal court. The court ordered the case remanded for trial of respondent's claim under § 703(a)(1).

---

[5]Respondent also contested the legality of his 1964 discharge by petitioner, but both courts held this claim barred by the statute of limitations. Respondent does not challenge those rulings here.

In remanding, the Court of Appeals attempted to set forth standards to govern the consideration of respondent's claim. The majority noted that respondent had established a *prima facie* case of racial discrimination; that petitioner's refusal to rehire respondent rested on "subjective" criteria which carried little weight in rebutting charges of discrimination; that, though respondent's participation in the unlawful demonstrations might indicate a lack of a responsible attitude toward performing work for that employer, respondent should be given the opportunity to demonstrate that petitioner's reasons for refusing to rehire him were mere pretext. In order to clarify the standards governing the disposition of an action challenging employment discrimination, we granted *certiorari*.

I

We agree with the Court of Appeals that absence of a Commission finding of reasonable cause cannot bar suit under an appropriate section of Title VII and that the District Judge erred in dismissing respondent's claim of racial discrimination under § 703(a)(1). Respondent satisfied the jurisdictional prerequisites to a federal action (i) by filing timely charges of employment discrimination with the Commission and (ii) by receiving and acting upon the Commission's statutory notice of the right to sue.

The Act does not restrict a complainant's right to sue to those charges as to which the Commission has made findings of reasonable cause, and we will not engraft on the statute a requirement which may inhibit the review of claims of employment discrimination in the federal courts. The Commission itself does not consider the absence of a "reasonable cause" determination as providing employer immunity from similar charges in a federal court, 29 CFR § 1601.30, and the courts of appeal have held that, in view of the large volume of complaints before the Commission and the non-adversary character of many of its proceedings, "court actions under Title VII are de novo proceedings and ... a Commission 'no reasonable cause' finding does not bar a lawsuit in the case." *Robinson v. Lorillard Corp.* 444 F.2d 791, 800 (4th Cir. 1971).

The critical issue before us concerns the order and allocation of proof in a private, non-class-action challenging employment discrimination....

...

The complainant in a Title VII trial must carry the initial burden under the statute of establishing a *prima facie* case of racial discrimination. This may be done by showing (i) that he belongs to a racial minority; (ii) that he applied and was qualified for a job for which the employer was seeking applicants; (iii) that, despite his qualifications, he was rejected; and (iv) that, after his rejection, the position remained open and the employer continued to seek applicants from persons of complainant's qualifications.[13] In the instant case, we agree with the Court of Appeals that respondent proved a *prima facie* case. Petitioner sought mechanics, respondent's trade, and continued to do so after respondent's rejection. Petitioner, moreover, does not dispute respondent's qualifications and acknowledges that his past work performance in petitioner's employ was "satisfactory."

The burden then must shift to the employer to articulate some legitimate, nondiscriminatory reason for the employee's rejection. We need not attempt in the instant case to detail every matter which fairly could be recognized as a reasonable basis for a refusal to hire. Here petitioner has assigned respondent's participation in unlawful conduct against it as the cause for his rejection. We think that this suffices to discharge petitioner's burden of proof at this stage and to meet respondent's *prima facie* case of discrimination.

The Court of Appeals intimated, however, that petitioner's stated reason for refusing to rehire respondent was a "subjective" rather than objective criterion which "carr[ies] little weight in rebutting charges of discrimination," 463 F.2d at 352. This was among the statements which caused the dissenting judge to read the opinion as taking "the position that such unlawful acts as Green committed against McDonnell would not legally entitle McDonnell to refuse to hire him, even though no racial motivation was involved...." *Id.* at 355. Regardless of whether this was the intended import of the opinion, we think the court below seriously underestimated the rebuttal weight to which petitioner's reasons were entitled. Respondent admittedly had taken part in a carefully planned "stall-in," designed to tie up access to and egress from petitioner's plant at a peak traffic hour. Nothing in Title VII compels an employer to absolve and rehire one who has engaged in such deliberate, unlawful activity against it. In upholding, under the National Labor Relations Act, the discharge of employees who had seized and forcibly retained an employer's factory buildings in an illegal sit-down strike, the Court noted pertinently:

> We are unable to conclude that Congress intended to compel employers to retain persons in their employ regardless of their unlawful conduct—to invest those who go on strike with an immunity from discharge for acts of trespass or violence against the employer's property.... Apart from the question of the constitutional validity of an enactment of that sort, it is enough to say that such a legislative intention should be found in some definite and unmistakable expression. *NLRB v. Fansteel Corp.*, 306 U.S. 240, 255.

---

[13]The facts necessarily will vary in Title VII cases, and the specification above of the *prima facie* proof required from respondent is not necessarily applicable in every respect to differing factual situations.

McDonnell Douglas v. Green

Petitioner's reason for rejection thus suffices to meet the *prima facie* case, but the inquiry must not end here. While Title VII does not, without more, compel rehiring of respondent, neither does it permit petitioner to use respondent's conduct as a pretext for the sort of discrimination prohibited by § 703(a)(1). On remand, respondent must, as the Court of Appeals recognized, be afforded a fair opportunity to show that petitioner's stated reason for respondent's rejection was in fact pretext. Especially relevant to such a showing would be evidence that white employees involved in acts against petitioner of comparable seriousness to the "stall-in" were nevertheless retained or rehired. Petitioner may justifiably refuse to rehire one who was engaged in unlawful, disruptive acts against it, but only if this criterion is applied alike to members of all races.

Other evidence that may be relevant to any showing of pretext includes facts as to the petitioner's treatment of respondent during his prior term of employment; petitioner's reaction, if any, to respondent's legitimate civil rights activities; and petitioner's general policy and practice with respect to minority employment. On the latter point, statistics as to petitioner's employment policy and practice may be helpful to a determination of whether petitioner's refusal to rehire respondent in this case conformed to a general pattern of discrimination against blacks. In short, on the retrial respondent must be given a full and fair opportunity to demonstrate by competent evidence that the presumptively valid reasons for his rejection were in fact a coverup for a racially discriminatory decision.

....

Comment

The Supreme Court tells us that the <u>McDonnell Douglas</u> formula is a prima facie case of disparate treatment. We must understand the Court to mean a prima facie case in the second sense, as footnote 13 makes clear. The formula could not be the prima facie-I of disparate treatment because the formula applies to a hiring case, whereas disparate treatment applies to all employment decisions; and even in a hiring case, a plaintiff could prove disparate treatment without using the formula, for example, by evidence that the employer said, "I would never hire a person of the plaintiff's race or sex."

If a plaintiff offers evidence of the facts in the <u>McDonnell Douglas</u> formula, an inference arises that the employer discriminated against the plaintiff. This is not to say that the plaintiff wins the case. The defendant may rebut the plaintiff's evidence or prove a defense. But if, at the end of the trial, the judge or jury believes the plaintiff's evidence and does not believe the defendant's, the formula is enough for the plaintiff to win the case.

The <u>McDonnell Douglas</u> formula is one prima facie-II of disparate treatment. Others exist. Indeed, a nearly infinite variety of prima facie-IIs exists for proving disparate treatment, as each case has its own adjudicative facts. Nonetheless, patterns of prima facie-IIs (patterns of adjudicative facts) can be identified. The <u>McDonnell Douglas</u> formula represents one pattern. The student has read examples of other patterns.

QUESTIONS FOR REFLECTION

1. In the <u>McDonnell Douglas</u> formula, what is the nature of the burden that shifts to the employer — a burden of production or of persuasion? How did the employer satisfy the burden in this case?

2. Which of the two types of defense did the employer attempt? Why?

Proof of Disparate Treatment
(continued)

STATISTICAL PROOF OF DISPARATE TREATMENT

Introduction

As we studied <u>McDonnell Douglas v. Green</u>, we focused on the prima facie-IIs that prove disparate treatment of individuals. The four patterns that we observed — the <u>McDonnell Douglas</u> formula, direct evidence of state of mind, comparison of similarly situated persons, and sexual harassment — are applicable to "one-on-one" cases, that is, cases in which an employer is alleged to have discriminated against one plaintiff (or a small number of plaintiffs). These patterns would be much less useful in a case in which an employer is alleged to have discriminated against many persons. Such a case, called a **class action**, is brought on behalf of a group (often a large group) of persons, and it would be impractical to repeat the <u>McDonnell Douglas</u> formula (or the other patterns) for each member of the class; indeed, the idea of a class action is to focus on the facts common to all members of the class and, as much as possible, to overlook the details. Statistics are well suited to describe common facts. The following case considers whether statistics can play a role in proving intentional discrimination against a class of persons, in other words, whether statistical evidence can constitute another pattern of proof for prima facie cases in the second sense of disparate treatment.

An element of disparate treatment is that the employer denied employment opportunities to the plaintiff(s). Statistics can obviously be helpful in determining whether an employer denied employment opportunities to members of a protected class. If 1,000 African-Americans apply for 1,000 vacant jobs at a firm and 200 of these applicants are hired, it is evident that the employer denied employment opportunities to 800 African-Americans.

Can statistics reveal anything else relevant to a disparate treatment case? In particular, can statistics help us determine whether an employer intentionally denied opportunities to a protected class? Can statistics help us to know whether the employer who denied opportunities to 800 African-Americans was motivated in any way by their race? The answer is a qualified yes: statistics can <u>help</u>, but they cannot carry the whole load.

Here is what statistics can do: they can convince us that an event is not a random variation in a fair process, in other words, that the event is so unlikely to occur by chance that it probably was influenced by a cause external to the process. But statistics cannot tell us what that cause is. They cannot reveal an employer's motivation. Only conventional evidence can do that.

Imagine that Groucho and Harpo are playing poker for money. Groucho shuffles the deck, deals, and wins the first hand with a royal flush. Groucho shuffles again, deals, and wins the second hand, also with a royal flush. Groucho shuffles a third time, deals, and once again wins with a royal flush. Harpo commences to think along these lines: "A player might get a royal flush in three consecutive hands, even in an honest game. This event happens by chance so rarely, however, that Groucho's 'good luck' probably had a cause external to the normal process of shuffling and dealing cards. Knowing that Groucho was dealing and that we were playing for money, I strongly suspect that he has been cheating ... so I'll never speak again."

Groucho's case shows that, when a process is supposed to be random and we get a result that is very unlikely to occur by chance, we can infer that an external cause is operating. Knowledge of the background can often suggest a likely cause. Harpo's knowledge that Groucho was dealing and winning money suggested that Groucho was cheating. Or suppose someone throws two dice a hundred times, and seven turns up on half the throws. This unlikely event most probably occurs because of a cause external to the normal process of throwing fair dice. Our knowledge that seven is an important number in craps would make us suspect that the dice are loaded. The same reasoning can be applied to discrimination cases.

Teamsters v. United States

In the following case, the government used statistical evidence as part of the proof that the employer intentionally discriminated against people of color. As you read the case, ask yourself to which elements of the prima facie-I of disparate treatment the government's statistics pertained. Also consider whether there were any flaws in the government's statistical evidence.

Int'l B'hood of Teamsters v. United States
431 U.S. 324 (1977)

Mr. Justice STEWART delivered the opinion of the Court.

{In 1968 the United States Department of Justice[a] sued T.I.M.E.-D.C., a national trucking company, alleging that it discriminated in the hiring and job assignment of African-Americans and Spanish-surnamed Americans. Specifically, the government claimed that the employer confined members of these groups to service in local (intra-city) driving jobs and reserved the higher paying line (inter-city) driving jobs for European-Americans.

{Having limited resources, the government usually brings suit only when a case raises an important issue or an employer appears to have discriminated against many people. This case satisfied both criteria: statistical evidence had proved to be highly useful in proving discrimination, and the employer had thousands of employees. This was a pattern-or-practice case, that is, the government alleged that the employer regularly discriminated against people of color over a substantial period of time. In such cases (or in class actions, which are like pattern-or-practice cases except the plaintiffs are private parties), the evidence must show that the employer discriminated against, not one or two, but many members of a protected class. To this end, the government relied heavily on statistical evidence, though conventional evidence, in the form of witnesses who testified to over 40 instances of discrimination against individuals, was also offered.

{The District Court found that many qualified people of color who sought line driving jobs had been ignored, given false or misleading information, or not considered on the same basis as whites. The same things happened to black and Latino city drivers who sought to transfer to line driving jobs. Both the District Court and the Court of Appeals for the Fifth Circuit held that the government proved that the employer had engaged in a pattern or practice of discrimination.}

...

In this Court the company and the union contend that their conduct did not violate Title VII in any respect, asserting first that the evidence introduced at trial was insufficient to show that the company engaged in a "pattern or practice" of employment discrimination....

---

[a] Since the 1972 amendments to Title VII, cases like this have been brought by the EEOC.

Teamsters v. United States

A

Consideration of the question whether the company engaged in a pattern or practice of discriminatory hiring practices involves controlling legal principles that are relatively clear. The Government's theory of discrimination was simply that the company, in violation of § 703(a) of Title VII, regularly and purposefully treated Negroes and Spanish-surnamed Americans less favorably than white persons. The disparity in treatment allegedly involved the refusal to recruit, hire, transfer, or promote minority group members on an equal basis with white people, particularly with respect to line-driving positions. The ultimate factual issues are thus simply whether there was a pattern or practice of such disparate treatment and, if so, whether the differences were "racially premised." *McDonnell Douglas Corp. v. Green*, 411 U.S. 792, 805 n. 18.[15]

As the plaintiff, the Government bore the initial burden of making out a prima facie case of discrimination. And, because it alleged a systemwide pattern or practice of resistance to the full enjoyment of Title VII rights, the Government ultimately had to prove more than the mere occurrence of isolated or "accidental" or sporadic discriminatory acts. It had to establish by a preponderance of the evidence that racial discrimination was the company's standard operating procedure — the regular rather than the unusual practice.

---

[15]"Disparate treatment" such as is alleged in the present case is the most easily understood type of discrimination. The employer simply treats some people less favorably than others because of their race, color, religion, sex, or national origin. Proof of discriminatory motive is critical, although it can in some situations be inferred from the mere fact of differences in treatment. Undoubtedly disparate treatment was the most obvious evil Congress had in mind when it enacted Title VII. See, e.g., 110 *Cong. Rec.* 13088 (1964) (remarks of Sen. Humphrey) ("What the bill does... is simply to make it an illegal practice to use race as a factor in denying employment. It provides that men and women shall be employed on the basis of their qualifications, not as Catholic citizens, not as Protestant citizens, not as Jewish citizens, not as colored citizens, but as citizens of the United States").

Claims of disparate treatment may be distinguished from claims that stress "disparate impact." The latter involve employment practices that are facially neutral in their treatment of different groups but that in fact fall more harshly on one group than another and cannot be justified by business necessity. Proof of discriminatory motive, we have held, is not required under a disparate-impact theory. Either theory may, of course, be applied to a particular set of facts.

We agree with the District Court and the Court of Appeals that the Government carried its burden of proof. As of March 31, 1971, shortly after the Government filed its complaint alleging systemwide discrimination, the company had 6,472 employees. Of these, 314 (5%) were Negroes and 257 (4%) were Spanish-surnamed Americans. Of the 1,828 line drivers, however, there were only 8 (0.4%) Negroes and 5 (0.3%) Spanish-surnamed persons, and all of the Negroes had been hired after the litigation had commenced. With one exception — a man who worked as a line driver at the Chicago terminal from 1950 to 1959 — the company and its predecessors did not employ a Negro on a regular basis as a line driver until 1969. And, as the Government showed, even in 1971 there were terminals in areas of substantial Negro population where all of the company's line drivers were white.[17] A great majority of the Negroes (83%) and Spanish-surnamed Americans (78%) who did work for the company held the lower paying city operations and serviceman jobs,[18] whereas only 39% of the nonminority employees held jobs in those categories.

The Government bolstered its statistical evidence with the testimony of individuals who recounted over 40 specific instances of discrimination. Upon the basis of this testimony the District Court found that "[numerous] qualified black and Spanish-surnamed American applicants who sought line driving jobs at the company over the years either had their requests ignored, were given false or misleading information about requirements, opportunities, and application procedures, or were not considered and hired on the same basis that whites were considered and hired." Minority employees who wanted to transfer to line-driver jobs met with similar difficulties.[19]

---

[17]In Atlanta, for instance, Negroes composed 22.35% of the population in the surrounding metropolitan area and 51.31% of the population in the city proper. The company's Atlanta terminal employed 57 line drivers. All were white. In Los Angeles, 10.84% of the greater metropolitan population and 17.88% of the city population were Negro. But at the company's two Los Angeles terminals there was not a single Negro among the 374 line drivers. The proof showed similar disparities in San Francisco, Denver, Nashville, Chicago, Dallas, and at several other terminals.

[18]Although line-driver jobs pay more than other jobs, and the District Court found them to be "considered the most desirable of the driving jobs," it is by no means clear that all employees, even driver employees, would prefer to be line drivers. Of course, Title VII provides for equal opportunity to compete for any job, whether it is thought better or worse than another.

[19]Two examples are illustrative:

George Taylor, a Negro, worked for the company as a city driver in Los Angeles, beginning late in 1966. In 1968, after hearing that a white city driver had transferred to a

(continued...)

The company's principal response to this evidence is that statistics can never in and of themselves prove the existence of a pattern or practice of discrimination, or even establish a prima facie case shifting to the employer the burden of rebutting the inference raised by the figures. But, as even our brief summary of the evidence shows, this was not a case in which the Government relied on "statistics alone." The individuals who testified about their personal experiences with the company brought the cold numbers convincingly to life.

In any event, our cases make it unmistakably clear that "[s]tatistical analyses have served and will continue to serve an important role" in cases in which the existence of discrimination is a disputed issue. *Mayor of Philadelphia v. Educational Equality League*, 415 U.S. 605, 620. We have repeatedly approved the use of statistical proof, where it reached proportions comparable to those in this case, to establish a prima facie case of racial discrimination in jury selection cases. Statistics are equally competent in proving employment discrimination.[20] We caution only that

---

(...continued)
line-driver job, he told the terminal manager that he also would like to consider line driving. The manager replied that there would be "a lot of problems on the road... with different people, Caucasian, et cetera," and stated: "I don't feel that the company is ready for this right now.... Give us a little time. It will come around, you know." Mr. Taylor made similar requests some months later and got similar responses. He was never offered a line-driving job or an application.

　　Feliberto Trujillo worked as a dockman at the company's Denver terminal. When he applied for a line-driver job in 1967, he was told by a personnel officer that he had one strike against him. He asked what that was and was told: "You're a Chicano, and as far as we know, there isn't a Chicano driver in the system."

[20]Petitioners argue that statistics, at least those comparing the racial composition of an employer's work force to the composition of the population at large, should never be given decisive weight in a Title VII case because to do so would conflict with § 703(j) of the Act, 42 U.S.C. § 2000e-2(j). That section provides:

> "Nothing contained in this subchapter shall be interpreted to require any employer ... to grant preferential treatment to any individual or to any group because of the race ... or national origin of such individual or group on account of an imbalance which may exist with respect to the total number or percentage of persons of any race ... or national origin employed by any employer ... in comparison with the total number or percentage of persons of such race ... or national origin in any community, State, section, or other area, or in the available work force in any community, State, section, or other area."

(continued...)

statistics are not irrefutable; they come in infinite variety and, like any other kind of evidence, they may be rebutted. In short, their usefulness depends on all of the surrounding facts and circumstances.

In addition to its general protest against the use of statistics in Title VII cases, the company claims that in this case the statistics revealing racial imbalance are misleading because they fail to take into account the company's particular business situation as of the effective date of Title VII. The company concedes that its line drivers were virtually all white in July 1965, but it claims that thereafter business conditions were such that its work force dropped. Its argument is that low personnel turnover, rather than post-Act discrimination, accounts for more recent statistical disparities. It points to substantial minority hiring in later years, especially after 1971, as showing that any pre-Act patterns of discrimination were broken.

The argument would be a forceful one if this were an employer who, at the time of suit, had done virtually no new hiring since the effective date of Title VII. But it is not. Although the company's total number of employees apparently dropped somewhat during the late 1960's, the record shows that many line drivers continued to be hired throughout this period, and that almost all of them were white. To be sure, there were improvements in the company's hiring practices. The Court of Appeals commented that "T.I.M.E.-D.C.'s recent minority hiring progress stands as a laudable

---

(...continued)

The argument fails in this case because the statistical evidence was not offered or used to support an erroneous theory that Title VII requires an employer's work force to be racially balanced. Statistics showing racial or ethnic imbalance are probative in a case such as this one only because such imbalance is often a telltale sign of purposeful discrimination; absent explanation, it is ordinarily to be expected that nondiscriminatory hiring practices will in time result in a work force more or less representative of the racial and ethnic composition of the population in the community from which employees are hired. Evidence of long-lasting and gross disparity between the composition of a work force and that of the general population thus may be significant even though § 703(j) makes clear that Title VII imposes no requirement that a work force mirror the general population. Considerations such as small sample size may, of course, detract from the value of such evidence, and evidence showing that the figures for the general population might not accurately reflect the pool of qualified job applicants would also be relevant.

> "Since the passage of the Civil Rights Act of 1964, the courts have frequently relied upon statistical evidence to prove a violation.... In many cases the only available avenue of proof is the use of racial statistics to uncover clandestine and covert discrimination by the employer or union involved."

United States v. Ironworkers Local 86, 443 F. 2d at 551.

Teamsters v. United States

good faith effort to eradicate the effects of past discrimination in the area of hiring and initial assignment." 517 F. 2d at 316. But the District Court and the Court of Appeals found upon substantial evidence that the company had engaged in a course of discrimination that continued well after the effective date of Title VII. The company's later changes in its hiring and promotion policies could be of little comfort to the victims of the earlier post-Act discrimination, and could not erase its previous illegal conduct or its obligation to afford relief to those who suffered because of it.[23]

The District Court and the Court of Appeals, on the basis of substantial evidence, held that the Government had proved a prima facie case of systematic and purposeful employment discrimination, continuing well beyond the effective date of Title VII. The company's attempts to rebut that conclusion were held to be inadequate.[24] For the reasons we have summarized, there is no warrant for this Court

---

[23]The company's narrower attacks upon the statistical evidence — that there was no precise delineation of the areas referred to in the general population statistics, that the Government did not demonstrate that minority populations were located close to terminals or that transportation was available, that the statistics failed to show what portion of the minority populations [was] located close to terminals or that transportation was available, that the statistics failed to show what portion of the minority population was suited by age, health, or other qualifications to hold trucking jobs, etc. — are equally lacking in force. At best, these attacks go only to the accuracy of the comparison between the composition of the company's work force at various terminals and the general population of the surrounding communities. They detract little from the Government's further showing that Negroes and Spanish-surnamed Americans who were hired were overwhelmingly excluded from line-driver jobs. Such employees were willing to work, had access to the terminal, were healthy and of working age, and often were at least sufficiently qualified to hold city-driver jobs. Yet they became line drivers with far less frequency than whites. See, e.g., Pretrial Stipulation 14, summarized in 517 F.2d at 312 n. 24 (of 2,919 whites who held driving jobs in 1971, 1,802 (62%) were line drivers and 1,117 (38%) were city drivers; of 180 Negroes and Spanish-surnamed Americans who held driving jobs, 13 (7%) were line drivers and 167 (93%) were city drivers).

In any event, fine tuning of the statistics could not have obscured the glaring absence of minority line drivers. As the Court of Appeals remarked, the company's inability to rebut the inference of discrimination came not from a misuse of statistics but from "the inexorable zero." *Id.*, at 315.

[24]The company's evidence, apart from the showing of recent changes in hiring and promotion policies, consisted mainly of general statements that it hired only the best qualified applicants. But "affirmations of good faith in making individual selections are insufficient to dispel a prima facie case of systematic exclusion." *Alexander v. Louisiana*, 405 U.S. 625, 632.

(continued...)

to disturb the findings of the District Court and the Court of Appeals on this basic issue.

....

(...continued)

The company also attempted to show that all of the witnesses who testified to specific instances of discrimination either were not discriminated against or suffered no injury. The Court of Appeals correctly ruled that the trial judge was not bound to accept this testimony and that it committed no error by relying instead on the other overpowering evidence in the case. The Court of Appeals was also correct in the view that individual proof concerning each class member's specific injury was appropriately left to proceedings to determine individual relief. In a suit brought by the Government under § 707(a) of the Act the District Court's initial concern is in deciding whether the Government has proved that the defendant has engaged in a pattern or practice of discriminatory conduct.

Comment

The prima facie case in the first sense of disparate treatment does not change, whether the proof is conventional or statistical. In other words, the elements of the claim of disparate treatment are constant, regardless of the nature of the proof. (This is true of every legal claim.) However, a variety of prima facie cases in the second sense exists. We have previously seen four varieties of prima facie-II of disparate treatment; all of them used conventional evidence. <u>Teamsters</u> introduces us to a fifth prima facie-II of disparate treatment, one that utilizes statistics to prove disparate treatment of a group of workers.

PROBABILITY ANALYSIS

Before we state the details of the prima facie-II of disparate treatment as proved by statistics, it will be useful to discuss the ideas that underlie this sort of evidence. We have already met Groucho and Harpo. Their game of cards introduces us to probability analysis. We use probability analysis without even thinking about it. For example, suppose one morning Inez notices that one of the tires of her car is low on air. She goes to Bill's Friendly Service Station; Bill finds a nail poking through the tread and repairs it. Inez is not concerned; tires pick up nails from time to time. The next morning she notices another tire is low on air. Bill finds another nail in the tread. Inez is unhappy, and she grumbles a bit; but she does nothing about it. After all, bad luck sometimes comes in streaks. But the following morning another tire is low on air and Bill finds yet another nail in it, and now Inez is rightly suspicious. Perhaps a load of nails had been spilled on a street which she uses regularly. Perhaps the adolescent who lives next door is taking revenge on her for informing the boy's parents that he had been smoking marijuana. Inez would reasonably begin to search for the cause of her problem.

Inez used a rough-and-ready form of probability analysis. Scientists use a more rigorous form of it. When a pharmaceutical company develops a new drug for treating a disease, the drug must be tested for efficacy and safety before the company is allowed to market the drug. In one rigorous procedure, known as a "double-blind trial," similar people who have the disease are divided into two groups. Physicians administer the new drug to one group and a placebo to the other ("the control") group, and neither the physicians nor the members of the groups know who is getting the drug and who is getting the placebo. After a period of time, the effects of the drug are compared to the effects of the placebo. If the drug works, there should be a difference between the groups.

For example, suppose a company develops a drug for Gold's disease[a] and arranges a trial of the drug. Let us say there were 1,000 students in each group. Suppose we know from past experience that, without treatment, approximately 60 percent of victims of the disease recover within a month. We observe that in the control group, 590 recovered and 410 were still sick, whereas in the group that was receiving the new drug, 700 recovered and 300 stayed sick. Do these numbers tell us whether or not the new drug is effective?

THE IDEA OF STATISTICAL SIGNIFICANCE

Our problem is that we know there is variability in natural phenomena. We want to ignore differences that occur within a phenomenon itself, and focus on differences that have causes outside the phenomenon. In the example of the drug trial, we expected 600 students in the control group to recover in a month; we observed that 590 did. This difference (10 fewer recoveries than expected) was within the natural range of variability of the disease; it was not caused by an agent outside the phenomenon. To say the same thing, the difference between 600 and 590 recoveries is not real; these numbers are identical for our purposes. Therefore, we conclude that our control group was not contaminated in any way.

---

[a]The symptoms of this disease, which seems to strike only students, are fatigue, boredom, headaches, eye strain, irritability, and cramps in the neck. The cause of the disease appears to be bending over a fat book of readings for excessive periods of time, sometimes exceeding 30 minutes.

But what of the group that received the new drug? Is the difference between the 600 recoveries that occur spontaneously, and the 700 recoveries that we observed, simply a natural variation within the normal variability of the disease, or is it a real difference? Should we ignore it, or does it mean something? Mathematical analysis reveals that the difference is real.[b]

The term of art used to describe a real difference in results is **statistical significance**. When a result is statistically significant, it is unlikely to be a natural variation in the phenomenon; rather, the result probably has a cause external to the phenomenon. Naturally, we want to know what the cause is, but we must postpone this inquiry for the moment.

THE QUALIFIED LABOR POOL

We cannot expect to reach the same level of precision in life, especially in a lawsuit over discrimination, as we can achieve in a scientific experiment, but we can approximate it. The first step is to determine our expectation. This is easily done in principle: we expect an employer to obey the law, which means to award jobs without regard to race or sex.[c] In

---

[b]A student either recovers within a month or does not; therefore, a binomial distribution can be expected. Applying the algorithm from <u>Castaneda v. Partida</u>, 430 U.S. 482 (1977) (discussed below), the standard deviation is ($\sqrt{(.6 \times .4)1,000}$ =) 15.5. The observed value is (700 − 600 = 100; 100 ÷ 15.5 =) 6.4 standard deviations from the expected value, which is a statistically significant result.

[c]Title VII prohibits discrimination based on race, color, religion, sex, or national origin; for convenience, we will shorten this list of protected characteristics to "race or sex." In addition, Title VII applies not only to jobs, but to all employment opportunities; for example, Title VII also prohibits discrimination in compensation, promotion, and fringe benefits like vacations and pensions. For this reason, it would be more accurate to say that we expect an employer to award employment opportunities without regard to race or sex. In the text we speak of jobs, rather than employment opportunities, because jobs are a typical focus of Title VII cases, and the prima facie-II of

(continued...)

practice, however, converting this general expectation into a specific number can be difficult.

Congress did not intend Title VII to compromise efficiency within a firm. Thus, an employer is never expected to hire a person who is not qualified for a job. Nor did Congress expect an employer to do the impossible. Thus, an employer is not expected to hire a person who is unwilling to accept the job. Putting these points into legal vocabulary, Title VII protects only workers who are willing and able to perform the job in question.

It follows that, as we determine our expectations about whom a law-abiding employer would hire, we must limit ourselves to the class of workers who are willing and able to perform the job. Let us call this class the **qualified labor pool.** A law-abiding employer will hire workers from the qualified labor pool without regard to their race or sex.

If every worker in the qualified labor pool is willing and able to perform the job, each worker is, for the employer's purposes, indistinguishable from each other worker. Therefore, each of them has an equal chance of being hired. In essence, an employer who pays attention only to qualifications hires at random from the qualified labor pool.

Of particular importance under Title VII, men and women, and whites and people of color, all look alike to a non-discriminatory employer. Consequently, in the qualified labor pool, each man and each woman, each white and each person of color, should have an equal chance of being hired. In essence, a non-discriminatory employer hires men and women, blacks and whites at random from the qualified labor pool. It follows that the proportion of a protected group in the qualified labor pool should match the proportion of the group who are hired for the job. Suppose 30 percent of the qualified labor pool for a job is male and 70 is female, and an employer is hiring 100 persons. We expect this employer to hire

---

^c(...continued)
disparate treatment as proved by statistics is most easily understood in the context of hiring, in which the employment opportunity is jobs.

approximately 30 men and 70 women.

PROXIES

The student should now be able to understand that if an employer is accused of race or sex discrimination, it is essential to determine the proportion of people of color or women in the qualified labor pool. But determining the racial or sexual characteristics of the qualified labor pool is nearly impossible to do directly. The following hypothetical case illustrates this and other problems.

The Good Foods Case

> Good Foods is a large chain of supermarkets in a metropolitan area. Last year, Good Foods received 10,000 applications for the job of full-time clerk in its stores, and it hired 780 white people and 220 people of color.

Suppose Good Foods is accused of discriminating against people of color in the hiring of full-time clerks. In order to use statistical evidence, we need to know the percentages of whites and people of color in the qualified labor pool for this job. As a practical matter, however, we cannot count the numbers of persons in the city who are qualified to be food clerks; and even if we could count them, we cannot learn which of them would accept the job with this particular employer. What can we do?

Similar difficulties occur in other contexts and are overcome by using proxies. A **proxy** stands in the place of something else. In statistics, a fair proxy has the same relevant characteristics as the universe for which the proxy stands; therefore, what is true of the proxy is true of the universe. For example, suppose a presidential candidate wants to know how the public feels about the party's foreign policy. The universe is the public, but it is impractical to ask every citizen in the nation; however, the answers given by a properly selected sample of between 1,000 and 1,500 persons will closely approximate what the entire population would answer. If two-thirds of the persons in the sample disapprove of the policy, two-thirds of the population also disapprove of the policy. The sample is a fair proxy for the population.

In employment discrimination cases, the relevant universe is the qualified labor pool. In the Good Foods Supermarket case, we want to know the percentages of whites and people of color in the pool. We cannot count them directly, and parties to litigation can rarely afford to commission a poll. But we need not lose hope, as other fair proxies exist.

Sometimes the population can serve as a proxy for the qualified labor pool for a job. The population is a fair proxy when the job in question is unskilled and the plaintiffs' group and the comparators are equally interested in the job.[d] This was so in <u>Teamsters</u>. The Court allowed the government to use the population surrounding the employer's terminals as a proxy for the qualified labor pool for the job of truck driver. The population was a fair proxy because no evidence in the case indicated that African-Americans were less qualified for, or less interested in, the job of truck driver than whites were. This is the reason that the Supreme Court noted that approximately half of the population of Atlanta was black. It followed that about half of the qualified labor pool was also black. Based on this fact, we would expect that about half of the company's drivers would be black.

The Good Foods case suggests another proxy, namely, the applicant pool. Applicants are an especially good proxy because we may safely assume that they are interested in the job. (Some are not, but we have no reason to believe that proportionally more black than white applicants would be unwilling to accept the job.) Also, because people usually do not bother to apply for

---

[d]If a job requires a high degree of education, we must take into account that proportionally more whites than people of color may have the appropriate training. The population would not be a fair proxy when the job in question is architect or physician. Similarly, we need to take into account that some jobs are less attractive to one group than to another. In a case alleging sex discrimination, the population would not be a fair proxy for the job of plumber because fewer women than men are interested in this trade.

jobs for which they are totally unqualified, we may assume that most applicants are qualified for the job. (At any rate, we have no reason to believe that proportionally more black than white applicants are unqualified.) Therefore, if 75 percent of applicants for the job of clerk in a Good Foods store are white and 25 percent are people of color, we may infer that the qualified labor pool is also 75 percent whites and 25 percent people of color. This fact creates the expectation that 75 percent of the clerks hired by Good Foods would be white and 25 percent, people of color.

EXPECTATIONS, OBSERVATIONS, AND DISPARITIES

The racial and sexual characteristics of a fair proxy for the qualified labor pool create our expectation. Our next step is to observe the employer's behavior. How many men and women, or whites and people of color, did the employer hire? These numbers are usually obtained from the employer's records.

Then we need to compare our expectation and our observation. We will be satisfied if we find no disparity. If 25 percent of the (proxy for) the qualified labor pool are people of color, and 25 percent of newly hired workers are also people of color, we will be content. The reason is not that the employer has satisfied a quota. Rather, the reason is that we have no reason to believe that race has influenced the hiring process. Think again of our example of the drug trial. In the normal process of Gold's disease, 60 percent of students recover within a month. If the rate of recovery in the group receiving the new drug is also approximately 60 percent, we must conclude that the drug had no effect; nothing outside the normal process of the disease influenced the students' recovery. In the context of employment, we expect employers to obey the law; therefore, we define non-discriminatory hiring as the normal process. If the employer's numbers meet our expectation, we conclude that illegal causes like race and sex had no effect; nothing outside the normal (non-discriminatory) process of hiring influenced the employer's decisions.

In the drug trial, if 700 of 1,000 students receiving the drug recover within a month, we must conclude that the drug was effective. The numbers convince us that a cause outside the normal process of the disease influenced the students' recovery; because of the rigorous structure of the double-blind trial, the only reasonable cause is the drug. Similarly, if the employer's numbers fall significantly beneath our expectation, we must conclude that a cause outside the normal hiring process contributed to the result. If we find a significant disparity between our expectation and our observation, race or sex may have influenced the employer's decisions.

Our conclusion, of course, must be based on a statistically significant disparity. An intuitive test of significance, such as Inez's judgment about the nails in her tires, is satisfactory for daily life, but liability in a law suit must be grounded on a more reliable standard because intuition can be misleading. Consider again the Good Foods case. The chain hires 1,000 persons, 220 of whom are persons of color. Because they are 25 percent of the (proxy for) the qualified labor pool, we expect people of color to receive (1,000 x .25 =) 250 jobs. The 220 jobs they get are (220 ÷ 250 =) 88 percent of what we expect. Intuition might lead us to conclude that this disparity is too small to worry about. After all, 88 percent is not far from our expectation. This result seems like flipping a coin 10 times and getting 6 heads and 4 tails. But such a conclusion would not be sound. A formal test of statistical significance will reveal that the result in the Good Foods case is a genuine disparity, not a random variation in a process that is indifferent to race.

A TEST OF STATISTICAL SIGNIFICANCE

There exist various tests of statistical significance, that is, of whether a disparity is real. One test that has been endorsed by the Supreme Court appears in <u>Castaneda v. Partida</u>, 430 U.S. 482 (1977).[e] The test is appropriately used when comparing two groups, for example, men versus women or, as in the Good Foods case, whites versus people of color. The test may be

---

[e]That the Court has not endorsed other tests of statistical significance does not mean that only this test is acceptable in the law. Indeed, the <u>Castaneda</u> test is not properly applicable to many other situations.

applied as follows:

Step 1

Identify a fair proxy for the qualified labor pool. In the Good Foods case, the proxy is applicants for the job.

Step 2

Determine the percentage of each of the two groups in the qualified labor pool. In the Good Foods case, whites are 75 percent of applicants, and people of color are 25 percent.[f]

Step 3

Calculate the product of these two percentages by multiplying them by each other. .75 x .25 = .1875.

Step 4

Determine the number of decisions the employer has made within the period covered by the statute of limitations.[g] Multiply this number by the product in step 3, and take the square root of the result. This number is the standard deviation for these numbers. In the Good Foods case, 1,000 persons were hired during the period covered by the statute of limitations. 1,000 x .1875 = 187.5. $\sqrt{187.5}$ = 13.7.

Step 5

Calculate the expected number of persons in the plaintiffs' group whom a non-discriminatory employer would have hired, that is, the number of persons in the plaintiffs' group who would have been hired if

---

[f]These percentages represent the probabilities of hiring each class in a random process. If 75 percent of the qualified labor pool is white, 75 percent of new hires will be white if hiring is performed at random.

[g]The statute of limitations in Title VII claims requires that a charge of discrimination be filed with the EEOC within 300 days of the alleged discriminatory act. An employer cannot be held liable for any decisions made more than 300 days before the charge was filed. Therefore, one must determine the date the charged was filed. Count back 300 days and, starting on this date and going forward, count the number of relevant decisions the employer made.

race had not been a causal factor in the hiring process.[h] To do this, multiply the percentage of plaintiffs in the qualified labor pool by the number of decisions the employer made. In the Good Foods case our expectation is that (.25 x 1,000 =) 250 persons of color should have been hired.

Step 6

Subtract the number of persons in the plaintiffs' group whom the employer actually hired from the number we expected in step 5. In the Good Foods case, the difference is (250 - 220 =) 30.

Step 7

Divide the difference calculated in step 6 by the standard deviation calculated in step 4. This quotient tells us the number of standard deviations by which the actual number of new hires from the plaintiff's group differs from the expected number. In the Good Foods case, 30 ÷ 13.7 = 2.2.

In Castaneda the Court said that if the actual number hired from the plaintiffs' group is two or three (or more) standard deviations below the expected number, we may conclude that the difference or disparity we have observed is unlikely to have occurred by chance in a non-discriminatory hiring process — in other words, that the

---

[h]This number is the same as the number of persons in the plaintiffs' group who would have been hired at random from the qualified labor pool. The reason is that all the whites and the people of color in the qualified labor pool are, by definition, qualified for the job and willing to accept it. Therefore, whites and people of color in the qualified labor pool look the same to a non-discriminatory employer. With no basis for distinguishing between whites and people of color, a non-discriminatory employer would hire them in proportion to their share of the pool. If 90 percent of the pool is white and 10 percent is people of color, 90 percent of the persons hired by a non-discriminatory employer would be white and 10 percent would be people of color. This result is equivalent to hiring at random from the pool.

result we have observed is statistically significant.[i]
According to statistical theory, if a result is
statistically significant, it probably has a specific
cause. Therefore, when the disparity between the number
of persons in the plaintiff's group whom we expect to
have been hired, and the number of persons in the
plaintiff's group who actually were hired, is
statistically significant, we know that this disparity is
real. It is not a random variation. It has a cause.
The next question is, what is the cause?

IDENTIFYING THE CAUSE OF A DISPARITY

Let us recur briefly to the experiment designed to
determine whether the drug to treat Gold's disease is
effective. We observed that 100 more persons taking the
drug recovered within a month than did persons taking the
placebo, and the next step was to determine why this
difference occurred. By themselves, statistics cannot
identify the cause.[j] Statistics can tell us that a
specific cause was probably at work, but they cannot
identify it. Other information, however, can. Our
experiment was carefully controlled so that the only
difference between the groups of patients was that one
group received the drug and the other received a placebo.
To the extent possible, every other cause was excluded.
For this reason, we may infer that the new drug was the
cause of the additional recoveries.

Unfortunately, life does not admit of double-blind
trials. We may feel confident that an event is so
unlikely to occur by chance that it probably has a

---

[i]This test of statistical significance may be expressed
directly in terms of probability: If the actual number
hired from the plaintiffs' group would occur by chance in a
non-discriminatory process less than one time in a hundred,
the disparity is statistically significant.

[j]In Teamsters the population of Atlanta was 51 percent
black; there were 57 line drivers at the Atlanta terminal,
but none was black or Latino. The corresponding numbers for
Los Angeles were 18 percent black population, 374 line
drivers, and, again, no black drivers. Such observations
would be extraordinarily improbable in a hiring system that
was indifferent to race. Nevertheless, the Court did not
infer intentional discrimination from these numbers.

specific cause, but we must acknowledge that many causes might be responsible. When Groucho dealt himself three consecutive royal flushes, Harpo had good reason to believe that a specific cause was at work; but, based only on this purely statistical information, he could not know what the cause was. Accordingly, he turned to what we may call background information. This is conventional (as opposed to statistical) evidence of the context in which the unlikely event occurred. Groucho and Harpo were playing cards for money; thus, Groucho had a reason to cheat. Groucho was dealing; thus, he had the opportunity to cheat. And Groucho was notorious for his bad character; thus, he had no compunctions about cheating. Using this background information, Harpo reasonably concluded that the most likely cause of Groucho's three royal flushes was his sharp dealing.

Under disparate treatment, which is intentional discrimination, only one cause is legally relevant: purpose. The plaintiffs must prove that the employer purposefully disadvantaged them. It follows that the last step in proving disparate treatment by statistics is the production of evidence of the employer's state of mind. Statistics cannot reveal state of mind, but conventional evidence — background information — can. In <u>Teamsters</u> the Court relied on evidence that people of color were given false information about job vacancies, and their applications were ignored. The Court was also aware of the long history of discrimination against people of color in the areas where the company's terminals were located. Such evidence revealed the employer's state of mind; it proved that the employer intentionally afforded people of color a lesser chance to become truck drivers than their white comparators.

THE PRIMA FACIE CASE IN THE SECOND SENSE
OF DISPARATE TREATMENT AS PROVED BY STATISTICS

To summarize briefly, there is only one prima facie-I of discrimination, but there are many prima facie-IIs. Some prima facie-IIs use only conventional evidence, e.g., the formula in <u>McDonnell Douglas v. Green</u>. Other prima facie-IIs use statistical evidence. We have been focusing in this comment on one of those statistical prima facie-IIs. Let us now summarize this pattern. It requires a plaintiff to

A)   identify a fair proxy for the qualified labor pool, e.g., the population or the applicant pool;

B)   identify an employment opportunity (e.g. being hired for a job) and establish a disparity between the percentages of the plaintiffs and the comparators who are in the proxy and who benefit from the opportunity;

C)   prove by conventional evidence that the disparity is caused by the employer's intent to disadvantage the plaintiffs because of their race or sex.

QUESTIONS FOR REFLECTION

1. Referring to the Teamsters case, was the evidence relevant that the company's predecessors had discriminated against people of color before Title VII took effect? Why or why not?

2. The company in Teamsters pointed out that the number of jobs for drivers declined in the late 1960s. Was this fact relevant? Why or why not?

3. The Court's opinion notes that the employer pointed out a number of supposed shortcomings in the government's statistics. What were they? Regardless of whether the government's evidence was in fact deficient in these ways, were they appropriate factors to take into account in evaluating statistical evidence?

Ω

Disparate Impact

Introduction

Prior to the 1960's, the only way to prove discrimination was to establish that the actor intended to disadvantage the victim because of one's race or sex. But during the 1960's a new way of proving discrimination evolved. Its genesis may have been the reconciliation of an old observation and a new theory. The observation was that people of color scored lower on intelligence tests than whites. The theory was that natural ability does not differ across racial groups. The reconciliation was the explanation that blacks' lower scores on intelligence tests were caused by cultural bias in the tests. Whether the explanation was valid or not (and it was highly controversial), it was widely propagated. Its chief importance for our purpose is twofold. The explanation focused on the outcome of the test, not the motivation of the people who designed or used the test. The designers (probably psychologists) and the users (schools and employers) may have acted in good faith, yet the test was unfair to people of color. And in focusing on outcome, the explanation was concerned with groups of people, not individuals. The test was unfair because blacks as a group scored lower than whites; there was no evidence that the score of any individual black was incorrect.

By the beginning of the 1970's, a new method of proving employment discrimination was being advanced. It focused on effects instead of motives and concerned groups instead of individuals. Under this method, which has come to be known as **disparate impact**, an act is discriminatory if its effect is to disadvantage a racial, sexual, or ethnic class unless the act can be justified by the legitimate needs of the business. The following case adopted the disparate impact method of proving discrimination. As you read the case, try to identify the elements of the prima facie case of disparate impact.

Griggs v. Duke Power Company
401 U.S. 424 (1971)

Mr. Chief Justice BURGER delivered the opinion of the Court.

We granted the writ in this case to resolve the question whether an employer is prohibited by the Civil Rights Act of 1964, Title VII, from requiring a high school education or passing of a standardized general intelligence test as a condition of employment in or transfer to jobs when (a) neither standard is shown to be significantly related to successful job performance, (b) both requirements operate to disqualify Negroes at a substantially higher rate than white applicants, and (c) the jobs in question formerly had been filled only by white employees as part of a longstanding practice of giving preference to whites.

Congress provided, in Title VII of the Civil Rights Act of 1964, for class actions for enforcement of provisions of the Act, and this proceeding was brought by a group of incumbent Negro employees against Duke Power Company. All the petitioners are employed at the Company's Dan River Steam Station, a power generating facility located at Draper, North Carolina. At the time this action was instituted, the Company had 95 employees at the Dan River Station, 14 of whom were Negroes; 13 of these are petitioners here.

The District Court found that prior to July 2, 1965, the effective date of the Civil Rights Act of 1964, the Company openly discriminated on the basis of race in the hiring and assigning of employees at its Dan River plant. The plant was organized into five operating departments: (1) Labor, (2) Coal Handling, (3) Operations, (4) Maintenance, and (5) Laboratory and Test. Negroes were employed only in the Labor Department where the highest paying jobs paid less than the lowest paying jobs in the other four "operating" departments in which only whites were employed.[1] Promotions were normally made within each department on the basis of job seniority. Transferees into a department usually began in the lowest position.

In 1955 the Company instituted a policy of requiring a high school education for initial assignment to any department except Labor, and for transfer from the Coal Handling to any "inside" department (Operations, Maintenance, or Laboratory). When the Company abandoned its policy of restricting Negroes to the Labor Department in 1965, completion of high school also was made a prerequisite to transfer from Labor to any other department. From the time the high school requirement was instituted to the time of trial, however, white employees hired before the time of the high school

---

[1] A Negro was first assigned to a job in an operating department in August 1966, five months after charges had been filed with the Equal Employment Opportunity Commission. The employee, a high school graduate who had begun in the Labor Department in 1953, was promoted to a job in the Coal Handling Department.

education requirement continued to perform satisfactorily and achieve promotions in the "operating" departments. Findings on this score are not challenged.

The Company added a further requirement for new employees on July 2, 1965, the date on which Title VII became effective. To qualify for placement in any but the Labor Department, it became necessary to register satisfactory scores on two professionally prepared aptitude tests, as well as to have a high school education. Completion of high school alone continued to render employees eligible for transfer to the four desirable departments from which Negroes had been excluded if the incumbent had been employed prior to the time of the new requirement. In September 1965 the Company began to permit incumbent employees who lacked a high school education to qualify for transfer from Labor or Coal Handling to an "inside" job by passing two tests—the Wonderlic Personnel Test, which purports to measure general intelligence, and the Bennett Mechanical Comprehension Test. Neither was directed or intended to measure the ability to learn to perform a particular job or category of jobs. The requisite scores used for both initial hiring and transfer approximated the national median for high school graduates.[2]

...

The District Court had found that while the Company previously followed a policy of overt racial discrimination in a period prior to the Act, such conduct had ceased. The District Court also concluded that Title VII was intended to be prospective only and, consequently, the impact of prior inequities was beyond the reach of corrective action authorized by the Act.

...

The objective of Congress in the enactment of Title VII is plain from the language of the statute. It was to achieve equality of employment opportunities and remove barriers that have operated in the past to favor an identifiable group of white employees over other employees. Under the Act, practices, procedures, or tests neutral on their face, and even neutral in terms of intent, cannot be maintained if they operate to "freeze" the status quo of prior discriminatory employment practices.

The Court of Appeals' opinion, and the partial dissent, agreed that, on the record in the present case, "whites register far better on the Company's alternative

---

[2]The test standards are thus more stringent than the high school requirement, since they would screen out approximately half of all high school graduates.

Griggs v. Duke Power Company

requirements" than Negroes.[6] This consequence would appear to be directly traceable to race. Basic intelligence must have the means of articulation to manifest itself fairly in a testing process. Because they are Negroes, petitioners have long received inferior education in segregated schools and this Court expressly recognized these differences in *Gaston County v. United States*, 395 U.S. 285 (1969). There, because of the inferior education received by Negroes in North Carolina, this Court barred the institution of a literacy test for voter registration on the ground that the test would abridge the right to vote indirectly on account of race. Congress did not intend by Title VII, however, to guarantee a job to every person regardless of qualifications. In short, the Act does not command that any person be hired simply because he was formerly the subject of discrimination, or because he is a member of a minority group. Discriminatory preference for any group, minority or majority, is precisely and only what Congress has proscribed. What is required by Congress is the removal of artificial, arbitrary, and unnecessary barriers to employment when the barriers operate invidiously to discriminate on the basis of racial or other impermissible classification.

Congress has now provided that tests or criteria for employment or promotion may not provide equality of opportunity merely in the sense of the fabled offer of milk to the stork and the fox.[a] On the contrary, Congress has now required that the posture

---

[6]In North Carolina, 1960 census statistics show that, while 34% of white males had completed high school, only 12% of Negro males had done so. U.S. Bureau of the Census, U.S. Census of Population: 1960 , Vol. 1, Characteristics of the Population, pt. 35, Table 47.

Similarly, with respect to standardized tests, the EEOC in one case found that use of a battery of tests, including the Wonderlic and Bennett tests used by the Company in the instant case, resulted in 58% of whites passing the tests, as compared with only 6% of the blacks. Decision of EEOC, CCH Empl. Prac. Guide, ¶17,304.53 (Dec. 2, 1966).

[a]   {"The Fox and the Crane
The fox the crane did solemnly invite
Only to tantalize her appetite,
For nothing he but liquid fare provides
That spreading o'er the table thinly glides,
Of which her spearlike beak could nothing sup,
Whilst the sly fox licks all unkindly up.
The crane, this false imposture to requite
The fox to new caresses did invite,
But a glass vial did her cates contain,
Which only she with length of bill could drain.
The fox, thus foiled with her more powerful arts,
To his own cell with scorn and shame departs.

(continued...)

and condition of the job-seeker be taken into account. It has–to resort again to the fable–provided that the vessel in which the milk is proffered be one all seekers can use. The Act proscribes not only overt discrimination but also practices that are fair in form, but discriminatory in operation. The touchstone is business necessity. If an employment practice which operates to exclude Negroes cannot be shown to be related to job performance, the practice is prohibited.

On the record before us, neither the high school completion requirement nor the general intelligence test is shown to bear a demonstrable relationship to successful performance of the jobs for which it was used. Both were adopted, as the Court of Appeals noted, without meaningful study of their relationship to job-performance ability. Rather, a vice president of the Company testified, the requirements were instituted on the Company's judgment that they generally would improve the overall quality of the work force.

The evidence, however, shows that employees who have not completed high school or taken the tests have continued to perform satisfactorily and make progress in departments for which the high school and test criteria are now used.[7] The promotion record of present employees who would not be able to meet the new criteria thus suggests the possibility that the requirements may not be needed even for the limited purpose of preserving the avowed policy of advancement within the Company. In the context of this case, it is unnecessary to reach the question whether testing requirements that take into account capability for the next succeeding position or related future promotion might be utilized upon a showing that such long-range requirements fulfill a genuine business need. In the present case the Company has made no such showing.

The Court of Appeals held that the Company had adopted the diploma and test requirements without any "intention to discriminate against Negro employees." We do not suggest that either the District Court or the Court of Appeals erred in examining the employer's intent; but good intent or absence of discriminatory intent

---

[a](...continued)
{The Moral:}

> Thus fraud t'entangle fraud is oft designed,
> And falsehood is by falsehood countermined."

--A fable by Aesop, translated by Thomas Philipott, 1666. — ed.}

[7]For example, between July 2, 1965, and November 14, 1966, the percentage of white employees who were promoted but who were not high school graduates was nearly identical to the percentage of non-graduates in the entire white work force.

Griggs v. Duke Power Company

does not redeem employment procedures or testing mechanisms that operate as "built-in head winds" for minority groups and are unrelated to measuring job capability.

The Company's lack of discriminatory intent is suggested by special efforts to help the undereducated employees through Company financing of two-thirds the cost of tuition for high school training. But Congress directed the thrust of the Act to the *consequences* of employment practices, not simply the motivation. More than that, Congress has placed on the employer the burden of showing that any given requirement must have a manifest relationship to the employment in question.

The facts of this case demonstrate the inadequacy of broad and general testing devices as well as the infirmity of using diplomas or degrees as fixed measures of capability. History is filled with examples of men and women who rendered highly effective performance without the conventional badges of accomplishment in terms of certificates, diplomas, or degrees. Diplomas and tests are useful servants, but Congress has mandated the common sense proposition that they are not to become masters of reality.

The Company contends that its general intelligence tests are specifically permitted by § 703(h) of the Act.[8]   That section authorizes the use of "any professionally developed ability test" that is not "designed, intended *or used* to discriminate because of race ...." (Emphasis added.)

The Equal Employment Opportunity Commission, having enforcement responsibility, has issued guidelines interpreting § 703(h) to permit only the use of job-related tests.[9] The administrative interpretation of the Act by the enforcing agency

---

[8]Section 703(h) applies only to tests. It has no applicability to the high school diploma requirement.

[9]EEOC Guidelines on Employment Testing Procedures, issued August 24, 1966, provide:

> "The Commission accordingly interprets "professionally developed ability test" to mean a test which fairly measures the knowledge or skills required by the particular job or class of jobs which the applicant seeks, or which fairly affords the employer a chance to measure the applicant's ability to perform a particular job or class of jobs. The fact that a test was prepared by an individual or organization claiming expertise in test preparation does not, without more, justify its use within the meaning of Title VII."

The EEOC position has been elaborated in the new Guidelines on Employee Selection Procedures, 29 CFR § 1607, 35 Fed. Reg. 12333 (Aug. 1, 1970). These guidelines demand
(continued...)

is entitled to great deference. Since the Act and its legislative history support the Commission's construction, this affords good reason to treat the guidelines as expressing the will of Congress.

...

Nothing in the Act precludes the use of testing or measuring procedures; obviously they are useful. What Congress has forbidden is giving these devices and mechanisms controlling force unless they are demonstrably a reasonable measure of job performance. Congress has not commanded that the less qualified be preferred over the better qualified simply because of minority origins. Far from disparaging job qualifications as such, Congress has made such qualifications the controlling factor, so that race, religion, nationality, and sex become irrelevant. What Congress has commanded is that any tests used must measure the person for the job and not the person in the abstract.

The judgment of the Court of Appeals is, as to that portion of the judgment appealed from, reversed.

✙

---

[9](...continued)
that employers using tests have available "data demonstrating that the test is predictive of or significantly correlated with important elements of work behavior which comprise or are relevant to the job or jobs for which candidates are being evaluated." *Id.* at § 1607.4(c).

QUESTIONS FOR REFLECTION

1. The employer in <u>Griggs</u> believed in good faith that workers with high school diplomas made better employees and that mechanical aptitude, as measured by the scored tests, was necessary for the jobs in question. It is true that the employer did not have evidence to support these beliefs, and that the diploma requirement and aptitude test disadvantaged blacks as compared to whites. Nevertheless, the employer did not intend to exclude blacks from jobs. Indeed, the employer paid most of the cost of tuition for employees who sought a high school education. Thus, it appears that the disparate impact definition of discrimination outlaws unintentional acts. Is it fair to hold employers liable for acts they do not intend to commit?

2. Should the Court have considered the evidence from the EEOC decision cited in n. 6?

3. The Supreme Court reversed the judgment of the lower court, that is, held the plaintiffs won on the issue of disparate impact. Should the Court instead have remanded the case to the trial court for further proceedings?

Comment

Section 703(a) of Title VII reads:

Sec. 703. (a) It shall be an unlawful employment practice for an employer —

(1) to fail or refuse to hire or to discharge any individual, or otherwise to discriminate against any individual with respect to his compensation, terms, conditions, or privileges of employment <u>because of</u> such individual's race, color, religion, sex, or national origin; or

(2) to limit, segregate, or classify his employees or applicants for employment in any way which would deprive or tend to deprive any individual of employment opportunities or otherwise adversely affect his status as an employee, <u>because of</u> such individual's race, color, religion, sex, or national origin.

Thus, the statute does not outlaw all discrimination. As far as Title VII is concerned, an employer is free to discriminate on the grounds of union activity, political beliefs, and so forth. The discrimination which is outlawed by the statute is limited to disadvantage of a worker because of one's race or sex.

This limitation gives rise to a difficult question. In disparate treatment, it is obvious that the employer disadvantages a worker because of the latter's race or sex. The employer intentionally denies opportunities to women and people of color; to say the same thing, the employer consciously uses race or sex as a selection criterion for awarding and denying employment opportunities to workers. In disparate impact, however, it is not obvious that the employer disadvantages a worker because of race or sex. The employer does not desire to deny opportunities to women or people of color. Rather than knowingly using race or sex as a selection criterion, the employer uses a criterion that is neutral on its face. And so the question arises: in a disparate impact case, how can we say that the employer denies opportunities to workers <u>because of</u> their race or sex?

We cannot answer this question now. Before we can, the student must understand the defense in disparate impact, which is our next topic.

$$\Omega$$

Business Necessity

Introduction

In a disparate impact case, the plaintiffs must prove that a specific employment practice has a disproportional adverse effect on their group; this is the essence of their prima facie case. For example, the plaintiffs in Griggs proved that the high school diploma requirement and the mechanical aptitude test disqualified proportionally more blacks than whites. Then the defendant has an opportunity to present a defense. An employer may defend a disparate impact case in the same ways that any other defendant may defend a case: the defendant may attack the plaintiff's prima facie case, prove an affirmative defense, or both.

Attacking the prima facie case of disparate impact is similar to attacking any other prima facie case. The employer typically attempts to discredit the plaintiffs' witnesses or evidence; thus an employer might try to show that the plaintiffs' statistics are inaccurate or the plaintiff's statistical methods are flawed.

The affirmative defense to disparate impact is, however, unique. Section 703(k)(1)(A)(i) of Title VII specifies this defense. An employment practice with a disproportional adverse effect is lawful if the practice is "job related for the position in question and is consistent with business necessity." This is known as the **business necessity defense**, and an employer can win a disparate impact case by establishing it.

One must be careful about the terms in section 703(k)(1)(A)(i), for they are terms of art; thus, they do not carry their ordinary English meanings. "Job related" does not mean merely connected in some way to a job, and "business necessity" does not mean indispensable to a business. Rather, these terms have acquired special meanings in the law. The meanings of these terms must be derived from the cases which apply the terms. In Griggs, the Supreme Court held that the diploma requirement and aptitude test were not job related and consistent with business necessity. The meaning of the terms "job related" and "consistent with business necessity" can be inferred from Griggs, at least in part,

by examining it to determine the deficiencies in the
criteria.

Before reading the following case, the student
should review Griggs and determine why the Court held
that the diploma requirement and aptitude test were not
"job related for the position in question" and not
"consistent with business necessity."

The following case, though decided before section
703(k)(1)(A)(i) was added to the Act, applied the
business necessity defense.

⚜

Spurlock v. United Airlines
475 F.2d 216 (10th Cir. 1972)

LEWIS, Chief Judge:– ...

The evidence established that on May 19, 1969, the appellant applied for the position of flight officer. At that time, appellant did not meet United's qualifications to be considered for flight officer. He was 29 years of age, had two years of college, principally in music education, had logged 204 hours of flight time, and had obtained a commercial pilot's license. United's minimum requirements for flight officer were 500 hours flight time, 21 to 29 years of age, a commercial pilot's license and instrument rating, and a college degree.

When appellant's application was received by mail in United's employment office, it was reviewed by a clerical employee. He circled in red the respects in which the appellant's qualifications were deficient. Appellant was then advised by letter that United had other applicants whose qualifications more nearly met United's requirements. No one at United saw or interviewed the appellant, and no one knew his race [African-American].

From the evidence, the trial court found an absence of an intent to discriminate on the part of United in hiring its flight officers. While it is important to examine the intent of a company charged with a Title VII violation, absence of discriminatory intent does not necessarily establish that the company's employment practices have no discriminatory *effect*. Title VII is aimed at the consequences of employment practices, not simply the motivation. Thus, when a plaintiff is claiming that the criteria used by a company in screening job applicants discriminate against a minority group, he needs only establish that the use of such criteria has a discriminatory *result*. It is not necessary to prove a discriminatory intent but only that the discriminatory criteria were used deliberately, not accidentally.

In order to establish that United's flight officer qualifications resulted in discrimination against blacks, the appellant showed that out of the approximately 5900 flight officers in United's employ at the time of the trial only 9 were blacks. Appellant contends that these statistics establish a prima facie case of racial discrimination. United claims that these bare statistics establish nothing unless accompanied by similar information as to the number of *qualified* black applicants for the flight officer position. The circuitousness of this bootstrap argument becomes obvious when one recalls that it is United's *qualifications* for flight officer that appellant claims are discriminatory against blacks. We hold, therefore, that by showing the minuscule number of black flight officers in United's employ, the appellant established a prima facie case of racial discrimination in hiring practices. This is true even though it is clear from the record that United applied its employment criteria without regard to race or color.

Employment practices which are inherently discriminatory may nevertheless be valid if a business necessity can be shown. And pre-employment qualifications which result in discrimination may be valid if they are shown to be job-related. Thus, once the appellant had established a prima facie case of racial discrimination, the burden fell upon United to show that its qualifications for flight officer were job-related. The trial court found that the burden had been met and that United's job qualifications were job-related. We agree.

The two job qualifications that appellant challenges are the requirements of a college degree and a minimum of 500 flight hours. The evidence at trial showed that United does not train applicants to be pilots but instead requires that their applicants be pilots at the time of their application. It cannot seriously be contended that such a requirement is not job-related. United also showed through the use of statistics that applicants who have higher flight hours are more likely to succeed in the rigorous training program which United flight officers go through after they are hired. The statistics clearly showed that 500 hours was a reasonable minimum to require of applicants to insure their ability to pass United's training program.[1] The evidence also showed that because of the high cost of the training program, it is important to United that those who begin its training program eventually become flight officers. This is an example of business necessity. We conclude that the evidence amply supports a finding that the requirement of 500 hours flight time is job-related.

---

[1]The statistics presented were for the period February 1965 through April 1967 and were based on United's experience with approximately 1300 trainees, 82 of whom did not complete the training program. The statistics produced the following results:

No. of Hours	No. of Trainees	No. of Failures	Failure Rate
200 or less	352	32	9%
201 to 500	128	19	14%
501 to 1,000	154	12	8%
1,001 to 1,500	175	9	5%
1,501 to 2,000	168	3	2%
2,001 to 2,500	119	2	2%
2,501 to 3,000	89	3	2%
3,001 to 5,001	118	2	2%

With regard to the college degree requirement, United officials testified that it was a requirement which could be waived if the applicant's other qualifications were superior, especially if he had a lot of high quality flight time, that is, flight time in high speed jet aircraft. The evidence showed that United flight officers go through a rigorous training course upon being hired and then are required to attend intensive refresher courses at six-month intervals to insure that all flight officers remain at peak performance ability. United officials testified that the possession of a college degree indicated that the applicant had the ability to understand and retain concepts and information given in the atmosphere of a classroom or training program. Thus, a person with a college degree, particularly one in the "hard" sciences, is more able to cope with the initial training program and the unending series of refresher courses than a person without a college degree. We think United met the burden of showing that its requirement of a college degree was sufficiently job-related to make it a lawful pre-employment standard....

When a job requires a small amount of skill and training and the consequences of hiring an unqualified applicant are insignificant, the courts should examine closely any pre-employment standard or criteria which discriminate against minorities. In such a case, the employer should have a heavy burden to demonstrate to the court's satisfaction that his employment criteria are job-related. On the other hand, when the job clearly requires a high degree of skill and the economic and human risks involved in hiring an unqualified applicant are great, the employer bears a correspondingly lighter burden to show that his employment criteria are job-related. The job of airline flight officer is clearly such a job. United's flight officers pilot aircraft worth as much as $20 million and transport as many as 300 passengers per flight. The risks involved in hiring an unqualified applicant are staggering. The public interest clearly lies in having the most highly qualified persons available to pilot airliners. The courts, therefore, should proceed with great caution before requiring an employer to lower his pre-employment standards for such a job. We conclude that United Airlines met its burden of proving that its employment requirements are job-related and the trial court's finding in that regard is not clearly erroneous.

AFFIRMED.

QUESTIONS FOR REFLECTION

1. Why were the diploma requirement and aptitude test in <u>Griggs</u> held to be not "job related ... and consistent with business necessity"?

2. Was the risk of a crash relevant to <u>Spurlock</u>?

3. Is <u>Spurlock</u> evidence that courts are friendlier to college diploma requirements than to high school diploma requirements?

4. Suppose the year is 1966. You have just been hired into the human resources department of the Duke Power Company. You quickly learn of the requirements for promotion to the inside departments, viz., a high school diploma and a satisfactory score on the mechanical aptitude test. You notice that these requirements have a disproportional adverse effect on African Americans. You cannot know what the Supreme Court will hold in 1971, but you do know that rational selection criteria are job related. What would you recommend to your superiors concerning the promotion requirements?

5. The EEOC Guidelines, mentioned in n. 9 of <u>Griggs</u>, state that a test that has an adverse effect on a protected class is discriminatory unless the test predicts success on important elements of the job for which the test is used. Determining whether a test predicts success on the job is called **validation**. Validation studies are expensive, often running into hundreds of thousands of dollars. How are cost-conscious employers likely to cope with the EEOC's guideline?

Ω

Proof of Disparate Impact

Introduction

We have looked, albeit briefly, at the prima facie case in the first sense of disparate impact (<u>Griggs v. Duke Power Co.</u>) and at the business necessity defense (<u>Spurlock v. United Air Lines</u>). Now we turn to the way disparate impact is proved. Unlike proof of disparate treatment, of which we found three patterns, we find that one pattern dominates the proof of disparate impact.[a] It requires plaintiffs to

A) identify a selection criterion (such as a written test, a diploma requirement, or an experience requirement) that is used to award an employment opportunity;

B) specify a proxy for the qualified labor pool (the group on whom the selection criterion operates)

C) demonstrate that the selection criterion has an adverse effect on the plaintiffs' group in (a proxy for) the qualified labor pool, in other words, that the criterion awards the employment opportunity to proportionally more comparators than plaintiffs.

The first requirement is straightforward, but the second requirement needs explanation.

The second requirement has two steps. The first step is to identify a fair proxy for the qualified labor pool. In a disparate treatment case proved by statistics, the plaintiff may have a choice from among several proxies, for example, the population of the area, applicants, or recent graduates of appropriate training programs. In a disparate impact case, the plaintiff also has a choice of proxies, but the choice is more limited. The proxy must be the group to which the selection

---

[a]This pattern applies to a variety of cases, including hiring, promotion, layoff, and discharge. Other patterns exist, however.

criterion is applied. Nevertheless, the specification of
that group may vary. In <u>Griggs</u> the plaintiffs challenged
a written test, and the proxy had to be test takers; but
the proxy could have been the persons who took the test
on a certain date at a certain place, or persons who took
the test on a range of dates at one place or in several
places. The plaintiffs in <u>Griggs</u> also challenged the
high school degree requirement. This requirement was
applied to applicants, so the proxy could have been the
applicant pool; but the proxy could also have been the
population of the area in which most of the defendant's
employees lived, or the population of the state. In
<u>Spurlock</u> the plaintiff challenged the requirement that
applicants have 500 hours of flight time. The
requirement was applied to applicants, so the proxy could
have been the applicant pool, or pilots with sufficient
experience to succeed in flight school.

After the proxy is identified, the second step of
the second requirement is for the plaintiffs to determine
the representation of their group and of the comparators
in the proxy. This is usually a matter of simple
arithmetic. Let us suppose, for example, that plaintiffs
(as in <u>Griggs</u>) are challenging a written test, so the
proxy is test takers. The plaintiffs need to calculate
the representation of their group and of the comparators
among test takers. Let us say that 80 percent of the
test takers are European-American and 20 percent are
Asian-American.

The third requirement calls for the plaintiffs to
prove that the challenged selection criterion
disproportionally disadvantages their group vis-a-vis the
comparators in the proxy. This step has three parts. In
the first part, the plaintiffs calculate their share of
the persons to whom the employer has awarded the
opportunity. This is also simple arithmetic. In our
example, the opportunity is passing a written test. The
plaintiffs would count the number of European-Americans
and Asian-Americans who achieved a passing score.

The second part of step three also requires nothing
but elementary arithmetic. The plaintiffs must compare
their share of the proxy with their share of the persons
who gain the opportunity. If these shares are the same,
no discrimination has occurred. In our example, Asians
are 20 percent of the proxy. If 20 percent (or more) of

the persons who pass the test are Asian, the plaintiffs have no cause to complain. But if the plaintiffs' share of the opportunity is less than their share of the proxy, they must proceed to the third part of step three.

If the plaintiffs' share of the opportunity is less than their share of the proxy, we must determine whether the disparity is real or only apparent - whether it is statistically significant or a random variation in a fair process. Suppose our plaintiffs constitute only 15 percent of the persons who pass the written test. Now the question arises, is the disparity between 20 percent (their share of the proxy) and 15 percent (their share of the opportunity) statistically significant? At this point, proof of disparate impact is identical to proof of disparate treatment by statistics, which we discussed above in connection with the <u>Teamsters</u> case. The **only** right way to answer this question is to apply a test of statistical significance.[b]

In the following case the court does not discuss whether the plaintiffs proved that the employer's selection criteria had an adverse effect. The reason is probably that the disparity is so large that it is obviously significant. The Court does, however, discuss whether the plaintiffs' proxy for the qualified labor pool was appropriate.

⚜

---

[b]Our reason for stressing the word "only" will become evident as the student reads the comment that follows this case.

Dothard v. Rawlinson
433 U.S. 321 (1977)

Mr. Justice STEWART delivered the opinion of the Court.

{The facts, which are stated more fully above in connection with bfoq's, were that Dianne Rawlinson was rejected as a "correctional counselor" in Alabama because she could not satisfy the state's requirement that prison guards weigh at least 120 pounds. The state also required that guards stand at least 5 feet 2 inches tall. The lower court ruled in Rawlinson's favor.}

...

II

In enacting Title VII, Congress required "the removal of artificial, arbitrary, and unnecessary barriers to employment when the barriers operate invidiously to discriminate on the basis of racial or other impermissible classification." *Griggs v. Duke Power Co.* 401 U.S. 424, 431. The District Court found that the minimum statutory height and weight requirements that applicants for employment as correctional counselors must meet constitute the sort of arbitrary barrier to equal employment opportunity that Title VII forbids. The appellants assert that the District Court erred both in finding that the height and weight standards discriminate against women, and in its refusal to find that, even if they do, these standards are justified as "job related."

A

The gist of the claim that the statutory height and weight requirements discriminate against women does not involve an assertion of purposeful discriminatory motive. It is asserted, rather, that these facially neutral qualification standards work in fact disproportionately to exclude women from eligibility for employment by the Alabama Board of Corrections. We dealt in *Griggs* and [in] *Albemarle Paper Co. v. Moody*, 422 U.S. 405, with similar allegations that facially neutral employment standards disproportionately excluded Negroes from employment, and those cases guide our approach here.

Those cases make clear that to establish a prima facie case of discrimination, a plaintiff need only show that the facially neutral standards in question select applicants for hire in a significantly discriminatory pattern. Once it is thus shown that the employment standards are discriminatory in effect, the employer must meet "the burden of showing that any given requirement [has] ... a manifest relationship to the employment in question." *Griggs* at 432. If the employer proves that the challenged requirements are job related, the plaintiff may then show that other selection devices without a similar discriminatory effect would also "serve the employer's legitimate interest in 'efficient and trustworthy workmanship.'" *Albemarle* at 425.

Although women 14 years of age or older comprise 52.75% of the Alabama population and 36.89% of its total labor force, they hold only 12.9% of its correctional counselor positions. In considering the effect of the minimum height and weight standards on this disparity in rate of hiring between the sexes, the District Court found that the 5'2" requirement would operate to exclude 33.29% of the women in the United States between the ages of 18-79, while excluding only 1.28% of men between the same ages. The 120-pound weight restriction would exclude 22.29% of the women and 2.35% of the men in this age group. When the height and weight restrictions are combined, Alabama's statutory standards would exclude 41.13% of the female population while excluding less than 1% of the male population. Accordingly, the District Court found that Rawlinson had made out a prima facie case of unlawful sex discrimination.

The appellants argue that a showing of disproportionate impact on women based on generalized national statistics should not suffice to establish a prima facie case. They point in particular to Rawlinson's failure to adduce comparative statistics concerning actual applicants for correctional counselor positions in Alabama. There is no requirement, however, that a statistical showing of disproportionate impact must always be based on analysis of the characteristics of actual applicants. The application process itself might not adequately reflect the actual potential applicant pool, since otherwise qualified people might be discouraged from applying because of a self-recognized inability to meet the very standards challenged as being discriminatory. A potential applicant could easily determine her height and weight and conclude that to make an application would be futile. Moreover, reliance on general population demographic data was not misplaced where there was no reason to suppose that physical height and weight characteristics of Alabama men and women differ markedly from those of the national population.

B

We turn, therefore, to the appellants' argument that they have rebutted the prima facie case of discrimination by showing that the height and weight requirements are job related. These requirements, they say, have a relationship to strength, a sufficient but unspecified amount of which is essential to effective job performance as a correctional counselor. In the District Court, however, the appellants produced no evidence correlating the height and weight requirements with the requisite amount of strength thought essential to good job performance. Indeed, they failed to offer evidence of any kind in specific justification of the statutory standards.

If the job-related quality that the appellants identify is bona fide, their purpose could be achieved by adopting and validating a test for applicants that measures strength directly. Such a test, fairly administered, would fully satisfy the standards of Title VII because it would be one that "measure[s] the person for the job and not the person in the abstract." *Griggs* at 436. But nothing in the present record even approaches such a measurement.

For the reasons we have discussed, the District Court was not in error in holding that Title VII of the Civil Rights Act of 1964, as amended, prohibits application of the statutory height and weight requirements to Rawlinson and the class she represents.

....

Comment

A little knowledge is dangerous, especially if it is old knowledge. Many people believe that whether a selection criterion has an adverse effect on a protected class is determined by the "eighty percent (or four-fifths) rule." The student will benefit from learning why this belief exists and why it is dangerous.

As is so often true, history illuminates the present. The history relevant to the Eighty Percent Rule began with a presidential order that all contracts with the federal government contain a non-discrimination clause; that is, in order to be awarded a contract to provide goods or services to the government, a contractor had to promise not to discriminate in employment on the basis of race or sex.[c] The federal government does business with thousands and thousands of private firms. From time to time (some would say, from moment to moment) federal contractors do not live up to their contractual obligations. The government knows this fact and has established compliance offices to monitor whether contractors are complying with their obligations. Beginning in the 1960s, the compliance offices began checking on whether contractors were keeping their promises not to discriminate on the basis of race or sex.

The number of federal contracts is huge. The number of employees of the federal compliance offices is small, and their resources are limited. The compliance offices made a fully rational decision: they decided to devote their scarce time and resources to investigating only the most serious violations of the duty not to discriminate. The compliance offices developed a simple test for deciding which contractors to investigate: if the success rate of women or people of color for a given opportunity is less than eighty percent of the success rate of the comparators for this opportunity, the

---

[c]This requirement remains in force today.

compliance office will investigate.[d] The greatest virtue
of the Eighty Percent Rule is that one does not need a
degree in statistics to apply it. The greatest vice of
the rule is the false belief that it reveals whether
discrimination has occurred.

As we mentioned in the introduction to this case,
whether discrimination has occurred depends on whether a
disparity is statistically significant. It follows that
if the Eighty Percent Rule were a proper test of
discrimination, the rule would be a test of statistical
significance. To say the same thing, the rule would
yield the same results as a recognized test of
statistical significance. The rule does not do this.

It is true that, in some cases involving small
groups, the Eighty Percent Rule yields the same result as
a test of statistical significance. In most cases,
however, the rule yields an erroneous result. Consider
two examples:

Example with a Small Set of Data

An employer wants to hire 100 new
workers; 100 men and 100 women apply, and the
employer hires 45 women and 55 men. The 80
Percent Rule asks, is the success rate of the
plaintiffs (women) at least 80 percent of the
success rate of the comparators (men)? The
rule is satisfied in this example because
women's success rate is (45 ÷ 100 =) 45
percent, men's success rate is (55 ÷ 100 =) 55
percent, and 45 percent is (45 ÷ 55 =) 82
percent of 55 percent. Testing for statistical
significance according to the method in
Castaneda v. Partida (see the Teamsters case

---

[d]For example, suppose a firm that builds houses hires
1,000 carpenters in a given year; 2,000 African-Americans and
6,000 European-Americans apply for these jobs, and 200
African-Americans and 800 European-Americans are hired. The
success rate of African-Americans is (200 ÷ 2,000) = 10
percent; the success rate of European-Americans is (800 ÷
6,000 =) 13 percent. The success rate of African-Americans is
(10 percent ÷ 13 percent =) 77 percent of the success rate of
European-Americans, and the Eighty Percent Rule is not
satisfied.

above) the probability of selecting a man in a sex-neutral process is (100 men ÷ 200 applicants =) .5; the probability of selecting a woman in a neutral process is the same. The number of decisions (persons hired) is 100. Therefore, the standard deviation is $\sqrt{(.5)(.5)(100)} = 5$. Thus, the result of 45 women is (50 - 45 = 5) one standard deviation below the expected result of 50; this result is not statistically significant because it could easily occur by chance in a selection process in which sex plays no role.

Example with a large set of data

Same as above with numbers larger by a factor of ten: 1,000 men and 1,000 women apply, and the employer hires 450 women and 550 men. Applying the Eighty Percent Rule yields the same result as above; adding a zero to the numbers does not change the proportions (450 ÷ 1,000 = 45 percent; 550 ÷ 1,000 = 55 percent; 45 percent ÷ 55 percent = 82 percent). The test for statistical significance, however, comes out differently. The probabilities of hiring men and women are the same as above (1,000 ÷ 2,000 = .5), but the number of decisions is much larger (1,000). The standard deviation is $(\sqrt{(.5)(.5)1,000} \approx)$ 16. The result of 450 women is (500 - 450 = 50; 50 ÷ 16 ≈ 3.1) more than 3 standard deviations below the expected result of 500; this result is statistically significant because it is unlikely to occur by chance in a selection process in which sex plays no role.

In the early days of Title VII, parties and some courts adopted the Eighty Percent Rule, partly because it appeared (albeit erroneously) to be approved by the federal government and partly because nearly anyone could apply the rule. It is clear today, however, that the Eighty Percent Rule is valid only for its original purpose — to help federal compliance offices to decide which contractors to investigate, and is not valid for determining whether a disparity is statistically significant.

QUESTIONS FOR REFLECTION

1. (a) What proxy for the qualified labor pool did the Court accept in <u>Dothard</u>? Was it a fair proxy? (b) What proxy did the employer argue should have been used? Should the employer's proxy have been accepted?

2. What evidence might the employer have introduced to vindicate its selection criteria (the height and weight requirements)?

Proof of Disparate Impact (cont'd)

Introduction

Like the preceding case, the following one pertains to proof of disparate impact. Note particularly the various ways in which, according to the court, disparate impact can be proved. Is the court correct? Then consider how the defendant might have proved the business necessity defense.

Green v. Missouri Pacific RR. Co.
523 F.2d 1290 (8th Cir. 1975)

BRIGHT, Circuit Judge:–The Missouri Pacific Railroad Company (MoPac) follows an absolute policy of refusing consideration for employment to any person convicted of a crime other than a minor traffic offense. Appellant Buck Green, who is black, raises the principal question of whether this policy violates Title VII of the Civil Rights Act of 1964, because this practice allegedly operates to disqualify blacks for employment at a substantially higher rate than whites and is not job related.

...

On September 29, 1970, Green, then 29 years of age, applied for employment as a clerk at MoPac's personnel office in the corporate headquarters in St. Louis, Missouri. In response to a question on an application form, Green disclosed that he had been convicted in December 1967 for refusing military induction. He stated that he had served 21 months in prison until paroled on July 24, 1970.[5] After reviewing the application form, MoPac's personnel officer informed Green that he was not qualified for employment at MoPac because of his conviction and prison record. Green, thereafter, sought relief under Title VII, and when administrative conciliation failed, he brought this action.

Since 1948, MoPac has followed the policy of disqualifying for employment any applicant with a conviction for any crime other than a minor traffic offense. Prior to 1972, MoPac also investigated an applicant's arrest record, but after the decision in *Gregory v. Litton Systems, Inc.*, 472 F.2d 631 (9th Cir. 1972), MoPac eliminated any arrest inquiry from its application form and ceased using arrest records as an employment criterion.

Green makes the following contentions on this appeal: (1) MoPac's policy of not hiring any person convicted of a criminal offense has a racially discriminatory effect and violates Title VII; (2) this policy is not justified by any business necessity....

_____

[5]Prior to Green's prosecution he had unsuccessfully sought classification as a conscientious objector by his draft board. Green did not appeal his conviction but sought post-conviction review. In proceedings which reached this court, the court, in a divided opinion, refused to review appellant's challenge to the alleged constitutional invalidity of his draft classification. *Cassidy v. United States*, 428 F.2d 585 (8th Cir. 1970). (Green's legal name at the time of these proceedings was Cassidy).

I. Whether Green proved a prima facie case of discrimination.

Although the employment practice in question is facially neutral, an employment test or practice which operates to exclude a disproportionate percentage of blacks violates Title VII unless the employer can establish that the practice is justified as a business necessity. Once a prima facie case of substantially disparate impact is made, the burden shifts to the employer to justify the employment practice or test as a business necessity.

Thus, we examine the threshold question of whether Green has presented a prima facie case. A disproportionate racial impact may be established statistically in any of three ways. The first procedure considers whether blacks as a class (or at least blacks in a specified geographical area) are excluded by the employment practice in question at a substantially higher rate than whites.

The second procedure focuses on a comparison of the percentage of black and white job applicants actually excluded by the employment practice or test of the particular company or governmental agency in question.

Finally, a third procedure examines the level of employment of blacks by the company or governmental agency in comparison to the percentage of blacks in the relevant geographical area.

Although Green alleged that MoPac discriminates against blacks generally in its employment practices, the district court focused only on whether a disparate impact could be statistically demonstrated by MoPac's policy of automatically rejecting all applicants with a conviction for an offense other than minor traffic infractions. Here, we consider a sweeping disqualification of all persons with a past record of some unlawful behavior, rather than a test directed at a precise measurement of intelligence or skills. The disparity of impact, if any, will be disclosed by an examination of how that policy affects applicants and potential applicants. We agree with the approach taken by the district court and primarily limit our statistical analysis to the effect of MoPac's policies against both blacks and whites in the general population in the area from which employees are drawn (metropolitan St. Louis), and the effect of this policy upon black and white applicants for employment with MoPac.

Initially, we note that the district court recognized statistical data and treatises offered into evidence by the plaintiff which indicate that blacks are convicted of crimes at a rate at least two to three times greater than the percentage of blacks in the populations of certain geographical areas. Dr. Ronald Christensen, a qualified expert witness for the plaintiff, concluded that it is between 2.2 and 6.7 times as likely that a black person will have a criminal conviction record during his lifetime than that a white person will have such a record. He further concluded that in urban areas from 36.9 percent to 78.1 percent of all black persons would incur a conviction during their lifetimes, but that from only 11.6 percent to 16.8 percent of all white persons would acquire a conviction.

MoPac's records of employment applications at its corporate headquarters during the period from September 1, 1971, through November 7, 1973, disclose that 3,282 blacks and 5,206 whites applied for employment. Of these individuals, 174 blacks (5.3 percent of the black applicants) and 118 whites (2.23 percent of the white applicants) were rejected because of their conviction records. Thus, statistically, the policy operated automatically to exclude from employment 53 of every 1,000 black applicants but only 22 of every 1,000 white applicants. The rejection rate for blacks is two and one-half times that of whites under this policy.

Although the district court recognized that these statistics denote a disparate impact, the court further compared the number of blacks rejected (174) to the total pool of applicants (8,488) and deemed the resulting figure of 2.05 percent as showing a "*de minimis* discriminatory effect" when compared to the percentage of blacks (16 percent) in the St. Louis metropolitan area. 391 F.Supp. at 996.

The trial court's use of additional statistics supporting a conclusion of a *de minimis* discriminatory effect suffers from two principal defects. First, comparing the number of black applicants rejected because of a conviction record to the total number of applicants does not reflect a disparity of impact separately against each race. Moreover, because more whites than blacks applied for employment (3,282 blacks and 5,206 whites) a comparison of the rejected blacks to the total number of applicants serves to dilute the actual discriminatory impact against blacks.

Second, comparing the resulting percentage of 2.05 against the percent of blacks in the relevant population area is of no assistance, for the issue in Title VII cases focuses on whether an employer has discriminated against any individual "because of such individual's race, color, religion, sex or national origin." The issue to be examined statistically is whether the questioned employment practice operates in a disparate manner upon a minority race or group, not whether the individuals actually suffering from a discriminatory practice are statistically large in number.

An employment criterion must be examined for its operation on a racially exclusionary basis—thus its effect must be measured upon blacks separately and upon whites separately.

The statistics establish that MoPac's employment practice under consideration disqualifies black applicants or potential black applicants for employment at a substantially higher rate than whites. Thus, Green has established a prima facie case of discrimination.

II. Is MoPac's employment practice justified by "Business Necessity"?

Once a prima facie case of discrimination has been established, the defendants must show that the employment practice in question is justified by "business necessity." The seminal decision for business necessity, of course, is *Griggs v. Duke Power Co.*, 401 U.S. 424 (1971), where the Court, in discussing the reach and intent of equal employment opportunity cases under Title VII said:

> [Title VII] proscribes not only overt discrimination but also practices that are fair in form, but discriminatory in operation. The touchstone is business necessity. If an employment practice which operates to exclude Negroes cannot be shown to be related to job performance, the practice is prohibited...

> ...

> What is required by Congress is the removal of artificial arbitrary, and unnecessary barriers to employment when the barriers operate invidiously to discriminate on the basis of racial or other impermissible classification. *Id.* at 431.

> ...

> What Congress has commanded is that any tests used must measure the person for the job and not the person in the abstract. *Id.* at 436.

> ...

In *Butts v. Nichols*, 381 F.Supp. 573 (S.D. Ia. 1974), the court ruled that a provision of the Iowa Code prohibiting the employment of felons in civil service positions violated the Equal Protection Clause of the Fourteenth Amendment. Although the case did not arise under Title VII, the language of the court in discussing the relationship of a conviction to employment is instructive:

> There is no doubt that the State could logically prohibit and refuse employment in certain positions where the felony conviction would directly reflect on the felon's qualifications for the job (e.g., conviction of embezzlement and a job requiring the handling of large

sums of money). The Iowa statutory scheme, however, has an across-the-board prohibition against the employment of felons in civil service positions. There is simply no tailoring in an effort to limit these statutes to conform to what might be legitimate state interests.

...

[The Iowa provision] suffers from a total lack of such narrowing criteria. As a result, the statute is both over and under inclusive: persons who clearly could serve the public interest are denied civil service jobs, while misdemeanants convicted of crimes indicating a lack of probity suffer no disqualification. In short, no consideration is given to the nature and seriousness of the crime in relation to the job sought. The time elapsing since the conviction, the degree of the felon's rehabilitation, and the circumstances under which the crime was committed are similarly ignored. *Id.* at 580-81.

The court in *Gregory v. Litton Systems, Inc.*, 316 F.Supp. 401 (C.D. Cal. 1970), determined that defendant's policy of barring from employment consideration anyone arrested on "a number of occasions" violated Title VII.

In *Wallace v. Debron Corp.*, 494 F.2d 674 (8th Cir. 1974), we reviewed an employer's policy of automatically discharging those individuals whose wages had been garnisheed more than once in a 12-month period. In remanding the factual question of whether this policy was justified by the business necessity test, we observed that all "artificial, arbitrary, and unnecessary racial barriers to employment" should be removed. *Id.* at 676.

These cases suggest that MoPac's procedure now at issue does not meet the requirements of the business necessity test. This test has been articulated in this circuit as follows:

It is likewise apparent that a neutral policy, which is inherently discriminatory, may be valid if it has overriding business justification.... However, this doctrine of business necessity, which has arisen as an exception to the amenability of discriminatory practices, "connotes an irresistible demand." The system in question must not only *foster* safety and efficiency, but must be *essential* to that goal.... In other words, there must be no acceptable alternative that will accomplish that goal "equally well with a lesser differential racial impact." *United States v. St. Louis-San Francisco Ry. Co.*, 464 F.2d 301, 308 (8th Cir. 1972) (emphasis in original).

Although this circuit's articulation of the business necessity test emphasizes the ability of a prospective employee to do the work, the second part of the test, that of "no acceptable alternative that will accomplish the goal equally well with a lesser differential racial impact," constitutes a general test which applies to an employment practice such as that in this case.

MoPac proffers a number of reasons for claiming that its policy is a business necessity: 1) fear of cargo theft, 2) handling company funds, 3) bonding qualifications, 4) possible impeachment of an employee as a witness, 5) possible liability for hiring persons with known violent tendencies, 6) employment disruption caused by recidivism, and 7) alleged lack of moral character of persons with convictions. But, as recognized by the district court, MoPac has not empirically validated its policy with respect to conviction records, nor shown that a less restrictive alternative with a lesser racial impact would not serve as well.

MoPac's witness, Dr. Robert N. McMurry, a consulting industrial psychologist to MoPac, testified that not every ex-offender will be a poor employee and that it would be preferable for a company to consider ex-offenders on an individual basis. He further acknowledged that an employment practice which excludes ex-offenders accentuates recidivism. Although the reasons MoPac advances for its absolute bar can serve as relevant considerations in making individual hiring decisions, they in no way justify an absolute policy which sweeps so broadly.

We cannot conceive of any business necessity that would automatically place every individual convicted of any offense, except a minor traffic offense, in the permanent ranks of the unemployed. This is particularly true for blacks who have suffered and still suffer from the burdens of discrimination in our society. To deny job opportunities to these individuals because of some conduct which may be remote in time or does not significantly bear upon the particular job requirements is an unnecessarily harsh and unjust burden.

Accordingly, we hold that appellant Green and all other blacks who have been summarily denied employment by MoPac on the basis of conviction records have been discriminated against on the basis of race in violation of Title VII and that the district court should enjoin MoPac's practice of using convictions as an absolute bar to employment. With respect to appellant Green, the district court should determine whether on the date of his application his background and experience qualified him for any position with MoPac.

⚜

QUESTIONS FOR REFLECTION

1. What are the other two ways, according to the court in <u>MoPac</u>, that a disproportional racial impact may be established? Are they sound?

2. What evidence might the employer have introduced to vindicate its selection criterion (the no-conviction requirement)?

Comment (continued)

CAUSATION IN DISPARATE IMPACT

Now that the student understands both the plaintiffs' and the defendant's evidence in a disparate impact case, we can answer the question we raised in our comment following <u>Griggs v. Duke Power</u>: in a disparate impact case, how can we say that the employer denies opportunities to workers because of their race or sex? The answer is revealed by the following reasoning.

1. A selection criterion that truly selects workers at random is not discriminatory. If an employer hires only Virgos, the work force will contain proportionally as many whites and people of color, men and women, as does the qualified labor pool.

RANDOM SELECTION CRITERION

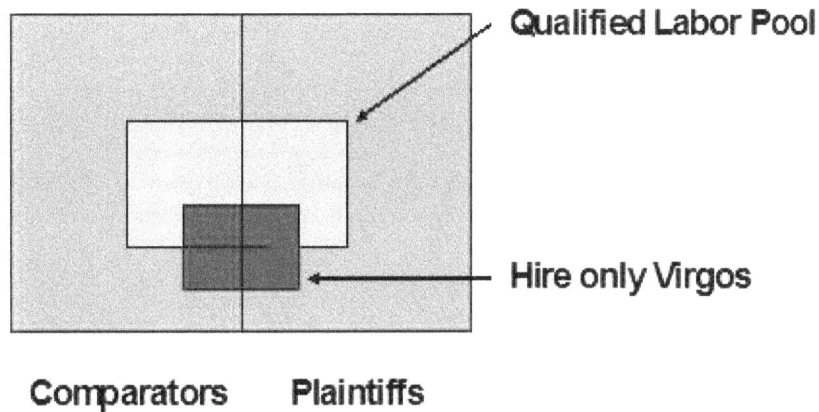

Qualified Labor Pool

Hire only Virgos

Comparators   Plaintiffs

Random selection criterion chooses randomly from inside and outside the qualified labor pool, and randomly across protected groups

    2. A job-related selection criterion does not select at random. It selects qualified workers. If qualifications are distributed equally across groups, a job-related selection criterion will not favor any group, but will select proportionally from each group.

JOB-RELATED SELECTION CRITERION AND EQUAL DISTRIBUTION OF QUALIFICATIONS

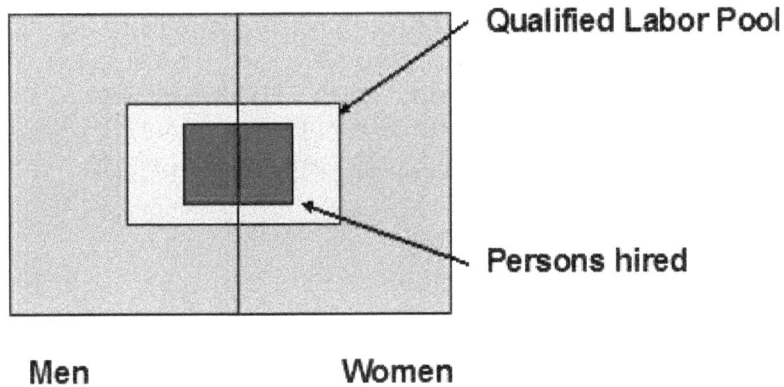

Job-related selection criterion chooses proportionally from among qualified persons. If qualifications are distributed equally across groups, the criterion chooses proportionally from each group

3. It is possible, however, that qualifications are not distributed equally across groups. If one group has more qualified members than another, a job-related selection criterion will appear to favor the larger group. In fact, however, a job-related criterion will select proportionally across groups in the qualified labor pool. For example, suppose the selection criteria in Dothard v. Rawlinson were job related. In this event, being at least 5 feet 2 inches tall and weighing at least 120 pounds would correlate with successful performance of the job; that is, taller, heavier persons would do the job better than smaller persons. It happens that men are taller and heavier than women. Suppose 99 percent of men but only 59 percent of women meet the height and weight criteria. This group constitutes the qualified labor pool. At first blush, it appears that the selection criteria favor men over women, but this appearance is misleading. The selection criteria will choose proportional numbers of qualified men and women.

JOB-RELATED SELECTION CRITERION
UNEQUAL DISTRIBUTION OF QUALIFICATIONS

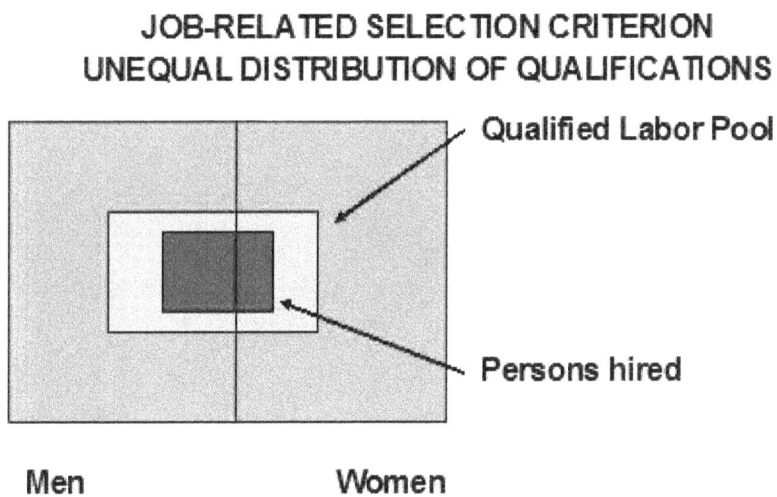

Job-related selection criterion chooses proportionally from among qualified persons. If proportionally more members of one protected group than another are qualified, the criterion chooses proportionally more of the former group

4. If a selection criterion is not job related, it does not select qualified workers. Indeed, a selection criterion that is not job related selects at random with respect to job performance.[f] If such a criterion also favors one group over another, the criterion neither selects qualified workers nor selects at random. **In this event, the criterion does one thing and one thing only: it favors one group over another on the basis of race or sex.** For example, suppose now that the height and weight selection criteria in <u>Dothard v. Rawlinson</u> were not job related. They selected at random with respect to job performance; taller, heavier persons did not make better guards than smaller persons. But the criteria favored men over women; 99 percent of men but only 59 percent of women satisfied the criteria. Therefore, these criteria actually did only one thing: they selected on the basis of sex.

---

[f]Conceivably, a criterion that is not job related could select, not at random, but inversely with respect to job performance. The criterion might favor unqualified workers over qualified workers. This possibility, which is probably rare, does not affect the argument in this note.

Causation in Disparate Impact and
Comparing Disparate Impact and Disparate Treatment

NONJOB-RELATED SELECTION CRITERION WITH AN ADVERSE EFFECT

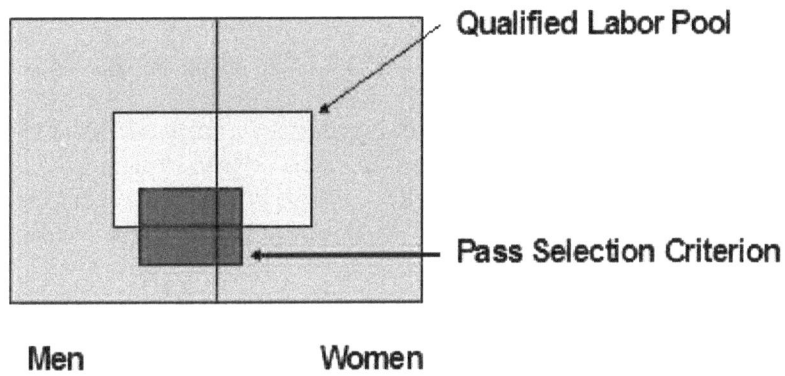

Qualified Labor Pool

Pass Selection Criterion

Men   **Women**

Nonjob-related selection criterion chooses randomly among qualified and unqualified persons, but favors one protected group over another

COMPARING DISPARATE TREATMENT AND DISPARATE IMPACT

A question may have come to the mind of the
reflective student: If there exists only one prima
facie-I of discrimination, and if there exist two methods
or prima facie-IIs for proving this prima facie-I (viz.,
disparate treatment and disparate impact), why are these
methods so different when they prove the same thing? The
answer is that they are more similar than they may seem.
In both of these methods of proving discrimination, the
plaintiffs —

- identify a fair proxy for the qualified labor
  pool. (In disparate treatment, the plaintiffs
  have a choice of proxies; in disparate impact,
  the proxy is the group on which the selection
  criterion operates.)

- calculate the plaintiffs' share of the proxy.

- identify an employment opportunity. (In
  disparate treatment, the opportunity is being
  hired or promoted; in disparate impact, the
  opportunity is satisfying the selection
  criterion.)

- calculate the plaintiffs' share of the
  beneficiaries of the opportunity.

- prove that a statistically significant
  disparity exists between the plaintiffs' share
  of the proxy and their share of the
  beneficiaries of the employment opportunity.

- establish that the cause of the disparity was
  race or sex. (In disparate treatment, the
  cause is the employer's intent to discriminate;
  in disparate impact, the cause is a selection
  criterion that has an adverse effect on the
  plaintiffs' group and is not job related.)

The foregoing list is organized according to the order of
proof in a disparate treatment case. The following list,
which contains the same information, is organized
according to the order of proof in a disparate impact
case. The plaintiffs —

- identify a selection criterion used by the employer. (In disparate impact, the criterion is not discriminatory on its face; in disparate treatment, the criterion is expressly race or sex.)

- identify a proxy for the qualified labor pool. (In disparate impact, the proxy is the group on which the selection criterion operates; in disparate treatment, the plaintiffs have a choice of proxies.)

- calculate the plaintiffs' share of the proxy.

- calculate the plaintiffs' share of the beneficiaries of the opportunity.

- prove that a statistically significant difference exists between the plaintiffs' share of the proxy and their share of the beneficiaries of the employment opportunity.

- establish that the cause of the disparity was race or sex. (In disparate treatment, the cause is race or sex because the selection criterion is expressly race or sex. In disparate impact, the cause is race or sex because the selection criterion has an adverse effect on the plaintiffs' group and is not job related.)

Thus, the only difference between disparate treatment as proved by statistics and disparate impact is that the selection criterion in the former is expressly race or sex, whereas the selection criterion in the latter is not race or sex on its face, but, because it has an adverse effect on the plaintiffs' group and is not job related, the criterion in operation is tantamount to race or sex.

$$\Omega$$

Affirmative Action

Introduction

The legitimacy of affirmative action is one of the great social questions of our era. Let us define affirmative action as the practice of granting preferences to "under-represented groups" (usually women and people of color) for opportunities like jobs and seats in educational programs. The degree of preference varies along a continuum, from, at one end, advertising opportunities in media that cater to under-represented groups, to, at the other end, reserving certain opportunities for members of under-represented groups (quotas). Between the ends of the continuum lie points such as giving credit to applicants who appear to have surmounted obstacles like racism and sexism, awarding extra points to each applicant from an under-represented group, and setting a target of a certain percentage of members of under-represented groups. The purpose of affirmative action also varies. Sometimes the purpose is to make up for the employer's or school's discrimination in the past. Other times the purpose is to modify the work or educational environment by introducing racial and sexual diversity, to manage effectively a diverse work force, to alter the nature of the enterprise's product or service, or to effect change in society at large.

The anti-discrimination statutes, such as Title VII, do not require affirmative action. Nor does the Constitution. Therefore, affirmative action is always voluntary. As a practical matter, however, affirmative action is often obligatory. For example, by executive order, federal contractors (primarily businesses that sell goods and services to the federal government) must engage in affirmative action. Many businesses depend on their trade with the government, with the result that they have little choice but to assent to affirmative action.

From the perspective of groups that are not under represented, affirmative action, except for its mildest forms, is tantamount to discrimination. Indeed, its opponents often call it "reverse discrimination," and on this basis it has been challenged in court on several occasions. The most famous case was Regents of the

Grutter v. Bollinger

<u>University of California v. Bakke</u>, in which the medical
school of the University of California at Davis reserved
16 of 100 seats in its entering class for members of
under-represented groups. The Supreme Court ruled on two
issues: Was the quota legal? If not, would a milder
form of affirmative action be permissible; in particular,
could the school in the future take race or ethnicity
into account in admitting students? The Court divided
sharply on each issue. Four Justices voted to answer
both questions yes; four voted to answer both questions
no. Justice Powell cast the deciding votes. He ruled
the quota was illegal, but taking race into account was
acceptable. Although there was a majority of the Court
on each issue, there was no majority opinion; indeed, the
Justices filed six separate opinions. Justice Powell's
opinion became the most influential.

The plaintiff in <u>Bakke</u> argued that the school's
affirmative action program was unconstitutional under the
Equal Protection Clause of the Fourteenth Amendment.[a]
Justice Powell applied the "strict scrutiny" test, which
is used when the government distinguishes among persons
on the basis of race or national origin.[b] Under this
test, a racial distinction is permissible only if it is
narrowly tailored to achieve a compelling interest of

---

[a]The plaintiff also challenged the program under Title VI of
the Civil Rights Act of 1964.

[b]Because the University of California at Davis was a public
school, its acts were subject to the Constitution.

government.[c] Justice Powell held that the quota failed
this test, but that a program that takes race into

---

[c]Note the continuing attention to means and ends. The end
is a compelling interest of the government; the mean is a
narrowly tailored distinction.

Three varieties of test are used to evaluate distinctions
when their constitutionality is challenged under the Equal
Protection Clause. Which test is used depends on the basis of
the distinction. When the basis of the distinction is
national origin or race, the test is strict scrutiny. Thus,
as mentioned in the text, strict scrutiny was applied in the
Bakke case.

When the basis of the distinction is sex, the test is
"intermediate (or mean) scrutiny," under which the distinction
is permissible if it bears a close and substantial
relationship to an important interest of the government. For
example, suppose a state law provided that, when a person
becomes legally incompetent, the court shall appoint as
guardian any willing adult son of the incompetent; but if no
adult son is willing to serve, the court shall appoint as
guardian any willing adult daughter of the incompetent. The
constitutionality of this distinction between men and women
would be decided under the intermediate scrutiny test. (We
predict the statute would be held unconstitutional.)

When the basis of the distinction is anything other than
race, national origin, or sex, the "rational basis" test is
used. Under this test, a distinction is permissible if it is
a rational step towards a legitimate objective of the
government. For example, suppose a state imposes a tax on
alcoholic beverages but not on soft drinks. The
constitutionality of this distinction between hard and soft
beverages would be decided under the rational basis test. (We
predict the tax would be held constitutional.)

Rational basis is the easiest test to satisfy, and strict
scrutiny is the hardest. There are more "legitimate"
interests of government than "important" interests, and more
"important" interests than "compelling" interests; similarly,
the latitude for a "rational step" is wider than for a "close
and substantial relationship," and wider for a "close and
substantial relationship" than for a "narrowly tailored" step.
Accordingly, distinctions based on race and national origin
are the hardest for the government to justify; distinctions
based on sex are in the middle; and distinctions based on
anything else are the easiest.

account as one factor among many would pass the test. He cited the admissions program of Harvard College as an example of the latter. Harvard's program, he argued, pursued the compelling end of achieving diversity among students, which contributed to their education. Harvard's program used permissible means because the factors that constituted diversity included not only race, but also geography, special talent, exceptional achievement, and so forth.

Two decades after Bakke, the Fifth Circuit Court of Appeals in Hopwood v. Texas struck down an affirmative action plan modeled on the Harvard program. The court argued that Bakke had been vitiated by subsequent decisions of the Supreme Court. Some other lower courts followed suit, generating the need for the Supreme Court to revisit the issue in Grutter v. Bollinger.

As it considered Grutter, the Court also considered Gratz v. Bollinger. Grutter challenged the affirmative action program of the law school of the University of Michigan, which counted race as one factor among others in pursuit of a diverse class. Gratz challenged the affirmative action program of the College of Literature, Science, and Arts of the same university, which, also in pursuit of a diverse class, awarded 20 extra points to applicants from under-represented groups.

Grutter v. Bollinger
539 U.S. 306 (2003)

JUSTICE O'CONNOR delivered the opinion of the Court.

This case requires us to decide whether the use of race as a factor in student admissions by the University of Michigan Law School (Law School) is unlawful.

I

A

The Law School ranks among the Nation's top law schools. It receives more than 3,500 applications each year for a class of around 350 students. Seeking to "admit a group of students who individually and collectively are among the most capable," the Law School looks for individuals with "substantial promise for success in law school" and "a strong likelihood of succeeding in the practice of law and contributing in diverse ways to the well-being of others."[d] More broadly, the Law School seeks "a mix of students with varying backgrounds and experiences who will respect and learn from each other." In 1992, the dean of the Law School charged a faculty committee with crafting a written admissions policy to implement these goals. In particular, the Law School sought to ensure that its efforts to achieve student body diversity complied with this Court's most recent ruling on the use of race in university admissions. See *Regents of Univ. of Cal. v. Bakke.* Upon the unanimous adoption of the committee's report by the Law School faculty, it became the Law School's official admissions policy.

The hallmark of that policy is its focus on academic ability coupled with a flexible assessment of applicants' talents, experiences, and potential "to contribute to the learning of those around them." The policy requires admissions officials to evaluate each applicant based on all the information available in the file, including a personal statement, letters of recommendation, and an essay describing the ways in which the applicant will contribute to the life and diversity of the Law School. In reviewing an applicant's file, admissions officials must consider the applicant's undergraduate grade point average (GPA) and Law School Admissions Test (LSAT) score because they are important (if imperfect) predictors of academic success in law school. The policy stresses that "no applicant should be admitted unless we expect that applicant to do well enough to graduate with no serious academic problems."

The policy makes clear, however, that even the highest possible score does not

---

[d]Citations to the record and the briefs in the Supreme Court and to the opinions of other Justices in this case are omitted.

guarantee admission to the Law School. Nor does a low score automatically disqualify an applicant. Rather, the policy requires admissions officials to look beyond grades and test scores to other criteria that are important to the Law School's educational objectives. So-called "soft' variables" such as "the enthusiasm of recommenders, the quality of the undergraduate institution, the quality of the applicant's essay, and the areas and difficulty of undergraduate course selection" are all brought to bear in assessing an "applicant's likely contributions to the intellectual and social life of the institution."

The policy aspires to "achieve that diversity which has the potential to enrich everyone's education and thus make a law school class stronger than the sum of its parts." The policy does not restrict the types of diversity contributions eligible for "substantial weight" in the admissions process, but instead recognizes "many possible bases for diversity admissions." The policy does, however, reaffirm the Law School's longstanding commitment to "one particular type of diversity," that is, "racial and ethnic diversity with special reference to the inclusion of students from groups which have been historically discriminated against, like African-Americans, Hispanics and Native Americans, who without this commitment might not be represented in our student body in meaningful numbers." By enrolling a "critical mass' of [underrepresented] minority students," the Law School seeks to "ensure their ability to make unique contributions to the character of the Law School."

The policy does not define diversity "solely in terms of racial and ethnic status." Nor is the policy "insensitive to the competition among all students for admission to the Law School." Rather, the policy seeks to guide admissions officers in "producing classes both diverse and academically outstanding, classes made up of students who promise to continue the tradition of outstanding contribution by Michigan Graduates to the legal profession."

B

Petitioner Barbara Grutter is a white Michigan resident who applied to the Law School in 1996 with a 3.8 grade point average and 161 LSAT score. The Law School initially placed petitioner on a waiting list, but subsequently rejected her application....

...

During the 15-day bench trial, the parties introduced extensive evidence concerning the Law School's use of race in the admissions process. Dennis Shields, Director of Admissions when petitioner applied to the Law School, testified that he did not direct his staff to admit a particular percentage or number of minority students, but rather to consider an applicant's race along with all other factors. Shields testified that at the height of the admissions season, he would frequently consult the so-called "daily reports" that kept track of the racial and ethnic composition of the class (along with other information such as residency status and gender). This was done, Shields testified, to ensure that a critical mass of underrepresented minority students would be reached so as to realize the educational benefits of a diverse student body. Shields stressed, however, that he did not seek to admit any particular number or percentage of underrepresented minority students.

Erica Munzel, who succeeded Shields as Director of Admissions, testified that "critical mass" means "meaningful numbers" or "meaningful representation," which she understood to mean a number that encourages underrepresented minority students to participate in the classroom and not feel isolated. Munzel stated there is no number, percentage, or range of numbers or percentages that constitute critical mass. Munzel also asserted that she must consider the race of applicants because a critical mass of underrepresented minority students could not be enrolled if admissions decisions were based primarily on undergraduate GPAs and LSAT scores.

The current Dean of the Law School, Jeffrey Lehman, also testified. Like the other Law School witnesses, Lehman did not quantify critical mass in terms of numbers or percentages. He indicated that critical mass means numbers such that underrepresented minority students do not feel isolated or like spokespersons for their race. When asked about the extent to which race is considered in admissions, Lehman testified that it varies from one applicant to another. In some cases, according to Lehman's testimony, an applicant's race may play no role, while in others it may be a "determinative" factor.

The District Court heard extensive testimony from Professor Richard Lempert, who chaired the faculty committee that drafted the 1992 policy. Lempert emphasized that the Law School seeks students with diverse interests and backgrounds to enhance classroom discussion and the educational experience both inside and outside the classroom. When asked about the policy's "commitment to racial and ethnic diversity with special reference to the inclusion of students from groups which have been historically discriminated against," Lempert explained that this language did not purport to remedy past discrimination, but rather to include students who may bring to the Law School a perspective different from that of members of groups which have not been the victims of such discrimination. Lempert acknowledged that other groups, such as Asians and Jews, have experienced discrimination, but explained they were not mentioned in the policy because individuals who are members of those groups were already being admitted to the Law School in significant numbers.

Grutter v. Bollinger

Kent Syverud was the final witness to testify about the Law School's use of race in admissions decisions. Syverud was a professor at the Law School when the 1992 admissions policy was adopted and is now Dean of Vanderbilt Law School. In addition to his testimony at trial, Syverud submitted several expert reports on the educational benefits of diversity. Syverud's testimony indicated that when a critical mass of underrepresented minority students is present, racial stereotypes lose their force because nonminority students learn there is no "minority viewpoint" but rather a variety of viewpoints among minority students.

In an attempt to quantify the extent to which the Law School actually considers race in making admissions decisions, the parties introduced voluminous evidence at trial. Relying on data obtained from the Law School, petitioner's expert, Dr. Kinley Larntz, generated and analyzed "admissions grids" for the years in question (1995-2000). These grids show the number of applicants and the number of admittees for all combinations of GPAs and LSAT scores. Dr. Larntz made "cell-by-cell" comparisons between applicants of different races to determine whether a statistically significant relationship existed between race and admission rates. He concluded that membership in certain minority groups "is an extremely strong factor in the decision for acceptance," and that applicants from these minority groups "are given an extremely large allowance for admission" as compared to applicants who are members of nonfavored groups. Dr. Larntz conceded, however, that race is not the predominant factor in the Law School's admissions calculus.

Dr. Stephen Raudenbush, the Law School's expert, focused on the predicted effect of eliminating race as a factor in the Law School's admission process. In Dr. Raudenbush's view, a race-blind admissions system would have a "very dramatic," negative effect on underrepresented minority admissions. He testified that in 2000, 35 percent of underrepresented minority applicants were admitted. Dr. Raudenbush predicted that if race were not considered, only 10 percent of those applicants would have been admitted. Under this scenario, underrepresented minority students would have comprised 4 percent of the entering class in 2000 instead of the actual figure of 14.5 percent.

In the end, the District Court concluded that the Law School's use of race as a factor in admissions decisions was unlawful. Applying strict scrutiny, the District Court determined that the Law School's asserted interest in assembling a diverse student body was not compelling because "the attainment of a racially diverse class ... was not recognized as such by *Bakke* and is not a remedy for past discrimination." The District Court went on to hold that even if diversity were compelling, the Law School had not narrowly tailored its use of race to further that interest. The District Court granted petitioner's request for declaratory relief and enjoined the Law School from using race as a factor in its admissions decisions. The Court of Appeals entered a stay of the injunction pending appeal.

Sitting en banc, the Court of Appeals reversed the District Court's judgment and vacated the injunction. The Court of Appeals first held that Justice Powell's opinion in *Bakke* was binding precedent establishing diversity as a compelling state interest.... The Court of Appeals also held that the Law School's use of race was narrowly tailored because race was merely a "potential 'plus' factor" and because the Law School's program was "virtually identical" to the Harvard admissions program described approvingly by Justice Powell and appended to his *Bakke* opinion.

...

We granted certiorari to resolve the disagreement among the Courts of Appeals on a question of national importance: Whether diversity is a compelling interest that can justify the narrowly tailored use of race in selecting applicants for admission to public universities. Compare *Hopwood v. Texas* (holding that diversity is not a compelling state interest), with *Smith v. University of Wash. Law School* (holding that it is).

II

A

We last addressed the use of race in public higher education over 25 years ago. In the landmark *Bakke* case, we reviewed a racial set-aside program that reserved 16 out of 100 seats in a medical school class for members of certain minority groups. The decision produced six separate opinions, none of which commanded a majority of the Court. Four Justices would have upheld the program against all attack on the ground that the government can use race to "remedy disadvantages cast on minorities by past racial prejudice." *Id.* at 325 (joint opinion of Brennan, White, Marshall, and Blackmun, JJ., concurring in judgment in part and dissenting in part). Four other Justices avoided the constitutional question altogether and struck down the program on statutory grounds. *Bakke* at 408 (opinion of Stevens, J., joined by Burger, C. J., and Stewart and Rehnquist, JJ., concurring in judgment in part and dissenting in part). Justice Powell provided a fifth vote not only for invalidating the set-aside program, but also for reversing the state court's injunction against any use of race whatsoever. The only holding for the Court in *Bakke* was that a "State has a substantial interest that legitimately may be served by a properly devised admissions program involving the competitive consideration of race and ethnic origin." *Id.* at 320. Thus, we reversed that part of the lower court's judgment that enjoined the university "from any consideration of the race of any applicant." *Ibid.*

Since this Court's splintered decision in *Bakke*, Justice Powell's opinion announcing the judgment of the Court has served as the touchstone for constitutional analysis of race-conscious admissions policies.... We therefore discuss Justice Powell's opinion in some detail.

Justice Powell began by stating that "the guarantee of equal protection cannot mean one thing when applied to one individual and something else when applied to a person of another color. If both are not accorded the same protection, then it is not equal." *Id.* at 289-290. In Justice Powell's view, when governmental decisions "touch upon an individual's race or ethnic background, he is entitled to a judicial determination that the burden he is asked to bear on that basis is precisely tailored to serve a compelling governmental interest." *Id.* at 299. Under this exacting standard, only one of the interests asserted by the university survived Justice Powell's scrutiny.

First, Justice Powell rejected an interest in "reducing the historic deficit of traditionally disfavored minorities in medical schools and in the medical profession" as an unlawful interest in racial balancing. *Id.* at 306-307. Second, Justice Powell rejected an interest in remedying societal discrimination because such measures would risk placing unnecessary burdens on innocent third parties "who bear no responsibility for whatever harm the beneficiaries of the special admissions program are thought to have suffered." *Id.* at 310. Third, Justice Powell rejected an interest in "increasing the number of physicians who will practice in communities currently underserved," concluding that even if such an interest could be compelling in some circumstances the program under review was not "geared to promote that goal." *Id.* at 306, 310.

Justice Powell approved the university's use of race to further only one interest: "the attainment of a diverse student body." *Id.* at 311. With the important proviso that "constitutional limitations protecting individual rights may not be disregarded," Justice Powell grounded his analysis in the academic freedom that "long has been viewed as a special concern of the First Amendment." *Id.* at 312, 314. Justice Powell emphasized that nothing less than the "'nation's future depends upon leaders trained through wide exposure' to the ideas and mores of students as diverse as this Nation of many peoples." *Id.* at 313 (quoting *Keyishian v. Board of Regents of Univ. of State of N. Y.* at 603 (1967)). In seeking the "right to select those students who will contribute the most to the 'robust exchange of ideas,'" a university seeks "to achieve a goal that is of paramount importance in the fulfillment of its mission." *Bakke* at 313. Both "tradition and experience lend support to the view that the contribution of diversity is substantial." *Ibid.*

Justice Powell was, however, careful to emphasize that in his view race "is only one element in a range of factors a university properly may consider in attaining the goal of a heterogeneous student body." *Id.* at 314. For Justice Powell, "it is not an interest in simple ethnic diversity, in which a specified percentage of the student body is in effect guaranteed to be members of selected ethnic groups," that can justify the use of race. *Id.* at 315. Rather, "the diversity that furthers a compelling state interest encompasses a far broader array of qualifications and characteristics of which racial or ethnic origin is but a single though important element." *Ibid.*

...

... [T]oday we endorse Justice Powell's view that student body diversity is a compelling state interest that can justify the use of race in university admissions.

B

The Equal Protection Clause provides that no State shall "deny to any person within its jurisdiction the equal protection of the laws." U.S. Const., Amdt. 14, § 2. Because the Fourteenth Amendment "protects *persons*, not *groups*," all "governmental action based on race — a group classification long recognized as in most circumstances irrelevant and therefore prohibited — should be subjected to detailed judicial inquiry to ensure that the *personal* right to equal protection of the laws has not been infringed." *Adarand v. Peña* at 227 (emphasis in original; internal quotation marks and citation omitted). We are a "free people whose institutions are founded upon the doctrine of equality." *Loving v. Virginia* at 11 (internal quotation marks and citation omitted). It follows from that principle that "government may treat people differently because of their race only for the most compelling reasons." *Adarand* at 227.

We have held that all racial classifications imposed by government "must be analyzed by a reviewing court under strict scrutiny." *Ibid.* This means that such classifications are constitutional only if they are narrowly tailored to further compelling governmental interests. "Absent searching judicial inquiry into the justification for such race-based measures," we have no way to determine what "classifications are 'benign' or 'remedial' and what classifications are in fact motivated by illegitimate notions of racial inferiority or simple racial politics." *Richmond v. J. A. Croson Co.* at 493 (plurality opinion). We apply strict scrutiny to all racial classifications to "'smoke out' illegitimate uses of race by assuring that [government] is pursuing a goal important enough to warrant use of a highly suspect tool." *Ibid.*

Strict scrutiny is not "strict in theory, but fatal in fact." *Adarand* at 237 (internal quotation marks and citation omitted). Although all governmental uses of race are subject to strict scrutiny, not all are invalidated by it. As we have explained, "whenever the government treats any person unequally because of his or her race, that person has suffered an injury that falls squarely within the language and spirit of the Constitution's guarantee of equal protection." *Id.* at 229-230. But that observation "says nothing about the ultimate validity of any particular law; that determination is the job of the court applying strict scrutiny." Id. at 230. When race-based action is necessary to further a compelling governmental interest, such action does not violate the constitutional guarantee of equal protection so long as the narrow-tailoring requirement is also satisfied.

Context matters when reviewing race-based governmental action under the Equal Protection Clause. See *Gomillion v. Lightfoot* at 343-344 (admonishing that, "in dealing with claims under broad provisions of the Constitution, which derive content by an interpretive process of inclusion and exclusion, it is imperative that generalizations, based on and qualified by the concrete situations that gave rise to them, must not be applied out of context in disregard of variant controlling facts"). In *Adarand* at 228, we made clear that strict scrutiny must take "'relevant differences' into account." Indeed, as we explained, that is its "fundamental purpose." *Ibid.* Not every decision influenced by race is equally objectionable and strict scrutiny is designed to provide a framework for carefully examining the importance and the sincerity of the reasons advanced by the governmental decisionmaker for the use of race in that particular context.

III

A

With these principles in mind, we turn to the question whether the Law School's use of race is justified by a compelling state interest. Before this Court, as they have throughout this litigation, respondents assert only one justification for their use of race in the admissions process: obtaining "the educational benefits that flow from a diverse student body." In other words, the Law School asks us to recognize, in the context of higher education, a compelling state interest in student body diversity.

...

The Law School's educational judgment that such diversity is essential to its educational mission is one to which we defer. The Law School's assessment that diversity will, in fact, yield educational benefits is substantiated by respondents and their *amici*. Our scrutiny of the interest asserted by the Law School is no less strict for taking into account complex educational judgments in an area that lies primarily within the expertise of the university. Our holding today is in keeping with our tradition of giving a degree of deference to a university's academic decisions, within constitutionally prescribed limits.

We have long recognized that, given the important purpose of public education and the expansive freedoms of speech and thought associated with the university environment, universities occupy a special niche in our constitutional tradition. In announcing the principle of student body diversity as a compelling state interest, Justice Powell invoked our cases recognizing a constitutional dimension, grounded in the First Amendment, of educational autonomy: "The freedom of a university to make its own judgments as to education includes the selection of its student body." *Bakke* at 312. From this premise, Justice Powell reasoned that by claiming "the right to select those students who will contribute the most to the 'robust exchange of ideas,'" a university "seeks to achieve a goal that is of paramount importance in the fulfillment of its mission." *Id.* at 313 (quoting *Keyishian* at 603). Our conclusion that the Law School has a compelling interest in a diverse student body is informed by our view that attaining a diverse student body is at the heart of the Law School's proper institutional mission, and that "good faith" on the part of a university is "presumed" absent "a showing to the contrary." *Id.* at 318-319.

As part of its goal of "assembling a class that is both exceptionally academically qualified and broadly diverse," the Law School seeks to "enroll a 'critical mass' of minority students." The Law School's interest is not simply "to assure within its student body some specified percentage of a particular group merely because of its race or ethnic origin." *Id.* at 307 (opinion of Powell, J.). That would amount to outright racial balancing, which is patently unconstitutional. *Freeman v. Pitts* at 494 ("Racial balance is not to be achieved for its own sake"). Rather, the Law School's concept of critical mass is defined by reference to the educational benefits that diversity is designed to produce.

These benefits are substantial. As the District Court emphasized, the Law School's admissions policy promotes "cross-racial understanding," helps to break down racial stereotypes, and "enables [students] to better understand persons of different races." These benefits are "important and laudable," because "classroom discussion is livelier, more spirited, and simply more enlightening and interesting" when the students have "the greatest possible variety of backgrounds."

The Law School's claim of a compelling interest is further bolstered by its *amici*, who point to the educational benefits that flow from student body diversity. In addition to the expert studies and reports entered into evidence at trial, numerous studies show that student body diversity promotes learning outcomes, and "better prepares students for an increasingly diverse workforce and society, and better prepares them as professionals."

These benefits are not theoretical but real, as major American businesses have made clear that the skills needed in today's increasingly global marketplace can only be developed through exposure to widely diverse people, cultures, ideas, and viewpoints. What is more, high-ranking retired officers and civilian leaders of the United States military assert that, "based on [their] decades of experience," a "highly qualified, racially diverse officer corps ... is essential to the military's ability to fulfill its principle mission to provide national security." The primary sources for the Nation's officer corps are the service academies and the Reserve Officers Training Corps (ROTC), the latter comprising students already admitted to participating colleges and universities. At present, "the military cannot achieve an officer corps that is both highly qualified and racially diverse unless the service academies and the ROTC used limited race-conscious recruiting and admissions policies." To fulfill its mission, the military "must be selective in admissions for training and education for the officer corps, and it must train and educate a highly qualified, racially diverse officer corps in a racially diverse setting." We agree that "it requires only a small step from this analysis to conclude that our country's other most selective institutions must remain both diverse and selective."

We have repeatedly acknowledged the overriding importance of preparing students for work and citizenship, describing education as pivotal to "sustaining our political and cultural heritage" with a fundamental role in maintaining the fabric of society. *Plyler v. Doe* at 221. This Court has long recognized that "education ... is the very foundation of good citizenship." *Brown v. Board of Education* at 493. For this reason, the diffusion of knowledge and opportunity through public institutions of higher education must be accessible to all individuals regardless of race or ethnicity. The United States, as *amicus curiae*, affirms that "ensuring that public institutions are open and available to all segments of American society, including people of all races and ethnicities, represents a paramount government objective." And, "nowhere is the importance of such openness more acute than in the context of higher education." Effective participation by members of all racial and ethnic groups in the civic life of our Nation is essential if the dream of one Nation, indivisible, is to be realized.

Moreover, universities, and in particular, law schools, represent the training ground for a large number of our Nation's leaders. *Sweatt v. Painter* at 634 (describing law school as a "proving ground for legal learning and practice"). Individuals with law degrees occupy roughly half the state governorships, more than half the seats in the United States Senate, and more than a third of the seats in the United States House of Representatives. The pattern is even more striking when it comes to highly selective law schools. A handful of these schools accounts for 25 of the 100 United States Senators, 74 United States Courts of Appeals judges, and nearly 200 of the more than 600 United States District Court judges.

In order to cultivate a set of leaders with legitimacy in the eyes of the citizenry, it is necessary that the path to leadership be visibly open to talented and qualified individuals of every race and ethnicity. All members of our heterogeneous society must have confidence in the openness and integrity of the educational institutions that provide this training. As we have recognized, law schools "cannot be effective in isolation from the individuals and institutions with which the law interacts." *Ibid.* Access to legal education (and thus the legal profession) must be inclusive of talented and qualified individuals of every race and ethnicity, so that all members of our heterogeneous society may participate in the educational institutions that provide the training and education necessary to succeed in America.

The Law School does not premise its need for critical mass on "any belief that minority students always (or even consistently) express some characteristic minority viewpoint on any issue." To the contrary, diminishing the force of such stereotypes is both a crucial part of the Law School's mission, and one that it cannot accomplish with only token numbers of minority students. Just as growing up in a particular region or having particular professional experiences is likely to affect an individual's views, so too is one's own, unique experience of being a racial minority in a society, like our own, in which race unfortunately still matters. The Law School has determined, based on its experience and expertise, that a "critical mass" of underrepresented minorities is necessary to further its compelling interest in securing the educational benefits of a diverse student body.

B

Even in the limited circumstance when drawing racial distinctions is permissible to further a compelling state interest, government is still "constrained in how it may pursue that end: [T]he means chosen to accomplish the [government's] asserted purpose must be specifically and narrowly framed to accomplish that purpose." *Shaw v. Hunt* at 908 (internal quotation marks and citation omitted). The purpose of the narrow tailoring requirement is to ensure that "the means chosen 'fit' ... the compelling goal so closely that there is little or no possibility that the motive for the classification was illegitimate racial prejudice or stereotype." *Richmond v. Croson* at 493 (plurality opinion).

...

To be narrowly tailored, a race-conscious admissions program cannot use a quota system — it cannot "insulate each category of applicants with certain desired qualifications from competition with all other applicants." *Bakke* at 315 (opinion of Powell, J.). Instead, a university may consider race or ethnicity only as a "'plus' in a particular applicant's file," without "insulating the individual from comparison with all other candidates for the available seats." *Id.* at 317. In other words, an admissions program must be "flexible enough to consider all pertinent elements of diversity in light of the particular qualifications of each applicant, and to place them on the same footing for consideration, although not necessarily according them the same weight." *Ibid.*

We find that the Law School's admissions program bears the hallmarks of a narrowly tailored plan. As Justice Powell made clear in *Bakke*, truly individualized consideration demands that race be used in a flexible, nonmechanical way. It follows from this mandate that universities cannot establish quotas for members of certain racial groups or put members of those groups on separate admissions tracks. Nor can universities insulate applicants who belong to certain racial or ethnic groups from the competition for admission. Universities can, however, consider race or ethnicity more flexibly as a "plus" factor in the context of individualized consideration of each and every applicant.

We are satisfied that the Law School's admissions program, like the Harvard plan described by Justice Powell, does not operate as a quota. Properly understood, a "quota" is a program in which a certain fixed number or proportion of opportunities are "reserved exclusively for certain minority groups." *Richmond v. Croson* at 496 (plurality opinion). Quotas "'impose a fixed number or percentage which must be attained, or which cannot be exceeded,'" *Local 28 of Sheet Metal Workers v. EEOC* at 495 (1986) (O'Connor, J., concurring in part and dissenting in part), and "insulate the individual from comparison with all other candidates for the available seats." *Bakke*, at 317 (opinion of Powell, J.). In contrast, "a permissible goal ... requires only a good-faith effort ... to come within a range demarcated by the goal itself," *Sheet Metal Workers* at 495, and permits consideration of race as a "plus" factor in any given case while still ensuring that each candidate "competes with all other qualified applicants," *Johnson v. Transportation Agency, Santa Clara Cty.* at 616, 638.

Justice Powell's distinction between the medical school's rigid 16-seat quota and Harvard's flexible use of race as a "plus" factor is instructive. Harvard certainly had minimum goals for minority enrollment, even if it had no specific number firmly in mind. See *Bakke* at 323 (opinion of Powell, J.) ("10 or 20 black students could not begin to bring to their classmates and to each other the variety of points of view, backgrounds and experiences of blacks in the United States"). What is more, Justice Powell flatly rejected the argument that Harvard's program was "the functional equivalent of a quota" merely because it had some "'plus'" for race, or gave greater "weight" to race than to some other factors, in order to achieve student body diversity. *Id.* at 317-318.

The Law School's goal of attaining a critical mass of underrepresented minority students does not transform its program into a quota. As the Harvard plan described by Justice Powell recognized, there is of course "some relationship between numbers and achieving the benefits to be derived from a diverse student body, and between numbers and providing a reasonable environment for those students admitted." *Id.* at 323. "Some attention to numbers," without more, does not transform a flexible admissions system into a rigid quota. *Ibid.* ... [B]etween 1993 and 2000, the number of African-American, Latino, and Native-American students in each class at the Law School varied from 13.5 to 20.1 percent, a range inconsistent with a quota.

...

That a race-conscious admissions program does not operate as a quota does not, by itself, satisfy the requirement of individualized consideration. When using race as a "plus" factor in university admissions, a university's admissions program must remain flexible enough to ensure that each applicant is evaluated as an individual and not in a way that makes an applicant's race or ethnicity the defining feature of his or her application. The importance of this individualized consideration in the context of a race-conscious admissions program is paramount. See *id.* at 318, n. 52 (opinion of Powell, J.) (identifying the "denial ... of the right to individualized consideration" as the "principal evil" of the medical school's admissions program).

Here, the Law School engages in a highly individualized, holistic review of each applicant's file, giving serious consideration to all the ways an applicant might contribute to a diverse educational environment. The Law School affords this individualized consideration to applicants of all races. There is no policy, either *de jure* or *de facto*, of automatic acceptance or rejection based on any single "soft" variable. Unlike the program at issue in *Gratz v Bollinger*, the Law School awards no mechanical, predetermined diversity "bonuses" based on race or ethnicity. See *Gratz* at 271 (distinguishing a race-conscious admissions program that automatically awards 20 points based on race from the Harvard plan, which considered race but "did not contemplate that any single characteristic automatically ensured a specific and identifiable contribution to a university's diversity"). Like the Harvard plan, the Law School's admissions policy "is flexible enough to consider all pertinent elements of diversity in light of the particular qualifications of each applicant, and to place them on the same footing for consideration, although not necessarily according them the same weight." *Bakke* at 317 (opinion of Powell, J.).

We also find that, like the Harvard plan Justice Powell referenced in *Bakke*, the Law School's race-conscious admissions program adequately ensures that all factors that may contribute to student body diversity are meaningfully considered alongside race in admissions decisions. With respect to the use of race itself, all underrepresented minority students admitted by the Law School have been deemed qualified. By virtue of our Nation's struggle with racial inequality, such students are both likely to have experiences of particular importance to the Law School's mission, and less likely to be admitted in meaningful numbers on criteria that ignore those experiences.

The Law School does not, however, limit in any way the broad range of qualities and experiences that may be considered valuable contributions to student body diversity. To the contrary, the 1992 policy makes clear "there are many possible bases for diversity admissions," and provides examples of admittees who have lived or traveled widely abroad, are fluent in several languages, have overcome personal adversity and family hardship, have exceptional records of extensive community service, and have had successful careers in other fields. The Law School seriously considers each "applicant's promise of making a notable contribution to the class by way of a particular strength, attainment, or characteristic — e.g., an unusual intellectual achievement, employment experience, nonacademic performance, or personal background." All applicants have the opportunity to highlight their own potential diversity contributions through the submission of a personal statement, letters of recommendation, and an essay describing the ways in which the applicant will contribute to the life and diversity of the Law School.

What is more, the Law School actually gives substantial weight to diversity factors besides race. The Law School frequently accepts nonminority applicants with grades and test scores lower than underrepresented minority applicants (and other nonminority applicants) who are rejected. This shows that the Law School seriously weighs many other diversity factors besides race that can make a real and dispositive difference for nonminority applicants as well. By this flexible approach, the Law School sufficiently takes into account, in practice as well as in theory, a wide variety of characteristics besides race and ethnicity that contribute to a diverse student body....

Petitioner and the United States argue that the Law School's plan is not narrowly tailored because race-neutral means exist to obtain the educational benefits of student body diversity that the Law School seeks. We disagree. Narrow tailoring does not require exhaustion of every conceivable race-neutral alternative. Nor does it require a university to choose between maintaining a reputation for excellence or fulfilling a commitment to provide educational opportunities to members of all racial groups. See *Wygant v. Jackson Bd. of Ed. at* 280, n. 6 (1986) (alternatives must serve the interest "'about as well'"); *Richmond v. Croson Co.* at 509-510 (plurality opinion) (city had a "whole array of race-neutral" alternatives because changing requirements "would have [had] little detrimental effect on the city's interests"). Narrow tailoring does, however, require serious, good faith consideration of workable race-neutral alternatives that will achieve the diversity the university seeks. *Id.* at 507 (set-aside plan not narrowly tailored where "there does not appear to have been any consideration of the use of race-neutral means"); *Wygant v. Jackson* at 280, n. 6 (narrow tailoring "requires consideration" of "lawful alternative and less restrictive means").

We agree with the Court of Appeals that the Law School sufficiently considered workable race-neutral alternatives. The District Court took the Law School to task for failing to consider race-neutral alternatives such as "using a lottery system" or "decreasing the emphasis for all applicants on undergraduate GPA and LSAT scores." But these alternatives would require a dramatic sacrifice of diversity, the academic quality of all admitted students, or both.

The Law School's current admissions program considers race as one factor among many, in an effort to assemble a student body that is diverse in ways broader than race. Because a lottery would make that kind of nuanced judgment impossible, it would effectively sacrifice all other educational values, not to mention every other kind of diversity. So too with the suggestion that the Law School simply lower admissions standards for all students, a drastic remedy that would require the Law School to become a much different institution and sacrifice a vital component of its educational mission. The United States advocates "percentage plans," recently adopted by public undergraduate institutions in Texas, Florida, and California to guarantee admission to all students above a certain class-rank threshold in every high school in the State. The United States does not, however, explain how such plans could work for graduate and professional schools. Moreover, even assuming such plans are race-neutral, they may preclude the university from conducting the individualized assessments necessary to assemble a student body that is not just racially diverse, but diverse along all the qualities valued by the university. We are satisfied that the Law School adequately considered race-neutral alternatives currently capable of producing a critical mass without forcing the Law School to abandon the academic selectivity that is the cornerstone of its educational mission.

We acknowledge that "there are serious problems of justice connected with the idea of preference itself." *Bakke* at 298 (opinion of Powell, J.). Narrow tailoring, therefore, requires that a race-conscious admissions program not unduly harm members of any racial group. Even remedial race-based governmental action generally "remains subject to continuing oversight to assure that it will work the least harm possible to other innocent persons competing for the benefit." *Bakke.* at 308. To be narrowly tailored, a race-conscious admissions program must not "unduly burden individuals who are not members of the favored racial and ethnic groups." *Metro Broadcasting, Inc. v. FCC* at 630 (1990) (O'Connor, J., dissenting).

We are satisfied that the Law School's admissions program does not. Because the Law School considers "all pertinent elements of diversity," it can (and does) select nonminority applicants who have greater potential to enhance student body diversity over underrepresented minority applicants. *Bakke* at 317 (opinion of Powell, J.). As Justice Powell recognized in *Bakke*, so long as a race-conscious admissions program uses race as a "plus" factor in the context of individualized consideration, a rejected applicant

> "will not have been foreclosed from all consideration for that seat simply because he was not the right color or had the wrong surname.... His qualifications would have been weighed fairly and competitively, and he would have no basis to complain of unequal treatment under the Fourteenth Amendment." *Id.* at 318.

We agree that, in the context of its individualized inquiry into the possible diversity contributions of all applicants, the Law School's race-conscious admissions program does not unduly harm nonminority applicants.

We are mindful, however, that "[a] core purpose of the Fourteenth Amendment was to do away with all governmentally imposed discrimination based on race." *Palmore v. Sidoti*. Accordingly, race-conscious admissions policies must be limited in time. This requirement reflects that racial classifications, however compelling their goals, are potentially so dangerous that they may be employed no more broadly than the interest demands. Enshrining a permanent justification for racial preferences would offend this fundamental equal protection principle. We see no reason to exempt race-conscious admissions programs from the requirement that all governmental use of race must have a logical end point. The Law School, too, concedes that all "race-conscious programs must have reasonable durational limits."

In the context of higher education, the durational requirement can be met by sunset provisions in race-conscious admissions policies and periodic reviews to determine whether racial preferences are still necessary to achieve student body diversity. Universities in California, Florida, and Washington State, where racial preferences in admissions are prohibited by state law, are currently engaged in experimenting with a wide variety of alternative approaches. Universities in other States can and should draw on the most promising aspects of these race-neutral alternatives as they develop. Cf. *United States v. Lopez* at 581 (Kennedy, J., concurring) ("The States may perform their role as laboratories for experimentation to devise various solutions where the best solution is far from clear").

The requirement that all race-conscious admissions programs have a termination point "assures all citizens that the deviation from the norm of equal treatment of all racial and ethnic groups is a temporary matter, a measure taken in the service of the goal of equality itself." *Richmond v. Croson* at 510 (plurality opinion); see also Nathanson & Bartnik at 293 ("It would be a sad day indeed, were America to become a quota-ridden society, with each identifiable minority assigned proportional representation in every desirable walk of life. But that is not the rationale for programs of preferential treatment; the acid test of their justification will be their efficacy in eliminating the need for any racial or ethnic preferences at all").

We take the Law School at its word that it would "like nothing better than to find a race-neutral admissions formula" and will terminate its race-conscious admissions program as soon as practicable. *Bakke* at 317-318 (opinion of Powell, J.) (presuming good faith of university officials in the absence of a showing to the contrary). It has been 25 years since Justice Powell first approved the use of race to further an interest in student body diversity in the context of public higher education. Since that time, the number of minority applicants with high grades and test scores has indeed increased. We expect that 25 years from now, the use of racial preferences will no longer be necessary to further the interest approved today.

IV

In summary, the Equal Protection Clause does not prohibit the Law School's narrowly tailored use of race in admissions decisions to further a compelling interest in obtaining the educational benefits that flow from a diverse student body.... The judgment of the Court of Appeals for the Sixth Circuit, accordingly, is affirmed.

It is so ordered.

JUSTICE SCALIA, with whom JUSTICE THOMAS joins, concurring in part and dissenting in part.

...

... The "educational benefit" that the University of Michigan seeks to achieve by racial discrimination consists, according to the Court, of "'cross-racial understanding'" and "'better prepar[ation of] students for an increasingly diverse workforce and society,'" all of which is necessary not only for work, but also for good "citizenship." This is not, of course, an "educational benefit" on which students will be graded on their Law School transcript (Works and Plays Well with Others: B+) or tested by the bar examiners (Q: Describe in 500 words or less your cross-racial understanding). For it is a lesson of life rather than law — essentially the same lesson taught to (or rather learned by, for it cannot be "taught" in the usual sense) people three feet shorter and twenty years younger than the full-grown adults at the

Grutter v. Bollinger

University of Michigan Law School, in institutions ranging from Boy Scout troops to public-school kindergartens. If properly considered an "educational benefit" at all, it is surely not one that is either uniquely relevant to law school or uniquely "teachable" in a formal educational setting. *And therefore:* If it is appropriate for the University of Michigan Law School to use racial discrimination for the purpose of putting together a "critical mass" that will convey generic lessons in socialization and good citizenship, surely it is no less appropriate — indeed, *particularly* appropriate — for the civil service system of the State of Michigan to do so. There, also, those exposed to "critical masses" of certain races will presumably become better Americans, better Michiganders, better civil servants. And surely private employers cannot be criticized — indeed, should be praised — if they also "teach" good citizenship to their adult employees through a patriotic, all-American system of racial discrimination in hiring. The nonminority individuals who are deprived of a legal education, a civil service job, or any job at all by reason of their skin color will surely understand.

Unlike a clear constitutional holding that racial preferences in state educational institutions are impermissible, or even a clear anticonstitutional holding that racial preferences in state educational institutions are OK, today's *Grutter-Gratz* split double header seems perversely designed to prolong the controversy and the litigation.... [O]ther suits may challenge the bona fides of the institution's expressed commitment to the educational benefits of diversity that immunize the discriminatory scheme in *Grutter*. (Tempting targets, one would suppose, will be those universities that talk the talk of multiculturalism and racial diversity in the courts but walk the walk of tribalism and racial segregation on their campuses — through minority-only student organizations, separate minority housing opportunities, separate minority student centers, even separate minority-only graduation ceremonies.) ... Finally, litigation can be expected on behalf of minority groups intentionally short changed in the institution's composition of its generic minority "critical mass." I do not look forward to any of these cases. The Constitution proscribes government discrimination on the basis of race, and state-provided education is no exception.

JUSTICE THOMAS, with whom JUSTICE SCALIA joins as to Parts I-VII, concurring in part and dissenting in part.

Frederick Douglass, speaking to a group of abolitionists almost 140 years ago, delivered a message lost on today's majority:

> "In regard to the colored people, there is always more that is
> benevolent, I perceive, than just, manifested towards us. What I ask
> for the negro is not benevolence, not pity, not sympathy, but simply
> *justice*. The American people have always been anxious to know what

they shall do with us.... I have had but one answer from the beginning. Do nothing with us! Your doing with us has already played the mischief with us. Do nothing with us! If the apples will not remain on the tree of their own strength, if they are worm-eaten at the core, if they are early ripe and disposed to fall, let them fall! ... And if the negro cannot stand on his own legs, let him fall also. All I ask is, give him a chance to stand on his own legs! Let him alone! ... Your interference is doing him positive injury. (Emphasis in original).

Like Douglass, I believe blacks can achieve in every avenue of American life without the meddling of university administrators. Because I wish to see all students succeed whatever their color, I share, in some respect, the sympathies of those who sponsor the type of discrimination advanced by the University of Michigan Law School (Law School). The Constitution does not, however, tolerate institutional devotion to the status quo in admissions policies when such devotion ripens into racial discrimination. Nor does the Constitution countenance the unprecedented deference the Court gives to the Law School, an approach inconsistent with the very concept of "strict scrutiny."

No one would argue that a university could set up a lower general admission standard and then impose heightened requirements only on black applicants. Similarly, a university may not maintain a high admission standard and grant exemptions to favored races. The Law School, of its own choosing, and for its own purposes, maintains an exclusionary admissions system that it knows produces racially disproportionate results. Racial discrimination is not a permissible solution to the self-inflicted wounds of this elitist admissions policy.

The majority upholds the Law School's racial discrimination not by interpreting the people's Constitution, but by responding to a faddish slogan of the cognoscenti....

I

The majority agrees that the Law School's racial discrimination should be subjected to strict scrutiny. Before applying that standard to this case, I will briefly revisit the Court's treatment of racial classifications.

The strict scrutiny standard that the Court purports to apply in this case was first enunciated in *Korematsu v. United States*. There the Court held that "pressing public necessity may sometimes justify the existence of [racial discrimination]; racial antagonism never can." Id. at 216. This standard of "pressing public necessity" has

Grutter v. Bollinger

more frequently been termed "compelling governmental interest," see, e.g., *Regents of Univ. of Cal. v. Bakke* at 299 (1978) (opinion of Powell, J.). A majority of the Court has validated only two circumstances where "pressing public necessity" or a "compelling state interest" can possibly justify racial discrimination by state actors. First, the lesson of *Korematsu* is that national security constitutes a "pressing public necessity," though the government's use of race to advance that objective must be narrowly tailored. Second, the Court has recognized as a compelling state interest a government's effort to remedy past discrimination for which it is responsible. *Richmond v. J. A. Croson Co.* at 504.

The contours of "pressing public necessity" can be further discerned from those interests the Court has rejected as bases for racial discrimination. For example, *Wygant v. Jackson Bd. of Ed.* found unconstitutional a collective-bargaining agreement between a school board and a teachers' union that favored certain minority races. The school board defended the policy on the grounds that minority teachers provided "role models" for minority students and that a racially "diverse" faculty would improve the education of all students. *Id.* at 315 (Stevens, J., dissenting) ("An integrated faculty will be able to provide benefits to the student body that could not be provided by an all-white, or nearly all-white faculty"). Nevertheless, the Court found that the use of race violated the Equal Protection Clause, deeming both asserted state interests insufficiently compelling. *Id.* at 275-276, (plurality opinion); *Id.* at 295 (White, J., concurring in judgment) ("None of the interests asserted by [the [school board] ... justify this racially discriminatory layoff policy").

An even greater governmental interest involves the sensitive role of courts in child custody determinations. In *Palmore v. Sidoti* the Court held that even the best interests of a child did not constitute a compelling state interest that would allow a state court to award custody to the father because the mother was in a mixed-race marriage. *Id.* at 433 (finding the interest "substantial" but holding the custody decision could not be based on the race of the mother's new husband).

Finally, the Court has rejected an interest in remedying general societal discrimination as a justification for race discrimination. "Societal discrimination, without more, is too amorphous a basis for imposing a racially classified remedy" because a "court could uphold remedies that are ageless in their reach into the past, and timeless in their ability to affect the future." *Wygant* at 276 (plurality opinion).

Where the Court has accepted only national security, and rejected even the best interests of a child, as a justification for racial discrimination, I conclude that only those measures the State must take to provide a bulwark against anarchy, or to prevent violence, will constitute a "pressing public necessity." Cf. *Lee v. Washington* at 334 (1968) (Black, J., concurring) (indicating that protecting prisoners from violence might justify narrowly tailored racial discrimination); *Croson* at 521 (Scalia, J., concurring in judgment) ("At least where state or local action is at issue, only a social emergency rising to the level of imminent danger to life and limb ... can justify [racial discrimination]").

The Constitution abhors classifications based on race, not only because those classifications can harm favored races or are based on illegitimate motives, but also because every time the government places citizens on racial registers and makes race relevant to the provision of burdens or benefits, it demeans us all. "Purchased at the price of immeasurable human suffering, the equal protection principle reflects our Nation's understanding that such classifications ultimately have a destructive impact on the individual and our society." *Adarand v. Peña* at 240 (Thomas, J., concurring in part and concurring in judgment).

II

Unlike the majority, I seek to define with precision the interest being asserted by the Law School before determining whether that interest is so compelling as to justify racial discrimination. The Law School maintains that it wishes to obtain "educational benefits that flow from student body diversity." This statement must be evaluated carefully, because it implies that both "diversity" and "educational benefits" are components of the Law School's compelling state interest. Additionally, the Law School's refusal to entertain certain changes in its admissions process and status indicates that the compelling state interest it seeks to validate is actually broader than might appear at first glance.

Undoubtedly there are other ways to "better" the education of law students aside from ensuring that the student body contains a "critical mass" of underrepresented minority students. Attaining "diversity," whatever it means,[5] is the

---

[5] "Diversity," for all of its devotees, is more a fashionable catchphrase than it is a useful term, especially when something as serious as racial discrimination is at issue. Because the Equal Protection Clause renders the color of one's skin constitutionally irrelevant to the Law School's mission, I refer to the Law School's interest as an "aesthetic." That is, the Law School wants to have a certain appearance, from the shape of the desks and tables in its classrooms to the color of the students sitting at them.

I also use the term "aesthetic" because I believe it underlines the ineffectiveness of racially discriminatory admissions in actually helping those who are truly underprivileged. Cf. *Orr v. Orr* at 283 (1979) (noting that suspect classifications are especially impermissible when "the choice made by the State appears to redound ... to the benefit of those without need for special solicitude"). It must be remembered that the Law School's racial

(continued...)

mechanism by which the Law School obtains educational benefits, not an end of itself....

...

The proffered interest that the majority vindicates today, then, is not simply "diversity." Instead the Court upholds the use of racial discrimination as a tool to advance the Law School's interest in offering a marginally superior education while maintaining an elite institution. Unless each constituent part of this state interest is of pressing public necessity, the Law School's use of race is unconstitutional. I find each of them to fall far short of this standard.

III

A

A close reading of the Court's opinion reveals that all of its legal work is done through one conclusory statement: The Law School has a "compelling interest in securing the educational benefits of a diverse student body." No serious effort is made to explain how these benefits fit with the state interests the Court has recognized (or rejected) as compelling....

Justice Powell's opinion in *Bakke* and the Court's decision today rest on the fundamentally flawed proposition that racial discrimination can be contextualized so that a goal, such as classroom aesthetics, can be compelling in one context but not in another. This "we know it when we see it" approach to evaluating state interests is not capable of judicial application. Today, the Court insists on radically expanding the range of permissible uses of race to something as trivial (by comparison) as the assembling of a law school class. I can only presume that the majority's failure to justify its decision by reference to any principle arises from the absence of any such principle.

B

Under the proper standard, there is no pressing public necessity in maintaining a public law school at all and, it follows, certainly not an elite law school. Likewise, marginal improvements in legal education do not qualify as a compelling state

---

[5](...continued)

discrimination does nothing for those too poor or uneducated to participate in elite higher education and therefore presents only an illusory solution to the challenges facing our Nation.

interest.

1

While legal education at a public university may be good policy or otherwise laudable, it is obviously not a pressing public necessity when the correct legal standard is applied....

...

IV

...

B

1

The Court's deference to the Law School's conclusion that its racial experimentation leads to educational benefits will, if adhered to, have serious collateral consequences. The Court relies heavily on social science evidence to justify its deference. But see also Rothman, Lipset, & Nevitte (finding that the racial mix of a student body produced by racial discrimination of the type practiced by the Law School in fact hinders students' perception of academic quality). The Court never acknowledges, however, the growing evidence that racial (and other sorts of) heterogeneity actually impairs learning among black students. See, e.g., Flowers & Pascarella at 674(concluding that black students experience superior cognitive development at Historically Black Colleges (HBCs) and that, even among blacks, "a substantial diversity moderates the cognitive effects of attending an HBC"); Allen (finding that black students attending HBCs report higher academic achievement than those attending predominantly white colleges).

At oral argument in *Gratz v. Bollinger*, counsel for respondents stated that "most every single one of [the HBCs] do have diverse student bodies." What precisely counsel meant by "diverse" is indeterminate, but it is reported that in 2000 at Morehouse College, one of the most distinguished HBC's in the Nation, only 0.1% of the student body was white, and only 0.2% was Hispanic. *College Admissions Data Handbook 2002-2003* at 613. And at Mississippi Valley State University, a public HBC, only 1.1% of the freshman class in 2001 was white. *Id.* at 603. If there is a "critical mass" of whites at these institutions, then "critical mass" is indeed a very small proportion.

The majority grants deference to the Law School's "assessment that diversity will, in fact, yield educational benefits." It follows, therefore, that an HBC's assessment that racial homogeneity will yield educational benefits would similarly be given deference. An HBC's rejection of white applicants in order to maintain racial homogeneity seems permissible, therefore, under the majority's view of the Equal Protection Clause. But see *United States v. Fordice* (Thomas, J., concurring) ("Obviously, a State cannot maintain ... traditions by closing particular institutions, historically white or historically black, to particular racial groups"). Contained within today's majority opinion is the seed of a new constitutional justification for a concept I thought long and rightly rejected — racial segregation.

2

Moreover one would think, in light of the Court's decision in *United States v. Virginia* that before being given license to use racial discrimination, the Law School would be required to radically reshape its admissions process, even to the point of sacrificing some elements of its character. In *Virginia*, a majority of the Court, without a word about academic freedom, accepted the [representation of] the all-male Virginia Military Institute (VMI) ... that some changes in its "adversative" method of education would be required with the admission of women, *id.* at 540, but did not defer to VMI's judgment that these changes would be too great. Instead, the Court concluded that they were "manageable." *Id.* at 551, n. 19. That case involved sex discrimination, which is subjected to intermediate, not strict, scrutiny. *Id.* at 533. So in *Virginia*, where the standard of review dictated that greater flexibility be granted to VMI's educational policies than the Law School deserves here, this Court gave no deference. Apparently where the status quo being defended is that of the elite establishment — here the Law School — rather than a less fashionable Southern military institution, the Court will defer without serious inquiry and without regard to the applicable legal standard.

C

Virginia is also notable for the fact that the Court relied on the "experience" of formerly single-sex institutions, such as the service academies, to conclude that admission of women to VMI would be "manageable." *Id.* at 544-545. Today, however, the majority ignores the "experience" of those institutions that have been forced to abandon explicit racial discrimination in admissions.

The sky has not fallen at Boalt Hall at the University of California, Berkeley, for example. Prior to Proposition 209's adoption of Cal. Const., Art. 1, § 31(a), which bars the State from "granting preferential treatment ... on the basis of race ... in the operation of ... public education," Boalt Hall enrolled 20 blacks and 28

Hispanics in its first-year class for 1996. In 2002, without deploying express racial discrimination in admissions, Boalt's entering class enrolled 14 blacks and 36 Hispanics. "University of California Law and Medical School Enrollments." Total underrepresented minority student enrollment at Boalt Hall now exceeds 1996 levels. Apparently the Law School cannot be counted on to be as resourceful. The Court is willfully blind to the very real experience in California and elsewhere, which raises the inference that institutions with "reputation[s] for excellence" rivaling the Law School's have satisfied their sense of mission without resorting to prohibited racial discrimination.

V

Putting aside the absence of any legal support for the majority's reflexive deference, there is much to be said for the view that the use of tests and other measures to "predict" academic performance is a poor substitute for a system that gives every applicant a chance to prove he can succeed in the study of law. The rallying cry that in the absence of racial discrimination in admissions there would be a true meritocracy ignores the fact that the entire process is poisoned by numerous exceptions to "merit." For example, in the national debate on racial discrimination in higher education admissions, much has been made of the fact that elite institutions utilize a so-called "legacy" preference to give the children of alumni an advantage in admissions. This, and other, exceptions to a "true" meritocracy give the lie to protestations that merit admissions are in fact the order of the day at the Nation's universities. The Equal Protection Clause does not, however, prohibit the use of unseemly legacy preferences or many other kinds of arbitrary admissions procedures. What the Equal Protection Clause does prohibit are classifications made on the basis of race. So while legacy preferences can stand under the Constitution, racial discrimination cannot.[10] I will not twist the Constitution to invalidate legacy preferences or otherwise impose my vision of higher education admissions on the Nation. The majority should similarly stay its impulse to validate faddish racial discrimination the Constitution clearly forbids.

In any event, there is nothing ancient, honorable, or constitutionally protected about "selective" admissions. The University of Michigan should be well aware that alternative methods have historically been used for the admission of students, for it brought to this country the German certificate system in the late-19th century.

---

[10]Were this Court to have the courage to forbid the use of racial discrimination in admissions, legacy preferences (and similar practices) might quickly become less popular — a possibility not lost, I am certain, on the elites (both individual and institutional) supporting the Law School in this case.

Wechsler at 16-39.   Under this system, a secondary school was certified by a university so that any graduate who completed the course offered by the school was offered admission to the university. The certification regime supplemented, and later virtually replaced (at least in the Midwest), the prior regime of rigorous subject-matter entrance examinations. *Id.* at 57-58. The facially race-neutral "percent plans" now used in Texas, California, and Florida are in many ways the descendants of the certificate system.

Certification was replaced by selective admissions in the beginning of the 20th century, as universities sought to exercise more control over the composition of their student bodies. Since its inception, selective admissions has been the vehicle for racial, ethnic, and religious tinkering and experimentation by university administrators. The initial driving force for the relocation of the selective function from the high school to the universities was the same desire to select racial winners and losers that the Law School exhibits today. Columbia, Harvard, and others infamously determined that they had "too many" Jews, just as today the Law School argues it would have "too many" whites if it could not discriminate in its admissions process. See *id.* at 155-168 (Columbia); Broun & Britt at 53-54 (Harvard).

Columbia employed intelligence tests precisely because Jewish applicants, who were predominantly immigrants, scored worse on such tests. Thus, Columbia could claim (falsely) that "'we have not eliminated boys because they were Jews and do not propose to do so. We have honestly attempted to eliminate the lowest grade of applicant [through the use of intelligence testing] and it turns out that a good many of the low grade men are New York City Jews.'" Hawkes. In other words, the tests were adopted with full knowledge of their disparate impact.

Similarly no modern law school can claim ignorance of the poor performance of blacks, relatively speaking, on the Law School Admissions Test (LSAT). Nevertheless, law schools continue to use the test and then attempt to "correct" for black underperformance by using racial discrimination in admissions so as to obtain their aesthetic student body. The Law School's continued adherence to measures it knows produce racially skewed results is not entitled to deference by this Court. The Law School itself admits that the test is imperfect, as it must, given that it regularly admits students who score at or below 150 (the national median) on the test. (Between 1995 and 2000, the Law School admitted 37 students — 27 of whom were black, 31 of whom were "underrepresented minorities" — with LSAT scores of 150 or lower.) And the Law School's *amici* cannot seem to agree on the fundamental question whether the test itself is useful. Compare Brief for Law School Admission Council as *Amicus Curiae* 12 ("LSAT scores ... are an effective predictor of students' performance in law school") with Brief for Harvard Black Law Students Association et al. as *Amici Curiae* 27 ("Whether [the LSAT] measures objective merit ... is certainly questionable").

Having decided to use the LSAT, the Law School must accept the constitutional burdens that come with this decision. The Law School may freely continue to employ the LSAT and other allegedly merit-based standards in whatever fashion it likes. What the Equal Protection Clause forbids, but the Court today allows, is the use of these standards hand-in-hand with racial discrimination. An infinite variety of admissions methods are available to the Law School. Considering all of the radical thinking that has historically occurred at this country's universities, the Law School's intractable approach toward admissions is striking.

The Court will not even deign to make the Law School try other methods, however, preferring instead to grant a 25-year license to violate the Constitution. And the same Court that had the courage to order the desegregation of all public schools in the South now fears, on the basis of platitudes rather than principle, to force the Law School to abandon a decidedly imperfect admissions regime that provides the basis for racial discrimination.

VI

The absence of any articulated legal principle supporting the majority's principal holding suggests another rationale. I believe what lies beneath the Court's decision today are the benighted notions that one can tell when racial discrimination benefits (rather than hurts) minority groups, and that racial discrimination is necessary to remedy general societal ills. This Court's precedents supposedly settled both issues, but clearly the majority still cannot commit to the principle that racial classifications are per se harmful and that almost no amount of benefit in the eye of the beholder can justify such classifications.

Putting aside what I take to be the Court's implicit rejection of *Adarand's* holding that beneficial and burdensome racial classifications are equally invalid, I must contest the notion that the Law School's discrimination benefits those admitted as a result of it. The Court spends considerable time discussing the impressive display of *amicus* support for the Law School in this case from all corners of society. But nowhere in any of the filings in this Court is any evidence that the purported "beneficiaries" of this racial discrimination prove themselves by performing at (or even near) the same level as those students who receive no preferences. Cf. Thernstrom & Thernstrom at 1605-1608 (discussing the failure of defenders of racial discrimination in admissions to consider the fact that its "beneficiaries" are underperforming in the classroom).

Grutter v. Bollinger

The silence in this case is deafening to those of us who view higher education's purpose as imparting knowledge and skills to students, rather than a communal, rubber-stamp, credentialing process. The Law School is not looking for those students who, despite a lower LSAT score or undergraduate grade point average, will succeed in the study of law. The Law School seeks only a facade — it is sufficient that the class looks right, even if it does not perform right.

The Law School tantalizes unprepared students with the promise of a University of Michigan degree and all of the opportunities that it offers. These overmatched students take the bait, only to find that they cannot succeed in the cauldron of competition. And this mismatch crisis is not restricted to elite institutions. See Sowell at 176-177 ("Even if most minority students are able to meet the normal standards at the 'average' range of colleges and universities, the systematic mismatching of minority students begun at the top can mean that such students are generally overmatched throughout all levels of higher education"). Indeed, to cover the tracks of the aestheticists, this cruel farce of racial discrimination must continue — in selection for the Michigan Law Review, see *University of Michigan Law School Student Handbook 2002-2003* at 39-40 (noting the presence of a "diversity plan" for admission to the review), and in hiring at law firms and for judicial clerkships — until the "beneficiaries" are no longer tolerated. While these students may graduate with law degrees, there is no evidence that they have received a qualitatively better legal education (or become better lawyers) than if they had gone to a less "elite" law school for which they were better prepared. And the aestheticists will never address the real problems facing "underrepresented minorities,"[11] instead continuing their social experiments on other people's children.

Beyond the harm the Law School's racial discrimination visits upon its test subjects, no social science has disproved the notion that this discrimination "engenders attitudes of superiority or, alternatively, provoke[s] resentment among those who believe that they have been wronged by the government's use of race." *Adarand* at 241 (Thomas, J., concurring in part and concurring in judgment). "These programs stamp minorities with a badge of inferiority and may cause them to develop dependencies or to adopt an attitude that they are 'entitled' to preferences." *Adarand* at 241.

---

[11]For example, there is no recognition by the Law School in this case that even with their racial discrimination in place, black men are "underrepresented" at the Law School. See *Law School Admissions Council Guide* at 426 (reporting that the Law School has 46 black women and 28 black men). Why does the Law School not also discriminate in favor of black men over black women, given this underrepresentation? The answer is, again, that all the Law School cares about is its own image among know-it-all elites, not solving real problems like the crisis of black male underperformance.

It is uncontested that each year, the Law School admits a handful of blacks who would be admitted in the absence of racial discrimination. Who can differentiate between those who belong and those who do not? The majority of blacks are admitted to the Law School because of discrimination, and because of this policy all are tarred as undeserving. This problem of stigma does not depend on determinacy as to whether those stigmatized are actually the "beneficiaries" of racial discrimination. When blacks take positions in the highest places of government, industry, or academia, it is an open question today whether their skin color played a part in their advancement. The question itself is the stigma — because either racial discrimination did play a role, in which case the person may be deemed "otherwise unqualified," or it did not, in which case asking the question itself unfairly marks those blacks who would succeed without discrimination. Is this what the Court means by "visibly open"?

Finally, the Court's disturbing reference to the importance of the country's law schools as training grounds meant to cultivate "a set of leaders with legitimacy in the eyes of the citizenry," through the use of racial discrimination deserves discussion. As noted earlier, the Court has soundly rejected the remedying of societal discrimination as a justification for governmental use of race. For those who believe that every racial disproportionality in our society is caused by some kind of racial discrimination, there can be no distinction between remedying societal discrimination and erasing racial disproportionalities in the country's leadership caste. And if the lack of proportional racial representation among our leaders is not caused by societal discrimination, then "fixing" it is even less of a pressing public necessity.

The Court's civics lesson presents yet another example of judicial selection of a theory of political representation based on skin color — an endeavor I have previously rejected. The majority appears to believe that broader utopian goals justify the Law School's use of race, but "the Equal Protection Clause commands the elimination of racial barriers, not their creation in order to satisfy our theory as to how society ought to be organized." *DeFunis v. Odegaard* at 342 (Douglas, J., dissenting).

VII

...

B

The Court also holds that racial discrimination in admissions should be given another 25 years before it is deemed no longer narrowly tailored to the Law School's fabricated compelling state interest. While I agree that in 25 years the practices of the

Law School will be illegal, they are, for the reasons I have given, illegal now. The majority does not and cannot rest its time limitation on any evidence that the gap in credentials between black and white students is shrinking or will be gone in that time frame. In recent years there has been virtually no change, for example, in the proportion of law school applicants with LSAT scores of 165 and higher who are black.[14] In 1993 blacks constituted 1.1% of law school applicants in that score range, though they represented 11.1% of all applicants. In 2000 the comparable numbers were 1.0% and 11.3%. *LSAC Statistical Report.* No one can seriously contend, and the Court does not, that the racial gap in academic credentials will disappear in 25 years. Nor is the Court's holding that racial discrimination will be unconstitutional in 25 years made contingent on the gap closing in that time.[15]

Indeed, the very existence of racial discrimination of the type practiced by the Law School may impede the narrowing of the LSAT testing gap. An applicant's LSAT score can improve dramatically with preparation, but such preparation is a cost, and there must be sufficient benefits attached to an improved score to justify additional study. Whites scoring between 163 and 167 on the LSAT are routinely rejected by the Law School, and thus whites aspiring to admission at the Law School have every incentive to improve their score to levels above that range. (In 2000, 209 out of 422 white applicants were rejected in this scoring range). Blacks, on the other hand, are nearly guaranteed admission if they score above 155. (In 2000, 63 out of 77 black applicants are accepted with LSAT scores above 155). As admission prospects approach certainty, there is no incentive for the black applicant to continue to prepare for the LSAT once he is reasonably assured of achieving the requisite score. It is far from certain that the LSAT test-taker's behavior is responsive to the Law School's

---

[14] I use a score of 165 as the benchmark here because the Law School feels it is the relevant score range for applicant consideration (absent race discrimination). (The median LSAT score for all accepted applicants from 1995-1998 was 168. The median LSAT score for accepted applicants was 167 for the years 1999 and 2000.) University of Michigan Law School Website (showing that the median LSAT score for accepted applicants in 2002 was 166).

[15] The majority's non sequitur observation that since 1978 the number of blacks that have scored in these upper ranges on the LSAT has grown says nothing about current trends. First, black participation in the LSAT until the early 1990's lagged behind black representation in the general population. For instance, in 1984 only 7.3% of law school applicants were black, whereas in 2000 11.3% of law school applicants were black. Today, however, unless blacks were to begin applying to law school in proportions greater than their representation in the general population, the growth in absolute numbers of high scoring blacks should be expected to plateau, and it has. In 1992, 63 black applicants to law school had LSAT scores above 165. In 2000, that number was 65.

admissions policies.[16]   Nevertheless, the possibility remains that this racial discrimination will help fulfill the bigot's prophecy about black underperformance — just as it confirms the conspiracy theorist's belief that "institutional racism" is at fault for every racial disparity in our society.

....

References

CASES

Adarand Constructors, Inc. v. Peña, 515 U.S. 200 (1995)
Brown v. Board of Education, 347 U.S. 483 (1954)
DeFunis v. Odegaard, 416 U.S. 312 (1974)
Freeman v. Pitts, 503 U.S. 467 (1992)
Gomillion v. Lightfoot, 364 U.S. 339 (1960)
Gratz v Bollinger, 539 U.S. 244 (2003)
Hopwood v. Texas, 78 F.3d 932 (5th Cir. 1996)
Johnson v. Transportation Agency, Santa Clara Cty., 480 U.S. 616 (1987).
Keyishian v. Board of Regents of Univ. of State of N. Y., 385 U.S. 589 (1967)
Korematsu v. United States, 323 U.S. 214 (1944)
Lee v. Washington, 390 U.S. 333 (1968) (*per curiam*)
Local 28 of Sheet Metal Workers v. EEOC, 478 U.S. 421 (1986)
Loving v. Virginia, 388 U.S. 1 (1967)
Metro Broadcasting, Inc. v. FCC, 497 U.S. 547 (1990)
Orr v. Orr, 440 U.S. 268 (1979)
Palmore v. Sidoti, 466 U.S. 429 (1984)
Plyler v. Doe, 457 U.S. 202 (1982)
Regents of Univ. of Cal. v. Bakke, 438 U.S. 265 (1978)
Richmond v. J. A. Croson Co., 488 U.S. 469 (1989)
Shaw v. Hunt, 517 U.S. 899 (1996)
Smith v. University of Wash. Law School, 233 F.3d 1188 (9th Cir. 2000)
Sweatt v. Painter, 339 U.S. 629 (1950)
United States v. Fordice, 505 U.S. 717 (1992)
United States v. Lopez, 514 U.S. 549 (1995)
United States v. Virginia, 518 U.S. 515 (1996)
Wygant v. Jackson Bd. of Ed., 476 U.S. 267 (1986)

---

[16]I use the LSAT as an example, but the same incentive structure is in place for any admissions criteria, including undergraduate grades, on which minorities are consistently admitted at thresholds significantly lower than whites.

Grutter v. Bollinger xxxvi

OTHER AUTHORITIES

Allen, "The Color of Success: African-American College Student Outcomes at Predominantly White and Historically Black Public Colleges and Universities," 62 Harv. Educ. Rev. 26 (1992)

Broun, H. & G. Britt, *Christians Only: A Study in Prejudice* (1931)

College Admissions Data Handbook 2002-2003 (43d ed. 2002)

Douglas, Frederick, "What the Black Man Wants: An Address Delivered in Boston, Massachusetts, on 26 January 1865," reprinted in 4 the *Frederick Douglass Papers* 59, 68 (J. Blassingame & J. McKivigan eds. 1991)

Flowers & Pascarella, "Cognitive Effects of College Racial Composition on African American Students After 3 Years of College," 40 J. of College Student Development 669 (1999), 669

Hawkes, Herbert E., dean of Columbia College, Letter to E. B. Wilson, June 16, 1922 (reprinted in *Qualified Student* 160-161)

Law School Admissions Council Guide

Law School Admissions Council Statistical Report (2001)

Nathanson & Bartnik, *The Constitutionality of Preferential Treatment for Minority Applicants to Professional Schools*, 58 Chicago Bar Rec. 282 (May-June 1977)

Rothman, Lipset, & Nevitte, "Racial Diversity Reconsidered," 151 Public Interest 25 (2003)

Sowell, *T., Race and Culture* (1994)

Thernstrom & Thernstrom, Reflections on the Shape of the River, 46 UCLA L. Rev. 1583 (1999)

"University of California Law and Medical School Enrollments," available at http://www.ucop.edu/acadadv/datamgmt/lawmed/law-enrolls-eth2.html

University of Michigan Law School Student Handbook 2002-2003

University of Michigan Law School Website, available at http://www.law.umich.edu/prospectivestudents/Admissions/index.htm

Wechsler, H., *The Qualified Student* 16-39 (1977)

Comment

As we noted in the introduction to <u>Grutter</u>, the Constitution was relevant because the University of Michigan is a public institution. The Constitution also applies to agencies of government in their capacity as employers. It is likely that <u>Grutter</u> will be precedent for affirmative action by public employers such as cities and states.

The Constitution does not apply to private employers. Of course, Title VII does, and it prohibits discrimination on the basis of race or sex. Does Title VII prohibit a private employer from engaging in affirmative action? The Supreme Court answered this question no in <u>United Steelworkers of America v. Weber</u>, 443 U.S. 193 (1979). Reasoning that affirmative action serves the central purpose of Title VII, which is to increase employment opportunities for women and people of color, the Court held Congress could not have intended to outlaw all affirmative action. The Court established four criteria that a lawful plan must satisfy:

First, a legitimate factual basis must exist for the plan. In <u>Weber</u> the evidence showed that, although African-Americans constituted nearly 40 percent of the labor market in the area, they held less than 2 percent of the skilled craft jobs in the company. As made clear in a subsequent case, <u>Johnson v. Transportation Agency, Santa Clara County</u>, 480 U.S. 616 (1987), the employer need not have been responsible (and, a fortiori, need not admit liability for) for the under representation.

Second, the plan must be fair to the disfavored class (usually European-American men). In <u>Weber</u> no whites were discharged, laid off, or overleaped in order to give opportunities to blacks. Instead, equal numbers of blacks and whites were accepted into a craft training program.

Third, a genuine plan must exist; an ad hoc decision to grant a preference will not suffice.

Finally, the plan must be temporary. The meaning of temporary is unclear. It plainly implies either a specific end date or an ending when a goal is achieved, but the Court did not indicate how many years a plan may persist. In <u>Weber</u> the plan was scheduled to terminate when blacks held 40 percent of the skilled craft jobs in the plant.

Question

When the morality of an act is being considered, disputes often arise between equity and justice. Equity is based on the consequences of an act, that is, on facts that occur afterwards. Justice is based on the antecedents of an act, that is, on facts that occur beforehand.[17] For example, a national debate is now occurring over how to treat illegal immigrants. Those who emphasize equity or consequences argue that illegal immigrants now in the country should be granted citizenship because their labor is important for some industries and because families should not be broken up. (Illegal immigrants often have children who, having been born in this country, are American citizens.) Those who emphasize justice or antecedents argue that illegal immigrants should not be granted citizenship because they knowingly violated the law when they entered the country.

We believe that both justice and equity are legitimate considerations. One does not trump the other. When they point in opposite directions, we have no accepted way to arbitrate between them.

To what extent is the disagreement over the constitutionality of affirmative action a conflict between justice and equity, between antecedents and consequences?

Ω

---

[17]Persons who emphasize the equity of an act are called "consequentialists" or "teleologists" (from the Greek word "telos," meaning end or purpose). Those who emphasize the justice of an act are called "non-consequentialists" or "deontologists" (from the Greek word "deon," meaning right.)

Reasonable Accommodation to Religion

Introduction

When Congress enacted Title VII, the law contained a simple prohibition on discrimination because of religion. As it administered the Act, the EEOC realized that a related problem was growing in importance: employment policies that seem to ignore religion often have ill effects on minority religions. One example is the business calendar. Most businesses are open on Monday through Friday, and many are open on Saturday. This calendar is problematic for Muslims, who observe the Sabbath on Friday, and for Jews and some Christians, who observe the Sabbath on Saturday. Similarly, most firms are open for business on religious holidays like Yom Kippur and Maulid al-Nabi (the birthday of the Prophet Mohammed). Another example is the work schedule. Many companies require their employees to work from 8:00 or 9:00 A.M. until 5:00 P.M. For Jews and some others, working until 5:00 P.M. on Friday in autumn and winter is problematic because their Sabbath begins at sundown on Friday.

Perhaps problems like these could have been dealt with under the disparate impact theory of discrimination. A prima facie case might be proved with evidence that an employment practice, such as being open for business on Saturday, has an adverse effect on members of certain religions. The problem was that disparate impact did not yet exist. The Equal Employment Opportunity Commission dealt with charges of religious discrimination almost from the day it opened its door, whereas the theory of disparate impact evolved in academic journals and the Commission in late 1960s. Indeed, it is likely that the Commission's approach to cases like the Saturday Sabbatarian contributed to (perhaps was the origin of) the theory of disparate impact.

In 1972 Congress added section 701(j) to Title VII. This section defines religion to include making reasonable accommodation to employees' religious observances. Thus, the duty in section 703 to refrain from discrimination on the basis of religion now includes

ii   *Hardison v. Trans World Airlines*

the duty to make reasonable accommodation. The following
two cases explore the scope of this duty.

Hardison v. Trans World Airlines

375 F. Supp. 877 (D.C. Mo. 1974)

JOHN W. OLIVER, District Judge:—This is an action by an individual plaintiff against his former employer, Trans World Airlines (TWA) and three labor organizations, International Association of Machinists and Aero Space Workers, District 142 [of the IAM], and Local 1650 [of the IAM], seeking redress from alleged religious discrimination in violation of the Civil Rights Act of 1964. Plaintiff asserts that his discharge from employment because of his refusal to work from sundown Friday to sundown Saturday pursuant to the tenets of his religion was a violation of his religious liberty. Plaintiff is a member of the Worldwide Church of God.

...

A. Union Responsibility

...

Although it is nowhere stated directly by plaintiff, it appears that he is complaining that the union discriminated against him because of its failure to [waive] the seniority provisions of the collective bargaining agreement between TWA and the International, which governed plaintiff's employment. A [waiver] of those provisions would have been required in order to adjust his schedule with one of the other workers on his shift so that he would be able to observe his Sabbath.

Plaintiff, in arguing that the union discriminated against him by "enforcing a collective bargaining agreement which was discriminatory against plaintiff in its application," is arguing that the union acted wrongly by standing by the contract and refusing actively to support plaintiff's efforts to avoid the seniority provisions of the contract. This actually amounts to an assertion that the union has a rather stringent duty to accommodate.

The duty to accommodate, which we shall discuss in more detail later in this opinion, at the time the alleged discrimination in this case took place, was required by EEOC guideline 29 C.F.R. § 1605.1:

> (b) The Commission believes that the duty not to discriminate on religious grounds, required by Section 703(a)(1) of the Civil Rights Act of 1964, includes an obligation *on the part of the employer* to make reasonable accommodations to the religious needs of employees and prospective employees where such accommodations can be made without undue hardship on the conduct of the employer's business. [Emphasis supplied.]

The unions interpret this language to mean that the duty is imposed only on the employer. They argue that that limitation was intentional because, they contend, a union has no power to accommodate. The union only has power to control its own organization, make collective bargaining agreements with the employer, and enforce those agreements. The employer, the unions conclude, is the only one who is in a position to accommodate.

We disagree. The language of the regulation does speak in terms of the employer but so have other provisions and regulations pursuant to the Act, which have been interpreted to include the union. For example, Section 703(h), the provision on seniority systems discussed below, has been applied to unions.

Furthermore, this case is a perfect example of a situation [in] which a union could accommodate a member if required to do so. TWA agreed that plaintiff could change shifts if the union approved. Such approval would mean that the union would have to suspend the operation of the seniority rules in plaintiff's case. Had the union made this accommodation, plaintiff would have been able to observe his Sabbath as he wished. The question, however, is whether Title VII imposed upon the unions the duty to ignore their contract under the circumstances of this particular case.

We do not believe that Title VII goes that far. We find and conclude that to require the union to ignore seniority in every case in which an employee with lesser seniority can observe his Sabbath only by changing shifts with a more senior employee would work an undue hardship on the union.

... Professor Harry T. Edwards and Mr. Joel H. Kaplan expressed concern that the EEOC regulation imposing the duty to accommodate places an intolerable burden on the employer. They described the burden of proving the absence of undue hardship as "nearly impossible to demonstrate if the work force is large enough." Edwards and Kaplan, *Religious Discrimination and the Role of Arbitration Under Title VII*, 69 Mich.L.Rev. 559, 628 (1971). They rightly argue that such an interpretation "imposes a priority of the religious over the secular" in that it might require an employer to favor employees whose religious beliefs require them to follow different schedules than the regular over other employees, even to the point of violating the other employees' bargained for rights. The same considerations apply in the case of the unions.

The labor-management contract to which the union is a party clearly sets out the seniority rules which are binding on the company and the union. That contract, of course, can not operate in violation of the laws of the United States, but we do not believe that Title VII requires that the seniority provisions be ignored. Professor Edwards and Mr. Kaplan discuss this problem at length:

> Assume that an employer operates a seven-day-a-week operation,
> that he has entered into a collective bargaining contract with the union, and

that the contract provides for shift preference by seniority. What if a low-seniority employee, who works a shift that includes Saturday and Sunday, converts to a religion that requires him not to work on one of those days? Must the employer then transfer this employee out of a Sunday or Saturday shift even though numerous employees with greater seniority are required to work over the weekend? Under the EEOC guidelines, the transfer of one employee could hardly be said to create an "undue hardship" for the employer, but what of the other employees? What of the hardship imposed on the employee who waited a long time to acquire sufficient seniority in order to avoid weekend work and is now forced back into it because of someone else's religious beliefs? Are the religious beliefs of one individual so weighty that they supersede the lack of religious beliefs of another? [69 Mich.L.Rev. at 628.]

Professor Edwards and Mr. Kaplan argue that the EEOC guidelines are confusing and could be construed to require the employer in every case to shift an employee out of seniority to accommodate religious beliefs. We do not believe that the EEOC guidelines require such a result. The hardship on [other] employees should certainly be considered as hardship on the conduct of business, for the management of employees is one of the chief concerns of a large business and, in the case of a labor union, is the chief concern. A hypertechnical application of the words "undue hardship of the employer's business" by ignoring this fact, would, as Professor Edwards and Mr. Kaplan argue, impose "a priority of the religious over the secular" [69 Mich.L.Rev. at 628] and would perhaps raise constitutional questions.[1] We find and conclude, therefore, that it would have been an undue hardship for the unions to have changed plaintiff's shift in violation of the seniority provisions of the labor management contract.

Finally, with reference to the seniority provisions, we find and conclude that § 703(h), if not absolutely controlling, at least indicates that Congress did not intend that unions or employers be required to take actions that could impinge upon *bona fide* seniority systems. That Section reads as follows:

---

[1]Professor Edwards and Mr. Kaplan direct attention to Judge Learned Hand's decision in *Otten v. Baltimore & Ohio R.R.,* 205 F.2d 58, 61, (2d Cir. 1953), in which he stated:

> The First Amendment protects one against action by the government ... but it gives no one the right to insist that in the pursuit of their own interests others must conform their conduct to his own religious necessities.... We must accommodate our idiosyncrasies, religious as well as secular, to the compromises necessary in communal life; and we can hope for no reward for the sacrifices this may require beyond our satisfactions from within, or our expectations of a better world.

Notwithstanding any other provision of this subchapter, it shall not be an unlawful employment practice for an employer to apply different standards of compensation, or different terms, conditions, or privileges of employment pursuant to a *bona fide* seniority or merit system ... provided that such differences are not the result of an intention to discriminate because of race, color, religion, sex, or national origin.

A significant judicial gloss has been placed on this language by courts processing racial discrimination cases. Consequently, a seniority system can not be "*bona fide*" if it perpetuates the consequences of past discrimination. In other words, a seniority system is not lawful if it freezes Negroes into past patterns of discrimination.

Plaintiff does not urge, nor, do we think, may he urge, that the seniority system in this case locked in any discrimination against individuals of plaintiff's or anyone else's religion. The seniority system was not designed with the intention to discriminate against religion nor did it act to lock members of any religion into a pattern wherein their freedom to exercise their religion was limited. It was coincidental that in plaintiff's case the seniority system acted to compound his problems in exercising his religion. He did not have sufficient seniority in the building to which he transferred to be able to impose his choice of days off over those of the other employees who had more seniority.

The duty to accommodate under the circumstances of this case, therefore, did not require the union to ignore its seniority system....

...

B. TWA Responsibility

Defendant TWA makes several arguments against plaintiff's contention that it violated Title VII of the Civil Rights Act of 1964 when it discharged him:

[1] A statutory requirement to accommodate religious needs of employees would violate the Establishment Clause of the First Amendment.

[2] Title VII of the Civil Rights Act of 1964 does not require employers to affirmatively accommodate employees' religious needs.

[3] TWA made reasonable accommodations to plaintiff's religious beliefs up to the point where further steps would have caused undue hardship.

[4] Plaintiff voluntarily placed himself in a position which he knew or should have known would diminish his chances for Sabbath observance.

[5] TWA did not "intentionally" discriminate against plaintiff on account of his religious beliefs.

The first question that must be resolved is indicated by #2 above, and that is, what kind of duty to avoid religious discrimination did Title VII of the Civil Rights Act of 1964 impose upon TWA? At the time of the acts complained of ... the statute did not provide for any duty on the part of an employer to accommodate the religious needs of employees.

...

The question, therefore, becomes whether the EEOC regulation [quoted above] is a proper interpretation of the Act before it was amended to specifically include a duty to accommodate. TWA cites *Dewey v. Reynolds Metals Co.,* 429 F.2d 324 (6th Cir. 1970), *aff'd per curiam by an equally divided court,* 402 U.S. 649 (1971), in support of its position that the Act did not impose a duty to accommodate. In *Dewey,* an employee alleged he had been wrongfully discharged from his employment because of his religious beliefs....

... [I]n *Dewey* the employer offered the plaintiff, as well as all other employees, the option of either working on Sunday or finding a replacement. The plaintiff did find replacements for five Sundays and then refused to find others, claiming that this practice was a sin. The Court of Appeals held that even if the 1967 regulation were applied, the employer made a reasonable accommodation by offering the replacement system.

Finally, *Dewey* was based in large part on the final award of a grievance arbitrator under the labor management contract, which has nothing to do with the question at issue here.

In *Riley v. Bendix Corp.,* 464 F.2d 1113 (5th Cir. 1972), the Court held flatly that the regulation was valid. It relied in part upon the amendment of the Act, which was approved by the Congress on March 8, 1972. Far from holding that the amendment indicates that the legislative intent of the old Act was not to include a duty

Hardison v. Trans World Airlines

to accommodate, as TWA argues we should conclude, the Court in *Riley* held the amendment validated and recognized the regulation as a proper interpretation of the old Act.

The amendment to § 703(j) is as follows:

> The term "religion" includes all aspects of religious observance and practice, as well as belief, unless an employer demonstrates that he is unable to reasonably accommodate to an employee's or prospective employee's religious observance or practice without undue hardship on the conduct of the employer's business.

...

The legislative history, reported at 118 *Congressional Record*, §§ 227-253, includes this statement by Senator Randolph of West Virginia, who sponsored the amendment:

> I think in the Civil Rights Act we thus intended to protect the same rights in private employment as the Constitution protects in Federal, State or local governments. Unfortunately, the courts have, in a sense, come down on both sides of the issue. The Supreme Court of the United States, in a case involving the observance of the Sabbath and job discrimination, divided evenly on this question.

> This amendment is intended, in good purpose, to resolve by legislation—and in a way I think was originally intended by the Civil Rights Act—that which the courts apparently have not resolved. [118 *Congressional Record* at § 228.]

The measure was passed in the Senate by unanimous vote.

The Chairman of the House Committee made this statement about the amendment:

> The purpose of this subsection is to provide the statutory basis for EEOC to formulate guidelines on discrimination because of religion such as those challenged in *Dewey v. Reynolds Metals Company,* 429 F.2d 325 [324], (6th Cir. 1970). [118 *Congressional Record*, pp. 1861-1862.]

The measure was also passed in the House by unanimous vote.

We find and conclude that the legislative history of the amendment of the Act, together with the fact that weight should be given to the administrative interpretation of the Act, as reflected by the regulation, indicate that regulation 29 C.F.R. § 1605.1(b) was facially valid and is controlling in this case.

We find TWA's argument that the duty to accommodate an employee's religious beliefs is a violation of the Establishment Clause of the First Amendment to be without merit....

...

We must now determine whether TWA did in fact take steps to make an accommodation to plaintiff's religious needs. The interpretation of the statutes embodied in the regulation requires that the employer show that it was unable to reasonably accommodate the employee's religious observance without undue hardship on the conduct of the employer's business.

TWA argues that it made three efforts to reasonably accommodate plaintiff's beliefs, that these were not successful from plaintiff's point of view, and that it was unable to make any further efforts. In April, 1968, plaintiff wrote Everett Kussmann, Manager of Stores Systems, asking for Friday sunset to Saturday sunset off. In response to that request Kussmann agreed (1) to [accept] the union steward seeking to swap days off; (2) to excuse time off on religious holidays if plaintiff agreed to work on "Christian" holidays if requested; and (3) to attempt to find plaintiff another job. On May 7, 1968, the steward reported that he was unable to work out scheduling changes and that he understood that no one was willing to swap days with plaintiff. TWA did not take part in the search for employees willing to swap shifts and it was admitted at trial that the union made no real effort. Plaintiff, however, was able for a period of time to work out his day off requirements within the framework of the seniority system.

On October 4, 1968, plaintiff wrote a letter to Kussmann, informing him that he had worked out his days off requirement by transfer to the 11-7 shift and renewing his request for specific religious holidays off. In response, Kussmann reiterated his offer to permit time off on plaintiff's religious holidays whenever possible and requested a list of those holidays. On October 20, 1968, plaintiff supplied such a list and expressed his gratitude for Kussmann's "understanding and cooperation."

On December 2, 1968 plaintiff transferred from Building 1, where he had sufficient seniority to maintain a shift in which he could observe his Sabbath, to Building 2, where he was near the bottom of the seniority list and could not be assured a satisfactory shift. His reason for the change was that he was married at that time and a change to Building 2 permitted him to work the day shift and have his evenings free. On March 7, 1969, a man of less seniority than plaintiff went on vacation and plaintiff

x   *Hardison v. Trans World Airlines*

was required to work in his position, which required him to work on Saturday.

Kussmann anticipated difficulties due to the events described above and so arranged a meeting on March 6 with plaintiff and the union steward, James Tinder. At that meeting Kussmann offered to accommodate plaintiff's religious observance by agreeing to any trade of shifts or change of sections that plaintiff and the union could work out. Any shift or change was impossible within the seniority framework and the union was not willing to violate the seniority provisions set out in the contract to make a shift or change.

TWA claims that any further action on its part would have caused undue hardship to the conduct of its business. First, had TWA forced another employee to trade shifts or jobs with plaintiff, such action would have violated the seniority provisions of the labor management contract and TWA would have been subjected to personnel problems and grievances.

Had TWA simply granted plaintiff days off on Saturday, it would have left TWA short of help in that position. Plaintiff worked in the Stores Department of TWA's facilities at Kansas City International Airport (KCI). That department is responsible for housing, retaining, and making available parts for use by TWA for use at its overhaul base at KCI and throughout its system. It operates on a twenty-four hour, seven-day-a-week basis. On weekends TWA worked a minimum number of employees, and plaintiff was the only person in his job on his shift during the weekends. To leave that position empty would have impaired the supplying of parts for essential airline operations. To fill plaintiff's position with someone from another area would deprive that area of its regular manpower. To bring in a man not working on that day would force TWA to pay premium wages for the time he filled in for plaintiff.

TWA argues also that if all employees were treated uniformly as to their religious beliefs and observances, it could be very difficult to perform seven-day-a-week airline operations.

We find and conclude that TWA's actions with respect to working out plaintiff's religious observance was a reasonable accommodation by TWA and that any further action by TWA would have worked an undue hardship on the conduct of its business. The duty to accommodate does not require that an employer make every effort short of going out of business to permit his employees to stay on the job and also to observe their religion. The term "*reasonable* accommodation" (emphasis added) should be read with the term "undue hardship" to arrive at the proper standard.

The duty imposed on an employer by Title VII is not a duty to impose hardships on the rest of his employees or members to accommodate the religious beliefs of a few. It is simply a duty to take affirmative action to try to find a way to permit the employee to observe his religion as he wishes, as opposed to a duty simply not to intentionally discriminate....

...

In none of the cases cited did the employer show that it had taken affirmative action on behalf of the employee. In this case, and in sharp contrast, TWA established as a matter of fact that it did take appropriate action to accommodate as required by Title VII. It held several meetings with plaintiff in which it attempted to find a solution to plaintiff's problems. It did accommodate plaintiff's observance of his special religious holidays. It authorized the union steward to search for someone who would swap shifts, which apparently was normal procedure. Witnesses for TWA testified that they attempted to work out plaintiff's problems in ways that had proved successful in similar cases.

TWA would not have been placed in a position where it could not work out plaintiff's problem [if] plaintiff, to suit his own convenience, [had not] transferred to Building 2 where he had insufficient seniority to bid on a suitable shift. That factor, however, should be viewed as a frustration of TWA's attempts to accommodate, and not as an action which relieved TWA of the duty to accommodate, as TWA argues.

We find and conclude that further accommodation by TWA would have worked an undue hardship on the conduct of its business. TWA had two choices for further accommodation: (1) to simply allow plaintiff to take his time off and attempt to replace him; or (2) to force another employee to change shifts.

TWA runs a twenty-four-hour-a-day, seven-day-a-week operation. Plaintiff performed an important job for TWA and was the only person performing his particular job on his shift during the weekend. To replace him with an employee from another area would leave that employee's work crew short. To replace him with an employee who was not regularly scheduled to work at that time would have caused TWA to pay premium wages. Both of these solutions would have created an undue burden on the conduct of TWA's business. Title VII cannot be interpreted to require that companies finance employees' religious beliefs.

TWA is a party to a labor-management contract which clearly sets out a seniority provision which is binding on the company and on the union. With respect to any asserted duty on the part of TWA to change plaintiff's shift in violation of the seniority provisions of the labor-management contract, the same considerations apply

Hardison v. Trans World Airlines

here as applied with respect to the union. Title VII does not force TWA to impose upon other employees because of one employee's religious belief. TWA's business includes the administration of its many employees, and to impose hardships upon them imposes hardships upon the company's business. We find and conclude, therefore, that it would have been an undue hardship for TWA to have changed plaintiff's shift in violation of the seniority provision of the labor-management contract.

Finally, we again make reference to the seniority provisions of Title VII, which exempt different treatment to different employees based upon a *bona fide* seniority system from the other provisions of § 703(a)(2). That section, as we stated in reference to the union's duty to accommodate, indicates that Congress did not intend that unions or employers be required to take actions that would impinge upon *bona fide* seniority systems.

For the reasons stated, we find and conclude that neither TWA nor any of the three unions violated Title VII of the Civil Rights Act of 1964 by reason of its discharge of plaintiff for his refusal to work on his Sabbath.

★ ★ ★ ★

Having lost, Hardison appealed. The decision of the Court of Appeals on his appeal follows.

★ ★ ★ ★

Hardison v. Trans World Airlines
527 F.2d 33 (8th Cir. 1975)

WEBSTER, Circuit Judge:—This appeal presents for our review important questions concerning the requirements of Title VII of the Civil Rights Act of 1964, and the guidelines on religious discrimination promulgated thereunder....

...

{The facts are stated in the opinion of the District Court.}

II. TWA Liability

29 C.F.R. § 1605.1, which we hold to be consistent with the statute, defines the parameters of the employer's duty. The company may not accept the role of a Pontius Pilate.[6] An effort to accommodate the employee's religious observances must be made. Such accommodation need only be a reasonable one. An accommodation alternative which imposes undue hardship upon the employer's business is unreasonable and not required. The burden of demonstrating its inability to reasonably accommodate falls upon the employer.

The record reflects a consistent effort by Hardison to acquaint TWA with his religious conversion and the effect of that commitment upon his ability to work during his Sabbath period and certain other religious holidays. He made no demands which were not consistent with his known religious beliefs. He was willing to work long weeks or short weeks provided his religious obligation to abstain from work on his Sabbath could be met. He even transferred to the twilight shift in order to minimize the impact of his absence on the company.

We cannot agree with the company's contention, apparently accepted by the District Court, that Hardison's transfer from Building No. 1 to Building No. 2 was evidence of a lack of cooperation on his part. The implication is that if Hardison had not transferred he would have retained enough seniority in Building No. 1 to protect himself against Sabbath day assignments. This is not accommodation. To limit Hardison's right of transfer within the company as a condition of accommodation would be "to discriminate against [him] with respect to his ... conditions, or privileges of employment, because of [his] ... religion ...." § 703(a)(1) The purpose of this transfer was to obtain a daytime shift, Hardison having recently married. While the regulation implies that the employee must be responsive to a reasonable accommodation, no such accommodation was ever offered by TWA, which at all times contended that it was precluded from accommodating Hardison's Sabbath observance by the collective bargaining agreement. Before an employer can assert the defense of non-cooperation, it is incumbent upon it to establish the accommodation which it has tendered and with which the employee refused to cooperate.

---

[6]Matthew 27:24.

> ["When Pilate saw that he was getting nowhere, but that instead an uproar was starting, he took water and washed his hands in front of the crowd. "I am innocent of this man's blood," he said. "It is your responsibility!"

[*The New Testament,* New International Version, the Free Bible Literature Society.—ed.]

Hardison's job assignment in Building No. 2 was to pick up or deliver parts needed by mechanics working in the building. He was to "run the train," that is, to continually make the rounds of the shops in the building. He was part of a work force of 38 to 40 people, although he would be the only person running the train during his particular shift on the weekend. TWA conceded that there were over 200 available employees who were capable of performing Hardison's work.

The District Court concluded that TWA had made a reasonable effort to accommodate Hardison's religious beliefs and that the alternatives rejected by TWA would have created an undue burden on TWA's business. Upon a full review of the record, we must respectfully disagree with both conclusions.

Alternatives Rejected

(1) Within the framework of the collective bargaining agreement, TWA could have permitted Hardison to work a four-day week. Hardison was willing to do this,[7] but the company would not agree because it would be short-handed during one shift. It conceded that a supervisor could be utilized or another worker on duty elsewhere could be transferred, but urged that this would cause some other shop function to suffer. Similar arguments have been rejected by the Equal Employment Opportunity Commission.

In determining whether a possible accommodation would result in undue hardship or mere inconvenience, we must look to the facts of each case. The burden of demonstrating undue hardship is upon the employer. In this case, the company contends that a short week for one man during the temporary period of Wyatt's vacation would have hampered its operations. Two company witnesses expressed such an opinion without any further evidence or factual support. We think the District Court erroneously drew an inference of undue hardship from such testimony. The actual hours involved in this case did not even amount to a full shift, since Hardison had transferred to the twilight shift and would have worked from 3:00 p.m. on Friday until sundown (approximately 6:30 p.m.), thus further reducing the impact upon the company's operations. Balanced against the interests to be protected by § 703(a), we cannot say such an accommodation would result in an undue hardship to the employer.

---

[7]Hardison was also willing to work a six-day week but this solution was in apparent violation of the 40 hour per week clause of the contract.

(2) Another alternative within the framework of the collective bargaining agreement was for TWA to fill Hardison's Sabbath shift from other available personnel. This could be accomplished by holding a worker over from the last shift, calling a worker in early, or, more logically, assigning a worker from the pool of 200 employees qualified to do the work. TWA contended that this alternative would be an undue hardship because such workers must be paid overtime compensation. The District Court said, "The duty to accommodate does not require that an employer make every effort short of going out of business to permit his employees to s[t]ay on the job and also to observe their religion", 375 F.Supp. at 889, and that "Title VII cannot be interpreted to require that companies finance employee's religious beliefs." 375 F.Supp. at 891. These general statements, while arguably correct, may tend to distort the actual hardship which overtime payments would have imposed upon TWA to fill Hardison's Sabbath shift under the facts of this case. The regulation does not preclude some cost to the employer any more than it precludes some degree of inconvenience to effect a reasonable accommodation. The regulation expressly casts upon the employer the burden of proving undue hardship upon its business. Each case must stand upon its own facts. The actual cost of accommodation by filling Hardison's Sabbath shift from available personnel is not clear from the record. We do know that in this case the cost would have ended upon Wyatt's return from his vacation. The company might well have concluded that the additional expense was preferable to getting along with one less man on the shift or suffering the administrative inconvenience of seeking a swap for Hardison. It does not appear from the record, however, that TWA gave any serious consideration to the reasonableness of such an alternative or to the extent of the burden it might create upon the business of TWA. We cannot say that its burden of proof has been met in this case.

(3) A third alternative considered was a swap between Hardison and another employee, either for another shift or for the Sabbath days. While both TWA and the union indicated no opposition to a voluntary swap, the acquiescence was clearly couched in terms of the limitations imposed by Article VI, the seniority clause of the collective bargaining agreement:

> (b)   The principle of seniority shall apply in the application of this Agreement in all reductions or increases of force, preference of shift assignment, vacation period selection, in bidding for vacancies or new jobs, and in all promotions, demotions, or transfers involving classifications covered by this Agreement.

Hardison v. Trans World Airlines

The company relied upon the union steward to handle the details. Every swap was technically at risk because the exchange was subject to the right of a senior worker to bump into the opening. Thus, the company and the union contended that they could not individually or jointly act to make a job exchange which would accommodate Hardison's religious need to be free of servile work on his Sabbath.

The proper relationship between a *bona fide* seniority system and the requirement of reasonable accommodation under 29 C.F.R. § 1605.1 has not yet been settled by the Supreme Court. The Equal Employment Opportunity Commission has taken the position that when the inflexibility of a collective bargaining agreement is raised as a defense to charges of religious discrimination, that inflexibility must be justified by substantial business necessity. At least one court has directed that an article in a collective bargaining agreement which would have required an employee to work occasional Saturdays in violation of his religious beliefs not be applied to such employee. It would seem that a collective bargaining agreement, the seniority provisions of which preclude *any* reasonable accommodation for religious observances by employees, is prima facie evidence of union and employer culpability under the Act.[12] We are not required to reach that point in this case, however, because the evidence is clear that TWA did not seek and the union therefore did not refuse to entertain a possible variance.

TWA did not even seek to find volunteers within the seniority system. It left that task to the union steward, who likewise did nothing. The matter was not referred to the Union Relief Committee, an informal organization of union members through which the union and TWA were normally able to avoid confrontations over seniority variances in special situations. This was the first Sabbath request which TWA and the union had received at the Kansas City operation. While company officials testified of their concern that giving Hardison a variance would irritate other union members, we find no evidence to support such an inference, nor are we convinced that such irritation, if real, would have been an undue hardship on the employer's business.

...

---

[12]If Saturday work inevitably falls to the employees with lowest seniority, one may well ask whether such seniority provisions would not effectively preclude TWA from ever hiring those Seventh Day Adventists, Orthodox Jews, and members of the Worldwide Church of God whose religious convictions preclude work from sundown on Friday until sundown on Saturday. It is no answer to such a person, or to the statute itself, that if he compromises his religious beliefs for a time he may develop enough seniority to practice them again.

IV. Constitutional Claim

... We find this reasoning persuasive, and we agree with the District Court's conclusion that the constitutional challenge must be rejected.

....

QUESTIONS FOR REFLECTION

1. Suppose an employer proposes an accommodation to a worker, and the worker accepts it; but it would violate a seniority provision of a collective bargaining agreement, and the union refuses to waive the contract. Is the accommodation unreasonable because it would violate the contract?

2. Suppose TWA did not have a union contract. In order to accommodate Hardison, TWA asked employee **A** to swap shifts with Hardison on the latter's Sabbath. When employee **A** refused to swap voluntarily, TWA ordered her to swap. Did TWA discriminate against employee **A**?

$$\Omega$$

Discrimination Based on Disability:

The Americans with Disabilities Act

file: Lab Cases\2013 Fall\Arline; August 3, 2013

What is a Handicap or Disability?

Introduction

The first step in interpreting civil rights (and some other kinds of) legislation is determining whom the legislation protects, in other words, the scope of the protected class. As we have noted, the Labor Act protects employees, but not supervisors, and Title VII protects workers in the labor force. The Rehabilitation Act of 1973 and the Americans with Disabilities Act of 1990 protect persons with disabilities. In order to apply the Rehabilitation and Disability Acts, therefore, it is necessary to decide what disabilities are.

School Board of Nassau County, Florida v. Arline
480 U.S. 273 (1987)

Justice BRENNAN delivered the opinion of the Court.

Section 504 of the Rehabilitation Act of 1973, as amended, (Act), prohibits a federally funded state program from discriminating against a handicapped individual solely by reason of his or her handicap. This case presents the questions whether a person afflicted with tuberculosis, a contagious disease, may be considered a "handicapped individual" within the meaning of § 504 of the Act, and, if so, whether such an individual is "otherwise qualified" to teach elementary school.

I

From 1966 until 1979, respondent Gene Arline taught elementary school in Nassau County, Florida. She was discharged in 1979 after suffering a third relapse of tuberculosis within two years. After she was denied relief in state administrative proceedings, she brought suit in federal court, alleging that the school board's decision to dismiss her because of her tuberculosis violated § 504 of the Act.

A trial was held in the District Court, at which the principal medical evidence was provided by Marianne McEuen, M.D., an assistant director of the Community Tuberculosis Control Service of the Florida Department of Health and Rehabilitative Services. According to the medical records reviewed by Dr. McEuen, Arline was hospitalized for tuberculosis in 1957. For the next 20 years, Arline's disease was in remission. Then, in 1977, a culture revealed that tuberculosis was again active in her system; cultures taken in March 1978 and in November 1978 were also positive.

The superintendent of schools for Nassau County, Craig Marsh, then testified as to the school board's response to Arline's medical reports. After both her second relapse, in the spring of 1978, and her third relapse in November 1978, the school board suspended Arline with pay for the remainder of the school year. At the end of the 1978-1979 school year, the school board held a hearing, after which it discharged Arline, "not because she had done anything wrong," but because of the "continued reoccurrence [sic] of tuberculosis."

In her trial memorandum, Arline argued that it was "not disputed that the [school board dismissed her] solely on the basis of her illness. Since the illness in this case qualifies the Plaintiff as a 'handicapped person' it is clear that she was dismissed solely as a result of her handicap in violation of Section 504." Record 119. The District Court held, however, that although there was "[no] question that she suffers a handicap," Arline was nevertheless not "a handicapped person under the terms of that statute." App. to Pet. for Cert. C-2. The court found it "difficult ... to conceive that Congress intended contagious diseases to be included within the definition of a handicapped person." The court then went on to state that, "even assuming" that a person with a contagious disease could be deemed a handicapped person, Arline was not "qualified" to teach elementary school. *Id.* at C-2-C-3.

The Court of Appeals reversed, holding that "persons with contagious diseases are within the coverage of section 504," and that Arline's condition "falls ... neatly within the statutory and regulatory framework" of the Act. 772 F.2d 759, 764 (CA11 1985). The court remanded the case "for further findings as to whether the risks of infection precluded Mrs. Arline from being 'otherwise qualified' for her job and, if so, whether it was possible to make some reasonable accommodation for her in that teaching position" or in some other position. *Id.,* at 765 (footnote omitted). We granted *certiorari* and now affirm.

II

In enacting and amending the Act, Congress enlisted all programs receiving federal funds in an effort "to share with handicapped Americans the opportunities for an education, transportation, housing, health care, and jobs that other Americans take for granted." 123 Cong. Rec. 13515 (1977) (statement of Sen. Humphrey). To that end, Congress not only increased federal support for vocational rehabilitation, but also addressed the broader problem of discrimination against the handicapped by including § 504, an antidiscrimination provision patterned after Title VI of the Civil Rights Act of 1964. Section 504 of the Rehabilitation Act reads in pertinent part:

> "No otherwise qualified handicapped individual in the United States, as defined in section 706(7) of this title, shall, solely by reason of his handicap, be excluded from participation in, be denied the benefits of, or be subjected to discrimination under any program or activity receiving Federal financial assistance...."

In 1974 Congress expanded the definition of "handicapped individual" for use in § 504 to read as follows:[3]

---

[3]The primary focus of the 1973 Act was to increase federal support for vocational rehabilitation; the Act's original definition of the term "handicapped individual" reflected this focus by including only those whose disability limited their employability, and those who could be expected to benefit from vocational rehabilitation. After reviewing the Department of Health, Education, and Welfare's subsequent attempt to devise regulations to implement the Act, however, Congress concluded that the definition of "handicapped individual," while appropriate for the vocational rehabilitation provisions in Titles I and III of the Act, was too narrow to deal with the range of discriminatory practices in housing, education, and health care programs which stemmed from stereotypical attitudes and ignorance about the handicapped.

"[Any] person who (i) has a physical or mental impairment which substantially limits one or more of such person's major life activities, (ii) has a record of such an impairment, or (iii) is regarded as having such an impairment." 29 U. S. C. § 706(7)(B).

The amended definition reflected Congress' concern with protecting the handicapped against discrimination stemming not only from simple prejudice, but also from "archaic attitudes and laws" and from "the fact that the American people are simply unfamiliar with and insensitive to the difficulties [confronting] individuals with handicaps." S. Rep. No. 93-1297, p. 50 (1974). To combat the effects of erroneous but nevertheless prevalent perceptions about the handicapped, Congress expanded the definition of "handicapped individual" so as to preclude discrimination against "[a] person who has a record of, or is regarded as having, an impairment [but who] may at present have no actual incapacity at all." *Southeastern Community College v. Davis*, 442 U.S. 397, 405-406, n. 6 (1979).

In determining whether a particular individual is handicapped as defined by the Act, the regulations promulgated by the Department of Health and Human Services are of significant assistance. As we have previously recognized, these regulations were drafted with the oversight and approval of Congress; they provide "an important source of guidance on the meaning of § 504." *Alexander v. Choate*, 469 U.S. 287, 304, n. 24 (1985). The regulations are particularly significant here because they define two critical terms used in the statutory definition of handicapped individual.[5] "Physical impairment" is defined as follows:

"[Any] physiological disorder or condition, cosmetic disfigurement, or anatomical loss affecting one or more of the following body systems:

---

[5]In an appendix to these regulations, the Department of Health and Human Services explained that it chose not to attempt to "set forth a list of specific diseases and conditions that constitute physical or mental impairments because of the difficulty of ensuring the comprehensiveness of any such list." 45 CFR pt. 84, Appendix A, p. 310 (1985). Nevertheless, the Department went on to state that "such diseases and conditions as orthopedic, visual, speech, and hearing impairments, cerebral palsy, epilepsy, muscular dystrophy, multiple sclerosis, cancer, heart disease, diabetes, mental retardation, [and] emotional illness" would be covered. *Ibid.* The Department also reinforced what a careful reading of the statute makes plain, "that a physical or mental impairment does not constitute a handicap for purposes of section 504 unless its severity is such that it results in a substantial limitation of one or more major life activities." *Ibid.* Although many of the comments on the regulations when first proposed suggested that the definition was unreasonably broad, the Department found that a broad definition, one not limited to so-called "traditional handicaps," is inherent in the statutory definition. *Ibid.*

neurological; musculoskeletal; special sense organs; respiratory, including speech organs; cardiovascular; reproductive, digestive, genitourinary; hemic and lymphatic; skin; and endocrine." 45 CFR § 84.3(j)(2)(i) (1985).

In addition, the regulations define "major life activities" as

"functions such as caring for one's self, performing manual tasks, walking, seeing, hearing, speaking, breathing, learning, and working."   § 84.3(j)(2)(ii).

III

Within this statutory and regulatory framework, then, we must consider whether Arline can be considered a handicapped individual.   According to the testimony of Dr. McEuen, Arline suffered tuberculosis "in an acute form in such a degree that it affected her respiratory system," and was hospitalized for this condition. Arline thus had a physical impairment as that term is defined by the regulations, since she had a "physiological disorder or condition ... affecting [her] ... respiratory [system]." 45 CFR § 84.3(j)(2)(i) (1985).   This impairment was serious enough to require hospitalization, a fact more than sufficient to establish that one or more of her major life activities were substantially limited by her impairment.   Thus, Arline's hospitalization for tuberculosis in 1957 suffices to establish that she has a "record of ... impairment" within the meaning of 29 U. S. C. § 706(7)(B)(ii), and is therefore a handicapped individual.

Petitioners concede that a contagious disease may constitute a handicapping condition to the extent that it leaves a person with "diminished physical or mental capabilities," Brief for Petitioners 15, and concede that Arline's hospitalization for tuberculosis in 1957 demonstrates that she has a record of a physical impairment. Petitioners maintain, however, that Arline's record of impairment is irrelevant in this case, since the school board dismissed Arline not because of her diminished physical capabilities, but because of the threat that her relapses of tuberculosis posed to the health of others.

We do not agree with petitioners that, in defining a handicapped individual under § 504, the contagious effects of a disease can be meaningfully distinguished from the disease's physical effects on a claimant in a case such as this.   Arline's contagiousness and her physical impairment each resulted from the same underlying condition, tuberculosis.   It would be unfair to allow an employer to seize upon the distinction between the effects of a disease on others and the effects of a disease on a patient and use that distinction to justify discriminatory treatment.[7]

Nothing in the legislative history of § 504 suggests that Congress intended such a result. That history demonstrates that Congress was as concerned about the effect of an impairment on others as it was about its effect on the individual. Congress extended coverage, in 29 U. S. C. § 706(7)(B)(iii), to those individuals who are simply "regarded as having" a physical or mental impairment. The Senate Report provides as an example of a person who would be covered under this subsection "a person with some kind of visible physical impairment which in fact does not substantially limit that person's functioning." S. Rep. No. 93-1297, at 64.[9] Such an impairment might not diminish a person's physical or mental capabilities, but could nevertheless substantially limit that person's ability to work as a result of the negative reactions of others to the impairment.[10]

---

[7]The United States argues that it is possible for a person to be simply a carrier of a disease, that is, to be capable of spreading a disease without having a "physical impairment" or suffering from any other symptoms associated with the disease. The United States contends that this is true in the case of some carriers of the Acquired Immune Deficiency Syndrome (AIDS) virus. From this premise the United States concludes that discrimination solely on the basis of contagiousness is never discrimination on the basis of a handicap. The argument is misplaced in this case, because the handicap here, tuberculosis, gave rise both to a physical impairment and to contagiousness. This case does not present, and we therefore do not reach, the questions whether a carrier of a contagious disease such as AIDS could be considered to have a physical impairment, or whether such a person could be considered, solely on the basis of contagiousness, a handicapped person as defined by the Act.

[9]Congress' desire to prohibit discrimination based on the effects a person's handicap may have on others was evident from the inception of the Act. For example, Representative Vanik, whose remarks constitute "a primary signpost on the road toward interpreting the legislative history of § 504," *Alexander v. Choate,* 469 U.S. 287, 295-296, and n. 13 (1985), cited as an example of improper handicap discrimination a case in which "a court ruled that a cerebral palsied child, who was not a physical threat and was academically competitive, should be excluded from public school, because his teacher claimed his physical appearance 'produced a nauseating effect' on his classmates." 117 Cong. Rec. 45974 (1971). See also 118 Cong. Rec. 36761 (1972) (remarks of Sen. Mondale) (a woman "crippled by arthritis" was denied a job not because she could not do the work but because "college trustees [thought] 'normal students shouldn't see her'"); *id.,* at 525 (remarks of Sen. Humphrey).

[10]The Department of Health and Human Services regulations, which include among the conditions illustrative of physical impairments covered by the Act "cosmetic disfigurement," lend further support to Arline's position that the effects of one's impairment on others is as relevant to a determination of whether one is handicapped as is the physical effect of one's handicap on oneself. 45 CFR § 84.3(j)(2)(i)(A) (1985). At oral argument,

(continued...)

Allowing discrimination based on the contagious effects of a physical impairment would be inconsistent with the basic purpose of § 504, which is to ensure that handicapped individuals are not denied jobs or other benefits because of the prejudiced attitudes or the ignorance of others. By amending the definition of "handicapped individual" to include not only those who are actually physically impaired, but also those who are regarded as impaired and who, as a result, are substantially limited in a major life activity, Congress acknowledged that society's accumulated myths and fears about disability and disease are as handicapping as are the physical limitations that flow from actual impairment. Few aspects of a handicap give rise to the same level of public fear and misapprehension as

---

[10] (...continued)
the United States took the position that a condition such as cosmetic disfigurement could not substantially limit a major life activity within the meaning of the statute, because the only major life activity that it would affect would be the ability to work. The United States recognized that "working" was one of the major life activities listed in the regulations, but said that to argue that a condition that impaired only the ability to work was a handicapping condition was to make "a totally circular argument which lifts itself by its bootstraps." Tr. of Oral Arg. 15-16. {The Solicitor General said that "there may be some conceptual difficulty in defining 'major life activities' to include work, for it seems 'to argue in a circle to say that if one is excluded, for instance, by reason of [an impairment, from working with others] ... then that exclusion constitutes an impairment, when the question you're asking is, whether the exclusion itself is by reason of handicap.'" Sutton v. United Air Lines, 119 S.Ct. 2139, 2151.} The argument is not circular, however, but direct. Congress plainly intended the Act to cover persons with a physical or mental impairment (whether actual, past, or perceived) that substantially limited one's ability to work. "[The] primary goal of the Act is to increase employment of the handicapped." *Consolidated Rail Corporation v. Darrone*, 465 U.S., at 633, n. 13; see also *id.* at 632 ("Indeed, enhancing employment of the handicapped was so much the focus of the 1973 legislation that Congress the next year felt it necessary to amend the statute to clarify whether § 504 was intended to prohibit other types of discrimination as well").

contagiousness.[12] Even those who suffer or have recovered from such noninfectious diseases as epilepsy or cancer have faced discrimination based on the irrational fear that they might be contagious.[13] The Act is carefully structured to replace such reflexive reactions to actual or perceived handicaps with actions based on reasoned and medically sound judgments: the definition of "handicapped individual" is broad, but only those individuals who are both handicapped and otherwise qualified are eligible for relief. The fact that some persons who have contagious diseases may pose a serious health threat to others under certain circumstances does not justify excluding from the coverage of the Act all persons with actual or perceived contagious diseases. Such exclusion would mean that those accused of being contagious would never have the opportunity to have their condition evaluated in light of medical evidence and a determination made as to whether they were "otherwise qualified." Rather, they would be vulnerable to discrimination on the basis of mythology — precisely the type of injury Congress sought to prevent.[14] We conclude that the fact that a person with a

---

[12]The isolation of the chronically ill and of those perceived to be ill or contagious appears across cultures and centuries, as does the development of complex and often pernicious mythologies about the nature, cause, and transmission of illness. Tuberculosis is no exception.

[13]Senator Humphrey noted the "irrational fears or prejudice on the part of employers or fellow workers" that make it difficult for former cancer patients to secure employment. 123 Cong. Rec. 13515 (1977). See also Feldman, Wellness and Work, in Psychosocial Stress and Cancer 173-200 (C. Cooper ed. 1984) (documenting job discrimination against recovered cancer patients); S. Sontag, Illness as Metaphor 6 (1978) ("Any disease that is treated as a mystery and acutely enough feared will be felt to be morally, if not literally, contagious. Thus, a surprisingly large number of people with cancer find themselves being shunned by relatives and friends ... as if cancer, like TB, were an infectious disease"); Dell, Social Dimensions of Epilepsy: Stigma and Response, in Psychopathology in Epilepsy: Social Dimensions 185-210 (S. Whitman & B. Hermann eds. 1986) (reviewing range of discrimination affecting epileptics); Brief for Epilepsy Foundation of America as Amicus Curiae 5-14 ("A review of the history of epilepsy provides a salient example that fear, rather than the handicap itself, is the major impetus for discrimination against persons with handicaps").

[14]Congress reaffirmed this approach in its 1978 amendments to the Act. There, Congress recognized that employers and other grantees might have legitimate reasons not to extend jobs or benefits to drug addicts and alcoholics, but also understood the danger of improper discrimination against such individuals if they were categorically excluded from coverage under the Act. Congress therefore rejected the original House proposal to exclude addicts and alcoholics from the definition of handicapped individual, and instead adopted the Senate proposal excluding only those alcoholics and drug abusers "whose current use of alcohol or drugs prevents such individual from performing the duties of the job in

(continued...)

X   *School Board of Nassau County v. Arline*

record of a physical impairment is also contagious does not suffice to remove that person from coverage under § 504.[15]

_____

[14] (...continued)

question or whose employment ... would constitute a direct threat to property or the safety of others." *29 U. S. C. § 706*(7)(B).

This approach is also consistent with that taken by courts that have addressed the question whether the Act covers persons suffering from conditions other than contagious diseases that render them a threat to the safety of others.

[15]The dissent implies that our holding rests only on our "own sense of fairness and implied support from the Act" .... It is evident, however, that our holding is premised on the plain language of the Act, and on the detailed regulations that implement it, neither of which the dissent discusses and both of which support the conclusion that those with a contagious disease such as tuberculosis may be considered "handicapped" under the Act. We also find much support in the legislative history, while the dissent is unable to find any evidence to support its view. Accordingly, the dissent's construction of the Act to exclude those afflicted with a contagious disease is not only arbitrary (and therefore unfair) but unfaithful to basic canons of statutory construction.

...

Nor is there any reason to think that today's decision will extend the Act beyond manageable bounds. Construing § 504 not to exclude those with contagious diseases will complement rather than complicate state efforts to enforce public health laws. As we state, courts may reasonably be expected normally to defer to the judgments of public health officials in determining whether an individual is otherwise qualified unless those judgments are medically unsupportable. Conforming employment decisions with medically reasonable judgments can hardly be thought to threaten the States' regulation of communicable diseases. Indeed, because the Act requires employers to respond rationally to those handicapped by a contagious disease, the Act will assist local health officials by helping remove an important obstacle to preventing the spread of infectious diseases: the individual's reluctance to report his or her condition. It is not surprising, then, that in their brief as amici curiae in support of respondent, the States of California, Maryland, Michigan, Minnesota, New Jersey, New York, and Wisconsin conclude that "inclusion of communicable diseases within the ambit of Section 504 does not reorder the priorities of state regulatory agencies ... [and] would not alter the balance between state and federal authority." Brief for State of California *et al.* 30.

IV

The remaining question is whether Arline is otherwise qualified for the job of elementary schoolteacher. To answer this question in most cases, the district court will need to conduct an individualized inquiry and make appropriate findings of fact. Such an inquiry is essential if § 504 is to achieve its goal of protecting handicapped individuals from deprivations based on prejudice, stereotypes, or unfounded fear, while giving appropriate weight to such legitimate concerns of grantees as avoiding exposing others to significant health and safety risks.[16] The basic factors to be considered in conducting this inquiry are well established.[17] In the context of the employment of a person handicapped with a contagious disease, we agree with amicus American Medical Association that this inquiry should include

> "[findings of] facts, based on reasonable medical judgments given the state of medical knowledge, about (a) the nature of the risk (how the disease is transmitted), (b) the duration of the risk (how long is the carrier infectious), (c) the severity of the risk (what is the potential harm to third parties) and (d) the probabilities the disease will be transmitted and will cause varying degrees of harm." Brief for American Medical Association as Amicus Curiae 19.

---

[16]A person who poses a significant risk of communicating an infectious disease to others in the workplace will not be otherwise qualified for his or her job if reasonable accommodation will not eliminate that risk. The Act would not require a school board to place a teacher with active, contagious tuberculosis in a classroom with elementary school children. Respondent conceded as much at oral argument.

[17]"An otherwise qualified person is one who is able to meet all of a program's requirements in spite of his handicap." *Southeastern Community College v. Davis,* 442 U.S. 397, 406 (1979). In the employment context, an otherwise qualified person is one who can perform "the essential functions" of the job in question. 45 CFR § 84.3(k) (1985). When a handicapped person is not able to perform the essential functions of the job, the court must also consider whether any "reasonable accommodation" by the employer would enable the handicapped person to perform those functions. *Ibid.* Accommodation is not reasonable if it either imposes "undue financial and administrative burdens" on a grantee, *Southeastern Community College v. Davis,* 442 U.S., at 412, or requires "a fundamental alteration in the nature of [the] program," *id.,* at 410. See 45 CFR pt. 84, Appendix A, p. 315 (1985) ("[Where] reasonable accommodation does not overcome the effects of a person's handicap, or where reasonable accommodation causes undue hardship to the employer, failure to hire or promote the handicapped person will not be considered discrimination").

In making these findings, courts normally should defer to the reasonable medical judgments of public health officials. The next step in the "otherwise-qualified" inquiry is for the court to evaluate, in light of these medical findings, whether the employer could reasonably accommodate the employee under the established standards for that inquiry.

Because of the paucity of factual findings by the District Court, we, like the Court of Appeals, are unable at this stage of the proceedings to resolve whether Arline is "otherwise qualified" for her job. The District Court made no findings as to the duration and severity of Arline's condition, nor as to the probability that she would transmit the disease. Nor did the court determine whether Arline was contagious at the time she was discharged, or whether the School Board could have reasonably accommodated her.[19] Accordingly, the resolution of whether Arline was otherwise qualified requires further findings of fact.

V

We hold that a person suffering from the contagious disease of tuberculosis can be a handicapped person within the meaning of § 504 of the Rehabilitation Act of 1973, and that respondent Arline is such a person. We remand the case to the District Court to determine whether Arline is otherwise qualified for her position. The judgment of the Court of Appeals is

Affirmed.

Chief Justice REHNQUIST, with whom Justice SCALIA joins, dissenting.

In *Pennhurst State School and Hospital v. Halderman,* 451 U.S. 1 (1981), this Court made clear that, where Congress intends to impose a condition on the grant of federal funds, "it must do so unambiguously." *id.* at 17. This principle applies with full force to § 504 of the Rehabilitation Act, which Congress limited in scope to "those who actually 'receive' federal financial assistance." *United States Department of Transportation v. Paralyzed Veterans of America,* 477 U.S. 597, 605 (1986). Yet, the Court today ignores this principle, resting its holding on its own sense of fairness and implied support from the Act. Such an approach, I believe, is foreclosed not only by *Pennhurst,* but also by our prior decisions interpreting the Rehabilitation Act.

---

[19]Employers have an affirmative obligation to take a reasonable accommodation for a handicapped employee. Although they are not required to find another job for an employee who is not qualified for the job he or she was doing, they cannot deny an employee alternative employment opportunities reasonably available under the employer's existing policies.

Our decision in *Pennhurst* was premised on the view that federal legislation imposing obligations only on recipients of federal funds is "much in the nature of a contract." 451 U.S. at 17. As we have stated in the context of the Rehabilitation Act, "'Congress apparently determined it would require ... grantees to bear the costs of providing employment for the handicapped as a quid pro quo for the receipt of federal funds.'" *United States Department of Transportation v. Paralyzed Veterans of America,* 477 U.S. 597, 605 (1986), quoting *Consolidated Rail Corporation v. Darrone,* 465 U.S. 624, 633, n. 13 (1984). The legitimacy of this quid pro quo rests on whether recipients of federal funds voluntarily and knowingly accept the terms of the exchange. *Pennhurst* at 17. There can be no knowing acceptance unless Congress speaks "with a clear voice" in identifying the conditions attached to the receipt of funds. *Ibid.*

The requirement that Congress unambiguously express conditions imposed on federal moneys is particularly compelling in cases such as this where there exists longstanding state and federal regulation of the subject matter. From as early as 1796, Congress has legislated directly in the area of contagious diseases. Congress has also, however, left significant leeway to the States, which have enacted a myriad of public health statutes designed to protect against the introduction and spread of contagious diseases. When faced with such extensive regulation, this Court has declined to read the Rehabilitation Act expansively. Absent an expression of intent to the contrary, "Congress ... 'will not be deemed to have significantly changed the federal-state balance.'" *Bowen v. American Hospital Assn.,* 476 U.S. 610, 644 (1986), quoting *United States v. Bass,* 404 U.S. 336, 349 (1971).

Applying these principles, I conclude that the Rehabilitation Act cannot be read to support the result reached by the Court. The record in this case leaves no doubt that Arline was discharged because of the contagious nature of tuberculosis, and not because of any diminished physical or mental capabilities resulting from her condition. Thus, in the language of § 504, the central question here is whether discrimination on the basis of contagiousness constitutes discrimination "by reason of ... handicap." Because the language of the Act, regulations, and legislative history are silent on this issue, the principles outlined above compel the conclusion that contagiousness is not a handicap within the meaning of § 504. It is therefore clear that the protections of the Act do not extend to individuals such as Arline.

In reaching a contrary conclusion, the Court never questions that Arline was discharged because of the threat her condition posed to others. Instead, it posits that the contagious effects of a disease cannot be "meaningfully" distinguished from the disease's effect on a claimant under the Act. To support this position, the Court observes that Congress intended to extend the Act's protections to individuals who have a condition that does not impair their mental and physical capabilities, but limits their major life activities because of the adverse reactions of others. This congressional recognition of a handicap resulting from the reactions of others, we are told, reveals that Congress intended the Rehabilitation Act to regulate discrimination on the basis of contagiousness.

This analysis misses the mark in several respects. To begin with, Congress' recognition that an individual may be handicapped under the Act solely by reason of the reactions of others in no way demonstrates that, for the purposes of interpreting the Act, the reactions of others to the condition cannot be considered separately from the effect of the condition on the claimant. In addition, the Court provides no basis for extending the Act's generalized coverage of individuals suffering discrimination as a result of the reactions of others to coverage of individuals with contagious diseases. Although citing examples of handicapped individuals described in the regulations and legislative history, the Court points to nothing in these materials suggesting that Congress contemplated that a person with a condition posing a threat to the health of others may be considered handicapped under the Act.[5] Even in an ordinary case of statutory construction, such meager proof of congressional intent would not be determinative. The Court's evidence, therefore, could not possibly provide the basis for "knowing acceptance" by such entities as the Nassau County School Board that their receipt of federal funds is conditioned on Rehabilitation Act regulation of public health issues.

In *Alexander v. Choate,* 469 U.S. at 299, this Court stated that "[any] interpretation of § 504 must ... be responsive to two powerful but countervailing considerations — the need to give effect to the statutory objectives and the desire to keep § 504 within manageable bounds." The Court has wholly disregarded this

---

[5]In fact, two of the examples cited by the Court may be read to support a contrary conclusion. The 1978 amendments to the Rehabilitation Act cited by the majority specifically exclude from the definition of a handicapped person alcoholics and drug abusers that "constitute a *direct threat to property or the safety of others.*" 29 U. S. C. § 706(7)(B) (emphasis added). If anything, this exclusion evinces congressional intent to avoid the Act's interference with public health and safety concerns. See Oversight Hearings on Rehabilitation Act of 1973 before the Subcommittee on Select Education of the House Committee on Education and Labor, 95th Cong., 2d Sess., 503 (1978) (statement of Rep. Hyde) ("Congress needs to give thoughtful and wide-ranging consideration to the needs of handicapped persons, balanced against the realities of public safety, economics, and commonsense"). This intent is also present in the statements of Representative Vanik relied on by the Court. Representative Vanik expressed apparent disapproval of a court ruling that "'a cerebral palsied child, *who was not a physical threat* and was academically competitive, should be excluded from public school, because his teacher claimed his physical appearance "produced a nauseating effect" on his classmates.'" 117 Cong. Rec. 45974 (1971) (emphasis added).

admonition here.

QUESTIONS FOR REFLECTION

1. In <u>Sutton v. United Air Lines</u>, 119 S.Ct. 2139 (1999), which follows below, Justice O'Connor reports that, during the oral argument of <u>Arline</u>, the Solicitor General said that "there may be some conceptual difficulty in defining 'major life activities' to include work, for it seems 'to argue in a circle to say that if one is excluded, for instance, by reason of [an impairment, from working with others] ... then that exclusion constitutes an impairment, when the question you're asking is, whether the exclusion itself is by reason of handicap.'" <u>Sutton</u> at 2151. Was there a conceptual difficulty? Should work count as major life activity?

2. The Court's holding does not mean that Ms. Arline won her case. Why not?

Exercise

The Supreme Court remanded the case to the district court. What further evidence would the parties want to present? See <u>Arline v. School Bd. of Nassau County</u>, 692 F. Supp. 1286 (M.D. FL, 1988).

What is a Handicap or Disability?
(continued)

Introduction

The Americans with Disabilities Act was patterned in substantial part on the Vocational Rehabilitation Act. Therefore, when an issue arises under the Disability Act, precedents under the Rehabilitation Act are usually applicable.

One issue common to both statutes is whether an individual's status as a handicapped or disabled person should be determined before or after mitigating measures have been taken. For example, suppose a person is severely hard of hearing; by use of a hearing aid (a mitigating measure), the person can hear almost normally. Judged before mitigation, the person is handicapped or disabled and, consequently, protected by law; judged after mitigation, the person is not. The following case addresses this issue in the context of the Disability Act.

Sutton v. United Air Lines
526 U.S. 1109 (1999)

Justice O'CONNOR delivered the opinion of the Court.

The Americans with Disabilities Act of 1990 (ADA or Act) prohibits certain employers from discriminating against individuals on the basis of their disabilities. See § 12112(a). Petitioners challenge the dismissal of their ADA action for failure to state a claim upon which relief can be granted. We conclude that the complaint was properly dismissed. In reaching that result, we hold that the determination of whether an individual is disabled should be made with reference to measures that mitigate the individual's impairment, including, in this instance, eyeglasses and contact lenses. In addition, we hold that petitioners failed to allege properly that respondent "regarded" them as having a disability within the meaning of the ADA.

I

Petitioners' amended complaint was dismissed for failure to state a claim upon which relief could be granted. Accordingly, we accept the allegations contained in their complaint as true for purposes of this case.

Petitioners are twin sisters, both of whom have severe myopia. Each petitioner's uncorrected visual acuity is 20/200 or worse in her right eye and 20/400 or worse in her left eye, but "with the use of corrective lenses, each ... has vision that is 20/20 or better." App. 23. Consequently, without corrective lenses, each "effectively cannot see to conduct numerous activities such as driving a vehicle, watching television or shopping in public stores," *id.* at 24, but with corrective measures, such as glasses or contact lenses, both "function identically to individuals without a similar impairment," *ibid.*

In 1992, petitioners applied to respondent for employment as commercial airline pilots. They met respondent's basic age, education, experience, and FAA certification qualifications. After submitting their applications for employment, both petitioners were invited by respondent to an interview and to flight simulator tests. Both were told during their interviews, however, that a mistake had been made in inviting them to interview because petitioners did not meet respondent's minimum vision requirement, which was uncorrected visual acuity of 20/100 or better. Due to their failure to meet this requirement, petitioners' interviews were terminated, and neither was offered a pilot position.

In light of respondent's proffered reason for rejecting them, petitioners filed a charge of disability discrimination under the ADA with the Equal Employment Opportunity Commission (EEOC). After receiving a right to sue letter, petitioners filed suit in the United States District Court for the District of Colorado, alleging that respondent had discriminated against them "on the basis of their disability, or because [respondent] regarded [petitioners] as having a disability" in violation of the ADA. App. 26. Specifically, petitioners alleged that due to their severe myopia they actually have a substantially limiting impairment or are regarded as having such an impairment, and are thus disabled under the Act.

The District Court dismissed petitioners' complaint for failure to state a claim upon which relief could be granted. Because petitioners could fully correct their visual impairments, the court held that they were not actually substantially limited in any major life activity and thus had not stated a claim that they were disabled within the meaning of the ADA. The court also determined that petitioners had not made allegations sufficient to support their claim that they were "regarded" by the respondent as having an impairment that substantially limits a major life activity. The court observed that "the statutory reference to a substantial limitation indicates ... that an employer regards an employee as handicapped in his or her ability to work by finding the employee's impairment to foreclose generally the type of employment involved." App. to Pet. for Cert. at A36 to A37. But petitioners had alleged only that respondent regarded them as unable to satisfy the requirements of a particular job, global airline pilot. Consequently, the court held that petitioners had not stated a claim that they were regarded as substantially limited in the major life activity of working. Employing similar logic, the Court of Appeals for the Tenth Circuit affirmed the District Court's judgment.

The Tenth Circuit's decision is in tension with the decisions of other Courts of Appeals. See, e.g., *Bartlett v. New York State Bd. of Law Examiners*, 156 F.3d 321, 329 (2d Cir. 1998) (holding self-accommodations cannot be considered when determining a disability), cert. pending, No. 98-1285; *Baert v. Euclid Beverage, Ltd.*, 149 F.3d 626, 629-630 (7th Cir. 1998) (holding disabilities should be determined without reference to mitigating measures); *Matczak v. Frankford Candy & Chocolate Co.*, 136 F.3d 933, 937-938 (3d Cir. 1997) (same); *Arnold v. United Parcel Service, Inc.*, 136 F.3d 854, 859-866 (1st Cir. 1998) (same); see also *Washington v. HCA Health Servs. of Texas, Inc.*, 152 F.3d 464, 470-471 (5th Cir. 1998) (holding that only some impairments should be evaluated in their uncorrected state). We granted *certiorari* and now affirm.

II

The ADA prohibits discrimination by covered entities, including private employers, against qualified individuals with a disability. Specifically, it provides that no covered employer "shall discriminate against a qualified individual with a disability because of the disability of such individual in regard to job application procedures, the hiring, advancement, or discharge of employees, employee compensation, job training, and other terms, conditions, and privileges of employment." § 102(a). A "qualified individual with a disability" is identified as "an individual with a disability who, with or without reasonable accommodation, can perform the essential functions of the employment position that such individual holds or desires." § 101(8). In turn, a "disability" is defined as:

> "(A) a physical or mental impairment that substantially limits one or more of the major life activities of such individual;

> "(B) a record of such an impairment; or

> "(C) being regarded as having such an impairment." § 3(2).

Accordingly, to fall within this definition one must have an actual disability (subsection (A)), have a record of a disability (subsection (B)), or be regarded as having one (subsection (C)).

The parties agree that the authority to issue regulations to implement the Act is split primarily among three Government agencies. According to the parties, the EEOC has authority to issue regulations to carry out the employment provisions in Title I of the ADA.... The Attorney General is granted authority to issue regulations with respect to Title II.... Finally, the Secretary of Transportation has authority to issue regulations pertaining to the transportation provisions of Titles II and III....

No agency, however, has been given authority to issue regulations implementing the generally applicable provisions of the ADA, which fall outside Titles I-V. Most notably, no agency has been delegated authority to interpret the term "disability." § 3(2).... The EEOC has, nonetheless, issued regulations to provide additional guidance regarding the proper interpretation of this term. After restating the definition of disability given in the statute, the EEOC regulations define the three elements of disability: (1) "physical or mental impairment," (2) "substantially limits," and (3) "major life activities." See 29 CFR §§ 1630.2(h)-(j). Under the regulations, a "physical impairment" includes "any physiological disorder, or condition, cosmetic disfigurement, or anatomical loss affecting one or more of the following body systems: neurological, musculoskeletal, special sense organs, respiratory (including speech organs), cardiovascular, reproductive, digestive, genito-urinary, hemic and lymphatic, skin, and endocrine." § 1630.2(h)(1). The term "substantially limits" means, among other things, "unable to perform a major life activity that the average person in the general population can perform;" or "significantly restricted as to the condition, manner or duration under which an individual can perform a particular major life activity as compared to the condition, manner, or duration under which the average person in the general population can perform that same major life activity." § 1630.2(j). Finally, "major life activities means functions such as caring for oneself, performing manual tasks, walking, seeing, hearing, speaking, breathing, learning, and working." §

1630.2(i). Because both parties accept these regulations as valid, and determining their validity is not necessary to decide this case, we have no occasion to consider what deference they are due, if any.

The agencies have also issued interpretive guidelines to aid in the implementation of their regulations. For instance, at the time that it promulgated the above regulations, the EEOC issued an "Interpretive Guidance," which provides that "the determination of whether an individual is substantially limited in a major life activity must be made on a case by case basis, without regard to mitigating measures such as medicines, or assistive or prosthetic devices." 29 CFR pt. 1630, App. § 1630.2(j) (1998). The Department of Justice has issued a similar guideline. See 28 CFR pt. 35, App. A, § 35.104 ("The question of whether a person has a disability should be assessed without regard to the availability of mitigating measures, such as reasonable modification or auxiliary aids and services"); pt. 36, App. B, § 36.104 (same). Although the parties dispute the persuasive force of these interpretive guidelines, we have no need in this case to decide what deference is due.

III

With this statutory and regulatory framework in mind, we turn first to the question whether petitioners have stated a claim under subsection (A) of the disability definition, that is, whether they have alleged that they possess a physical impairment that substantially limits them in one or more major life activities. Because petitioners allege that with corrective measures their vision "is 20/20 or better," see App. 23, they are not actually disabled within the meaning of the Act if the "disability" determination is made with reference to these measures. Consequently, with respect to subsection (A) of the disability definition, our decision turns on whether disability is to be determined with or without reference to corrective measures.

Petitioners maintain that whether an impairment is substantially limiting should be determined without regard to corrective measures. They argue that, because the ADA does not directly address the question at hand, the Court should defer to the agency interpretations of the statute, which are embodied in the agency guidelines issued by the EEOC and the Department of Justice. These guidelines specifically direct that the determination of whether an individual is substantially limited in a major life activity be made without regard to mitigating measures.

Respondent, in turn, maintains that an impairment does not substantially limit a major life activity if it is corrected. It argues that the Court should not defer to the agency guidelines cited by petitioners because the guidelines conflict with the plain meaning of the ADA. The phrase "substantially limits one or more major life activities," it explains, requires that the substantial limitations actually and presently

Sutton v. United Air Lines

exist. Moreover, respondent argues, disregarding mitigating measures taken by an individual defies the statutory command to examine the effect of the impairment on the major life activities "of such individual." And even if the statute is ambiguous, respondent claims, the guidelines' directive to ignore mitigating measures is not reasonable, and thus this Court should not defer to it.

We conclude that respondent is correct that the approach adopted by the agency guidelines — that persons are to be evaluated in their hypothetical uncorrected state — is an impermissible interpretation of the ADA. Looking at the Act as a whole, it is apparent that if a person is taking measures to correct for, or mitigate, a physical or mental impairment, the effects of those measures — both positive and negative — must be taken into account when judging whether that person is "substantially limited" in a major life activity and thus "disabled" under the Act. The dissent relies on the legislative history of the ADA for the contrary proposition that individuals should be examined in their uncorrected state. Because we decide that, by its terms, the ADA cannot be read in this manner, we have no reason to consider the ADA's legislative history.

Three separate provisions of the ADA, read in concert, lead us to this conclusion. The Act defines a "disability" as "a physical or mental impairment that *substantially limits* one or more of the major life activities" of an individual. § 3(2)(A) (emphasis added). Because the phrase "substantially limits" appears in the Act in the present indicative verb form, we think the language is properly read as requiring that a person be presently — not potentially or hypothetically — substantially limited in order to demonstrate a disability. A "disability" exists only where an impairment "substantially limits" a major life activity, not where it "might," "could," or "would" be substantially limiting if mitigating measures were not taken. A person whose physical or mental impairment is corrected by medication or other measures does not have an impairment that presently "substantially limits" a major life activity. To be sure, a person whose physical or mental impairment is corrected by mitigating measures still has an impairment, but if the impairment is corrected it does not "substantially limit" a major life activity.

The definition of disability also requires that disabilities be evaluated "with respect to an individual" and be determined based on whether an impairment substantially limits the "major life activities of such individual." § 3(2). Thus, whether a person has a disability under the ADA is an individualized inquiry....

The agency guidelines' directive that persons be judged in their uncorrected or unmitigated state runs directly counter to the individualized inquiry mandated by the ADA. The agency approach would often require courts and employers to speculate about a person's condition and would, in many cases, force them to make a disability determination based on general information about how an uncorrected impairment usually affects individuals, rather than on the individual's actual condition. For instance, under this view, courts would almost certainly find all diabetics to be disabled, because if they failed to monitor their blood sugar levels and administer insulin, they would almost certainly be substantially limited in one or more major life activities. A diabetic whose illness does not impair his or her daily activities would therefore be considered disabled simply because he or she has diabetes. Thus, the guidelines approach would create a system in which persons often must be treated as members of a group of people with similar impairments, rather than as individuals. This is contrary to both the letter and the spirit of the ADA.

The guidelines approach could also lead to the anomalous result that in determining whether an individual is disabled, courts and employers could not consider any negative side effects suffered by an individual resulting from the use of mitigating measures, even when those side effects are very severe. See, e.g., Johnson, Antipsychotics: Pros and Cons of Antipsychotics, RN (Aug. 1997) (noting that antipsychotic drugs can cause a variety of adverse effects, including neuroleptic malignant syndrome and painful seizures); Liver Risk Warning Added to Parkinson's Drug, FDA Consumer (Mar. 1, 1999) (warning that a drug for treating Parkinson's disease can cause liver damage); Curry & Kulling, Newer Antiepileptic Drugs, American Family Physician (Feb. 1, 1998) (cataloging serious negative side effects of new antiepileptic drugs). This result is also inconsistent with the individualized approach of the ADA.

Finally, and critically, findings enacted as part of the ADA require the conclusion that Congress did not intend to bring under the statute's protection all those whose uncorrected conditions amount to disabilities. Congress found that "some 43,000,000 Americans have one or more physical or mental disabilities, and this number is increasing as the population as a whole is growing older." § 2(a)(1). This figure is inconsistent with the definition of disability pressed by petitioners.

Although the exact source of the 43 million figure is not clear, the corresponding finding in the 1988 precursor to the ADA was drawn directly from a report prepared by the National Council on Disability.... That report detailed the difficulty of estimating the number of disabled persons due to varying operational definitions of disability. National Council on Disability, Toward Independence 10 (1986). It explained that the estimates of the number of disabled Americans ranged from an overinclusive 160 million under a "health conditions approach," which looks at all conditions that impair the health or normal functional abilities of an individual, to an underinclusive 22.7 million under a "work disability approach," which focuses on individuals' reported ability to work. *Id*. at 10-11. It noted that "a figure of 35 or 36 million [was] the most commonly quoted estimate." *Id*. at 10. The 36 million number included in the 1988 bill's findings thus clearly reflects an approach to defining disabilities that is closer to the work disabilities approach than the health conditions approach.

This background also provides some clues to the likely source of the figure in the findings of the 1990 Act. Roughly two years after issuing its 1986 report, the National Council on Disability issued an updated report. See On the Threshold of Independence (1988). This 1988 report settled on a more concrete definition of disability. It stated that 37.3 million individuals have "difficulty performing one or more basic physical activities," including "seeing, hearing, speaking, walking, using stairs, lifting or carrying, getting around outside, getting around inside, and getting into or out of bed." *Id*. at 19. The study from which it drew this data took an explicitly functional approach to evaluating disabilities. It measured 37.3 million persons with a "functional limitation" on performing certain basic activities when using, as the questionnaire put it, "special aids," such as glasses or hearing aids, if the person usually used such aids. U.S. Dept. of Commerce, Bureau of Census, Disability, Functional Limitation, and Health Insurance Coverage: 1984/85, p. 1, 47 (1986). The number of disabled provided by the study and adopted in the 1988 report, however, includes only noninstitutionalized persons with physical disabilities who are over age 15. The 5.7 million gap between the 43 million figure in the ADA's findings and the 37.3 million figure in the report can thus probably be explained as an effort to include in the findings those who were excluded from the National Council figure. {The Court mentioned persons not in institutions but with activity limitations due to mental illnesses and mental retardation, persons under 18 with activity limitations, and residents in nursing and related care facilities}.

Regardless of its exact source, however, the 43 million figure reflects an understanding that those whose impairments are largely corrected by medication or other devices are not "disabled" within the meaning of the ADA....

By contrast, nonfunctional approaches to defining disability produce significantly larger numbers. As noted above, the 1986 National Council on Disability report estimated that there were over 160 million disabled under the "health conditions approach." Toward Independence at 10.... {The Court stated that the number of people with vision impairment is 100 million, with hearing impairment is 28 million, and with high blood pressure, 50 million.}

Because it is included in the ADA's text, the finding that 43 million individuals are disabled gives content to the ADA's terms, specifically the term "disability." Had Congress intended to include all persons with corrected physical limitations among those covered by the Act, it undoubtedly would have cited a much higher number of disabled persons in the findings. That it did not is evidence that the ADA's coverage is restricted to only those whose impairments are not mitigated by corrective measures. The dissents suggest that viewing individuals in their corrected state will exclude from the definition of "disabled" those who use prosthetic limbs. This suggestion is incorrect. The use of a corrective device does not, by itself, relieve one's disability. Rather, one has a disability under subsection A if, notwithstanding the use of a corrective device, that individual is substantially limited in a major life activity. For example, individuals who use prosthetic limbs or wheelchairs may be mobile and capable of functioning in society but still be disabled because of a substantial limitation on their ability to walk or run. The same may be true of individuals who take medicine to lessen the symptoms of an impairment so that they can function but nevertheless remain substantially limited. Alternatively, one whose high blood pressure is "cured" by medication may be regarded as disabled by a covered entity, and thus disabled under subsection C of the definition. The use or nonuse of a corrective device does not determine whether an individual is disabled; that determination depends on whether the limitations an individual with an impairment actually faces are in fact substantially limiting.

Applying this reading of the Act to the case at hand, we conclude that the Court of Appeals correctly resolved the issue of disability in respondent's favor. As noted above, petitioners allege that with corrective measures, their visual acuity is 20/20 and that they "function identically to individuals without a similar impairment," App. at 24, Amended Complaint P37e. In addition, petitioners concede that they "do not argue that the use of corrective lenses in itself demonstrates a substantially limiting impairment." Brief for Petitioners 9, n. 11. Accordingly, because we decide that disability under the Act is to be determined with reference to corrective measures, we agree with the courts below that petitioners have not stated a claim that they are substantially limited in any major life activity.

IV

Our conclusion that petitioners have failed to state a claim that they are actually disabled under subsection (A) of the disability definition does not end our inquiry. Under subsection (C), individuals who are "regarded as" having a disability are disabled within the meaning of the ADA. Subsection 3 provides that having a disability includes "being regarded as having" "a physical or mental impairment that substantially limits one or more of the major life activities of such individual." There are two apparent ways in which individuals may fall within this statutory definition: (1)

a covered entity mistakenly believes that a   person has a physical impairment that substantially limits one or more major life activities, or (2) a covered entity mistakenly believes that an actual, nonlimiting impairment substantially limits one or more major life activities. In both cases, it is necessary that a covered entity entertain misperceptions about the individual — it must believe either that one has a substantially limiting impairment that one does not have or that one has a substantially limiting impairment when, in fact, the impairment is not so limiting. These misperceptions often "result from stereotypic assumptions not truly indicative of ... individual ability." See 42 U.S.C. § 12101(7). See also *School Bd. of Nassau Cty. v. Arline*, 480 U.S. 273, 284 (1987) ("By amending the definition of 'handicapped individual' to include not only those who are actually physically impaired, but also those who are regarded as impaired and who, as a result, are substantially limited in a major life activity, Congress acknowledged that society's accumulated myths and fears about disability and disease are as handicapping as are the physical limitations that flow from actual impairment"); 29 CFR pt. 1630, App. § 1630.2(l) (explaining that the purpose of the regarded as prong is to cover individuals "rejected from a job because of the 'myths, fears and stereotypes' associated with disabilities").

There is no dispute that petitioners are physically impaired. Petitioners do not make the obvious argument that they are regarded due to their impairments as substantially limited in the major life activity of seeing. They contend only that respondent mistakenly believes their physical impairments substantially limit them in the major life activity of working. To support this claim, petitioners allege that respondent has a vision requirement, which is allegedly based on myth and stereotype. Further, this requirement substantially limits their ability to engage in the major life activity of working by precluding them from obtaining the job of global airline pilot, which they argue is a "class of employment." See App. 24-26, Amended Complaint P38. In reply, respondent argues that the position of global airline pilot is not a class of jobs and therefore petitioners have not stated a claim that they are regarded as substantially limited in the major life activity of working. Standing alone, the allegation that respondent has a vision requirement in place does not establish a claim that respondent regards petitioners as substantially limited in the major life activity of working. Post-Argument Brief for the United States et al. as Amici Curiae 5-6 ("Under the EEOC's regulations, an employer may make employment decisions based on physical characteristics"). By its terms, the ADA allows employers to prefer some physical attributes over others and to establish physical criteria. An employer runs afoul of the ADA when it makes an employment decision based on a physical or mental impairment, real or imagined, that is regarded as substantially limiting a major life activity. Accordingly, an employer is free to decide that physical characteristics or medical conditions that do not rise to the level of an impairment — such as one's height, build, or singing voice — are preferable to others, just as it is free to decide that some limiting, but not substantially limiting, impairments make individuals less than ideally suited for a job.

Considering the allegations of the amended complaint in tandem, petitioners have not stated a claim that respondent regards their impairment as substantially limiting their ability to work. The ADA does not define "substantially limits," but "substantially" suggests "considerable" or "specified to a large degree." ... The EEOC has codified regulations interpreting the term "substantially limits" in this manner, defining the term to mean "unable to perform" or "significantly restricted." See 29 CFR §§ 1630.2(j)(1)(i),(ii) (1998).

When the major life activity under consideration is that of working, the statutory phrase "substantially limits" requires, at a minimum, that plaintiffs allege they are unable to work in a broad class of jobs. Reflecting this requirement, the EEOC uses a specialized definition of the term "substantially limits" when referring to the major life activity of working:

> "significantly restricted in the ability to perform either a class of jobs or a broad range of jobs in various classes as compared to the average person having comparable training, skills and abilities. The inability to perform a single, particular job does not constitute a substantial limitation in the major life activity of working." § 1630.2(j)(3)(i).

The EEOC further identifies several factors that courts should consider when determining whether an individual is substantially limited in the major life activity of working, including the geographical area to which the individual has reasonable access, and "the number and types of jobs utilizing similar training, knowledge, skills or abilities, within the geographical area, from which the individual is also disqualified." §§ 1630.2(j)(3)(ii)(A), (B). To be substantially limited in the major life activity of working, then, one must be precluded from more than one type of job, a specialized job, or a particular job of choice. If jobs utilizing an individual's skills (but perhaps not his or her unique talents) are available, one is not precluded from a substantial class of jobs. Similarly, if a host of different types of jobs are available, one is not precluded from a broad range of jobs.

Because the parties accept that the term "major life activities" includes working, we do not determine the validity of the cited regulations. We note, however, that there may be some conceptual difficulty in defining "major life activities" to include work, for it seems "to argue in a circle to say that if one is excluded, for instance, by reason of [an impairment, from working with others] ... then that exclusion constitutes an impairment, when the question you're asking is, whether the exclusion itself is by reason of handicap." Tr. of Oral Arg. in *School Bd. of Nassau Co. v. Arline*, 481 U.S. 1024, 1987 U.S. LEXIS 1785, O. T. 1986, p. 15 (argument of Solicitor General). Indeed, even the EEOC has expressed reluctance to define "major life activities" to include working and has suggested that working be viewed as a residual life activity, considered, as a last resort, *only* "if an individual is not substantially limited with respect to *any other* major life activity." 29 CFR pt. 1630, App. § 1630.2(j) (1998) (emphasis added) ("If an individual is substantially limited in *any other* major life activity, no determination should be made as to whether the individual is substantially limited in working" (emphasis added)).

Assuming without deciding that working is a major life activity and that the EEOC regulations interpreting the term "substantially limits" are reasonable, petitioners have failed to allege adequately that their poor eyesight is regarded as an impairment that substantially limits them in the major life activity of working. They allege only that respondent regards their poor vision as precluding them from holding positions as a "global airline pilot." Because the position of global airline pilot is a single job, this allegation does not support the claim that respondent regards petitioners as having a substantially limiting impairment. See 29 CFR § 1630.2(j)(3)(i) ("The inability to perform a single, particular job does not constitute a substantial limitation in the major life activity of working"). Indeed, there are a number of other positions utilizing petitioners' skills, such as regional pilot and pilot instructor to name a few, that are available to them. Even under the EEOC's Interpretative Guidance, to which petitioners ask us to defer, "an individual who cannot be a commercial airline pilot because of a minor vision impairment, but who can be a commercial airline co-pilot or a pilot for a courier service, would not be substantially limited in the major life activity of working." 29 CFR pt. 1630, App. § 1630.2.

Petitioners also argue that if one were to assume that a substantial number of airline carriers have similar vision requirements, they would be substantially limited in the major life activity of working. Even assuming for the sake of argument that the adoption of similar vision requirements by other carriers would represent a substantial limitation on the major life activity of working, the argument is nevertheless flawed. It is not enough to say that if the physical criteria of a single employer were imputed to all similar employers one would be regarded as substantially limited in the major life activity of working only as a result of this imputation. An otherwise valid job requirement, such as a height requirement, does not become invalid simply because it would limit a person's employment opportunities in a substantial way if it were adopted by a substantial number of employers. Because petitioners have not alleged, and cannot demonstrate, that respondent's vision requirement reflects a belief that petitioners' vision substantially limits them, we agree with the decision of the Court of Appeals affirming the dismissal of petitioners' claim that they are regarded as disabled.

For these reasons, the decision of the Court of Appeals for the Tenth Circuit is affirmed.

It is so ordered.

Justice STEVENS, with whom Justice BREYER joins, dissenting.

When it enacted the Americans with Disabilities Act in 1990, Congress certainly did not intend to require United Air Lines to hire unsafe or unqualified pilots. Nor, in all likelihood, did it view every person who wears glasses as a member of a "discrete and insular minority." Indeed, by reason of legislative myopia it may not have foreseen that its definition of "disability" might theoretically encompass, not just "some 43,000,000 Americans," § 2(a)(1), but perhaps two or three times that number. Nevertheless, if we apply customary tools of statutory construction, it is quite clear that the threshold question whether an individual is "disabled" within the meaning of the Act — and, therefore, is entitled to the basic assurances that the Act affords — focuses on her past or present physical condition without regard to mitigation that has resulted from rehabilitation, self-improvement, prosthetic devices, or medication. One might reasonably argue that the general rule should not apply to an impairment that merely requires a nearsighted person to wear glasses. But I believe that, in order to be faithful to the remedial purpose of the Act, we should give it a generous, rather than a miserly, construction.

There are really two parts to the question of statutory construction presented by this case. The first question is whether the determination of disability for people that Congress unquestionably intended to cover should focus on their unmitigated or their mitigated condition. If the correct answer to that question is the one provided by eight of the nine Federal Courts of Appeals to address the issue, and by all three of the Executive agencies that have issued regulations or interpretive bulletins construing the statute — namely, that the statute defines "disability" without regard to ameliorative measures — it would still be necessary to decide whether that general rule should be applied to what might be characterized as a "minor, trivial impairment." *Arnold v. United Parcel Service, Inc.*, 136 F.3d 854, 866, n. 10 (1st Cir. 1998) (holding that unmitigated state is determinative but suggesting that it "might reach a different result" in a case in which "a simple, inexpensive remedy," such as eyeglasses, is available "that can provide total and relatively permanent control of all symptoms"). I shall therefore first consider impairments that Congress surely had in mind before turning to the special facts of this case.

I

"As in all cases of statutory construction, our task is to interpret the words of [the statute] in light of the purposes Congress sought to serve." *Chapman v. Houston Welfare Rights Organization*, 441 U.S. 600, 608 (1979). Congress expressly provided that the "purpose of [the ADA is] to provide a clear and comprehensive national

Sutton v. United Air Lines

mandate for the elimination of discrimination against individuals with disabilities." § 2(b)(1). To that end, the ADA prohibits covered employers from "discriminating against a qualified individual *with a disability* because of the disability" in regard to the terms, conditions, and privileges of employment. § 102(a) (emphasis added).

The Act's definition of disability is drawn "almost verbatim" from the Rehabilitation Act of 1973. The ADA's definition provides:

"The term 'disability' means, with respect to an individual —

"(A) a physical or mental impairment that substantially limits one or more of the major life activities of such individual;

"(B) a record of such an impairment; or

"(C) being regarded as having such an impairment." § 3(2).

The three parts of this definition do not identify mutually exclusive, discrete categories. On the contrary, they furnish three overlapping formulas aimed at ensuring that individuals who now have, or ever had, a substantially limiting impairment are covered by the Act.

An example of a rather common condition illustrates this point: There are many individuals who have lost one or more limbs in industrial accidents, or perhaps in the service of their country in places like Iwo Jima. With the aid of prostheses, coupled with courageous determination and physical therapy, many of these hardy individuals can perform all of their major life activities just as efficiently as an average couch potato. If the Act were just concerned with their present ability to participate in society, many of these individuals' physical impairments would not be viewed as disabilities. Similarly, if the statute were solely concerned with whether these individuals viewed themselves as disabled — or with whether a majority of employers regarded them as unable to perform most jobs — many of these individuals would lack statutory protection from discrimination based on their prostheses.

The sweep of the statute's three-pronged definition, however, makes it pellucidly clear that Congress intended the Act to cover such persons. The fact that a prosthetic device, such as an artificial leg, has restored one's ability to perform major life activities surely cannot mean that subsection (A) of the definition is inapplicable. Nor should the fact that the individual considers himself (or actually is) "cured," or that a prospective employer considers him generally employable, mean that subsections (B) or (C) are inapplicable. But under the Court's emphasis on "the present indicative verb form" used in subsection (A), that subsection presumably would not apply. And under the Court's focus on the individual's "present — not potential or hypothetical" —

condition and on whether a person is "precluded from a broad range of jobs," subsections (B) and (C) presumably would not apply.

In my view, when an employer refuses to hire the individual "because of" his prosthesis, and the prosthesis in no way affects his ability to do the job, that employer has unquestionably discriminated against the individual in violation of the Act. Subsection (B) of the definition, in fact, sheds a revelatory light on the question whether Congress was concerned only about the corrected or mitigated status of a person's impairment. If the Court is correct that "[a] 'disability' exists only where" a person's "present" or "actual" condition is substantially impaired, there would be no reason to include in the protected class those who were once disabled but who are now fully recovered. Subsection (B) of the Act's definition, however, plainly covers a person who previously had a serious hearing impairment that has since been completely cured. Still, if I correctly understand the Court's opinion, it holds that one who continues to wear a hearing aid that she has worn all her life might not be covered — fully cured impairments are covered, but merely treatable ones are not. The text of the Act surely does not require such a bizarre result.

The three prongs of the statute, rather, are most plausibly read together not to inquire into whether a person is currently "functionally" limited in a major life activity, but only into the existence of an impairment — present or past — that substantially limits, or did so limit, the individual before amelioration. This reading avoids the counterintuitive conclusion that the ADA's safeguards vanish when individuals make themselves more employable by ascertaining ways to overcome their physical or mental limitations.

To the extent that there may be doubt concerning the meaning of the statutory text, ambiguity is easily removed by looking at the legislative history. As then-Justice REHNQUIST stated for the Court in *Garcia v. United States*, 469 U.S. 70 (1984): "In surveying legislative history we have repeatedly stated that the authoritative source for finding the Legislature's intent lies in the Committee Reports on the bill, which 'represent the considered and collective understanding of those Congressmen involved in drafting and studying the proposed legislation.'" 469 U.S. at 76 (quoting *Zuber v. Allen*, 396 U.S. 168, 186 (1969)). The Committee Reports on the bill that became the ADA make it abundantly clear that Congress intended the ADA to cover individuals who could perform all of their major life activities only with the help of ameliorative measures.

The ADA originated in the Senate. The Senate Report states that "whether a person has a disability should be assessed without regard to the availability of mitigating measures, such as reasonable accommodations or auxiliary aids." S. Rep. No. 101-116, p. 23 (1989). The Report further explained, in discussing the "regarded as" prong:

> "[An] important goal of the third prong of the [disability] definition is to ensure that persons with medical conditions that are under control, and that therefore do not currently limit major life activities, are not discriminated against on the basis of their medical conditions. For example, individuals with controlled diabetes or epilepsy are often denied jobs for which they are qualified. Such denials are the result of negative attitudes and misinformation." *Id.* at 24.

When the legislation was considered in the House of Representatives, its Committees reiterated the Senate's basic understanding of the Act's coverage, with one minor modification: They clarified that "correctable" or "controllable" disabilities were covered in the first definitional prong as well. The Report of the House Committee on the Judiciary states, in discussing the first prong, that, when determining whether an individual's impairment substantially limits a major life activity, "the impairment should be assessed without considering whether mitigating measures, such as auxiliary aids or reasonable accommodations, would result in a less-than-substantial limitation." H. R. Rep. No. 101-485, pt. III, p. 28 (1990). The Report continues that "a person with epilepsy, an impairment which substantially limits a major life activity, is covered under this test," *ibid.*, as is a person with poor hearing, "even if the hearing loss is corrected by the use of a hearing aid." *Id.* at 29.

The Report of the House Committee on Education and Labor likewise states that "whether a person has a disability should be assessed without regard to the availability of mitigating measures, such as reasonable accommodations or auxiliary aids." *Id.* pt. II, at 52. To make matters perfectly plain, the Report adds:

> "For example, a person who is hard of hearing is substantially limited in the major life activity of hearing, *even though the loss may be corrected through the use of a hearing aid.* Likewise, persons with impairments, such as epilepsy or diabetes, which substantially limit a major life activity are covered under the first prong of the definition of disability, *even if the effects of the impairment are controlled by medication.*" *Ibid.* (emphasis added).

All of the Reports, indeed, are replete with references to the understanding that the Act's protected class includes individuals with various medical conditions that ordinarily are perfectly "correctable" with medication or treatment. See 469 U.S. at 74 (citing with approval *Strathie v. Department of Transportation*, 716 F.2d 227 (3d Cir. 1983), which held that an individual with poor hearing was "handicapped" under the Rehabilitation Act even though his hearing could be corrected with a hearing aid); H. R. Rep. No. 101-485, pt. III, at 51 ("the term" disability includes "epilepsy, ... heart disease, diabetes"); *id.* pt. III, at 28 (listing same impairments); S. Rep. No. 101-116, at 22 (same).[2]

In addition, each of the three Executive agencies charged with implementing the Act has consistently interpreted the Act as mandating that the presence of disability turns on an individual's uncorrected state. We have traditionally accorded respect to such views when, as here, the agencies "played a pivotal role in setting [the statutory] machinery in motion." *Ford Motor Credit Co. v. Milhollin*, 444 U.S. 555, 566 (1980) (brackets in original; internal quotation marks and citation omitted). At the very least, these interpretations "constitute a body of experience and informed judgment to which [we] may properly resort" for additional guidance. *Skidmore v. Swift & Co.*, 323 U.S. 134, 139-140 (1944). See also *Bragdon v. Abbott*, 524 U.S. 624, 642 (1998) (invoking this maxim with regard to the Equal Employment Opportunity Commission's (EEOC) interpretation of the ADA).

The EEOC's Interpretive Guidance provides that "the determination of whether an individual is substantially limited in a major life activity must be made on a case by case basis, without regard to mitigating measures such as medicines, or assistive or prosthetic devices." 29 CFR pt. 1630, App. § 1630.2(j) (1998). The EEOC further explains:

> "An individual who uses artificial legs would ... be substantially limited in the major life activity of walking because the individual is unable to walk without the aid of prosthetic devices. Similarly, a diabetic who without insulin would lapse into a coma would be substantially limited because the individual cannot perform major life activities without the aid of medication." *Ibid.*

The Department of Justice has reached the same conclusion. Its regulations provide that "the question of whether a person has a disability should be assessed without regard to the availability of mitigating measures, such as reasonable modification or auxiliary aids and services." 28 CFR pt. 35, App. A, § 35.104 (1998). The Department of Transportation has issued a regulation adopting this same definition of "disability." See 49 CFR pt. 37.3 (1998).

---

[2]The House's decision to cover correctable impairments under subsection (A) of the statute seems, in retrospect, both deliberate and wise. Much of the structure of the House Reports is borrowed from the Senate Report; thus it appears that the House Committees consciously decided to move the discussion of mitigating measures. This adjustment was prudent because in a case in which an employer refuses, out of animus or fear, to hire an individual who has a condition such as epilepsy that the employer knows is controlled, it may be difficult to determine whether the employer is viewing the individual in her uncorrected state or "regards" her as substantially limited.

In my judgment, the Committee Reports and the uniform agency regulations merely confirm the message conveyed by the text of the Act — at least insofar as it applies to impairments such as the loss of a limb, the inability to hear, or any condition such as diabetes that is substantially limiting without medication. The Act generally protects individuals who have "correctable" substantially limiting impairments from unjustified employment discrimination on the basis of those impairments. The question, then, is whether the fact that Congress was specifically concerned about protecting a class that included persons characterized as a "discrete and insular minority" and that it estimated that class to include "some 43,000,000 Americans" means that we should construe the term "disability" to exclude individuals with impairments that Congress probably did not have in mind.

II

The EEOC maintains that, in order to remain allegiant to the Act's structure and purpose, courts should always answer "the question whether an individual has a disability ... without regard to mitigating measures that the individual takes to ameliorate the effects of the impairment." Brief for United States and EEOC as Amicus Curiae 6. "There is nothing about poor vision," as the EEOC interprets the Act, "that would justify adopting a different rule in this case." *Ibid.*

If a narrow reading of the term "disability" were necessary in order to avoid the danger that the Act might otherwise force United to hire pilots who might endanger the lives of their passengers, it would make good sense to use the "43,000,000 Americans" finding to confine its coverage. There is, however, no such danger in this case. If a person is "disabled" within the meaning of the Act, she still cannot prevail on a claim of discrimination unless she can prove that the employer took action "because of" that impairment, and that she can, "with or without reasonable accommodation ... perform the essential functions" of the job of a commercial airline pilot. Even then, an employer may avoid liability if it shows that the criteria of having uncorrected visual acuity of at least 20/100 is "job-related and consistent with business necessity" or if such vision (even if correctable to 20/20) would pose a health or safety hazard.

This case, in other words, is not about whether petitioners are genuinely qualified or whether they can perform the job of an airline pilot without posing an undue safety risk. The case just raises the threshold question whether petitioners are members of the ADA's protected class. It simply asks whether the ADA lets petitioners in the door in the same way as the Age Discrimination in Employment Act of 1967 does for every person who is at least 40 years old, and as Title VII of the Civil Rights Act of 1964 does for every single individual in the work force. Inside that door lies nothing more than basic protection from irrational and unjustified discrimination because of a characteristic that is beyond a person's control. Hence, this particular case, at its core, is about whether, assuming that petitioners can prove that they are "qualified," the airline has any duty to come forward with some legitimate explanation for refusing to hire them because of their uncorrected eyesight, or whether the ADA leaves the airline free to decline to hire petitioners on this basis even if it is acting purely on the basis of irrational fear and stereotype.

I think it quite wrong for the Court to confine the coverage of the Act simply because an interpretation of "disability" that adheres to Congress' method of defining the class it intended to benefit may also provide protection for "significantly larger numbers" of individuals than estimated in the Act's findings. It has long been a "familiar canon of statutory construction that remedial legislation should be construed broadly to effectuate its purposes." *Tcherepnin v. Knight*, 389 U.S. 332, 336 (1967). Congress sought, in enacting the ADA, to "provide a ... comprehensive national mandate for the discrimination against individuals with disabilities." § 2(b)(1). The ADA, following the lead of the Rehabilitation Act before it, seeks to implement this mandate by encouraging employers "to replace ... reflexive reactions to actual or perceived handicaps with actions based on medically sound judgments." *Arline*, 480 U.S. at 284-285. Even if an authorized agency could interpret this statutory structure so as to pick and choose certain correctable impairments that Congress meant to exclude from this mandate, Congress surely has not authorized us to do so.

When faced with classes of individuals or types of discrimination that fall outside the core prohibitions of anti-discrimination statutes, we have consistently construed those statutes to include comparable evils within their coverage, even when the particular evil at issue was beyond Congress' immediate concern in passing the legislation. Congress, for instance, focused almost entirely on the problem of discrimination against African-Americans when it enacted Title VII of the Civil Rights Act of 1964. But that narrow focus could not possibly justify a construction of the statute that excluded Hispanic-Americans or Asian-Americans from its protection — or as we later decided (ironically enough, by relying on legislative history and according "great deference" to the EEOC's "interpretation"), Caucasians.

We unanimously applied this well-accepted method of interpretation last Term with respect to construing Title VII to cover claims of same-sex sexual harassment. *Oncale v. Sundowner Offshore Services, Inc.*, 523 U.S. 75 (1998). We explained our holding as follows:

> "As some courts have observed, male-on-male sexual harassment in the workplace was assuredly not the principal evil Congress was concerned with when it enacted Title VII. But statutory prohibitions often go beyond the principal evil to cover reasonably comparable evils, and it is ultimately the provisions of our laws rather than the principal concerns of our legislators by which we are governed. Title VII prohibits 'discrimination ... because of ...

Sutton v. United Air Lines

sex' in the 'terms' or 'conditions' of employment. Our holding that this includes sexual harassment must extend to sexual harassment of any kind that meets the statutory requirements." *Id*. 469 U.S. at 79-80.

This approach applies outside of the discrimination context as well. In *H. J. Inc. v. Northwestern Bell Telephone Co.*, 492 U.S. 229 (1989), we rejected the argument that the Racketeer Influenced and Corrupt Organization Act (RICO) should be construed to cover only "organized crime" because Congress included findings in the Act's preamble emphasizing only that problem. After surveying RICO's legislative history, we concluded that even though "the occasion for Congress' action was the perceived need to combat organized crime, ... Congress for cogent reasons chose to enact a more general statute, one which, although it had organized crime as its focus, was not limited in application to organized crime." 492 U.S. at 248.[3]

Under the approach we followed in *Oncale* and *H. J. Inc.*, visual impairments should be judged by the same standard as hearing impairments or any other medically controllable condition. The nature of the discrimination alleged is of the same character and should be treated accordingly.

Indeed, it seems to me eminently within the purpose and policy of the ADA to require employers who make hiring and firing decisions based on individuals' uncorrected vision to clarify why having, for example, 20/100 uncorrected vision or better is a valid job requirement. So long as an employer explicitly makes its decision based on an impairment that in some condition is substantially limiting, it matters not under the structure of the Act whether that impairment is widely shared or so rare that it is seriously misunderstood. Either way, the individual has an impairment that is covered by the purpose of the ADA, and she should be protected against irrational stereotypes and unjustified disparate treatment on that basis.

I do not mean to suggest, of course, that the ADA should be read to prohibit discrimination on the basis of, say, blue eyes, deformed fingernails, or heights of less than six feet. Those conditions, to the extent that they are even "impairments," do not substantially limit individuals in any condition and thus are different in kind from the impairment in the case before us. While not all eyesight that can be enhanced by glasses is substantially limiting, having 20/200 vision in one's better eye is, without

---

[3]The one notable exception to our use of this method of interpretation occurred in the decision in *General Elec. Co. v. Gilbert*, 429 U.S. 125, (1976), in which the majority rejected an EEOC guideline and the heavy weight of authority in the federal courts of appeals in order to hold that Title VII did not prohibit discrimination on the basis of pregnancy-related conditions. Given the fact that Congress swiftly "overruled" that decision in the Pregnancy Discrimination Act of 1978, I submit that the views expressed in the dissenting opinions in that case should be followed today.

treatment, a significant hindrance. Only two percent of the population suffers from such myopia. Such acuity precludes a person from driving, shopping in a public store, or viewing a computer screen from a reasonable distance. Uncorrected vision, therefore, can be "substantially limiting" in the same way that unmedicated epilepsy or diabetes can be. Because Congress obviously intended to include individuals with the latter impairments in the Act's protected class, we should give petitioners the same protection.

III

The Court does not disagree that the logic of the ADA requires petitioner's visual impairment to be judged the same as other "correctable" conditions. Instead of including petitioners within the Act's umbrella, however, the Court decides, in this opinion and its companion, *Murphy v. United Parcel Service, Inc.*, 119 S.Ct. 2133 (1999) to expel all individuals who, by using "measures [to] mitigate [their] impairments" are able to overcome substantial limitations regarding major life activities. The Court, for instance, holds that severe hypertension that is substantially limiting without medication is not a "disability,"*ibid.*, and — perhaps even more remarkably — indicates (directly contrary to the Act's legislative history, see supra, at 7) that diabetes that is controlled only with insulin treatments is not a "disability" either.

The Court claims that this rule is necessary to avoid requiring courts to "speculate" about a person's "hypothetical" condition and to preserve the Act's focus on making "individualized inquiries" into whether a person is disabled. The Court also asserts that its rejection of the general rule of viewing individuals in their unmitigated state prevents distorting the scope of the Act's protected class to cover a "much higher number" of persons than Congress estimated in its findings. And, I suspect, the Court has been cowed by respondent's persistent argument that viewing all individuals in their unmitigated state will lead to a tidal wave of lawsuits. None of the Court's reasoning, however, justifies a construction of the Act that will obviously deprive many of Congress' intended beneficiaries of the legal protection it affords.

The agencies' approach, the Court repeatedly contends, "would create a system in which persons often must be treated as members of a group of people with similar impairments, rather than individuals, [which] is both contrary to the letter and spirit of the ADA." The Court's mantra regarding the Act's "individualized approach," however, fails to support its holding. I agree that the letter and spirit of the ADA is designed to deter decision making based on group stereotypes, but the agencies' interpretation of the Act does not lead to this result. Nor does it require courts to "speculate" about people's "hypothetical" conditions. Viewing a person in her "unmitigated" state simply requires examining that individual's abilities in a different state, not the abilities of every person who shares a similar condition. It is just as easy individually to test petitioners' eyesight with their glasses on as with their glasses off.[5]

Ironically, it is the Court's approach that actually condones treating individuals merely as members of groups. That misdirected approach permits any employer to dismiss out of hand every person who has uncorrected eyesight worse than 20/100 without regard to the specific qualifications of those individuals or the extent of their abilities to overcome their impairment. In much the same way, the Court's approach would seem to allow an employer to refuse to hire every person who has epilepsy or diabetes that is controlled by medication, or every person who functions efficiently with a prosthetic limb.

Under the Court's reasoning, an employer apparently could not refuse to hire persons with these impairments who are substantially limited even with medication, but that group-based "exception" is more perverse still. Since the purpose of the ADA is to dismantle employment barriers based on society's accumulated myths and fears, it is especially ironic to deny protection for persons with substantially limiting impairments that, when corrected, render them fully able and employable. Insofar as the Court assumes that the majority of individuals with impairments such as prosthetic limbs or epilepsy will still be covered under its approach because they are substantially limited "notwithstanding the use of a corrective device," I respectfully disagree as an empirical matter. Although it is of course true that some of these individuals are substantially limited in any condition, Congress enacted the ADA in part because such individuals are not ordinarily substantially limited in their mitigated condition, but rather are often the victims of "stereotypic assumptions not truly indicative of the individual ability of such individuals to participate in, and contribute to, society." § 2(a)(7).

It has also been suggested that if we treat as "disabilities" impairments that may be mitigated by measures as ordinary and expedient as wearing eyeglasses, a flood of

---

[5]For much the same reason, the Court's concern that the agencies' approach would "lead to the anomalous result" that courts would ignore "negative side effects suffered by an individual resulting from the use of mitigating measures" is misplaced. It seems safe to assume that most individuals who take medication that itself substantially limits a major life activity would be substantially limited in some other way if they did not take the medication. The Court's examples of psychosis, Parkinson's disease, and epilepsy certainly support this presumption. To the extent that certain people may be substantially limited only when taking "mitigating measures," it might fairly be said that just as contagiousness is symptomatic of a disability because an individual's "contagiousness and her physical impairment each [may result] from the same underlying condition," *School Bd. of Nassau Cty. v. Arline*, 480 U.S. 273, 282 (1987), side effects are symptomatic of a disability because side effects and a physical impairment may flow from the same underlying condition.

litigation will ensue. The suggestion is misguided. Although vision is of critical importance for airline pilots, in most segments of the economy whether an employee wears glasses — or uses any of several other mitigating measures — is a matter of complete indifference to employers. It is difficult to envision many situations in which a qualified employee who needs glasses to perform her job might be fired — as the statute requires — "because of" the fact that she cannot see well without them. Such a proposition would be ridiculous in the garden-variety case. On the other hand, if an accounting firm, for example, adopted a guideline refusing to hire any incoming accountant who has uncorrected vision of less than 20/100 — or, by the same token, any person who is unable without medication to avoid having seizures — such a rule would seem to be the essence of invidious discrimination.

In this case the quality of petitioners' uncorrected vision is relevant only because the airline regards the ability to see without glasses as an employment qualification for its pilots. Presumably it would not insist on such a qualification unless it has a sound business justification for doing so (an issue we do not address today). But if United regards petitioners as unqualified because they cannot see well without glasses, it seems eminently fair for a court also to use uncorrected vision as the basis for evaluating petitioners' life activity of seeing.

Under the agencies' approach, individuals with poor eyesight and other correctable impairments will, of course, be able to file lawsuits claiming discrimination on that basis. Yet all of those same individuals can already file employment discrimination claims based on their race, sex, or religion, and — provided they are at least 40 years old — their age. Congress has never seen this as reason to restrict classes of antidiscrimination coverage. Indeed, it is hard to believe that providing individuals with one more antidiscrimination protection will make any more of them file baseless or vexatious lawsuits. To the extent that the Court is concerned with requiring employers to answer in litigation for every employment practice that draws distinctions based on physical attributes, that anxiety should be addressed not in this case, but in one that presents an issue regarding employers' affirmative defenses.

In the end, the Court is left only with its tenacious grip on Congress' finding that "some 43,000,000 Americans have one or more physical or mental disabilities," § 2(a)(1) — and that figure's legislative history extrapolated from a law review "article authored by the drafter of the original ADA bill introduced in Congress in 1988." We previously have observed that a "statement of congressional findings is a rather thin reed upon which to base" a statutory construction. *National Organization for Women, Inc. v. Scheidler*, 510 U.S. 249, 260 (1994). Even so, as I have noted above, I readily agree that the agencies' approach to the Act would extend coverage to more than that number of people (although the Court's lofty estimates may be inflated because they do not appear to exclude impairments that are not substantially limiting). It is equally undeniable, however, that "43 million" is not a fixed cap on the Act's protected class: By including the "record of" and "regarded as" categories, Congress fully expected the Act to protect individuals who lack, in the Court's words, "actual" disabilities, and therefore are not counted in that number.

What is more, in mining the depths of the history of the 43 million figure — surveying even agency reports that predate the drafting of any of this case's controlling legislation — the Court fails to acknowledge that its narrow approach may have the perverse effect of denying coverage for a sizeable portion of the core group of 43 million. The Court appears to exclude from the Act's protected class individuals with controllable conditions such as diabetes and severe hypertension that were expressly understood as substantially limiting impairments in the Act's Committee Reports — and even, as the footnote in the margin shows, in the studies that produced the 43 million figure. Given the inability to make the 43 million figure fit any consistent method of interpreting the word "disabled," it would be far wiser for the Court to follow — or at least to mention — the documents reflecting Congress' contemporaneous understanding of the term: the Committee Reports on the actual legislation.

IV

Occupational hazards characterize many trades. The farsighted pilot may have as much trouble seeing the instrument panel as the near sighted pilot has in identifying a safe place to land. The vision of appellate judges is sometimes subconsciously obscured by a concern that their decision will legalize issues best left to the private sphere or will magnify the work of an already-overburdened judiciary. Although these concerns may help to explain the Court's decision to chart its own course — rather than to follow the one that has been well marked by Congress, by the overwhelming consensus of circuit judges, and by the Executive officials charged with the responsibility of administering the ADA — they surely do not justify the Court's crabbed vision of the territory covered by this important statute.

Accordingly, although I express no opinion on the ultimate merits of petitioners' claim, I am persuaded that they have a disability covered by the ADA. I therefore respectfully dissent.

QUESTIONS FOR REFLECTION

1. When Congress gives an administrative agency the power to issue regulations, those regulations have virtually the same force as a statute passed by Congress itself. The Disability Act empowered the EEOC and Departments of Justice and Transportation to issue regulations, and each agency issued a regulation saying that disability should be judged without regard to possible mitigation. On what reasoning does the majority in Sutton reject these regulations? How could one reply to the Court's reasoning?

2. The majority in Sutton disregards legislative history that explicitly addresses mitigation by arguing that, when the text of a statute is unambiguous, legislative history should not be consulted. If a statute is unambiguous, interpretation of its words should be unnecessary; reasonable persons should agree on their meaning. Thus, if the majority holds to its position that the statute is unambiguous, the majority should not need to interpret any words or phrases in the statute; certainly the majority should not seek guidance as to the meaning of the statute in its legislative history. Does the majority in fact hold to its position, or does it consult legislative history or otherwise interpret the words of the statute?

$$\Omega$$

APPENDIX

Constitution and Statutes

Glossary

Excerpts from

the Constitution of the United States

and Various Statutes

The Constitution of the United States

Excerpts

Preamble

We the People of the United States . . . do ordain and establish this Constitution for the United States of America.

Article III

Section 1. The judicial Power of the United States, shall be vested in one supreme Court, and in such inferior Courts as the Congress may from time to time ordain and establish. The Judges, both of the supreme and inferior Courts, shall hold their Offices during good Behavior....

Section 2. The judicial Power shall extend to all Cases, in Law and Equity, arising under this Constitution, the Laws of the United States....

Amendments

V

No person shall be held to answer for a capital, or otherwise infamous crime, unless on a presentment or indictment of a Grand Jury, except in cases arising in the land or naval forces, or in the Militia, when in actual service in time of War or public danger; nor shall any person be subject for the same offence to be twice put in jeopardy of life or limb; nor shall be compelled in any criminal case to be a witness against himself, nor be deprived of life, liberty, or property, without due process of law; nor shall private property be taken for public use, without just compensation.

IX

The enumeration in the Constitution, of certain rights, shall not be construed to deny or disparage others retained by the people.

X

The powers not delegated to the United States by the Constitution, nor prohibited by it to the States, are reserved to the States respectively, or to the people.

XIV

Section 1. All persons born or naturalized in the United States and subject to the jurisdiction thereof, are citizens of the United States and of the State wherein they reside. No State shall make or enforce any law which shall abridge the privileges or immunities of citizens of the United States; nor shall any State deprive any person of life, liberty, or property, without due process of law; nor deny to any person within its jurisdiction the equal protection of the laws.

Americans with Disabilities Act

Excerpts

GENERAL PROVISIONS

Sec. 2. DEFINITIONS — As used in this Act

(1) DISABILITY. The term "disability" means, with respect to an individual —

    (A) a physical or mental impairment that substantially limits one or more major life activities of such individual;

    (B) a record of such an impairment; or

    (C) being regarded as having such an impairment (as described in paragraph (3)).

(2) MAJOR LIFE ACTIVITIES.

    (A) IN GENERAL. For purposes of paragraph (1), major life activities include, but are not limited to, caring for oneself, performing manual tasks, seeing, hearing, eating, sleeping, walking, standing, lifting, bending, speaking, breathing, learning, reading, concentrating, thinking, communicating, and working.

    (B) MAJOR BODILY FUNCTIONS. For purposes of paragraph (1), a major life activity also includes the operation of a major bodily function, including but not limited to, functions of the immune system, normal cell growth, digestive, bowel, bladder, neurological, brain, respiratory, circulatory, endocrine, and reproductive functions.

(3) REGARDED AS HAVING SUCH AN IMPAIRMENT. For purposes of paragraph (1)(C):

    (A) An individual meets the requirement of "being regarded as having such an impairment" if the individual establishes that he or she has been subjected to an action prohibited under this Act because of an actual or perceived physical or mental impairment whether or not the impairment limits or is perceived to limit a major life activity.

(B)   Paragraph (1)(C) shall not apply to impairments that are transitory and minor. A transitory impairment is an impairment with an actual or expected duration of six months or less.

(4)   RULES OF CONSTRUCTION REGARDING THE DEFINITION OF DISABILITY. The definition of "disability" in paragraph (1) shall be construed in accordance with the following:

    (A)   The definition of disability in this Act shall be construed in favor of broad coverage of individuals under this Act, to the maximum extent permitted by the terms of this Act.

    (B)   The term "substantially limits" shall be interpreted consistnetly with the findings and purposes of the ADA Amendments Act of 2008.

    (C)   An impairment that substantially limits one major life activity need not limit other major life activities in order to be considered a disability.

    (D)   An impairment that is episodic or in remission is a disability if it would substantially limit a major life activity when active.

    (E)

       (i)   The determination of whether an impairment substantially limits a major life activity shall be made without regard to the ameliorative effects of mitigating measures such as —

          (I)   medication, medical supplies, equipment, or appliances, low-vision devices (which do not include ordinary eyeglasses or contact lenses), prosthetics including limbs and devices, hearing aids and cochlearn immplants or other implanable hearing devices, mobility devices, or oxygen therapy equipment and supplies;

          (II)   use of assistive technology;

          (III)   reasonable accommodations or auxiliary aids or services; or

          (IV)   learned behavioral or adaptive neurological modifications.

(ii) The ameliorative effects of mitigating measures of ordinary eyeglasses or contact lenses shall be considered in determining whether an impairment substantially limits a major life activity.

(iii) As used in this subparagraph —

(I) the term "ordinary eyeglasses or contact lenses" means lenses that are intended to fully correct visual acuity or eliminate refractive error; and

(II) the term "low-vision devices" means devices that magnify, enhance, or otherwise augment a visual image.

Sec. 3. ADDITIONAL DEFINITIONS

As used in this Act:

(1) AUXILIARY AIDS AND SERVICES. The term "auxiliary aids and services" includes —

(A) qualified interpreters or other effective methods of making aurally delivered materials available to individuals with hearing impairments;

(B) qualified readers, taped texts, or other effective methods of making visually delibered materials available to individuals with visual impairments;

(C) acquisition or modification of equipment or devices; and

(D) other similar services and actions.

TITLE I — EMPLOYMENT

Sec. 101. DEFINITIONS — As used in this title:

(1) COMMISSION. The term "Commission" means the Equal Employment Opportunity Commission established by section 705 of the Civil Rights Act of 1964.

(2) COVERED ENTITY. The term "covered entity" means an employer, employment agency, labor organization, or joint labor-management committee.

(3) DIRECT THREAT. The term "direct threat" means a significant risk to the health or safety of others that cannot be eliminated by reasonable accommodation.

(4)   EMPLOYEE. The term "employee" means an individual employed by an employer. With respect to employment in a foreign country, such term includes an individual who is a citizen of the United States.

(5)   EMPLOYER.

    (A)   IN GENERAL. The term "employer" means a person engaged in an industry affecting commerce who has 15 or more employees for each working day in each of 20 or more calendar weeks in the current or preceding calendar year, and any agent of such person ... and any agent of such person.

    (B)   EXCEPTIONS. The term "employer" does not include —

        (i)   the United States, a corporation wholly owned by the government of the United States, or an Indian tribe; or

        (ii)   a bona fide private membership club (other than a labor organization) that is exempt from taxation under section 501(c) of the Internal Revenue Code of 1986.

(6)   ILLEGAL USE OF DRUGS —

    (A)   IN GENERAL. The term "illegal use of drugs" means the use of drugs, the possession or distribution of which is unlawful under the Controlled Substances Act. Such term does not include the use of a drug taken under supervision by a licensed health care professional, or other uses authorized by the Controlled Substances Act or other provisions of Federal law.

    (B)   DRUGS. The term "drug" means a controlled substance, as defined in schedules I through V of section 202 of the Controlled Substances Act.

(8)   QUALIFIED INDIVIDUAL WITH A DISABILITY. The term "qualified individual with a disability" means an individual with a disability who, with or without reasonable accommodation, can perform the essential functions of the employment position that such individual holds or desires. For the purposes of this title, consideration shall be given to the employer's judgment as to what functions of a job are essential; and if an employer has prepared a written description before advertising or interviewing applicants for the job, this description shall be considered evidence of the essential functions of the job.

(9)   REASONABLE ACCOMODATION.   The   term "reasonable accommodation" may include —

(A)   making existing facilities used by employees readily accessible to and usable by individuals with disabilities; and

(B)   job restructuring, part-time or modified work schedules, reassignment to a vacant position, acquisition or modification of equipment or devices, appropriate adjustment or modifications of examinations, training materials or policies, the provision of qualified readers or interpreters, and other similar accommodations for individuals with disabilities.

(10) UNDUE HARDSHIP.

(A)   IN GENERAL. The term "undue hardship" means an action requiring significant difficulty or expense, when considered in light of the factors set forth in subparagraph (B).

(B)   FACTORS TO BE CONSIDERED. In determining whether an accommodation would impose an undue hardship on a covered entity, factors to be considered include —

(i)   the nature and cost of the accommodation needed under this Act;

(ii)   the overall financial resources of the facility or facilities involved in the provision of the reasonable accommodation; the number of persons employed at such facility; the effect on expenses and resources, or the impact otherwise of such accommodation upon the operation of the facility;

(iii)   the overall financial resources of the covered entity; the overall size of the business of a covered entity with respect to the number of its employees; the number, type, and location of its facilities; and

(iv)   the type of operation or operations of the covered entity, including the composition, structure, and functions of the workforce of such entity; the geographic separateness, administrative, or fiscal relationship of the facility or facilities in question to the covered entity.

Sec. 102. DISCRIMINATION.

(a)   GENERAL RULE. No covered entity shall discriminate against a qualified individual with a disability because of the disability of such individual in regard to job application procedures, the hiring, advancement, or discharge of employees, employee compensation, job training, and other terms, conditions, and privileges of employment.

(b)   CONSTRUCTION. As used in subsection (e), the term "discriminate" includes —

(1)   limiting, segregating, or classifying a job applicant or employee in a way that adversely affects the opportunities or status of such applicant or employee because of the disability of such applicant or employee;

(2)   participating in a contractual or other arrangement or relationship that has the effect of subjecting a covered entity's qualified applicant or employee with a disability to the discrimination prohibited by this title (such relationship includes a relationship with an employment or referral agency, labor union, an organization providing fringe benefits to an employee of the covered entity, or an organization providing training and apprenticeship programs);

(3)   utilizing standards, criteria, or methods of administration —

(A)   that have the effect of discrimination on the basis of disability; or

(B)   that perpetuate the discrimination of others who are subject to common administrative control;

(4)   excluding or otherwise denying equal jobs or benefits to a qualified individual because of the known disability of an individual with whom the qualified individual is known to have a relationship or association;

(5)

(A)   not making reasonable accommodations to the known physical or mental limitations of an otherwise qualified individual with a disability who is an applicant or employee, unless such covered entity can demonstrate that the accommodation would impose an undue hardship on the operation of the business of such covered entity; or

(B)   denying employment opportunities to a job applicant or employee who is an otherwise qualified individual with a disability, if such denial is based on the need of such covered entity to make reasonable accommodation to the physical or mental impairments of the employee or applicant;

(6)   using qualification standards, employment tests or other selection criteria that screen out or tend to screen out an individual with a disability or a class of individuals with disabilities unless the standard, test or other selection criteria, as used by the covered entity, is shown to be job-related for the position in question and is consistent with business necessity; and

(7)   failing to select and administer tests concerning employment in the most effective manner to ensure that, when such test is administered to a job applicant or employee who has a disability that impairs sensory, manual, or speaking skills, such test results accurately reflect the skills, aptitude, or whatever other factor of such applicant or employee that such test purports to measure, rather than reflecting the impaired sensory, manual, or speaking skills of such employee or applicant (except where such skills are the factors that the test purports to measure).

(d)   MEDICAL EXAMINATIONS AND INQUIRIES.

(2)   PREEMPLOYMENT.

(A)   PROHIBITED EXAMINATION OR INQUIRY. Except as provided in paragraph (3), a covered entity shall not conduct a medical examination or make inquiries of a job applicant as to whether such applicant is an individual with a disability or as to the nature or severity of such disability.

(B)   ACCEPTABLE INQUIRY. A covered entity may make preemployment inquiries into the ability of an applicant to perform job-related functions.

(3)   EMPLOYMENT ENTRANCE EXAMINATION. A covered entity may require a medical examination after an offer of employment has been made to a job applicant and prior to the commencement of the employment duties of such applicant, and may condition an offer of employment on the results of such examination, if —

(A) all entering employees are subjected to such an examination regardless of disability;

(B) information obtained regarding the medical condition or history of the applicant is collected and maintained on separate forms and in separate medical files and is treated as a confidential medical record, except that —

(i) ssupervisors and managers may be informed regarding necessary restrictions on the work or duties of the employee and necessary accommodations;

(ii) first aid and safety personnel may be informed, when appropriate, if the disability might require emergency treatment; and

(iii) government officials investigating compliance with this Act shall be provided relevant information on request; and

(C) the results of such examination are used only in accordance with this title.

(4) EXAMINATION AND INQUIRY.

(A) PROHIBITED EXAMINATION AND INQUIRIES. A covered entity shall not require a medical examination and shall not make inquiries of an employee as to whether such employee is an individual with a disability or as to the nature or severity of the disability, unless such examination or inquiry is shown to be job-related and consistent with business necessity.

(B) ACCEPTABLE EXAMINATIONS AND INQUIRIES . A covered entity may conduct voluntary medical examinations, including voluntary medical histories, which are part of an employee health program available to employees at that work site. A covered entity may make inquiries into the ability of an employee to perform job-related functions.

(C) REQUIREMENT. Information obtained under subparagraph (B) regarding the medical condition or history of any employee are subject to the requirements of subparagraphs (B) and (C) of paragraph (3).

Sec. 103 — DEFENSES

    (a)   IN GENERAL. It may be a defense to a charge of discrimination under this Act, that an alleged application of qualification standards, tests, or selection criteria that screen out or tend to screen out or otherwise deny a job or benefit to an individual with a disability has been shown to job-related and consistent with business necessity, and such performance cannot be accomplished by reasonable accommodation, as required under this title.

    (b)   QUALIFICATION STANDARDS. The term "qualification standards" may include a requirement that an individual shall not pose a direct threat to the health or safety of other individuals in the workplace.

    (c)   QUALIFICATION STANDARDS AND TESTS RELATED TO UNCORRECTED VISION. Notwithstanding section 3(4)(E)(ii), a covered entity shall not use qualification standards, employment tests, or other selectiaon criteria based on an individual's uncorrected vision unless the standard, test,or other selection criteria, as used by the covered entity, is shown to be job-rleated for the position in question and consistent with business necessity.

Sec. 104. ILLEGAL USE OF DRUGS AND ALCOHOL

    (a)   QUALIFIED INDIVIDUAL WITH A DISABILITY. For purposes of this title, the term "qualified individual with a disability" shall not include any employee or applicant who is currently engaging in the illegal use of drugs, when the covered entity acts on the basis of such use.

    (b)   RULES OF CONSTRUCTION. Nothing in subsection (a) shall be construed to exclude as a qualified individual with a disability an individual who—

        (1)   has successfully completed a supervised drug rehabilitation program and is no longer engaging in the illegal use of drugs, or has otherwise been rehabilitated successfully and is no longer engaging in such use;

        (2)   is participating in a supervised rehabilitation, program and is no longer engaging in such use; or

        (3)   is erroneously regarded as engaging in such use, but is not engaging in such use;

    except that it shall not be a violation of this Act for a covered entity to adopt or administer reasonable policies or procedures, including but not limited to drug testing, designed to ensure that an individual described in paragraph (1) or (2) is no longer engaging in the illegal use of drugs.

(c)   AUTHORITY OF COVERED ENTITY. A covered entity —

   (1)   may prohibit the illegal use of drugs and the use of alcohol at the workplace by all employees

   (2)   may require that employees shall not the under the influence of alcohol or be engaging in the illegal use of drugs at the workplace;

   (3)   may require that employees behave in conformance with the requirements established under the Drug-Free Workplace Act of 1988;

   (4)   may hold an employee who engages in the illegal use of drugs or who is an alcoholic to the same qualification standards for employment or job performance and behavior that such entity holds other employees, even if any unsatisfactory performance or behavior is related to the drug use or alcoholism of such employee....

(d)   DRUG TESTING.

   (1)   IN GENERAL. For purposes of this title, a test to determine the illegal use of drugs shall not be considered a medical examination.

Antitrust Acts

Excerpts

Sherman Act

Sec. 1. Every contract, combination in the form of trust or otherwise, or conspiracy, in restraint of trade or commerce among the several States, or with foreign nations, is declared to be illegal. Every person who shall make any such contract or engage in any such combination or conspiracy hereby declared to be illegal shall be deemed guilty of a felony, and on conviction thereof, shall be punished by fine not exceeding one million dollars if a corporation, or, in any other person, one hundred thousand dollars, or by imprisonment not exceeding three years, or by both said punishments, in the discretion of the court.

Sec. 2. Every person who shall monopolize, or attempt to monopolize, or combine or conspire with any other person or persons, to monopolize any part of the trade or commerce among the several States, or with foreign nations, shall be punished by fine not exceeding one million dollars, or by imprisonment not exceeding three years, or by both said punishments, in the discretion of the court.

Sec. 4. The several district courts of the United States are invested with jurisdiction to prevent and restrain violations of this act; and it shall be the duty of the several United States attorneys, in their respective districts, under the direction of the Attorney General, to institute proceedings in equity to prevent and restrain {i.e., issue injunctions against) such violations.

Sec. 7. Any person who shall be injured in his business or property by any other person or corporation by reason of anything forbidden or declared to be unlawful by this act, may sue therefor ... and recover three fold the damages by him sustained, and the costs of suit, including a reasonable attorney's fee.

Clayton Act

Sec. 6. That the labor of a human being is not a commodity or article of commerce. Nothing contained in the antitrust laws shall be construed to forbid the existence and operation of labor ... organizations ... or to forbid or restrain individual members of such organizations from lawfully carrying out the legitimate objects thereof; nor shall such organizations, or the members thereof, be held or construed to be illegal combinations or conspiracies in restraint of trade, under the antitrust laws.

Sec. 16. That any person, firm, corporation, or association shall be entitled to sue for and have injunctive relief ... against threatened loss or damage by a violation of the antitrust laws....

Sec. 20. That no restraining order or injunction shall be granted by any court of the United States, or a judge or the judges thereof, in any case between an employer and employees, or between employers and employees, or between employees, or between persons employed and persons seeking employment, involving, or growing out of, a dispute concerning terms or conditions of employment, unless necessary to prevent irreparable injury to property, or to a property right, of the party making application, for which injury there is no adequate remedy at law....

And no such restraining order or injunction shall prohibit any person or persons, whether singly or in concert, from terminating any relation of employment, or from ceasing to perform any work or labor, or from recommending, advising, or persuading others by peaceful means so to do; or from attending at any place where any such person or persons may lawfully be, for the purpose of peacefully obtaining or communicating information, or from peacefully persuading any person to work or to abstain from working; or from ceasing to patronize or to employ any party to such dispute, or from recommending, advising, or persuading others by peaceful and lawful means so to do; or from paying or giving to, or withholding from, any person engaged in such dispute, any strike benefits or other moneys or things of value; or from peaceably assembling in a lawful manner, and for lawful purposes; or from doing any act or thing which might lawfully be done in the absence of such dispute by any party thereto; nor shall any of the acts specified in this paragraph be considered or held to be violations of any law of the United States.

⚜

Civil Rights Act of 1964, Title VII
as amended

Excerpts

DEFINITIONS

Sec. 701. For the purposes of this title —

(b) The term "employer" means a person engaged in an industry affecting commerce who has fifteen or more employees for each working day in each of twenty or more calendar weeks in the current or preceding calendar year, and any agent of such person....

…

(k) The terms "because of sex" or "on the basis of sex" include, but are not limited to, because of or on the basis of pregnancy, childbirth, or related medical conditions; and women affected by pregnancy, childbirth, or related medical conditions shall be treated the same for all employed-related purposes, including receipt of benefits under fringe benefits programs, as other persons not so affected but similar in their ability or inability to work....

DISCRIMINATION BECAUSE OF RACE, COLOR, RELIGION, SEX, OR NATIONAL ORIGIN

Sec. 703. It shall be an unlawful employment practice for an employer —

(a)(1) to fail or refuse to hire or to discharge any individual, or otherwise to discriminate against any individual, with respect to his compensation, terms, conditions, or privileges of employment, because of such individual's race, color, religion, sex, or national origin; or

(2) to limit, segregate, or classify his employees or applicants for employment in any way which would deprive or tend to deprive any individual of employment opportunities or otherwise adversely affect his status as an employee, because of such individual's race, color, religion, sex, or national origin.

(b) It shall be an unlawful employment practice for an employment agency to fail or refuse to refer for employment, or otherwise to discriminate against, any individual because of his race, color, religion, sex, or national origin, or to classify or refer for employment any individual on the basis of his race, color, religion, sex, or national origin.

(c) It shall be an unlawful employment practice for a labor organization —

(1) to exclude or to expel from its membership, or otherwise to discriminate against, any individual because of his race, color, religion, sex, or national origin;

(2) to limit, segregate, or classify its membership or applicants for membership, or to classify or fail or refuse to refer, for employment any individual, in any way which would deprive or tend to deprive any individual of employment opportunities, or would limit such employment opportunities or otherwise adversely affect his status as an employee or as an applicant for employment, because of such individual's race, color, religion, sex, or national origin; or

(3) to cause or attempt to cause an employer to discriminate against an individual in violation of this section.

(d) It shall be an unlawful employment practice for any employer, labor organization, or joint labor-management committee controlling apprenticeship or other training or retraining, including on-the-job training programs to discriminate against any individual because of his race, color, religion, sex, or national origin in admission to, or employment in, any program established to provide apprenticeship or other training.

(e) Notwithstanding any other provision of this title, (1) it shall not be an unlawful employment practice for an employer to hire and employ employees, for an employment agency to classify, or refer for employment any individual, for a labor organization to classify its membership or to classify or refer for employment any individual, or for an employer, labor organization, or joint labor-management committee controlling apprenticeship or other training or retraining programs to admit or employ any individual in any such program, on the basis of his religion, sex, or national origin in those certain instances where religion, sex, or national origin is a bona fide occupational qualification reasonably necessary to the normal operation of that particular business or enterprise, and (2) it shall not be an unlawful employment practice for a school, college, university, or other educational institution or institution of learning to hire and employ employees of a particular religion if such school, college, university, or other educational institution or institution of learning is, in whole or in substantial part, owned, supported, controlled, or managed by a particular religion or by a particular religious corporation, association, or society, or if the curriculum of such school, college, university, or other educational institution or institution of learning is directed toward the propagation of a particular religion.

(h) Notwithstanding any other provision of this title, it shall not be an unlawful employment practice for an employer to apply different standards of compensation, or different terms, conditions, or privileges of employment pursuant to a bona fide seniority or merit system, or a system which measures earnings by quantity or quality of production or to employees who work in different locations, provided that such differences are not the result of an intention to discriminate because of race, color, religion, sex, or national origin, nor shall it be an unlawful employment practice for an employer to give and to act upon the results of any professionally developed ability test provided that such test, its administration or action upon the results is not designed, intended or used to discriminate because of race, color, religion, sex or national origin. It shall not be an unlawful employment practice under this title for any employer to differentiate upon the basis of sex in determining the amount of the wages car compensation paid or to be paid to employees of such employer of such employer is authorized by the provisions of section 206(d) of Title 29 {the Equal Pay Act}.

(j) Nothing contained in this title shall be interpreted to require any employer, employment agency, labor organization, or joint labor management committee subject to this title to grant preferential treatment to any individual or to any group because of the race, color, religion, sex, or national origin of such individual or group on account of an imbalance which may exist with respect to the total number or percentage of persons of any race, color, religion, sex, or national origin employed by any employer, referred or classified for employment by any employment agency or labor organization, admitted to membership or classified by any labor organization, or admitted to, or employed in, any apprenticeship or other training program, in comparison with the total number or percentage of persons of such race, color, religion, sex, or national origin in any community, State, section, or other area, or in the available work force in any community, State, section, or other area.

(k)(1)(A) An unlawful employment practice based on disparate impact is established under this title only if —

(i) a complaining party demonstrates that a respondent uses a particular employment practice that causes a disparate impact on the basis of race, color, religion, sex, or national origin and the respondent fails to demonstrate that the challenged practice is job related for the position in question and consistent with business necessity; or

(ii) the complaining party makes the demonstration described in subparagraph (C) {below} with respect to an alternative employment practice and the respondent refuses to adopt such alternative employment practice.

(B) (i) With respect to demonstrating that a particular employment practice causes a disparate impact as described in subparagraph (A)(i), the complaining party shall demonstrate that each particular challenged employment practice causes a disparate impact, except that if the complaining party can demonstrate to the court that the elements of respondent's decisionmaking process are not capable of separation for analysis, the decisionmaking process may be analyzed as one employment practice.

(ii) If the respondent demonstrates that a specific employment practice does not cause the disparate impact, the respondent shall not be required to demonstrate that such practice is required by business necessity.

(C) The demonstration referred to by subparagraph (A)(ii) {above} shall be in accordance with the law as it existed on Jane 4, 1989, with respect to the concept of "alternative employment practice."

(2) A demonstration that an employment practice is required by business necessity may not be used as a defense against a claim of intentional discrimination under this title.

(3) Notwithstanding any other provision of this title, a rule barring the employment of an individual who currently and knowingly uses or possesses a controlled substance, as defined in schedules I and II of section 102(6) of the Controlled Substances Act (21 U.S.C. 802(6)), other than the use or possession of a drug taken under the supervision of a licensed health care professional, or any other use or possession authorized by the Controlled Substances Act or any other provision of Federal law, shall be considered an unlawful employment practice under this title only if such rule is adopted or applied with an intent to discriminate because of race, color, religion, sex, or national origin.

(l) It shall be an unlawful employment practice for a respondent, in connection with the selection or referral of applicants or candidates for employment or promotion, to adjust the scores of, use different cutoff scores for, or otherwise alter the results of, employment-related tests on the basis of race, color, religion, sex, or national origin.

(m) Except as otherwise provided in this title, an unlawful employment practice is established when the complaining party demonstrates that race, color, religion, sex, or national origin was a motivating factor for any employment practice, even though other factors also motivated the practice.

PREVENTION OF UNLAWFUL EMPLOYMENT PRACTICES

Sec. 706. (a) The Commission is empowered, as hereinafter provided, to prevent any person from engaging in any unlawful employment practice as set forth in section 703 or 704 of this title.

(b) Whenever a charge is filed by or on behalf of a person claiming to be aggrieved, or by a member of the Commission, alleging that an employer, employment agency, labor organization, or joint labor-management committee controlling apprenticeship or other training or retraining, including on-the-job training programs has engaged in an unlawful employment practice, the Commission shall serve a notice of the charge (including the date, place and circumstances of the alleged unlawful employment practice) on such employer, employment agency, labor organization, or joint labor-management committee (hereinafter referred to as the "respondent") within ten days, and shall make an investigation thereof. Charges shall be in writing under oath or affirmation and shall contain such information and be in such form as the Commission requires. Charges shall not be made public by the Commission. If the Commission determines after such investigation that there is not reasonable cause to believe that the charge is true, it shall dismiss the charge and promptly notify the person claiming to be aggrieved and the respondent of its action. In determining whether reasonable cause exists, the Commission shall accord substantial weight to final findings and orders made by State or local authorities in proceedings commenced under State or local law pursuant to the requirements of subsections (c) and (d) of this section. If the Commission determines after such investigation that there is reasonable cause to believe that the charge is true, the

Commission shall endeavor to eliminate such alleged unlawful employment practice by informal methods of conference, conciliation, and persuasion. Nothing said or done during and as a part of such informal endeavors may be made public by the Commission, its officers or employees, or used as evidence in a subsequent proceeding without the written consent of the persons concerned. Any person who makes public information in violation of this subsection shall be fined not more than $1000 or imprisoned for not more than one year, or both. The Commission shall make its determination on reasonable cause as promptly as possible and, so far as practicable, not later than one hundred and twenty days from the filing of the charge or, where applicable under subsection (c) or (d) of this section, from the date upon which the Commission is authorized to take action with respect to the charge.

(c) In the case of an alleged unlawful employment practice occurring in a State, or political subdivision of a State, which has a State or local law prohibiting the unlawful employment practice alleged and establishing or authorizing a State or local authority to grant or seek relief from such practice or to institute criminal proceedings with respect thereto upon receiving notice thereof, no charge may be filed under subsection (b) or this section by the person aggrieved before the expiration of sixty days after proceedings have been commenced under the State or local law, unless such proceedings have been earlier terminated, provided that such sixty-day period shall be extended to one hundred and twenty days during the first year after the effective date of such State or local law. If any requirement for the commencement of such proceedings is imposed by a State or local authority other than a requirement of the filing of a written and signed statement of the facts upon which the proceeding is based, the proceeding shall be deemed to have been commenced for the purposes of this subsection at the time such statement is sent by registered mail to the appropriate State or local authority.

(d) In the case of any charge filed by a member of the Commission alleging an unlawful employment practice occurring in a State or political subdivision of a State which has a State or local law prohibiting the practice alleged and establishing or authorizing a State or local authority to grant or seek relief from such practice or to institute criminal proceedings with respect thereto upon receiving notice thereof, the Commission shall, before taking any action with respect to such charge, notify the appropriate State or local officials and, upon request, afford them a reasonable time, but not less than sixty days (provided that such sixty-day period shall be extended to one hundred and twenty days during the first year after the effective day of such State or local law), unless a shorter period is requested, to act under such State or local law to remedy the practice alleged.

(e)(1) A charge under this section shall be filed within one hundred and eighty days after the alleged unlawful employment practice occurred, and notice of the charge (including the date, place and circumstances of the alleged unlawful employment practice) shall be served upon the person against whom such charge is made within then days thereafter, except that in a case of an unlawful employment practice with respect to which the person aggrieved has initially instituted proceedings with a State or local agency with authority to grant or seek relief from such practice or to institute criminal proceedings with respect thereto upon receiving notice thereof, such charge shall be filed by or on behalf of the person aggrieved within three hundred days after the alleged unlawful employment practice occurred, or within thirty days after receiving notice that the State or local agency has terminated the proceedings under the State or local law, whichever is earlier, and a copy of such charge shall be filed by the Commission with that State or local agency.

(2) For purposes of this section, an unlawful employment practice occurs with respect to a seniority system that has been adopted for an intentionally discriminatory purpose in violation of this title (whether or not that discriminatory purpose is apparent on the face of the seniority provision), when the seniority system is adopted, when an individual becomes subject to the seniority system, or when a person aggrieved is injured by the application of the seniority system or provision of the system.

(f)(1) If within thirty days after a charge is filed with the Commission or within thirty days after expiration of any period of reference under subsection (c) or (d) of this section, the Commission has been unable to secure from the respondent a conciliation agreement acceptable to the Commission, the Commission may bring a civil action against any respondent not a government, governmental agency, or political subdivision named in the charge. In the case of a respondent which is a government, governmental agency or political subdivision, if the Commission has been unable to secure from the respondent a conciliation agreement acceptable to the Commission, the Commission shall take no further action and shall refer the case to the Attorney General, who may bring a civil action against such respondent in the appropriate United States district court. The person or persons aggrieved shall have the right to intervene in a civil action brought by the Commission or the Attorney General in a case involving a government, governmental agency, or political subdivision. If a charge filed with the Commission pursuant to subsection (b) of this section is dismissed by the Commission, or if within one hundred and eighty days from the filing of such charge or the expiration of any period of reference under subsection (c) or (d) of this section, whichever is later, the Commission has not filed a civil action under this section or the Attorney General has not filed a civil action in a case involving a government, governmental agency, or political subdivision, or the Commission has not entered into a conciliation agreement to which the person aggrieved is a party, the Commission, or the Attorney General in a case involving a government, governmental agency, or political subdivision, shall so notify the person aggrieved and within ninety days after the giving of such notice a civil action may be brought against the respondent named in the charge (A) by the person claiming to be aggrieved or (B) if such a charge was filed by a member of the Commission, by any person whom the charge alleges was aggrieved by the alleged unlawful employment practice.

(g)(1) If the court finds that the respondent has intentionally engaged in or is intentionally engaging in an unlawful employment practice charged in the complaint, the court may enjoin the respondent from engaging in such unlawful employment practice, and order such affirmative action as may be appropriate, which may include, but is not limited to, reinstatement or hiring of employees, with or without back pay (payable by the employer, employment agency, or labor organization, as the case may be, responsible for the unlawful employment practice), or any other equitable relief as the court deems appropriate. Back pay liability shall not accrue from a date more than two years prior to the filing of a charge with the Commission. Interim earnings or amounts earnable with reasonable diligence by the person or persons discriminated against shall operate to reduce the back pay otherwise allowable.

(2)(A) No order of the court shall require the admission or reinstatement of an individual as a member of a union, or the hiring, reinstatement, or promotion of an individual as an employee, or the payment to him of any back pay, if such individual was refused admission, suspended, or expelled, or was refused employment or advancement or was suspended or discharged for any reason other than discrimination on account of race, color, religion, sex, or national origin or in violation of section 703 or 704 of this title.

(B) On a claim in which an individual proves a violation under section 703(m) and a respondent demonstrates that the respondent would have taken the same action in the absence of the impermissible motivating factor, the court —

(i) may grant declaratory relief, injunctive relief (except as provided in clause (ii)), and attorney's fees and costs demonstrated to be directly attributable only to the pursuit of a claim under section 703(m); and

(ii) shall not award damages or issue an order requiring any admission, reinstatement, hiring, promotion, or payment, described in subparagraph (A).

The Equal Pay Act of 1963
29 U.S.C. § 206(d)(1)

No employer having employees subject to any provisions of this section shall discriminate, within any establishment in which such employees are employed, between employees on the basis of sex by paying wages to employees in such establishment at a rate less than the rate at which he pays wages to employees of the opposite sex in such establishment for equal work on jobs the performance of which requires equal skill, effort, and responsibility, and which are performed under similar working conditions, except where such payment is made pursuant to (i) a seniority system; (ii) a merit system; (iii) a system which measures earnings by quantity or quality of production; or (iv) a differential based on any other factor other than sex: *Provided*, That an employer who is paying a wage rate differential in violation of this subsection shall not, in order to comply with the provisions of this subsection, reduce the wage rate of any employee.

National Labor Relations Act
Labor Management Relations Act

Excerpts

Sec. 1. The denial by some employers of the right of employees to organize and the refusal by some employers to accept the procedure of collective bargaining lead to strikes and other forms of industrial strife or unrest, which have the intent or the necessary effect of burdening or obstructing commerce by (a) impairing the efficiency, safety, or operation of the instrumentalities of commerce; (b) occurring in the current of commerce; (c) materially affecting, restraining, or controlling the flow of raw materials or manufactured or processed goods from or into the channels of commerce, or the prices of such materials or goods in commerce; or (d) causing diminution of employment and wages in such volume as substantially to impair or disrupt the market for goods flowing from or into the channels of commerce.

The inequality of bargaining power between employees who do not possess full freedom of association or actual liberty of contract and employers who are organized in the corporate or other forms of ownership association substantially burdens and affects the flow of commerce, and tends to aggravate recurrent business depressions, by depressing wage rates and the purchasing power of wage earners in industry and by preventing the stabilization of competitive wage rates and working conditions within and between industries.

Experience has proved that protection by law of the right of employees to organize and bargain collectively safeguards commerce from injury, impairment, or interruption, and promotes the flow of commerce by removing certain recognized sources of industrial strife and unrest, by encouraging practices fundamental to the friendly adjustment of industrial disputes arising out of differences as to wages, hours, or other working conditions, and by restoring equality of bargaining power between employers and employees.

Experience has further demonstrated that certain practices by some labor organizations, their officers, and members have the intent or the necessary effect of burdening or obstructing commerce by preventing the free flow of goods in such commerce through strikes and other forms of industrial unrest or through concerted activities which impair the interest of the public in the free flow of such commerce. The elimination of such practices is a necessary condition to the assurance of the rights herein guaranteed.

It is declared to be the policy of the United States to eliminate the causes of certain substantial obstructions to the free flow of commerce and to mitigate and eliminate these obstructions when they have occurred by encouraging the practice and procedure of collective bargaining and by protecting the exercise by workers of full freedom of association, self-organization, and designation of representatives of their own choosing, for the purpose of negotiating the terms and conditions of their employment or other mutual aid or protection.

DEFINITIONS

Sec. 2. When used in this Act—

(2) The term "employer" includes any person acting as an agent of an employer, directly or indirectly, but shall not include the United States or any wholly owned Government corporation, or any Federal Reserve Bank, or any State or political subdivision thereof, or any person subject to the Railway Labor Act, as amended from time to time, or any labor organization (other than when acting as an employer), or anyone acting in the capacity of officer or agent of such labor organization.

(3) The term "employee" shall include any employee, and shall not be limited to the employees of a particular employer, unless the Act explicitly states otherwise, and shall include any individual whose work has ceased as a consequence of, or in connection with, any current labor dispute or because of any unfair labor practice, and who has not obtained any other regular and substantially equivalent employment, but shall not include any individual employed as an agricultural laborer, or in the domestic service of any family or person at his home, or any individual employed by his parent or spouse, or any individual having the status of an independent contractor, or any individual employed as a supervisor, or any individual employed by an employer subject to the Railway Labor Act, as amended from time to time, or by any other person who is not an employer as herein defined.

(9) The term "labor dispute" includes any controversy concerning terms, tenure or conditions of employment, or concerning the association or representation of persons in negotiating, fixing, maintaining, changing, or seeking to arrange terms or conditions of employment, regardless of whether the disputants stand in the proximate relation of employer and employee.

(11) The term "supervisor" means any individual having authority, in the interest of the employer, to hire, transfer, suspend, lay off, recall, promote, discharge, assign, reward, or discipline other employees, or responsibly to direct them, or to adjust their grievances, or effectively to recommend such action, if in connection with the foregoing the exercise of such authority is not of a merely routine or clerical nature, but requires the use of independent judgment.

RIGHTS OF EMPLOYEES

Sec. 7. Employees shall have the right to self-organization, to form, join, or assist labor organizations, to bargain collectively through representatives of their own choosing, and to engage in other concerted activities for the purpose of collective bargaining or other mutual aid or protection, and shall also have the right to refrain from any or all such activities except to the extent that such right may be affected by an agreement requiring membership in a labor organization as a condition of employment as authorized in section 8(a)(3).

UNFAIR LABOR PRACTICES

Sec. 8. (a) It shall be an unfair labor practice for an employer—

(1) to interfere with, restrain, or coerce employees in the exercise of the rights guaranteed in section 7;

(2) to dominate or interfere with the formation or administration of any labor organization or contribute financial or other support to it: *Provided,* That subject to rules and regulations made and published by the Board pursuant to section 6, an employer shall not be prohibited from permitting employees to confer with him during working hours without loss of time or pay;

(3) by discrimination in regard to hire or tenure of employment or any term or condition of employment to encourage or discourage membership in any labor organization: *Provided,* That nothing in this Act, or in any other statute of the United States, shall preclude an employer from making an agreement with a labor organization (not established, maintained, or assisted by any action defined in section 8(a) of this Act as an unfair labor practice) to require as a condition of employment membership therein on or after the thirtieth day following the beginning of such employment or the effective date of such agreement, whichever is the later, (i) if such labor organization is the representative of the employees as provided in section 9(a), in the appropriate collective-bargaining unit covered by such agreement when made, and (ii) unless following an election held as provided in section 9(e) within one year preceding the effective date of such agreement, the Board shall have certified that at least a majority of the employees eligible to vote in such election have voted to rescind the authority of such labor organization to make such an agreement: *Provided further,* That no employer shall justify any discrimination against an employee for non-membership in a labor organization (A) if he has reasonable grounds for believing that such membership was not available to the employee on the same terms and conditions generally applicable to other members, or (B) if he has reasonable grounds for believing that membership was denied or terminated for reasons other than the failure of the employee to tender the periodic dues and the initiation fees uniformly required as a condition of acquiring or retaining membership;

(4) to discharge or otherwise discriminate against an employee because he has filed charges or given testimony under this Act;

(5) to refuse to bargain collectively with the representatives of his employees, subject to the provisions of section 9(a).

(b) It shall be an unfair labor practice for a labor organization or its agents—

(1) to restrain or coerce (A) employees in the exercise of the rights guaranteed in section 7: *Provided,* That this paragraph shall not impair the right of a labor organization to prescribe its own rules with respect to the acquisition or retention of membership therein; or (B) an employer in the

selection of his representatives for the purposes of collective bargaining or the adjustment of grievances;

(2) to cause or attempt to cause an employer to discriminate against an employee in violation of subsection (a)(3) or to discriminate against an employee with respect to whom membership in such organization has been denied or terminated on some ground other than his failure to tender the periodic dues and the initiation fees uniformly required as a condition of acquiring or retaining membership;

(3) to refuse to bargain collectively with an employer, provided it is the representative of his employees subject to the provisions of section 9(a);

(c) The expressing of any views, argument, or opinion, or the dissemination thereof, whether in written, printed, graphic, or visual form, shall not constitute or be evidence of an unfair labor practice under any of the provisions of this Act, if such expression contains no threat of reprisal or force or promise of benefit.

(d) For the purposes of this section, to bargain collectively is the performance of the mutual obligation of the employer and the representative of the employees to meet at reasonable times and confer in good faith with respect to wages, hours, and other terms and conditions of employment, or the negotiation of an agreement or any question arising thereunder, and the execution of a written contract incorporating any agreement reached if requested by either party, but such obligation does not compel either party to agree to a proposal or require the making of a concession: *Provided,* That where there is in effect a collective-bargaining contract covering employees in an industry affecting commerce, the duty to bargain collectively shall also mean that no party to such contract shall terminate or modify such contract, unless the party desiring such termination or modification—

(1) serves a written notice upon the other party to the contract of the proposed termination or modification sixty days prior to the expiration date thereof, or in the event such contract contains no expiration date, sixty days prior to the time it is proposed to make such termination or modification;

(2) offers to meet and confer with the other party for the purpose of negotiating a new contract or a contract containing the proposed modifications;

(3) notifies the Federal Mediation and Conciliation Service within thirty days after such notice of the existence of a dispute, and simultaneously therewith notifies any State or Territorial agency established to mediate and conciliate disputes within the State or Territory where the dispute occurred, provided no agreement has been reached by that time; and

(4) continues in full force and effect, without resorting to strike or lockout, all the terms and conditions of the existing contract for a period of sixty days after such notice is given or until the expiration date of such contract, whichever occurs later.

The duties imposed upon employees, and labor organizations by paragraphs (2), (3), and (4) shall not be construed as requiring either party to discuss or agree to any modification of the terms and conditions contained in a contract for a fixed period, if such modification is to become effective before such terms and conditions can be reopened under the provisions of the contract. Any employee who engages in a strike within any notice period specified in this subsection, shall lose his status as an employee of the employer engaged in the particular labor dispute, for the purposes of sections 8, 9, and 10 of this Act, but such loss of status for such employee shall terminate if and when he is reemployed by such employer.

REPRESENTATIVES AND ELECTIONS

Sec. 9. Representatives designated or selected for the purposes of collective bargaining by the majority of the employees in a unit appropriate for such purposes, shall be the exclusive representatives of all the employees in such unit for the purposes of collective bargaining in respect to rates of pay, wages, hours of employment, or other conditions of employment: *Provided,* That any individual employee or a group of employees shall have the right at any time to present grievances to their employer and to have such grievances adjusted, without the intervention of the bargaining representative, as long as the adjustment is not inconsistent with the terms of a collective-bargaining contract or agreement then in effect: *Provided further,* That the bargaining representative has been given opportunity to be present at such adjustment.

LIMITATIONS

Sec. 13. Nothing in this Act, except as specifically provided for herein, shall be construed so as either to interfere with or impede or diminish in any way the right to strike or to affect the limitations or qualifications on that right.

Sec. 14. (a) Nothing herein shall prohibit any individual employed as a supervisor from becoming or remaining a member of a labor organization, but no employer subject to this Act shall be compelled to deem individuals defined herein as supervisors as employees for the purpose of any law, either national or local, relating to collective bargaining.

(b) Nothing in this Act shall be construed as authorizing the execution or application of agreements requiring membership in a labor organization as a condition of employment in any State or Territory in which such execution or application is prohibited by State or Territorial law.

SUITS BY AND AGAINST LABOR ORGANIZATIONS

Sec. 301. (a) Suits for violation of contracts between an employer and a labor organization representing employees in an industry affecting commerce as defined in this Act, or between any such labor organizations, may be brought in any district court of the United States having jurisdiction of the parties, without respect to the amount in controversy or without regard to the citizenship of the parties.

(b) Any labor organization which represents employees in an industry affecting commerce as defined in this Act and any employee whose activities affect commerce as defined in this Act shall be bound by the acts of its agents. Any such labor organization may sue or be sued as an entity and in behalf of the employees whom it represents in the courts of the United States. Any money judgment against a labor organization in a district court of the United States shall be enforceable only against the organization as an entity and against its assets, and shall not be enforceable against any individual member or his assets.

SAVING PROVISION

Sec. 502. Nothing in this Act shall be construed to require an individual employee to render labor or service without his consent, nor shall anything in this Act be construed to make the quitting of his labor by an individual employee an illegal act; nor shall any court issue any process to compel the performance by an individual employee of such labor or service, without his consent; nor shall the quitting of labor by an employee or employees in good faith because of abnormally dangerous conditions of work at the place of employment of such employee or employees be deemed a strike under this Act.

Norris-LaGuardia Act

Excerpts

Sec. 1. No court of the United States ... shall have jurisdiction to issue any restraining order or temporary or permanent injunction in a case involving or growing out of a labor dispute, except in a strict conformity with the provisions of this Act ....

Sec. 2. In the interpretation of this Act and in determining the jurisdiction and authority of the courts of the United States ... the public policy of the United States is hereby declared as follows:

Whereas under prevailing economic conditions, developed with the aid of governmental authority for owners of property to organize in the corporate and other forms of ownership association, the individual unorganized worker is commonly helpless to exercise actual liberty of contract and to protect his freedom of labor, and thereby to obtain acceptable terms and conditions of employment, wherefore, though he should be free to decline to associate with his fellows, it is necessary that he have full freedom of association, self-organization, and designation of representatives of his own choosing, to negotiate the terms and conditions of his employment, and that he shall be free from the interference, restraint, or coercion of employers of labor, or their agents, in the designation of such representatives or in self-organization or in other concerted activities for the purpose of collective bargaining or other mutual aid or protection; therefore, the following definitions of, and limitations upon, the jurisdiction and authority of the courts of the United States are hereby enacted.

Sec. 3. Any undertaking or promise, such as is described in this section ... is hereby declared to be contrary to the public policy of the United States, shall not be enforceable in any court of the United States and shall not afford any basis for the granting of legal or equitable relief by any such court, including specifically the following:

Every undertaking or promise hereafter made, whether written or oral, express or implied, constituting or contained in any contract or agreement of hiring or employment between any individual, firm, company, association, or corporation, and any employee or prospective employee of the same whereby

(a) Either party to such contract or agreement undertakes or promises not to join, become, or remain a member of any labor organization or of any employer organization; or

(b) Either party to such contract or agreement undertakes or promises that he will withdraw from an employment relation in the event that he joins, becomes, or remains a member of any labor organization or of any employer organization.

Sec. 4. No court of the United States shall have jurisdiction to issue any restraining order or temporary or permanent injunction in any case involving or growing out of any labor dispute to prohibit any person or persons participating or interested in such dispute from doing, whether singly or in concert, any of the following acts:

(a) Ceasing or refusing to perform any work or to remain in any relation of employment;

(b) Becoming or remaining a member of any labor organization or of any employer organization...;

(c) Paying or giving to, or withholding from, any person participating or interested in such labor dispute, any strike or unemployment benefits or insurance, or other moneys or things of value;

(d) By all lawful means aiding any person participating or interested in any labor dispute who is being proceeded against in, or is prosecuting, any action or suit in any court of the United States or of any State;

(e) Giving publicity to the existence of, or the facts involved in, any labor dispute, whether by advertising, speaking, patrolling, or by any other method not involving fraud or violence;

(f) Assembling peaceably to act or to organize to act in promotion of their interests in a labor dispute;

(g) Advising or notifying any person of an intention to do any of the Acts heretofore specified;

(h) Agreeing with other persons to do or not to do any of the acts heretofore specified; and

(i) Advising, urging, or otherwise causing or inducing without fraud or violence the acts heretofore specified, regardless of any such undertaking or promise as is described in section 3 of this Act.

Sec. 5. No court of the United States shall have jurisdiction to issue a restraining order or temporary or permanent injunction upon the ground that any of the persons participating or interested in a labor dispute constitute or are engaged in an unlawful combination or conspiracy because of the doing in concert of the acts enumerated in section 4 of this Act.

...

Sec. 7. No court of the United States shall have jurisdiction to issue a temporary or permanent injunction in any case involving or growing out of a labor dispute ... except after hearing the testimony of witnesses in open court (with opportunity for cross-examination) in support of the allegations of a complaint made under oath, and testimony in opposition thereto, if offered, and except after findings of fact by the court, to the effect —

(a) That unlawful acts have been threatened and will be committed unless restrained or have been committed and will be continued unless restrained ....

(b) That substantial and irreparable injury to complainant's property will follow;

(c) That as to each item of relief granted greater injury will be inflicted upon complainant by the denial of relief than will be inflicted upon defendants by the granting of relief;

(d) That complainant has no adequate remedy at law; and

(e) That the public officers charged with the duty to protect complainant's property are unable or unwilling to furnish adequate protection.

Such hearing shall be held after due and personal notice thereof has been given, in such manner as the court shall direct, to all known persons against whom relief is sought, and also to the chief of those public officials of the county and city within which the unlawful acts have been threatened or committed charged with the duty to protect complainant's property: *Provided, however,* That if a complainant shall also allege that, unless a temporary restraining order shall be issued without notice, a substantial and irreparable injury to complainant's property will be unavoidable, such a temporary restraining order may be issued upon testimony under oath, sufficient, if sustained, to justify the court in issuing a temporary injunction upon a hearing after notice. Such a temporary restraining order shall be effective for no longer than five days and shall become void at the expiration of said five days....

...

Sec. 11. In all cases arising under this Act in which a person shall be charged with contempt in a court of the United States ... the accused shall enjoy the right to a speedy and public trial by an impartial jury of the State and district wherein the contempt shall have been committed....

...

Sec. 13. When used in this Act, and for the purposes of this Act

(a) A case shall be held to involve or to grow out of a labor dispute when the case involves persons who are engaged in the same industry, trade, craft, or occupation; or have direct or indirect interests therein; or who are employees of the same employer; or who are members of the same or an affiliated organization of employers or employees; whether such dispute is (1) between one or more employers or associations of employers and one or more employees or associations of employees; (2) between one or more employers or associations of employers and one or more employers or associations of employers; or (3) between one or more employees or associations of employees and one or more employees or associations of employees; or when the case involves any conflicting or competing interests in a "labor dispute" ... of "persons participating or interested" therein....

(b) A person or association shall be held to be a person participating or interested in a labor dispute if relief is sought against him or it, and if he or it is engaged in the same industry, trade, craft, or occupation in which such dispute occurs, or has a direct or indirect interest therein, or is a member, officer, or agent of any association composed in whole or in part of employers or employees engaged in such industry, trade, craft, or occupation.

(c) The term "labor dispute" includes any controversy concerning terms or conditions of employment, or concerning the association or representation of persons in negotiating, fixing, maintaining, changing, or seeking to arrange terms or conditions of employment, regardless of whether or not the disputants stand in the proximate relation of employer and employee.

...

Sec. 15. All Acts and parts of Acts in conflict with the provisions of this Act are hereby repealed.

$$\Omega$$

Glossary

A Glossary of Legalisms

The following definitions are written for non-law students. The definitions are accurate, but not always complete. They are drawn from *Ballentine's Law Dictionary*, 3d ed.(1969); Bryan A. Garner, *A Dictionary of Modern Legal Usage (Oxford Univ. Press, 1987);* as well as the author's experience. Most of the examples are the author's.

alter ego: literally, "the other I," "the other self." In Labor Law, the term usually refers to a new business that is substantially identical (same owner, same product, etc.) to one that has just closed, the purpose being to evade the duty to bargain with a union. "Jesse's Tours," which opened a mile away from and a month after (1) the union won the right to represent the employees of "Jesse's Junkets" and (2) Jesse closed the latter, was the latter's alter ego; in consequence, Jesse was obliged to bargain with the union regarding the terms and conditions of employment of the employees of the former.

ab initio (ab i-NISH-ē-ō): from the beginning. A trusteeship imposed for illegal reasons is void *ab initio*.

a fortiori (ā-for-she-ARE-ē): literally, "from the stronger"; by the force of logic; for a stronger reason. Who would steal from a friend *a fortiori* would steal from a stranger.

> Death, be not proud, though some have called thee
> Mighty and dreadful, for thou art not so;
> For those whom thou think'st thou doest overthrow
> Die not, poor Death; nor yet canst thou kill me.
> From rest and sleep, which but they pictures be,
> Much pleasure, then from thee much more must flow ....

—John Donne, *Holy Sonnets. Annunciation x*

amicus curiae (ah-ME-kus CURE-ē-ī) *(*pl. ***amici*** (a-ME-ki) ***curiae):*** literally, "friend of the court"; a party who has no direct stake in the outcome of a case but files a brief with a court. Studying cases in labor and employment law, one finds *amicus curiae* briefs filed by the AFL-CIO, the American Civil Liberties Union, the Business Roundtable, the Equal Employment Advisory Council, the NAACP Legal Defense Fund, the NOW Legal Defense Fund, the U.S. Chamber of Commerce, etc.

appellant: the party who lost in the court below and is seeking to reverse the judgment of that court. Suppose Jones sues Smith. In the trial court, the name of the case is *Right v. Wrong*; Right is the plaintiff and Wrong is the defendant. Suppose Right wins and Wrong appeals. In the appellate court, the name of the case might change to *Wrong v. Right*; Wrong is the appellant, and Right is the respondent. Suppose, instead, that Wrong wins in the trial court and Right appeals. In the appellate court, the name of the case would remain *Right v. Wrong*; Right is the appellant, and Wrong is the respondent. If the decision of the appellate court is appealed to a still higher court, the same process occurs again.

appellee: the party who won in the court below and who is defending the judgment of that court.

arguendo: for the sake of argument only. "My client was in Chicago when the victim was murdered," argued the defendant's attorney; "but assuming *arguendo* that he was present at the scene of the murder, he could not have stabbed her with this knife because his arm was broken."

case at bar: the case presently being decided. Synonyms include the "case at hand," the "instant case," the "present case," and (confusingly) "this case."

cause of action: a legal claim; the grounds that entitled one person to obtain legal relief against another. "Tom, Tom, the piper's son/ Stole a pig and away he run/ The pig was eat and Tom was beat/ And Tom went crying down the street." The owner of the pig had a cause of action against Tom.

caveat (KA-vē-at): literally, "let him beware"; therefore, a warning. "My advice to students is that they should always do the assigned reading before class, with one *caveat:* they should also take care of their health by sleeping enough."

certiorari (sir-sure-ARE-ē): a writ or order in which the U.S. Supreme Court agrees to allow a party who has lost in a lower court to present one's case to the Supreme Court. The writ of *certiorari* is discretionary; in labor cases, there is no right of appeal to the Supreme Court. One may file a petition for a writ of *certiorari* and, if four Justices of the Court vote to hear the case, the writ is granted.

condition precedent (pre-SĒ-dent)**:** a condition (or event) that must occur before an obligation (such as a contract) arises. On September 1st, *A* agreed to pay *B* $50 if *B* would ride a tray down Libe Slope during a blizzard. The next day, *B* rode a tray down the Slope and demanded the money: whereupon *A* said, "I owe you nothing. There was no blizzard today; therefore, the condition precedent to my obligation has not occurred."

court of equity: a court that can issue an injunction. Until at least the 1930s, the judicial systems of most states and of the federal government were bifurcated. Depending on the nature of the plaintiff's claim, a case went to a "court of law" or a "court of equity." Only a court of equity could issue injunctions. (The origin of this dual structure was the judicial system of medieval England, in which courts of law were the king's courts and courts of equity were ecclesiastical courts.) Today nearly all American judicial systems are unified with respect to law and equity (though special courts remain for specific purposes, e.g., family courts).

damnum absque injuria (DAM-num AB-skay in-JUR-ē-ah): damage without legal injury. When Mary returned the engagement ring that Harry had given her, it cut him to the quick but was *damnum absque injuria*.

de facto**:** in fact (as distinguished from *de jure, q.v.*). Public schools in the North are often segregated *de facto* because of housing patterns and the desire for neighborhood schools.

defendant: the party in court who is accused of having done something wrong to the party who brought the case

defendant in error: an older term for the appellee, *q.v.*

*de jure***:** by law (as distinguished from *de facto, q.v.*). In the past, Southern public schools were commonly segregated *de jure.*

de minimus: too small to matter; trifling. The contract called for the seller to deliver 10,000 trees, in exchange for which the buyer agreed to pay $500,000. The seller delivered 9,999 trees. This *de minimus* difference may have justified the buyer's withholding $50, but did not justify the buyer's renouncing the contract.

dictum (pl. *dicta):* a statement by a court on an issue not necessary to the holding of the case; an unnecessary statement. The lower federal courts are not technically bound by *dicta* in the opinions of the Supreme Court, but one is an adventurous trial judge who ignores them.

en banc: decided by all of the judges of the court, rather than by a panel of the judges. A federal Circuit Court of Appeals may be comprised of 5 to 10 or more judges. They normally decide cases in panels of three judges, and a decision of a panel is binding precedent on subsequent panels. Occasionally, however, all of the judges of the court hear a case and, sitting *en banc,* they may overrule a panel's decision. The U.S. Supreme Court always sits *en banc.*

equity: see "court of equity" in this glossary.

ex parte: in the absence of one of the parties to the case. Some courts will issue an *ex parte* restraining order against a strike, relying on the employer's representations and without hearing from the union.

expressio unius est exclusio alterius: the expression of one thing implies the exclusion of another thing. If a statute states a rule of law as well as a list five exceptions to the rule, it is assumed that no further exceptions were intended.

id.: abbreviation for *idem.* Used in legal writing as a citation meaning "the same as the previous citation. This court has held that birds can fly. *Right v. Wrong,* 123 F.2d 456 (99th Cir. 1999). However, as Justice Serçan has noted, "The penguin can't." *Id. at 789.*

inclusio unius est exclusio alterius: the inclusion of one thing implies the exclusion of other things. If a statute states a general rule and lists three exceptions, the principle of *inclusio unius est exclusio alterius* suggests that no further exceptions were intended.

infra: below, usually in the same document. The term *supra* is defined *infra.*

in limine (in LIM-in-ē): at the outset. Let us agree *in limine* not to condemn each other for the arguments we make in class.

in pari materia (in-pear-ē ma-TARE-ē-ah): in relation to the same matter or subject; having due regard for related issues. Statutes on the same subject must be read *in pari materia.*

in point: see *"on point"* in this glossary

inter alia (inter Ā-lee-ah): among other things. This glossary contains, *inter alia*, some bad jokes.

in terrorem: by way or warning or intimidation; tending to inspire fear or dread. A no-contest clause in a will, which provides that anyone who contests the validity of the will is automatically disinherited, operates *in terrorem* and should be construed narrowly.

ipse dixit: literally," he himself said it"; thus, a statement made but not supported; an arbitrary claim. Never let your adversary get away with an *ipse dixit*; always insist that a claim be supported by evidence, authority, or argument.

issue: (1) a point of disagreement. Tom wanted pizza for dinner, and Jerry wanted Chinese. The issue was, what shall Tom and Jerry eat for dinner? (2) offspring. Huey, Dewey, and Louie are the issue of issue of Donald's sister, Della.

judicial notice: a legal doctrine that allows a judge of a court (or a member of any other sort of tribunal) to rely on a fact even though the parties to the case have not introduced evidence of that fact. Judicial notice is appropriate for facts that are common knowledge, e.g., the time the sun rose in Ithaca, New York on June 21st, and for other facts that are within the knowledge of a person in the judge's position, e.g., the date on which a paper was filed with the court.

malum in se: evil in itself; refers to an act so obviously bad that everyone knows it is bad. This state needs no statute against torture to make it a crime because torture is *malum in se*.

mutatis mutandis: with appropriate but unimportant changes. The President's criticism of the Senate applied, *mutatis mutandis*, to the House of Representatives.

on point or **in point:** apposite; pertinent; dealing with or discussing the same issue as the issue under consideration. A precedent on point controls the outcome of the issue at hand.

per curiam (per-CURE-ē-um): literally, "by the court"; used to refer to an opinion not signed by an individual judge. *Per curiam* opinions are often brief.

per se: in or by itself. Losing a leg is *per se* disabling to a soccer player.

plaintiff: the party who complains in court to have been wronged by some other party.

plaintiff in error: an older term for the appellant, *q.v.*

police power: the power of the government to administer the community. This term is broader than the word "police" suggests to a modern reader; the police power extends to areas beyond the responsibility of a police officer. A better sense of the term can be seen in the military phrase, "to police an area," which means to make the area clean and orderly. The scope of the police power is suggested by the etymology of the word "police," which derives from the Greek word polis, meaning city or political community. Polis is also the source of our word "policy."

precedent on point: *see "on point"* in this glossary.

prima facie (PRY-mah FĀ-shah; PREE-mah FAH-she): literally, "at first view."
Prima facie case: (1) The ultimate facts which a plaintiff must prove in order to win relief; the elements of a claim. If the plaintiff proves a *prima facie* case, the plaintiff will win unless the defendant proves a defense. (2) The evidence that establishes the existence of the ultimate facts or elements of a claim. The plaintiff's *prima facie* case failed because her evidence on a crucial element of her claim was unbelievable.

pro tanto: literally, "for so much"; thus, to the extent that. Twenty months ago, the employer discharged a worker because of the latter's concerted activity. The worker had been earning $2,000 per month. On first inspection, therefore, the employer owes the worker back pay in the amount of $40,000. But the worker was ill and out of the labor market for two months; thus, even if she had not been unlawfully discharged, she would not heave earned $4,000. In addition, for 4 months she held a job paying $1,500 per month (= $6,000). The amount due the worker must be reduced *pro tanto* (in this case, by $10,000).

quid pro quo: literally, "this for that"; thus, a thing which is exchanged for something else. Arbitration is the *quid pro quo* for a no-strike clause.

respondeat superior (re-SPON-dē-at superior): an employer is responsible for the wrongful acts of one's employee. When Jane, in the course of making a scheduled delivery, negligently drove the Ives Co.'s truck over my big toe, Ives was liable to me by virtue of *respondeat superior*.

sine qua non (SĒ-nah kwa non) literally, "without which it is not"; a necessary prerequisite. Regular attendance to lectures is a *sine qua non* of success in this course.

stare decisis (STAR-ē dē-SIGH-sus): the doctrine of precedent. A court is obliged by *stare decisis* to follow its previous decisions.

sua sponte: by itself; on its own motion; without being asked to. Although both parties were willing to go to trial, the court dismissed the case *sua sponte*.

sub nom.: abbreviation of *sub nomine*, which means under the name of. The case of *Round v. About* was decided by the appellate court sub nom. *Back v. Forth*.

sub judice (sub jew-DĒ-see): presently under consideration by this court. The case of *Right v. Wrong* must be distinguished from the case *sub judice*.

sui generis (SUE-ē generous) literally, "of its own kind" or self generating; thus, unique. Labor law is neither tort nor contract, but *sui generis*.

supra: above, usually in the same document. The term *infra* is defined *supra*.

tort: a violation of a duty that is imposed by law (as opposed to a duty imposed by contract) but is not a crime. Negligence, trespass to property, and battery are torts.

vel non: or not. The liability *vel non* of the employer turns on the supervisor's knowledge.

writ of *certiorari*: see *"certiorari"* in this glossary.

$$\Omega$$

www.ingramcontent.com/pod-product-compliance
Lightning Source LLC
Chambersburg PA
CBHW082115210326
41599CB00031B/5770